EU Law

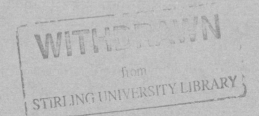

EU Law

Dr Iyiola Solanke

PEARSON

Harlow, England • London • New York • Boston • San Francisco • Toronto • Sydney • Auckland • Singapore • Hong Kong
Tokyo • Seoul • Taipei • New Delhi • Cape Town • São Paulo • Mexico City • Madrid • Amsterdam • Munich • Paris • Milan

Pearson Education Limited
Edinburgh Gate
Harlow CM20 2JE
United Kingdom
Tel: +44 (0)1279 623623
Web: www.pearson.com/uk

First Published 2015 (print and electronic)

© Pearson Education Limited 2015 (print and electronic)

ISBN: 978-1-4082-2833-3 (print)
        978-1-4082-2834-0 (PDF)
        978-1-292-08558-6 (eText)

British Library Cataloguing-in-Publication Data
A catalogue record for the print edition is available from the British Library

Library of Congress Cataloging-in-Publication Data
Solanke, Iyiola, author.
EU law/Iyiola Solanke. — First Edition.
     pages cm
  ISBN 978-1-4082-2833-3
1. Law—European Union countries. I. Title. II. Title: Exploring European Union law.
  KJE947.S66 2015
  341.242'2—dc23

                                                                    2015009808

10 9 8 7 6 5 4 3 2 1
19 18 17 16 15

Print edition typeset in 10/12pt Sabon MT Pro by 71
Printed by Ashford Colour Press Ltd, Gosport

NOTE THAT ANY PAGE CROSS REFERENCES REFER TO THE PRINT EDITION

Brief contents

Part IV   EU Internal Market and Competition Law 355

Contents

List of Abbreviations

ADR Alternative dispute resolution
AFJS Area of Freedom, Justice and Security
AG Advocate General
AsG Advocates-General
AM Absolute majority
CAP Common Agricultural Policy
CC Conciliation Committee
CCP Central contact point
CCP Common Commercial Policy
CD Citizenship Directive
CEE Charges having equivalent effect
CEEC Committee of European Economic Co-operation
CFI Court of First Instance
CFP Common Fisheries Policy
CFR Charter of Fundamental Rights
CFSP Common Foreign and Security Policy
CHR Commission on Human Rights
CISA Convention Implementing the Schengen Convention
CJ Court of Justice
CJEU Court of Justice of the European Union
CM Council of Ministers
COMREG Committee of the Regions
COOL Country of origin labelling
COREPER The Permanent Representatives Committee of the EU
CP Common Position
CSFP Common and Foreign Security Policy
CST Civil Service Tribunal
CT Constitutional Treaty
DG Directorate General
EC European Council
ECHR European Court of Human Rights
ECI European Citizen's Initiative
ECJ European Court of Justice
ECN European Competition Network
ECOSOC Economic and Social Committee
ECSC European Coal and Steel Community
ECtHR European Court of Human Rights
ECU European Currency Unit
EEA European Economic Area

EEC European Economic Community
EFTA European Free Trade Association
EMU European and Monetary Union
EO European Ombudsman
EP European Parliament
EPI European Parliament Initiative
EPPO European Public Prosecutor's Office
GAC General Affairs Council
GATT General Agreement on Tariffs and Trade
GC General Court
GCC German Constitutional Court
HR High Representative of the Union for Foreign Affairs and Security Policy
IAB Impact Assessment Board
ICCPR International Covenant on Civil and Political Rights
ICERD International Convention on the Elimination of All Forms of Racial Discrimination
ICTY UN International Criminal Tribunal on Former Yugoslavia
IGC Intergovernmental conference
IMPALA Independent Music Publishers and Labels Association
INTI Integration of Third Country National
JCMS *Journal of Common Market Studies*
JHA Justice and Home Affairs
LT Lisbon Treaty
MEP Member of the European Parliament
MEQR Measures Equivalent to a Quantitative Restriction
MS Member state
NGO Non-governmental organisation
OEEC Organisation of European Economic Co-operation
OFM Other family members
OJ Official Journal of the European Union
OLP Ordinary Legislative Procedure
OMC Open method of coordination
OOPEC Office for Official Publications of the EC

PCI Parliamentary Committee of Inquiry
QMV Qualified majority voting
QR Quantitative restrictions
SEA Single European Act
SGEI Services of general economic interest
SIS Schengen Information System
SSGI Social services of general interest

TCN Third country national
TEU Treaty on European Union
TFEU Treaty on the Functioning of the
European Union
UNDHR United Nations Declaration of
Human Rights
UNSC United Nations Security Council

Preface

The CJEU is the busiest court in the world, producing up to and sometimes more than 500 decisions in a single year. The student of EU law should be clear that they are about to enter a world of law that has its own legal instruments, law-making rules, principles and concepts and priorities. Yet this world is not totally unknown: EU law covers topics familiar from the first year of an undergraduate law degree, such as administrative law, institutional law and constitutional law. At the same time, EU law introduces learners to new areas of law that may be pursued in later years at undergraduate or postgraduate level, such as competition law, immigration law, trade law or equality and human rights law. Study of EU law therefore builds upon past learning while creating a base for future studies.

The study of EU law can be a challenge. These topics are often modules and degree programmes in their own right. Furthermore, European integration is an ongoing project thus change is continual and keeping abreast of the judicial decisions requires stamina and determination. In addition, misleading reports in the press can create confusion.[1] Despite these challenges, the material can be mastered. The purpose of this book is to help you to succeed in this, by encouraging reflection, debate and practical application alongside assimilation of new rules, concepts and principles.

The legal framework that has supported and sometimes led European integration is the focus of this book. The exploration will of necessity consider more than EU law: EU integration is both politics and economics:[2] economics and politics are both method and motivation. Law has been effective in perforating the boundaries of the nation state, making them permeable to create the internal market, yet has not fully erased them. All three – law, politics and economics – have played a role in the complex process by which the member states have partially opened up their markets and welfare systems. Member states have used European institutions to both promote and prevent over-intrusion of global forces (internationalisation and liberalisation)[3] thus national differences persist, even if the challenges are common.[4] Law has also in particular played a role where compromise and negotiation has failed or stalled.

My objective in writing this book was to present EU law in a way that is detailed and comprehensive, enjoyable to read and clear to understand. The story of the EU and EU law is full of controversy, conflict and change. However, we can only read about the lawmakers of the past – we live EU law: it is being made and remade in our lifetime. Whether it concerns family reunification or the sale of seal products, smoking or what

---

[1] http://www.thesun.co.uk/sol/homepage/news/4984447/Correction.html, http://ukhumanrightsblog.com/2013/06/26/the-sun-gets-regulator-reprimand-and-apologises-for-misleading-on-european-human-rights/#more-18879
[2] Erik Jones and Amy Verdun (eds) 'The Political Economy of European Integration: theory and analysis', Routledge, 2005, p. 1
[3] Maria Green Cowles, in Jones and Verdun, 2005, p. 26
[4] Scharpf and Schmidt 'Welfare and Work in the Open Economy, Vol 2: Diverse responses to Common Challenges' Oxford University Press, 2000

we eat, EU law affects how we live and what we do – as individuals and through our politicians – affects it. It is a topic that demands the attention of any aspiring lawyer, CEO or politician within the EU as well as beyond.

In order to remind the reader of the world within which EU law lives, each chapter begins with an opening 'scenario': this might be the details of a case, a quote from a newspaper or journal article or an extract from an EU legal instrument or official report. The purpose of this opening is to provide a context for the legal information that follows and a backdrop for the rules to be discussed. Throughout the chapter you will be invited to reflect upon the rules presented, often in light of this opening setting. These moments of reflection enable you to practise the application of EU law, to analyse it or – equally important – encourage you to develop an opinion. They also offer a possibility for discussion of a specific issue with your peers, either in class or in the cafe. Finally, they act as an intellectual hiatus, enabling you to ensure understanding of the material just read before moving onto the next section. In summary, the opening scenario acts as a factual background upon which to engage with EU law and the moments of reflection offer points for application, analysis and debate. By making EU law less abstract in this way, my hope is to make it more approachable and engaging. It may never become your favourite area of law, but I hope that you enjoy exploring it.

A quick word on terminology: you will note as you read through the text that both 'European Community' and 'European Union' are used. The word 'Community' appears where it is used in older case law and in some scholarly works. However this is a historic term and the current title is now 'European Union'. Also, a word is necessary on the Union courts: when there was just one court it was called the 'ECJ' (European Court of Justice) – this name appears in some extracts. The current collective name for all three European Courts is the Court of Justice of the European Union (CJEU). Abbreviations such as CJ (Court of Justice), GC (General Court) or CST (Civil Service Tribunal) are used when referring to decisions of a specific court. Likewise, the pre-Lisbon Treaty numbering has only been used in extracts and citations, with the new Treaty numbering provided alongside.

With the CJEU producing so many decisions annually, writing a single-author tome covering the core constitutional, institutional and substantive aspects of EU law gets harder every year. If I have managed to do this at all successfully, it has only been due to the support of many people, especially my ever-patient editors at Pearson Press – Cheryl Cheasley, Holly Gardner, Owen Knight, Helen Leech, Roxanne Selby and Jennifer Sargunar: a big thanks to all of you for your care for this project. I am also grateful for the team of anonymous reviewers whose encouraging comments accompanied me as I wrote. My efficient editors–Jim Cauter and Linda Dhondy–added important final touches. Beyond the editorial team, I would like to thank my students for trusting me to teach them something worthwhile, as well as colleagues, collaborators and friends in academia, civil society and legal practice who have nurtured my passion for this topic – a special thank you goes to Professor Damian Chalmers, who many years ago inspired me to explore EU law. Finally, heartfelt thanks go to my family near and far, for inspiring me everyday with their faith, courage and love.

Publisher's acknowledgements

We are grateful to the following for permission to reproduce copyright material:

Figures
Figure 2.1 after *Eurobarometer, 2009*, © European Union, 1995–2015; Figure 8.1 from Commission Staff Working Document on the Application of the EU Charter of Fundamental Rights in 2011, Brussels: SWD (2012) 84 final, p.3, © European Union, 1995–2014; Figure 12.1 adapted from *The European Union*, 9th ed., Cambridge University Press (El-Agraa, A. M. (ed.) 2011) p.2.

Table
Table on pages xli–lix from *Consolidated Treaties: Charter of Fundamental Rights*, March 2010, Luxembourg: Publications Office of the European Union, © European Union, 2010.

Text
Extract on page 23 from *Laeken Declaration on the Future of the European Union* at http://european-convention.eu.int/pdf/LKNEN.pdf [Accessed 29 July 2009], © European Union, 1995–2015; Epigraph on page 167 from German court is not the ultimate authority on EU, *Financial Times*, 07/07/2011 (Eeckhout, P.), © Piet Eeckhout; Epigraph on page 325 from A fact finding analysis on the impact on the Member States' social security systems of the entitlements of non-active intra-EU migrants to special non-contributory cash benefits and healthcare granted on the basis of residence, *DG Employment, Social Affairs and Inclusion via DG Justice Framework Contract* (Final report submitted by ICF GHK in association with Milieu Ltd), © European Union, 1995–2014. Contains public sector information – © European Union, 1995–2014

In some instances we have been unable to trace the owners of copyright material, and we would appreciate any information that would enable us to do so.

Table of Cases

Competition Law Decisions

Table of European Union Treaties

Table of Equivalences

Attached to the consolidated version of the Treaty on Europea Union (OJ C 326, 26.10.2012) at pg 196.

Treaty on European Union

Old numbering of the Treaty on European Union	New numbering of the Treaty on European Union
TITLE I – COMMON PROVISIONS	TITLE I – COMMON PROVISIONS
Article 1	Article 1
	Article 2
Article 2	Article 3
Article 3 (repealed) [2]	
	Article 4
	Article 5 [3]
Article 4 (repealed) [4]	
Article 5 (repealed) [5]	
Article 6	Article 6
Article 7	Article 7
	Article 8
TITLE II – PROVISIONS AMENDING THE TREATY ESTABLISHING THE EUROPEAN ECONOMIC COMMUNITY WITH A VIEW TO ESTABLISHING THE EUROPEAN COMMUNITY	TITLE II – PROVISIONS ON DEMOCRATIC PRINCIPLES
Article 8 (repealed) [6]	Article 9
	Article 10 [7]
	Article 11
	Article 12

(1) Tables of equivalences as referred to in Article 5 of the Treaty of Lisbon. The original centre column, which set out the intermediate numbering as used in that Treaty, has been omitted.

(2) Replaced, in substance, by Article 7 of the Treaty on the Functioning of the European Union ("TFEU") and by Articles 13(1) and 21, paragraph 3, second subparagraph of the Treaty on European Union ("TEU").

(3) Replaces Article 5 of the Treaty establishing the European Community ("TEC").

(4) Replaced, in substance, by Article 15.

(5) Replaced, in substance, by Article 13, paragraph 2.

(6) Article 8 TEU, which was in force until the entry into force of the Treaty of Lisbon (hereinafter "current"), amended the TEC. Those amendments are incorporated into the latter Treaty and Article 8 is repealed. Its number is used to insert a new provision.

(7) Paragraph 4 replaces, in substance, the first subparagraph of Article 191 TEC.

(*continued*)

Treaty on European Union (*continued*)

TITLE III - PROVISIONS AMENDING THE TREATY ESTABLISHING THE EUROPEAN COAL AND STEEL COMMUNITY	TITLE III – PROVISIONS ON THE INSTITUTIONS
Article 9 (repealed) [8]	Article 13
	Article 14 [9]
	Article 15 [10]
	Article 16 [11]
	Article 17 [12]
	Article 18
	Article 19 [13]
TITLE IV - PROVISIONS AMENDING THE TREATY ESTABLISHING THE EUROPEAN ATOMIC ENERGY COMMUNITY	TITLE IV – PROVISIONS ON ENHANCED COOPERATION
Article 10 (repealed) [14] Articles 27a to 27e (replaced) Articles 40 to 40b (replaced) Articles 43 to 45 (replaced)	Article 20 [15]

(8) The current Article 9 TEU amended the Treaty establishing the European Coal and Steel Community. This latter expired on 23 July 2002. Article 9 is repealed and the number thereof is used to insert another provision.

(9)

  ● Paragraphs 1 and 2 replace, in substance, Article 189 TEC;

  ● paragraphs 1 to 3 replace, in substance, paragraphs 1 to 3 of Article 190 TEC;

  ● paragraph 1 replaces, in substance, the first subparagraph of Article 192 TEC;

  ● paragraph 4 replaces, in substance, the first subparagraph of Article 197 TEC.

(10) Replaces, in substance, Article 4.

(11)

  ● Paragraph 1 replaces, in substance, the first and second indents of Article 202 TEC;

  ● paragraphs 2 and 9 replace, in substance, Article 203 TEC;

  ● paragraphs 4 and 5 replace, in substance, paragraphs 2 and 4 of Article 205 TEC.

(12)

  ● Paragraph 1 replaces, in substance, Article 211 TEC;

  ● paragraphs 3 and 7 replace, in substance, Article 214 TEC.

  ● paragraph 6 replaces, in substance, paragraphs 1, 3 and 4 of Article 217 TEC.

(13)

  ● Replaces, in substance, Article 220 TEC.

  ● the second subparagraph of paragraph 2 replaces, in substance, the first subparagraph of Article 221 TEC.

(14) The current Article 10 TEU amended the Treaty establishing the European Atomic Energy Community. Those amendments are incorporated into the Treaty of Lisbon. Article 10 is repealed and the number thereof is used to insert another provision.

(15) Also replaces Articles 11 and 11a TEC.

Treaty on European Union (*continued*)

TITLE V – PROVISIONS ON A COMMON FOREIGN AND SECURITY POLICY	TITLE V – GENERAL PROVISIONS ON THE UNION'S EXTERNAL ACTION AND SPECIFIC PROVISIONS ON THE COMMON FOREIGN AND SECURITY POLICY
	Chapter 1 – General provisions on the Union's external action
	Article 21
	Article 22
	Chapter 2 – Specific provisions on the common foreign and security policy
	Section 1 – Common provisions
	Article 23
Article 11	Article 24
Article 12	Article 25
Article 13	Article 26
	Article 27
Article 14	Article 28
Article 15	Article 29
Article 22 (moved)	Article 30
Article 23 (moved)	Article 31
Article 16	Article 32
Article 17 (moved)	Article 42
Article 18	Article 33
Article 19	Article 34
Article 20	Article 35
Article 21	Article 36
Article 22 (moved)	Article 30
Article 23 (moved)	Article 31
Article 24	Article 37
Article 25	Article 38
	Article 39
Article 47 (moved)	Article 40
Article 26 (repealed)	
Article 27 (repealed)	
Article 27a (replaced) [16]	Article 20
Article 27b (replaced) [16]	Article 20
Article 27c (replaced) [16]	Article 20
Article 27d (replaced) [16]	Article 20
Article 27e (replaced) [16]	Article 20

(16) The current Articles 27a to 27e, on enhanced cooperation, are also replaced by Articles 326 to 334 TFEU.

(*continued*)

Treaty on European Union (*continued*)

Article 28	Article 41
	Section 2 – Provisions on the common security and defence policy
Article 17 (moved)	Article 42
	Article 43
	Article 44
	Article 45
	Article 46
TITLE VI – PROVISIONS ON POLICE AND JUDICIAL COOPERATION IN CRIMINAL MATTERS (repealed) [17]	
Article 29 (replaced) [18]	
Article 30 (replaced) [19]	
Article 31 (replaced) [20]	
Article 32 (replaced) [21]	
Article 33 (replaced) [22]	
Article 34 (repealed)	
Article 35 (repealed)	
Article 36 (replaced) [23]	
Article 37 (repealed)	
Article 38 (repealed)	
Article 39 (repealed)	
Article 40 (replaced) [24]	Article 20
Article 40 A (replaced) [24]	Article 20
Article 40 B (replaced) [24]	Article 20
Article 41 (repealed)	
Article 42 (repealed)	

(17) The current provisions of Title VI of the TEU, on police and judicial cooperation in criminal matters, are replaced by the provisions of Chapters 1, 5 and 5 of Title IV of Part Three of the TFEU.

(18) Replaced by Article 67 TFEU.

(19) Replaced by Articles 87 and 88 TFEU.

(20) Replaced by Articles 82, 83 and 85 TFEU.

(21) Replaced by Article 89 TFEU.

(22) Replaced by Article 72 TFEU.

(23) Replaced by Article 71 TFEU.

(24) The current Articles 40 to 40 B TEU, on enhanced cooperation, are also replaced by Articles 326 to 334 TFEU.

Treaty on the Functioning of the European Union (*continued*)

TITLE VII – PROVISIONS ON ENHANCED COOPERATION (replaced) [25]	TITLE IV – PROVISIONS ON ENHANCED COOPERATION
Article 43 (replaced) [25]	Article 20
Article 43 A (replaced) [25]	Article 20
Article 43 B (replaced) [25]	Article 20
Article 44 (replaced) [25]	Article 20
Article 44 A (replaced) [25]	Article 20
Article 45 (replaced) [25]	Article 20
TITRE VIII – FINAL PROVISIONS	TITLE VI – FINAL PROVISIONS
Article 46 (repealed)	
	Article 47
Article 47 (replaced)	Article 40
Article 48	Article 48
Article 49	Article 49
	Article 50
	Article 51
	Article 52
Article 50 (repealed)	
Article 51	Article 53
Article 52	Article 54
Article 53	Article 55

Treaty on the Functioning of the European Union

Old numbering of the Treaty establishing the European Community	New numbering of the Treaty on the Functioning of the European Union
PART ONE – PRINCIPLES	PART ONE – PRINCIPLES
Article 1 (repealed)	
	Article 1
Article 2 (repealed) [26]	
	Title I – Categories and areas of union competence
	Article 2
	Article 3
	Article 4
	Article 5

(25) The current Articles 43 to 45 and Title VII of the TEU, on enhanced cooperation, are also replaced by Articles 326 to 334 TFEU.

(26) Replaced, in substance, by Article 3 TEU.

(*continued*)

Treaty on the Functioning of the European Union (*continued*)

	Article 6
	Title II – Provisions having general application
	Article 7
Article 3, paragraph 1 (repealed) [27]	
Article 3, paragraph 2	Article 8
Article 4 (moved)	Article 119
Article 5 (replaced) [28]	
	Article 9
	Article 10
Article 6	Article 11
Article 153, paragraph 2 (moved)	Article 12
	Article 13 [29]
Article 7 (repealed) [30]	
Article 8 (repealed) [31]	
Article 9 (repealed)	
Article 10 (repealed) [32]	
Article 11 (replaced) [33]	Articles 326 to 334
Article 11a (replaced) [33]	Articles 326 to 334
Article 12 (repealed)	Article 18
Article 13 (moved)	Article 19
Article 14 (moved)	Article 26
Article 15 (moved)	Article 27
Article 16	Article 14
Article 255 (moved)	Article 15
Article 286 (moved)	Article 16
	Article 17
PART TWO – CITIZENSHIP OF THE UNION	PART TWO – NON-DISCRIMINATION AND CITIZENSHIP OF THE UNION
Article 12 (moved)	Article 18
Article 13 (moved)	Article 19
Article 17	Article 20
Article 18	Article 21

(27) Replaced, in substance, by Articles 3 to 6 TFEU.
(28) Replaced, in substance, by Article 5 TEU.
(29) Insertion of the operative part of the protocol on protection and welfare of animals.
(30) Replaced, in substance, by Article 13 TEU.
(31) Replaced, in substance, by Article 13 TEU and Article 282, paragraph 1, TFEU.
(32) Replaced, in substance, by Article 4, paragraph 3, TEU.
(33) Also replaced by Article 20 TEU.

Treaty on the Functioning of the European Union (*continued*)

Article 19	Article 22
Article 20	Article 23
Article 21	Article 24
Article 22	Article 25
PART THREE – COMMUNITY POLICIES	PART THREE – POLICIES AND INTERNAL ACTIONS OF THE UNION
	Title I – The internal market
Article 14 (moved)	Article 26
Article 15 (moved)	Article 27
Title I – Free movement of goods	Title II – Free movement of goods
Article 23	Article 28
Article 24	Article 29
Chapter 1 – The customs union	Chapter 1 – The customs union
Article 25	Article 30
Article 26	Article 31
Article 27	Article 32
Part Three, Title X, Customs cooperation (moved)	Chapter 2 – Customs cooperation
Article 135 (moved)	Article 33
Chapter 2 – Prohibition of quantitative restrictions between Member States	Chapter 3 – Prohibition of quantitative restrictions between Member States
Article 28	Article 34
Article 29	Article 35
Article 30	Article 36
Article 31	Article 37
Title II - Agriculture	Title III – Agriculture and fisheries
Article 32	Article 38
Article 33	Article 39
Article 34	Article 40
Article 35	Article 41
Article 36	Article 42
Article 37	Article 43
Article 38	Article 44
Title III – Free movement of persons, services and capital	Title IV – Free movement of persons, services and capital
Chapter 1 – Workers	Chapter 1 – Workers
Article 39	Article 45
Article 40	Article 46
Article 41	Article 47
Article 42	Article 48

(*continued*)

Treaty on the Functioning of the European Union (*continued*)

Chapter 2 – Right of establishment	Chapter 2 – Right of establishment
Article 43	Article 49
Article 44	Article 50
Article 45	Article 51
Article 46	Article 52
Article 47	Article 53
Article 48	Article 54
Article 294 (moved)	Article 55
Chapter 3 – Services	Chapter 3 – Services
Article 49	Article 56
Article 50	Article 57
Article 51	Article 58
Article 52	Article 59
Article 53	Article 60
Article 54	Article 61
Article 55	Article 62
Chapter 4 – Capital and payments	Chapter 4 – Capital and payments
Article 56	Article 63
Article 57	Article 64
Article 58	Article 65
Article 59	Article 66
Article 60 (moved)	Article 75
Title IV – Visas, asylum, immigration and other policies related to free movement of persons	Title V - Area of freedom, security and justice
	Chapter 1 – General provisions
Article 61	Article 67 [34]
	Article 68
	Article 69
	Article 70
	Article 71 [35]
Article 64, paragraph 1 (replaced)	Article 72 [36]
	Article 73
Article 66 (replaced)	Article 74
Article 60 (moved)	Article 75
	Article 76

(34) Also replaces the current Article 29 TEU.
(35) Also replaces the current Article 36 TEU.
(36) Also replaces the current Article 33 TEU.

Treaty on the Functioning of the European Union (*continued*)

	Chapter 2 – Policies on border checks, asylum and immigration
Article 62	Article 77
Article 63, points 1 et 2, and Article 64, paragraph 2 [37]	Article 78
Article 63, points 3 and 4	Article 79
	Article 80
Article 64, paragraph 1 (replaced)	Article 72
	Chapter 3 – Judicial cooperation in civil matters
Article 65	Article 81
Article 66 (replaced)	Article 74
Article 67 (repealed)	
Article 68 (repealed)	
Article 69 (repealed)	
	Chapter 4 – Judicial cooperation in criminal matters
	Article 82 [39]
	Article 83 [39]
	Article 84
	Article 85 [39]
	Article 86
	Chapter 5 – Police cooperation
	Article 87 [40]
	Article 88 [40]
	Article 89 [41]
Title V – Transport	Title VI – Transport
Article 70	Article 90
Article 71	Article 91

(37) Points 1 and 2 of Article 63 EC are replaced by paragraphs 1 and 2 of Article 78 TFEU, and paragraph 2 of Article 64 is replaced by paragraph 3 of Article 78 TFEU.

(38) Replaces the current Article 31 TEU.

(39) Replaces the current Article 30 TEU.

(40) Replaces the current Article 32 TEU.

(41)

- Article 140, paragraph 1 takes over the wording of paragraph 1 of Article 121.
- Article 140, paragraph 2 takes over the second sentence of paragraph 2 of Article 122.
- Article 140, paragraph 3 takes over paragraph 5 of Article 123.

(continued)

Treaty on the Functioning of the European Union (*continued*)

Article 72	Article 92
Article 73	Article 93
Article 74	Article 94
Article 75	Article 95
Article 76	Article 96
Article 77	Article 97
Article 78	Article 98
Article 79	Article 99
Article 80	Article 100
Title VI – Common rules on competition, taxation and approximation of laws	Title VII – Common rules on competition, taxation and approximation of laws
Chapter 1 – Rules on competition	Chapter 1 – Rules on competition
Section 1 – Rules applying to undertakings	Section 1 – Rules applying to undertakings
Article 81	Article 101
Article 82	Article 102
Article 83	Article 103
Article 84	Article 104
Article 85	Article 105
Article 86	Article 106
Section 2 – Aids granted by States	Section 2 – Aids granted by States
Article 87	Article 107
Article 88	Article 108
Article 89	Article 109
Chapter 2 – Tax provisions	Chapter 2 – Tax provisions
Article 90	Article 110
Article 91	Article 111
Article 92	Article 112
Article 93	Article 113
Chapter 3 – Approximation of laws	Chapter 3 – Approximation of laws
Article 95 (moved)	Article 114
Article 94 (moved)	Article 115
Article 96	Article 116
Article 97	Article 117
	Article 118
Title VII – Economic and monetary policy	Title VIII – Economic and monetary policy
Article 4 (moved)	Article 119
Chapter 1 – Economic policy	Chapter 1 – Economic policy
Article 98	Article 120
Article 99	Article 121

Treaty on the Functioning of the European Union (*continued*)

Article 100	Article 122
Article 101	Article 123
Article 102	Article 124
Article 103	Article 125
Article 104	Article 126
Chapter 2 – monetary policy	Chapter 2 – monetary policy
Article 105	Article 127
Article 106	Article 128
Article 107	Article 129
Article 108	Article 130
Article 109	Article 131
Article 110	Article 132
Article 111, paragraphs 1 to 3 and 5 (moved)	Article 219
Article 111, paragraph 4 (moved)	Article 138
	Article 133
Chapter 3 – Institutional provisions	Chapter 3 – Institutional provisions
Article 112 (moved)	Article 283
Article 113 (moved)	Article 284
Article 114	Article 134
Article 115	Article 135
	Chapter 4 – Provisions specific to Member States whose currency is the euro
	Article 136
	Article 137
Article 111, paragraph 4 (moved)	Article 138
Chapter 4 – Transitional provisions	Chapter 5 – Transitional provisions
Article 116 (repealed)	
	Article 139
Article 117, paragraphs 1, 2, sixth indent, and 3 to 9 (repealed)	
Article 117, paragraph 2, first five indents (moved)	Article 141, paragraph 2
Article 121, paragraph 1 (moved) Article 122, paragraph 2, second sentence (moved) Article 123, paragraph 5 (moved)	Article 140 [42]
Article 118 (repealed)	

(42)

Article 141, paragraph 1 takes over paragraph 3 of Article 123.

Article 141, paragraph 2 takes over the first five indents of paragraph 2 of Article 117.

(*continued*)

Treaty on the Functioning of the European Union (*continued*)

Article 123, paragraph 3 (moved) Article 117, paragraph 2, first five indents (moved)	Article 141 [43]
Article 124, paragraph 1 (moved)	Article 142
Article 119	Article 143
Article 120	Article 144
Article 121, paragraph 1 (moved)	Article 140, paragraph 1
Article 121, paragraphs 2 to 4 (repealed)	
Article 122, paragraphs 1, 2, first sentence, 3, 4, 5 and 6 (repealed)	
Article 122, paragraph 2, second sentence (moved)	Article 140, paragraph 2, first subparagraph
Article 123, paragraphs 1, 2 and 4 (repealed)	
Article 123, paragraph 3 (moved)	Article 141, paragraph 1
Article 123, paragraph 5 (moved)	Article 140, paragraph 3
Article 124, paragraph 1 (moved)	Article 142
Article 124, paragraph 2 (repealed)	
Title VIII – Employment	Title IX – Employment
Article 125	Article 145
Article 126	Article 146
Article 127	Article 147
Article 128	Article 148
Article 129	Article 149
Article 130	Article 150
Title IX – Common commercial policy (moved)	Part Five, Title II, common commercial policy
Article 131 (moved)	Article 206
Article 132 (repealed)	
Article 133 (moved)	Article 207
Article 134 (repealed)	
Title X – Customs cooperation (moved)	Part Three, Title II, Chapter 2, Customs cooperation
Article 135 (moved)	Article 33
Title XI – Social policy, education, vocational training and youth	Title X – Social policy
Chapter 1 – social provisions (repealed)	
Article 136	Article 151
	Article 152
Article 137	Article 153
Article 138	Article 154

(43) Replaced, in substance, by the second sentence of the second subparagraph of paragraph 1 of Article 208 TFUE.

Treaty on the Functioning of the European Union (*continued*)

(continued)

Treaty on the Functioning of the European Union (*continued*)

Article 165	Article 181
Article 166	Article 182
Article 167	Article 183
Article 168	Article 184
Article 169	Article 185
Article 170	Article 186
Article 171	Article 187
Article 172	Article 188
	Article 189
Article 173	Article 190
Title XIX – Environment	Title XX – Environment
Article 174	Article 191
Article 175	Article 192
Article 176	Article 193
	Titre XXI – Energy
	Article 194
	Title XXII – Tourism
	Article 195
	Title XXIII – Civil protection
	Article 196
	Title XXIV – Administrative cooperation
	Article 197
Title XX – Development cooperation (moved)	Part Five, Title III, Chapter 1, Development cooperation
Article 177 (moved)	Article 208
Article 178 (repealed) [44]	
Article 179 (moved)	Article 209
Article 180 (moved)	Article 210
Article 181 (moved)	Article 211
Title XXI – Economic, financial and technical cooperation with third countries (moved)	Part Five, Title III, Chapter 2, Economic, financial and technical cooperation with third countries
Article 181a (moved)	Article 212
PART FOUR – ASSOCIATION OF THE OVERSEAS COUNTRIES AND TERRITORIES	PART FOUR - ASSOCIATION OF THE OVERSEAS COUNTRIES AND TERRITORIES
Article 182	Article 198
Article 183	Article 199

(44) The second sentence of the second subparagraph of paragraph 1 replaces, in substance, Article 178 TEC.

Treaty on the Functioning of the European Union (*continued*)

Article 184	Article 200
Article 185	Article 201
Article 186	Article 202
Article 187	Article 203
Article 188	Article 204
	PART FIVE - EXTERNAL ACTION BY THE UNION
	Title I – General provisions on the union's external action
	Article 205
Part Three, Title IX, Common commercial policy (moved)	Title II – Common commercial policy
Article 131 (moved)	Article 206
Article 133 (moved)	Article 207
	Title III – Cooperation with third countries and humanitarian aid
Part Three, Title XX, Development cooperation (moved)	Chapter 1 – development cooperation
Article 177 (moved)	Article 208 [45]
Article 179 (moved)	Article 209
Article 180 (moved)	Article 210
Article 181 (moved)	Article 211
Part Three, Title XXI, Economic, financial and technical cooperation with third countries (moved)	Chapter 2 – Economic, financial and technical cooperation with third countries
Article 181a (moved)	Article 212
	Article 213
	Chapter 3 – Humanitarian aid
	Article 214
	Title IV – Restrictive measures
Article 301 (replaced)	Article 215
	Title V – International agreements
	Article 216
Article 310 (moved)	Article 217
Article 300 (replaced)	Article 218
Article 111, paragraphs 1 to 3 and 5 (moved)	Article 219
	Title VI – The Union's relations with international organisations and third countries and the Union delegations
Articles 302 to 304 (replaced)	Article 220

(45) Replaced, in substance, by Article 14, paragraphs 1 and 2, TEU.

(*continued*)

Treaty on the Functioning of the European Union (*continued*)

	Article 221
	Title VII – Solidarity clause
	Article 222
PART FIVE – INSTITUTIONS OF THE COMMUNITY	PART SIX – INSTITUTIONAL AND FINANCIAL PROVISIONS
Title I – Institutional provisions	Title I – Institutional provisions
Chapter 1 – The institutions	Chapter 1 – The institutions
Section 1 – The European Parliament	Section 1 – The European Parliament
Article 189 (repealed) [46]	
Article 190, paragraphs 1 to 3 (repealed) [47]	
Article 190, paragraphs 4 and 5	Article 223
Article 191, first paragraph (repealed) [48]	
Article 191, second paragraph	Article 224
Article 192, first paragraph (repealed) [49]	
Article 192, second paragraph	Article 225
Article 193	Article 226
Article 194	Article 227
Article 195	Article 228
Article 196	Article 229
Article 197, first paragraph (repealed) [50]	
Article 197, second, third and fourth paragraphs	Article 230
Article 198	Article 231
Article 199	Article 232
Article 200	Article 233
Article 201	Article 234
	Section 2 – The European Council
	Article 235
	Article 236
Section 2 – The Council	Section 3 – The Council
Article 202 (repealed) [51]	
Article 203 (repealed) [52]	
Article 204	Article 237

(46) Replaced, in substance, by Article 14, paragraphs 1 to 3, TEU.
(47) Replaced, in substance, by Article 11, paragraph 4, TEU.
(48) Replaced, in substance, by Article 14, paragraph 1, TEU.
(49) Replaced, in substance, by Article 14, paragraph 4, TEU.
(50) Replaced, in substance, by Article 16, paragraph 1, TEU and by Articles 290 and 291 TFEU.
(51) Replaced, in substance, by Article 16, paragraphs 2 and 9 TEU.
(52) Replaced, in substance, by Article 16, paragraphs 4 and 5 TEU.

Treaty on the Functioning of the European Union (*continued*)

Article 205, paragraphs 2 and 4 (repealed) [53]	
Article 205, paragraphs 1 and 3	Article 238
Article 206	Article 239
Article 207	Article 240
Article 208	Article 241
Article 209	Article 242
Article 210	Article 243
Section 3 – The Commission	Section 4 – The Commission
Article 211 (repealed) [55]	
	Article 244
Article 212 (moved)	Article 249, paragraph 2
Article 213	Article 245
Article 214 (repealed) [57]	
Article 215	Article 246
Article 216	Article 247
Article 217, paragraphs 1, 3 and 4 (repealed) [58]	
Article 217, paragraph 2	Article 248
Article 218, paragraph 1 (repealed) [59]	
Article 218, paragraph 2	Article 249
Article 219	Article 250
Section 4 – The Court of Justice	Section 5 – The Court of Justice of the European Union
Article 220 (repealed) [60]	
Article 221, first paragraph (repealed) [61]	
Article 221, second and third paragraphs	Article 251
Article 222	Article 252
Article 223	Article 253
Article 224 [62]	Article 254

(53) Replaced, in substance, by Article 295 TFEU.
(54) Replaced, in substance, by Article 17, paragraph 1 TEU.
(55) Replaced, in substance, by Article 19, paragraph 2, first subparagraph, of the TEU.
(56) Replaced, in substance, by Article 17, paragraphs 3 and 7 TEU.
(57) Replaced, in substance, by Article 17, paragraph 6, TEU.
(58) Replaced, in substance, by Article 295 TFEU.
(59) Replaced, in substance, by Article 19 TEU.
(60) Replaced, in substance, by Article 19, paragraph 2, first subparagraph, of the TEU.
(61) The first sentence of the first subparagraph is replaced, in substance, by Article 19, paragraph 2, second subparagraph of the TEU.
(62) Replaces, in substance, the third indent of Article 202 TEC.

(*continued*)

Treaty on the Functioning of the European Union (*continued*)

	Article 255
Article 225	Article 256
Article 225a	Article 257
Article 226	Article 258
Article 227	Article 259
Article 228	Article 260
Article 229	Article 261
Article 229a	Article 262
Article 230	Article 263
Article 231	Article 264
Article 232	Article 265
Article 233	Article 266
Article 234	Article 267
Article 235	Article 268
	Article 269
Article 236	Article 270
Article 237	Article 271
Article 238	Article 272
Article 239	Article 273
Article 240	Article 274
	Article 275
	Article 276
Article 241	Article 277
Article 242	Article 278
Article 243	Article 279
Article 244	Article 280
Article 245	Article 281
	Section 6 – The European Central Bank
	Article 282
Article 112 (moved)	Article 283
Article 113 (moved)	Article 284
Section 5 – The Court of Auditors	Section 7 – The Court of Auditors
Article 246	Article 285
Article 247	Article 286
Article 248	Article 287
Chapter 2 – Provisions common to several institutions	Chapter 2 – Legal acts of the Union, adoption procedures and other provisions
	Section 1 – The legal acts of the Union

Treaty on the Functioning of the European Union (*continued*)

Article 249	Article 288
	Article 289
	Article 290 [63]
	Article 291 [63]
	Article 292
	Section 2 – Procedures for the adoption of acts and other provisions
Article 250	Article 293
Article 251	Article 294
Article 252 (repealed)	
	Article 295
Article 253	Article 296
Article 254	Article 297
	Article 298
Article 255 (moved)	Article 15
Article 256	Article 299
	Chapter 3 – The Union's advisory bodies
	Article 300
Chapter 3 – The Economic and Social Committee	Section 1 – The Economic and Social Committee
Article 257 (repealed) [64]	
Article 258, first, second and fourth paragraphs	Article 301
Article 258, third paragraph (repealed) [65]	
Article 259	Article 302
Article 260	Article 303
Article 261 (repealed)	
Article 262	Article 304
Chapter 4 – The Committee of the Regions	Section 2 – The Committee of the Regions
Article 263, first and fifth paragraphs (repealed) [66]	
Article 263, second to fourth paragraphs	Article 305
Article 264	Article 306
Article 265	Article 307
Chapter 5 – The European Investment Bank	Chapter 4 – The European Investment Bank

(63) Replaced, in substance, by Article 300, paragraph 2 of the TFEU.
(64) Replaced, in substance, by Article 300, paragraph 4 of the TFEU.
(65) Replaced, in substance, by Article 300, paragraphs 3 and 4, TFEU.
(66) Replaced, in substance, by Article 310, paragraph 4, TFEU.

(continued)

Treaty on the Functioning of the European Union (*continued*)

Article 266	Article 308
Article 267	Article 309
Title II – Financial provisions	Title II – Financial provisions
Article 268	Article 310
	Chapter 1 – The Union's own resources
Article 269	Article 311
Article 270 (repealed) [67]	
	Chapter 2 – The multiannual financial framework
	Article 312
	Chapter 3 – The Union's annual budget
Article 272, paragraph 1 (moved)	Article 313
Article 271 (moved)	Article 316
Article 272, paragraph 1 (moved)	Article 313
Article 272, paragraphs 2 to 10	Article 314
Article 273	Article 315
Article 271 (moved)	Article 316
	Chapter 4 – Implementation of the budget and discharge
Article 274	Article 317
Article 275	Article 318
Article 276	Article 319
	Chapter 5 – Common provisions
Article 277	Article 320
Article 278	Article 321
Article 279	Article 322
	Article 323
	Article 324
	Chapter 6 – Combating fraud
Article 280	Article 325
	Title III – Enhanced cooperation
Articles 11 and 11a (replaced)	Article 326 [68]
Articles 11 and 11a (replaced)	Article 327 [68]
Articles 11 and 11a (replaced)	Article 328 [68]
Articles 11 and 11a (replaced)	Article 329 [68]
Articles 11 and 11a (replaced)	Article 330 [68]
Articles 11 and 11a (replaced)	Article 331 [68]

(67) Also replaces the current Articles 27a to 27e, 40 to 40b, and 43 to 45 TEU.

Treaty on the Functioning of the European Union (*continued*)

Articles 11 and 11a (replaced)	Article 332 [68]
Articles 11 and 11a (replaced)	Article 333 [68]
Articles 11 and 11a (replaced)	Article 334 [68]
PART SIX – GENERAL AND FINAL PROVISIONS	PART SEVEN – GENERAL AND FINAL PROVISIONS
Article 281 (repealed) [69]	
Article 282	Article 335
Article 283	Article 336
Article 284	Article 337
Article 285	Article 338
Article 286 (replaced)	Article 16
Article 287	Article 339
Article 288	Article 340
Article 289	Article 341
Article 290	Article 342
Article 291	Article 343
Article 292	Article 344
Article 293 (repealed)	
Article 294 (moved)	Article 55
Article 295	Article 345
Article 296	Article 346
Article 297	Article 347
Article 298	Article 348
Article 299, paragraph 1 (repealed) [70]	
Article 299, paragraph 2, second, third and fourth subparagraphs	Article 349
Article 299, paragraph 2, first subparagraph, and paragraphs 3 to 6 (moved)	Article 355
Article 300 (replaced)	Article 218
Article 301 (replaced)	Article 215
Article 302 (replaced)	Article 220
Article 303 (replaced)	Article 220
Article 304 (replaced)	Article 220
Article 305 (repealed)	

(68) Replaced, in substance, by Article 47 TEU.
(69) Replaced, in substance by Article 52 TEU.
(70) Replaced, in substance by Article 51 TEU.

(*continued*)

Treaty on the Functioning of the European Union (*continued*)

Article 306	Article 350
Article 307	Article 351
Article 308	Article 352
	Article 353
Article 309	Article 354
Article 310 (moved)	Article 217
Article 311 (repealed) [71]	
Article 299, paragraph 2,first subparagraph, and paragraphs 3 to 6 (moved)	Article 355
Article 312	Article 356
Final Provisions	
Article 313	Article 357
	Article 358
Article 314 (repealed) [72]	

Source: © European Union, 1995–2014.

(71) Replaced, in substance by Article 55 TEU.
(72) Replaced, in substance by Article 55 TEU.

Table of European Union Regulations

Table of European Union Directives

Table of European Union Decisions

International Legislation

UK Legislation

1 The history and development of the European Union

Setting the scene

In 2011, Greece, a long-term member of the European Union and the single European currency (the Eurozone) was on the verge of bankruptcy. After many long, heated and controversial debates at 'Euro-rescue-summits', the EU and the European Central Bank agreed a rescue plan to 'bail out' Greece. Under the plan, Greece was relieved of a debt in the region of 200 million euros but in turn would have to drastically cut public spending by removing jobs and public services as well as increasing taxes. On 1 November 2011 the Greek Prime Minister, Papandreou, announced that the bail-out plan would be put to a national referendum, allowing the Greek people to agree to the austerity measures to be imposed upon them. The EU leaders reacted with horror; under pressure from France and Germany, Papandreou cancelled the referendum on 4 November 2011. He subsequently resigned.

1. Introduction

European integration is not *per se* an anti-poverty project, yet poverty – both individual and social – was one problem to which integration was the answer. It is hard to imagine the desolate and desperate conditions that prevailed throughout Europe after the Second World War. Even in the countries that won the war, millions of people were hungry and homeless, with no means to provide for themselves or their dependants. In Britain, basic commodities were in such short supply that rationing had to be introduced after the war. Movement was difficult as roads and railway networks were largely destroyed. The need to address this devastation was one major reason why, five years after the end of the war, on 6 May 1950,[1] six European nations – France, West Germany, Italy, Belgium, the Netherlands and Luxembourg – signed an agreement to pool coal and steel resources in a new organisation: the European Coal and Steel Community (ECSC). It has been said that the journey towards 'an ever closer union' between the peoples of Europe began on that day.

The Greek bail-out indicates both how far European integration has travelled and also the limits of European integration. The distrust and resentment, especially between Greece and Germany, that emerged during the Eurozone crisis threatened to split the EU. However, both the EU and the euro survived the crisis, suggesting that after just six decades of cooperation a solid foundation underpins EU integration. For all the posturing and controversies, there is a commitment to this process.

This chapter will explore why this is so. It will provide a background to European integration, from the creation of the ECSC and the European Economic Community (EEC or the 'Community') to its evolution into the present day European Union (EU). There is much that has been and can be said on this topic but I have chosen to focus on three things: first, patterns of post-war regional cooperation, of which the EEC was just one example; second, the enlargement of the EEC, which saw it grow from six members in 1957 to an EU of 28 member states in 2013; and third, the process of Treaty reform and development from the Treaty of Rome in 1957 to the Treaty of Lisbon in 2009.

2. Post-war regional cooperation: from the CEEC to the EEC

The nation state has been the dominant form of political, economic and social organisation in Western Europe since the sixteenth century. However, the Second World War demonstrated the dangers and limits of the nation state – the violence and mass destruction carried out in its name between 1939 and 1945 undermined the legitimacy of this organisational form. To many the nation state represented a failed form: it had failed to defend or protect its citizens and had repeatedly brought about war rather than stability. What was its use? In particular, what was its future – could it sustain peace in Europe, especially when the Allied occupation of Germany and management of the German economy came to an end? The evidence suggested that the nation state endangered rather than sustained peace.

In order to secure peace a more cooperative form of political organisation that prioritised mutual cooperation instead of national self-interest was needed. Thus regional cooperation became an answer to practical and pressing social, economic and geopolitical issues.

---

[1]Since the Milan Summit in 1985, 9 May is celebrated as 'Europe Day'.

It was a means to reconstruct the European continent. It did not signify the disappearance of the nation state. On the contrary, it has been convincingly argued that regional cooperation 'rescued' the nation state. Milward argues that the EEC and the process of European integration, was:

> A part of that post-war rescue of the European nation state, because the new political consensus on which this rescue was built required the process of integration, the surrender of limited areas of national sovereignty to the supranation.[2]

Regional cooperation was not a unique answer: it was not and is not confined to Europe,[3] and the European Coal and Steel Community (ECSC) created by the Treaty of Paris in 1950[4] was just one of many international organisations created to coordinate reconstruction and growth of sovereign nation states. For example, it was preceded in 1947 by the Committee of European Economic Cooperation (CEEC) and in 1948 by the Organisation of European Economic Cooperation (OEEC). These three organisations illustrate the different levels of cooperation that existed at the time to promote regional reconstruction. Together, they paved the way to the EEC.

i.   The CEEC

The Committee of European Economic Cooperation (CEEC) was created in 1947 with a single goal: to coordinate the requests of all countries seeking financial aid from the United States offered under the Marshall Plan. The Marshall Plan was a package of aid from the United States to Europe, announced in June 1947, on the eve of the beginning of the Cold War. It was designed to enable Europe to revive a working economy 'so as to permit the emergence of political and social conditions in which free institutions can exist'.[5] However, the United States gained as well – European unity was also a route to transfer US goods, political organisation, production methods and consumer behaviour to Europe.[6] Much of the money went 'back to the United States for the purchase of food, raw materials and capital goods' thereby stimulating the US economy as well as European recovery.[7]

Participation in CEEC was international – it included the neutral countries of the Second World War (Ireland, Sweden and Switzerland) as well as Austria, Britain, France, Belgium, the Netherlands and Luxembourg, Italy and Portugal, Greece, Turkey, Denmark, Norway and Iceland.[8] Eastern European countries, including the Soviet Union, were also invited to join, and the Czech Republic initially accepted but later withdrew

---

[2]Alan Milward, *The European Rescue of the Nation State*, Routledge, 2nd edn, 2000, pp. 3–4
[3]The CMEA (1949) comprised Bulgaria, Czechoslovakia, the GDR, Hungary, Poland, Romania and the USSR, Mongolia, Cuba and Vietnam; in West Africa the UDEAC comprised Zaire, Gabon, Cameroon and the Central African Republic; the CEAO (1973) comprised Cote D'Ivoire, Mali, Mauritania, Niger, Senegal, Burkina Faso and Benin; in South Africa SACU (1969) comprised Botswana, Lesotho, Swaziland and South Africa. See Ali M. El-Agraa (ed), *The European Union: History, Institutions, Economics and Policies*, 5th edn, Prentice Hall Europe, 1998, p. 7
[4]The Treaty of Paris had a lifespan of 50 years; the Treaty of Rome was left open-ended.
[5]See John Killick, *The United States and European Reconstruction 1945-1960*, Keele University Press, 1997, Chapter 8, p. 81
[6]Killick 1997, p. 167; Derek H. Aldcroft and Anthony Sutcliffe (eds), *Europe in the International Economy: 1500-2000*, Edward Elgar, 1999, p. 188
[7]John Kenneth Galbraith, *The World Economy Since the Wars: A Personal View*, Sinclair-Stevenson, 1994, p. 160
[8]Henry Pelling, *Britain and The Marshall Plan*, MacMillan Press, 1988, pp. 12–16

when the Soviet Union declined to join.[9] The CEEC was an international organisation that existed solely to facilitate cooperation and did not affect the sovereignty of each participating state. Each nation formulated its own goals for recovery which were compiled in a single combined aid bill submitted to the United States via the CEEC.

ii. The OEEC

Another new international organisation, the Organisation of European Economic Cooperation (OEEC)[10] was created in 1948 to distribute the Marshall Plan aid[11] and supervise a programme of trade liberalisation.[12] Like the CEEC, the OEEC focused on coordination: before receiving aid, each member country was required to sign an individual Letter of Intent and a Bilateral Agreement containing various reciprocal obligations.[13] The OEEC did not impinge upon national autonomy which may explain why so many states were keen to join it, yet so few sought to join the ECSC. The OEEC was especially important for West Germany: it was the only international organisation on which it sat as a full member and interacted on a basis of equality.[14] International cooperation generated a great deal of optimism and hope for the future during an otherwise bleak period. An article in the London *Times* noted in 1949 that:

> When the cooperative efforts of the last year are contrasted with the intense economic nationalism of the inter-war years, it is surely permissible to suggest that the Marshall Plan is initiating a new and hopeful era in European history.[15]

iii. The ECSC

It was the level of coordination that made the ECSC different. The Schuman Plan, upon which the ECSC was based, was the vision of Jean Monnet, a French minister who had spent time in the United States and was deeply influenced by US federalism.[16] The idea of a 'United States of Europe', where governmental power was distributed between different levels of political administration, was Monnet's brainchild. The Schuman Plan provided for a coal and steel community under the control of a 'High Authority', that is a 'supranational' body which would be independent of member governments yet take decisions that would be binding upon the member governments. The High Authority would have power over prices, investment, cartels, external tariffs, taxation, transport and labour. Thus unlike the intergovernmental coordination that characterised the CEEC and OEEC, the ECSC would affect the sovereignty of the participating states by acting on a supranational basis beyond the nation state.

---

[9]Paul Kapteyn, *The Stateless Market: The European Dilemma of Integration and Civilisation,* Routledge, 1996, p. 51
[10]Paul Henri Spaak, PM of Belgium, was its first Chair. It is now known as the Organisation for Economic Cooperation and Development (OECD) and focuses on global liberalisation.
[11]It also streamlined and screened future annual requests. Pelling 1988, p. 53; Aldcroft and Sutcliffe 1999, p. 187
[12]Milward 2000, p. 132
[13]Pelling 1988, p. 34
[14]Pelling 1988, p. 107
[15]Pelling 1988, p. 54. See also pp. 103–105. American disappointment gave rise to plans to establish a European defence organisation, which ultimately failed due to French refusal of German rearmament.
[16]Killick 1997, p. 143. The speech that Schuman read was written by Monnet (Gillingham 2003, p. 22).

The ECSC was an unprecedented experiment.[17] Its key supranational element, the proposed High Authority, prompted a variety of reactions. The ECSC was similar to the Benelux customs union created by Belgium, the Netherlands and Luxembourg in 1948,[18] thus these countries, together with Germany and Italy, accepted the proposal despite not surrendering all national sovereignty.[19] Outright opposition was voiced by Britain, the Scandinavian countries, the Swiss and the Portuguese.[20] Britain was twice invited to join the ECSC (in 1950 and 1953) but declined.

Ultimately, the ECSC had limited success in taking Europe beyond traditional inter-governmentalism – the High Authority was unable to exercise the powers conferred on it: 'it could annoy, harass, and threaten but it lacked the enforcement machinery to inflict much real pain. Supranationalism in practice was a paper tiger.'[21] This may be because by the time it was created, it was seen to address a 'non-problem':[22] the Franco-German conflict over European coal and steel had reduced and these products had lost their strategic importance due to cheap coal imports from the United States and oil from the Middle East.

Nonetheless, the ECSC brought about important transformations in terms of political relationships and models of regional economic organisation. First, it continued the rehabilitation of West Germany in European affairs: there was no repeat of its 'pariah' status suffered after the First World War. On the contrary, West German participation was crucial – it was 'the core of the system' and 'quickly became the most important supplier and also the most important market for most other western European countries' with all other countries exporting more to West Germany than anywhere else.[23] Yet West Germany exported more to the rest of the world than to its neighbours. Germany continues to be the strongest economy in the EU.

Second, the ECSC established the idea of common markets, integration and independent international bodies in the public mind[24] and so was an important precursor to the EEC. Nonetheless, the EEC was so radical that it stimulated competition in the organisation of regional cooperation – our discussion will now turn to EFTA, which was created in 1960 to challenge it.

Iv. The EEC and EFTA

It should by now be clear that there is no single model for regional cooperation: it can include or exclude anything that participants agree to accept. Political cooperation can be intergovernmental or supranational or have elements of both. The scope of economic cooperation can include primary products alone (raw materials, energy, agricultural produce) or manufactured products (such as toys, cars, mobile phones, computers) or both.

---

[17]Bruno de Witte 'The European Union as an International Legal Experiment', in de Burca and Weiler (eds) *The Worlds of European Constitutionalism,* Cambridge University Press, 2011

[18]Aldcroft and Sutcliffe 1999, p. 205

[19]Belgian Foreign Minister Paul van Zeeland disagreed with Monnet on the level of national autonomy that had to be relinquished to regulate coal. Milward, 2000, p. 65; Gillingham, *European Integration 1950–2003: superstate or new market economy?,* Cambridge University Press 2003, p. 27.

[20]Pelling, p. 126

[21]Gillingham 2003, p32

[22]Gillingham 2003, p. 23

[23]Milward 2000, pp. 134-135

[24]Gillingham 2003, p. 26

The EEC was a more ambitious form of regional organisation: it took regional cooperation to a new level by both expanding the scope of activity beyond raw materials and deepening the political ties between cooperating states. It included a customs duty as well as the creation of a 'common market' in a range of sectors including agriculture, goods, services, transport and capital.

The aims of the EEC were predominantly economic. They included the elimination of customs duties and quantitative restrictions on imported and exported goods; the establishment of a common customs tariff and common commercial policy; the achievement of free movement for persons, services and capital; the adoption of common agricultural policy (CAP), common transport policy, common competition policy; coordination of economic policies and legal harmonisation; and the creation of the European Investment Bank. Just two social goals were listed: the creation of a European Social Fund and promotion of economic and social development overseas.[25]

Having formed their own customs union 10 years earlier, the Benelux countries had few issues with the EEC customs union. This simply meant that products would not be taxed when crossing borders of those within the union. France, however, feared a customs union would flood the country with foreign products and reduce it to a 'European backwater'. France agreed to the removal of protections of industrial products in return for its preferences being met in agricultural policy[26] – the EEC incorporated the French agricultural policy of high import duties and high export subsidies. Under the controversial Common Agricultural Policy (CAP) – 'the giveaway programme for farmers'[27] – farming and related activities were protected and the costs of this protection were shared. Germany was prepared to pay for this because in return it gained an internal market for its thriving industry.[28]

The 'common market' was to be created by the 'removal' of borders. Economic integration can proceed using one of two methods: a) the removal of borders and the setting of a single standard, or b) reducing the impact of borders so that there is equal treatment despite different standards. Removal of the border means that the same rights are enjoyed throughout the market area: rights are equal because they are the same. Ignoring the border retains distinctive national rights (as territorial rights) but allowing non-nationals to have equal access to these rights and therefore enjoy the same rights.[29] The EEC common market envisaged in the 1957 Treaty of Rome was therefore more controversial than the ECSC. Rather than just reject it, in 1960 the opponents of the EEC actually created another organisation to compete with it – the European Free Trade Association (EFTA).

The key organiser of EFTA was Britain. Although Britain rejected the invitation to join the EEC, it did recognise the benefits of economic integration. However, for Britain, economic coordination needed to be organised in a way which did not disturb its interests in the larger Commonwealth and position in the world.[30] The problem lay in both the scope and method of coordination. It preferred coordination which focused on

---

[25]Article 3 EC (Treaty of Rome). Compare with the goals listed in Article 3 TEU.

[26]Kapteyn 1996, p. 56. The agricultural vote was especially important in France, where 30 per cent of the active labour force (7.5 million persons) worked on the land. Milward 2000, p. 244, citing M. Pierre Pflimlin.

[27]Gillingham 2003, p. 81

[28]Kapteyn 1996, p. 57

[29]F.V. Meyer *The Seven: A Provision Appraisal of the European Free Trade Association*, Barrie and Rockliff with Pall Mall Press, 1960, p. 3

[30]Ali M. El-Agraa (ed) *The European Union: History, Institutions, Economics and Policies,* 5th edn, Prentice Hall Europe, 1998, p. 6

manufactured goods only – a common policy for agriculture (as seen above a fundamental interest for France), was out of the question – and a looser form of cooperation that ignored borders instead of removing them.

Britain therefore proposed an alternative free trade area to rival the EEC. This idea did garner support from most OEEC members, but talks stalled over the issue of agriculture. Nonetheless, in 1960 seven OEEC countries – Austria, Denmark, Norway, Portugal, Sweden, Switzerland and the United Kingdom – signed the Convention of Stockholm to create a separate community for free trade in manufactured goods alone, thus creating the European Free Trade Association.[31] EFTA focused on the removal of tariffs, quotas and export duties – it was a scheme of 'mutual non-annoyance'.[32] 'Mutual non-annoyance' means that states *reduce* the relevance and impact of the border; by removing rules that annoy, especially tariffs and fees pushing up product prices, states can cooperate with each other for mutual benefit. However, 'mutual non-annoyance' does not *remove* the national frontier, nor require any harmonisation of standards and policies.

EFTA met the disparate needs of its members: Britain was able to maintain its leadership position in Europe; Austria and Switzerland were able to participate in trade liberalisation without threat to their neutrality or sovereignty; and Portugal, Denmark, Norway and Sweden gained a more flexible structure for their existing trade relations with Britain.[33] Unlike the EEC, it had no broad economic or political goals. Entry was voluntary and Article 42 of the Stockholm Convention provided for withdrawal – such a provision was absent from the EU until the Treaty of Lisbon in 2009. The Stockholm Convention created only one institution, a Council comprising representatives of each member state. Unanimity was required for action. Its purpose was more limited and interaction more informal than the EEC. It was so successful that it became a competitor to the EEC.[34]

Yet, by 1963, competition between the EEC Six and EFTA Seven was crumbling: Britain – the nucleus of EFTA – had applied to join the EEC along with two other EFTA members – Denmark and Ireland. Why did membership of the EEC became desirable – what can explain this development? Why did those countries that originally shunned membership then seek it? Why did the former Soviet-nations also want to become part of this 'club' after 1989?

These questions will be answered in more detail in the section on enlargement but one general explanation could be that internationalisation is an unavoidable evolution of a capitalist market trading system: it is inevitable that products will be traded across national frontiers and enterprises will span those frontiers. This gives birth to the 'transnational' or international corporation: such global entities will have limited identification with any one country or government and their activities will require rules that span nation states. As a consequence, national identities and passions will diminish along with national tensions. The transnational corporation will in its own interests promote friendship between nations and encourage 'freedom of movement of people, components and products. Communications, travel, finance, add to the sense of association.'[35]

---

[31]Finland joined in 1961, Iceland in 1970.
[32]Meyer 1960, p. 45
[33]Christopher Preston, *Enlargement and Integration in the European Union,* Routledge/UACES, 1997, p. 26
[34]Gillingham 2003, Chapter 3
[35]Galbraith 1994, pp. 167-168

The strong and persistent Eurosceptic sentiments expressed across Europe during the European Parliament (EP) elections of May 2014 may undermine this theory. Passions associated with the nation state remain strong. Economies may have become interdependent across borders but the EU, as argued by Milward, has not made the nation state meaningless. Likewise the eurozone crisis of 2008 provides a clear illustration that European integration does not travel along 'an unavoidable linear continuum'[36] propelled by increasing international contact and familiarity: when the Greek economy failed, Germans rejected the idea that their taxes should bail out Greece and the Greeks resented the economic high-handedness of Germany.

As will be seen in the following section, there is no single answer to explain why countries join this political edifice – each has its own reasons and illustrate that accession is a choice rather than a submission to the inevitable. Accession also does not dampen national self-interest – in fact, for the majority of its existence, integration has been rejected either by the member states (using the national veto from 1965–86) or their citizens (via Treaty rejections in 1992, 2004 and 2007).

VIEWPOINT

Which form of regional cooperation do you think is most a) useful and b) sustainable?

3. Enlargement of the EEC and the EU

Territorial expansion was integral to the integration agenda – without new nations joining, there could be no large common market. The six founders made it clear that the new EEC was open to members: the preamble called upon other peoples of Europe who shared their ideals to join their efforts, while Article 271 TFEU stated that 'any European state may apply to become a member of the Community'. And join they did, even though by the time of the first accession in 1973, the judicial doctrines of supremacy and direct effect had made it clear that the EEC was much more than a traditional intergovernmental organisation like, for example, the United Nations.

As a result of the constantly evolving characteristics of the European polity, each joining state enters a slightly different entity. Entry has never been automatic – Britain, Ireland and Denmark are the only countries to have been explicitly rejected, Turkey the only applicant not to have been fully accepted. The Norwegians and the Swiss are the only countries to refuse membership.[37] Also, states which join together rarely apply together. Britain finally joined in 1973, together with Ireland and Denmark, at a time when the foundations of the EEC legal system were being consolidated; Greece joined in 1981, following the collapse of its dictatorship; Spain and Portugal followed in 1986, just as a new period of integration was beginning; Finland, Austria and Sweden joined in 1994, after 'completion' of the Single Market, creation of the European Union and European Citizenship; following a long period of preparation in 2004, 10 countries – Cyprus and Malta plus eight former members of the USSR (the Czech Republic, Hungary, Estonia, Latvia, Lithuania, Poland, Slovakia and Slovenia) – joined during the phase of

---

[36]Milward 2000, p. 6
[37]The Swiss rejected membership of the EEA in 1992. Morocco's application was rejected in 1987 on the grounds that it is not a European country.

Constitutional Europe; and, just before the global financial meltdown, in 2007 Romania and Bulgaria brought the number up to 27. The last two rounds of growth have occurred during a period where political union has been resolutely rejected by the peoples of Europe. Finally, Croatia joined in 2013 bringing the membership to 28.[38]

This expansion has been both triggered and accompanied by seismic political changes within Europe but outside the EU. The oil crisis of 1973, for instance, 'reminded western Europe of its common interest',[39] while the political regimes in the Mediterranean and the USSR forced it to respond to the collapse of military dictatorships in southern Europe during the 1970s and the collapse of communism in Eastern Europe in the late 1980s and 90s. Enlargement has also established the EU – paradoxically given its own non-democratic origins – as the guarantor of democracy in Europe. For countries in these regions, membership was also a reinvention: joining guaranteed a liberal democratic future. As the EU has grown, it has also rebranded itself, shedding the skin of an elite political club to become a protector of liberal democratic values in Europe.

i.   The abandonment of EFTA: Britain, Ireland and Denmark

In the 1950s, Britain believed that it could recover economically via trading relationships with the former colonies in Africa, Asia and the Caribbean in the Commonwealth. Britain refused to join the ECSC and the EEC. When invited to Messina in 1955, it sent a lower rated 'representative' rather than a 'delegate' and withdrew from the talks by the end of the year.[40] In 1960, it established EFTA, which was a partnership based on trade autonomy rather than harmonisation.[41] At that time, British living standards were still the highest in Europe. However, this decade also brought with it the beginning of the decline.

The decision to join the EEC was the beginning of 'a process of reassessment and readjustment'[42] of its relationships with the Commonwealth, the United States and Europe. Already in 1957, Ghana had successfully gained its independence from Britain: other colonies rapidly followed suit and by the mid-1960s most were free of overseas rule. US support under Kennedy for the EEC also indicated a weakening of the 'special' Anglo-American relationship. Membership of the EEC was a strategy to reverse declining British influence in world affairs.

Yet this was not straightforward. Due to their close trade links, Ireland, Denmark and Norway applied together with Britain. This first application in 1961 was robustly rejected by one member state: France. In 1963, President de Gaulle publicly expressed clear doubts about Britain's ability to play a full role in the Community:

> England in effect is insular, she is maritime. She is linked through her exchanges, her markets, her supply lines to the most diverse and, often, the most distant countries. She pursues essentially industrial and commercial activities, and only slight agricultural ones. She has in all her doings very marked and very original habits and traditions. In short, the very nature, the structure, the very situation that are England's differ profoundly from most of the Continental's.[43]

---

[38]At time of writing, applications to join the EU had been received from Albania, Iceland, Macedonia, Montenegro, Serbia and Turkey who are considered to be 'on the road' to membership.
[39]Aldcroft and Sutcliffe 1999, p. 212
[40]Preston 1997, p. 25
[41]Preston 1997, p. 26
[42]Aldcroft and Sutcliffe 1999, p. 194
[43]Preston 1997, p. 29

These are wide-ranging objections and may have masked an unexpressed fear that British entry would help the United States exert influence in the Community to the detriment of France.

Britain's fortunes continued to decline, leading to another application in 1967. It was vetoed again by de Gaulle, this time on the basis of Britain's poor economic condition. If de Gaulle had not resigned in 1969, and been replaced by Georges Pompidou who was more amenable to British entry, it is debatable when Britain would have joined the EEC. At the Hague Summit in December 1969 it was agreed to commence accession talks with the four applicant countries. Negotiations were concluded by 1971 and, after a last-minute disagreement on the Common Fisheries Policy (CFP), an Accession Treaty was signed in January 1972 for activation 12 months later. Of the four applicants, only Norway failed to join – the arrangements for agriculture and fisheries were strongly opposed and when asked in a referendum about ratification of the Accession Treaty, 53.5 per cent of Norwegians voted 'no'.[44] Norway's rejection was the first time that the voice of citizens had determined European integration.

What of the remaining EFTA members? Four of them followed Britain to join the EEC – Portugal in 1986 and Austria, Finland and Sweden in 1994. As the latter three were politically and economically stable, and through ties with EFTA already had open economies, their accession raised relatively few concerns. The Norwegians were again offered the option of membership in 1992 and again refused – albeit by a fractionally smaller majority (52.3 per cent). The CFP continued to be an issue and the newly created European Union citizenship raised concerns for Norwegian identity. The Swiss declined due to concerns with neutrality and sovereignty. Iceland remained outside of European integration, but following its financial meltdown submitted an application for membership in July 2009.[45] Iceland and Norway nonetheless enjoy the benefits of EU membership as they are part of the European Economic Area (EEA), a separate organisation which includes the 28 EU member states and Liechtenstein.

ii. The escape from dictatorships: Greece, Spain and Portugal

Greece had signed an Association Agreement with the EEC in July 1961. This was, however, frozen after the military coup in April 1967. Following the Turkish occupation of Cyprus in 1974, the dictatorship collapsed. Full Community membership was seen as a way for Greece to strengthen its 'Western political orientation whilst distancing itself from the US'.[46] Accession was therefore part of a strategy for national reorientation. A formal application was submitted in June 1975, but Greek enthusiasm was met with a lukewarm reaction in the EEC: this was due to the situation in Cyprus and also because the Community had in 1964 signed an Association Agreement with Turkey.[47] While the two nations had identical status the delicate balance could be maintained: Greek accession would upset this balance. The Commission ultimately said 'not yet'. Delay was, however, rejected by the Council of Ministers and negotiations were opened in July 1976. The final Accession Conference convened in May 1979, and Greece became a member in

---

[44]Preston 1997, p. 44

[45]Accession negotiations started in July 2010 but were put on hold by the Icelandic government in May 2013.

[46]Preston 1997, p. 49

[47]Turkey applied for full membership in 1987. Preston 1997, p. 215

January 1981. In total, the Greek accession took about 3 years, a short period when compared with the 12 years of the first enlargement and 10 years of the CEECs.[48]

Spain had also signed an Association Agreement with the EEC in 1970 but under Franco's rule was largely isolated from trade liberalisation. The Spanish socialists saw membership of the EEC as key to national political self-respect,[49] as the route to modernisation and democratisation, away from the 'anti-European Hispanidad so beloved by Francoism' and the traditionalism that characterised his rule. Spain embraced the Community[50] and following Franco's death in November 1975, resumed trade relations with it in 1976, becoming a member in 1981. European integration remains popular: in 2002, Spain was the most Eurocentric country after Italy and Luxembourg – 77 per cent of Spanish voters approved of the Constitution.[51]

Likewise, the Salazar and Caetano dictatorships effectively isolated Portugal until the 'Red Carnation' revolution of 1974.[52] Political stability did not return until 1976. As a member of EFTA since 1960, Portugal enjoyed trade links with Britain and benefited from a Special Relations Agreement with the EEC. An application for membership was submitted in March 1977. As with Greece, EEC membership was ultimately to become a guarantee of domestic democratic stability,[53] although the Communist Party saw membership as a luxury.

Greece, Spain and Portugal benefited from a positive Community response to their applications, even though their membership required significant financial transfers which had not arisen during the previous enlargements. With the SEA underway as they joined, they also gained from being at the table during negotiations. As with Ireland, Greece, Spain and Portugal were designated 'Objective 1' areas in the regional policy, making them eligible to receive significant funds from the Community. By 1987, these four countries recorded annual growth of 2.87 per cent, higher than the EEC average.[54] As mentioned above, in 2011 Greece benefited from the largest direct financial transfer in the history of EU integration – the Eurozone members essentially created a 'Marshall Plan' for Greece.

iii. The escape from communism: Central and Eastern European accession

The response was more conditional following the collapse of communism in Eastern Europe, by which time the European Union had been created. When the barbed-wire border between Hungary and Austria was dismantled on 2 May 1989, the communist regimes in central and Eastern Europe – Poland, Hungary, East Germany, Czechoslovakia, Bulgaria and Romania – quickly collapsed. By 1991, both the Iron Curtain and the Berlin

---

[48]Preston 1997, Chapter 3

[49]Preston 1998, p. 85

[50]Sebastian Balfour and Alejandro Quiroga, *The Reinvention of Spain: Nation and Identity Since Democracy*, Oxford University Press, 2007, pp. 82-83

[51]Balfour and Quiroga 2007, p. 162

[52]Preston 1998, p. 65

[53]Preston, 1998, pp. 68-69

[54]'The Single Market and Tomorrow's Europe: A Progress Report from the European Commission', Office for Official Publications of the European Communities (OOPEC), 1996, p. 110

Wall were gone: the Soviet Union had disintegrated and the two halves of Germany had been reunified:

> borders which had been set in stone by the Yalta and Potsdam Treaties after the Second World War suddenly became changeable. The geo-political order based on bloc logic was ended, and the multi-national states in which ideological orientation had served as a basis for cohesion (the USSR, Yugoslavia and CSSR) disintegrated.[55]

The fall of the Iron Curtain brought conflict back to European soil: in 1990 war broke out in Yugoslavia. By 1995, nine communist countries[56] had mushroomed into 27 sovereign states.[57] For these fledgling states, membership of the EU – synonymous with democracy and market liberalisation – became the key foreign policy goal.

The immediate reaction of the EU was ad hoc and hesitant.[58] Europe was uncertain how to respond and controversially, shied away from a home-grown 'Marshall Plan' to finance the costly reconstruction of Eastern Europe.[59] Piecemeal aid and technical support was extended via specific EU programmes but it was only in 1999 that a long-term strategy was announced with the publication of the Stability Pact. In the Sarajevo Summit Declaration, the EU member states reaffirmed their responsibility to 'build a Europe that is at long last undivided, democratic and at peace' and promised to 'work together to promote the integration of South Eastern Europe into a continent where borders remain inviolable but no longer denote division and offer the opportunity of contact and cooperation'. However, entry into the EU was not going to happen in a hurry to those seeking 'integration into Euro-Atlantic structures' – the Summit gave only a lukewarm commitment to make 'every effort to assist them to make speedy and measurable progress along this road'. Far stronger was the desire for regional cooperation: 'it is our strong wish that all the countries of the region work together in a spirit of cohesion and solidarity through the Stability Pact to build a common, prosperous and secure future.'[60]

This lukewarm response to the enthusiastic candidates may explain the extended and intrusive accession process. Admission was harder: conditions were higher and more approvals required. The Treaty on European Union (TEU) inserted a new clause on accession to the EU.[61] The EU also developed mechanisms of 'passive' and 'active' leverage to entice applicants and exercise control.[62] Passive levers included the political and economic benefits of membership as opposed to the costs of exclusion. Active levers were laid out in the pre-accession process: these included political, economic, legal and administrative[63] conditions.[64] Implementation of administrative reform became a priority at Gothenburg

---

[55]Brigitta Busch and Michal Krzyzanowski, 'Inside/Outside the European Union', in Warwick Armstrong and James Anderson (eds) *Geopolitics of European Union Enlargement: the fortress empire,* Routledge, 2007, p. 108

[56]Poland, Hungary, East Germany, Czechoslovakia, Bulgaria and Romania, the Soviet Union, Albania and Yugoslavia

[57]Milada Anna Vachudova, *Europe Undivided,* Oxford University Press, 2005, p. 1

[58]Mary Farrell, 'The EU and inter-regional cooperation', in Erik Jones and Amy Verdun (eds) *The Political Economy of European Integration: theory and analysis,* Routledge, 2005, p. 141

[59]Estimates varied from 27 to 63.5 billion ecus (15–25 per cent of the total EU budget). Gillingham 2003, p. 414

[60]Sarajevo Summit Declaration at http://www.stabilitypact.org/constituent/990730-sarajevo.asp

[61]According to Article 49, any European state that respected fundamental and human rights could become a member of the Union. In order to do so, it needed to apply to the Council of Ministers, which would decide by unanimous vote after consulting the Commission and receiving the assent of the European Parliament.

[62]Vachudova 2005, p. 63

[63]Added at Madrid in 1995.

[64]The Copenhagen Criteria. Online at http://www.consilium.europa.eu/ueDocs/cms_Data/docs/pressData/en/ec/72921.pdf

in 2001. These criteria have become powerful tools for 'europeanisation'[65] – the adoption of EU values and rules – in central and Eastern Europe.[66] They illustrate the growing concern about effective implementation of EU rules by new member states.

The accession process is described in terms of partnership but in reality the Commission and the Council decide the terms and the pace of progress towards full membership. This is illustrated by the experience of Croatia. In 2002, the country declared that full membership of the EU was a basic foreign policy aim. It applied in 2003, and hoped that its application would be fast tracked, enabling it to join in 2004. Despite an internal cross-parliamentary consensus and high popular support (70 per cent of Croatians were in favour), and support from a range of member states including Ireland, Belgium, the Netherlands and Britain, this timetable was not achieved. Concerns existed as to the pace of reforms to administrative and judicial systems and the question of cooperation with the UN International Criminal Tribunal on Former Yugoslavia (ICTY). Ultimately, Bulgaria and Romania, where opposition to communism had been weak,[67] joined before Croatia. Croatia became a full member in July 2013.

Vachudova describes enlargement as the EU's 'best foreign policy tool'.[68] However, the large number of new entrants crystallised looming problems concerning values, institutions and policy. The 2004 enlargement in particular raised the issue of the existing structures and forced the question of institutional change. In becoming the target of hopes for democracy in these regions, the EEC itself was forced to become more democratic. Enlargement posed challenges to which the EEC could only respond by changing itself, while the accession negotiations triggered a 'mutual adjustment process'.[69] The way in which the EU changed will be discussed in the next section.

VIEWPOINT

What do you think are the key reasons for joining the EU?

---

4. From the Treaty of Rome to the Treaty of Lisbon

The Treaty of Rome was the primary source of Community (now Union) law thus any change to the Treaty changes the law upon which the European Union acts and adopts legislation. The Treaty was first changed in 1986 and most recently in 2009. A new Treaty, creating a new structure and introducing new powers was agreed in 1992 – this Treaty created the European Union and EU law. EU law is now the term used for all law related to the European Union. The European Economic Community or European Community no longer exist. This section will set out the key moments of Treaty reform since 1986.

Treaty reform is a long and labour-intensive affair. Although the Treaty changes are formally agreed by Heads of State at a two- or three-day lavish Summit, known as an

---

[65]Frank Schimmelfennig and Ulrich Sedelmeier (eds) *The Europeanisation of Central and Eastern Europe*, Cornell University Press, 2005
[66]See for example the 'Communication from the Commission – Commission Opinion on the application from the former Yugoslav Republic of Macedonia for membership of the European Union' (COM/2005/0562 final)
[67]Vachudova 2005, p. 39
[68]Vachudova 2005, p. 247
[69]Preston 1998, p. 86

Intergovernmental Conference, they are thrashed out by diplomats and civil servants in negotiations that take place in the preceding year or years. The hard work, however, does not end when a compromise is reached – a Treaty agreed in Maastricht, Nice or Lisbon must then be sent back to the member states for ratification. Some member states are constitutionally required to hold a referendum and as history has shown, European citizens are not averse to telling their leaders 'No thank you!' This happened most recently with the Lisbon Treaty. However, long before European citizens sent their leaders back to the drawing board, a member state (France) did this and in so doing, set the scene for the first major Treaty reform in 1986.

i.   De Gaulle says 'No' and the Luxembourg Compromise

The cooperation agreed in the text of the Treaty of Rome was immediately followed by refusals to cooperate in practice. Less than 10 years after the Treaty was signed, cooperation came to a grinding halt when, in 1965, President de Gaulle instructed the French delegation to walk out of the Council of Ministers. The reason was increasing supranationalism – the voting procedure in the Council of Ministers was set to change from unanimity (one member, one vote and one veto) to qualified majority voting (QMV) where no member would have a veto. Under majority voting, member states could be outvoted – an unwilling nation would be unable to prevent adoption of a proposal harmonising a policy field and its country would have to implement the policy. QMV means that any member state can be overruled in the adoption of a proposal. De Gaulle refused to accept this, frightened at what might be forced upon his nation. The French chair was left empty for seven months during which time the EEC could not adopt any measures. The French delegates did not return until each member state had been guaranteed a veto: the 'Luxembourg Compromise' of 1966 stated that:

> Where, in the case of decisions which may be taken by majority vote on a proposal of the Commission, very important interests of one or more partners are at stake, the Members of the Council will endeavour, within a reasonable time, to reach solutions which can be adopted by all the Members of the Council while respecting their mutual interests and those of the Community.[70]

Although as a political Declaration, it did not amend the Treaty and has no legally binding status,[71] the Luxembourg Compromise placed Community action firmly within the sphere of intergovernmental cooperation.[72]

This had at least three long term consequences. First, French behaviour indicated to Britain that the EEC was not on a fixed path to supranationalism – this may have encouraged Britain to apply again in 1969. Second, the French 'No' kept decision-making tied to the unanimity traditional to international organisations: every member state had a vote and

---

[70]http://europa.eu/scadplus/glossary/luxembourg_compromise_en.htm

[71]In Case 68/86 *UK* v *Council* [1988] ECR 855, the Court held that decision-making procedures in the Treaty 'are not at the disposal of the Member States or of the institutions themselves'. The ECJ held that the Member States or EU institutions may not adopt an ad hoc approach to these.

[72]Gilbert argues that de Gaulle made the EC 'grow up' – Gilbert, 'Narrating the Process: Questioning the Progressive Story of European Integration,' *JCMS* 46(3), 2008, pp. 641–662

could veto any action with which it did not agree. Unanimous voting significantly slowed the pace of plans for economic interdependence and 'many of the freedoms prescribed in the Treaty of Rome for capital, goods, services and people remained a dead letter.'[73] Autonomous action by the Commission was effectively curbed, and integration was arguably stalled for the next 20 years. Thus the Luxembourg Compromise immobilised the EEC at a time when trade around the world was becoming increasingly transnational. By 1986, the EEC had 12 members and a total population of 370 million people yet the common market remained underdeveloped and performed poorly compared to Japan and the USA, who were making inroads into important European industries such as cars and electronics.[74] It was to bring the Community back up to the level of its global competitors that the Single European Act was created in 1986. This was the third consequence of the Luxembourg Compromise.

ii. The Single European Act (1986)

The Single European Act was the first major revision to the Treaty of Rome. Industry was a major driver, encouraging the Commission to kick-start integration. Multinational companies were calling for removal of barriers – these hindered transnational trade and undermined their global competitiveness. Accelerated integration was needed as Europe would 'lose out in the competitive world economy if internal markets were not freed of the multitude of duties and control measures, and if these were not integrated . . . to form a single internal free market, similar to those in the United States and Japan'.[75] Technical barriers – such as different national rules on product specifications, labelling, health and safety – were an impediment, discouraging producers from selling goods abroad. The Commission produced a White Paper in 1985 to address this. The White Paper set out 282 directives and proposals necessary to complete the Common Market. It formed the basis of the Single European Act which aimed to create by 1992 an 'area without internal frontiers in which the free movement of goods, peoples, services and capital is assured'. The Common Market was renamed the Single Market.

Among its key proposals was a plan to replace unanimous voting with majority voting in almost every area of Community activity concerned with the single market. Extension of majority voting essentially enabled the Council to take binding decisions which might conflict with the preferences of a nation state – in other words, it acted as a supranational body.[76] This by-passed rather than removed the Luxembourg Compromise. The introduction of majority voting released decision-making and resulted in five years of frenzied activity: Regulations and Directives could be approved by the Council of Ministers at a significant pace. A second important innovation was the introduction of the 'cooperation' legislative procedure, which gave more power to the European Parliament in law-making. These changes simultaneously enhanced both the democratic and supranational character of Community legislation.

The single market programme can be described as harmonisation in a hurry: commercial behaviour in the Community had to catch up with the rest of the world. By 1993, most of the legislation needed to complete the single market had been passed.

---

[73]OOPEC 1996, p. 7

[74]Preston 1997, p. 147

[75]Kapteyn 1996, p. 63

[76]See Robert O. Keohane and Stanley Hoffman (eds), *The New European Community – Decision Making and Institutional Change,* Westview Press, 1991, p. 16

On 1 January 1993, customs checks on goods at borders were abolished: this alone reportedly saved importers and exporters billions per year. National deregulation and reregulation at the European level addressed the patchwork of technical standards in areas such as road transportation, telecommunications, and construction: between 1992 to 1994, 1,136 regulations and directives were passed (compared to just 315 from 1957–92).[77] The Toy Safety Directive, for example, freed toy manufacturers from having to satisfy a number of different national tests on their products. The final key element of the SEA was official incorporation of the principle of mutual recognition (see Chapter 13), reinforcing the *Cassis de Dijon*[78] judgment of the ECJ.

However, the haste in Brussels was not reflected in the member states. National regulators remained focused on protecting their own markets and citizens. From 1992 to 1994, when the single market was due to be complete, member states incorporated into national law just 430–470 new proposed national regulations.[79] Thus while the Community and commerce sought more opportunities to liberalise trade, national administrations sought to protect domestic jobs and tax revenue. Results were therefore limited. This tension between responding to globalisation and protecting national wealth is a constant companion to integration in Europe. The tension exists because European leaders are reluctant to relinquish traditional policy instruments[80] used to control the economy, such as state subsidies and public sector jobs. Completion of the single market raised several challenges: it exposed vulnerable economic sectors to transnational competition, restricted aids to industry, introduced competition to public services, increased professional mobility, and reduced tax income by increasing the ability of capital to flee.[81]

Sensitive issues, such as social and fiscal policy, were not included in the programme and remained subject to unanimity.[82] In addition, border checks on persons remained. These have proved to be enduring, especially in relation to those who do not 'look' European (because they have a different skin colour) or who do not have the citizenship of a member state.[83] The single market programme did not focus on citizens: it was also not designed to improve free movement of workers – the Community accepted that the mobile factor was capital rather than labour and that EU Social Funds made it possible to find a living at home rather than emigrate.[84] It can be argued that the direct beneficiaries of the 1986 single market programme were the companies of Europe rather than its peoples; persons only came to the fore in 1992 at Maastricht.

ANALYSING THE LAW

Did the Single European Act reduce the impact of the border or remove the border?

---

[77]Gillingham 2003, p. 240

[78]C-120/78 [1979] ECR 649, [1979] 3 CMLR 494

[79]OOPEC 1996, p. 29

[80]Kapteyn 1996, p. 64

[81]Gillingham 2003, p. 257

[82]Andrew Moravcsik, 'Negotiating the Single European Act', in Keohane and Hoffmann (eds), 1991, pp. 41–84

[83]Estimated to be 12.2 million in 1996, see OOPEC 1996, p. 121

[84]OOPEC 1996, p. 119

iii. The Treaty of Maastricht (1992) and the Danish 'No'

Just as the SEA was for business, the Treaty on European Union (TEU) signed at Maastricht, sought to engage citizens in the process of European integration. This meant addressing the social issues excluded from the SEA in 1986. Of the few Treaty provisions concerned with social policy, the strongest was Article 157 TFEU (Treaty on the Functioning of the European Union), which entrenched the traditional international labour law standard of equal pay between women and men.[85] This was developed via litigation at the Court of Justice. The Single European Act had included some social initiatives, such as vocational training and health and safety standards but these were unpopular with some member states (especially Britain) and so minimalist in orientation.

The idea of developing a stronger social element to the single market took clearer form in May 1988, when the President of the Commission, Jacques Delors, announced a plan to draw up a Social Charter. He stated that 'there can be no progress without economic progress, and no economic progress without social cohesion'. At its Summit meeting in Madrid in June 1989, the European Council stated that:

> In the course of construction of the single European market social aspects should be given the same importance as economic aspects and should accordingly be developed in a balanced fashion.

A step forward was taken that same year when at the Strasbourg Summit all member states – except Britain – adopted the Social Charter. The Charter had no legal force but was nonetheless an important political statement. It lay out areas which formed the basis of the social dimension: the improvement of living and working conditions, free movement of workers, the right to join trade unions, social protection, equal pay, freedom of association and collective bargaining, the right to information, consultation and participation, and vocational training.[86] However, the social dimension was double-edged: on the one hand it moved towards the creation of social protection but on the other it served economic needs of avoiding 'social dumping' which might hinder the operation of the market.[87] It was therefore designed to protect commerce as much as people.

These developments ran alongside the slow resurrection of the idea of a political union. At the Paris Summit of 1972, the Community had not only promised action in the social field but also set itself the ambitious objective to 'transform, before the end of this decade and in strict conformity with the treaties already concluded, all member states' relations into a European Union' which embraced economic and monetary union (EMU).'[88] Lord Ralf Dahrendorf,[89] a liberal federalist working as a European Commissioner, suggested that integration towards a political union should proceed from the bottom up, promoting participation in the development of a democratic Europe, rather than using the

---

[85]Ruth Nielsen and Erika Szyszczak, *The Social Dimension of the European Community*, 2nd edn, Handelshojskolens Forlag, 1993, p. 109

[86]Marie-Elisabeth Maes, *Building a People's Europe: 1992 and the Social Dimension*, Whurr Publishers, 1990, p. 4

[87]Nielsen and Szyszczak, 1993, p. 46

[88]Aldcroft and Sutcliffe 1999, p. 222

[89]Ralf Dahrendorf, *Plaeydoyer fuer die Europaeische Union*, Piper Verlag, 1973

top-down, elitist and bureaucratic model envisaged by Jean Monnet. Dahrendorf also argued for an 'a la carte' Europe where states participated by choice rather than coercion.

The plans dissipated until events in Eastern Europe after 1989 resurrected the appeal of political union. After the collapse of communism, the reunification of Germany became very likely. Worried again by the potential of its neighbour, President François Mitterand of France seized upon the idea of a European political union to anchor the more populous and powerful reunited German nation. Two intergovernmental conferences (IGC) were planned for December 1990, one to deal with monetary union, the other with political union and the social dimension. Agreement on these issues resulted in the 1992 Treaty on European Union (TEU), signed at Maastricht, the second major amendment to the original Treaty of Rome.

The TEU redefined and expanded Community competence in a wide range of areas including social and industrial policy, communications and energy networks, environmental and consumer protection, development aid, culture, health, education and training. Three major innovations were also launched at Maastricht. The first was financial – a phased timetable was laid out for the creation of the single European currency and the introduction of EMU as the major monetary system of the EU by January 1999. The second was structural: the Treaty on European Union created a new edifice – the European Union (EU) – which comprised three distinct 'pillars.' Each pillar contained a distinct set of policies. Pillar One housed the renamed 'European Community' – the original Community institutions and competences laid out in the Treaty of Rome; Pillar Two became the home of the new Common and Foreign Security Policy (CFSP); and all issues relating to Justice and Home Affairs (JHA) were placed in Pillar Three. Pillar One remained subject to Community rules and law-making procedures, Pillars Two and Three were not. These were domains in which the member states could negotiate and compromise free from any level of democratic scrutiny and beyond even the reach of the CJEU. Action in these Pillars dealing with issues of central importance to citizens' everyday lives – policing, cross-border crime, civil and criminal justice – was even less transparent than in Pillar One.

The third change was political – the creation of 'European Union Citizenship'. European Union citizenship extended a range of rights to all those holding the nationality of a member state. These included the right to move freely and reside in another member state; the right to vote and stand in municipal elections in another member state; passive and active voting rights in EP elections in another member state; the right to diplomatic and consular protection when in a third country where the home member state is not represented and the right to petition the EP and complain to the European Ombudsman.[90] Given that its monopoly on legislative initiative remained intact, it can also be argued that the Commission gained power at Maastricht via the ability to introduce legislation in these important areas.

Notwithstanding this, a further way in which European leaders sought to appeal to Europeans and increase the legitimacy of EU authority was by increasing the power of the only directly elected Community institution – the European Parliament. The institutions will be discussed in full in Chapter 2 but it is worth briefly mentioning how they were affected by the TEU. The EP was given oversight in areas similar to that held by a traditional legislative body, but not the same powers. In relation to the Community budget, it was given a final say on non-compulsory expenditure; control of compulsory expenditure

---

[90]Articles 17–21 TEU

remained with the Council of Ministers. The EP also received more legislative powers: under the co-decision procedure, it worked on a more equal basis with the Commission and Council, although it still could not initiate or block measures. Its powers to scrutinise the other institutions were also enhanced in two ways: first, under Article 263 TFEU, it became a semi-privileged actor with standing before the Court to request annulment of Council and Commission acts which threatened its powers. Second, Article 228 TFEU created an Ombudsman, through which the Parliament could investigate citizen's complaints of maladministration by the Commission.

Despite Dahrendorf's goals, these TEU reforms were not informed by popular action. Integration by edict from above remained the standard operating procedure: there was little public engagement in the process, and the dramatic structural change placed important issues far beyond the reach of democratic scrutiny. It can be argued that Maastricht gave the appearance of democratisation but in fact promoted the opposite. The pillar structure seemed to contradict Article 1 TEU which stated that the objective of EU integration is 'an ever closer union among the people of Europe in which decisions are taken as openly as possible and as closely as possible to the citizens'.[91] However, without the shield offered by the pillar structure, it is unlikely that the member states would have agreed to cooperate in these policy areas. Pillar One housed the history, Pillars Two and Three the future of European integration. There was interaction between the three pillars: member states relied upon institutions created in the Treaty of Rome to coordinate their activities in Pillars Two and Three. The Pillar structure may have guaranteed subsidiarity — that action would be taken as closely as possible to the citizen – but it undermined transparency: that decision-making would be as open as possible.

The TEU was to enter into force when ratified by all the member states. However, this was stalled when Denmark rejected it, citing concerns over sovereignty and neutrality. It was also subject to a legal challenge before the German Constitutional Court[92] and the British High Court.[93] The problem centred upon the use of the word 'federal' – this was deliberately not defined so that it could mean anything to everybody. For some the image of federal multi-level law-making meant greater centralisation, for others greater autonomy. Germany claimed that the TEU symbolised a victory for European federalism while Britain asserted that the pillar structure ruled out any hope of a federal Europe.[94] For the European voters this created a ball of confusion. However, after receiving assurances that its national identity would be protected, Danish voters accepted the Treaty at a second ballot in October 2002. Worre argues that this was a vote in favour of intergovernmental cooperation.[95] In both Germany and Britain, the applications for judicial review were dismissed.[96]

---

[91]Article 1 TEU

[92]German Constitutional Court decision from 12 October 1993, BVerfGE 89, 155; *Brunner v European Union Treaty* CMLR [1994] 57

[93]*R v Secretary of State for Foreign and Commonwealth Affairs, ex parte Rees-Mogg* (1994) 1 All ER 457

[94]Louise B. van Tartwijk-Novey, *The European House of Cards: towards a United States of Europe?*, MacMillan Press, 1995, p. 21

[95]Torben Worre 'First No, Then Yes: The Danish Referendums on the Maastricht Treaty 1992 and 1993', *JCMS* 33(2), 1995, pp. 235–257

[96]J. Weiler 'The State "über alles": Demos, Telos and the German Maastricht Decision', Jean Monnet Working Paper, 1995; Lenz, 'Der Vertrag von Maastricht nach dem Urteil des Bundesverfassungsgerichts', *NJW* 1993, p. 3038; Wieland, 'Germany in the EU – The Maastricht Decision of the Bundesverfassungsgericht', *European Journal of International Law* 1994, p. 259; Rick Rawlings, 'Legal Politics: the United Kingdom and Ratification of the Treaty on European Union' *PL*, 1994, p. 367; Szyszczak, 'Ratifying the Treaty on European Union: a final report', *ELR* 1993, p. 541

> **VIEWPOINT**
>
> Which of the three main reforms do you think was most important? Why?

iv. The Treaty of Amsterdam (1997)

The last-minute brokering and tinkering which characterised the TEU process made a further review inevitable. Article N TEU provided for this. Article N contained a review clause and scheduled an Intergovernmental Conference for 1996 to consider which provisions of the Treaty of Maastricht needed to be revised, as well as other issues which might affect the effective operation of the Union. The IGC agenda was limited to existing issues rather than new ones. The accession of 10 new members was also pending. The Reflection Group, under the then Spanish President Carlos Westendorp, established five broad themes for the IGC.[97]

Changes were made which suggested a retreat from closer integration. For example, the enhancement of the principle of subsidiarity – that decisions be taken as closely as possible to the persons affected – meant a closer scrutiny of action at the EU level.[98] Also, new provisions were introduced allowing for 'enhanced cooperation'[99] if a group of member states wished to pursue further integration in a number of policy areas within the Treaty institutional framework.[100] These provisions served multiple political purposes: the vocabulary of flexibility covered:

> changes in the context and conditions for integration; variations in the objectives of the actors; differences in the interests of the actors; controversies about which values and norms should be embedded in the process; debates about the feasible and desirable policy scope for shared regimes; and questioning of the institutional rules and practices through which to develop policy regimes.[101]

They simultaneously protected the process of integration by allowing a vanguard of member states to press ahead with integration yet also opened the door to a Europe of 'bits and pieces'. The Annexation of the Schengen Agreement[102] to the Treaty via a Protocol, and the opt-out of Schengen by Denmark, Britain and Ireland further suggested that the 'multi-speed' EU envisaged by Dahrendorf in 1972 was coming into being.

---

[97]'An area of freedom, security and justice; the Union and the citizen; an effective and coherent foreign policy; the Union's institutions; enhanced cooperation', CONF 2500/96, Brussels, 5 December 1996

[98]Article 1 Protocol on the application of the principles of subsidiarity and proportionality

[99]See C-274/11 and C-295/11 *Spain and Italy* v *Council* on the use of enhanced cooperation under Articles 20 TEU and 329 TFEU for creation of the 'unitary patent'.

[100]Alexander C.G. Stubb, 'Negotiating Flexible Integration', in K. Neunreither and A. Wiener (eds), *European Integration After Amsterdam: institutional dynamics and prospects for democracy*, Oxford University Press, 2000, p. 155

[101]Helen Wallace, 'Flexibility: integration or disintegration?' in Neunreither and Wiener 2000, p. 178

[102]The Schengen Agreement dates back to 1985 when five member states (Belgium, Netherlands, Luxembourg, Germany and France) agreed to abolish border checks at their common frontiers. The agreement was only implemented in 1990 following the signing of the Convention implementing Schengen (CIS). By 1997 it had been adopted by 13 member states: Belgium, Denmark, the Federal Republic of Germany, Greece, Spain, France, Italy, Luxembourg, the Netherlands, Austria, Portugal, Finland and Sweden. The Protocol authorised the signatories to 'establish closer cooperation among themselves within the scope of those agreements and related provisions . . . within the institutional and legal framework of the European Union'.

Again, brief mention must be made of the institutions. Sadly, little progress was made in relation to urgent institutional reforms — the size of the Commission, reweighting of votes in the Council of Ministers, and the redistribution of seats in the EP were postponed. There were nonetheless, some important changes, such as the right of assent over the College of Commissioners given to the Commission president;[103] simplification and extension of the co-decision procedure; the transfer of matters concerning visas, immigration and asylum issues located in Pillar Three to Pillar One.

The Amsterdam Treaty was therefore both a success and a failure – there was no 'qualitative leap towards a more democratic system of EU governance'[104] but it could be argued that there was creep towards more legitimacy via a subtle shift in the balance of institutional power between the EP and the Commission. A further attempt was made to address the pressing institutional issues in 2000. The result was the Treaty of Nice.

VIEWPOINT

Is the Schengen Agreement a sign of an 'à la carte' or 'multi-speed' Europe?

---

v. The Treaty of Nice (2000) and the Irish 'No'

By 2000 the question of enlargement loomed large. A very practical question needed to be resolved – how to ensure that the institutions designed for six could continue to work with 25 member states? While these institutional reforms were on the one hand simply a practical matter, they were also very political questions: reform redistributed power between the institutions and the member states, as well as between the member states themselves. Reforms were proposed to the three main institutions, but those suggested to the Council of Ministers and the Commission were the most controversial.

Reform to the voting procedure in the Council of Ministers produced heated debate, as did plans to reduce the size of the Commission. Ultimately it was agreed that the number of votes allocated to each member state in the Council of Ministers would change, as would the definition of a 'qualified majority' – the number of votes needed to adopt a measure. Henceforth a qualified majority would consist of two parts: a specific number of votes and approval by a majority of member states representing at least 62 per cent of the total EU population. Furthermore, it was proposed to extend the use of qualified majority voting to 27 new areas.[105] The most contentious aspect concerning the Commission was the idea that as soon as the Union reached 27 member states, there

---

[103]Paragraph 2, Declaration No. 32 on the organisation and functioning of the Commission attached to the Amsterdam Treaty. Online at http://eur-lex.europa.eu/en/treaties/dat/11997D/htm/11997D.html

[104]Gerda Falkner and Michael Nentwich, 'The Future Institutional Balance?', in Neunreither and Wiener 2000, p. 18

[105]Free movement of citizens (Article 21 TFEU), judicial co-operation in civil matters (Article 81 TFEU); international agreements in trade in services and the commercial aspects of intellectual property (Article 207 TFEU); industrial policy (Article 173 TFEU); economic, financial and technical cooperation with third countries (Article 212 TFEU); approval of rules governing members of the EP (Article 223 TFEU); the statute of European political parties (Article 224 TFEU); the rules of procedure of the ECJ and GC (Articles 253 and 254 TFEU). QMV was also partially extended to areas dealing with visas, asylum and immigration. Unanimity was maintained in five broad areas – taxation, social policy, cohesion policy, asylum and immigration policy and the common commercial policy. The ordinary legislative procedure was also extended to some of the new areas subject to QMV. See Lisbon Treaty Table of Equivalences OJ C115/361.

would be fewer Commissioners than member states – that is some member states would not have a Commissioner. There was no detail as to how this would be achieved except a provision whereby a system of rotation would be introduced.

It may be an understatement that the consensus reached at Nice 'produced suboptimal solutions to the institutional challenges raised by the prospect of an enlarged membership'.[106] Deep distrust and dissatisfaction was expressed, in particular by the citizens of Ireland who rejected the Treaty due to a number of concerns. Objections were raised about the growing 'democratic deficit':[107] the loss of the right to nominate a Commissioner, loss of MEPs as well as votes and the veto in the Council of Ministers. In addition, they raised concerns that the new arrangements for qualified majority voting in the Council and the flexibility clauses would lead to a 'two-tier' Europe. Finally, Ireland's involvement in the proposed 'Rapid Reaction Force' was seen as an embryonic European Army that would end the country's neutral status.[108]

Focused measures were taken to address Irish concerns. First, the Irish government established a 'National Forum on Europe'; second, a more rigorous parliamentary structure for European scrutiny was created; and third, the Seville Declaration on neutrality was agreed. At the Seville European Council in June 2002, the member states accepted an Irish Declaration that 'spelled out the "triple lock" – UN mandate; cabinet approval; Dáil approval – on Irish participation in EU military activities'.[109] These measures reassured voters and they accepted the Treaty at a second ballot in October 2002.

However, the process and its results left a long shadow. European leaders were as disillusioned and frustrated as the Irish voters – the summary of the Treaty reforms presented here belies the year-long activities behind every agreement, the months of negotiation and bargaining in Brussels and other European capitals. As seen, after all the compromise, a Treaty could still be jettisoned into history if a nation rejected it. The method of reform via intergovernmental conference was inefficient: the process was labour-intensive, dominated by power questions, a lack of transparency and late-night bargaining yet for all that failed to deliver the fundamental changes required.

The disappointment among the member states created the context for a major project – the creation of a Convention and the Constitutional Treaty for Europe. A 'post-Nice' process was set in motion by Declaration 23 Annexed to the Nice Treaty to foster a 'deeper and wider debate about the future of the European Union' and to bring integration 'closer to the citizens'.[110] Consequently, by the time the Treaty of Nice entered into force, it was already overshadowed by a much larger and grander project.

vi. The Constitutional Treaty: France and the Netherlands say 'No'

In 2001 at Laeken, in an attempt to restore confidence in European integration, the European Council took the momentous decision to establish a Convention to debate the

---

[106]David Phinemore, 'Towards European Union', in Michelle Cini (ed), *European Union Politics*, 2nd edn, OUP, 2007, p. 40

[107]The 'democratic deficit' refers to the idea that the EU lacks democratic legitimacy. See http://europa.eu/legislation_summaries/glossary/democratic_deficit_en.htm

[108]Peter Doyle, 'Ireland and the Nice Treaty,' Centre for European Integration Studies, Discussion Paper C115, 2002

[109]Karin Gilland, 'Referendum Briefing No 1 – Ireland's Second Referendum On The Treaty Of Nice', October 2002, http://www.sussex.ac.uk/sei/documents/irelandno1.pdf

[110]Thomas Christiansen and Christine Reh, *Constitutionalizing the European Union*, Palgrave MacMillan, 2009, p. 78

future of Europe. The Laeken Declaration took the optimistic view that after 50 years, 'Europe is on its way to becoming one big family' but faced two specific challenges: internally there was deep disengagement with citizens; externally, Europe had still not established its role in the post-Cold War world. The task of the Union was therefore to design a response to these challenges in a way that met with the expectations of citizens. Internal changes focused on the institutions – these were to become more efficient, open and participatory as well as less interventionist:

> Within the Union, the European institutions must be brought closer to its citizens. Citizens undoubtedly support the Union's broad aims, but they do not always see a connection between those goals and the Union's everyday action. They want the European institutions to be less unwieldy and rigid and, above all, more efficient and open. Many also feel that the Union should involve itself more with their particular concerns, instead of intervening, in every detail, in matters by their nature better left to Member States' and regions' elected representatives. This is even perceived by some as a threat to their identity. More importantly, however, they feel that deals are all too often cut out of their sight and they want better democratic scrutiny.
>
> [. . .]
>
> Now that the Cold War is over and we are living in a globalised, yet also highly fragmented world, Europe needs to shoulder its responsibilities in the governance of globalisation. The role it has to play is that of a power resolutely doing battle against all violence, all terror and all fanaticism, but which also does not turn a blind eye to the world's heartrending injustices. In short, a power wanting to change the course of world affairs in such a way as to benefit not just the rich countries but also the poorest. A power seeking to set globalisation within a moral framework, in other words to anchor it in solidarity and sustainable development.
>
> [. . .]
>
> What they expect is more results, better responses to practical issues and not a European superstate or European institutions inveigling their way into every nook and cranny of life. In short, citizens are calling for a clear, open, effective, democratically controlled Community approach, developing a Europe which points the way ahead for the world. An approach that provides concrete results in terms of more jobs, better quality of life, less crime, decent education and better health care. There can be no doubt that this will require Europe to undergo renewal and reform.
>
> [. . .]
>
> The Union needs to become more democratic, more transparent and more efficient. It also has to resolve three basic challenges: how to bring citizens, and primarily the young, closer to the European design and the European institutions, how to organise politics and the European political area in an enlarged Union and how to develop the Union into a stabilising factor and a model in the new, multipolar world.[111]

---

[111]Laeken Declaration On The Future Of The European Union at http://european-convention.eu.int/pdf/LKNEN.pdf

A number of questions on the future of Europe were laid out in the Laeken Declaration, covering four main themes:

1 the division and definition of powers;
2 the simplification of the treaties;
3 the institutional set-up;
4 moving towards a Constitution for European citizens.

Not only did the existing Treaties need to be tidied up, but the institutions still needed to be prepared for enlargement. Added to these needs were a myriad of objectives, including the desire to bring Europe closer to its citizens, reduce the democratic deficit by making its institutions more accountable, and for some, move the Union closer to a federal entity. It therefore established the Convention on the Future of Europe 'in order to pave the way for the next Intergovernmental Conference as broadly and openly as possible'.[112]

The Convention held its first meeting in March 2002, almost exactly a year after the Treaty of Nice had been signed. It was steered by a 'Praesidium' of 13 Convention members including a President, two Vice-Presidents, two European Commissioners, two MEPs, three government representatives, two national parliamentarians[113] and a representative from the candidate countries.[114] Its task was to lead the process. Valéry Giscard d'Estaing, described by the right-wing *Daily Telegraph* as a 'lordly septuagenarian and vivid raconteur',[115] was appointed President of the Convention.

A great deal of interest was stimulated by the Convention composition, which included two key features setting it apart from the top-down closed procedures of the past. First, the Convention sought to be representative – all existing (15) and candidate countries (13) [116] sent one government and two parliamentary representatives; there were 16 representatives from the EP and two from the Commission. Every full member of the Convention had an 'alternate' to ensure that representation remained high.[117] A number of organisations had observer status: the European Ombudsman, the Economic and Social Committee (three representatives), the Committee of the Regions (six representatives), and the social partners (three representatives). The Presidents of the Court of Justice and of the Court of Auditors could be invited by the Praesidium to address the Convention.

Second, the Convention provided for a 'Forum', in order to create a popular debate involving all citizens. The Forum was open to organisations representing civil society (the social partners, the business world, non-governmental bodies, academia, etc.). It was primarily a virtual network: organisations would receive 'regular information' on the Convention's proceedings to which they could respond using a procedure set out by the Praesidium.

---

[112]Laeken Declaration

[113]Gisela Stuart represented Britain and recorded her views of the Convention process in *The Making of Europe's Constitution,* Fabian Society, 2003, p. 17

[114]This was not mentioned in the declaration but added later 'in response to pressure'– Stuart 2003, p. 24

[115]Ambrose Evans-Pritchard, 'Giscard d'Estaing is now so grand he really seems to think he is Louis XIV', 20 May 2003, http://www.telegraph.co.uk/news/uknews/1430576/Giscard-dEstaing-is-now-so-grand-he-really-seems-to-think-he-is-Louis-XIV.html

[116]The Laeken Declaration provided for the candidate countries to fully participate in proceedings but they were unable 'to prevent any consensus which may emerge among the Member States'. http://european-convention.eu.int/organisation.asp?lang=EN

[117]http://european-convention.eu.int/organisation.asp?lang=EN

From the outside, this process appeared remarkably open especially in contrast to the secrecy and closed atmosphere of traditional intergovernmental conferences. Over the 16 months of its existence, the Convention sat in 26 plenary sessions, established 11 working groups and held 50 meetings of the Praesidium. The wide representation within the Convention members suggested broad discussion and debate incorporating a plurality of perspectives. Documents were posted online allowing those not present to follow and engage with the proceedings. Of course, only those who knew about the Convention, and had the time to engage with it could do so. As it failed to attract media or public attention,[118] it is questionable whether it succeeded in the declared aim of citizen engagement.

From the inside, engagement was also a problem. Many of those involved lacked time – government representatives were not always well prepared, national parliamentarians were sidelined by the European Parliament, plenary debates were in reality short speeches, and decision-making in the Praesidium was more diplomatic in character than democratic. The volume of material produced meant that large amounts of the text were actually passed without detailed discussion. New provisions were sometimes introduced without translation and at late stages: ultimately, 'from its high minded beginnings, the Convention became a mixture of individual idiosyncracies, principled positions and political horse-trading'.[119]

It has since been argued that the 'Convention process' was dominated by one man – Giscard d'Estaing. Tsebelis argues that d'Estaing was able to produce a text due to successful institutional and positional agenda setting:

> When a text is composed, the person holding the 'pen' usually has a significant impact on the content of the document . . . Giscard d'Estaing was the 'agenda-setter' in the Convention and for the Intergovernmental Conference 2003–2004. An agenda-setter is a politician who is able to control the agenda during the deliberations and make proposals to the decision making body.

Institutional agenda setting refers to the rules permitting certain actors to make proposals and others to be unable to modify them before final passage. Positional agenda setting refers to the number of actors that have to agree for a proposal, and the number of actors occupying the middle of their ideological space. Giscard d'Estaing made use of these components of agenda setting when he presided over the EU Convention. According to Tsebelis, d'Estaing was successful for two main reasons. First, because he expanded the authority of the convention and shaped the document that it produced by entrenching his own preference for producing a single proposal rather than several alternatives expected for the IGC. Second, the avoidance of open votes in the Convention, empowered him to summarise debates and determine 'consensus'. Also, by imposing time limits on convention participants he was able to 'reduce or even eliminate the input of other actors to the final document'. As a result he had a large success rate in his proposals.[120] As a

---

[118]Church and Phinnemore in Cini 2007, p. 49

[119]Gisela Stuart 2003, pp. 19–23

[120]George Tsebelis, 'Agenda Setting In The EU Constitution: From The Giscard Plan To The Pros Ratification(?) Document', Paper presented at the DOSEI conference, Brussels 2005, http://sitemaker.umich.edu/tsebelis/files/giscardagenda.pdf

number of the proposals in d'Estaing's text[121] remained, the Lisbon Treaty which entered into force in December 2009 is ultimately also the work of one man.

a) The Constitution for Europe

The Convention did produce two texts. First, in July 2002 a European Youth Convention, an initiative of d'Estaing, was agreed.[122] Its substance is questionable given that it was drawn up in three days by 210 representatives from 28 countries. Second, less than a year later, in June 2003, the Convention presented the Draft Treaty Establishing a Constitution for Europe (CT), a single text containing four major parts plus Protocols, Annexes and Declarations which added detail to the contents of the major parts.

D'Estaing's text contained many significant reforms. It is worth highlighting the key changes because many of these remained in the Lisbon Treaty which entered into force in December 2009. By combining all previous treaties, the Constitutional Treaty text merged the EEC and the EU, removing the Pillar structure. Article I-2 CT added new values of human dignity, equality, the rights of minorities and the characterisation of the values upheld by the societies of the member states. Article I-3 CT merged the objectives of the EEC and EU, and added some new ones such as the promotion of scientific and technological advance, of solidarity between generations and of the protection of children's rights. A new Article I-6 entrenched the principle of primacy of EU law over the law of the member states – while this had been asserted by the CJEU since the 1960s, it had never been articulated in the Treaty. Article I-7 gave the Union legal personality: this enables the EU to enter into international agreements covering all areas of Union activity, including security and defence, civil and criminal justice. Article I-8 gave constitutional status to the existing symbols (flag, motto, anthem, etc.) of the Union.

Fundamental rights were enhanced by Article I-9 CT which incorporated the EU Charter of Human Rights adopted at Nice in 2000.[123] This entrenchment in the Convention gave the Charter binding legal status. The role of citizens was enhanced by Article I-47 (now Article 11 TEU; Article 24 TFEU), which gave them a conditional right to initiate legislation based on the submission of a petition of at least one million signatures obtained from a number of member states. The Commission retained the discretion to act upon this invitation to create a legislative proposal.

Article I-11 established that the exercise of the Union's competences is governed not only by the principle of conferral but also by the principles of subsidiarity and proportionality. Monitoring of this principle was to be strengthened by the involvement of the national parliaments and use of an 'early warning' card system. Articles I-12 to I-17 CT (Articles 3–4 TFEU) lay out a 'catalogue' of competence, distributing them among the EU and the member states. Article I-18 gave the Commission power to act in the absence of a specific Treaty basis. This was broader than its predecessor in Article 308 EC because it was not limited to action pertaining to the common market but covered the scope of areas

---

[121]Treaty Establishing A Constitution for Europe, OJ C310/47 2004, http://eur-lex.europa.eu/JOHtml.do?uri=OJ:C: 2004:310:SOM:EN:HTML

[122]http://register.consilium.eu.int/pdf/en/02/cv00/00205en2.pdf

[123]The Cologne European Council had in 1999 established a 'Convention' to prepare a text focusing on human rights. This became a 'Charter of Fundamental Rights'. The Charter set out in a single text the range of civil, political, economic and social rights of European citizens and all persons resident in the EU. The rights are laid out in six sections: Dignity, Freedoms, Equality, Solidarity, Citizens' rights, and Justice. It was presented at Nice, where it was signed by the Presidents of the European Parliament, the Council and the Commission. Despite the cross-institutional support, its status was not clarified by the Heads of Governments and States http://www.europarl.europa.eu/charter/default_en.htm

in Part III. The Article also obliged the Commission to inform national parliaments of proposals based on the flexibility clause, so that they could monitor compliance with the subsidiarity principle. Article 24(4) CT contained the 'Passarelle Clause' which allows the Council of Ministers to move from the national veto to QMV, subject to governmental but not necessarily parliamentary approval. This provision was controversial, not only because it was not fully debated, but also because the CT did not propose a mechanism to determine when and how power should be returned from the EU to the member states.

A new typology of legal acts was established in Article I-33 CT (Article 290 and 291 TFEU). The six new legal acts were separated into 'legislative' and 'non-legislative' acts. Article I-34 CT contained two legislative acts – laws and framework laws – and lay down the procedure for their adoption. Non-legislative acts – European regulations, European decisions, recommendations and opinions – were laid out in Article I-35 CT. These were similar in character to the Rome Treaty measures. With the disappearance of the Pillar structure, this typology would also apply to action concerning justice, security, policing and related issues, although only European decisions were to be used in the fields of security and defence.

Two final proposals are worth highlighting for their attempt to appeal to citizens and Euro-sceptics: in order to promote transparency, Article 15(2) CT lay out that both the EP and the Council of Ministers would meet in public, but only 'considering and voting on a draft legislative act'. In addition, a new rule was added which allowed members to exit: Article I-60 CT established that withdrawal could take place at any time, and a state which had withdrawn could rejoin without going through the accession procedure.

As the following table shows, some institutional proposals in the CT were adopted in the Lisbon Treaty:

CT Institutional Proposals in the Lisbon Treaty	COMPOSITION	PROCESS	POWERS
EUROPEAN PARLIAMENT	Capped at 732 members	Extended use of co-decision => co-legislator in 70 areas	Final say on EU budget, veto on Commission spending programme
EUROPEAN COUNCIL	Appointment of a new Foreign Minister for CFSP (Baroness Catherine Ashton)	Chair held for 2.5 years instead of 6 months (Art.15(5) TEU)	No legislative powers
COUNCIL OF MINISTERS	Unchanged	Will meet in public; use of 'double majority' for QMV	Redistributed but large states have more say
COMMISSION	1 per MS; rotating nomination	2 tiers: voting (15) and non-voting	Unchanged
NEW: 'Euro-Group' (Art. 137 TFEU)	Ministers of MS that have adopted the euro		Coordination of economic policies
NEW: 'European External Action Service'	Officials from Council of Ministers, the Commission, MS diplomatic corps		Duties to assist the new Foreign Minister

VIEWPOINT

Would you have voted for or against the Constitutional Treaty? Why?

b) National responses to the constitutional treaty

The Convention Process turned out to be more time consuming than the traditional process. Negotiations on the Constitutional Treaty opened in September 2003 and a final amended version was signed by the newly enlarged EU25 at the Rome Summit in October 2004. In order to enter into force all 25 member states had to ratify it. Many countries did so in 2005, including Germany, Italy and Spain, where 77 per cent of voters approved it. Problems emerged when voters in France and the Netherlands rejected it. On 29 May 2005, the French public rejected the Constitution by a margin of 55 per cent to 45 per cent on a turnout of 69 per cent; just three days later the Dutch rejected the Constitution by a margin of 61 per cent to 39 per cent on a turnout of 62 per cent. This did not stall the ratification process in other member states: Luxembourg held a referendum on 10 July 2005 approving the Constitution by 57 per cent to 43 per cent. However, other member states[124] cancelled planned referendums and although by February 2007, 18 member states had accepted the Constitutional Treaty, given the need for unanimity, the Constitution was unable to enter into force.

According to a European Commission survey, the reasons for rejection were varied. In both countries very few rejected the Treaty due to opposition to European integration in general or EU enlargement.[125] In the Netherlands the key factor was lack of information (31 per cent of respondents), followed by fears for loss of national sovereignty (19 per cent), political opposition (14 per cent) and considerations of the expense of Europe. In France, the overwhelming factor was concern for employment and enterprise (31 per cent of respondents) followed closely by worry about the national economic situation (26 per cent), concern that the text was too liberal (19 per cent), political opposition (18 per cent), and welfare issues (16 per cent). Joerges has 'little doubt that this perceived dismantling of the French welfare state through the integration process, the portrayal of Europe as a neo-liberal deregulation machinery, the anxieties such as Europeanisation and globalisation provoked amongst the French had a substantial impact on their "*non*"'.[126]

Lack of clarity was an issue: in France 12 per cent of respondents claimed that the text was too complex; this was an issue for just 5 per cent of respondents in the Netherlands. Much of the problem was attributed to the misinformation fed to the public by an ill-informed press and anti-European organisations. Added to this, governments themselves did too little to 'sell' the text to their electorates. When they did discuss the text, the focus fell on what it did not do rather than what it did.[127]

---

[124]Sweden, Denmark, the UK, Poland, the Czech Republic and Ireland.

[125]Flash Eurobarometer 171: 'Post-referendum survey in France, May 2005', Question 5; Flash Eurobarometer 172: 'The European Constitution: Post-Referendum Netherlands', Question 5

[126]Christian Joerges, 'On the Disregard for History in the Convention Process', *European Law Journal* 12(1), January 2006, pp. 2–5

[127]Stuart 2003

In June 2007, the Constitutional project was officially abandoned in favour of a new 'Reform Treaty'. Questions were raised as to whether full-scale institutional and constitutional reform was actually needed, and why. Shaw identified strong arguments against: first, EU reform was an unnecessary distraction and ultimately unable to address problems that lay within the national arena: it was not clear that reform of the majority voting system would change either the incidence or contents of EU legislation. Second, the French and Dutch polls demonstrated that further developments to democratise the EU were clearly unpopular and risked 'upsetting the delicate balance that has been worked out over many years'. Finally, governments and citizens alike were now sensitive to the 'constitutional pretensions' of the Constitutional Treaty and would reject any attempt to replicate it. However, Shaw also presented strong arguments in favour of this: first, the institutions designed for six members states cooperating across a limited range of issues were close to collapse; second, renovation was necessary to 'restore citizens' faith in the European Union and its capacity to deliver'; and third, she argued: ' . . . it seems irrational to toss away such hard won agreements and compromises and . . . it seems conversely rational to relocate those compromises into a legal instrument which does not attract such controversy, and to try to recapture that spirit of compromise'.[128]

vii. The Lisbon Treaty and the second Irish 'No'

A Reform Treaty was finally agreed in Lisbon in December 2007. The Lisbon Treaty (LT)[129] was a traditional amending Treaty instead of a single Constitution. It amended both the 1957 Treaty of Rome and the 1992 Treaty on European Union (TEU) signed at Maastricht. The Treaty of Rome was given a new name: the Treaty on the Functioning of the European Union (TFEU).[130] The TFEU now organises the functioning of the Union and sets out 'the areas of, delimitations of and arrangements for exercising its competences'.[131] Henceforth there will be only these two Treaties, the TEU (55 provisions) and the TFEU (358 provisions) both of which are the legal bases of the Union and are of equal legal value.[132] The awkward distinction between the EC and the EU, and the pillar structure are removed.

The Lisbon Treaty maintained many of the initiatives in the Constitutional Treaty. Essentially it adopted the substance of the Constitutional Treaty but dropped the symbolism – the name of 'Constitution', the flag, anthem, etc.[133] As Shaw noted, voters were vigilant: the Irish recognised this and in June 2008, 53.4 per cent of the electorate rejected it.[134] Clarity was again an issue – the key factor mentioned was lack of information (34.9 per cent), followed by concerns for Irish identity (19.5 per cent) but just over 10 per cent also cited a lack of trust in their politicians.[135] The result was a major blow: all member states were required to ratify the Lisbon Treaty and 14 had already done so.

---

[128]Jo Shaw, 'The Constitutional Treaty: Resuscitation, Long Term Hibernation or Death?', 2007, pp. 2-4 http://www.um.edu.mt/europeanstudies/books/CD_MESA07/pdf/jshaw.pdf

[129]Consolidated versions of the Treaty on European Union and the Treaty on the Functioning of the European Union, OJ C115 2008, http://eur-lex.europa.eu/JOHtml.do?uri=OJ:C:2008:115:SOM:EN:HTML

[130]http://eur-lex.europa.eu/LexUriServ/LexUriServ.do?uri=OJ:C:2008:115:0047:0199:EN:PDF

[131]Article 1(1) TFEU

[132]Article 1(2) TFEU

[133]George Tsebelis, 'Thinking About the Recent Past and the Future of the EU', *JCMS* 46(2), March 2008, pp. 265–292

[134]Turnout for the Nice Treaty referendum was by contrast 35 per cent.

[135]Flash Eurobarometer 245: 'Post-referendum survey in Ireland', Question 9

Only Ireland had held a referendum, necessary because constitutional amendments were required to accommodate the Treaty. All three main Irish parties called for a 'Yes' vote but again a vigorous 'No' campaign had been mounted by well-organised groups from across the political spectrum.[136]

Securing a 'Yes' for the Lisbon Treaty required more work. As the new Treaty was due to come into force on 1 January 2009, time was of the essence. It was difficult to promote because it was complex and 'lacked a compelling rationale, such as the single market and structural funds in the case of the Single European Act, or economic and monetary union in the case of the Maastricht Treaty'.[137] The Irish Foreign Ministry set out to clarify it, issuing a document to set out out the scope of the Treaty and the proposed changes.[138] The document included a glossary and contained numerous Annexes, laying out the Protocols attached to the Lisbon Treaty, Declarations made by the member states and concerning provision of the Treaty and its Protocols, new areas of EU competence, key changes in the voting procedure (from unanimity to majority voting) and law-making (use of co-decision).

This transparency may explain why – even though the Lisbon Treaty retained many of the key amendments concerning law-making, majority voting, external action and freedom, security and justice proposed by the Constitutional Treaty – it was accepted by 67 per cent of Irish voters in a second referendum in October 2009. Irish voters were also pacified by a political decision to allow Ireland to attach a Protocol to the next amendment of the founding treaties. However, the most compelling explanation for the change of heart may have been the deepening global economic crisis, which hit Ireland particularly hard.[139] The Lisbon Treaty also gave assurances to other member states in the Protocols and Declarations. Britain, Poland and the Czech Republic, for example, were especially concerned about the impact of the EU Charter of Fundamental Rights, which was to become binding and of equal status to the Treaties. Statements were therefore attached in Protocols to limit any potential impact.[140]

VIEWPOINT

What do you think are the strongest reasons in support of and against complete institutional and constitutional reform in the EU?

---

5. Conclusion: Regional reconstruction – why bother?

Sixty years after World War II and in a Union with so many new members with such divergent histories and memories it is still necessary but no longer sufficient to pay tribute to the memories and motives that guided the founders in the 1950s.[141]

---

[136]'Ireland rejects EU reform Treaty', http://news.bbc.co.uk/1/hi/world/europe/7453560.stm; Henry McDonald and Allegra Stratton, 'Irish voters reject EU Treaty', Friday 13 June 2008 at http://www.guardian.co.uk/world/2008/jun/13/ireland

[137]Desmond Dinan, 'Institutions and Governance: Saving the Lisbon Treaty – An Irish Solution to a European Problem', *JCMS* 47, 2009 Annual Review, pp. 113–132

[138]Department of Foreign Affairs (2009) The Lisbon Treaty: White Paper – An explanation of changes to the functioning of the European Union made by the Lisbon Treaty.

[139]Dinan 2009, p. 166

[140]Protocols attached to the Lisbon Treaty

[141]Joerges 2006, p. 4

The EU is increasingly recognised as a successful, but just one, option for regional cooperation.[142] There is no easy way to explain its evolution: the origins of the EEC bears the hallmarks of 'monnetism';[143] liberal intergovernmentalism would argue that EU integration is a 'series of rational choices made by national leaders';[144] a sociological institutional, or constructivist perspective would highlight that these choices were made in specific opportunity contexts, which did not simply appear but were constructed. No single theory can capture the whole story of the 'European adventure'.

Its survival is even harder to explain – given that it has enjoyed just one relatively short period of intensive harmonisation (1986–1992), and has been rocked to its foundations by the 2008 financial crisis, an intriguing question is why the Union is so resilient? One answer to this question might be that the Treaty of Rome created a uniquely strong framework for regional cooperation within which the 'clash of national interests could occur without being pushed to the point of mutual destruction. Unless they wished to break the edifice, member states were forced to find agreement.'[145] At time of writing, no member state has yet left the Union, so this may be a good explanation. The edifice has teetered towards collapse many times and remains vulnerable to exogenous factors, but thus far is clearly strong enough to withstand rejection and crisis.

The resilience may also be because of, or in spite of, the fact that what began as 'an elitist blueprint' is steadily involving more people. Despite pioneering supranationalism, democracy was not a concern for the six founders of the EEC. The key institutions created – the European Commission, the Council of Ministers and the Assembly – were not constituted, for example, to promote participation, representation, transparency or accountability. All members of these institutions were identified and nominated by the member states – none were elected or hired independently of national governments. The process of European integration is now determined by many more factors than the preferences of the member states and the Commission.[146] Agriculturalists remain a powerful lobbying group in many member states. Likewise 'business activism',[147] such as the European Round Table of Industrialists, plays a role – this was central to member states acceptance of the Single Market programme of the late 1980s to early 1990s.[148] Increasingly other non-state actors, such as non-governmental organisations (NGOs), consumer groups, trade unionists can also determine the direction and pace of integration.

Citizens have also started to raise their voices. When asked about the Treaty of Maastricht, the Constitution and the Treaty of Lisbon, significant numbers of citizens have shown that they are not yet ready to transfer their trust from the nation state to the EU – the TEU was rejected by Danish voters in 1992[149] and challenged before the German Constitutional Court; the Constitution was rejected by the Dutch and French in 2004; and the Lisbon Treaty was initially rejected by the Irish in 2008. The Reform Treaty marks a retreat to implicit and informal constitutionalisation. Yet many citizens still want

---

[142]Laurence Henry, 'The ASEAN Way and Community Integration: Two Different Models of Regionalism', *European Law Journal* 13(6), November 2007, pp. 857–879

[143]See Gillingham 2003, Chapter 2

[144]Andrew Moravscik, *The Choice for Europe*, Routledge, 1998, p. 18

[145]El Agraa 1998, p. 24

[146]See Gillingham 2003, Chapter 4

[147]Gillingham 2003, p. 237

[148]Maria Green Cowles, 'Non-State Actors and False Dichotomies – Reviewing IR/IPE Approaches to European Integration', in Jones and Verdun 2005, pp. 2628–2629

[149]It was accepted in 1993, when 56.8 per cent voted in favour.

their country in or to join the EU[150] – Ukraine, for instance, erupted in violence over President Yanukovych's refusal in November 2013 to sign a trade and association agreement with the EU.[151]

From the outside, this turbulence in European integration is perplexing: an American, for example, might ask why 'do the states compete so much with one another, when their true competition is often with non-European entities? Why does the European Council never seem to act in a timely manner? Why do Euro-citizens have so poor of an appreciation of what the Community does for them?' [152] These are complex questions with no easy answer. It is true that thanks to EU integration, the average standard of living of most citizens in all EU member states, prior to the global financial collapse of 2008, had risen. Prices did fall as cross-border trade flourishes and national regulation is replaced by harmonised European rules. However, citizens are unlikely to know the details of where the EU has directly improved their lives. The 'Roaming Regulation'[153] for example compelled mobile network operators to reduce the cost of using mobiles abroad – none explained that they did so due to the intervention of the European Commission. This Regulation was an initiative of the Commission designed to reduce the high cost of using mobile phones abroad, first highlighted by a Commission study in October 2005[154] and in a subsequent Eurobarometer survey in 2006, where 70 per cent of respondents agreed with the introduction of EU rules to lower roaming costs across the EU.[155]

Yet not all European Union initiatives have been beneficial, and some advocate for the return of certain areas to the nation state. The Common Agricultural Policy (CAP) so key in 1957 remains one of the most controversial issues. It has been described as a hidden tax and Gillingham suggests it be restored to national control.[156] It is also increasingly clear that trade liberalisation has not brought benefits for everyone – non-citizens, those with few domestic rights, pay perhaps the heaviest price of global competitiveness. They and the low-skilled suffer most from the demise of national industries and disappearance of jobs. This can lead paradoxically to a retreat to the very sentiments that integration was designed to avoid: nationalism, accompanied by growing xenophobia and racism. These after-effects have only latterly been considered and the resurgence of sovereignty they cause remains to be effectively addressed.

Nonetheless, there remain compelling reasons for European nations to cooperate closely and act as friends. As the United States continues to retreat, Europe is forced to act together. This is as true today as in the 1950s.[157] European integration has made

---

[150]Rachid Azrout, Joost van Spanje and Claes de Vreese 'When News Matters: Media Effects on Public Support for European Union Enlargement in 21 countries', *JCMS* 50(5), 2012, p. 691

[151]http://www.nytimes.com/2013/12/24/opinion/kauffmann-how-europe-can-help-kiev.html?_r=0

[152]Thomas C. Fischer, An American Looks at the European Union, *European Law Journal* 12(2), March 2006, pp. 226–278

[153]Regulation (EC) No 544/2009 Of The European Parliament And Of The Council of 18 June 2009, http://eur-lex. europa.eu/LexUriServ/LexUriServ.do?uri=OJ:L:2009:167:0012:0023:EN:PDF

[154]Proposal for a Regulation Of The European Parliament And Of The Council on roaming on public mobile networks within the Community and amending Directive 2002/21/EC on a common regulatory framework for electronic communications networks and services. COM(2006) 382 final, p. 3

[155]The Roaming Regulation, which limits the prices of using mobile phones abroad, came into effect on 1 July 2009.

[156]Gillingham 2003, p. 123

[157]The development of a European defence policy became necessary when after the end of the Cold War and the collapse of the USSR, the United States made it clear that it would play less of a role in European defence issues. Van Tartwijk-Novey 1995, p. 74

war less likely; yet US withdrawal makes a European common foreign and security policy necessary. An older generation might see the rationale for this but a younger generation may not. Paradoxically, Europeans want the security that the EU can offer, but hesitate to provide the EU with the tools to deliver this effectively.[158] This may also be in part because although younger generations benefit most from European integration, they also have the weakest understanding of its original motivations: the avoidance of war, which continues to decline as a significant motivation for integration. Yet there remain substantial security issues that are best tackled in cooperation: regulation of the trading practices and behaviour of financial institutions, trafficking of persons, especially young girls and international crime. Environmental degradation and climate change are also issues that may be best addressed at a regional rather than a national level.

Regional integration thus continues to be of relevance, even if the nature of its relevance has changed. Clarity of purpose and transparency in action will be vital if future reform is to avoid the drama of the Lisbon Treaty. Indeed, it has been argued that the ability of the integration project to respond to new challenges, such as those mentioned above, is critical for its credibility – if 'the European Union fails to react, it can be quickly portrayed as irrelevant, an organisation that was useful in the past, but is no longer able to tackle the issues of the 21st century'.[159] It has to avoid the fate of the ECSC – of solving 'non-problems'. Strain and tension will inevitably accompany almost everything that the EU does. Perhaps this friction should be seen as polishing rather than problematic – the Eurostar, the euro and the EU are as much products of tension as cooperation.

Despite the inclusion in the Treaty of a clause to leave the EU, European integration seems more likely to continue than end, even if this is faster and deeper between eurozone states than those outside the eurozone.[160] Now as in the past, France and Germany still need each other: 'France needs Germany to hide its weakness and Germany needs France to disguise its strength'.[161] In a display of intimacy and understanding, in 2003 France represented German interests at an EU summit meeting.[162] Despite fighting to get in, Britain continues to display equivocal commitment to the EU promising its electorate a referendum on membership and frustrating its European partners.[163] For others, EU accession remains a route to the resolution of national problems, be they economic or political. This was as true for Britain in the 1960s as it is now for Macedonia and Kosovo, new applicants in the twenty-first century.

---

[158]Philippe C. Schmitter, *How to Democratize the European Union . . . and Why Bother?*, Rowan and Littlefield Publishers, 2000

[159]Jukka Snell, ' "European constitutional settlement", an ever closer union, and the Treaty of Lisbon: democracy or relevance?', *European Law Review* 33(5), 2008, p. 9

[160]17 at time of writing. See 'The Divisiveness Pact' and 'Outs and Ins', *Economist*, 12–18 March 2011, p. 46 and p. 41 respectively

[161]*Economist*, 12–18 March 2011, p. 46

[162]Stephen Castle, 'Chirac represents Germany at EU summit, setting alarm bells ringing at Number 10', *Independent*, 16 October 2003, http://www.independent.co.uk/news/world/europe/chirac-represents-germany-at-eu-summit-setting-alarm-bells-ringing-at-number-10-583520.html

[163]Comment by Michel Roucard at http://www.theguardian.com/commentisfree/2014/jun/06/french-message-britain-get-out-european-union

Further reading

On the methods and process of regional integration:

Rachid Azrout, Joost van Spanje and Claes de Vreese, 'When News Matters: Media Effects on Public Support for European Union Enlargement in 21 countries', *JCMS* 50(5), 2012, p. 691

Thomas C. Fischer, 'An American Looks at the European Union', *European Law Journal* 12(2), March 2006, pp. 226–278

Laurence Henry, 'The ASEAN Way and Community Integration: Two Different Models of Regionalism', *European Law Journal* 13(6), 2007, pp. 857–879

Bruno de Witte, 'The European Union as an International Legal Experiment', in de Burca and Weiler (eds), *The Worlds of European Constitutionalism*, Cambridge University Press, 2011

On the Treaty of European Union:

Erika Szyszczak, 'Ratifying the Treaty on European Union: a final report', *ELR* 541, 1993

On the Constitutional Treaty:

Clive Church and David Phinnemore, 'The Rise and Fall of the Constitutional Treaty', in Michelle Cini (ed), *European Union Politics*, 2nd edn, Oxford University Press, 2007

Christian Joerges, On the Disregard for History in the Convention Process, *European Law Journal* 12(1), January 2006, pp. 2–5

George Tsebelis, 'Agenda Setting In The EU Constitution: From The Giscard Plan To The Pros Ratification(?) Document', Paper presented at the DOSEI conference, Brussels 2005; http://sitemaker.umich.edu/tsebelis/files/giscardagenda.pdf

On the Lisbon Treaty:

Desmond Dinan, 'Institutions and Governance: Saving the Lisbon Treaty – An Irish Solution to a European Problem', *JCMS* 47, Annual Review 2009, pp. 113–132

Jukka Snell, '"European constitutional settlement", an ever closer union, and the Treaty of Lisbon: democracy or relevance?', *European Law Review* 9, 2008

Daniel Thym, 'In the Name of Sovereign Statehood: A Critical Introduction to the Lisbon Judgement of the German Constitutional Court', *CMLR* 46, 2009, p. 1795

Part I

The EU Institutional Setting

2 The central institutions of the EU

Setting the scene

With the Treaty of Lisbon, the European Council has solidified as one of the official EU institutions, ostensibly nestling itself at the top of the political hierarchy. Some commentators assert that the law has already taken over from the facts here, and that the body may justifiably be perceived as the 'European government'.

de Waele and Broeksteeg, 2012

1. Introduction

A new Article 13 was inserted into the TEU by the Treaty of Lisbon. It states that:

(1) The Union shall have an institutional framework which shall aim to promote its values, advance its objectives, serve its interests, those of its citizens and those of the Member States, and ensure the consistency, effectiveness and continuity of its policies and actions.

This paragraph opens Title III TEU on the institutions, which can be described as the culmination of the concerns and objectives expressed in the Laeken Declaration of 2000 and the White Paper on Governance in 2001. Both documents identified the need to change internal procedures in order to improve the role of Europe in the lives of its residents and citizens, thus it emphasises the *raison d'être* of the Union in the twenty-first century – to promote the Treaty values and objectives; to serve the interests of the citizen and the member states; and to ensure the consistency, impact and sustainability of its actions. The institutions are designed to pursue these goals.

Article 13 TEU lists the Union's institutions as: the European Parliament, the European Council, the Council, the European Commission, the Court of Justice of the European Union, the European Central Bank, and the Court of Auditors. These institutions are obliged to 'practice mutual sincere cooperation'.[1] The first five bodies form what Hix[2] also calls the 'government' of the European Union political system. He argues that:

the EU need not be a state to fulfil many of the traditional functions of government . . . the EU certainly possesses all the classic characteristics of a political system . . . Executive, legislative and judicial powers are exercised 'jointly' by the EU institutions. Nevertheless, instead of a classic 'organic' separation of powers into three different institutions, there is a 'functional' separation of powers across several institutions . . . [3]

Farrell and Heretier disagree with this:

the European Union is neither a standard democratic nation state, nor an intergovernmental organization, but something in between. There is no 'government' as such in the European Union, with a party to support it in Parliament; rather, there are fifteen governments, each with specific mandates from their domestic population.[4]

Are these institutions and their procedures adequate to be called a 'government'? If not that, what else? As the quote at the beginning of the chapter suggests, does the European Council sit atop this political hierarchy?

This debate will form the backdrop to an exploration of the key policy and law-making institutions – the European Parliament (the EP), the European Council (the EC), the

---

[1]Article 13(1)(2)
[2]Simon Hix, *The Political System of the European Union*, MacMillan, 1999
[3]Hix 1999, p. 344
[4]Henry Farrell and Adrienne Héritier, 'The Invisible Transformation of Codecision: Problems of Democratic Legitimacy', SIEPS Paper 2003, pp. 7, 27

Council of Ministers (the Council) and the European Commission (the Commission). The advisory committees – the Economic and Social Committee (ECOSOC) and the Committee of the Regions (COMREG)[5] – will not be examined. The CJEU will be dealt with in a separate chapter.

The elements of the exploration will be taken from Article 13(2) TEU, where each institution is mandated to act 'within the limits of the powers conferred on it in the Treaties, and in conformity with the procedures, conditions and objectives set out in them'. The chapter will outline the powers: what authority does each institution have, for what functions and how is it exercised? It will discuss their composition and identify supervisory relationships between the institutions.

One thing that the EU seems to have in excess are senior officers. Each institution has at least one President and Vice-President. The Lisbon Treaty changed the presidencies of the institutions and created a new one. Examination of the presidencies may shed light on the nature of 'government' in the EU and the place of the European Council within it. The final section will be devoted to understanding the powers, roles and accountability of these senior officers of the EU. Perhaps clear leadership makes the EU more 'governmental'?

2. The key institutions: powers, tasks and composition

i.   The European Parliament

According to Article 14(1), the European Parliament (EP) has three main functions. First, it 'shall, jointly with the Council, exercise legislative and budgetary functions'; second, it 'shall exercise functions of political control and consultation as laid down in the Treaties'; and finally, it 'shall elect the President of the Commission' – the Commission President is the head of the EU executive and possibly the most powerful position in EU policymaking. These will each be examined in turn.

a) Legislative functions

The current European Parliament has little in common with the Assembly created by the Treaty of Rome in 1957. That body had very limited functions while the current EP performs significant roles in relation to the adoption of legislation and the EU annual budget. It is a body with important responsibilities – after exploring these we will consider the extent to which its composition helps or hinders it in the fulfilment of these tasks. Its composition was less important in 1957, when it was an Assembly appointed by the member states.

Under the Treaty of Rome, it performed a marginal function in the adoption of legislation[6] but the introduction and development of co-decision[7] has made it a powerful co-legislator. Under co-decision (now known as the ordinary legislative procedure or OLP), legislation may only be adopted with the approval of the EP. Article 14 TEU entrenches this status in the Treaty. Nonetheless, the EP lacks a function usually associated

---

[5]See Articles 300–307 TFEU
[6]C-138/79 *Roquette Frères* v *Council* [1980] ECR 3333
[7]Article 294 TFEU – as this chapter focuses on functions, the legislative procedures will be discussed in a subsequent chapter.

with a legislature – the responsibility to propose legislation. Only the Commission may propose new legislation. The Maastricht Treaty created a limited EP right of initiative – Article 225 TFEU allows the EP to request that the Commission submit a proposal, subject to the support of a majority of the EP members, if it considers a Union act is required in order to implement the Treaties. However, the Commission is under no obligation to do so, in which case it must only inform the EP of its reasons. The EP has no further recourse under the Treaty, unless it can bring an action for failure to act under Article 266 TFEU. Paradoxically for a law-making chamber, the EP has a stronger power to veto legislation than to propose it. Its power to propose legislation is on a par with that set out in the European Citizen's Initiative (ECI) in Article 11(4) TEU.

The EP also now performs a role as a supervisor of the exercise of executive power. Previously, it was a semi-privileged applicant under Article 263 TFEU thus unable to automatically intervene or bring actions for annulment before the Court of Justice. The decision in *Chernobyl*[8] gave the EP limited additional authority to intervene only in order to protect its interests.[9] Under the Lisbon Treaty it is now a fully privileged applicant before the CJEU, sharing the same status as the member states, Council of Ministers (CM) and Commission to bring an action for judicial review:

> The Court of Justice of the European Union shall review the legality of legislative acts, of acts of the Council, of the Commission and of the European Central Bank, other than recommendations and opinions, and of acts of the European Parliament and of the European Council intended to produce legal effects *vis-à-vis* third parties. It shall also review the legality of acts of bodies, offices or agencies of the Union intended to produce legal effects *vis-à-vis* third parties. It shall for this purpose have jurisdiction in actions brought by a Member State, the European Parliament, the Council or the Commission.

This is a significant power, as it enables the EP to intervene at another stage – after the adoption of legislation – to influence the political content of EU law and policy.

b) Budgetary control

In relation to the budget, Article 314 TFEU states that the EP now shares equal control with the Council of Ministers on all aspects of EU spending. Before 1970, the Council was the sole budgetary authority, with the EP having a consultative role. This changed with the Treaties of 1970 and 1975:[10] the former gave the EP the last word on 'non-compulsory' expenditure (around 8 per cent of the budget) – 'compulsory expenditure' on items related to Treaty obligations or arising from legislative initiatives remained under the control of the Council. The 1975 Treaty gave the EP a right to reject the budget as a whole.

The Lisbon Treaty removed this distinction between compulsory and non-compulsory costs – the full budget must now be agreed by the European Parliament before it can be adopted. The draft annual budget is prepared by the Commission and sent simultaneously to the Council and EP. The Council adopts a position which it sends to the Parliament for amendment or approval. The EP has 42 days to approve or amend the Council Position.

---

[8]See C-302/87 *Parliament v Council* (Comitology) [1988] ECR 5615 and C-70/88 *Parliament v Council* (Chernobyl) [1991] ECR I-4529
[9]C-181 and 248/91 *Parliament v Council* (Aid to Bangladesh) [1993] ECR I-3685
[10]Treaties of 22 April 1970 and 22 July 1975

In the event that the EP does not adopt a position on the Council draft, the budget is deemed to be adopted. Thus the EP only has a veto power where it is united. If the Council disagrees with the EP amendments, discussions will be taken to a Conciliation Committee, where 28 members of the Council and EP work together to produce a joint text. The budget for 2014 went into this conciliation process and was agreed only in November 2013. The 2014 budget is 142.6 billion euros. The budgetary power is therefore significant.

The responsibility to draft the Parliament's position falls upon the EP Budgets Committee. This Committee is also responsible for preparing the framework for the seven-year budgetary exercise from 2014 to 2020 (the 'Multiannual Financial Framework'). It also has the task of fulfilling the Lisbon Treaty goal that the EU budget be fully financed by own resources. Own resources, comprising customs duties, VAT and a proportion of national income as well as taxes on staff salaries and infringement fines, flow directly to the EU. They account for 99 per cent of the EU income.

c) Political control and consultation

The EP exercises political control in a variety of ways. Its strongest form of control is perhaps the 'Investiture of the Commission' – since the Maastricht Treaty in 1992, the Commission President and the Commissioners can only be appointed after they have been approved by the EP as a whole. Although the EP has held hearings[11] for the individual Commissioner-designates since 1999, MEPs cannot veto individual Commissioners. They can only block all members of a new Commission from taking up their duties. The EP threatened to exercise these powers in 2004 due to the Italian nominee for Justice Commissioner, Rocco Buttiglione – a devout Catholic, Buttiglione had 'described homosexuality as "a sin" and slighted unmarried mothers and working wives'.[12] Chaos was only averted when Buttiglione withdrew. For some commentators this highlighted the need to revise 'ridiculous' rules preventing the EP from vetting individual nominees.[13]

Election of the Commission President is another form of political control. Under Article 17(7) TEU, the European Council shall propose a candidate for the President of the Commission to the EP. The proposal 'shall take into account the elections to the European Parliaments'. This connection has been introduced to add meaning and relevance to the EP elections but also to strengthen the political legitimacy of the Commission President. Legitimacy is further enhanced as the candidate must be elected by a majority of the EP. In 2012, the EP adopted a resolution stressing the importance of connecting the elections to the Commission 'more directly to the choice of the voters'. The resolution also called for members of the next Commission to be drawn from the EP and suggested that in order to secure a gender balance in the European Commission, member states should propose a female and male candidate.[14]

The linkage is therefore intended to illustrate that the chosen Commission President is a response to the preferences of the electorate but the strength of this link remains to be seen. The EP elections of May 2014 were the first time that this was put into practice. The lack of commitment to this principle was immediately apparent – following these

---

[11]http://www.europarl.europa.eu/hearings//default.htm;jsessionid=D4C2F1525AF70A86A48D38BE4BC6B79B?language=EN
[12]Stephen Castle, 'Defiant MEPs on course to vote out new Commission', *Independent,* 27 October 2004, p. 21
[13]Stephen Castle, 'European democracy would be advanced by a vote against the Commission', *Independent,* 27 October 2004, p. 30
[14]European Parliament resolution of 22 November 2012 on the elections to the European Parliament in 2014 (2012/2829(RSP))

elections, Jean-Claude Juncker emerged as the favourite candidate among the member states[15] but Britain strongly opposed this and, in an unprecedented move, British Prime Minister David Cameron published a newspaper article in which he appealed directly to voters not to support Juncker's candidature.[16]

The Commission as a body is responsible to the EP – this is manifested in a somewhat extreme power – the power to sack the Commission as a whole. This motion of censure existed in the Treaty of Rome:

Article 17(8) TEU: The Commission, as a body, shall be responsible to the European Parliament. In accordance with Article 234 of the Treaty on the Functioning of the European Union, the European Parliament may vote on a motion of censure of the Commission. If such a motion is carried, the members of the Commission shall resign as a body and the High Representative of the Union for Foreign Affairs and Security Policy shall resign from the duties that he carries out in the Commission.

Article 234 TFEU requires the entire Commission to resign if a two-thirds majority of the votes cast by the EP support this. There have been only eight motions of censure since 1957: none has been adopted – in 1999, the threat of censure following findings of fraud and cronyism by Commissioner Edith Cresson[17] led to the resignation en masse of the Santer Commission.

Political control is also exerted via the submission of written and oral Parliamentary questions (Article 230 TFEU) to the Commission. The Commission must reply either orally or in writing. In addition, Article 233 TFEU calls for the EP to discuss in open session the annual general report submitted to it by the Commission. This public review of the Commission performance may enhance overall transparency of the EU.

In relation to consultation, the EP enjoys scrutiny over the common foreign and security policy. Article 36 TEU states that the High Representative for Foreign Affairs must regularly consult the EP on the 'main aspects and basic choices' of the common foreign and security policy and keep it informed on the evolution of policies. This enables the EP to formulate questions and make recommendations to the High Representative and Council.

Beyond this, the EP can establish temporary parliamentary committees of inquiry (PCIs) to investigate allegations of maladministration in the implementation of Union law (Art. 226 TFEU). This power was introduced at Maastricht and allows these Committees to be set up at any time for an unspecified duration. PCIs can be used to conduct an in-depth investigation into a particular issue. In theory, they can be very useful not only to enhance the EP powers of control but also to draw public attention to specific issues and place topics on the political agenda. Previous Committees have been established to investigate cross-national problems such as the Community Transit System, BSE or the Equitable Life Pension scandal.[18] In practice they are weak – the exercise of these powers was set out in an inter-institutional agreement of 1995.[19] Except with regard to

---

[15]http://www.bbc.co.uk/news/u http://www.europeanvoice.com/elections-2014-possible-presidents/k-politics-27827729
[16]David Cameron, 'Invented Process to appoint President of the European Commission is damaging to democracy', Letter to *Irish Times*, 13 June 2014
[17]C-432/04 *Commission* v *Edith Cresson* [2006] ECR I-6387
[18]http://www.europarl.europa.eu/parlArchives/comArch/staticDisplay.do?language=EN&id=157
[19]Decision 95/167 of the EP, the Council and the Commission of 19 April 1995 on the detailed provisions governing the exercise of the European Parliament's right of Inquiry. A Regulation to improve the power of PCIs was proposed in 2012: http://www.publications.parliament.uk/pa/cm201213/cmselect/cmeuleg/86xxv/8608.htm

the European Commission, the committee cannot summon witnesses, punish refusals to cooperate or give evidence. It cannot subpoena documents or request assistance from a national court.[20]

Finally, the EP can receive individual or group petitions on matters falling within the scope of the Union's activity from any citizen, natural or legal person residing in the EU (Art. 227 TFEU) – these are addressed to the EP President.

ANALYSING THE LAW

Is the provision of political and supervisory powers for the EP an adequate alternative to a law-making initiative?

---

d) Composition

These are significant powers and tasks – what is the nature of the body to which they are entrusted? The EP is unique organisation. Since 1979 it has been the only directly elected institution of the European Union, and the only directly elected international parliament in the world. When created as an appointed Assembly in 1957, it was one of many such parliaments established after the Second World War. Such 'transnational parliaments' have mushroomed since the end of the Cold War – by now there are about 50 worldwide.[21]

Article 14(2) TEU: The European Parliament shall be composed of representatives of the Union's citizens. They shall not exceed seven hundred and fifty in number, plus the President. Representation of citizens shall be degressively proportional, with a minimum threshold of six members per Member State. No Member State shall be allocated more than ninety-six seats.

The EP is no longer composed of non-elected national officials: elections are held every five years[22] thus there have been seven elections to this body (EP7 began its term in May 2014). At 35 per cent, the EP now has a higher share of women members than all of the parliaments in the member states. However, its performance in relation to other indices of diversity, such as race and ethnicity, are low. Diversity in the EP is important because when the EU accedes to the European Convention on Human Rights, it will also join the Council of Europe: the EP will send a delegation representing its interests to the Parliamentary Assembly of the Council.[23] Homogeneity needs to be addressed so that shortcomings in one institution are not replicated in others.

---

[20]Report on the crisis of the Equitable Life Assurance Society (2006/2199(INI)) by the Committee of Inquiry into the crisis of the Equitable Life Assurance Society. Rapporteur: Diana Wallis. FINAL A6-0203/2007, p. 340, http://www.europarl.europa.eu/comparl/tempcom/equi/report_en.pdf
[21]Christiane Kraft-Kasack, 'Transnational Parliamentary Assemblies: A Remedy for the Democratic Deficit of International Governance?', *West European Politics* 31(3), May 2008, pp. 534–557
[22]Article 14(3) 'The members of the European Parliament shall be elected for a term of five years by direct universal suffrage in a free and secret ballot.'
[23]Jean Paul Jacqué, 'The Accession of the European Union to the European Convention on Human Rights and Fundamental Freedoms', *Common Market Law Review* 48, 2011, p. 995

A numerical maximum was inserted at Lisbon due to a concern that a more numerous body might lose its capacity to work effectively. The European Council Summit in June 2013 adopted a decision bringing the size of the next EP down to 750 members by redistributing the number of seats: the lowest number of seats is increased to six but the highest number is reduced from 99 to 96. This will be reviewed again prior to the elections for EP8 in 2019.[24] Following the accession of Croatia on 1 July 2013 there were 766 Members of the European Parliament (MEPs); since the May 2014 elections this has gone back down to 751.

The EP represents citizens, while the European Council represents the member states and the Council of Ministers represents national governments – this is entrenched in Article 10(1) TEU. Degressive proportionality refers to the unfortunate circumstance that MEPs in larger member states have more constituents than those in smaller ones. This is unsatisfactory as it means that citizens in smaller member states in theory enjoy better representation which produces 'unbalanced representation.'[25] It can be argued that a method needs to be developed to allocate seats between member states in a fair, objective and transparent manner.

Beyond this, it is questionable how 'representative' the EP actually is of the European citizens: turnout at elections in 2009 and 2014 was just 43 per cent (down from 62 per cent in 1979).[26] Eurobarometer results for 2009 reported a steep drop in confidence in the European Parliament, describing the results as 'the worst in ten years': as Figure 2.1 shows, the proportion of Europeans who express trust in the European Parliament stood at 45 per cent (−6 points) while the proportion who tend not to trust it increased from 31 per cent in Autumn 2008 to 37 per cent in January–February 2009.

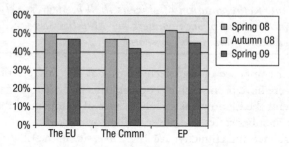

FIGURE 2.1   Trust in the EU

Source: Eurobarometer 76: Public Opinion in the EU, December 2011, p. 21 http://ec.europa.eu/public_opinion/archives/eb/eb76/eb76_first_en.pdf

---

[24]European Council, 'The European Council decides on the composition of the European Parliament 2014–2019', Press Release, 28 June 2013, http://www.consilium.europa.eu/uedocs/cms_data/docs/pressdata/en/ec/137648.pdf
[25]Juan Mayoral, 'Democratic improvements in the European Union under the Lisbon Treaty: Institutional changes regarding democratic government in the EU', Robert Schuman Centre for Advanced Studies, University European Institute, February 2011, p. 2
[26]Eurobarometer 2009

Although by Autumn 2010 this had improved – 48 per cent tended to trust the EP – trust levels fell to 41 per cent by Autumn 2011. The Commission suffered a similar downfall, with levels of trust dropping from 44 per cent to 36 per cent in the same timeframe.[27] It is noticeable, however, that the EP retained higher levels of trust than the Commission.

Arrangement of the EP elections may affect both turnout and trust. MEPs are elected during national competitions organised by the Member states, often alongside local elections. There is no pan-European format for this. EP elections are often seen as secondary national competitions, as they are fought on national rather than European issues. Attention has been paid to the lack of real EU level elections for the EP in the context of concerns for the substance of EU citizenship. The Commission has argued that in the current state of affairs it is difficult for citizens to exercise basic rights of political expression, and in 2012 submitted a proposal to improve the link between European political parties and European citizens and civil society:

2.4. Participation in the democratic life of the Union

The right to vote and to stand as a candidate in municipal and European elections in the host Member State is the political expression of the concept of European citizenship. Yet, in practice, the exercise of this right leaves much to be desired, and must be facilitated by communication and information campaigns on the rights associated with citizenship of the Union. With a view to the European elections of 2014, careful thought should be given to measures to encourage citizens: an ambitious approach based on electoral campaigns that focus on genuine European debates must be facilitated. It will be helpful if it can be made easier for citizens to take part in all stages of the voting procedure and to register on the electoral roll, and if the elections can be held in the week of 9 May. More generally, ways of adding to the electoral rights of citizens residing in another Member State should be studied, on the basis of periodic reports submitted in accordance with the Treaty, in order to increase the participation of citizens in the democratic life of their Member State of residence.[28]

European leaders were too preoccupied with the challenges of fiscal Union to pay much attention to this request prior to the 2014 elections.[29]

Furthermore, MEPs do not sit in party formations, but in broad political groupings, each with its own Chair. Every national party represented must therefore identify a formation within which its national and European political agenda will best fit. Prior to 2009, there were seven such political groupings: European People's Party (EPP); Group of the Progressive Alliance of Socialists and Democrats (S&D); Group of the Alliance of Liberals and Democrats for Europe (ALDE); Group of the Greens/European Free Alliance Greens (EFA); Confederal Group of the European United Left – Nordic Green Left (GUE/NDL); Europe of Freedom and Democracy Group (EFD) (where the UK Independence Party sits).

---

[27]See Eurobarometer 76: 'Public Opinion in the EU', December 2011, p. 21, http://ec.europa.eu/public_opinion/archives/eb/eb76/eb76_first_en.pdf. Subsequent data are not available as the survey question changed.

[28]European Commission, 'An area of freedom, security and justice serving the citizen', Brussels, COM(2009) 262 final, p. 10

[29]European Commission, 'Proposal for a Regulation of the European Parliament and of the Council on the statute and funding of European political parties and European political foundations', COM(2012) 499 final

Their much larger number means that the EPP and S&D dominate the plenary sessions, where votes are taken after the work of the Committees is discussed. Their size also allows these groupings to dominate the EP committees, where the real work of dealing with legislation is conducted.

The election of 2009 saw a shift to the right in the EP and resulted in the creation of a new grouping known as the European Conservatives and Reformists Group (ECR), within which the British Conservatives now sit. That year also saw the British National Party (BNP), 'on a sad day for Britain'[30] send its first two MEPs to Strasbourg. It is ironic that a polity designed to defeat fascism now hosts those same ideas in its most democratic institution. The 2014 elections increased the representation of right-wing Eurosceptic views in the EP.

The organisational structure may also seem impenetrable: in addition to a Secretariat of around 5,400 officials (excluding temporary and contract staff), the MEPs form one level of a bureaucracy that includes a President and 14 Vice-Presidents; a Bureau of the Parliament (consisting of the President, VPs and five quastors); a Conference of Presidents (made up of EP Presidents, EP party chairs, chairman of the Conference of Committee Chairmen); and a Conference of Committee Chairmen (which includes all of the Committee Chairs). Finally, MEPs are less stationary than their national counterparts. They endure a nomadic existence: the EP meets in Brussels, Luxembourg and Strasbourg. It also works in 20 official languages.[31]

VIEWPOINT

Do you think that the internal organisation of the EP contributes to the low levels of trust in the EP?

Contrary to popular perception, the political composition of the EP is important. There is a direct relationship between the outcome of EP elections and key EP 'product': amendments to Commission proposals. According to its size, each political grouping will chair one of the 20 committees that produces these amendments. A committee consists of 24 to 76 MEPs, and has valuable administrative resources including a bureau

TABLE 2.1   Distribution of seats and committee chairmanship in EP8 (2014–2019)

EP 2014 (EP 2009)	EPP	S&D	ECR	ALDE	GREENS/EFA	GUE/NDL	EFD	NI
Parliamentary seats	221 (265)	191 (184)	64 (54)	59 (84)	54 (55)	52 (35)	32 (32)	43 (27)
Committees chaired	(8)	(6)	(1)	(3)	(1)	(1)	(0)	(0)

---

[30]Martin Wainwright, 'EU elections: BNP's Nick Griffin wins seat in European parliament', *Guardian*, 3 December 2011, http://www.guardian.co.uk/politics/2009/jun/07/european-elections-manchester-liverpool; Bruno Waterfield, 'BNP take their seats in European Parliament', *Telegraph*, 3 December 2011, http://www.telegraph.co.uk/news/world-news/europe/eu/5824547/BNP-take-their-seats-in-European-Parliament.html
[31]http://www.elections2014.eu/en/new-parliament

and a secretariat. They are open to the public and cover topics from women's rights to security and defence, and the budget.[32]

The Committees are the heart of the EP.[33] Members are drawn from all political groupings. It is here that specialists who undertake the detailed scrutiny of proposals for legislation and design amendments which are then presented to the EP plenary for public discussion and debate (Art. 16(8) TEU). Preparatory work for the Parliament's plenary sittings takes place at this level. Given the specialised nature of the committee composition, proposed amendments are rarely challenged at plenary sessions. The Plenary has limited exposure to the issues and little time to conduct business so Committee decisions are unlikely to be questioned when presented to the plenary. Consequently, the organisation of and decision-making within the committees is of crucial importance for effective representation of diverse voices in agenda setting.

The Committees have a common structure: each has its own Chair, bureau and secretariat. Some have sub-committees, focusing on specific issues. Because of their central role in the exercise of EP authority and 'legislative entrepreneurship',[34] the Committee Chair is a powerful, highly honoured and prized position. The Committee Chair exerts significant influence on the contents of these amendments and their political colour – red, yellow, green, blue or black – matters.[35] As the largest political grouping, the EPP will chair the most committees; the EFD do not chair any. The ECR, a Eurosceptic Conservative grouping that is now the third largest in the EP, chairs one Committee. Chairmanships are reallocated at the beginning of every EP term. Distribution is determined by the 'D'hondt method', which awards the role according to the overall number of EP seats secured by the group.

APPLYING THE LAW

Who is the MEP for your constituency? What political party do they belong to? Where does that party sit in the EP? Does that grouping chair any committees?

---

ii. The European Council

When created in 1974, the European Council (EC) was an informal body meeting as a subset of the Council of Ministers. It was not mentioned in the Treaty of Rome and was only formalised by the Single European Act.[36] The duties of the EC were not outlined in the Single European Act but its general function was to set a strategic direction for the EU and tackle issues over which there was stagnation in the Council of Ministers. In order

---

[32]At present there are 22 standing committees as well as two ad hoc committees on 'Financial, Economic and Social Crisis' and a 'Policy Challenges Committee'. See http://www.europarl.europa.eu/activities/committees/committeesList.do?language=EN

[33]Gail McElroy, 'Committee Representation in the European Parliament', *European Union Politics* 7(1), 2006, pp. 5–29

[34]C. Anthony di Benedetto, *Journal of Product Innovation Management* 23(1), January 2006, p. 1

[35]Roger Scully, Simon Hix and David M. Farrell, 'National or European Parliamentarians? Evidence from a New Survey of the Members of the European Parliament', *JCMS* 50(4), 2012, pp. 670–683

[36]Article 2

to fulfil this general role it met twice a year. It did not have an administration of its own: meetings were prepared by the General Secretariat of the Council of Ministers, in conjunction with the Foreign Ministries in the Member states. Its role was first explicitly stated in the TEU as being 'to provide the Union with political direction and impetus (as for example with EMU or the Employment strategy); second to be a forum for political decision in sensitive areas (e.g. CFSP); third to discuss the budget; and finally to set the agenda for major reforms, such as constitutional changes.

A key proposal to change its status was introduced by the Constitutional Treaty. The CT proposal became Article 15(1) TEU:

Article 15(1): The European Council shall provide the Union with the necessary impetus for its development and shall define the general political directions and priorities thereof. It shall not exercise legislative functions.

In performing these duties, it has no legislative role – this remains the responsibility of the Council of Ministers. Its key job is strategic policy guidance rather than law making. Nonetheless, the EC has at least three further critical tasks: the first is to act as an arbiter when there is stalemate within the Council; the second is to accept applications and set out the conditions of eligibility for countries wishing to join the EU;[37] and the third is to consider a new option – requests to leave the EU.

a) Strategic political guidance

The European Council has to take a long-term and strategic view of the activities and objectives of the EU in all of its areas of competence:

Article 22(1) TEU: On the basis of the principles and objectives set out in Article 21, the European Council shall identify the strategic interests and objectives of the Union. Decisions of the European Council on the strategic interests and objectives of the Union shall relate to the common foreign and security policy and to other areas of the external action of the Union. Such decisions may concern the relations of the Union with a specific country or region or may be thematic in approach. They shall define their duration, and the means to be made available by the Union and the Member States.

In order to complete these tasks the EC can set up ad hoc committees, such as the Dooge Committee that planned the political edifice which became the EU. More recently it established the Task Force on Economic Governance in response to the debt crisis engulfing EU member states.[38] The objective of the Task Force is to 'devise proposals for better budgetary discipline and an improved crisis resolution framework' – its report 'Strengthening Economic Governance in the EU'[39] was presented to the EC in October 2011 by the EC President, Hermann Van Rompuy. Its recommendations included creation of an 'early warning system' fiscal surveillance system, deeper coordination of financial policy in the 'European semester',[40] creation of a crisis resolution framework for the eurozone to

---

[37]Article 49 TFEU
[38]http://www.european-council.europa.eu/the-president/taskforce.aspx?lang=en
[39]http://www.consilium.europa.eu/uedocs/cms_data/docs/pressdata/en/ec/117236.pdf
[40]This is the new annual cycle of economic policy coordination, established in the wake of the eurozone crisis. See http://ec.europa.eu/europe2020/making-it-happen/index_en.htm

address financial distress and containment, a stronger institutional framework for economic governance and, of course, tighter fiscal discipline. As the EC works on an intergovernmental basis, all 27 heads of state and government have to agree for any of this action to be taken: decisions are based on unanimity. It can only act when all members agree to do so on the recommendation of the CM.[41]

b) Arbitration of stalemates

The EC now has the task of managing inter-institutional relations: it is to set out the configurations of the Council (Art. 236 TFEU), determine the presence of a human rights breach by a member state (Art. 7(2) TEU) and is the final referee in relation to disputes between the member states. This role is now formalised in Article 82(3) TFEU:

> *Article 82(3) TFEU: Where a member of the Council considers that a draft directive as referred to in paragraph 2 would affect fundamental aspects of its criminal justice system, it may request that the draft directive be referred to the European Council. In that case, the ordinary legislative procedure shall be suspended. After discussion, and in case of a consensus, the European Council shall, within four months of this suspension, refer the draft back to the Council, which shall terminate the suspension of the ordinary legislative procedure.*

Other previously informal arrangements were also formalised by the Lisbon Treaty. For example, prior to the Lisbon Treaty, some supervisory responsibility over the EC was exercised by the EP, to whom the EC had to report after each meeting and annually: this arrangement is now entrenched in Article 15 TEU, as a duty upon the President of the EC.

c) Overseeing membership of the EU

Under Article 49 TEU, applications made to join the EU are conditional upon eligibility conditions agreed upon by the European Council (as well as the consent of the EP). A new power was bestowed upon the EC at Lisbon:

> *Article 50(1) TEU: Any Member State may decide to withdraw from the Union in accordance with its own constitutional requirements. 2. A Member State which decides to withdraw shall notify the European Council of its intention. In the light of the guidelines provided by the European Council, the Union shall negotiate and conclude an agreement with that State, setting out the arrangements for its withdrawal, taking account of the framework for its future relationship with the Union. That agreement shall be negotiated in accordance with Article 218(3) of the Treaty on the Functioning of the European Union. It shall be concluded on behalf of the Union by the Council, acting by a qualified majority, after obtaining the consent of the European Parliament.*

Article 50 TEU also sets out that withdrawal from the EU will be set out in an agreement, which can enter into force up to two years later. A state that withdraws may rejoin albeit subject to the same accession procedure used by new members. Had Scotland voted for independence in September 2014, it would therefore have been significant whether it was treated as a new or continuing member – there is only one way in the Treaty to join the EU.

---

[41]Article 22(1) TEU

> **APPLYING THE LAW**
>
> What conditions should the European Council set on states wishing to leave
> the EU?

d) Composition

Its composition continues to be drawn directly from the governments of the member
states:

---

*Article 15(2) TEU: The European Council shall consist of the Heads of State or
Government of the Member States, together with its President and the President
of the Commission. The High Representative of the Union for Foreign Affairs and
Security Policy shall take part in its work.*

The only member of this formation who does not represent a member state is the High
Representative of the Union for Foreign Affairs and Security Policy (HR). The High
Representative is a new position, created by the Lisbon Treaty. The HR is appointed by
the European Council using qualified majority voting, with the agreement of the President
of the Commission, and can be removed from office using the same procedure.[42] The role
of the High Representative is to conduct and contribute to the Union's common foreign
and security policy, and its security and defence policy.[43] The post-holder is also a Vice-
President of the Commission and shares with it responsibility for ensuring consistency in
the Union's external relations and coordinating other aspects of the Unions external
action.[44] As the HR is also Chair of the Foreign Policy Council in the Council of Ministers,
this is the only senior EU post that straddles three of the central institutions.

Under Article 13(1) TEU, the EC is now a full institution of the EU. As a formal EU
institution, all of its work and decisions are within the jurisdiction of the CJEU. It can
therefore also be the target of an action under Article 263 TFEU, although it is not clear
which of its decisions will be 'acts' for the purpose of that provision. Its role under Article
17(7) TEU in the appointment of the President of the Commission and the Commissioners may fall into this category, as well as its decisions relating to accessions and Treaty
reforms. It can be assumed that those decisions published in the *Official Journal* will fall
under the scope of the CJEU.

Article 15(3) TEU provides that the European Council 'shall meet twice every six
months, convened by its President'. These meetings are the so-called 'Summits', where
leaders of European governments meet to discuss immediate problems (such as the crisis
in the eurozone), determine strategy, adopt amendments to the Treaties and find agreement on long-term policies. However, as the summits to discuss the euro crisis in 2011
demonstrated, any firm decision to act may be elusive – except where the Treaties provide
otherwise, decisions of the European Council must be taken by consensus.[45] Summits can

---

[42]Article 18 TEU
[43]Article 18(2) TEU
[44]Article 18(4) TEU
[45]Article 15(4) TEU. See also European Council Decision of 1 December 2009 adopting its Rules of Procedure (RP)
(2009/882/EU) Article 6

be held more regularly – if the situation so requires, the President is called upon to convene a special meeting of the European Council under Article 15 (3) TEU). Unlike the Council of Ministers, all of its meetings are closed to the public although the EC is bound by general provisions concerning access to Council documents. It may also choose to make public the result of votes.[46] Heads of state are therefore shielded from public view when they sit in the European Council.

iii. The Council of Ministers

The Council of Ministers (the Council or CM) is the key decision-making organ of the EU. The Council of Ministers should not be confused with the European Council, although the formal titles of these institutions are very similar. They are distinct both in relation to their tasks, powers and composition.

Article 16 1 TEU: The Council shall, jointly with the European Parliament, exercise legislative and budgetary functions. It shall carry out policy-making and coordinating functions as laid down in the Treaties.

It was designed in 1957 as the central forum for debate and decision-making and has retained that position. The Council is responsible for the day-to-day pursuit of all aspects of the EU work agenda, from appointments to social security policy, and thus must work closely with the Commission. For example, it adopts, together with the Commission President-elect, the list of the other persons proposed for appointment as members of the Commission;[47] it determines the rules governing the committees provided for in the Treaties (Article 242 TFEU); and all the salaries, allowances and pensions of all senior EU officials – the Presidents of the European Council and the Commission, the High Representative, the Members of the Commission, the Presidents, Members and Registrars of the Court of Justice of the European Union, and the Secretary-General of the Council. It also determines any payment to be made instead of remuneration (Article 243 TFEU).

a) Legislative and budgetary functions

All consultations for any measure pass through the Council, whether it be a proposal for a legal instrument or consideration of soft law measures. Until the Lisbon Treaty, the CM had final say on proposals from the Commission: the situation is now different in that it can only adopt a Commission proposal if the EP agrees. The two institutions must therefore work together to ensure laws are made as necessary. The Council may exercise its powers jointly with the EP, but the Treaty gives it much more individual autonomy. It can for example, delegate its law-making powers to the Commission;[48] the EP cannot do this. The CM can also request the Commission to undertake studies in specific areas or submit a proposal. Unlike such requests from the EP, the Commission must respond positively.

---

[46]Rules of Procedure Articles 4 and 10

[47]Article 17(7)(2) – 'They shall be selected, on the basis of the suggestions made by Member States'

[48]C-9/56 *Meroni & Co., Industrie Metallurgiche, SpA v High Authority of the European Coal and Steel Community;* [1957-1958] ECR 133 Articles 290 and 291 on delegated and implementing legislation

Furthermore, there is still an area where the CM can act alone:

Article 29 TEU: The Council shall adopt decisions which shall define the approach of the Union to a particular matter of a geographical or thematic nature. Member States shall ensure that their national policies conform to the Union positions.

The pillar structure introduced by the TEU gave the CM exclusive competence over Common Foreign and Security Policy (CFSP) and Justice and Home Affairs (JHA). Under Article 26(2) TEU, the Council has the duty to frame the CFSP and must implement it according to strategic guidance from the European Council. Any decisions relating to the CFSP, including those initiating a mission, must be adopted unanimously by the CM on a proposal from the High Representative or an initiative of a member state.[49] Despite abolition of the pillar structure, the member states retain control over this area of policy by virtue of its exclusion from the jurisdiction of the CJEU. No legislative acts may be adopted.[50]

The CM holds a great deal of power but it does not formally oversee or 'supervise' any other institution. As the tasks of the Union have mushroomed over the last 50 years – not only have they become broader, but more sensitive and requiring a faster response – it probably has enough to do managing its own affairs. Additionally, in relation to accountability, it is increasingly anomalous that the CM does not answer to any higher body. However, as all of its members are indirectly elected, it can be argued that it is also indirectly held accountable by the electorates in the member states.

b) Composition

The CM has a very different composition to the European Council:

Article 16(2) TEU: The Council shall consist of a representative of each Member State at ministerial level, who may commit the government of the Member State in question and cast its vote.

This point is emphasised in Article 203(1) TFEU raising the possibility that the representative need not necessarily be a minister, but must have the authority to commit their government. However, the Council is a more complex institution than its name suggests: it is named after these ministers because they form the most visible and senior layer, but it has three other layers: COREPER I and II, the working groups as well as the Presidencies. Much of the daily work in Brussels is conducted by the permanent representatives in COREPER, the full-time heads of national missions to the EU:

Article 16(7) TEU: A Committee of Permanent Representatives of the Governments of the Member States shall be responsible for preparing the work of the Council.

COREPER has two sections: COREPER II, which deals with horizontal and politically sensitive issues is where the permanent representatives themselves sit. They prepare the ministerial meetings of the GAER, JHA and ECOFIN.[51] Their deputies sit in COREPER I, which handles all dossiers for the remaining Council configurations.[52] COREPER has two main tasks: the first is to scrutinise Commission proposals; the second is to prepare

---

[49] Article 42(4)
[50] Article 24 (ex Article 11 TEC)
[51] see below on configurations of the Council
[52] M. Westlake and D. Galloway, *The Council of the European Union*, John Harper, 2004, p. 204

the agenda for the Ministerial meetings. It will then produce two lists of items: 'A' items are those which need no discussion and have been agreed; 'B' items are those which require discussion.[53]

COREPER coordinates a further layer of over 200 working groups, which help it to fulfil its tasks.[54] This layer of the Council is not mentioned in the Treaty but these working groups function at the heart of EU law. They are the real problem-solving forums of the Council – this is where most of the vital work on legislation is done. Members of the working groups tend to be civil servants from the member states. They work in a consensual atmosphere trying to smooth out problems arising from Commission proposals before they are passed on to the relevant council via COREPER for formal approval or in rare circumstances a vote by the Ministers.

c) Policy-making and coordinating functions

The ministers meet in nine different configurations determined by policy area:

Article 16(6) TEU: The Council shall meet in different configurations, the list of which shall be adopted in accordance with Article 236 of the Treaty on the Functioning of the European Union. The General Affairs Council shall ensure consistency in the work of the different Council configurations. It shall prepare and ensure the follow-up to meetings of the European Council, in liaison with the President of the European Council and the Commission. The Foreign Affairs Council shall elaborate the Union's external action on the basis of strategic guidelines laid down by the European Council and ensure that the Union's action is consistent.

The Finance ministers from the 28 member states will meet in the Economic and Financial Affairs Council; national interior and justice ministers will meet in the Justice and Home Affairs Council; labour ministers will meet in the Employment, Social Policy and Consumer Affairs council; likewise, the relevant ministers will meet in the Councils for Competitiveness; Transport, Telecommunications and Energy; Agriculture and Fisheries; Environment; Education, Youth and Culture. As mentioned above, the General Affairs and Foreign Affairs councils have more horizontal functions.

Unlike the other Council configurations, the Foreign Affairs Council has a permanent Chair, who is in fact not a minister from a member state: the High Representative of the Union for Foreign Affairs and Security Policy (HR) created by the Lisbon Treaty has specific responsibility for foreign, security and defence policy:

Article 27(1) TEU: The High Representative of the Union for Foreign Affairs and Security Policy, who shall chair the Foreign Affairs Council, shall contribute through his proposals to the development of the common foreign and security policy and shall ensure implementation of the decisions adopted by the European Council and the Council. 2. The High Representative shall represent the Union for matters relating to the common foreign and security policy. He shall conduct political dialogue with third parties on the Union's behalf and shall express the Union's position in international organisations and at international conferences.

---

[53]R. van Schendelen, *Machiavelli in Brussels: The Art of Lobbying the EU Amsterdam,* Amsterdam University Press, 2002
[54]A list of preparatory groups is now available at: http://register.consilium.europa.eu/pdf/en/13/st05/st05581.en13.pdf

The Chair of the Foreign Affairs Council is 'assisted' by a European External Action Service, which works alongside national diplomatic services. Members include officials from the national diplomatic corps, as well as persons from relevant departments of the Council General Secretariat and the Commission.[55] The HR, who is also a Vice-Commissioner in the Commission, is to work with the Council to 'ensure the unity, consistency and effectiveness of action by the Union'.[56] The HR links the European Council, the Council and Commission – the only institution in which she has no seat is the EP. This is the only EU role that straddles three of the main institutions.

Legislative measures agreed by the EU are therefore in practice adopted by the relevant sectoral Council rather than the Council as a whole. Within this, however, there is scope for the Council to act across the formations: for example agricultural decisions can be adopted by the transport council. This is a practical necessity because these ministers do not spend their working lives in Brussels – they are based in the member states and must attend to their EU duties alongside the numerous tasks arising in the national arena.

VIEWPOINT

Should there be a permanent Council of Ministers in the EU?

---

d) Council voting methods

The voting system was updated in the Lisbon Treaty to make qualified majority voting the normal mode of adopting decisions in the Council. According to Article 16(3) TEU, the Council must now adopt measures according to QMV unless the Treaty provides otherwise. Under this system of voting, each member state has a set number of votes allocated according to its population size. This means that countries like Germany, Poland and the UK have the largest number of votes, while states such as Luxembourg and Malta have the smallest.[57] This distribution also applies to the European Council when it is acting under QMV.[58] When unanimous voting is used, abstention is futile – it counts as a yes (Art. 238(4) TFEU).

This is a stark contrast to voting under the Treaty of Rome, where majority voting was the exception and unanimity the norm. It is a strong indication that the EU has moved beyond its intergovernmentalist origins – under QMV, member states can be forced to accept measures with which they do not agree. The transition to QMV as the norm has a number of important consequences. It removes the national veto – business within the Council of Ministers can no longer be held to ransom by an intransigent member state.

---

[55]Article 27 (3) TEU 'The organisation and functioning of the European External Action Service shall be established by a decision of the Council. The Council shall act on a proposal from the High Representative after consulting the European Parliament and after obtaining the consent of the Commission.'
[55]Article 26(2) TEU
[57]The other arrangements governing the qualified majority are laid down in Article 238(2) TFEU.
[58]Article 235 TFEU

A new system came into force from 1 November 2014 that changed the calculation of the qualified majority. A qualified majority vote is now based upon a 'double majority':

> *Article 16(4) TEU: As from 1 November 2014, a qualified majority shall be defined as at least 55% of the members of the Council, comprising at least fifteen of them and representing Member States comprising at least 65% of the population of the Union.*

A higher threshold applies in two circumstances: first, where the Council acts on its own initiative or on a proposal from the EP, and second, where not all members of the Council participate in the voting, for example when the Council votes on the request of a member state to leave the Union (Art. 238(3)(b) TFEU). In these circumstances:

> *Article 238 TFEU: . . . the qualified majority shall be defined as at least 72% of the members of the Council, representing Member States comprising at least 65% of the population of the Union.*

However a well-functioning democracy should not be a tyranny of the majority – a mechanism to *prevent* the adoption of legislation is required. The TEU has made provision for measures to be halted by a 'blocking minority'.

> *Article 16(4) TEU: A blocking minority must include at least four Council members, failing which the qualified majority shall be deemed attained.*

An observant reader may wonder how the voting system operates in practice – as proposals can be adopted across the council configurations, who is voting? The question is, however, even more fundamental: how often does the Council vote? This depends upon how often topics reach the ministerial meetings for discussion and decision: according to Hage,[59] ministers will decide between 35 per cent and 48 per cent of all Council matters. The frequency of voting depends upon the workload of the Council configuration:

> the proportion of decisions that are directly taken by ministers seems to be related to the workload of a certain Council configuration. The fewer acts that are dealt with in a certain policy area, the higher the proportion decided on the ministerial level. For example, three out of the four decisions in Education were made by ministers and five out of the six in Employment. Notable exceptions to this pattern are Transport, with an overall number of 21 decisions, of which 14 (67 per cent) were made on the political level of the Council, and GAER, in which only 1 out of 17 decisions (roughly 6 per cent) 20 was decided by the ministers.[60]

The existence of a 'compliance paradox' means that voting is likely to be avoided: whether ministers agree or not they will have to implement the decision at home if the measure is adopted. If they openly oppose it in Brussels, they will encourage pressure at home for

---

[59]Frank Hage, 'Who Decides in the Council of the European Union?', *JCMS* 46(3), 2008, pp. 533–558
[60]Hage 2008, p. 547

non-implementation. It is therefore in their best interests to avoid explicit voting and to seek consensus, as consensus in Brussels will ease compliance at home.[61]

Voting may be further avoided as the Council proceedings become more transparent. In line with the Laeken Declaration, changes have been made to improve openness in the ministerial meetings. Under Article 16(8) TFEU final voting on draft legislation is to be conducted in public view. These sessions are now recorded and broadcast over the internet.[62] Voting patterns are also published for those interested to consult.[63] As a result of these changes, the working atmosphere in the Council should become slightly less secretive – national ministers may become more accountable but also this access may help the public to understand the processes by which important decisions are made.

VIEWPOINT

Should all Ministerial Councils be open to the public? Consider the advantages and disadvantages of making the adoption of EU law more transparent.

iv. The European Commission

The European Commission (the Commission) emerged from the 'High Authority' created by the Treaty of Paris for the ECSC. It was envisioned as the 'embryonic federal government' for Europe. It was given a wide range of significant tasks from internal budgetary management to external representation. It is therefore no wonder that it is seen as the civil service of the EU. Perhaps most importantly of all, it is the 'guardian' of the Treaty: it not only oversees compatibility of national action with EU law but has the power to bring member states before the CJEU if it feels this is warranted by an infringement. It determines this alone, after communication with the relevant national authorities. The decision is made by the Commission as a whole, based upon its working principle of collective decision-making and responsibility.

Article 17(1) TEU: The Commission shall promote the general interest of the Union and take appropriate initiatives to that end. It shall ensure the application of the Treaties, and of measures adopted by the institutions pursuant to them. It shall oversee the application of Union law under the control of the Court of Justice of the European Union. It shall execute the budget and manage programmes. It shall exercise coordinating, executive and management functions, as laid down in the Treaties. With the exception of the common foreign and security policy, and other cases provided for in the Treaties, it shall ensure the Union's external representation. It shall initiate the Union's annual and multiannual programming with a view to achieving interinstitutional agreements.

---

[61]van Schendelen 2002; Thomas König and Sven-Oliver Proksch, 'Exchanging and voting in the Council: endogenizing the spatial model of legislative politics', *Journal of European Public Policy* 13(5), August 2006, pp. 647–669
[62]http://video.consilium.europa.eu/
[63]http://video.consilium.europa.eu/index.php?pl=2&sessionno=3506&lang=EN

a) Enforcement

The Commission is described as the 'guardian' of the Treaties. As such, it oversees the *acquis communitaire:* the Treaties plus 9,576 regulations and 1,989 directives[64] as well as the case law of the CJEU. Compliance is a continual problem and the Commission is responsible for initiating and ensuring enforcement of Union law. Together with the CJEU, it must oversee the application of the Treaties and secondary legislation not only in the member states but also by its co-institutions.

The procedures by which it does this have developed over the years. Management modes have developed since 1957. A direct centralised mode of enforcement is pursued under Articles 258–260 TFEU, which allows the Commission to commence infringement proceedings for faulty or late transposition and non-transposition of directives, backed up by the threat of a judicial and financial sanction. Newer, non-Treaty, forms of indirect arms length enforcement (EU PILOT and SOLVIT) have been introduced to make the system more efficient. These systems have introduced 'co-administration' – they are implemented together with agencies in the member states.

Article 105 TFEU makes the Commission solely responsible for enforcement of EU competition law – the European Competition Network (ECN), set up under Regulation 1/2003, helps it to fulfil this duty. Finally, the Commission has standing to request annulment of a measure before the CJEU under Article 263 TFEU.

The Commission pursues its role as guardian zealously and has sometimes overstepped its Treaty remit for this role. On such occasions the CJEU and national judges have reprimanded it. In *Commission* v *Portugal,* the CJEU annulled a Commission decision that Portugal had failed to comply with an infringement decision – the CJEU held that the Commission acted beyond its powers.[65] In *Newby Foods*[66] a national court described as 'improper' the Commission intention to encourage disregard for a court order in the member states. This case is worthy of further discussion as it gave rise to the novel question on the extent to which the Commission is obliged to enforce decisions of a national court.

Regulation 853/2004 sets out classifications for 'mechanically separated meat' (MSM) – under Article 1(14) product removed using mechanical means 'resulting in the loss or modification of the muscle fibre structure' is MSM. The Commission interpreted this provision as applying to *any* meat mechanically separated, even though Article 1(15) of the regulation defined meat as those products which had 'undergone processes insufficient to modify the internal muscle fibre structure of the meat.' Newby Foods argued that its products fell under Article 1(15). The national judge asked the CJEU to comment on the Commission interpretation and in the meantime suspended the enforcement of the national measure implementing the EU regulation by granting Newby Foods interim relief.[67] This allowed Newby Foods to continue selling its product in the internal market without labelling it as MSM. However, Newby Foods produced evidence suggesting that the Commission was taking action to ensure that Newby Foods could only sell its meat outside the UK if labelled as MSM, thus undermining the effectiveness of the interim order.

Newby Foods sought a declaration that the Commission action was contempt of court. This led to two novel questions relating to the accountability of the Commission: first,

---

[64]European Commission Annual Report 2012, http://ec.europa.eu/eu_law/docs/docs_infringements/annual_report_30/com_2013_726_en.pdf

[65]C-292/11P

[66]*Newby Foods* v *Food Standards Agency* [2014] EWHC 1340 (Admin)

[67]As set out in C-143/88 and C-92/89, *Zuckerfabrik Süderdithmarschen* v *Hauptzollamt Itzehoe* and *Zuckerfabrik Soest GmbH* v *Hauptzollamt Paderborn* (1991) (ECR I-415) [33]

was the Commission (or a national court in any other member state) bound by the interim relief granted by a national court; and second, was the Commission under any duty to respect the order? Is the Commission bound to 'guard' the decisions of a national court in the same way as decisions of the CJEU? The Commission argued that the national court lacked jurisdiction 'to control or otherwise seek to sanction' its exercise of the powers conferred on it by the Treaties.[68] The national judge agreed but added a provision – while it lacked jurisdiction to 'determine the lawfulness or otherwise' of the acts of the Commission, the duty of sincere cooperation laid out in Article 4(3) TEU and discussed in *Zwartveld*[69] applied to the behaviour of the Commission:

> [57] As a corollary of the obligation that rests on national courts it seems to me that the duty of sincere cooperation owed by Commission institutions must extend to according full and proper respect to orders made by the courts of Member States that are intended to secure or preserve individual rights under Community [Union] law. In my view, the exercise of that duty involves avoiding conduct that is deliberately directed at undermining an order of a national court made after due inquiry into the relevant facts. All the more so where the Commission has intervened in the relevant proceedings before a national court and has been given a full opportunity to put forward its position.

> [58] It appears to have been common ground, at least at one stage, and, if it is not any longer, it is my view that if a product is lawfully produced in accordance with an order of a national court it follows that it is, in principle, entitled to be put into free circulation in other Member States unless and until the Court of Justice, or a national court acting within its own jurisdiction, declares otherwise. It is not in my view proper for a Commission institution itself to declare that the decision of the national court is of no effect outside the jurisdiction of the Member State concerned, if that is done in a manner that implies that the court order can just be ignored. That is the function of the appropriate court (whether that is a national court or the Court of Justice will depend on circumstances).

The national judge held that the Commission role as guardian of the Treaties does not exempt it from the duty of sincere cooperation laid out in the TEU unless it is acting in good faith to, for example, protect human and animal health. Encouraging disregard for a court order was described as 'improper' rather than 'contempt.' It remains to be seen whether the CJ agrees with this assessment of the duty of the Commission to comply with decisions of a national court but the Court seems in no hurry to address the question – it declined the request to expedite the case.[70]

APPLYING THE LAW

Find and read Article 4(3) TEU and *Newby* v *FSA* – what is meant by the principle of 'sincere cooperation' and how is it relevant in this case?

---

[68][47]

[69]C-2/88 *Zwartveld and others* [1990] ECR I-3365

[70][17]. The CJ decided against Newby Foods on 16th October 2014. See C-453/13 *Newby Foods Ltd* v *Food Standards Agency* (nyr). The CJ made no comment on the obligations of the Commission.

b) Short- and long-term planning

The Commission is responsible for ensuring that the Union works to achieve the goals set out in the Treaty. It does this by setting out its work agenda in an annual Work Programme. This programme identifies the priorities for the Commission, the activities it will undertake and the policies which it will present to the Council and EP for adoption. Priorities are widespread – for 2014 they include, for example, finalisation of measures to promote growth and job creation, investment in innovation and research, enhancing the fight against undeclared work, tax fraud and tax evasion, reinforcement of economic governance through completion of the Banking Union, implementation of the Single Supervisory Mechanism and agreement on the Single Resolution Mechanism and preparation for a new international climate agreement.

c) Legislative

In addition, the Commission holds the monopoly on initiating new EU laws:

Article 17(2) TEU: Union legislative acts may only be adopted on the basis of a Commission proposal, except where the Treaties provide otherwise. Other acts shall be adopted on the basis of a Commission proposal where the Treaties so provide.

It initiates legislation at the request of the CM in almost all areas of EU competence. Legislative acts can usually only be adopted on the basis of a Commission proposal. It is expected to use its huge resources of expertise to draft proposals which will then be amended by the CM and EP. It is to function here as a 'neutral broker' or civil service, allowing the CM and EP to play the more political roles. It can, however, also exercise powers delegated to it by the CM and EP under Articles 290 and 291 TFEU – the powers delegated must be clearly set out in law if they are not to be revoked by the CJEU.

Its role is therefore multifaceted: it does more than execute policy, but also plans, designs, coordinates, manages and enforces it, not only within the EU but also beyond in countries where the EU pursues its development policy and humanitarian activities. External representation is now shared with the High Representative for Foreign Affairs. The other institutions depend upon the Commission to initiate and manage these activities, and oversee the budget that it is given to do so. The Commission must ensure that the money is spent as planned and that all expenditure is accounted for. Its workload continues to grow: for example, by the end of 2014, police and judicial cooperation in criminal matters will be fully integrated into EU law – the Commission must therefore set out a vision for the evolution of justice and home affairs policies as the Stockholm programme comes to an end.[71] Small wonder perhaps that it has a staff of over 30,000 employees.

ANALYSING THE LAW

Consider which body/ bodies perform these tasks in a member state? Is the Commission doing too much?

---

[71]Communication from the Commission to the European Parliament, the Council, the European Economic and Social Committee and the Committee of the Regions: Commission Work Programme 2014, COM(2013) 739 final, p. 9

d) Composition

What organisational framework supports this activity? The European Commission is separated into distinct departments, or 'Directorates General' (DGs). Each DG has its own Commissioner; every member state also has its own Commissioner (reduced from two per member state to just one in 1992) thus at present there are 28 DGs.[72] The 'Commission' refers therefore to the 28 Commissioners and their Directorates. The task of these Commissioners is to protect the interests of the EU as a whole. Decisions are taken on a collegiate basis – all must agree for Commission action to be taken. This applies to its law-making as well as its enforcement role.

These Commissioners are not elected, and although nominated by their member state, they are to be independent of it and act in the interests of the EU during their term of office:

Article 17(3) TEU: The Commission's term of office shall be five years. The members of the Commission shall be chosen on the ground of their general competence and European commitment from persons whose independence is beyond doubt. In carrying out its responsibilities, the Commission shall be completely independent. Without prejudice to Article 18(2), the members of the Commission shall neither seek nor take instructions from any Government or other institution, body, office or entity. They shall refrain from any action incompatible with their duties or the performance of their tasks.

There has been little research on the actual nature of the independence of the Commissioners. One evaluation focused on the *anatomy* of the Commission in order to assess the *autonomy* of its officials. Focusing on the temporary officials employed in the Commission, who have an 'ambiguous affiliation towards the Commission' the study concluded that their specific position allowed them to 'blend departmental, epistemic and supranational behavioural dynamics, thereby safeguarding their behavioural autonomy'.[73]

This is an important finding because the Treaty is silent on the recruitment of Commission officials, and is even somewhat ambiguous on the precise nature of the appointment of Commissioners. This has altered over the years, in an attempt to address criticisms that the Commission is an unelected behemoth and prevent occurrences of nepotism. Under the Maastricht Treaty, the Commissioners were nominated by the member states in consultation with the proposed Commission President. This changed slightly at Amsterdam, when the Commission President gained a right to veto the national nominee. Since Maastricht, the Commission has had to be approved *en bloc* by the European Parliament. This procedure is still in place and has been extended to include the High Rep:

Article 17(7)(3) TEU: The President, the High Representative of the Union for Foreign Affairs and Security Policy and the other members of the Commission shall be subject as a body to a vote of consent by the European Parliament. On the basis of this consent the Commission shall be appointed by the European Council, acting by a qualified majority.

---

[72]http://ec.europa.eu/commission_2010-2014/index_en.htm
[73]Jarle Trondal, 'The anatomy of autonomy: Reassessing the autonomy of the European Commission, *European Journal of Political Research* 47, 2008, pp. 467–488

As already mentioned, the EP may invite Commissioner-designates to hearings, but it cannot veto individual Commissioners.[74] This level of political control may not appear in the near future given the significant structural change that took place in 2014.

This change is 10 years overdue. As the EU prepared to receive 10 new member states in 2004, it was widely agreed that an institution with 25 Commissioners would be unwieldy. There are now 28 Commissioners. Agreement that change was necessary did not quickly translate into agreement on the nature of that change. Modifying the original design eluded EU leaders prior to the 2004 enlargement and agreement had to be reached with 27 rather than 15 member states. A proposal contained in the Constitutional Treaty suggested that by 2009 there be just 13 Commissioners rather than one per member state, selected according to 'equal rotation' to reflect the demographic and geographical range of the Member States'. While the Constitution failed, parts of this proposal were in fact adopted. The change was instituted at the end of 2014:

Article 17(5) TEU: As from 1 November 2014, the Commission shall consist of a number of members, including its President and the High Representative of the Union for Foreign Affairs and Security Policy, corresponding to two thirds of the number of Member States, unless the European Council, acting unanimously, decides to alter this number. The members of the Commission shall be chosen from among the nationals of the Member States on the basis of a system of strictly equal rotation between the Member States, reflecting the demographic and geographical range of all the Member States. This system shall be established unanimously by the European Council in accordance with Article 244 of the Treaty on the Functioning of the European Union.

The new Commission could therefore have had between 18–20 members[75] but the Heads of State and Government agreed not to make this change. This may be because it remains unclear whether those member states without Commissioners will have any representation in a smaller configuration of this institution. The Lisbon Treaty did not go as far as the Constitution: it made no mention of gender representation or of 'non-voting Commissioners' that would sit alongside the voting members.

VIEWPOINT

Who is the Commissioner for your member state? Would the popular election of Commissioners enhance democracy in the EU?

---

3. Senior leadership in the EU: Presidential powers

This section will explore the power of the EU Presidents. The EU has many senior officials – each institution has at least one President and some in addition have several

---

[74]http://www.europarl.europa.eu/hearings//default.htm;jsessionid=D4C2F1525AF70A86A48D38BE4BC6B79B?
language=EN
[75]Croatia became the 28th member state of the EU in July 2013.

Vice-Presidents. Leadership is fragmented and power is unequal. Their tasks vary and merit separate consideration but there are at least three functions common to all:

- establishment of work programmes;
- everyday supervision; and
- public representation.

They differ significantly, however, in their: length of term of office; powers over internal members and their workload; powers over other institutions. Within the institutions, the most powerful President is the Commission President: neither the Trio of Presidents in the Council of Ministers nor the President of the European Council can compete with this position in terms of the key factors of leadership: transparency, visibility, playing an educational role, clarity, setting out a direction, credibility and continuity.[76] As Table 2.2 below shows, only the Commission President has the full range of tasks:

i.   The President of the European Commission

The President of the European Commission is perhaps the most democratically legitimate role in the EU. This person is proposed by the European Council to the European Parliament. In choosing a candidate, the EC must take into account the results of the EP elections. This candidate must be elected by the European Parliament by a majority of its component members. If the candidate does not obtain the required majority, the

TABLE 2.2   The EU presidents and their tasks

The EU presidents	Commission	Parliament	Council of Ministers	European Council
TERM	5 YEARS	5 YEARS	18/6 MTHS	2.5 YEARS
POWER TO SET WORK PROGRAMME	YES	NO	YES	NO
DETERMINATION OF VICE-PRESIDENTS	YES	Only with Heads of State	NA	NA
APPOINTMENT OF MEMBERS	YES	NO	NO	NO
RESIGNATION OF MEMBERS	YES	NO	NO	NO
INTERNAL TASK DISTRIBUTION	YES	NO	NO	NO
EXTERNAL EU REPRESENTATION	YES	YES	NO	YES

---

[76]Torun Dewan and David P. Myatt, 'The Qualities of Leadership: Direction, Communication, and Obfuscation', *American Political Science Review*, 102(3), August 2008

procedure must be repeated.[77] This means that in theory, the leader of the Commission will share the political ideology of the largest grouping in the EP.

This appointment procedure makes the Commission President the most powerful institutional President with the widest range of powers allocated by the Treaty. The 28 Commissioners work directly under her authority. The President of the Commission has a number of important responsibilities. The President has authority to lay down guidelines within which the Commission and its Commissioners will work and decides upon the internal organisation of the Commission, 'ensuring that it acts consistently, efficiently and as a collegiate body'. Beyond this administrative power, the Commission President also appoints all Commission Vice-Presidents from the ranks of the members of the Commission. The only VP not appointed by the President is the High Representative.[78] A member of the Commission must resign if the President so requests; the same applies to the High Representative, although a separate procedure is set out for this.[79]

The responsibility of the Commission President for the Commissioners is further emphasised by the fact that she not only sets out the structure of the Commission's responsibilities but also allocates them among the members. Commissioners are clearly placed under the authority of the President:

> *Article 248 TFEU: The responsibilities incumbent upon the Commission shall be structured and allocated among its members by its President, in accordance with Article 17(6) of that Treaty. The President may reshuffle the allocation of those responsibilities during the Commission's term of office. The Members of the Commission shall carry out the duties devolved upon them by the President under his authority.*

No other President exerts such control over the portfolios of members of their institution. The very public debate in 2014 over the nomination of Jean-Claude Juncker for this position is a clear indication of its importance.

ii.   The Council Presidency

The role of the President of the Council of Ministers is laid out in Article 16(9) TEU:

> *The Presidency of Council configurations, other than that of Foreign Affairs, shall be held by Member State representatives in the Council on the basis of equal rotation, in accordance with the conditions established in accordance with Article 236 of the Treaty on the Functioning of the European Union.*

The rotation is set out in a formal decision.[80] As previously noted, the Foreign Affairs Council has a permanent Chair – the High Representative shall preside over the Foreign Affairs Council for the term of that office.[81] Very little else is said in the TEU on the

---

[77] Article 17(7)
[78] Article 17(6)
[79] See Article 18(1)
[80] Council Decision of 1 January determining the order in which the office of President of the Council shall be held (OJ L1/11 2007). This will have to be amended to include Croatia, which formally joined the EU in July 2013.
[81] Article 18(3)

President of the Council of Ministers. This was, however, seen as a very prestigious role, especially for the smaller member states – it is a time when they have a chance to 'lead' the polity of 500 million people on a world stage. It has also been argued that the role holds significant agenda shaping – setting, structuring and exclusion – power. Vigorous agenda-shaping is tolerated in the expectation that each member state will have a chance to pursue their own objectives:

> When you are not the Presidency, you are swallowing bitter pills every day, only because you know that you will have the Presidency one day and the others will have to swallow their bitter pills. You suffer for six years and in the seventh you get to bash the others. The Presidencies are always overstepping the limits [of neutral behaviour]. What you want is a Presidency that is skilfully violating you so that it is not publicly visible.[82]

Of course, with 28 member states, each now has to 'suffer' the others for a little longer.

The traditional pattern has been that the Council Presidents rotated every six months. While holding this office, a minister of that member state chairs meetings of each of the Council configurations. The responsibilities of the Chair includes:

- arranging the meetings, setting the agenda and agenda priorities;
- developing political initiatives;
- liaising with the Commission and the EP Presidents;
- representing the Council in the other institutions;
- leading OLP procedures;
- signing agreed acts; and
- chairing the CM councils.

These are each significant tasks and despite the support of the General Secretariat of the Council, much of the work has to be conducted in the member states. This can cause a number of problems, not least of which is lack of continuity: six months was seen to be too short a time frame for any significant objectives to be achieved.

The single six-month rotation has therefore now been replaced by a group Presidency lasting for 18 months. During these 'Team Presidencies' the three member states develop a common programme which lays out the agenda for the term of the trio. This may reduce the influence that any single member state can exert over agenda setting, agenda structuring and agenda exclusion. Some scope remains – each of the trio will still have a six-month window to decide which Commission proposals go forward and which do not – but there is less likelihood that the Council agenda will swing from one issue to the other as was the case previously.

The Team Presidency assumes, however, that all member states are equally well organised. This is not the case – some national administrations are less well run for a number of different reasons. In addition, domestic political matters can confound the best laid plans for a productive Presidency. This was the problem during the Spain–Belgium–Hungary presidency from January 2010 to June 2011. A work programme was developed which set out a number of priorities in the areas of justice and home affairs, the internal market,

---

[82]Jonas Tallberg, 'The agenda-shaping powers of the EU Council Presidency', *Journal of European Public Policy* 10(1), February 2003, pp. 1–19, 16. See also Andreas Warntjen, 'Steering the Union. The Impact of the EU Presidency on Legislative Activity in the Council', *JCMS* 45(5), 2007, pp. 1135–1157; Robert Thomson, 'The Council Presidency in the European Union: Responsibility with Power', *JCMS* 46(3), 2008, pp. 593–617

external affairs and employment. Creation of an internal digital market was a priority. Spain had outlined legislative plans during its six months in office but these were not realised. As President-in-Office it was also down to Spain to provide the EU response to the volcanic ash cloud which floated across Europe during spring 2010 – it was slow to do so. By the time it handed over to Belgium it had improved somewhat but the period had not been highly productive. Belgium took over at a time when it was beset by domestic problems which hindered its effectiveness presiding over the CM.

The reforms have highlighted the limitations of the CM as a leadership rather than a law-making forum[83] and may explain the decision to create a 'permanent' President of the European Council: this was the office to provide the 'leadership' Henry Kissinger first sought in the 1970s when he asked 'Who do I call if I want to call Europe?

iii. The European Council President

The European Council President is the most senior figure in the European Council. The EC President previously shadowed the Council of Ministers presidency, rotating every six months. The same member state would therefore lead both Councils, which offered some level of coordination and cohesion but could also become a strain on national resources. There was also some overlap as the duties of the President were not outlined in the Single European Act. In general, the President was to guide the Council as it sought to set a strategic direction for the EU.

The first major proposal to change the role of the EC President arose from the Convention on the Future of the EU in 2001. It suggested that the President be elected by QMV on a term of two years, renewable once. Removal from office was to be by the same process. This suggestion was formalised in Art 15(5) TEU:

The European Council shall elect its President, by a qualified majority, for a term of two and a half years, renewable once. In the event of an impediment or serious misconduct, the European Council can end the President's term of office in accordance with the same procedure.

Article 15 TEU also gives the President specific tasks:

- to chair the Council and 'drive forward' its work;
- to ensure the preparation and continuity of the work of the European Council;
- to find cohesion and consensus within the European Council.

These tasks are expanded upon in the Rules of Procedure.[84] Reading them clarifies the administrative nature of the role. The EC President is to prepare for and follow up on the Council meetings. He has limited autonomy in this as it must be done on the basis of the work of the General Affairs Council (GAC).[85] This includes preparation of the agenda, which must be submitted to the GAC at least four weeks before the meeting, and preparation of the draft guidelines for the European Council conclusions, draft conclusions and

---

[83]O. Young, 'Political Leadership and Regime Formation: On the Development of Institutions in International Society', *International Organization* 45(3), 1991, pp. 281–308
[84]European Council Decision of 1 December 2009 adopting its Rules of Procedure (RP) (2009/882/EU)
[85]Article 2(1) RP

draft decisions.[86] Adopted decisions are signed by the EC President which suggests that s/he has some authority in determining their content.[87] During meetings, the EC President oversees the conduct of proceedings, ensuring that the rules are applied and discussions are conducted smoothly.[88] The Rules of Procedure call for 'close cooperation and coordination with the Presidency of the Council and the President of the Commission, particularly by means of regular meetings',[89] but requires only that EC President presents a report to the EP 'after each of the meetings of the European Council.[90]

The President may be the most senior figure but it is clear that this is not the most influential post on the EC.[91] For example, a major initiative chaired by the EC President was the recent Task Force on Economic Governance.[92] This was, however, very clearly dominated and driven by the member states, who as elected heads of state have a democratic mandate that the EC President lacks. The EC President also lacks access to administrative resources. There is no equivalent to COREPER in the EC. The exclusion from eligibility of a person holding a national office also means that the EC President will not have any national resources at his availability. Instead the President is 'assisted' by the General Secretariat of the Council.[93]

Does this matter? One advantage from the perspective of the EU is that it saves costs: no new administration is created to require additional resources. The absence of a new layer of bureaucracy also avoids any exacerbation of the democratic deficit. Yet there are some significant disadvantages – the General Secretariat already has its hands full in servicing the Council configurations, COREPER and the Working Groups – what guarantee is there that the work of the EC President will be given priority? The absence of an independent administration may also reduce the scope of autonomy of the EC President and undermine the effectiveness of the office in providing structural, entrepreneurial and intellectual leadership.[94] The lack of administrative support raises the question of whether there was any intention for the EC President to conduct substantive political tasks.

While there may be good reasons to avoid the clash of personalities that could arise with an EC President who enjoys a strong national profile, it is doubtful that a person without this can be a leader at the EU level. A national leader could bring a strong identity to the role from which the EU could benefit. A disadvantage may be that a strong leader from a member state will convey a strong national identity – the EC President should promote the EU identity not the national one. However, avoidance of a person with a strong national profile risks the EC President being a person with no international profile at all. This has been identified as a weakness of the current EC President, Hermann van Rompuy. In bringing anonymity to the office, the office itself is anonymous and overshadowed by national figures.

---

[86]Article 3 RP
[87]Article 12 RP. They are also signed by the Secretary General of the Council of Ministers.
[88]Article 4 RP
[89]Article 2(3) RP
[90]Article 5 RP
[91]Henri Dewaele and Hansko Broeksteeg, 'The Semi-Permanent European Council Presidency: Some Reflections On The Law and Early Practice', *Common Market Law Review* 49, 2012, pp. 1039–1074
[92]http://www.european-council.europa.eu/the-president/taskforce.aspx?lang=en
[93]Article 13 RP states: 'The European Council and its President shall be assisted by the General Secretariat of the Council, under the authority of its Secretary-General.'
[94]Spyros Blavoukos, Dimitris Bourantonis and George Pagoulatos, 'A President for the European Union: A New Actor in Town?' *JCMS* 45(2), 2007, pp. 231–252

At present therefore the EC President is not the 'go to' person sought by Henry Kissinger all those years ago. The absence of practical support and political authority makes van Rompuy a moderator rather than the initiator envisaged. He must not only vie with the Council of the Ministers – whose power was in no way diminished by the Treaty – but also with the member states: it is noticeable that the Team-Presidency of Spain, Belgium and Hungary prepared a mandate even though it is van Rompuy who should 'drive forward' the work of the EU[95] – it appears that the member states interpret this as meaning he is to be their political chauffeur rather than leader.

There is therefore little reason to mistake this new office as creating a President of the European Union. Observers may have assumed that the EC President was to take a leadership role but it is clear that a leader was not what the member states sought. This may seem illogical as the EC President will provide more continuity than the Council presidencies: over a span of five years, the European Council could have just one President compared to 9 in the Council of Ministers. However, in terms of legitimacy, being less accountable the EC President cannot challenge the more autonomous CM Presidencies. The role even shares tasks with the High Representative:

> *Article 15(6)(d)(2) TEU: The President of the European Council shall, at his level and in that capacity, ensure the external representation of the Union on issues concerning its common foreign and security policy, without prejudice to the powers of the High Representative of the Union for Foreign Affairs and Security Policy.*

The value of this role is therefore questionable. The EU may gain from the more corporate air offered by the EC President. Also, even if the EC President has little power to set or direct the agenda at least van Rompuy and his successors can exercise some oversight which may mean that the member states are held more accountable. The transfer of more managerial tasks to the EC President frees the national leaders to get on with the business of politics. However, if the EC is to set the strategic direction for the EU then its President should be given the resources for this significant task.

ANALYSING THE LAW

Who has more authority over EU law – the Commission President or the Council President?

iv. The European Parliament President

> *Article 14(4) TEU: The European Parliament shall elect its President and its officers from among its members.*

The EP has had its own President since 1952. It is the only institution to have had two female Presidents – Simone Veil (1979–82) and Nicole Fontaine (1999–02). Interestingly, unlike the Presidents of the other three institutions, the Treaty sets out no role for

---

[95]Christian Tomuschat, 'Calling Europe by Phone', *CMLR* 47, 2010, p. 3 (Editorial)

the EP President. However, an outline of the tasks associated with this office can be found on the EP President's web page: the President chairs the plenary sittings of Parliament, the Conference of the Presidents of Political Groups (seven) and the Bureau of Parliament (including 14 Vice-Presidents).

- the President chairs the plenary sittings of Parliament,
- the Conference of the Presidents of Political Groups (seven), and
- the Bureau of Parliament (including 14 Vice-Presidents).

She is also responsible for the application of the Rules of Procedure of Parliament, and, to this end, oversees all the activities of Parliament and its bodies.

The President plays an important representative role, both within the EU and beyond:

- she represents the EP perspective within the European Council, addressing this body before each of its meetings to lay out the EP position on the matters due to be discussed;
- will participate in the IGC alongside member state ministers;
- chairs the EP/CM conciliation delegations[96] on discussion of the EU budget; and
- signs it on behalf of the EP.

The EP President will also sign all legislative acts adopted under the ordinary legislative procedure. Externally, the President will represent the EP in all legal matters, and in its international relations: like the Commission President she will conduct official visits within and outside the EU. In order to fulfil these tasks, the EP Presidency has its own sizeable Cabinet, which it can commission to conduct strategic studies.

VIEWPOINT

Does the silence of the Treaty on the EP President undermine the authority of this institution?

4. A government for the EU?

Do these institutional configurations and roles equate to the government outlined by Hix? Taken altogether, what do these powers, roles and leaders tell us about the existence of a 'government? And do they fulfil the ambitions laid at Laeken, in the White Paper on Governance and perhaps most importantly in Article 13 TEU – are they organised to 'serve the interest' of the citizen?

As argued by Hix, the main institutions perform the key functions of government: they adopt law and policy to protect and enhance the lives of those that they govern. Using Hix's functional definition, the EU therefore has a government. However, Farell and Heretier are also correct – there is no party to support this government. Yet, it does operate according to a mandate – the Treaties. The aims and objectives laid out in the Treaties could only be adopted at Lisbon with the agreement of the member states and (as seen in Chapter 1) in many cases the direct approval of national electorates in the member

---

[96]The President may, under the EP/Council ordinary legislative procedure, chair the EP/Council conciliation committee.

states. Furthermore, as they say, the EU is neither an intergovernmental organisation nor a 'standard' nation state but the relevance of the political form is questionable – as the nation state emerged from the city state, this does not per se prevent the EU – a 'post-nation state' – from having a government.

However, the absence of a clear leader may undermine the claim that the EU has a government. Kissinger's question was insightful and remains to be answered adequately. Leadership in the EU is fragmented and constantly contested by the member states. If we were to ask who leads the government of the EU, the answer may well be – the President of the Commission, who exerts the most political authority over the EU bureaucracy and the most control over the EU's work programme. Whether this is a democratically legitimate state of affairs is a different question. It is indicative of the non-democratic aspirations of the Treaty that the EP President, leader of the only directly elected institution, has the fewest powers. The noble goals of linkage between the EU voters and EU political leadership set out in the Lisbon Treaty have been tarnished by the arguments over the next Commission President.[97]

Majone questions whether a 'government' can be defined by functions alone: does it need to have a clear source of powers – i.e. the citizens – in order to be worthy of this name? In the absence of legitimate powers derived from citizens, is the EU just 'a web of national and supranational regulatory institutions held together by shared values and objectives, and by a common style of policymaking'?[98] This question will be taken up in the discussion on the law-making powers of the EU.

The EU institutions are much changed from the time of their inception – Monnet would not recognise the bodies that he is credited with designing. Yet change inevitably begets other problems:

> Supranational power breeds secrecy yet it impedes processes that are commonly regarded as essential in a democracy, namely the possibility of citizens holding politicians and government officials accountable for their actions, and the possibility of having a public debate on government policy ... At the same time, certain democratic policies require secrecy in order to be effective at all.[99]

Transparency and accountability have improved to some extent:

- the Commission publishes its Rules of Procedure and an annual report on the activities of the Union;[100]
- the European Parliament must publish its proceedings;[101]
- the European Council must 'present a report to the European Parliament after each of the meetings of the European Council';[102] and
- the Council of Ministers must now 'meet in public when it deliberates and votes on a draft legislative act. To this end, each Council meeting shall be divided into two

---

[97]http://www.economist.com/news/europe/21604180-angela-merkel-constrained-search-compromise-over-appointment-next

[98]G. Majone, *Regulating Europe,* Routledge, 1996 cited in Hix 2006, p. 344

[99]Dierdre Curtin, 'Judging EU Secrecy', Amsterdam Law School Legal Studies Research Paper No. 2012-103; Amsterdam Centre for European Law and Governance Research Paper No. 2012-07

[100]Article 249 TFEU

[101]Article 232 TFEU

[102]Article 15(6)(d) TEU

parts, dealing respectively with deliberations on Union legislative acts and non-legislative activities.'[103]

This is unlikely to satisfy Majone. Do these reforms satisfy you?

VIEWPOINT

To what extent does the European Council sit at the top of the EU political hierarchy?

5. Conclusion

The institutions of the European Union are laid out in primary EU law – the Treaties. They have been reformed with every Treaty amendment yet have not changed their basic design since 1957. They were not designed to represent, engage or endear the public or serve the citizen – the bureaucratic apparatus created to pursue economic union 'did not operate properly, were unstable or did not work at all'.[104] In addition the institutional methods designed by Jean Monnet have been criticised as elitist and undemocratic. Nonetheless, the institutions perform functions of a government, and perhaps it should be no surprise that they suffer similar shortcomings as national governments – inefficiency, opaque procedures, unwieldy institutions and a surfeit of senior roles with overlapping and vague powers. The EU probably has more 'Presidents' and 'Vice-Presidents' than any national polity but their powers added together do not equate to that of any national head of state or government.

The EU institutions have consequently suffered from a poor public image that seems to have changed little despite the reforms over the years: not only is the EP seen as ineffective, cumbersome and expensive, but the Commission is still seen as power hungry and unaccountable, perhaps because it is the only body that has a central role in both law-making and enforcement of EU law. Surprisingly, given its centrality in the adoption of EU measures, the Council of Ministers has had to bear little criticism of its practices. This may be because it is comprised of Ministers who are duly elected in their respective member states.

The public image deficit suffered by the Commission and European Parliament may be due to their undemocratic origins and operational methods – transparency and accountability of these institutions was not part of the design concept. This has slowly been introduced in a gradual move away from Monnet's methods while maintaining the basic institutional structure. It is unlikely that he would recognise the supervisory roles which have been introduced to put in place checks and balances so that the institutions are more accountable to each other and to citizens in the member states.

Retention of the basic design may explain why attempts to reform the institutions since 2000 have had only slow success. These reforms have predominantly involved an incremental empowerment of the European Parliament. Yet despite the changes, the EP

---

[103]Article 16(8) TEU
[104]John Gillingham, *European Integration 1950–2003: superstate or new market economy?*, Cambridge University Press, 2003, p. 4

remains the weakest of the three main law-making bodies.[105] A sceptic might argue that this was intentional: although 'pro-integrationist' member states might prioritise granting more power to the Parliament 'member states less inclined towards integration might grant more power to the Parliament if they perceive no de facto change in the existing power distribution linked to the formalisation'.[106] This may explain why the changes to the EP have not had a dramatic effect on the democratic legitimacy of the EU as a whole.

There is little that can be changed in the Commission except to reduce its size or powers. It has been argued that such change is overdue:

> In EU lore, it is axiomatic that the European Commission has suffered from increasing overload. The conventional wisdom is that, over the years, the Commission picked up new responsibilities in different policy areas without the matching increases in available resources to develop and manage them. By the time of the fall of the Santer Commission in March 1999, tasks had outstripped capacity to the point where many were convinced that the management system in key areas had broken down irretrievably. The two reports by the Committee of Independent Experts (CIE) both documented these failures and suggested a comprehensive programme of management reform.[107]

Some of these suggestions, such as the introduction of impact and risk assessment procedures, have found their way into the Treaty of Lisbon. Whether they have actually reduced the workload of the Commission is another question. None of them have reduced its pre-eminence among the EU institutions that govern Europe.

---

[105]Christine Kraft-Kasak, 'Transnational Parliamentary Assemblies: A Remedy for the Democratic Deficit of International Governance?' *West European Politics*, 31(3) May 2008, pp. 534–557; 'European Elections: Is the European Parliament Important today?', *CMLR* 46, 2008, p. 767 (Editorial)
[106]Catherine Moury, 'Explaining the European Parliament's Right to Appoint and Invest the Commission', *West European Politics* 30(2), March 2007, pp. 367–391
[107]Roger P . Levy, 'European Commission Overload And The Pathology Of Management Reform: Garbage Cans, Rationality And Risk Aversion', *Public Administration* 84(2), June 2006, pp. 423–439

Further reading

On the institutions and democracy:

Juan Mayoral, 'Democratic improvements in the European Union under the Lisbon Treaty: Institutional changes regarding democratic government in the EU', Robert Schuman Centre for Advanced Studies, University European Institute, February 2011

Wolfgang Streeck, 'Markets and Peoples: Democratic Capitalism and European Integration', *New Left Review* 73, 2012

On the European Parliament:

Christiane Kraft-Kasack, 'Transnational Parliamentary Assemblies: A Remedy for the Democratic Deficit of International Governance?', *West European Politics* 31(3), May 2008, pp. 534–557

Roger Scully, Simon Hix and David M. Farrell, 'National or European Parliamentarians? Evidence from a New Survey of the Members of the European Parliament', *JCMS* 50(4), 2012, pp. 670–683

Christian Tomuschat, 'European Elections: Is the European Parliament Important today?', *CMLR* 46, 2008, p. 767 (Editorial)

On the European Commission:

Roger P. Levy, 'European Commission Overload And The Pathology Of Management Reform: Garbage Cans, Rationality And Risk Aversion', *Public Administration* 84(2), 2006, pp. 423–439

On the Council of Ministers:

Henri Dewaele and Hansko Broeksteeg, 'The Semi-Permanent European Council Presidency: Some Reflections On The Law and Early Practice' *Common Market Law Review* 49, 2012, pp. 1039–1074

Frank Hage 'Who Decides in the Council of the European Union?', *JCMS* 46(3), 2008, pp. 533–558

Robert Thomson, 'The Council Presidency in the European Union: Responsibility with Power', *JCMS* 46(3), 2008, pp. 593–617

Andreas Warntjen, 'Between bargaining and deliberation: decision-making in the Council of the European Union', *JEPP* 17(5), 2010, p. 665

On leadership in the EU:

Dierdre Curtin, 'Judging EU Secrecy', Amsterdam Law School Legal Studies Research Paper No. 2012-103; Amsterdam Centre for European Law and Governance Research Paper No. 2012-07

Torun Dewan and David P. Myatt, 'The Qualities of Leadership: Direction, Communication, and Obfuscation', *American Political Science Review* 102(3), August 2008

Christian Tomuschat, 'Calling Europe by Phone', *CMLR* 47, 2010, p. 3 (Editorial)

3 Legislative processes

Setting the scene

According to conservative estimates, over 79,000 adults, including 19,000 non-smokers, died in the EU-25 in 2002 due to exposure to tobacco smoke at home (72,000) and in their workplace (7,300). A Eurobarometer survey of March 2009 found 84 per cent of EU citizens in favour of smoke-free offices and other indoor workplaces, 77 per cent in favour of smoke-free restaurants, and 61 per cent supporting smoke-free bars and pubs. In 2014, 15 EU countries had comprehensive smoke-free laws in place. Ireland, the UK, Greece, Spain and Hungary have the strictest smoke-free provisions with a complete ban on smoking in enclosed public places, on public transport and in workplaces. In April 2014, the EP and Council adopted Directive 2014/40/EU on the approximation of the laws, regulations and administrative provisions of the member states concerning the manufacture, presentation and sale of tobacco and related products.

1. Introduction

Who makes the laws that govern the European Union, and how? Law-making is perhaps the most important function in a democracy: laws affect almost every aspect of life from where we park our cars to what we eat and the chemicals in our cosmetics. They regulate product content as well as behaviour and relationships of both the state and individuals. However, as important as the rules themselves is that they are followed. So it is not just the rules themselves that are important but how they are made, for this secures their credibility. Laws need to be fair, clear and comprehensible and in addition made according to procedures that are seen to be legitimate. Legitimate procedures must underpin rule-making if laws are to be considered credible by the populace who must follow them. This chapter will explore the typology of laws made in the EU and the procedures by which they are made.

A key question in relation to credibility is the source of authority used to make EU law – does this come from the 'people' of Europe? This question lies at the heart of the so-called 'democratic deficit'[1] at the centre of the EU regulatory environment, the law- and policy-making fora and procedures in a polity. The 'democratic deficit' has many aspects, such as the disengagement of the 'peoples' of Europe from law-making, the limited public debate and the marginal role of elected representatives in law-making. As the EP is the only directly elected body in the EU it was logical that this 'deficit' could be addressed by enhancing its role. This conclusion was arguably based upon an assumption that democracy in the EU was analogous to that in the nation state and would be improved by strengthening the role of elected representatives. The success of the democratic approach is questionable. This chapter will suggest an alternative approach to assessing this deficit that does not focus on elected representatives.

The chapter begins with an exploration of the law-making procedures themselves, looking at the different procedures for legislative and non-legislative measures. It then sets these within the regulatory environment of the EU to discuss the democratic deficit and a potential alternative. Finally, it analyses the EU law-making environment from the perspective of 'electocracy' – when viewed through this lens, does the EU look more legitimate?

2. The legal acts of the Union

The Treaty on the Functioning of the European Union (TFEU) lists five distinct forms of Union law, of which three are binding:

Article 288 TFEU: To exercise the Union's competences, the institutions shall adopt regulations, directives, decisions, recommendations and opinions. A regulation shall have general application. It shall be binding in its entirety and directly applicable in all Member States. A directive shall be binding, as to the result to be achieved, upon each Member State to which it is addressed, but shall leave to the national authorities the choice of form and methods. A decision shall be binding in its

---

[1]Giandomenico Majone, 'Europe's "Democratic Deficit": The Question of Standards', *European Law Journal* 4(1), 2002, pp. 5–28; Andrew Moravcsik, 'In Defence of the "Democratic Deficit": Reassessing the Legitimacy of the European Union', *Journal of Common Market Studies* 40(4), pp. 603–634; Andreas Follesdal and Simon Hix, 'Why There is a Democratic Deficit in the EU: A Response to Majone and Moravcsik', *JCMS* 44(3), 2006, pp. 533–562

entirety. A decision which specifies those to whom it is addressed shall be binding only on them. Recommendations and opinions shall have no binding force.

The Treaties constitute the primary source of Union law; these secondary forms have not changed since their introduction in 1957. The majority of laws made are regulations – 31 per cent of all EU legal measures take this form; 27 per cent are directives and only 9 per cent are decisions. Regulations are used where a rule needs to be implemented in the same way and at the same time in all of the member states. Agricultural measures are often laid out in regulations. Directives give member states more discretion: they can be implemented according to the culture and values of the member state as long as they satisfy the obligation set out in it. A timeframe of two years is usually given for this implementation to be completed.

Directives often deal with sensitive social issues such as health and safety, non-discrimination, or burden of proof. As such issues are differently addressed across the EU, Union law allows national administrations flexibility in how to achieve the aims laid out in them. As seen in the opening scenario, the new EU rules on smoking have been set out in a directive, allowing member states to adopt them in the most fitting way for their legal system. This may be via a new law or the amendment of an existing law. Either way, the national act must make clear that it is intended to implement the contents of an EU directive. Finally, a decision is a narrow legal tool which only applies to those to whom it is addressed – competition law findings under Article 9 of Regulation 1/2003 are often laid out in a decision. Non-binding instruments – recommendations and opinions – have also not changed.

The Lisbon Treaty retained all five forms but introduced is a new hierarchy of EU acts. Under Article 289(3) TFEU, 'legal acts adopted by legislative procedure shall constitute legislative acts'. This divides legal acts into two categories: those adopted by legislative procedure (*legislative* acts) and those which are not (*non-legislative* acts). This structural change was introduced to clarify the different *levels* of EU legal acts. Prior to Lisbon, the Treaties did not establish a hierarchy of secondary Union law. This has now been rectified: the binding forms of secondary Union law – regulations, directives and decisions – will now be either legislative or non-legislative. These non-legislative acts can be seen as a third or tertiary level of EU law.

The distinction between secondary and tertiary legal acts lies in the content and the law-making procedure. Legislative acts are now mainly created using the 'ordinary legislative procedure' (OLP – previously known as co-decision); non-legislative acts are made using other procedures. Legislative acts contain the 'essential' elements of the act while non-legislative acts can only address the non-essential elements of legislative acts.[2] The 'essential' elements consist of the normative content and direction of the policy; the 'non-essential' elements are, for example, classifications and lists.[3] Non-legislative acts are therefore complementary to legislative acts. They will complement the basic legislative acts in two ways: 'implementing acts'[4] are designed to secure a uniform implementation in the member states; 'delegated acts'[5] adapt or supplement existing legislation.

---

[2]C-355/10 *European Parliament* v *Council of the European Union*, Judgment of the Court of Justice (Grand Chamber) of 5 September 2012. For comment see Merijn Chamon, 'How the concept of essential elements of a legislative act continues to elude the Court. *Parliament* v *Council*', *Common Market Law Review* 50, 2013, pp. 849–860

[3]For example, the lists at issue in T-262/10 *Microban International and Microban* (Europe) v *Commission* [2011] ECR II-7697

[4]Article 291(2)

[5]Article 290

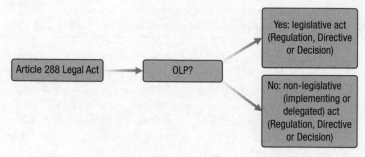

FIGURE 3.1   Article 288 TFEU Legislative and Non-legislative Acts

It is unhelpful that both legislative and non-legislative acts can appear in the same forms, that is as regulations, directives or decisions.[6] However, according to Article 291(4) TFEU the measure itself will make clear whether it is a legislative act or a non-legislative (implementing or delegated) act.[7] The procedure for adopting legal acts will be discussed in the following section.

ANALYSING THE LAW

What legal form does the smoking ban use? What must member states do to give it legal force in national law?

---

3. The legislative procedures

The procedures used to create Union law have been subject to continual change. Over the years they had expanded to a total number of 22 but this has now been significantly reduced and simplified. The main procedure is now known as the 'ordinary legislative procedure' (OLP). It is the default method for making EU law. The 'special' legislative procedures to be discussed in this chapter are consultation and consent.

i.   The ordinary legislative procedure (OLP)

Article 289(1): The ordinary legislative procedure shall consist in the joint adoption by the European Parliament and the Council of a regulation, directive or decision on a proposal from the Commission.

This procedure is defined in Article 294 TFEU. The ordinary legislative procedure laid out here was previously known as 'co-decision'. It provides for up to three readings of a

---

[6]Herwig Hoffman, 'Legislation, Delegation and Implementation under the Treaty of Lisbon: Typology Meets Reality', *European Law Journal*, 15(4), July 2009, pp. 482–505
[7]See, for example, Commission Delegated Regulation (EU) No 1268/2012 of 29 October 2012 on the rules of application of Regulation (EU, Euratom) No 966/2012 of the European Parliament and of the Council on the financial rules applicable to the general budget of the Union and Commission Implementing Decision of 18.4.2012 establishing a questionnaire for Member States reports on the implementation of Directive 2008/98/EC of the European Parliament and of the Council on waste

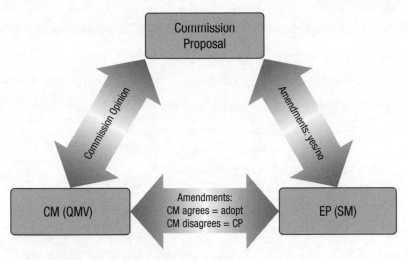

FIGURE 3.2 First reading under the OLP

proposed measure by the EP and the Council. The content of a legislative act has therefore potentially been extensively debated and amended by the EP and Council.

In this procedure, the EP operates as a co-legislator. The Commission will send its proposal to the Council and EP at the same time. The EP cannot reject the proposal at the first reading, only make amendments. However, if the EP and Council agree the proposal can be adopted at the first reading by the CM using Qualified Majority Voting (QMV). This is encouraged – the inter-institutional agreement states that 'the institutions shall cooperate in good faith with a view to reconciling their positions as far as possible so that, wherever possible, acts can be adopted at first reading'.[8] In 2009, 75 per cent of proposals were adopted at first reading; only 8 per cent passed through three readings.[9]

A 'fast track' first reading emerged in the late 1990s.[10] This procedure calls for the involvement of limited actors from the EP, CM and Commission. The EP committee rapporteur and shadow rapporteur are entrusted to conduct negotiations with the Council (Presidency representatives). The EP committee produces a report that acts as its mandate for negotiations with the Council. Once the report has been adopted by the committee, the Council's representatives open informal negotiations with the EP's rapporteur. The result is a compromise that is endorsed by the Council and submitted to the EP plenary, usually as a package of endorsed amendments.

If the draft is not adopted, the Council will set out a 'Common Position' (CP). This is reviewed by the responsible EP Committee. The EP has three months to respond to the Common Position. It can act in three ways:

- it may reject the CP, in which case it is not adopted;
- it may also do nothing or approve – the CP is adopted;
- it may amend the CP – these amendments are sent back to the CM and Commission, who give their opinions.

---

[8]Joint Declaration of the European Parliament, the Council and the Commission of 13 June 2007 on practical arrangements for the codecision procedure (Article 251 of the EC Treaty) OJ C 145/5
[9]General Activity Report 2009
[10]1998 Codecision Dorsale

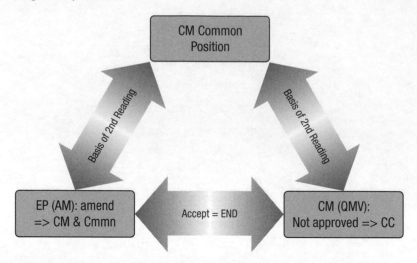

FIGURE 3.3   Second reading under the OLP

The CM then has three months to approve the EP amendments: if it does so the act can be adopted by QMV (or unanimity if the Commission opposes the EP amendments). A fast-track second reading procedure has emerged which allows the EP to open negotiations with the CM before the Common Position is produced. The EP and CM delegations will agree a final text that is recommended to the EP plenary for a second reading.

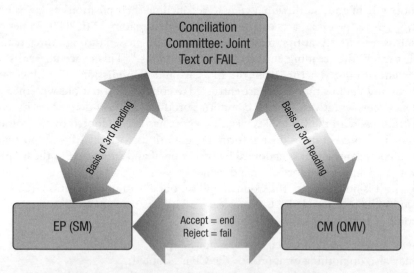

FIGURE 3.4   Third reading in the Conciliation Committee

Should agreement not be reached after the second reading, the CM has six weeks to decide if the proposal will go to the Conciliation Committee (CC) for its third and final reading. The EP President must give approval for this. The Conciliation Committee consists of equal numbers of national COREPER representatives and MEPs. The EP delegation to the Conciliation Committee has no set number – it must simply 'consist of a number of members equal to the number of members of the Council delegation'.[11] Its composition must reflect the political composition in the EP. It signifies the worst possible outcome for the Commission as this institution plays no part in the discussions – its role is to broker a deal between the preferences of the EP and CM. The CC has six weeks to agree a joint text (based upon an amended Common Position), using a simple majority in the EP and QMV in the CM. This timeframe can be extended by one month and two weeks respectively. However, if ultimately either institution fails to approve the proposed text, the act cannot be adopted. The Conciliation Committee is usually effective in arriving at a consensus.[12] It is likely that the text is formulated to achieve a minimum consensus and because the text is not referred back to the CC, the subject experts are not part of the negotiation.[13] The deliberations are not made public.[14]

APPLYING THE LAW

Under the OLP, can the EP adopt a measure without the agreement of the Council?

---

ii.   The 'special' legislative procedures – consultation and consent

In 1957, the Rome Treaty gave the parliamentary assembly an outsider advisory role in the legislative process: the Commission proposed and the Council adopted legislation. Consultation was only introduced in 1979, when the first direct elections to the EP were held. The key actors in the consultation procedure remain the Commission and the CM. Consultation has three basic steps:

1   The Commission submits a proposal to the Council.
2   The Council consults the Parliament.
3   The Council adopts the measure, either by qualified majority or by unanimity, depending upon the field.

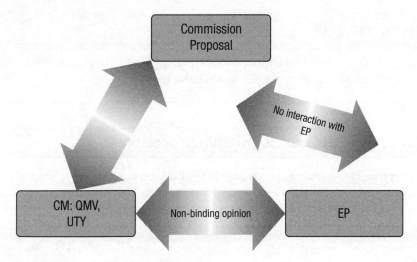

FIGURE 3.5   The consultation procedure

---

[11]Rule 68(1) EP Rules of Procedure
[12]In EP6, 23 out 24 conciliation committees were successful
[13]Rule 43(3)
[14]Rule 68(7) EP Rules of Procedure

Under Article 289(2) TFEU, consultation is now a 'special legislative procedure' where the Parliament is asked for its opinion on proposed legislation before the Council adopts it. The EP still plays a marginal role – it is not required to carry out any detailed legislative work. However, it has always taken its role in consultation seriously and has turned to the Court of Justice to force the Council to respects its rights under this procedure. In *Isoglucose* the Council was reprimanded for not awaiting the opinion of the EP: the Court stated that even if this were not binding, the democratic legitimation of EU laws required this formality to be respected. However, in *Roquette,* the CJ likewise stressed to the EP that it had an obligation to 'co-operate sincerely' and could not abuse its role by delaying its response.

Consultation gives the EP a strong power to delay, especially where the measure is part of a package.[15] The balance of power lies clearly in the horizontal inter-institutional relationships between the CM and the Commission but the EP can also be influential where the CM and Commission disagree. Despite working together, the CM (representing the member states) and Commission (representing the interests of the EU) have different priorities – the CM is strongest where it is unanimous; the Commission will prevail where QMV is used in the CM.

The use of this procedure is now limited to a small number of legislative areas, such as internal market and competition law. Consultation of the EP is also required, as a non-legislative procedure, where international agreements are being adopted under the Common Foreign and Security Policy.

Consent[16] provides the EP with a veto power where it is required to give its consent to certain legislative proposals. The Council cannot overrule the EP on this matter. Consent applies to accession agreements and association agreements. Consent is required as a non-legislative procedure when the EU wishes to ratify and adopt international agreements, such as the ECHR or in arrangements for withdrawal from the EU. It is used in the legislative procedure in the adoption of measures to combat discrimination and when Article 352 TFEU is used as a subsidiary legal basis.

APPLYING THE LAW

Identify the Treaty Article mentioned in the Preamble of Directive 2014/40. Which procedure was used to adopt the Tobacco Directive?

---

4. Analysis of the non-legislative procedures

Just as the primary law-making procedures in the EU have been subject to change, so have the procedures at the secondary level of law-making in the EU. This section examines the new rules for the exercise of delegated and implementing powers.

---

[15]Raya Kardasheva, 'The Power to Delay: The European Parliament's Legislative Influence', *JCMS* 47(2), March 2009, pp. 385–409
[16]Previously known as 'assent', this procedure was introduced by the SEA in 1986.

i.   Delegated acts

The European Parliament and the Council of Ministers may delegate law-making powers to the Commission. To do so lawfully, they must explicitly define the 'objectives, content, scope and duration' of the delegation of power in the legislative act. The 'essential elements' or political content cannot be delegated.[17]

Article 290(1): A legislative act may delegate to the Commission the power to adopt non-legislative acts of general application to supplement or amend certain non-essential elements of the legislative act.

In order to retain oversight and control, the legislative act must clearly state the precise conditions of the delegation and the circumstances under which it can be revoked by the EP or Council. Under Article 290(2) there are two forms of control:

- the European Parliament or the Council may decide to revoke the delegation; or
- the delegated act may enter into force only if no objection has been expressed by the European Parliament or the Council within a period set by the legislative act.

Either institution may decide to revoke a delegation and prevent a delegated act from entering into force on any ground – if they object to it within a certain timeframe, it will fail. In order for these options to be exercised, the EP and Council must vote on the draft presented by the Commission: the European Parliament shall act by a simple majority and the Council by a qualified majority.

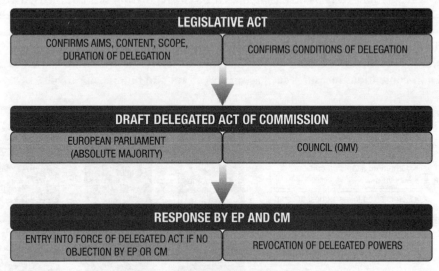

FIGURE 3.6   Law-making procedure under Article 290(2)

---

[17]See the non-binding Common Understanding between the institutions on how to use Delegated Acts: Communication from the Commission of 9 December 2009 on the implementation of Article 290 TFEU.

ii. Implementing acts

A different procedure is used for implementing acts. These acts are used to ensure that legislation is adopted by all 28 member states in a uniform way. Implementing powers can be conferred on the Commission or the Council:

> *Article 291(1): Member States shall adopt all measures of national law necessary to implement legally binding Union acts.*
>
> *(2) Where uniform conditions for implementing legally binding Union acts are needed, those acts shall confer implementing powers on the Commission, or, in duly justified specific cases and in the cases provided for in Articles 24 and 26 of the Treaty on European Union, on the Council.*

Article 290(3) calls for the exercise of implementing powers to be set down in further rules, agreed by the EP and the Council. These rules set out the so-called 'comitology' procedures. They only apply to implementing powers when they are being exercised by the Commission. Comitology refers to the network of committees used to oversee Commission action when exercising implementing powers under Article 291. This network of over 200 committees acts as a system of control whereby committees of national experts, acting as *national* representatives on behalf of the member states, scrutinise Commission drafts and adopt formal positions.

Comitology is not new – Article 291 TFEU has replaced and modernised the previous system.[18] These committees have been reduced from five configurations to just two. In order to implement the simplified comitology procedures associated with Article 291 TFEU a regulation[19] was passed using the OLP. The regulation sets out the two procedures and the possibility of referral to an appeal body (essentially the Council). The advisory procedure, also known as the 'basic' procedure, offers the most flexibility and freedom of action – the Committee adopts an opinion and may vote; the Commission must only take 'utmost account' of the Committee view. This procedure is used to deal with non-contentious measures such as surveys, grant and funding approvals.

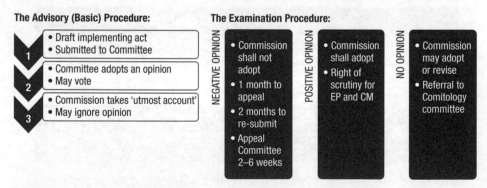

FIGURE 3.7 The advisory and examination procedures

---

[18]Comitology Decision 1999/468/EC of 28 June 1999, amended by Council Decision 2006/512/EC of 18 July 2006
[19]Regulation (EU) No 182/2011 of the EP and Council of 16 February 2011 laying down the rules and general principles concerning mechanisms for control by Member States of the Commission's exercise of implementing powers and repealing Decision 1999/468/EC

The examination procedure is more involved – under it the Committee must adopt an opinion using qualified majority voting. This will be used for implementing acts of general scope, programmes with substantial budgetary implications, measures related to the CAP and fisheries, taxation and the Common Commercial Policy (CCP), a new policy area. The new examination procedure offers the Commission both additional constraints and flexibility. The Commission must secure a qualified majority vote in favour in order to adopt the implementing act; if a simple majority opposes it, it shall not be adopted. However, more flexibility exists if there is stalemate in the Committee: should it be unable to achieve a qualified majority for or against (hence issues no opinion), the Commission is not obliged to adopt the implementing act (as happened previously with authorisations for genetically modified organisms (GMOs)). The Commission can reconsider and resubmit a modified act to the committee. If no opinion is issued in relation to implementing acts on taxation, financial services, health and safety, or safeguard measures, the Commission may not adopt it. The Parliament and the Council have the right of scrutiny (Article 11) whereby they may at any time pass a non-binding resolution, stating that the draft implementing act exceeds the implementing powers provided for in the basic act.[20]

The need for comitology can be summarised as speed, flexibility, control and efficiency. It is a faster procedure, allowing legislation to be updated in line with events, technology or markets; it enables a more flexible response than the legislative procedures; it allows the legislator to retain control over the delegation of power – the more sensitive the measure, the more control exerted; it promotes efficiency by freeing the legislator to concentrate on core work while leaving technical aspects to the Commission supported by experts in the area. Simplification was necessary because the system became bloated: in 2009, there were 266 comitology committees, 894 comitology committee meetings overseeing 1,808 implementing measures.[21]

A tension that is likely to resurface is the question of 'essential elements.' This idea has been used in the Union law-making vernacular without the benefit of a clear definition. Advocate General Geelhoed offered an interpretation of this phrase in *Forest Focus*:

[27] Where Article 2(b) of the second comitology decision mentions 'measures of general scope designed to apply essential provisions of basic instruments', including 'measures concerning the protection of the health or safety of humans, animals or plants', the choice of wording leads one to deduce that the basic instrument itself is already presumed to have a normative content or scope and that the implementing actions can be binding on natural and legal persons . . .

The CJ provided some guidance on the scope of that 'normative content.' In its ruling, it described the 'essential elements' of the *Forest Focus* scheme as being:

- observation and tools to improve and develop the scheme;
- provisions relating to national programmes which required detailed rules for implementation to be laid down, taking into account national, European and international monitoring mechanisms so as to avoid any additional administrative burden;
- the scientific advisory group; the manuals laying down the monitoring methods referred to in the regulation;

---

[20]EIPA 2011, pp. 17–18
[21]Alan Hardacre and Michael Kaeding, 'Delegated and Implementing Acts – The New Comitology, 2011, pp. 7–8

- approval criteria for private entities designated by the member states as bodies competent to manage the activities included in the approved national programmes;
- general monitoring of the scheme and the management of the Community contribution by the member states; and
- the obligations on the member states to provide information intended to promote integrated data evaluation at Community level and facilitate monitoring of the efficiency of the scheme.[22]

This may give indication of the *necessary* content of the basic legislative instrument, but the *minimum* content remains unclear – what is the essence of the essential elements?

ANALYSING THE LAW

Read the Tobacco Directive – is it a legislative or non-legislative act? Identify three provisions that you think are its 'essential elements'.

---

5. Understanding the regulatory environment of the EU

The key motivation for the reduction of legislative and non-legislative procedures has been the 'better' and 'smarter' regulation agenda.[23] Since 2002, the Commission has worked to simplify and improve the regulatory environment (the law- and policy-making fora and procedures in a polity) in the EU. In order to be seen as democratic, the regulatory environment must possess certain qualities. It is expected, for example, that there is a clear separation of powers, so that the legislature and the executive can operate independently of each other but also that the judiciary can oversee both. It is also expected that the rules made in any regulatory environment reflect the 'will of the people' as expressed and protected by their elected representatives in the legislature. Furthermore, there are important aspects such as diversity, transparency, accountability and efficiency. Diversity ensures that all voices are heard; transparency facilitates oversight over the exercise of public power and so facilitates control by the electorate; transparency in turn promotes accountability, as those who are making crucial decisions can be identified and made to answer for their actions; this in turn promotes efficiency – decisions are made in good time, for the right reasons using valid information. The regulatory environment that bears these characteristics is seen as credible and the law made in it respected as legitimate.

i.   The 'democratic deficit'

These underpinnings of democratic credibility and legitimacy are hard to achieve in a non-national regulatory environment such as the EU. Democracy has come to be defined in relation to the nation state despite its origins in the city of Athens.[24]

---

[22]C-122/04 *Commission v Parliament and Council* [2006] ECR I-2001 [43]
[23]EU Regulatory Fitness of December 2012 (COM(2012) 746). See in general materials at http://ec.europa.eu/smart-regulation/better_regulation/key_docs_en.htm
[24]Plato and Aristotle were critics not supporters of Athenian democracy.

However, the EU arguably does not have a 'demos', a citizenry which can be identified as the source of its law-making powers. This absence of a 'demos' is one of the key aspects of the so-called 'democratic deficit' in the EU. It has been argued instead that the EU has a 'demoi-cracy' – that the political community that underpins the purpose of the political infrastructure is not singular (*demos*) but multiple (*demoi*).[25] However, this does not address the underlying issue which is that the EU is neither a nation nor a state nor a nation state, thus an evaluation of democracy arising from these ideas will always discover a deficit. Nonetheless, the EU is also weak on other indicators of democracy such as a clear separation of powers – the Commission, for example, has a key role in law initiation, law-making, implementation and enforcement. Its dominance undermines democracy.

Enhancement of the EP role has done little to improve this. Arguably, it has worsened the deficit: as the status of the EP in Union law-making has improved, the turnout to EP elections has declined, as illustrated by Table 3.1 which shows a continued steady disengagement of the European electorate:

TABLE 3.1   The EP status in law-making compared with participation in EP elections (1979–2014)

Year	Procedure	EP election turnout (%)
EP1 1979 (EU9)	Consultation	61.99
EP2 1984 (EU10)		58.98
EP3 1989 (EU12)	Cooperation	58.41
EP4 1994 (EU12)	Co-decision I	56.67
EP5 1999 (EU15)	Co-decision II	49.51
EP6 2004 (EU25)		45.47
EP7 2009 (EU27 – 28 from July 2013)	Co-decision = OLP	43
EP8 (2014–2019)		43

This clear disengagement, put together with the data on distrust, indicates that all is not well with the state of democracy in the EU.[26] The success of the Far Right at the 2014 EP elections, which gained 10 seats to become the third largest grouping, more seriously indicates a level of voter disgust with the EU as a whole.

ii.   Electocracy

Guinier argues that the three 'D's' (disengagement, distrust and disgust) are characteristic of an 'electocracy'. An electocracy is a:

> political environment that defines itself by sacred moments of choice. The act of choosing in a competitive contest produces a clear winner. By casting their ballots, citizens bestow democratic accountability on the victor. At the same time, who wins the contest is even more important than who votes. And who votes is more important than the quality and quantity of citizen participation in, or the policy consequences of, other

---

[25] Kalypso Nicolaïdis, 'European Demoicracy and Its Crisis', *JCMS* 51(2), 2013, pp. 351–369
[26] The Europeans in 2009

important political acts of self-government such as deliberation, persuasion or collective mobilisation.[27]

In an electocracy, rule is by elections and power is exercised by 'powerful strangers',[28] perhaps a fitting description for the current relationship between Union citizens and their law-makers in the Commission as well as the EP. In order to return to a deeper democracy where elected representatives act as 'catalysts for citizen involvement not just surrogates for citizen views or identities', she suggests three alternative 'D's' – dialogue, debate and diversity – as a new metric of democratic accountability.

This focus on engagement in public debate is shared by Amartya Sen, who argues that:

> democracy must also be seen more generally in terms of the capacity to enrich reasoned engagement through enhancing informational availability and the feasibility of interactive discussions. Democracy has to be judged not just by the institutions that formally exist but by the extent to which different voices from diverse sections of the people can actually be heard.[29]

This is, he continues, a post-statist way of seeing democracy which 'can have an impact on the pursuit of it at the global level – not just within a nation state'.

Sen's definition highlights four aspects: engagement, diversity, information and interaction. Like Guinier, this conception of democracy has a grander vision: its goal is the advancement of public reasoning rather than the perfecting of specific institutions (like a democratic global government or global elections). However, unlike Guinier, Sen looks beyond the nation state: improvement of the 'possibility and reach of public reasoning' transforms both global democracy and global justice into 'eminently understandable ideas that can plausibly inspire and influence practical actions across borders'.[30]

These ideas may be just what the EU needs. Such conceptions of democracy can be usefully applied to the EU. They change the question of democracy in the EU to 'what are the procedures for ensuring that the quality of law-making is informed by interaction, dialogue and debate, that is engaged, pluralistic and informed?' It is perhaps less important which institution conducts these and more important that they are conducted. The exploration that follows will look for evidence of these aspects in law-making in the EU. However, in order to get a good grip on the problem, it will begin by examining electocracy in the EP.

iii. Electocracy in the EP

Article 10(1) TEU: The functioning of the Union shall be founded on representative democracy.

(2) Citizens are directly represented at Union level in the European Parliament. Member States are represented in the European Council by their Heads of State or Government and in the Council by their governments, themselves democratically accountable either to their national Parliaments, or to their citizens.

---

[27]Lani Guinier, 'Beyond Electocracy: Rethinking the Political Representative as Powerful Stranger', *MLR* 1(71), 2008, p. 2
[28]Guinier 2008, p. 3
[29]Amartya Sen, *The Idea of Justice,* Allen Lane, 2009, preface p. xiii
[30]Sen 2009, p. xiii

(3) Every citizen shall have the right to participate in the democratic life of the Union. Decisions shall be taken as openly and as closely as possible to the citizen.

(4) Political parties at European level contribute to forming European political awareness and to expressing the will of citizens of the Union.

This unique body is therefore now officially the voice of the EU citizen. This lends weight to its role as co-legislator and supervisor of the EU budget and, on the face of it, adds to the democratic legitimacy of the EU. The adoption of the OLP as the default law-making procedure further centralises the role of the EP.

It is clear that the OLP has enhanced the position of the EP in EU law-making but has it advanced the democratic legitimacy of EU laws? The answer appears to be no – data shows that engagement, measured by participation in EP elections, has declined. In addition, inclusion and interaction are undermined by the fast-track procedures which are often used on complex legislative packages such as the Climate Change Package of 2008. These procedures also reduce external engagement – insider relationships between rapporteurs and committee chairs are crucial to fast-track agreement.

The EP is dependent for success on the vigour with which the committee chairs and rapporteurs adopt an entrepreneurial stance to their role. Under OLP, rapporteurs write a report on the legislative proposal and in so doing set the agenda for the EP opinion. It has also been argued that rapporteurs influence EP opinions when legislative proposals are subject to consultation and fast-track readings under OLP, as they have an information advantage and negotiating position that other MEPs lack.[31] EP coordinators equally play a key role – they act as 'watchdogs' for the grouping or 'intra committee whips' making sure that members say the same thing. These actors are powerful because they also allocate tasks.[32] Committee chairs and coordinators, rapporteurs and shadow rapporteurs are used to find consensus within committees, as well as at fast-track readings:

> Shadow *rapporteurs* can also play a role in the quest of finding consensus within committee. These players are appointed by opposed political group(s) not only to monitor the work of the *rapporteur* and to report back to their respective political group but also to find agreement on political issues *across* the boundaries of political groups.[33]

The advantage of the cooperation between shadow rapporteurs and rapporteur is that time can be saved if all agree; the disadvantage is that not every shadow rapporteur is skilful enough to convince their political group to accept the compromise reached with the rapporteur. Settembri and Neuhold conclude that the EP has developed new norms to facilitate internal cooperation and become a more cohesive actor to meet the demands of the OLP.[34]

---

[31]Rory Costello and Robert Thomson, 'The Policy impact of leadership in committees: Rapporteurs influence on the European parliaments opinions', *European Union Politics* 11(2), 2010, pp. 219–240

[32]Charlotte Burns, 'Co-decision and Inter-Committee Conflict in the European Parliament Post-Amsterdam', *Government and Opposition* 41(2), Spring 2006, pp. 230–248; Torsten J. Selck and Bernard Steunenberg, 'Between Power and Luck – The European Parliament in the EU Legislative Process', *European Union Politics* 5(1), 2004, pp. 25–46

[33]Pierpaolo Settembri and Christine Neuhold, 'Achieving Consensus Through Committees: Does the European Parliament Manage?', *JCMS* 47(1), 2009, p. 142. The Bolkestein Directive attempted to set out new rules for the free movement of services in the EU.

[34]Settembri and Neuhold 2009, p.148

The EP has been described as a 'non-unitary' institution with internal rivalries.[35] This internal structure means that in order to meet first reading timeframes, debate must be truncated. The truncation of debate undermines the role of the national parliaments in holding their governments to account: it places national delegations under pressure to reach agreements under a very tight timetable, allowing limited scope for discussion. This is not corrected by the EP Plenary, which rarely makes any changes to the package. While they may be good for efficiency, it is questionable whether the fast-track procedures enhance democratic legitimacy. However, they are set to continue and be reinforced.[36]

In addition, negotiation can now take place in meetings known as 'trilogues'.[37] These are informal tripartite meetings which facilitate cooperation between the EP, Commission and CM in the OLP. They can be called at any reading and include any level of representation, as required by the discussion. Participation is limited but can include the Council Presidency, the Commission and the chairs of the relevant committees, rapporteurs of the European Parliament as well as the co-chairs of the Conciliation Committee. Trilogues are compulsory during conciliation – they must take place throughout the conciliation committee to resolve issues and prepare agreement. Each institution sets its own negotiation mandate and transmits this to the other institutions. There is a great deal of satisfaction with the system:

> This trilogue system has demonstrated its vitality and flexibility in increasing significantly the possibilities for agreement at first and second reading stages, as well as contributing to the preparation of the work of the Conciliation Committee.[38]

The main advantage is that ideas can be exchanged without formal decisions being taken. Each side simply accepts ideas to refer back to their delegation.

Again, these informal talks do not necessarily advance democracy – trilogues in the EP and CM shall be announced 'where practicable'[39] but this does not mean that they are open to the public. The small size and composition may allow for effective intensive dialogue but their informality harkens back to the days of opaque diplomacy in the early years of the EEC: if overused, they may unwittingly take law-making back to elitism rather than pull it forward into the twenty-first century. Although the 2008 negotiating code of conduct aims to increase transparency and accountability, especially at an early stage of the procedure, these informal practices may have the opposite effect.[40] As these are forums to find compromise, they also undermine the presence and audibility of minority voices. The commitment to an early consensus challenges the EP ability to fully represent the richness and diversity of debate in the EU. Is this acceptable for the sake of efficiency? Paradoxically, EP prominence in Union law-making may have weakened its voice.

---

[35]Settembri and Neuhold 2009, pp. 127–151

[36]EP 2009 Codecision Report, p. 9

[37]See Rule 70, EP Rules of Procedure; Joint Declaration of the European Parliament, the Council and the Commission of 13 June 2007 on practical arrangements for the codecision procedure (Article 251 of the EC Treaty) OJ C145/5

[38]Annex XX (7). See also EP Rules of Procedure ANNEX XXI Code of conduct for negotiating in the context of the ordinary legislative procedures agreed by the Conference of Presidents 21 September 2008

[39]Annex XX (9) EP Rules of Procedure

[40]Further procedures used in specific areas include the opinion in Article 140 TFEU (economic and monetary union), the dialogue with industry under Articles 154 and 155 TFEU (agreements between management and labour). Codification (consolidation of repealed and modified acts) is provided for in Rule 46 EP rules of procedure and the adoption of voluntary agreements instead of legislation under Rules 48 and 85 EP rules of procedure.

It may be odd to highlight consensus as a problem undermining democracy, but it has been argued that the EP is too consensual. Settembri and Neuhold, while finding conflict in some committees, suggest high levels of consensus both within the committees and the EP as a whole: voting practice in EP committees tend towards unanimity. Consensual deals are common – the average majorities endorsing a text in the first two years of EP5 and EP6 were 94.8 per cent and 95.1 per cent respectively. This means that behind any vote lies a 'giant coalition'.

Some committees (such as Employment, Environment, Liberty and Justice) are more consensual than others, thus use of OLP in these areas give the EP strong powers. Environment (ENV) which deals with measures as varied as the Waste Shipment Regulation, the Ecodesign Directive and the Soil Directive, is a good example of a highly consensual committee. In EP6 it was involved in 400 procedures, and led on 172. Of these 114 were dealt with under OLP: of the 96 concluded in EP6, 61 per cent were concluded at the first reading, 29 per cent at second reading and just 9 per cent went to conciliation.

The early search for consensus associated with OLP ties in with the drive for better regulation. Efficiency is an important element for democracy – citizens are not well served by procedures that prolong or stifle the expression of their will. The majority of legislation is now passed at first reading. Yet it is questionable whether it adds to or detracts from plurality and the richness of EU democracy – cohesion in the EP is higher than in the US Congress. This may make it a reliable and cooperative legislative partner, but undermines its representative role – 'democracy is about more than respecting the views of the majority. It is also about safeguarding the rights of minorities, including unpopular minorities – democracy 'values everyone equally even if the majority does not'.[41] Democracy requires the opportunity for debate and dialogue.

These institutional constraints of the EP suggest that upon balance, the member states remain the most strongly represented cohort in the EU democracy. Selck and Steunenberg (2004) and Burns (2006) come to the counterintuitive conclusion that the EP was able to secure its preferences more using its influence under consultation rather than the formal powers under OLP. Under its marginal role in consultation the EP had no need to conduct detailed legislative work and could therefore concern itself more with expressing public opinion. They argue that under the OLP, the EP is hampered by informational deficits.

The remedying of the democratic deficit is therefore perhaps limited. The question remains – how does the EU polity get the best from its EP? If its institutional form hinders it in certain roles should the form be changed or the responsibilities shaped to fit? The reform of the EP has in fact been as much informed by its rivalry with the Council of Ministers and the Commission as by the need to give its role as representative more weight. These constraints limit the EP exploitation of its new position and the full exercise of the new powers.[42] Members may now operate more as 'powerful strangers' than before.

The route to maximise the potential of the EP may be to focus less on horizontal relationships (i.e. inter-institutional at the EU level) and more on vertical relationships[43] (i.e. between

---

[41]Lord Reed in R (on the application of Chester) (Appellant) v Secretary of State for Justice (Respondent) and McGeoch (AP) (Appellant) v The Lord President of the Council and another (Respondents) (Scotland) Michaelmas Term [2013] UKSC 63 [88] citing Ghaidan v Godin-Mendoza [2004] 2 AC 557 [132]
[42]Robert Thomson and Madeleine Hosli, 'Who Has Power in the EU? The Commission, Council and Parliament in Legislative Decision-making', JCMS 44(2), 2006, pp. 391–417
[43]Guinier 2008, p. 22

the EP and EU residents and citizens). As Guinier argues, 'the representative alone does not stand for democracy'. Citizens, she stresses need to be given more opportunities to be active agenda setters not just voters at elections. Under her vision, elections are a process rather than a single act and parliamentary representatives are held to account continuously rather than at specific moments. This may be the way to add weight the words of Article 10(2) TEU whereby 'Citizens are directly represented at Union level in the European Parliament'.

VIEWPOINT

How can too much consensus be bad for democracy?

---

6. Thinking beyond electocracy

Having explored the limitations of the EP, the following section will examine opportunities for debate, dialogue and diversity in the EU beyond this institution. Opportunity for dialogue and debate in the democratic life of the EU can be assessed via, for example, the principles of subsidiarity and proportionality, and the national parliaments or the European Citizen's Initiative (ECI) and the European Parliament Initiative (EPI) under Article 225 TFEU. Fundamental principles informing the procedure of EU law-making – such as conferral of powers and the legal basis – also contribute to the democratic legitimacy of Union acts. The section begins with an examination of the most fundamental issue: the source of law-making authority in the EU and the doctrine of conferred powers.

i.   Conferred powers

A fundamental principle of law-making authority is use of a clear source of authority. A common challenge to EU rules is the lack of competence, or power to take formal action in a specific area. Such challenges may be ad hoc, dependent upon chance litigation, but they nonetheless present an opportunity for debate on a fundamental issue. This issue was, for example, a key argument in *Vodafone*[44] where mobile operators unsuccessfully challenged the Commission proposal for a regulation setting a cap on roaming rates. Although the EU is an autonomous legal entity, the source of its authority lies in an international Treaty, which confers powers upon it to act. When they signed up to the 'common exercise of sovereign powers'[45] the six signatory states set this out in a Treaty. These origins in an international Treaty mean that the 'DNA' of the EU lies in international law even if the EU is a non-traditional international organisation. When the CJ declared in *van Gend* that the EU constituted a 'new legal order' it did not remove it from these moorings in international law. On the contrary, it specifically anchored it there,

---

[44]C-58/8 *Vodafone Ltd, Telefónica O2 Europe plc, T-Mobile International AG, Orange Personal Communications Services Ltd* v *Secretary of State for Business, Enterprise and Regulatory Reform* about EC Regulation No. 717/2007
[45]Neil Walker, 'The European Union as an International Legal Experiment', in G. de Burca and J.H.H. Weiler (eds), *The Worlds of European Constitutionalism*, Cambridge University Press, 2011, pp. 19–56

describing the EU as a legal order of 'international law' and identifying the Treaties – international legal instruments – as the source of rights in EU law:

> ... the EEC [Union] constitutes a new legal order of international law ... Independently of the legislation of Member States, Community law therefore not only imposes obligations on individuals but is also intended to confer upon them rights which become part of their legal heritage. These rights arise not only where they are expressly granted by the Treaty, but also by reason of obligations which the Treaty imposes in a clearly defined way upon individuals as well as upon the MS and upon the institutions of the Community ...

This case did not therefore take the EU beyond the realms of international law, but broadened the definitions of the types of organisation that could be created thereunder. As the CJ declared, thenceforth the subjects of Union (then Community) law would be not only the signatory states, as per traditional international law, but also the citizens in those states, and the institutions of the newly created organisation. The seven judges at the CJ were not acting alone – this may explain why despite the complaints of many member states the basic idea of a 'new legal order' was able to take hold and flourish.[46]

These origins in international law mean that some international law principles remain relevant, in particular the idea of conferral of powers. Title I of the TFEU sets out the terms of action for the Union, establishing conferral of powers as a foundational principle of the EU. According to Article 5 TEU:

---

(1) The limits of Union competences are governed by the principle of conferral ...

(2) Under the principle of conferral, the Union shall act only within the limits of the competences conferred upon it by the Member States in the Treaties to attain the objectives set out therein. Competences not conferred upon the Union in the Treaties remain with the Member States.

The centrality of this principle is again underlined in Article 7 TFEU, which obliges the Union to act in a consistent manner in consideration of all of its objectives and ' . . . in accordance with the principle of conferral of powers'. When the Treaties confer powers, their use is subject to conditions. These conditions are also laid out in the Treaties and include the use of a legal basis, provision of reasons, as well as the principles of subsidiarity and proportionality.[47]

ii. The catalogue of competences

The scope of conferred powers is now set out in a 'catalogue of competences'. Article 2 TFEU introduces the idea of two 'categories' of competence: 'exclusive' and 'shared'. It states that:

---

(1) When the Treaties confer on the Union exclusive competence in a specific area, only the Union may legislate and adopt legally binding acts, the Member States being able to do so themselves only if so empowered by the Union or for the implementation of Union acts.

---

[46]Antoine Vauchez, 'The transnational politics of judicialisation. *Van Gend en Loos* and the making of EU polity', *European Law Journal*, 16(1), January 2010, pp. 1–28
[47]Article 5 (1) TEU. See 'Report from the Commission on Subsidiarity and Proportionality' COM(2010) 547 final

> *(2) When the Treaties confer on the Union a competence shared with the Member States in a specific area, the Union and the Member States may legislate and adopt legally binding acts in that area. The Member States shall exercise their competence to the extent that the Union has not exercised its competence. The Member States shall again exercise their competence to the extent that the Union has decided to cease exercising its competence.*

'Exclusive competence' refers to areas where the member states have agreed not to undertake independent initiatives because only the Union may act. These fields include the areas that also formed the core of the EEC: the common customs union; the establishment of competition rules necessary for the functioning of the internal market; monetary policy for the member states in the eurozone; conservation of marine biological resources under the common fisheries policy; the common commercial policy.[48]

In these fields, the Union has full competence but may relinquish its competence to act to the member states. When the Union legislates in these areas it is not subject to the tests of subsidiarity or proportionality. The Union also continues to enjoy exclusive competence for the conclusion of international agreements under three circumstances: first, when this is laid out in a legislative act of the Union, that is an act adopted by the Council of Ministers, European Parliament or the Commission; second, when it is necessary to enable the Union to exercise its internal competence; and third, when its conclusion has an impact upon common rules, by for example reducing or expanding their scope. Power for the EU to accede to the ECHR, for example, arises from this provision.

If competency to act is imagined as a continuum, these rules fall at one extreme. They form the core of the areas where the EU is at its most supranational. At the other end of the continuum are the areas from which EU action is barred, other than in order to 'support, coordinate or supplement the actions of the Member States'. These include: protection and improvement of human health; industry; culture; tourism; education, vocational training, youth and sport; civil protection; administrative cooperation. Fields at this end of the continuum therefore represent the EU at its most intergovernmental, where action by the EU is 'by invitation only'.

The centre of the continuum is occupied by those fields where both EU and national action is permissible. Shared competency means that the:

> . . . Union and the Member States may legislate and adopt legally binding acts in that area. The Member States shall exercise their competence to the extent that the Union has not exercised its competence. The Member States shall again exercise their competence to the extent that the Union has decided to cease exercising its competence.

This recognises the action of the EU, and allows the member states to act where the EU has not or has ceased to be active. It seems therefore to envisage a scenario where the EU will abandon a policy area. To date, this has not been done but the provision suggests that this may occur in the future.[49] It is here that the subsidiarity and proportionality tests play a key role to determine not only whether action by the EU or member states is more appropriate but also the form of such action.

---

[48]Article 3 TFEU
[49]Article 2(2) TFEU

Under Article 4(2) TFEU, 'shared competence' applies in the following key areas:

- internal market;
- social policy, for the aspects defined in this Treaty;
- economic, social and territorial cohesion;
- agriculture and fisheries, excluding the conservation of marine biological resources;
- environment;
- consumer protection;
- transport;
- trans-European networks;
- area of freedom, security and justice;
- common safety concerns in public health matters.

These areas are described as 'principal': if they are of such importance, the question is why the member states agreed for competence here to be shared? The answer may lie in the fact that the EU already enjoys competence in many of these areas and it would have been futile to try to limit its scope for action.

More specific caveats are given in fields concerning research and humanitarian aid. In these fields, the TFEU states clearly that the EU has competence but the 'exercise of that competence shall not result in Member States being prevented from exercising theirs'. This also applies to areas of research, technological development and space,[50] and development cooperation and humanitarian aid.[51] In the former, the EU may conduct activities to 'define and implement programmes' but in relation to development and humanitarian aid the scope is wider – here the Union may 'conduct a common policy'. Under Article 4(4), for example, bilateral development can continue alongside EU development programmes. It is questionable whether this also applies to the 'principal' areas of shared competence.

ANALYSING THE LAW

Where on the continuum does competence for the Tobacco Directive fall?

Activities falling under the previous second pillar of the EU – common foreign and security policy (CFSP) – are mentioned in Article 2(4) TFEU: the Union is given competence to 'define and implement a common foreign and security policy, including the progressive framing of a common defence policy'. Title V of the Treaty on European Union (TEU) contains the General Provisions on the Union's External Action and Specific Provisions on the Common Foreign and Security Policy. Article 24 TEU lays out specific conditions for action in this area. While the Union competence is broad, covering all areas of foreign policy and questions relating to the Union's security, the way in which it may act is restricted. Specific rules are laid out which make unanimous voting in the Council of Ministers the norm, exclude the conclusion of any legislative instruments and curtail the jurisdiction of the CJEU.

---

[50]Article 4(3) TFEU
[51]Article 4(4) TFEU

Where, therefore would competency for CFSP fall on the continuum? It is not specifically mentioned. Article 24(1) suggests that it remains intergovernmental, yet consideration of Article 24(2) might lead to the conclusion that it falls in the middle:

> *Within the framework of the principles and objectives of its external action, the Union shall conduct, define and implement a common foreign and security policy, based on the development of mutual political solidarity among Member States, the identification of questions of general interest and the achievement of an ever-increasing degree of convergence of Member States' actions.*

The status of the field is further complicated by the fact that under Article 26(3) TEU responsibility for its implementation falls to the High Representative and the member states, using both national and EU resources. Article 352 TFEU is also used to control Union action in this area – Article 352(4) TFEU excludes its 'use as a basis for attaining objectives pertaining to the common foreign and security policy . . . '.

The catalogue of competences tries to formalise the breadth of EU action and also its depth: in some fields all types of action is possible; in others more minimal engagement is permissible. Its existence enhances transparency and therefore the democratic legitimacy of EU law. However, it does not fully resolve the question of where power to act resides – the so-called 'residual clause' still exists. Under Article 352 TFEU, if action is required to attain an objective of the Union and the Treaty has not provided 'the necessary powers the Council shall take . . . the appropriate measures'. The interpretation given to this provision continues to be controversial.[52] Its use as an alternative legal basis for harmonisation measures is also curtailed by Article 352(3) TFEU. However, it still provides scope for competence to 'creep'.

A further check against competence creep in exclusive areas exists in Article 4 TEU:

> (1) *In accordance with Article 5, competences not conferred upon the Union in the Treaties remain with the Member States.*
>
> (2) *The Union shall respect the equality of Member States before the Treaties as well as their national identities, inherent in their fundamental structures, political and constitutional, inclusive of regional and local self-government. It shall respect their essential State functions, including ensuring the territorial integrity of the State, maintaining law and order and safeguarding national security. In particular, national security remains the sole responsibility of each Member State.*

The conferral of powers and catalogue of competences appear to be defensive concepts used to shield national democracy from ever-widening EU powers.

ANALYSING THE LAW

Read Article 288 TFEU – What is the relationship between EU legal acts and the competences of the Union?

---

[52]Compare C-8/73 *Hauptzollamt Bremerhaven* v *Massey Ferguson* [1973] ECR 897 with C-402/05 P and C-415/05 P *Kadi and Al Barakaat International Foundation* v *Council and Commission* [2008] ECR I-6351

The discussion above and cases such as *Vodafone*[53] show that competence is an issue with legal and political dimensions.[54] Article 4 TEU notwithstanding, the question of *Kompetenz Kompetenz* (competence competence) – who has the authority to decide where authority in the EU lies – has not yet been definitely answered. The German Constitutional Court rejected this explicitly in its Maastricht judgment and repeated it in a more qualified way in its more recent Lisbon judgment. Yet as Beck points out, there is still no clear answer.[55]

However, there is a positive aspect to this conflict – it 'polishes' democracy in the EU by forcing into existence certain procedures that promote interaction, debate and therefore transparency. There are at least three practical consequences to the conferral of powers: first, any law must state clearly the legal provision upon which it is based – monitoring of this promotes engagement through judicial review; second, all action by the EU must be proportionate – this promotes constant reflection on the design of legislation; and third, action in areas of shared competence must satisfy the subsidiarity test, requiring on-going engagement with and reflection upon the best interests of the citizen.

iii. The legal basis

A procedural check on law-making in the EU is provided by the conditions of legality. These include the requirement for a legal basis and the obligation to give reasons.[*] In order to act legitimately in relation to its tasks, the EU must have been given the power to act. This power resides in the provisions of the Treaty. If a power is not mentioned, the EU 'cannot' legitimately act. This was an argument used in relation to the introduction of legal protection against discrimination in the 1990s – it was argued that without a Treaty provision mentioning discrimination, an EU anti-discrimination measure would be unlawful.

The Treaty provision is therefore an essential aspect of legitimate law-making in the EU. The legal basis acts as the source of authority and legitimacy, laying out the scope of EU action. In addition to this political relevance, it also performs the practical task of providing the Commission with a mandate for action. The legal basis sets out the law-making procedure that is to be used and the forms of law that can be adopted. Even proposals for the European Citizens Initiative (ECI) must identify the legal basis upon which the draft proposal will be based. This has been the most popular reason for rejection by the Commission:

> **Title of proposed citizens' initiative: *'Minority Safe Pack – one million signatures for diversity in Europe'***
>
> The main objective of your proposed initiative is the adoption by the EU of a set of legal acts to improve the protection of persons belonging to national and linguistic minorities and strengthen cultural and linguistic diversity in the Union. You propose Articles 167, 165, 177, 178, 173, 182, 25, 20, 19, 79, 118, 53, 62, 109, 108, 107 of the Treaty on the Functioning of the European Union (TFEU), Articles 2 and 3 of the Treaty on the European Union (TEU) and Articles 21 and 22 of the Charter of Fundamental Rights as possible

---

[53]This case concerned the validity of Regulation No 717/2007
[54]See *Spain v Council* (UPC)
[55]Gunnar Beck, 'The Lisbon Judgment of the German Constitutional Court, the Primacy of EU Law and the Problem of *Kompetenz-Kompetenz*: A Conflict between Right and Right in Which There is No *Praetor*', *European Law Journal* 17(4), 2011, p. 470
[*]Article 296 TFEU

legal bases for your initiative. First of all, while the respect for rights of persons belonging to minorities is one of the values of the Union referred to in Article 2 TEU, neither the Treaty on European Union, nor the Treaty on the Functioning of the European Union provide for a legal base as regards the adoption of legal acts aiming at promoting the rights of persons belonging to minorities [. . .] In conclusion, the Commission considers that there is no legal basis in the Treaties which would allow the Commission to present a complete set of proposals for the 'Minority Safe Pack' as defined in your application.

Debate is often provoked over the Commission choice of a legal basis. The legal basis is subject to judicial review, thus the Commission must give reasons for its choice. The EP and other applicants will use this as the first challenge to any EU act. When a proposal arrives at the EP, the responsible committee must first verify the legal basis. The responsible committee or legal affairs committee may table amendments in the EP to change the legal basis of a proposal.[56]

When examining such cases, the CJEU will identify the core purpose of the act in an attempt to ensure that the most appropriate legal basis has been chosen.[57] Prior to the Lisbon Treaty, it was possible – sometimes necessary[58] – to combine a number of provisions to construct a strong legal basis for action. Combination in the Treaties may still be necessary; however, in so doing, the Commission may not select dual bases with conflicting procedures[59] which undermine participation rights.[60] Where this is incorrect the results can be fatal – in *Ship Pollution*, the Commission adopted an act which used criminal measures as sanctions for environmental pollution and the CJ held that:

[74] In the light of the foregoing, it must be concluded that Framework Decision 2005/667, in encroaching on the competence which Article 80(2) EC [100 TFEU] attributes to the Community, infringes Article 47 EU [40 TEU] and, being indivisible, must be annulled in its entirety.

Action is not completely prohibited in the absence of specific base – there is no Treaty provision dealing specifically with nanomaterials but general action (such as funding of research into nanotechnology) has been possible under the general legislative framework on environmental protection, worker protection and product legislation.

APPLYING THE LAW

Find and read the various Articles listed in the above-mentioned proposal for an ECI. Why are these inadequate legal bases for the proposal?

---

[56]Rule 37 EP Rules of Procedure 2013
[57]C-338/01 *Commission* v *Council* (Indirect Taxes) [2004] ECR I-4829
[58]In *Kadi*, Regulations 881/2002/12 and 561/2003 implementing the UN Security Council Decisions were based upon Articles 75, 215 and 352 TFEU. A key question was whether the Community had competence to adopt economic sanctions against individuals.
[59]C-338/01 *Indirect Taxes* [57]
[60]C-300/89 *Commission* v *Council* (Titanium Dioxide) [1991] ECR I-2867

This linkage between the Treaty and acts of the institutions is therefore an essential requirement to demonstrate and advance the legitimacy of law-making in the EU.

iv. Subsidiarity and proportionality

An important question in law-making concerns the motivation for legislation – is it needed and why? Who will benefit from it? Related to this question of necessity is the issue of proximity: if the law is needed, what is the best level to make it? The procedures for answering these questions potentially advance democratic legitimacy in the EU. The two fundamental principles that focus on these questions are subsidiarity and proportionality. They are laid out in Article 5 TEU:

> *(1) The use of Union competences is governed by the principles of subsidiarity and proportionality . . .*
>
> *(2) Under the principle of subsidiarity, in areas which do not fall within its exclusive competence, the Union shall act only if and in so far as the objectives of the proposed action cannot be sufficiently achieved by the Member States, either at central level or at regional and local level, but can rather, by reason of the scale or effects of the proposed action, be better achieved at Union level.*
>
> *(3) Under the principle of proportionality, the content and form of Union action shall not exceed what is necessary to achieve the objectives of the Treaties.*

Subsidiarity applies to fewer areas than proportionality. In those areas of non-exclusive competence where it applies,[61] it is used to define the boundary between member state and EU tasks. It guides an answer to the question 'who should act?' In areas of shared competence, the principle establishes a clear presumption in favour of member state action: the Union should only act if member states first, cannot achieve the objectives sufficiently and second, by the reason of the scale or effects, the Union can achieve them better.[62] Both elements must be satisfied.

In contrast, the proportionality test seeks to ensure that the means used are balanced in relation to the goals articulated. It applies to both areas of shared and exclusive competence and defines the character of action. It is a guiding principle to answer the question of what the form and nature of EU action should be. Under Article 5(4) the content and form of Union action shall not exceed that which is 'necessary' and 'appropriate' to achieve the objectives of the Treaties – all action must favour the least restrictive option. Proportionality can be summarised as a means–ends test: are the means used necessary and appropriate to achieve the stated aims? Prior to this, the measure must be seen to be 'legitimate', that is targeted towards aims that have a clear 'public interest nature distinguishable from purely individual reasons' such as cost reduction or improving competitiveness.[63]

Invocation of these principles can halt the law-making procedure in the EU. The institutions of the Union must apply the subsidiarity principle as laid out in the Lisbon

---

[61]C-288/11 P *Mitteldeutsche Flughafen* confirmed that the principle does not apply to areas of exclusive competence, in this case state aid.
[62]17th Report from the Commission on Subsidiarity and Proportionality COM(2010) 547 final, Brussels, p. 2
[63]C-159/10 *Fuchs and Köhler* [2011] ECR I-6919 [52]; C-388/07 *Age Concern England* [2009] ECR I-1569 [46]

Treaty Protocol. The Commission must consult widely before proposing legislation and include a compliance statement in each legislative proposal; a different level of analysis is conducted at three stages, starting with a 'road-map' and ending with a detailed impact assessment.[64] In 2012, the Impact Assessment Board (IAB) examined 97 impact assessments and issued 144 opinions. Comments on issues of subsidiarity were included in 33 per cent of its opinions.[65] The European Parliament and Council (COREPER) must also justify any amendments affecting the scope of Union action. Finally, the Court of Justice can review the legality of acts of the institutions for compliance with the principle of subsidiarity. In *Vodafone*[66] the Court held that the proposal respected both subsidiarity and proportionality. More recently, the Court confirmed that the subsidiarity principle does not give rise to individual rights.[67]

Responsibility for compliance with subsidiarity is scattered. The EP, ECOSOC and COMREG monitor compliance using their own mechanisms. COSAC and the European Parliament have called for the establishment of EU-level criteria to evaluate compliance with the principles of subsidiarity and proportionality. Responsibility now also lies with the national Parliaments[68] – they are to 'ensure compliance' with the principle in using a procedure set out in Protocol 2 attached to the Lisbon Treaty.

In order to enable the national parliaments to conduct a subsidiarity review, the Protocol lays out a specific procedure. The Commission, EP and Council are to send to them all drafts and adopted resolutions. The national parliaments must then express their view on compliance with subsidiarity. If they find non-compliance, they now have a right to send a 'reasoned opinion' indicating non-compliance of the draft with the subsidiarity principle, to the Commission. The number of negative opinions determines which compulsory review procedure will apply – a 'yellow card' or 'orange card' mechanism. The yellow card is the weaker of the two: it leads only to amendment or withdrawal. Under the 'orange card' mechanism the EP or Council can in addition stop the legislative procedure. The yellow card requires the number of negative opinions from national parliaments to represent at least one third of all the votes allocated to them[69] (or one quarter for proposals in the area of judicial cooperation in criminal matters and police cooperation); the orange card requires the number of negative opinions to represent a simple majority under OLP.[70]

Between 2010 and 2013, 1,506 submissions were received from the national parliaments under Protocol 2, in relation to 429 draft proposals. Of these, around 15 per cent (269) were 'reasoned opinions'. The majority (1,237) were deemed to be 'contributions', that is other submissions that did not fulfil the criteria to be a reasoned opinion. This can occur because the submission was sent to the EP by the Commission rather than the national parliament, or because the national chamber sent two submissions in respect of the same draft legislative act. Also, a reasoned opinion that goes beyond the issue of subsidiarity to discuss the substantive merits of proposals will be deemed a 'contribution'.

---

[64]COM(2010) 547, p. 4. See the impact assessment guidelines at SEC(2009) 92 and the Impact assessment summary at http://ec.europa.eu/health/archive/ph_determinants/life_style/tobacco/documents/tobacco_ia2009_exs_en.pdf
[65]Annual Report from the Commission on Subsidiarity And Proportionality COM(2013) 566 final, p. 3
[66]C-58/8 *Vodafone Ltd, Telefónica O2 Europe plc, T-Mobile International AG, Orange Personal Communications Services Ltd v Secretary of State for Business, Enterprise and Regulatory Reform* about EC Regulation No 717/2007
[67]C-221/10 P *Artegodan*
[68]Lisbon Treaty Protocol (No 2) on Subsidiarity and Proportionality replacing Protocol (No 30) on the application of the principles of subsidiarity and proportionality (1997)
[69]The current threshold is 18 votes – COM(2013) 566 final, p. 7
[70]Each national parliament has two votes; in bicameral systems each of the two chambers has one vote.

A national parliament may therefore think that it has sent a reasoned opinion, only for it to be downgraded to a contribution. Some national parliaments seem to consistently send 'contributions' suggesting unfamiliarity with the procedure or a resistance to the control exerted by the EP.[71]

The first yellow card was used by the national parliaments in 2012:[72] it is noticeable that national parliaments were able to achieve a collaborative response for the first time on the Commision 'Monti II' proposal. Twelve reasoned opinions (and four contributions) were sent against a proposal for a regulation on the exercise of the right to take collective action within the context of the freedom of establishment and the freedom to provide services. The regulation would have established in law that there is no primacy between economic freedoms and the right to strike.[73] The yellow card indicates how effective national parliaments can be when they cooperate – the Commission initially argued that the subsidiarity principle had not been breached but concluded that the response made the proposal unlikely to succeed before the European Parliament and CM. The Monti II proposal was withdrawn.[74] In 2013, the yellow card was triggered when 13 reasoned opinions (and four contributions) were received against the proposal for a Council regulation on the establishment of the European Public Prosecutor's Office (EPPO). These represented more than 25 per cent (18 out of 56) of the votes allocated to national parliaments/chambers. As the proposal fell into the area of freedom, security and justice, a fourth of the total number of votes suffices to reach the threshold.[75] A high number of reasoned opinions (11) were also sent in relation to a proposal for maritime spatial planning and integrated coastal management[76] but no yellow card was triggered as the threshold was not reached.

In practice, it is questionable how far the subsidiarity parliamentary review procedure advances debate, dialogue or diversity in EU law-making. Berman argues that the EU is 'remarkable' for its approach to subsidiarity policing and its introduction of the 'early warning' mechanism. This has the advantage of galvanising parliaments to influence their own governments[77] but it is questionable how busy legislatures, including subnational parliaments, will find time to respond to the many proposals sent by the Commission within eight weeks.[78] Reports are not encouraging: briefing sessions can be very short – for instance, in Ireland:

> The longest session was the first before the *Dail*'s Select Committee on European Affairs which lasted about two hours. The norm is about one hour. One session lasted

---

[71]Directorate-General for the Presidency – Directorate for Relations with National Parliaments Legislative Dialogue Unit 'State of Play on reasoned opinions and contributions submitted by national Parliaments under Protocol No 2 of the Lisbon Treaty' 2013 at www.presnet.ep.parl.union.eu/presnet/cms/Legislative-Activities/Subsidiarity

[72]COM(2013) 566 final, p. 3

[73]This concern was raised by trade unions subsequent to the *Viking* and *Laval* cases.

[74]COM(2013) 566 final, pp. 7–8. Fabbrini and Granat argue the Commission was wrong to do so – Federico Fabbrini and Katarzyna Granat, '"Yellow card, but no foul": The role of the national parliaments under the subsidiarity protocol and the Commission proposal for an EU regulation on the right to strike', *Common Market Law Review* 50(1), 2013, pp. 115–143

[75]See note 74

[76]Figures from the Directorate General for the Presidency – Directorate for relations with national parliaments – Legislative Dialogue Unit, 2012 and 2013

[77]George A. Bermann, 'National Parliaments and Subsidiarity: An Outsider's View', in Ingolf Pernice and Evgeni Tanchev (eds), 'Ceci N'est Pas Une Constitution – Constitutionalisation Without a Constitution?', 7th International ECLN-Colloquium, Sofia 17–19 April 2008 (Nomos Verlag), 2009

[78]Article 4, Lisbon Treaty Protocol 1 on the national parliaments

only 30 minutes because the Minister was under severe time pressure. It is hardly surprising, therefore, that very little time is devoted to any single issue. Several measures received no real discussion at all. This is disturbing given that these briefing sessions are the only real opportunity that the Committee and the *Oireachtas* have to influence the shape or content of these measures.[79]

In addition, given their different procedures[80] and cultures, it is questionable how diligently each will approach this task: in 2012, 50 per cent of all opinions came from just three legislatures: the Swedish *riskdag*, the French *senat* and the German *Bundestag*. It is also very unlikely that legislatures will share priorities, thus the card mechanisms will be used rarely. When a yellow card is used, the Commission can manipulate the consequence to pursue its own agenda: it agreed to withdraw the Monti II proposal but only in order to secure cooperation on other measures. The Commission was able to use the procedure to gain leverage – it gave ground on one measure; the national parliaments gave ground on two.[81] Thus while the subsidiarity and proportionality reviews have the potential to advance democracy in the EU, organisational constraints may at present hinder this.

ANALYSING THE LAW

Read the preamble of the Tobacco Directive – how does it respect the principles of subsidiarity and proportionality?

---

v.   The European Citizen's Initiative (ECI)

A valuable aspect of engagement is the ability to set the legislative agenda. The determination of the priorities of the EU has been an area where the legitimacy of its law-making has been called into question. In a traditional international organisation this would be the remit of the signatory member states; in a nation state this would be determined by the 'people' as expressed at general elections. Within the EU this has since 1957 been the monopoly of the Commission. Despite the improvements to its role as co-legislator, the EP still does not have this power: under Article 225 TFEU, it may request that the Commission present a proposal on a particular topic, but the Commission is under no obligation to comply. However, the Lisbon Treaty introduced a further procedure to give citizens to have a minimal level of control over the legislative agenda. In order to stimulate engagement, diversity and interaction, the Treaty created a 'European Citizens Initiative' (ECI) to facilitate direct international democracy.

The ECI offers EU citizens a form of direct democracy[82] – it introduces a political procedure whereby a significant number of eligible individuals may trigger a process

---

[79]Dermot Walsh, 'Parliamentary scrutiny of EU criminal law in Ireland', *ELR* 31, 2006, p. 48

[80]See COSAC, '18th Bi-annual Report: Developments in European Union Procedures and Practices Relevant to Parliamentary Scrutiny', 2012

[81]Proposal for a Directive of the European Parliament and the Council on the enforcement of Directive 96/71/EC, and enforcement of posted workers' rights as underlined in point 3 l) of the 'Compact for Growth and Jobs' adopted by the European Council on 28–29 June 2012 – COM(2013) 0566 final

[82]Korea Democracy Foundation (KDF), *Global Citizens in Charge: How Modern Direct Democracy Can Make Our Representative Democracies Truly Representative*, 2009

leading to the adoption of a legal act. It is a procedure that exists in many countries, including EU member states such as Austria, Hungary, Italy, Latvia, Lithuania, Poland, Romania, Slovakia, Slovenia and Spain.[83] In the United States, such 'citizens' ballot initiatives' have given rise to new programmes, for example, in early childhood services[84] and mental health,[85] with their own dedicated source of tax revenue: tobacco taxes for early childhood and an income tax surcharge on millionaires for mental health.[86]

There are many advantages to direct democracy: they have the potential to enhance mass participation in the exercise of public power, thus enhancing the sense of ownership of legislation and draw attention to areas – for example, those affecting black, minority ethnic and other marginalised groups – that law-makers may choose to ignore if left to their own devices. However, Californian Proposition 209[87] demonstrates that direct democracy can also be used to undo progressive action. This voter initiative changed state law to prohibit the use of positive action to address the continuing effects of racial, ethnic and gender underrepresentation in public education, employment and contracting.

Provision for direct democracy was not made in the original or amended EU treaties. Concrete proposals first appeared in the Convention on the Future of Europe and were carried over into the Lisbon Treaty. Article 11(4) TEU is the first transnational instrument for direct democracy. It provides that:

> *Not less than one million citizens who are nationals of a significant number of Member States may take the initiative of inviting the European Commission, within the framework of its powers, to submit any appropriate proposal on matters where citizens consider that a legal act of the Union is required for the purpose of implementing the Treaties.*

A regulation laying out the details of this mechanism was adopted in February 2011.[88] The opportunity given by the ECI for direct input at the European level also releases – albeit slightly – the grip of the Commission and Council on the EU legislative agenda and so may 'nurture the feeble 'European *demos*'.[89] It may be that the ECI is a non-electoral form of political participation[90] that can address the lack of engagement with the EP.

The provisions of the regulation can be analysed in terms of four specific elements: *personal, quantitative, territorial* and *temporal*. The personal element deals with who may participate in an ECI; the quantitative addresses how many must participate; the territorial looks at the location of the participants, and the temporal element considers

---

[83]'Direct democracy and the EU . . . Is that a threat or a promise?', *CMLR* 45, 2008, p. 929 (editorial comments); see also Theo Schiller, 'Modern Direct Democracy in Europe: Dynamic Development on All Levels' in KDF 2009, p. 135
[84]Proposition 10, 1998
[85]Proposition 63, 2004
[86]Joe Mathews 'Initiative Blues: The North American Experience with Initiatives and Referendums' in KDF 2009, p. 118
[87]This voter initiative in California changed state law to prohibit use of positive action to address the continuing effects of racial, ethnic and gender under-representation in public education, employment and contracting.
[88]Regulation on the citizens initiative, COM(2010) p. 119. For comment see Jaroslav Suchman, 'European Citizens (may soon take the) Initiative', *Columbia Journal of Law Online* 16, 2010 p. 59
[89]*CMLR*, 2008, p. 932 (editorial comments)
[90]Hanspeter Kriesi, 'Political Mobilisation, Political Participation and the Power of the Vote', *West European Politics*, 31(1–2), January–March 2008, pp. 147–168

the timeframe for an ECI.[91] A fifth element for consideration is *topical:* what may be the subject of an ECI?

The **personal** element shows an exclusive approach to direct democracy. Under Article 3, 'The organisers shall be *citizens* of the Union and be of the age to be entitled to vote in elections to the European Parliament.' They must 'form a citizens' committee of at least seven persons who are residents of at least seven different Member States'. Organisers are responsible for the collection of signatures[92] – signatories must also be natural persons[93] who are EU *citizens* who are entitled to vote in EP elections. This raises a serious concern: EU residents, who are not EU citizens, including those recognised as long-term[94] and permanent residents,[95] are totally excluded from this form of participatory democracy. It is regrettable that, its title notwithstanding, such a categorical restriction was imposed on a mechanism intended to enhance participation. It adds to the second-class status of third country nationals, many of whom will belong to black and minority ethnic groups. The EP initially raised concerns about this but dropped its misgivings at an early stage. The ECI is therefore limited in promoting plurality and audibility of marginal voices.

The **quantitative** element, however, promotes participation – in an EU of 500 million: a valid ECI requires a minimum of just 1 million signatures. According to the **territorial** element, the signatories must come from at least one quarter of the member states.[96] An Annex sets out the minimum number of citizens per member state: this ranges from 74,250 in Germany to 4,500 in Malta and Estonia. The **temporal** aspect is set out in Article 5(5) – the ECI must reach the target signatures within 12 months: this will mean that ECIs including Germany will have more to do than those concerning smaller member states. The time period begins as soon as the ECI has been registered:

> *All statements of support shall be collected after the date of registration of the proposed citizens' initiative and within a period not exceeding 12 months. At the end of that period, the register shall indicate that the period has expired and, where appropriate, that the required number of statements of support was not collected.*

Finally, Article 4(2) lays out that the **topic** of the ECI must fall within the framework of EU competency: it does not specify whether this must be an area of exclusive or shared competency. The proposed ECI will be rejected if it is 'manifestly abusive, frivolous or vexatious' or 'manifestly contrary to the values of the Union as set out in Article 2 TEU'. This is expected to prevent proposals by extremist groups from gaining attention, however the regulation does not exclude political parties such as the BNP from initiating ECIs.

Obligations are placed upon the Commission, the organisers and the member states. The Commission must within two months of receipt of an intention to launch an ECI verify the eligibility of an initiative before signatures are collected and register it.[97] In particular, the Commission must 'provide accurate information', create and keep updated a user-friendly guide in all of the EU official languages, which will be available on the

---

[91]Andreas Auer, 'European Citizens Initiative', *European Constitutional Law Review* 1(1), 2005, pp. 79–86
[92]Article 5(1). This may be done on paper or electronically (5(2)).
[93]Article 6(4)(a)
[94]Council Directive 2003/109 on third country nationals who are 'long term residents', OJ L16
[95]See Directive 2004/38, Article 16
[96]Article 7(1)
[97]ECI Regulation Article 4

Commission's ECI website,[98] it will guide and support organisers of the ECI during the process, and upon request during the collection of signatures, include translations of the ECI proposal in the register.[99]

The organisers of the ECI also have significant responsibilities with regard to protection of data, and are made liable for any damages arising from an ECI.[100] They must declare the source of funding for the ECI.[101] If successful, they shall under Article 11 enjoy the opportunity to present the ECI at a public hearing, if appropriate at the EP, together with other EU bodies. The member states must verify the signatories by conducting a random sample.

The ECI Regulation has already been criticised for being overly-bureaucratic and raising expectations that cannot be fulfilled. Concerns have also been raised about costs, the protection of data (given the varying laws in the member states) and the administrative burden placed on member states.[102] Questions on the discretion given to the Commission under Article 4(2) and the impact of a proposed ECI on another member state also remain unanswered.[103] Safeguards remain conspicuously absent from the regulation – this was highlighted during parliamentary debate on the ECI.[104] It is assumed that aggrieved citizens can turn either to the European Ombudsman or the CJEU.

There is no guarantee that it will work or work well, but the ECI provides a constitutional potential for the citizens of Europe to set the EU agenda. Many have been encouraged to do so – there are currently 17 open initiatives. However, Article 11(4) is only an invitation – the Commission retains the power to decline, although it must provide reasons. Twelve have been refused registration: in all cases the refusal was because the proposal fell outside the scope of EU powers. Nonetheless the ECI has significant potential to stimulate not only cross-national dialogue but also diversity and cross-generational interaction.

APPLYING THE LAW

Could the Tobacco Directive be the basis of an ECI? What must you take into consideration?

vi. The European Parliament Initiative (EPI)

A problem with the ECI is that a signature does not equate to deliberation – the ECI will promote horizontal engagement between citizens in different member states but ultimately these are electronic networks rather than forums for personal debate

---

[98]http://ec.europa.eu/citizens-initiative/public/welcome
[99]ADDENDUM TO "I/A" ITEM NOTE, 'Proposal for a Regulation of the European Parliament and of the Council on the citizens' initiative (first reading), Interinstitutional file: 2010/0074 (COD), Brussels, 7 February 2011
[100]Article 13
[101]Article 4(1)
[102]Under Article 5(3) member states will have to verify that the petition is accurate by conducting a random sample of statements.
[103]House of Commons European Committee: General Committee Debate on the Citizens Initiative, Session 2010-11.
[104]http://www.publications.parliament.uk/pa/cm201011/cmgeneral/euro/110117/110117s01.htm

and discussion. An ECI may also only reach those who are already engaged in civil society.[105] The legislative initiative extended to EU citizens via the ECI is therefore not a complete alternative to a legislative initiative for the EP. At least the MEPs have space to debate at some length.

Article 225 TFEU gives the EP a right to propose legislation:

The European Parliament may, acting by a majority of its component Members, request the Commission to submit any appropriate proposal on matters on which it considers that a Union act is required for the purpose of implementing the Treaties. If the Commission does not submit a proposal, it shall inform the European Parliament of the reasons.

The proposal must indicate its legal basis and may include a short explanatory statement. Any request must respect fundamental rights and subsidiarity. The EP does not have a right to have any proposal adopted. As with the ECI, the Commission must provide reasons for its refusal. This seems to place both on an equal footing: it is debateable whether an ECI or an EPI has more chance of success.

The EP has interpreted this power to mean it may request the Commission to submit a proposal for the adoption of a new act or for the amendment of an existing act. The basis of its request will be a report by the relevant committee, which will be voted upon in Plenary. The assumption is that the higher the consensus in the EP, the harder it will be for the Commission to refuse to submit a proposal. This suggests that the measures with the highest chance of success will be ideologically consistent with the largest political grouping in the EP, currently the centre-right EPP or a compromise between it and the second largest grouping, the centre-left S&D. The EP may set a deadline which will prevent the Commission from ignoring the request indefinitely and force it to give a timely response.[106] The EP resolution containing the request must also contain detailed recommendations as to the content of the required proposals and indication of how the financial resources for these will be secured.

Any MEP or group of up to 10 MEPs[107] may table a proposal for a Union act under Article 225 TFEU but the EP President and the committee chairs play central roles. The EP President must receive the proposal and verify its adherence to the formal legal requirements, thereafter announcing it in the Plenary. Prior to referring it to the relevant committee, the proposal will be translated into those languages deemed necessary by the chair of that committee. The committee will draft a report 'after having heard'[108] the authors of the proposal. This suggests that the authors may not be closely involved after submission of the proposal. It is the committee that makes the recommendation that a proposal be opened for signature by MEPs. Signature by a majority of MEPs equates to authorisation of the proposal report by the Conference of Presidents. The committee must follow the progress of preparation of any proposed legislative act drawn up following a particular request by the EP. If the committee decides not to open the report for signature or the requisite number of signatures is not achieved, the committee has three months to decide what to do.

---

[105]Michael Dougan, 'What are we to make of the citizens' initiative?', *Common Market Law Review* 48(6), 2011, pp. 1807–1848
[106]Rule 42(1) EP Rules of Procedure: Initiative pursuant to Article 225 of the Treaty on the Functioning of the European Union
[107]The authors are named in the title of the report (Rule 42(3) EP RP)
[108]Rule 42(3) EP RP

Which has the stronger power: the European Parliament Initiative or the European Citizen Initiative?

7. Conclusion: Who makes EU law?

This chapter explored the law-making procedures in the EU and their exercise by the institutions to discover not only how Union law is made but who makes it. Union law comes in different forms: it can be binding (regulations, directives and decisions) or non-binding (opinions and recommendations); and, since Lisbon, legal acts can be legislative (made using OLP or one of the special procedures) or non-legislative (made using delegated or implementing powers). Implementing acts are made together with the comitology committees, bodies of experts from the member states who advise the Commission on proposals. The Committees act on behalf of the member states to scrutinise the exercise of these implementing powers.

The idea that the power to govern is *granted* to public authorities by the people who are the subjects of its acts remains central. The powers exercised by the EU to make legislative acts are conferred via the Treaties. Their exercise is conditional upon compliance with the principles of legality, subsidiarity and proportionality: they must be based upon an appropriate provision in the Treaties; the Union must be the most appropriate level to adopt the act; and the type of action must be necessary, targeted and the least onerous possible. All three principles are justiciable before the CJEU and are often used by parties to challenge a measure with which they disagree.

Nonetheless, the EU regulatory environment within which these acts are made is subject to constant criticism for lack of adherence to basic democratic principles. EU law remains predominantly driven and made by the Commission, an unelected body of civil servants. Despite the introduction of checks and balances, the Council–Commission tandem remains central: the Commission proposes and the Council adopts. It was in order to address this that the European Parliament has been given status as equal legislator with the Council. The EP has gained from changes to the law-making procedures yet the one area in which its powers diverge most starkly from a national parliament is in relation to the initiation of legislation. It has a right to request the Commission adopts a proposal but still cannot determine the legislative agenda.

Empowerment of the EP has arguably re-created an 'electocracy' rather than a deep democracy: law-making efficiency may be improved but turnout for the EP elections indicate that it has not translated into greater engagement with the 'peoples of Europe'. Its new responsibilities in law-making are a doubled-edged sword: they have increased its status but also its workload – its role in the OLP requires formation of a 'position' rather than just an opinion.[109] In order to fulfil its new tasks its orientation has shifted from championing open debate with the public to building horizontal policy networks and insider consensus via bureaucrats. The increase in informal trilogues undermines its

---

[109]Desmond Dinan, 'Institutions and Governance: Saving the Lisbon Treaty – An Irish Solution to a European Problem', JCMS 47, Annual Review 2009, pp. 113–132

task to represent the peoples of Europe. The declining turnout at EP elections suggests a decreasing interest in the EU as a representative democracy. Transparency is another casualty when more actors are involved – this is a noticeable problem in comitology[110] and the OLP.[111]

Democracy in the EU remains important, even if it is not a nation state,[112] but the democratic norm adopted may be faulty.[113] A real re-engagement cannot focus on elections alone but needs to promote the three 'D's' of dialogue, debate and diversity. There are promising signs in the EU for the promotion of these three 'D's' – in particular, the European Citizen's Initiative (ECI) offers a way for citizens to interact with each other across borders (horizontal engagement) and also with the EU legislator (vertical engagement). The ECI can be criticised for its complexity and superficiality – interaction is predominantly electronic – but the initiative creates an opportunity for the dialogue and debate called for by Guinier and Sen. The European Parliament Initiative (EPI) is also a step towards greater engagement as it enables the EP to set the legislative agenda for the EU. To highlight the EP alone is also to overlook potentially positive aspects of the practice of democracy in the EU.[114]

Democratisation[115] of the EU is an ongoing and long-term project, like European integration itself. The key question is whether, when put together, the reforms made thus far are robust enough to ensure that Union law is not only legitimate but also credible. Emulation of national democracy makes it inevitable that the EP will also mirror their fundamental problems. This has greater consequences for the EU given the limited opportunities for direct engagement with the people of Europe. As an innovative regulatory space, the EU can find new answers, such as using Article 11(4) TEU to develop new metrics of democracy based on the three D's. This may prove a more fruitful way to advance democracy – there are limits to incremental improvements to the OLP. Reimagining democracy may also produce a more self-confident EU that is connected to citizens on its own terms rather via analogy with the nation state.

---

[110]These have been reduced by the European Commission Comitology Register: http://ec.europa.eu/transparency/regcomitology/index.cfm and the European Commission Expert Group Register: http://ec.europa.eu/transparency/regexpert

[111]Access to conciliation documents was addressed in C-39/05 P and C-52/05 P *Sweden and Turco v Council* [2008] ECR I-4723

[112]Phillipe Schmitter, 'Democracy in Europe and Europe's Democracy', *Journal of Democracy* 14(4), 2003, p. 71

[113]de Witte suggests that we think of the EU as an 'advanced international organisation' – B. De Witte, 'The European Union as an International Legal Experiment', in G. de Búrca and J. Weiler, *The Worlds of European Constitutionalism*, Cambridge University Press, 2012

[114]Francis Cheneval and Frank Schimmelfennig, 'The Case for Democracy in the European Union', *JCMS* 51(2), 2013, pp. 351–369

[115]Schmitter 2003, pp. 71–85

Further reading

On forms of acts:

Alan Hardacre and Michael Kaeding, Delegated and Implementing Acts - The New Comitology', *EIPA*, 2011, pp. 7-8

On the democratic deficit:

Francis Cheneval and Frank Schimmelfennig, 'The Case for Democracy in the European Union', *JCMS* 51(2), 2013, pp. 351-369

Andreas Follesdal and Simon Hix, 'Why There is a Democratic Deficit in the EU: A Response to Majone and Moravcsik', *JCMS* 44(3), 2006, pp. 533-562

Giandomenico Majone, 'Europe's "Democratic Deficit": The Question of Standards', *European Law Journal* 4(1), 1998, pp. 5-28

Andrew Moravcsik, 'In Defence of the "Democratic Deficit": Reassessing the Legitimacy of the European Union', *Journal of Common Market Studies*, 40(4), 2002, pp. 603-634

Kalypso Nicolaïdis, 'European Democracy and Its Crisis', *JCMS* 51(2), 2013, pp. 351-369

Phillipe Schmitter, 'Democracy in Europe and Europe's Democratisation', *Journal of Democracy*, 14(4) October 2003, pp. 71-85

On the committees and law-making:

Rory Costello and Robert Thomson, 'The Policy impact of leadership in committees: Rapporteurs influence on the European parliaments opinions', *European Union Politics* 11(2), 2010, pp. 219-240

Pierpaolo Settembri and Christine Neuhold, 'Achieving Consensus Through Committees: Does the European Parliament Manage?', *JCMS* 47(1), 2009, pp. 127-151

On the representation and legislative initiative:

Andreas Auer, 'European Citizens Initiative', *European Constitutional Law Review* 1(1), 2005, pp. 79-86

Michael Dougan, 'What are we to make of the citizens' initiative?', *Common Market Law Review* 48(6), 2011, pp. 1807-1848

Lani Guinier 'Beyond Electocracy: Rethinking the Political Representative as Powerful Stranger', *MLR* 71(1), 2008, p. 22

Hanspeter Kriesi, 'Political Mobilisation, Political Participation and the Power of the Vote', *West European Politics*, 31(1-2), January–March 2008, pp. 147-168

On subsidiarity:

Fabbrini, Katarzyna Granat, '"Yellow card, but no foul": The role of the national parliaments under the subsidiarity protocol and the Commission proposal for an EU regulation on the right to strike', *Common Market Law Review* 50(1), 2013, pp. 115-143

4 The Court of Justice of the European Union (CJEU) – direct and indirect access

Setting the scene

Canada's seal industry has been dealt a blow by an EU regulation banning seal products. A group that includes the Canadian Fur Institute, the seal processing industry and one of Canada's largest Inuit groups sought to challenge the Commission ban before the General Court. However, the General Court decision in favour of the regulation was subsequently upheld by the Court of Justice, making the import of seal products into the EU unlawful in the absence of an exemption. The Inuit Tapiriit Kanatami have an exemption but oppose the ban due to the effects it may have on the wider market: the price for sealskins has collapsed since the ban despite the exemption, not only damaging Canada's 300-year-old commercial sealing industry but also jeopardising the jobs and livelihood of 6,000 workers.

1. Introduction

The 'European Court of Justice' (ECJ) was 'established for a community of six Member States with a population of around 140 million citizens';[1] the current 'Court of Justice of the European Union' (CJEU) – the collective name[2] for the courts of the European Union judicial order – now 'serves' a Union of 28 member states and over 500 million residents and citizens. The ECJ received four cases in 1954; in one single year (2010) a total of 1,406 cases were brought before the three courts of the CJEU.

Under Article 19(1) TEU the CJEU as well as the courts and tribunals of the member states are the guardians of the EU legal order. The CJEU is the final authority on EU law, which judges must apply in national courts.[3] The tasks of the CJEU are also laid out in Article 19 TEU:

> *(1) It shall ensure that in the interpretation and application of the Treaties the law is observed [. . .]*
>
> *(3) The Court of Justice of the European Union shall, in accordance with the Treaties:*
>
> > *(a) rule on actions brought by a Member State, an institution or a natural or legal person;[4]*
> >
> > *(b) give preliminary rulings, at the request of courts or tribunals of the Member States, on the interpretation of Union law or the validity of acts adopted by the institutions;[5]*
> >
> > *(c) rule in other cases provided for in the Treaties.*

This latter category includes, for example, jurisdiction over the legality of acts adopted by the European Council or by the Council pursuant to Article 7 TEU,[6] jurisdiction in disputes relating to compensation for damage[7] or concerning the fulfilment by member states of obligations under the Statute of the European Investment Bank.[8] It also oversees personnel matters – disputes between the Union and its employees – under Article 270 TFEU.[9] Most personnel cases are now dealt with solely by the Civil Service Tribunal (CST) but cases concerning the compulsory retirement of members of the Commission

---

[1] Bo Vesterdorf, 'The Community court system ten years from now and beyond: challenges and possibilities', *ELR* 28, 2003, p. 303
[2] Article 19 TEU
[3] 'Since the *Factortame* cases in the 1990s, that other European aspect of our government, EU law, has meant that Judges have a duty effectively to override legislation when it does not comply with EU law' – Lord Neuberger Of Abbotsbury, 'Is The House Of Lords "Losing Part Of Itself"?', The Young Legal Group Of The British Friends Of The Hebrew University, Lecture 2 December 2009, Para 21, p. 10
[4] Article 234 TFEU concerning actions brought on grounds of lack of competence, infringement of an essential procedural requirement, infringement of the Treaties or of any rule of law relating to their application, or misuse of powers; Article 265 TFEU on failure to act
[5] Article 267 TFEU
[6] Article 269 TFEU
[7] Article 268 TFEU, as specified in Article 340
[8] Article 271 TFEU
[9] This provision was used in *Commission v Cresson*. The Court met as a full plenary of 27.

are sent to the CJ.[10] The CJEU also acts as an appeal court on Article 263 TFEU and Article 267 TFEU cases from the General Court (GC), and can review appeals to the GC from CST (questions on the unity or consistency of EU law only).

The CJEU has long ceased to be a monolithic institution 'tucked away in the duchy of Luxembourg'.[11] As it has grown, there is increasing concern over the way in which the CJEU functions. Despite managing an extraordinary caseload over the last 60 years, there are some practices which grow ever more anomalous in the age of transparency and the citizen-centric post-Lisbon CJEU: tasks are conducted behind closed doors; recruitment remains largely closed to the public; the decision-making process is lengthy; rulings have not always been clear and new procedures have been implemented without clear guidance.[12]

To what extent therefore does it act as the 'third branch' of government, ensuring that public powers are exercised in the interests of the 'peoples' of Europe, or even those people beyond affected by EU law such as the Inuits of Canada? A court is said to be the last branch of government because it is the first defence of the individual – individuals rely on the judiciary to protect their rights and freedoms from intrusion by the exercise of public power.[13] Does this apply to the CJEU – does it protect individuals and Union citizens? These questions highlight the main themes in this chapter. They can only be partly answered by examining the organisation of the CJEU – its tasks and composition. A fuller answer requires further exploration of the extent to which individuals can access the Court to challenge Union legal acts. This chapter will therefore focus on the two main procedures to bring actions before the CJEU: direct actions via Article 263 TFEU and indirect actions under Article 267 TFEU.

2. The organisation of the CJEU

The structure of the CJEU is laid out in Article 19 TEU:

> *The Court of Justice of the European Union shall include the Court of Justice, the General Court and specialised courts . . .*

The Union judicial system currently includes three separate courts: the Court of Justice (CJ)[14], the General Court[15] (GC – formerly the Court of First Instance) and the Civil Service Tribunal (CST)[16] created in 2008. There are now 71 full members in the Union judiciary. All members are responsible for ensuring respect for the autonomy of the

---

[10]Article 247 TFEU (ex Article 216 TEC) states that 'If any Member of the Commission no longer fulfils the conditions required for the performance of his duties or if he has been guilty of serious misconduct, the Court of Justice may, on application by the Council acting by a simple majority or the Commission, compulsorily retire him.'

[11]Eric Stein, Lawyers, Judges and the Making of a Transnational Constitution, *American Journal of International Law* 75(1), 1981, p. 1

[12]The expedited procedures such as Article 267(4)

[13]See for example *Secretary of State for the Home Department* v *Al -Jedda* [2013] UKSC 62, [2013] WLR(D) 371, [2013] 3 WLR 1006 where the UK Supreme Court prevented the Home Secretary from stripping a man of his British citizenship.

[14]Article 251–253 TFEU

[15]Article 254 TFEU

[16]N. Lavranos, (2005) 'The New Specialised Courts within the European Judicial System', *ELR* 30, 2005, p. 261.

European Union legal order created by the Treaties.[17] They are assisted by an army of legal clerks and translators.[18]

The CJ (the only court mentioned in the Treaty of Rome) and the GC each comprise one judge from the member states – they have 28 full members each, although the CJ has proposed an increase in the number of GC judges to 39.[19] In addition, the CJ has eight Advocates-General (AsG), who are mandated to 'assist the court' but have no judicial decision-making power. Every national legal and judicial system within the EU is represented in these two courts. The CST is different – it has only seven judges. This court is not constructed on the basis of national representation.

In comparison to the US federal system, which has 94 district courts (each with between 2 and 28 judges) and 13 circuit courts (comprising 179 judges),[20] this is perhaps a small system for use by up to 500 million people.[21] A comparison with the USA also shows that the CJEU is highly – perhaps overly – productive: in 2013, the CJ alone completed 701 cases (595 in 2012) and had 699 new cases brought before it (632 in 2012) with in addition to 884 cases pending. In just over 50 years of existence it has produced over 9,000 judgments and opinions. In comparison, the US Supreme Court – taking an average of 100 decisions per year – has produced perhaps 20,000 judgments in 200 years.

i.   The structure of judicial deliberation

The CJEU is a unique court – its composition is international yet its decisions are as binding as those of a national court. Unlike other supreme courts, the appellate function is a minor part of its role[22] – the majority of its work arises from requests to interpret the Treaty or the validity of secondary legislation under Article 267 TFEU. Furthermore, unlike other supreme courts, no member of the CJEU is permanent. Judges and AsG are appointed for a term of six years, although this is renewable at the discretion of the member states. In addition, unlike most Supreme Courts, all of the CJEU rulings are unanimous – the CJEU may function in many different languages, but it is both unanimous (it produces a single decision) and univocal (if there is reasoning, it follows one line).[23]

Judicial deliberation takes place inside the 'delibere' – this is where decisions are formulated. The judges in all three courts now meet in small 'chambers' or groups of three

---

[17]See Opinion 1/91 [35]. Restated in Opinion 1/09 Of The Court (Full Court) on the creation of a European and Community Patents Court, 8 March 2011.

[18]The language of a case is chosen by the applicant or referring court. They can choose from Bulgarian, Czech, Danish, Dutch, English, Estonian, Finnish, French, German, Greek, Hungarian, Irish, Italian, Latvian, Lithuanian, Maltese, Polish, Portuguese, Romanian, Slovak, Slovene, Spanish or Swedish.

[19]CJEU Annual Activity Report 2011, p. 4

[20]Sandra Day O Connor, *The Majesty of the Law: Reflections of a Supreme Court Justice*, Random House, 2004, pp. 208-209

[21]Niamh Nic Shuibhne, 'A court within a court: is it time to rebuild the Court of Justice?', *ELR* 34(2), 2009, pp. 173–174 (Editorial); Arjen Meij, 'Courts in transition: Administration of justice and how to organize it – Celebrating six decades of the Court of Justice in a close community of Magistrates', *Common Market Law Review* 50(3), 2013, pp. 3–14 (Guest Editorial)

[22]Cases may be appealed on their facts from the CST to the General Court and from the General Court to the Court of Justice.

[23]James Lee, 'A Defence of Concurring Speeches', *Public Law*, 2009, pp. 305–331. Between 1970 and 2000, rates of unanimity were as follows: USA 42.9 per cent; Australia 58.9 per cent; Canada 75.6 per cent; UK 81.2 per cent; South Africa 90.9 per cent. See blog by Chris Hanratty at: http://ukscblog.com/dissenting-opinons-in-the-uksc

or five[24] to decide upon cases; on very important cases the CJ will meet as a Grand Chamber of 11 or 15.[25] As stated by Lazowski,[26]

> The Grand Chamber cases are supposed to be crème de la crème of case law of the Court of Justice. They are meant to serve as precedents and to provide ultimate guidance to national courts under the preliminary ruling procedure. In case of actions for annulment and infringement proceedings they also settle constitutional disputes and institutional battles within the European Union's institutional framework and challenges to Member States' compliance with EU law (respectively).

When a Court opinion is required, the CJ can meet in a formation of 28.[27]

All chambers produce collective decisions. Under the Rules of Procedure[28] that set out its mode of operation, the Court shall deliberate in closed session. The judges participating in the delibere will be those who were present at the oral proceedings as well as the assistant rapporteur, if used. Although every judge taking part in the deliberations shall state his opinion and the reasons for it, this is never made public. Thus while the Rules state that the 'conclusions reached by the majority of the Judges after final discussion shall determine the decision of the Court', the size of the majority is never known beyond the Court.

This closure has increasingly been sharply criticised. Hepple and Barnard, for example, argued that the 'strong stench of compromise' pervading the decision of the then 15 men at the CJ in *Seymour Smith* lent 'weight to those arguing for the Court to allow for dissenting opinions'.[29] National judges are equally disgruntled – in the UK, Lord Mance argues that the CJEU should allow separate opinions to avoid 'jurisprudence that is both obscure and rigid' – 'readers and users of the European Court's jurisprudence would benefit by a change which would allow individual freedom of expression to its judges and make the Court's decision-making and reasoning more transparent, flexible and perhaps paradoxically, coherent'.[30] The CJEU's pursuit of univocality and unanimity has been described as 'artificial'[31] and out of tandem with the member states: according to a poll taken prior to enlargement on the use of dissenting opinions in the CJEU, nine member states were in favour of their use, and six were against.[32]

Separate – dissenting or concurring – opinions are controversial. It is rare to find an ambivalent position on their use. The arguments on either side to some extent mirror each other – on the one hand dissent reveals the 'deliberative nature of the court' which

---

[24]Article 11(a) RP

[25]The last Grand Chamber of 13 sat on 24 September 2011. It will now meet in a formation of 15 – CJEU Annual Report 2011, p. 9. The full text of proposals is available at: http://curia.europa.eu/jcms/jcms/Jo2_7031

[26]Adam Łazowski, 'Advocates General and Grand Chamber Cases: Assistance with the Touch of Substitution', in Catherine Barnard, Markus Gehring and Iyiola Solanke (eds), *Cambridge Yearbook of European Law Studies* 14, 2012, p. 635

[27]See for example Opinion 2/13 of the Court (Full Court) on accession to the European Convention of Human Rights, 18 December 2014. A formation of 27 will also meet to decide upon the Article 267 reference on the ESM from Ireland.

[28]Article 27

[29]B. Hepple and C. Barnard 'Indirect Discrimination: Interpreting Seymour Smith', *Cambridge Law Journal* 58(2), 1999, p. 399

[30]Lord Mance in Lee 2009, pp. 325–326

[31]J. Laffranque 'Dissenting Opinions in the European Court of Justice – Estonia's possible contribution to the democratisation of the European Judicial System', *Juridica International* IX, 2004, p. 21

[32]In favour: Germany, Finland, Sweden, Denmark, Spain, UK, Ireland, Greece, Portugal; Against: France, Italy, Netherlands, Belgium, Luxembourg, Austria. See Laffranque 2004, fn 29.

strengthens its institutional authority and legitimacy' in governance, but on the other dissent may 'detract from the legitimacy of a court'. Where for some, dissent allows judges to contribute to 'the marketplace of competing ideas' and produce the 'best possible rule', for others it weakens the court by undermining unanimity and weakens judicial decisions by undermining legal certainty. While for some, dissent is a 'healthy, even necessary practice that improves the way law is made' and reinforces collegiality by ensuring all points of view are articulated equally, for others it weakens judgments by obviating the need to find consensus. If for some, dissent strengthens public confidence in the judiciary by showing reasoning and debate, for others they weaken judges by undermining the secrecy that protects independence. Finally, the argument that dissent contributes to the education of judges and observers so that 'today's dissent might become tomorrow's majority' is countered with the view that they are inefficient and waste time.[33]

VIEWPOINT

Read the Editorial by Nic Shuibhne – does the EU need to be rebuilt to create a bigger court? Should a new court allow separate opinions?

---

a) The Advocates General – beyond the delibere

The members of the CJEU can be divided into two categories – those full members who sit inside the delibere and participate in the decision-making, and those full members who do not sit in the delibere. Only the 28 judges in the CJ and GC are the decision-making members, as are the seven judges in the CST; the eight Advocates General in the CJ are outside the delibere – they do not sit in the decision-making chamber. They are non-decision-making members in the CJ.

Nonetheless, judges and AsG are equal: they are appointed in the same manner by 'common accord of the Governments of the Member States for a term of six years from persons whose independence and competence are beyond doubt;' they are also subject to a partial replacement every three years, and eligible for reappointment.[34] At present, the formal criteria for an Advocate General (AG) is the same as for a CJEU judge and both share the same status.[35] They make the same oath to perform 'duties impartially and conscientiously and to preserve the secrecy of the deliberations of the Court',[36] enjoy immunity from legal proceedings during and after office and Community privileges in all of the member states,[37] may not hold any political or administrative post or

---

[33]For representations of these views see: John Alder, 'Dissents in Courts of Last Resort: Tragic Choices?', in *Oxford Journal of Legal Studies* 20, 2000, pp. 238–244; J. Rivers, 'Proportionality and variable intensity of review', *Cambridge Law Journal* 65(1), 2006, p. 174; M. Todd Henderson 'From *Seriatim* to Consensus and Back Again: A Theory Of Dissent', John M. Olin Law and Economics Working Paper No. 363, Chicago Law School, October 2007, pp. 1–2; G. Harpaz (2006) 'The Israeli Supreme Court in search of universal legitimacy' *Cambridge Law Review* 65(1), 2006, p. 7
[34]Article 32 Treaty establishing the European Steel and Coal Community (ECSC), Paris, 18 April 1951
[35]Rules of Procedure, Article 6. The status of Advocates General was formalised in 1974 when the Rules of Procedure declared that they are of equal rank to judges.
[36]Protocol on the Statute of the Court of Justice (hereafter 'Protocol'), Article 2, ECSC
[37]Protocol, Article 3

gainful occupation,[38] and are remunerated in a similar fashion.[39] Both judges and AsG are removed from the CJEU by the member states, primarily by non-renewal of tenure. Their duties terminate upon resignation, or death.[40] Both tend to come from the higher ranks of the national judiciary and civil service, legal practice and the higher tier of academia.[41] The development of a judicial profile for members enhances the independent image of the CJEU and its legal authority, although the Treaty has never explicitly excluded non-lawyers from membership.[42]

There are at present eight Advocates General. The Rules of Procedure state that the 'Court shall take its decision in closed session after hearing the Advocate General'.[43] The AG has no judicial decision-making power in the CJEU or elsewhere. What then do they do? Their duty remains to act with 'complete impartiality and independence' in making 'in open court, reasoned submissions on cases which . . . require his involvement': the AG no longer gives an opinion on every case that comes before the CJ[44] – the Court decided to rule without it in *Asociatia ACCEPT*[45] – and only rarely provides an opinion for the General Court. The AG can be compared to a trial judge in the United States, who has more independence than US appellate judges:

> He knows that if he cannot convince the higher courts, he can be overruled, thus preventing damage to the system. He need not modify his opinions to garner the votes of others on the panel. In a sense he is, by analogy to what Justice Brandeis described as the laboratories of the states, in a position to experiment, to push the envelope of the law in the direction of what he conceives to be justice.[46]

Importantly, the AG is the only visible member of the CJEU – every opinion is signed by its author – and therefore provides some transparency at the Court. It is primarily via the AG opinion that those who are subject to the decisions of the CJEU are able to understanding its thinking.

The AG 'assists' the Court by providing an 'opinion' prior to the determination of the judges. This is neither a 'separate opinion' nor a draft judgment. The opinion produced by the AG is an independent and impartial assessment of the facts in a case assigned to them.[47] The opinion is a self-styled,[48] self-standing and complete document which expresses a personal opinion of the AG. It is not subject to deliberation, discussion and/ or later amendment. There is no right to reply to the opinion.[49] Unlike Judges who have

---

[38]Protocol, Article 4

[39]Protocol, Article 5

[40]Protocol, Article 12

[41]A number have written textbooks on EU law – K. Lenartes, D. Arts and I. Maselis, *Procedural Law of the European Union,* 2nd edn, Sweet & Maxwell, 2006; G. Tesauro, *Diritto comunitario,* 5th edn, CEDAM, 2008; Allan Rosas and Lorna Armati, *EU Constitutional Law,* Hart Publishing, 2012

[42]Judge Vesterdorf, House of Lords European Union Scrutiny Commitee, 15th Report (2006–7), HL 75 [99]

[43]Article 3 Rules of Procedure

[44]In addition, the AG opinion is not published when provided in a case dealt with under the accelerated procedure. See C. Barnard, 'The PPU: is it worth the candle? An early assessment', *European Law Review* 34(2), 2009, p. 281

[45]C-81/12 *Asociatia ACCEPT* v *Consiliul National pentru Combaterea Discriminarii*

[46]Jack B. Weinstein, 'The Role Of Judges In A Government Of, By, And For The People: Notes For the 58th Cardozo Lecture', *Cardozo Law Review* 30(1), 2008, p. 32

[47]Online at http://curia.europa.eu/en/instit/presentationfr/index_savoirplus.htm

[48]There is no standard style for presentation of an opinion.

[49]This was conclusively ruled out by the Court in the *Emesa Sugar* ruling, where it said that the ruling by the European Court of Human Rights (ECtHR) in the *Vermeulen* case concerning the Belgian *Procueur General* was not transferable to the AG at the Court C-17/98 *Emesa Sugar* [2000] ECR I-665.

to negotiate and compromise[50] in order to reach a collective decision, the Advocate General does not have to accommodate the views of others. The Advocates General are free to determine the boundaries of their investigations: the opinion may place the questions presented to the Court within a broader geographical, economic or social context. Thus the opinions can contain considerations not developed by the parties which the Court may adopt.[51] Sometimes the Court has referred national judges to the conclusions of the Advocates General for answers to issues which the Court itself is not empowered to consider.[52] It has been argued that this facilitates a certain amount of bold exploration of legal reasoning and logic on the part of Advocates General, which in turn can embolden the CJEU to make rulings it may not have otherwise taken.[53] The personal nature of the opinion is underlined by the fact that it is neither amended nor corrected by anybody other than the AG, it is not negotiated,[54] and the AG signs her name beneath it. Such autonomy could hardly be imagined in the four words describing their formal task – 'to assist the Court'.

There is no equivalent to the AG in any legal system of the member states.[55] The Advocate General first appeared in Article 10 of the Protocol attached to the Treaty of Paris (Protocol), which established the European Coal and Steel Community (ECSC): it set out that 'the Court shall be assisted by two Advocates-General (AsG) and a Registrar'. Under Article 11 Protocol, the AG was mandated to act with 'complete impartiality and independence' and make 'in open court, oral and reasoned submissions on cases brought before the Court, in order to assist the Court in the performance of the task assigned to it . . . ' This role of assistance excluded participation in the delibere: the AG could help the Court find a decision, but not decide.

As with judges, the Council can increase the number of AsG by unanimity. The number of judges has increased with every enlargement but the number of Advocates General increased only with the enlargements of 1973, 1981 and 1986, when new seats were created to accommodate large acceding states. Apart from a brief period in the 1990s when the number increased to nine, there have been eight AsG for the last two decades. The Lisbon Treaty has opened an opportunity for this to change: Article 252 TFEU[56] states that the Court should be 'assisted by eight Advocates-General' but Article 19(2) TEU[57] removes any numerical limit.[58] Under Article 252 TFEU the number of AsG can be increased following a request of the Court of Justice and a unanimous decision by the Council.[59] It would not be surprising if the number were increased as of the current 28 member states, only five – France, Italy, Germany, Spain and the UK – have a

---

[50]Barnard and Hepple 1999, p. 411

[51]P.J.G. Kapteyn and P. Verloren van Themaat, *Introduction to the law of the European Communities,* 3rd edn, Kluwer Law International, 1998, p. 250, fn 393

[52]P.S.R.F. Mathijsen, *A Guide To European Union Law,* 8th edn, Sweet & Maxwell, 2004, p. 106; Renaud Dehousse, *The European Court of Justice. The politics of judicial integration,* Macmillan Press, 1998, p. 9

[53]Neville March Hunnings, *The European Courts,* John Harper Publishing, 1996, pp. 57–58

[54]C-17/98 *Emesa Sugar (Free Zone) N.V v Aruba* [2000] ECR I-675

[55]K. Borgsmidt, 'The Advocate General at the European Court of Justice: A Comparative Study', *European Law Review,* 1988, p. 106

[56]Treaty on the Functioning of the European Union, OJ C115/158, 9 May 2008. Formerly Article 222 TEC

[57]Treaty on the European Union, OJ C115/13, 9 May 2008

[58]Poland now has a permanent AG.

[59]The proposal to increase the number of Advocates General to 9 from 1 July 2013 and to 11 from 7 October 2015 was debated in the UK House of Lords on 10 June 2013.

permanent AG. The remaining 23 countries share three seats which are allocated on an alphabetical rotating basis.[60]

ii.   Recruitment of CJEU members

Judges administer a public good – justice – which courts exist to protect. As the judiciary is the central actor in the justice system, judges without credibility result in a justice system without legitimacy.[61] The composition of the judiciary is therefore important. An important question is who can become a judge in the CJEU, delivering justice to the peoples of Europe?

It may help to reflect upon what judges do to answer this question. Although there is no definitive outline for the judicial role, the tasks allocated to the judiciary in the post-war period have become broader and more complex, due both to an increase in the number of courts and tribunals,[62] more legal and more technical[63] rules and the wider reach of regulation. Public expectation is also higher: courts around the world are called upon to respond to a broad range of social, political and economic questions. It has been argued that judicial decisions are replacing political debate in mature democracies:[64] law has displaced politics and religion as the language of power because politicians and the clergy have become discredited. More than ever, legal opinions are therefore a 'normalising force'.[65] Several authors describe courts as 'the most powerful political force in the nation.'[66]

Access to courts is therefore more important than ever:

> . . . the principle of public access to the Courts is an essential element in our system. Nor are the reasons in the slightest degree difficult to find. The Judges speak and act on behalf of the community. They necessarily exercise great power in order to discharge heavy responsibilities. The fact that they do it under the eyes of their fellow citizens means that they must provide daily and public assurance that so far as they can manage it what they do is done efficiently if possible, with human understanding it may be hoped, but certainly by a fair and balanced application of the law to the facts as they really appear to be. Nor is it simply a matter of providing just answers for individual cases, important though that always will be. It is a matter as well of maintaining a system of justice which requires that the judiciary will be seen day by day attempting

---

[60]I. Solanke, 'Diversity and Independence in the European Court of Justice', *Columbia Journal of European Law* 15(1), 2009, p. 89

[61]After losing a big case in Ecuador, Chevron sought to put the nation's judiciary on trial in the United States –'The Really Long Arm of American Justice', *Bloomberg Business Week,* 2011, p. 27

[62]For example, the Court of Protection created in England in 2007 to make decisions on the lives of vulnerable people, or more recently, the special tribunal created to resolve the Qantas dispute.

[63]In *Human Genome Sciences Inc (Appellant)* v *Eli Lilly and Company (Respondent)* [2011] UKSC 51 the UK Supreme Court considered the validity of a patent which claims the nucleotide sequence of the gene which encodes for a novel protein; in C-34/10 *Bruestle* v *Greenpeace plc,* the Court of Justice had to determine whether precursor cells from human stem cells could be patented.

[64]See C. Guarnieri and P. Pederzolli, *The Power of Judges: A comparative study of courts and democracy,* Oxford University Press, 2002. See also R. Hirschl, *Towards Juristocracy: the origin and consequences of the new constitution,* Harvard University Press, 2004; K. Malleson, and P. Russell, *Appointing Judges in an Age of Judicial Power,* University of Toronto Press, 2006

[65]M. Todd Henderson, 'From *Seriatim* to consensus and Back Again: A Theory of Dissent', John M. Olin Law and Economics Working Paper No. 363, October 2007, pp. 5–7

[66]Virginia A. Hettinger, Stefanie A. Lindquist and Wendy L. Martinek, 'Comparing Attitudinal and Strategic Accounts of Dissenting Behavior on the U.S. Courts of Appeals', *AJPS* 48, 2004, p. 123

to grapple in the same even fashion with the whole generality of cases. To the extent that public confidence is then given in return so may the process may be regarded as fulfilling its purposes.[67]

VIEWPOINT

To what extent do you agree with P. Woodhouse? Do judges simply provide answers or are they a political force?

There are now two procedures to appoint members to the CJEU: the original intergovernmental procedure for the CJ and the GC, and a new supranational one for the CST. The Treaties give little guidance on methods of recruitment to the CJ and GC: Article 253 TFEU simply states that:

The Judges and Advocates-General of the Court of Justice shall be chosen from persons whose independence is beyond doubt and who possess the qualifications required for appointment to the highest judicial offices in their respective countries or who are jurisconsults of recognised competence; they shall be appointed by common accord of the governments of the Member States for a term of six years, after consultation of the panel provided for in Article 255.

The criteria in Article 254 TFEU for members of the GC differ in just one respect: members shall be persons who 'possess the *ability* required for appointment to *high* judicial office'.

There is no formal 'lower level'[68] from which to recruit members of the CJ in the way that national constitutional courts recruit members from a state court. Some member states – notably Italy – have used the GC as a feeder court for the CJ.[69] Recruitment is conducted solely at the national level (although there is now a judicial panel to oversee this at the EU level)[70] and is generally a closed affair – nominees are rarely openly sought nor publicly scrutinised. All members of the CJ and GC are selected and nominated by the member states using self-determined methods, under the control of the national political leadership. Some member states advertise vacancies in daily newspapers and a few hold some form of hearing – most do not. Member states are also responsible for reappointment and removal. The role played by the EU is symbolic, at the moment of formal appointment by the European Council. The European Council may take time to consider a nominee but refusal of a candidate is unlikely. Scrutiny is minimal, informal and highly confidential.[71] It may be that the freedom of member states to appoint, reappoint and remove members at their whim impinges upon the independence of the EU judiciary.

---

[67]Words of the President of the Court of Appeal, P. Woodhouse, in *Broadcasting Corporation of New Zealand v Attorney General* [1982] 1 NZLR 120, 122 as quoted in *The Queen (on the application of Guardian News and Media Limited) and City of Westminster Magistrates' Court* [2012] EWCA Civ 420 [3]
[68]The new civil service tribunal might also fulfil this role in the future.
[69]David Edward, Romain Schintgen and Antonio La Pergola were also initially members of the CFI before joining the ECJ.
[70]Article 225 TFEU
[71]Solanke 2009, p. 89

By contrast, there is a central nomination and appointment process at the European level for the CST. Under Article 257 TFEU specialised courts may be created by regulation on a proposal from the Commission after consultation with the Court of Justice or at the request of the Court of Justice after consultation with the Commission. The regulation establishing a specialised court must set out the rules for its organisation and its jurisdiction. The CST Regulation established that recruitment to the CST is organised and managed by the General Secretariat of the Council of Ministers: it publishes and circulates vacancies and candidates send their *curriculum vitaes* and supporting materials directly to it. Unlike for the CJ and GC, there are more eligibility criteria: applicants are to be persons whose independence is beyond doubt, who possess the ability required for appointment to national judicial office. In addition, however, the decision states that they 'must be citizens of the Union' who are able to work within a 'collegiate structure in a multinational, multilingual environment'.[72]

A key innovation for the CST was the creation of a consultation committee. All application materials are considered by this committee, whose task is to identify and shortlist candidates,[73] compile from the applications a shortlist of at least 14 names, and to assist the Council by providing 'an opinion on candidates' suitability to perform the duties of judge at the Civil Service Tribunal'.[74] The committee comprises 'seven persons chosen from among former members of the Court of Justice and the Court of First Instance and lawyers of recognized competence'.[75] Its members are appointed by the Council, acting by a qualified majority on a recommendation of the President of the CJEU, for a four-year term. The Council appoints the President of the committee.[76] The committee met in May and June 2005 to reduce the 243 applications received to a list of 14 'candidates having the most suitable high-level experience' for the Council of Ministers.[77] As the committee has only consultative status, its opinion is not binding.

Nonetheless, witnesses to the House of Lords Select Committee on the European Union described the CST procedure as a 'useful and encouraging precedent'.[78] The CST method was the first time that appointments to a Union court departed from the principle of one judge per member state and that the procedure was managed at the EU level. Both of these initiatives are to be welcomed and would have to be extended were separate opinions to be introduced. It is not inconceivable that a similar method could be extended to determine the composition of the CJ and GC but to do this these courts must like the CST discard the principle of member state representation.[79] Selection and appointment at the

---

[72]Article 3(4) of Annex I to Protocol on the Statute of the Court of Justice
[73]Council Decision of 22 July 2005 on appointing Judges of the European Union Civil Service Tribunal OJ L197/28 2005; Council Decision of 18 January 2005 concerning the conditions and arrangements governing the submission and processing of applications for appointment as a judge of the European Union Civil Service Tribunal OJ L50/9 2005
[74]Article 3(4) of Annex I to Protocol on the Statute of the Court of Justice
[75]Article 2, Annex, Council Decision of 18 January [2005] OJ L50/7
[76]OJ L50/9. The first members included one former AG, Giuseppe Tesauro, and Leif Sevón (President), Christopher Bellamy, Yves Galmot, Peter Grilc, Gabriele Kucsko-Stadlmayer and Miroslaw Wyrzykowski, OJ L197/29 2005. Article 2 Council Decision of 18 January 2005 concerning the conditions and arrangements governing the submission and processing of applications for appointment as a judge of the European Union Civil Service Tribunal OJ L50/7 2005
[77]Article 5, Annex, Council Decision of 18 January OJ L50/7 2005
[78]Sir Christopher Bellamy in House of Lords EU Committee (2006–7) 'An EU Competition Court', HL 75, *HL Fifteenth Report,* para. 97
[79]A lesson could be learned in the long term from the African Court of Justice (ACJ): although the African Union has 53 member states, the ACJ has only 11 judges. Each member state of the African Union may nominate one candidate from any of the member states. See K. Magliveras and G. Naldi, 'The African Court of Justice', *Heidelberg Journal of International Law/ ZaöRV* 66, 2006, p. 187

European level would allow for closer control at the European level, preventing decisions being taken at the national level which may have a negative impact upon the day-to-day business of the Court. Additional distance from their national governments would increase the independence of the members and the legitimacy of the Court.

APPLYING THE LAW

Can the CST appointment procedure be used for the CJ and GC? Consider the advantages and disadvantages of this.

The creation of the Judicial Panel in Article 255 TFEU has potentially started this shift by introducing an element of scrutiny at the European level prior to the appointment of CJ and GC members. This panel is to be composed of 'seven persons chosen from among former members of the Court of Justice and the General Court, members of national supreme courts and lawyers of recognised competence, one of whom shall be proposed by the European Parliament'. Although the Council is again given authority to establish and choose these persons, the panel is to 'act on the initiative of President of the Court of Justice'. This suggests a more active responsibility for the Court in relation to the panel and its tasks. Its main duty is to 'give an opinion on candidates' suitability to perform the duties of Judge and Advocate General of the Court of Justice and the General Court' prior to their appointment. The status of the opinion is not outlined but since its creation candidates rejected by the Panel have also been found unsuitable by the Council.

3. Access to the CJEU

Article 13 TEU declares that:

The Union shall have an institutional framework which shall aim to promote its values, advance its objectives, serve its interests, those of its citizens and those of the Member States, and ensure the consistency, effectiveness and continuity of its policies and actions.

This provision is also addressed to the Court of Justice of the European Union. The idea of a court serving the interests of citizens is novel:[80] what does such a duty for a court mean within the democratic government of the EU? At a minimum, it must mean that citizens can bring their matters before such a court.

Access is determined primarily by judges: judges in national courts and tribunals decide whether a question should be referred via the preliminary reference procedure under Article 267 TFEU; EU judges determine admissibility and standing under Article 263 TFEU. From the perspective of the CJEU, Articles 263 TFEU and 267 TFEU work in tandem to ensure access. If a party has been informed of the direct route, they are not

---

[80]B. de Witte 'Democratic Adjudication in Europe. Is the European Court of Justice Responsive to the Citizens?', in Michael Dougan, Niamh Nic Shuibhne and Eleanor Spaventa (eds), *Empowerment and Disempowerment of the European Citizen,* Hart Publishing, 2012

allowed to use the indirect route[81] but standing under Article 263 is not a bar to Article 267 action.[82] There is no individual right to have a case heard by the CJ or GC. In *Kadi* the GC held that there is no absolute right of access to the courts.[83] It is questionable whether this is necessary for a court that oversees the EU Treaties and is therefore effectively a constitutional court, especially as it is now to 'serve'[84] the interests of the citizen.

i.   Direct actions: direct access under Article 263 TFEU

One of the most important aspects determining who may bring a case before the courts are the rules of standing, or *locus standi*. Standing has been called one of the most amorphous concepts in the entire domain of public law. The vagueness of the doctrine is said to impose 'a hurdle on the path of public access to the courts'.[85] The question of standing has been a controversial issue for the EU judicial order. Direct access is difficult for individuals – it is possible only for 'natural and legal persons'[86] if they can demonstrate an unbroken connection between an institutional act and their personal situation, which must be unique. As will be seen below, this was a hurdle for the Inuit Tapiriit Kanatami who wanted to challenge the EU ban on seal products.

Article 263(1) TFEU gives the CJEU authority to:

> . . . *review the legality of legislative acts, of acts of the Council, of the Commission and of the European Central Bank, other than recommendations and opinions, and of acts of the European Parliament and of the European Council intended to produce legal effects vis-à-vis third parties. It shall also review the legality of acts of bodies, offices or agencies of the Union intended to produce legal effects vis-à-vis third parties.*

What is a 'legislative act'? A legislative act includes regulations, directives and decisions. In *Calpak*[87] the CJ made clear that 'the choice of form cannot alter the nature of a measure'. This phrase applies to any act which has binding force or produces legal effects, such as the Council negotiating procedure,[88] a letter from the Commission[89] or a Commission sanction decision under Article 260(2) TFEU.[90] The Court will always examine the substance of the challenged measure. In addition, the CJEU may review acts of Council, the Commission, European Central Bank (ECB), the European Council as well as acts of bodies, offices or agencies of the Union exercising delegated powers, such as the Fundamental Rights Agency.[91] Article 263 may not be used to review acts of the member states.

---

[81]C-188/92 *TWD*

[82]C-241/95 *Accrington Beef;* C-50/00 P *Unión de Pequeños Agricultores* v *Council* [2002] ECR I-0000 [40]

[83]T-315/01 *Yassin Abdullah Kadi* v *Council of the European Union and Commission of the European Communities* and C-402/05 *Kadi Yassin Abdullah Kadi and Al Barakaat International Foundation* v *Council of the European Union and Commission of the European Communities.*

[84]Article 13 TEU

[85]Weinstein 2008, p. 76

[86]Article 263(4)

[87]C-789 and 790/79 *Calpak* v *Commission* [1980] ECR 1949

[88]C-22/70 *Commission* v *Council* (ERTA) [1971] ECR 263

[89]C-60/81 *IBM* v *Commission* [1981] ECR and C-39/93 *S.F.E.I. and others* v *Commission* [1994] ECR I-2681

[90]C-292/11 P *Commission* v *Portugal*

[91]For comment on bodies not subject to CJ review prior to Lisbon see Jill Wakefield 'Good Governance and the European Anti-fraud Office', *European Law Journal* 15(4), July 2009, pp. 425–441

A consequence of review is annulment – under Article 264 TFEU an act can be declared void. Why should an act be declared invalid? Five grounds are laid out: lack of competence, infringement of an essential procedural requirement, infringement of the Treaties or of any rule of law relating to their application, or misuse of power. Lack of competence can arise when there is no legal base in the Treaty conferring the authority to act in a particular area or when the measure is tainted by an unlawful delegation of power. In the *Tobacco Advertising* case, the CJ annulled a measure which it deemed designed to regulate public health, an area in which the EU (then) lacked competence.[92] An infringement of an essential procedural requirement includes 'technical' defects such as a failure to give reasons under Article 296 TFEU or to consult.[93] These must be of an 'essential' nature', as determined by the CJEU. An infringement of the Treaty or any rule of law relating to its application is a very general ground which could include a breach of any rule of EU law not found in the Treaties (e.g. general principles of EU law). Misuse of power refers to an evasion of a procedure prescribed by the Treaty or the adoption of a Union act for reasons other than those stated.[94]

Who may ask the Court to review these acts? The Article creates three categories of standing. Privileged applicants are listed in 263(2):

> *It shall for this purpose have jurisdiction in actions brought by a Member State, the European Parliament, the Council or the Commission on grounds of lack of competence, infringement of an essential procedural requirement, infringement of the Treaties or of any rule of law relating to their application, or misuse of powers.*

Member states have always been able to bring an action for annulment. In 2011, Spain and Italy used Article 263 to request annulment of a Council decision authorising the use of enhanced cooperation in unitary patent protection.[95] The EP has had to fight for privileged status[96] – previously, as a 'semi-privileged applicant', it could only bring cases before the CJ to protect its prerogatives. It used actions against the Council of Ministers to add substance to its role under the consultation procedure. Currently, the Court of Auditors and the ECB are semi-privileged applicants. The third group comprises 'non-privileged applicants – under Article 263(4):

> *Any natural or legal person may, under the conditions laid down in the first and second paragraphs, institute proceedings against an act addressed to that person or which is of direct and individual concern to them, and against a regulatory act which is of direct concern to them and does not entail implementing measures.*

This provision extends to the 'peoples' of Europe – as individuals or commercial entities – only limited direct access to the CJEU to seek review of Union acts. This group can only challenge an act that is

1 addressed to them,
2 or if not addressed to them of 'direct' and 'individual' concern, or
3 is a regulatory act of direct concern to them which does not require transposition into national law.

[92]C-9/56 *Meroni* v *ECSC High Authority* [1957-1958] ECR 133; C-376/98 *Germany* v *EP and Council* [2000] ECR I-008419 (Tobacco Advertising Judgement)
[93]C-138/79 *Roquette Freres* v *Council* (Isoglucose)
[94]C-105/75 *Guiffrida* – purpose of recruitment procedures
[95]C-274/11 *Spain* v *Council* and C-295/11 *Italy* v *Council*
[96]C-388/92 *EP* v *Council*; C-65/93 *EP* v *Council*

Before exploring this provision, it is important to understand how it differs from the text in place prior to the Lisbon Treaty. Direct access was arguably more restricted under the previous wording, which allowed non-privileged applicants to only challenge a decision addressed to them or a decision not addressed to them which was of direct and individual concern, even if this was presented in the form of a regulation or a decision addressed to another person.[97] This meant that a person who was not the addressee of a decision or regulation had to satisfy three distinct court-made tests: that the measure was reviewable;[98] that it was of direct concern; *and* individual concern. The new wording is more flexible in that it does not specify the type of act that can be challenged – it is no longer necessary to prove that a regulation is in fact a decision, for example[99] – but the tests of direct and individual concern remain and continue to restrict access.

a) The tests of direct and individual concern

In order to demonstrate direct concern applicants must show uninterrupted causality: that the measure affects their legal position regardless of any action by the addressees of the measure.[100] The impact has to be 'automatic . . . without the application of other intermediate rules'. A regulation could be of direct concern if, as in *International Fruit*,[101] it leaves little discretion to the member states and the scope of action left to them makes little difference to the legal position of the applicants. If a decision leaves sufficient room for discretion, it will not be of direct concern.[102] A good example of direct concern is found in *Sony*,[103] where the global electronics giant sought to challenge a regulation adopted by the Commission to regulate items such as the PlayStation.

ANALYSING THE LAW

Read T-243/01 Sony – how did the Court find direct concern?

The test for individual concern was developed during the same timeframe that the CJ lay out the ideas of supremacy and direct effect. While strengthening enforcement in the member states, the CJ restricted access in Luxembourg. The restrictive standing test was created in *Plaumann*[104] decided five months after *van Gend*.[105] In *Plaumann*, it decided that:

persons other than those to whom a decision is addressed may only claim to be individually concerned if that decision affects them by reason of certain attributes which

---

[97]'. . . a decision which, although in the form of a regulation or a decision addressed to another person, is of direct and individual concern to the former.'
[98]T-243/01 *Sony* [58-60]
[99]C-11/82 *Piraiki-Patraiki*; C-152/88 *Sofrimport*; C-358/89 *Extramet*; C-309/89 *Codorniu*. In *Codorniu* the Court found a genuine regulation of direct and individual concern in a case on infringement of trademark rights. Likewise in C-480 and 483/93 *Antillean Rice*, a true regulation was found to be of direct and individual concern where the Commission had breached its duty by failing to consider those in the position of the applicants.
[100]C-386/96 P *Dreyfus*
[101]C-41-44/70 *International Fruit* (regulation limiting the import of apples from third countries)
[102]C-222/83 *Municipality of Differdange*: a decision addressed to Luxembourg left sufficient discretion to the national authority thus the action was inadmissible
[103]T-243/01 *Sony* [61-62]
[104]C-25/62 *Plaumann*
[105]Decided 5 February 1963

are peculiar to them or by reason of circumstances in which they are differentiated from all other persons, and by virtue of these factors distinguishes them individually just as in the case of the person addressed.

This test was not determined based upon economic impact per se – standing would only be granted if the applicant were effectively a mirror image of the addressee by virtue of character or context. *Sony* provides a good example of this: the CJ decided that although the contested regulation was written in a general and abstract manner, it focused specifically on the classification of the PlayStationR2 because:

[72] . . . [the technical description is] so specific that it could not have applied to any products other than the PlayStationR2, at least not at the time the contested regulation entered into force.

Applicants who, like Sony, can demonstrate a level of involvement in the consultation process leading up to adoption of a measure can nearly always show individual concern. Another example is provided by the application by the Independent Music Publishers and Labels Association (IMPALA) for review of the Commission decision approving the merger between Bertelsmann and Sony Group: standing was given because IMPALA had not only responded to Commission questionnaires in 2004 but had also made a separate submission in 2005 on why the Commission should declare the merger incompatible with the common market, citing concerns about further concentration in the market and the impact that this would have on market access, including in the retail sector, the media, the internet and consumer choice.[106]

ANALYSING THE LAW

Which is the harder test to satisfy – direct or individual concern? Why?

There were many problems with this test: applicants not only had to prove they were in a similar position to the addressee, but also that they were the only persons in that position – the more others could claim the same, the less likely that standing would be granted. This led to the perverse position that the larger number of persons negatively affected by a decision, the harder it was to challenge. The timeframe is another barrier – claims must be lodged within two months:[107] it will not always be possible for small businesses, for example, to know the impact of a measure upon them within this timeframe let alone if others were equally affected. The CJEU recently confirmed that the clock begins to run regardless of where the act is published – in hard print or on the internet.[108] It was also problematic that if direct access were not afforded to an affected party, a national measure was absent to challenge the only route to review was to break the law.[109]

---

[106]T-464/04 *Impala* v *Commission* [2006] 5 CMLR 19
[107]C-188/92 *TWD Textilwerke Deggendorf*
[108]C-626/11P *Polyelectrolyte Producers Group GEIE (PPG) and another* v *European Chemicals Agency (ECHA), Kingdom of Netherlands and another, intervening* [2013] WLR (D) 365
[109]See Cornelia Koch 'Locus Standi of Private Applicants Under the EU Constitution: Preserving Gaps in the Protection of Individuals' Right to an Effective Remedy, *ELRev* 30(4), 2005, pp. 511–527

The latter in particular brought the completeness of the judicial system elaborated in *Les Verts* under question.[110] In 2002, alternative formulations of the test for standing under Article 263(4) were proposed by the (then) Court of First Instance (CFI) and AG Jacobs in the CJ. In *UPA*, AG Jacobs proposed that ' . . . a person is to be regarded as individually concerned by a Community measure where, by reason of his particular circumstances, the measure has, or is liable to have, a substantial adverse effect on his interests'.[111] Less than two months later the CFI suggested in *Jego Quere* that 'a natural or legal person is to be regarded as individually concerned by a Community measure of general application that concerns him directly if the measure in question affects his legal position, in a manner which is both definite and immediate, by restricting his rights or by imposing obligations on him. The number and position of other persons who are likewise affected by the measure, or who may be so, are of no relevance in that regard.'[112]

VIEWPOINT

How do these tests differ from a) *Plaumann* and b) from each other?

The CJ response was negative: the judges refused on both occasions to modify the test. In answer to AG Jacobs it invited the member states to reform the system;[113] in *Jego Quere* two years later it more or less repeated *Plaumann*.

> In particular, natural or legal persons cannot be individually concerned by such a measure unless they are affected by it by reason of certain attributes peculiar to them, or by reason of a factual situation which differentiates them from all other persons and distinguishes them individually in the same way as an addressee.[114]

The member states did respond to the invitation in UPA – the wording was revised in the Lisbon Treaty[115] to introduce a third route to gain standing. What, however, are the consequences of this reform? It is not clear that access is broader now that individual applicants need only show *direct* concern for regulatory acts. Two new questions arose: first, what is a 'regulatory act', and second, did the new test introduce a new meaning of 'direct' concern? Answers were given in *Inuit* v *Commission*.[116]

In *Inuit,* the Commission adoption of a regulation on the management of products made from seal was challenged by a number of companies (legal persons) trading in such products. As the action was brought after the entry into force of the TFEU, it was governed by the new wording in Article 263(4). The question was therefore whether the

---

[110]Koen Lenaerts, 'The Rule of Law and the Coherence of the Judicial System of the European Union', *CMLR* 44, 2007, pp. 1625–1659

[111]C-50/00 *UPA* 21 March 2002 [60]

[112]T-177/01 3 May 2002 [51]

[113]UPA 25 July 2002 [44]

[114]C-263/02 *Jego Quere* 1 April 2004 [45]

[115]The new wording applies only to new cases – T-532/08 *Norilsk Nickel Harjavalta Oy & Umicore SA/NV v Commission.*

[116]T-18/10 *Inuit Tapiriit Kanatami and Others* v *Parliament and Council* [2011] ECR II-0000 on Regulation (EC) No 1007/2009 of the European Parliament and of the Council of 16 September 2009 on trade in seal products (OJ L286 2009, p. 36). The case has been appealed to the CJ – C-605/10.

applicants had to prove only direct concern or both direct and individual concern. In order to benefit from the easier standing rules, the regulation would have to be deemed a 'regulatory act'.

The meaning of a 'regulatory act' is not defined in the Treaty. The GC therefore conducted a 'literal, historical and teleological' survey to determine this and came to three conclusions. First, it decided that 'regulatory acts' are a special category of acts of general application that do not call for implementation:

> [45] It must be concluded that the fourth paragraph of Article 263 TFEU, read in conjunction with its first paragraph, permits a natural or legal person to institute proceedings against an act addressed to that person and also (i) against a legislative or regulatory act of general application which is of direct and individual concern to them and (ii) against certain acts of general application, namely regulatory acts which are of direct concern to them and do not entail implementing measures.

Yet a regulatory act is not confined to delegated acts under Article 290 TFEU.[117]

Guidance was taken from the Convention discussions on this phrase to reach the second conclusion that there is a distinction between legislative acts and regulatory acts: the former, which enjoy stronger democratic legitimacy, are subject to the dual conditions of direct and individual concern; the latter were not. The GC thus concluded:

> [56] In view of the foregoing, it must be held that the meaning of 'regulatory act' for the purposes of the fourth paragraph of Article 263 TFEU must be understood as covering all acts of general application apart from legislative acts. Consequently, a legislative act may form the subject-matter of an action for annulment brought by a natural or legal person only if it is of direct and individual concern to them.

As the contested regulation was adopted using the ordinary legislative procedure in Article 294 TFEU, it was a legislative act; the applicants would thus have to show both direct and individual concern in order to gain standing. The Advocate General agreed with the GC conclusion that the 'high democratic legitimation' of legislative acts sets these apart and the CJ dismissed the appeal, holding that the General Court had not erred.[118] It is now agreed that a 'regulatory act' does not cover all regulations or acts of general application but relates to a narrow category of acts. Arguably, applying a broader interpretation would erode the distinction between the term 'acts' and 'regulatory acts' in Article 263(4) TFEU.[119]

Furthermore it was clarified that there is no right of access to the CJEU:

> [105] Article 47 of the Charter does not require that an individual should have an unconditional entitlement to bring an action for annulment of European Union legislative acts directly before the Courts of the European Union.

---

[117][48]

[118]C-583/11P *Inuit Tapiriit Kanatami and others* v *European Parliament, Commission of the European Union and another intervening* [2013] WLR (D) 370

[119][58]

A second relevant case for understanding Article 263(4) TFEU is *Microban*.[120] It adds clarity to the nature of the tests to be applied in the assessment of a 'regulatory act'. Microban, a company based in the United States, challenged the validity of Commission Decision 2010/169/EU which did not authorise the use of a particular product – triclosan – in plastics designed to wrap or store food. This was previously a tolerated substance following guidance of the Scientific Committee on Food/European Food Safety Authority. In 2010, however, triclosan was removed from the list: the consequence of this removal was that triclosan could no longer be marketed in the EU. As Microban were not the addressees of the decision, their claim for standing would have to be based on the third route – a regulatory act that does not require implementing measures which is of direct concern. The GC began by referring back to the conclusion in *Inuit* that a 'regulatory act' must be understood as covering all acts of general application apart from legislative acts[121] and found that the contested decision was adopted by the Commission in the exercise of implementing powers and not in the exercise of legislative powers.[122] It also was universally applicable:

[23] Moreover, the contested decision is of general application in that it applies to objectively determined situations and it produces legal effects with respect to categories of persons envisaged in general and in the abstract.

It could therefore be considered to be a regulatory act under Article 263(4). Having passed this hurdle, the GC then had to decide if the decision was of direct concern to *Microban*. The test remained the same and *Microban* passed it:

[32] . . . it must be observed that, according to case-law, by allowing a natural or legal person to institute proceedings against regulatory acts of direct concern to them which do not entail implementing measures, the fourth paragraph of Article 263 TFEU pursues an objective of opening up the conditions for bringing direct actions . . . Accordingly, the concept of direct concern, as recently introduced in that provision cannot, in any event, be subject to a more restrictive interpretation than the notion of direct concern as it appeared in the fourth paragraph of Article 230 EC.

As the applicants passed the test of direct concern under the former Article 230(4), they also did so under direct concern in the new Article 263(4). It was also found that the decision entailed no implementing measures.[123] Standing was thus granted: the next challenge was to win on substance. The GC held that the Commission had erred by choosing the wrong legal basis, and also that it had breached procedure by failing to undertake a proper risk assessment. The decision was therefore annulled.

It remains to be seen whether these changes have made 'peoples lives easier' as per the goal declared by the Commission in 2009.[124] Access is improved only in relation to non-legislative acts, which do not pertain to the essential elements of EU legislation. For legislative acts, both tests of direct and individual concern must be satisfied – *Plaumann* remains in place in relation to these basic legal acts.

---

[120]T-262/10 *Microban International and Microban (Europe)* v *Commission* [2011] ECR II-7697
[121][21]
[122][22]
[123][35-38]
[124]An area of freedom, security and justice serving the citizen, COM(2009) 262 final

Legislative acts may henceforth be as difficult to change as constitutional law in the member states. Furthermore only those with significant resources like Mr Kadi, a billionaire who brought cases in the United States and EU, will be able to do so. While it is important to avoid excessive challenge to legal measures, the ability to hold the EU legislator to account must not become a privilege for the wealthy. Between 2009 and 2013 new direct actions before the CJ has fallen from 149 to 72 (although during the same timeframe they increased from 214 to 319 before the GC).

VIEWPOINT

Summarise the test for direct access under Article 263(4) TFEU. In your view, is access easier or more restricted?

---

ii. Preliminary rulings: indirect access under Article 267 TFEU

Article 267 TFEU sets out the procedure whereby national judges can send questions[125] to the CJEU for interpretation of the Treaty and adopted measures, and the validity of the latter. The questions sent can concern technical matters such as the classification of pyjamas,[126] constitutional issues dealing with EU citizenship[127] or the validity of the European Stability Mechanism.[128]

Article 267 TFEU states that:

---

1 *The Court of Justice shall have jurisdiction to give preliminary rulings concerning:*

   a the interpretation of this Treaty

   b the validity and interpretation of acts of the Institutions.

2 *Where such a question is raised before a court or tribunal of a Member State, that court or tribunal may, if it considers that a decision on the question is necessary to enable it to give judgment, request the Court of Justice to give a ruling thereon.*

3 *Where any such question is raised in a case pending before a court or tribunal of a Member State against whose decisions there is no judicial remedy under national law that court or tribunal shall bring the matter before the Court of Justice.*

The CJEU has jurisdiction to interpret international agreements.[129] A national court or tribunal cannot declare an EU act invalid of its own volition but must refer the matter to the CJEU.[130] This is not an appellate procedure.

---

[125]For example, see the question sent from the Commerical Court in *Depfa Bank Plc v Provincia Di Pisa and Dexia Crediop S.P.A v Provincia Di Pisa* [2012] EWHC 687 (Comm) 2 March 2012
[126]For example C-338/95 *Wiener S.I. GmbH v Hauptzollamt Emmerich* [1997] ECR I-6495 where AG Jacobs discussed a rationalisation of cases dealt with under Article 234
[127]C-413-01 *Franca Ninni Orasche v Bundesminister fuer Wissenschaft, Verkehr und Kunst* [2003] ECR 1-13187 where AG Geelhoed discussed the consequences of economic inactivity in relation to European Union citizenship
[128]C-370/12 *Thomas Pringle v Governement of Ireland, Ireland and The Attorney General*
[129]C-240/09 *Lesoochranárske zoskupenie VLK v Ministerstvo životného prostredia Slovenskej republiky,* [2011] ECR I-1255 stating that Article 9 (3) of the Aarhus Convention does not enjoy direct effect
[130]C-314/85 *Firma Fotofrost v HZA Lubeck Ost* [1987] ECR 4199, [1988] 3 CMLR 57

There is no definition in the Treaty of the meaning or characteristics of a 'court or tribunal'. Some guidance was laid out in *El Yassini:*[131]

> In order to determine whether a body making a reference is a court or tribunal for the purposes of Article 177 of the Treaty [Art 267 TFEU], which is a question governed by Community law alone, the Court takes account of a number of factors, such as whether the body is established by law, whether it is permanent, whether its jurisdiction is compulsory, whether its procedure is inter partes, whether it applies rules of law and whether it is independent.

However, even if a body satisfies all of these characteristics, it will not be seen as a court or tribunal unless it is required to determine a legal dispute or exercise a judicial function: when a body makes an administrative decision 'without being required to decide a legal dispute' it cannot be regarded as exercising a judicial function, even if it satisfies the other conditions mentioned above.[132] Furthermore, in addition to meeting these criteria, the body must fall within the remit of a member state: in *Miles* v *Others*[133] the Complaints Board 'belonged' to an international organisation and thus could not refer a question under Article 267 TFEU.

The CJEU does not consider the scope of activity of the body concerned or the national judicial hierarchies. Bodies that may be established as courts or tribunals in the national legal system will not automatically be accorded this status under Article 267, while those that do not have this status may gain it. For example, in a reference from the Greek statutory competition law authority, the 'Epitropi Antagonismou', it held that although this was a statutory body it did not have compulsory jurisdiction – in accordance with Regulation 1/2003, the Commission could relieve the Epitropi of its competence to pursue competition law breaches. For this reason it was held not to be a court or tribunal under Article 267 TFEU:

> Whenever the Commission relieves a national competition authority such as the Epitropi Antagonismou of its competence, the proceedings initiated before that authority will not lead to a decision of a judicial nature.[134]

This breadth means Article 267 TFEU is potentially a more accessible route to the CJEU but it cannot be used directly by individual applicants – it creates a channel for court to court dialogue. Individual access is therefore indirect. When they so desire, judges may 'shield'[135] national legislation from EU law. It is left to the discretion of the individual judge as to whether a reference should be sent and what should be asked.[136] A judge faced with this request may ignore it,[137] agree[138] or refuse: in *Mid Sussex Advice Bureau* Elias

---

[131]C-416/96 *El Yassini*. See also C-246/80 *Broekmeulen* [1981] ECR 2311 and C-54/96 *Dorsch Consult*

[132]C-178/99 *Doris Salzman* [2001] ECR I-04421 [15]. See also C-60/02 X (*Montres Rolex*) [2004] ECR I-651 C-3/03 *SYFAIT*

[133]C-196/ 09 *Miles and Others* v *European Schools* [2011] ECR I-5105

[134]C-53/03 *SYFAIT and others* [2005] ECR I-4609

[135]Andreas J. Obermaier, 'The National Judiciary – Sword of European Court of Justice Rulings: The Example of the *Kohll/Decker* Jurisprudence', *European Law Journal* 14(6), November 2008, pp. 735–752

[136]C-36/80 *Irish Creamery Milk Suppliers* [1981] ECR 735

[137]*Samin* v *Westminster* [2012] EWCA Civ 1468; *Sandiford* v *Foreign Secretary* [2013] EWHC 168 (Admin)

[138]In *MR and Others Bangladesh* [2010] UKUT 449 (IAC) (C-83/11 *Rahman*) Justice Blake concluded in a case before the Immigration and Asylum Tribunal that an interpretation by the CJ was necessary and referred to a series of questions on Article 3(2) of the Citizenship Directive.

LJ believed that the referral asking whether a volunteer was a 'worker' who could access rights in the Disability Discrimination Act 1995[139] when read with the Framework Directive,[140] would fail:

> I do not accept that there is sufficient doubt as to the outcome to merit a reference to Europe on the substantive issue. Certain French authorities relied on by Mr O'Dempsey to create that doubt did not on careful analysis lend real support to his submissions. I am satisfied that the appellant's case would fail before the ECJ.[141]

Alternatively a judge may decide not to refer because they can interpret the issue adequately themselves[142] or to avoid delay.[143] However, the national court must give reasons for its refusal – in *Dhahbi*,[144] the European Court of Human Rights (ECtHR) in Strasbourg held that where a national court of last instance fails to explain its refusal to refer under EU law, this could violate the right to a fair trial in Article 6 ECHR. The Italian Court of Cassation, against whose decisions there is no appeal under domestic law, had refused to refer a question to the CJEU on whether the refusal of household allowance to a Tunisian resident in Italy was compatible with the Euro-Mediterranean Agreement. Drawing from *Vergauwen*,[145] the ECtHR held that national courts must say why the question is not relevant, or if the provision has already been interpreted or is so clear as to not require interpretation. The judgment must enable determination of how the request was addressed – it can no longer be simply ignored, as in *Samin* or *Sandiford*.

The national judge cannot of course determine the response of the CJEU. While it is the responsibility of the national court to specify clearly the question(s) on which it needs assistance and the facts to which they refer, the CJEU will not accept all references.[146] Initially it took the position that it would not check the reference closely, as long as there were two sides to the dispute[147] but this position has changed. The CJ has gradually set out conditions on when it will reply to a question. These were summarised in *Bacardi*: first, the national judge who is facing the dispute must determine both the need for a preliminary ruling and the relevance of the questions which it submits to the Court. The national judge must explain why a reply to their questions is necessary to enable them to give judgment.[148] Second, the CJ may exceptionally examine the conditions in which the case was referred by the national court – the CJ has no jurisdiction to give a preliminary ruling where the questions do not relate to the facts of the main action or its purpose, or where the problem is hypothetical, or where the Court does not have before it the factual or legal material necessary to give a useful answer to the questions submitted to it.

---

[139]Now the Equality Act 2010
[140]EU Directive 2000/78/EEC establishing a general framework for equal treatment in employment and occupation
[141]X v *Mid Sussex Citizens Advice Bureau & Ors* [2011] EWCA Civ 28 (26 January 2011)
[142]Mr Justice Singh in *The Queen (on the application of Jaspers (Treburley) Ltd and others)* v *Food Standards Agency* [2013] EWHC 1788 (Admin) [58–59]; Lord Justice Beatson in *Evans* v *Community Secretary* [2012] EWHC 1830 (Admin) [43]
[143]*Oboh et al & Halauder* v *Home Secretary* [2013] EWCA Civ 1525 [61]
[144]*Dhahbi* v *Italy*, 8 April 2014
[145]*Vergauwen* v *Belgium*, No. 4832/04, 10 April 2012 – in this case the Belgium Constitutional Court had fully justified its refusal to refer.
[146]Between 1990 and 1997, the CJ rejected 20 references. See Catherine Barnard and Eleanor Sharpston, 'The Changing Face Of Article 177 References', *Common Market Law Review* 34, 1997, pp. 1113–1171
[147]C-104/79 *Foglia* v *Novello* [1980] ECR 745, [1981] 1 CMLR 585; C-261/81 *Rau* v *De Schmedt* [1982] ECR 3961
[148]C-104/79 *Foglia*

Finally, the CJ will reject any questions which may permit a national judge to decide whether national legislation is in accordance with Community law.[149] Inadmissible questions include those referred by a representative of the Public Prosecutor's Office who was acting as a party to the proceedings and who had merely requested the court concerned to examine evidence.[150]

There is no time limit associated with the procedure: the question can be sent as soon as need becomes apparent to the member state court or tribunal.[151] However, it must relate to a pending dispute – it must be sent before a decision has been made. This was made clear in *Salzmann*:

> [14] Furthermore, while Article 177 of the Treaty [now Article 267 TFEU] does not make the reference to the Court subject to there having been an inter partes hearing in the proceedings in the course of which the national court refers a question for a preliminary ruling, it follows, none the less, from that Article that a national court may refer a question to the Court only if there is a case pending before it and if it is called upon to give judgment in proceedings intended to lead to a decision of a judicial nature.[152]

Beyond this, however, there is no limit to the number of questions that may be contained in a reference,[153] or the number of references that a court can make prior to its decision: a national court can seek multiple interpretations from the Court before the main proceedings are decided, as long as these are new questions or considerations which might give rise to a different answer.[154] The CJ will also add to the questions sent if it deems this appropriate:

> [44] The fact that the question of the application of Directive 83/183 was canvassed only by Mr and Mrs Weigel and by the Commission and was not actually submitted to the Court by the national court does not prevent the Court from considering it. Even though, strictly speaking, the national court has directed its question solely to the interpretation of Articles 39 EC [Art. 45 TFEU] and 12 EC [Art. 19 TFEU], the Court is not thereby precluded from providing the national court with all those elements for the interpretation of Community law which may be of assistance in adjudicating on the case pending before it, whether or not that court has specifically referred to them in its questions.[155]

It is not necessary that the measure concerned is directly applicable, or if a directive that the transposition period has expired: the Court has jurisdiction to give preliminary rulings on validity and interpretation of these acts.[156]

---

[149]C-318/00 *Bacardi-Martini SAS* [41–45]; C 14/86 *X* [1987] ECR 2545 [15]; C-347/06 *ASM Brescia SpA v Comune di Rodengo Saiano*
[150]C-60/02 *Montres Rolex* [2004] ECR I-651
[151]Court of Justice Recommendations to national courts and tribunals in relation to the initiation of the preliminary ruling procedure C-338/01 2012
[152]C-178/99 *Doris Salzman* [2001] ECR I-0442 [14]. See also C-318/85 *Greis Unterweger* and C-134/97 *Victoria Film*
[153]A total of 24 questions were sent in C-159 and 160/10 *Gerhard Fuchs & Peter Köhler v Land Hessen*, 2nd chamber
[154]C-292/04 *Meilicke* [23–25]
[155]C-387/01 *Weigel*. See also C-241/89 *SARPP* [1990] ECR I 4695 [8], C-315/92 *Verband Sozialer Wettbewerb* ('*Clinique*') [1994] ECR I-317 [7] and C-87/97 *Consorzio per la tutela del formaggio Gorgonzola* [1999] ECR I-1301 [16]
[156]C-491/01 *British American Tobacco* ECR 2002 I-11453 [32–33]

The provision sets out a clear division of labour: the national court determines the questions that its needs answered, the CJEU answer those questions on EU law; the national court applies this interpretation to the facts before it. The relationship between the national and EU courts is ostensibly heterarchical. However, as seen above, the CJEU will sometimes refuse a reference or answer questions beyond those referred. It has also recently produced guidance on how to use the procedure, covering topics such as when to refer and the format of the reference (typed, with numbered pages). This has led some to question whether a hierarchy is creeping into the relationship: has the Treaty dialogue been transformed into a monologue?

Weiler's 'judicial empowerment'[157] thesis veers towards the latter: under this theory, both EU and national judges have been empowered, but due to the doctrine of supremacy the former gained more than the latter. His argument suggests that national judges have been complicit in the transformation of the procedure and their own disempowerment:

(a) the ECJ's constitutional jurisprudence and (b) the incentive structures in place for most national judges pushed in the same pro-integrative direction. Most important, national judges could acquire, many for the first time, the power to control the legality of state acts previously beyond their reach, such as statutes. Article 267 not only legitimized what would become a complicit relationship between the ECJ and the national courts, it also afforded both judicial levels a good deal of protection from potential political fallout.[158]

The process is indeed driven by the national courts – they decide when to refer and what to ask. Perhaps the key question is whether Article 267 in general serves the interests of the peoples of Europe, and which type of relationship does so more effectively.

VIEWPOINT

Does Article 267 TFEU serve the interests of the peoples of Europe in access to justice?

Yes	No
Wide access for national judicial authorities	Lack of independent access for individuals; too many references
Any question can be sent at any time before a decision	The court will decide which questions it answers
The use of the system is free	The additional time added to the domestic case may incur costs
The references go to different chambers	A similar question may give rise to a different interpretation

---

[157]Joseph H.H. Weiler, 'The Transformation of Europe', *Yale Law Journal* 100(8), 1991, pp. 2403–2483; Joseph H.H Weiler, 'A Quiet Revolution: The European Court of Justice and its Interlocutors', *Comparative Political Studies* 26(4), 1994, pp. 510–534

[158]Alec Stone Sweet, 'The European Court of Justice and the judicialisation of EU governance', *Living Reviews in European Governance* 5(2), 2010, p. 29. The *Sunday Trading* cases are an example of this.

Limited access reduces opportunities for the CJEU. As noted by former US Supreme Court Justice Sandra Day O'Connor:

> Courts . . . are mainly reactive institutions . . . courts are rarely the first to ponder the constitutional questions that come before them . . . the judiciary has no role to play until someone with a personal stake in the matter challenges the government action or practice in court. Thus a courts agenda is critically shaped by the issues and concerns of individual litigants.[159]

The opportunity for the CJEU to tackle important matters is therefore compromised. Concerns have also been raised by the committee overseeing compliance with the Aarhus Convention. It stated in its Report for 2011 that:

> [94] With regard to access to justice by members of the public, the Committee is convinced that if the jurisprudence of the EU Courts, as evidenced by the cases examined, were to continue, unless fully compensated for by adequate administrative review procedures, the Party concerned would fail to comply with Article 9, paragraphs 3 and 4, of the [Aarhus] Convention.[160]

4. Improving access and the quality of dialogue

The Article 267 TFEU procedure provides the CJ with most of its work and continues to be highly used: in 2011, 'the number of references for a preliminary ruling submitted was, for the third year in succession, the highest ever reached, and it exceeded the number in 2009 by almost 41 per cent (423 cases in 2011 compared with 302 cases in 2009)'.[161] There are at least two key tensions in the Article 267 procedure: between the individual and the national judge; and between the national judge and the CJ. The individual may feel that rights are being denied due to underuse by national judges while the CJ struggles to respond to too many references on increasingly complex issues. These tensions – underuse and overuse – will be discussed in the following sections.

i.   Underuse by courts of last instance

The Treaty tries to manage the use Article 267 TFEU by separating national courts and tribunals into two categories: those with a discretion to refer (para 2) and those who are obliged to refer (para 3). The dialogue is therefore open to all judges who care to enter into it; only those in courts of last instance *must* refer.[162] This obligation has, however, lacked enforcement – although many such courts, predominantly constitutional courts,

---

[159]O'Connor 2004, pp. 166–167
[160]See David Hart, 'No standing for the Inuit in Luxembourg', http://ukhumanrightsblog.com/2013/10/12/no-standing-for-the-inuit-in-luxembourg/\#more-19779
[161]CJEU Annual Report 2011, p. 10
[162]C-314/85 *Firma Fotofrost v HZA Lubeck Ost* [1987] ECR 4199, [1988] 3 CMLR 57

adhered to the obligation,[163] others simply refused to comply.[164] The Treaty provided no tools to address circumstances such as these. The CJ eventually took steps to stem the potential damage to its authority. In *CILFIT*[165] it introduced two caveats to the obligation – *acte clair* and *acte éclairé*. The doctrine of *acte clair* removed the obligation where the answer to the question is very clear while *acte éclairé* removed the obligation by directing the national court to previous cases where the court had answered an identical question. Neither of these attempts to address underuse have worked very well.

The first reason why these doctrines have not satisfactorily addressed underuse is because of the fairly tight conditions attached to the use of *acte clair*. In *CILFIT*, the CJ explained that in order to determine that the interpretation was obvious, national judges would have to compare all language versions of the provision, in the context of the terminology used in EU law and in the light of the EU *acquis communitaire*. This is somewhat impossible given that there are 23 official languages used at the CJEU and the *acquis* contains almost 10,000 pieces of secondary legislation as well as the Treaties. The limits of *acte éclairé* can be seen in *Koebler*,[166] where the national court did as it was told – looked at a case where an identical question had been answered – but came to the wrong conclusion. The CJ used this opportunity to add to the Article 267(3) obligation by linking non-compliance to state liability.[167] It is questionable how powerful a deterrent this extension of state liability is: as seen in the CAB case,[168] the Court of Appeal dismissed the appeal without giving permission to go any further.

ii.   Overuse by lower courts

Paradoxically, despite the issues outlined in the previous section, the system is very well used by courts and tribunals who enjoy discretion to refer. According to Obermeier, they have helped to effectively redesign national law:

> the national judiciary was the sword of the ECJ in implementing the *Kohll/Decker* jurisprudence. This Article clearly indicates that national courts are a key variable for understanding and explaining national implementation: they are able to accelerate implementation. As soon as national courts accept and apply the doctrines elaborated by the ECJ, governments face accomplished facts.[169]

The bulk of the workload of the CJEU arrives via referrals from lower courts.[170] The problem is that there are too many and as a result they take too long to be disposed of. In 2010, the average time for the CJEU to deal with a referral was 16.1 months. This is a clear improvement upon previous years (see Table 4.1) but remains a significant length

---

[163]Elke Cloots, 'Germs of Plurlist Judicial Adjudication: Advocaten voor de Wereld and other references from the Belgian constitutional court', *CMLR* 47, 2010, pp. 645–672

[164]Filippo Fontanelli and Giuseppe Martinico, 'Between Procedural Impermeability and Constitutional Openness: The Italian Constitutional Court and Preliminary References to the European Court of Justice', *European Law Journal* 16(3), May 2010, pp. 345–364

[165]C-283/81

[166]C-224/01 *Köbler v Austria*

[167]C-6 and 9/90 *Francovich; Brasserie Du Pecheur/Factortame III*

[168]*X v Mid Sussex Citizens Advice Bureau & Others* [2011] EWCA Civ 28 (26 January 2011)

[169]p. 751

[170]Seminal cases such as *van Gend en Loos* and *Simmenthal* were sent by lower national courts.

TABLE 4.1   Average length of time for completion of a preliminary reference

	New references	Completed references	Average length of time
2008	288	301	16.8 months
2009	302	259	17.1 months
2010	385	339	16.1 months
Source: Data taken from CJEU Annual Reports			

of time, potentially adding costs for the parties who have already waited for their case to wind its way through the national system once and will still have to wait for the national judge to apply the CJ interpretation. In 2013, the average time went up to 16.3 months. It has been argued that the system is crumbling due to its own success.[171]

Bearing in mind the pending accession of 10 new member states, reforms began to be made to the procedure in the Nice Treaty in 2000. An option was to increase the delivery of judgments. This could be done in one of two ways. One was to transfer jurisdiction of preliminary rulings to the GC, an idea that was supported by the then President of that court, Judge Vesterdorf:

> It is surely no longer desirable that the judges of the highest Community [Union] law court have to deal with a large number of essentially technical cases and because of this burden find themselves under such a pressure of case-load that they have insufficient time for treating the really important cases.

However, it was argued that it would be dangerous to 'transfer competence in this area to the CFI [GC] thus putting the unity and consistency of Community [Union] law and, it is argued, the coherence of the preliminary reference system itself, at risk'.[172]

Nonetheless, this option was adopted in the Nice Treaty – the General Court was given jurisdiction to hear preliminary references in specified areas; at the same time provision was made in Article 257 TFEU to reduce the GC workload with the creation of a new judicial panel – the Civil Service Tribunal – which would take over its personnel cases. More recently, the creation of a Patent Court has been proposed to further relieve the CJ.[173] Finally, the Nice Treaty introduced scope for future expansion of the GC: Article 19(2) TEU states that it must comprise 'at least one judge from each Member State'. Capacity to produce judgments at the CJ was also increased by the creation of Chambers.

VIEWPOINT

Do you agree that the judges in the highest courts should not deal with technical questions or with the threat to coherence argument?

---

[171]Report by the Working Party on the Future of the European Communities' Court System January 2000, http://ec.europa.eu/dgs/legal_service/pdf/due_en.pdf
[172]Vesterdorf 2003, pp. 314–315
[173]A new tribunal, the Unified Patents Court, has already been agreed and at time of writing was due to open its doors: http://www.unified-patent-court.org/ and see Commission press release: http://europa.eu/rapid/pressReleases Action.do?reference=MEMO/12/509&format=HTML&aged=0&language=EN&guiLanguage=en; and article in the *Guardian:* http://www.guardian.co.uk/law/2012/jul/03/unified-patent-court-london

a) The *procedure préjudicielle d'urgence* (PPU)

A further option was to amend the Article 267 procedure in specific cases so that decisions could be produced more speedily. As summarised by Barnard:

> Courts, litigants and commentators have long lamented the slowness of the Art.234 EC [Article 267 TFEU] reference procedure: at their worst, reference times before the Court of Justice reached over two years. When this was added to the period that litigation had taken to wind its way through the national system, cases could last for over 10 years. Litigants died in that time and courts, particularly higher courts, became disinclined to make references, whatever the formal requirements of Art.234 EC. The image of *Jarndyce v Jarndyce* haunted the procedure and the Court of Justice was subject to much criticism. This problem has been exacerbated by two factors: first, the rapid enlargement of the Union since 1993; and secondly, the possibility for the ECJ to hear references under both Title IV of the EC Treaty on visas, asylum, immigration and other policies related to free movement of persons (but only from courts of last resort) and Title VI TEU on provisions on police and judicial cooperation (but only where the Member State has opted to take advantage of this possibility. The ECJ has long been aware of the problem and has done much to tighten up its internal processes so that reference times are now down to below 20 months (and much of this time is taken up with the onerous process of translation). Nevertheless, this is still clearly too long in disputes involving real urgency, in particular cases involving child abduction and cases where the defendant is in prison.[174]

In 2000, two new procedures were introduced to address these concerns:

- an expedited procedure for direct actions under Article 263;[175] and
- an accelerated procedure for indirect references under Article 267.[176]

National judges may request that a case be fast-tracked under one of these procedures, but the CJEU may and often does decline.[177] The expedited procedure removes some stages from the process, but the accelerated procedure simply allows a case to jump to the top of the list: once there the normal procedure is followed. The accelerated procedure was not found to cut down the duration of the proceedings – speed was secured by displacing other pending cases – hence it was used in just three cases.[178] However, the need for an effective system for faster delivery of preliminary rulings did not disappear: it became more urgent as the court received questions in the area of freedom, security and justice.[179] Such questions, which could concern persons in detention, requires quick decisions.

---

[174]Catherine Barnard, 'The PPU: is it worth the candle? An early assessment', *ELR* 34(2), 2009, pp. 281–297

[175]Pursuant to the provision of Article 62a of the Rules of Procedure. This procedure was used in *Mojahedin Organisation* (1 day); and the *Stability Pact* case C-27/04.

[176]Pursuant to the provision of Article 104a of the Rules of Procedure

[177]*The Queen (on the Application of Newby Foods Ltd) v The Food Standards Agency (No.7)* [2014] EWHC 1340 (Admin) [17]

[178]C-189/01 *Jippes*; C-66/08 *Kozlowski*; C-127/08 *Metock* which respectively took 76, 149 and 122 days to judgment.

[179]These were initially dealt with under Article 35 TEU and Article 68 EC [both now repealed]. Article 68 EC allowed courts of last resort to refer cases concerning migration of TCNs (UK and Ireland opted out of this). The Council of Ministers, Commission or member states can also ask for rulings in this area (68(3)). It was highly problematic that individuals had no standing although this area deeply concerns them. Article 35 TEU allowed national courts to make references in cases falling under the competence of Pillar Three (PJCC) as long as their member state had opted in to this provision. Six member states did so: Belgium, NL, LUX, Greece, Germany and Austria. See C-467/04 *Gasparini*

The *procedure préjudicielle d'urgence* (PPU) was therefore introduced in 2008 for certain types of cases.[180] Article 267(4) TFEU states explicitly that this procedure should be used in custody cases:

If such a question is raised in a case pending before a court or tribunal of a Member State with regard to a person in custody, the Court of Justice of the European Union shall act with the minimum of delay.

The PPU removes certain stages found in the ordinary procedure and is thus both shorter and faster. The procedure features limited interventions and written observations are limited to the member state sending the question(s), the parties and the EU institutions. The case is allocated to a dedicated chamber of five judges. The referring national court must request its use and justify the request. It may also suggest an answer to the questions it poses. As with the ordinary legislative procedure, the CJEU will determine how to respond to this request – there have been at least three occasions[181] where use of the PPU was seen as inappropriate. Recent guidance indicates that it will be applied in cases concerning detainees (asylum seekers), questions decisive of an individual's legal situation and, of course, custody cases.[182]

The PPU improves access and disposal of a case. The consequence of this simplification of Article 267 is that these references have been disposed of within 2.1 months on average: the recent case of *McBride*[183] is a good example of the speed with which the court can work. The case concerned three children aged three, seven and nine years old who were separated from their father for more than a year. Given that continued separation might irreparably harm the relationships with their father, the Court decided, on the Judge-Rapporteur's proposal and after hearing the Advocate General, to grant the referring court's request that the reference for a preliminary ruling be dealt with under the urgent procedure.[184] The reference was received at the CJEU Registry on 6 August 2010 and accepted under the PPU five days later on 11 August 2010. The hearing took place the following month on 20 September and a decision was given on 5 October 2010.[185] Cases are not always dealt with at this speed: in *El Dridi*[186] the reference was received on 10 February 2011; the PPU was approved on 17 February 2011; a hearing took place on 30 March 2011; and the decision was delivered on 28 April 2011.

However, speed is not the only advantage: the quality of decision-making can also improve:

> . . . at present there is one, perhaps unexpected, beneficial side effect of the short timeframe between hearing and judgment: the facts and legal issues remain fresh in the

---

[180]Pursuant to the provisions of Article 104b of the Rules of Procedure, available for cases falling within the area of freedom, security and justice. See Council Decision of 20 December 2007 amending the Protocol on the Statute of the Court of Justice (2008/79/EC, Euratom) OJ L24/42 29 Jan 2008

[181]C-123/08 *Wolzenburg* (no urgency); C-375/08 *Pontini* (agriculture); C-66/08 *Kozlwski* (pre-PPU)

[182]CJEU Annual Activity Report 2011, p. 99

[183]C-400/10 PPU *McBride*

[184][28–29]

[185]See also C-195/08 PPU *Rinau*; C-296/08 PPU *Goicoechea*; C-388/08 PPU *Leymann & Pustarov*

[186]C-61/11 PPU *Hassen El Dridi, alias Soufi Karim* – a third-country national, El Dridi, entered Italy illegally. In 2004 a deportation decree was issued against him, on the basis of which an order to leave the national territory within five days was issued in 2010. As he did not comply with that order, Mr El Dridi was sentenced by the District Court, Trento (Italy) to one year's imprisonment.

judges' minds. The judges can remain focused on the particular case in a way that might not be possible when they are juggling a large case load and having to revisit cases sometimes years after the hearing. This may help to improve the quality of the discussion and the decision-making, and go some way towards speeding up the process. This brings us to the final and fundamental question: how urgent is urgent?[187]

Is the CJEU now a court which citizens can trust to look after their interests, especially now that the Lisbon Treaty,[188] in removing the pillar structure introduced at Maastricht, has endowed the Court with responsibility for all areas previously in Pillar Three?[189] There is a concern that the PPU undermines the rule of law – it is still not completely clear when will it be applied. In addition, transparency is lost due to non-publication of the AG opinion. This is ironic, as the areas of law in which the PPU is used are central to individual interests. In addition, human rights questions are multiplying at the CJEU. Such cases raise complex questions. The level of concern outside the Court was reflected in an unprecedented letter from a number of academics to the CJEU making the cogent case for the restoration of transparency via publication of the Advocate General opinion.[190]

ANALYSING THE LAW

Why is transparency important for a court?

b) A Court that protects individuals?

The long-term impact of the responses to underuse and overuse remain unclear. Problems with efficiency remain: although the backlog is not getting any worse, current figures show that it continues. The chamber system introduced in 2000 has perhaps fragmented the system without delivering the much-sought gains: in 2009, over 90 per cent of cases were heard in chambers (33.54 per cent 3 judges; 57.17 per cent 5 judges). In the context where 630 cases are dealt with in one year (2010), the chamber system has perhaps only endangered chamber coordination and created more opportunity for legal fragmentation.

These issues can be addressed by reducing access so that fewer courts can request a preliminary ruling. This could allow the court to focus on its 'fundamental' task – 'ensuring that in the interpretation and application of the Treaties the law is observed' – and speak with the clarity and persuasiveness required to provide authoritative guidance, which cannot be done if it pulverises its authority into hundreds of (sometimes) contradictory and (often) insufficiently reasoned answers. Komarek proposes the introduction of a hierarchy so that access by the lowest national courts is removed. However, CJ data shows that in some member states up to 75% of questions come from lower courts and tribunals.

Reducing access to the Article 267 procedure cannot, however, address the continued wide variation in the use of this important dialogue: in 2008 four member states (Czech

[187]Barnard 2008
[188]For a summary of the impact of Lisbon Treaty changes on the CJEU, see Rene Barents, 'The Court of Justice After the Treaty of Lisbon', *CMLR* 47, 2010, pp. 709–728
[189]The exceptions are CFSP, internal policing and law enforcement (excluded under Articles 275 and 276 TFEU respectively).
[190]Barnard 2008

Republic, Ireland, Cyprus, Portugal) sent just one reference while Germany sent 71, Italy 39 and the Netherlands sent 34. A survey on the use of Article 267 TFEU conducted by the European Parliament in 2007[191] found that only around 5 per cent of respondents said that they had made at least one reference for a preliminary ruling in the course of their professional career. This figure was divided unequally among the member states, with Hungary being the only 'new' member state represented, with six references.[192]

The survey covered a wide variety of courts, with the largest contingents being administrative, employment, financial, social and labour courts. Thirty-seven per cent of responses came from member states that joined the EU in 2004; 63 per cent came from those joining before. It highlighted many problems in EU-MS judicial dialogue, many of which compromise the ability of this system to deliver justice. It is shocking to note that of the respondents, 65 per cent rarely accessed the case law of the CJEU, even though only 8 per cent claimed that they did not know how to do so – while 17 per cent never did so. Judges working in the fields of intellectual property, finance or taxation, and administrative judges (75 per cent, 60 per cent and 46 per cent respectively) were much more likely to consult EU law regularly than those dealing with labour/employment issues or social law (20 per cent and 25 per cent respectively). Not a single responding judge dealing with family or criminal law claimed to consult CJEU case law regularly.

The limited use of EU law is harder to understand given that a majority of responding judges (54 per cent) considered themselves familiar with the preliminary ruling procedure. Yet a significant number – 32 per cent – felt unfamiliar with it and only 14 per cent felt very familiar with it. Again, wide discrepancies were found between the member states: in Bulgaria, Belgium and France for instance, the vast majority of respondents (84 per cent, 87 per cent and 94 per cent respectively) considered themselves unfamiliar with the preliminary ruling procedure. Austrian, Czech and German respondents considered themselves the least unfamiliar with the procedure (12 per cent, 13 per cent and 18 per cent of 'unfamiliar' responses respectively). Interestingly, the member states with the largest proportion of respondents who considered themselves very familiar with the procedure were Denmark, Austria and Sweden, that is not founding member states. Fortunately, those that did use the system seemed satisfied with the reply from the Court: 89 per cent found the CJEU's ruling readily applicable to the facts of the case, thus enabling a reasonably unproblematic conclusion to the preliminary reference procedure – one judge even said that the judgment was so clear that only the costs were left to be decided at national level. Whether this goes beyond dialogue is another question.

The report highlights a number of areas needing attention to improve the operation of the procedure. These included the significant disparities in national judges' knowledge of Union law across the EU; the limited foreign language skills of national judges; the difficulties experienced by national judges in accessing specific and current information on EU law; the need to improve and intensify the initial and further training of national judges in EU law; the judges' relative lack of familiarity with the preliminary ruling procedure, and the need to reinforce the dialogue between national judges and the Court of Justice. In particular, a number of judges called for closer involvement of the referring

---

[191]Report on the role of the national judge in the European judicial system (2007/2027(INI)), Committee on Legal Affairs. Rapporteur: Diana Wallis. RR\402874EN.doc PE402.874v02-00

[192]Michal Bobek, 'Learning to talk: preliminary rulings, the courts of the new member states and the court of justice', *CMLR* 45, 2008, pp. 1611–1643

judges in the preliminary reference procedure. There was a sense in which the procedure should be 'renationalised' by prioritising the role of the national judge. Most recently, the EP called for creation of forums:

> at which judges of all levels of seniority in areas of law where domestic and cross-border issues frequently arise can hold discussions on a recent area or areas of legal controversy or difficulty, in order to encourage discussion, build contacts, create channels of communication and build mutual confidence and understanding.[193]

In 2012, the CJEU issued new rules of procedure to address the continued rise in its workload.[194] These focused on maintenance of efficiency of the referral procedure. A series of recommendations were made to the national courts and tribunals on how to use the procedure. The guidance gives some insight into the practical challenges arising from this dialogue and how the CJEU hopes to work with the national courts in the future. There have clearly been basic presentational issues undermining administration of the procedure. The reminder to type references on numbered pages suggests that some handwritten questions are sent on pages that may not be in order. The mention that 10 pages may suffice suggests some references are much longer. Guidance on the positioning of the questions at the beginning or end indicates that these are not always set out clearly.

Delays may also be due to premature referral. Although the question may be sent at any time, the CJEU suggests this be postponed until the national proceedings have reached a stage at which the referring court or tribunal is able to define the legal and factual context of the case. It also suggests that in the interests of the proper administration of justice, the reference be made only after both sides have been heard. This seems to arise from a managerial rationale – it would ensure that the CJEU has all the information necessary to check that Union law does apply to the main proceedings. An increased interest in its role as a manager is also apparent from the concern with the impact of its rulings – the guidance states the CJEU 'would welcome information from that court or tribunal on the action taken upon its ruling in the main proceedings, and communication of the referring court's or tribunal's final decision'. Also, national courts and tribunals are encouraged to briefly propose solutions to the questions referred.

ANALYSING THE LAW

Where should the balance of power be in the Article 267 procedure? Should national judges be encouraged to adopt a more independent role? At this stage of integration of EU law, and given the goal to create a single judicial area, should national judges be encouraged more to talk to each other?

---

[193]European Parliament resolution of 14 March 2012 on judicial training (2012/2575(RSP)) at http://www.europarl.europa.eu/sides/getDoc.do?pubRef=-//EP//TEXT+TA+P7-TA-2012-0079+0+DOC+XML+V0//EN
[194]Court of Justice Recommendations to national courts and tribunals in relation to the initiation of the preliminary ruling procedure C-338/01 2012

5. Conclusion

The CJEU has proved itself to be a successful judicial authority, but it remains somewhat opaque and distant from those it is supposed to protect and 'serve'. Its judges are largely unknown, their reasoning sometimes unclear and deliberation remains impenetrable. Like the Commission, the CJEU has a low 'public salience' securing media attention primarily when journalists criticise a ruling.[195] This negative press matters – it manufactures scepticism and distrust in the minds of the general public which the CJEU is ill-placed to counter.

Unnecessarily secretive procedures will do little to ensure or enhance the legitimacy of the CJEU in the eyes of the Union citizens it is now meant to serve. A more open selection procedure, less directly controlled by the member states, could increase the legitimacy of the CJEU. The legitimacy of the Court is determined not only by its decisions but also its composition – it is broadly acknowledged that courts derive legitimacy from the extent to which their composition reflects those they serve. Progress has been made on the composition of the Court in relation to gender[196] but there has been little movement in relation to the equally important areas of race and religion. This will be more relevant as the CJEU develops constitutional principles for the EU in relation to race, ethnicity and religion under Article 19 TFEU.

Access for litigants needs to be kept under review. Standing rules have been described as a 'door-closing technique' that violate the fundamental principle of transparency – as Weinstein writes, if people 'cannot discover what is going on in our government through litigation, how can they control officials?'[197] Despite recent changes, direct access under Article 263 TFEU remains a prohibitively expensive option for most people in the EU. Standing rules under the Treaty therefore limit the ability of the peoples of Europe to hold the EU institutions to account.

Article 267 offers more access, albeit indirect. The preliminary ruling procedure has been highly successful in the development and dissemination of EU law. It has been used to pose both categorical[198] and interpretative questions before the CJEU. From just 5 out of 35 cases in 1962, Article 267 TFEU in 2010 produced 385 out of 631 incoming cases.[199] The use of Article 263 is much less: in 2010 there were 136 new cases – most concerning the environment.[200] In order to maintain the efficacy of this procedure, some attention needs to be paid to the CJEU 'judicial economy'.[201]

---

[195]'An obscurantist and absurd judgment', Comment in the *Independent* on the Advocate General opinion in C-34/10 *Brustle* v *Greenpeace* on stem cells, *Independent*, 29 April 2011

[196]On the appearance of female members at the Court see Sally J. Kenney, 'Breaking the Silence: Gender Mainstreaming and the Composition of the European Court of Justice', *Feminist Legal Studies* 10, 2002, pp. 257–270. Curiously, although the majority of judges on continental Europe are women, the majority of members at the CJEU are men. John Bell, *Judiciaries Within Europe: A comparative review*, Cambridge University Press, 2006, p.1

[197]Weinstein 2008, p. 62

[198]For example C-138/11 *Compass-Datenbank GmBH* v *Republik Oesterreich* [2012] WLR (D) 202 on the definition of an 'undertaking' in Article 102 TFEU.

[199]The absolute data for cases lodged between 1953 and 2010 show that, out of a total of 16,828, 7,005 were questions referred for preliminary rulings. See Daniele P. Domenicucci, 'The role of national courts and presentation of the preliminary reference procedure', Paper presented at ERA – Academy of European Law Seminar on 'The Anti-Discrimination Directives 2000/43 and 2000/78 in Practice', Trier, 9–10 May 2011

[200]CJEU Annual Activity Report 2011

[201]Marc L. Busch and Krzysztof J. Pelc, 'The Politics of Judicial Economy at the World Trade Organisation', *International Organisation* 64, Spring 2010, pp. 257–279

The challenge is to find the right balance in the use of these provisions to secure full access to the Court – a credible area of 'freedom, security and justice' requires no less. Direct access needs to be opened up; indirect access needs to be reorganised, perhaps to encourage greater use by courts of last instance and less use by lower courts. An answer to problems of transparency and access may be to incorporate some use of majority opinions. Article 257 TFEU allows the former; interestingly, the second new panel to be created includes use of dissenting opinions. The use of these opinions was suggested in the draft statute for the 'European Patent Court' (which has now been found compatible with the Treaty) – it states that 'in exceptional circumstances any judge of the panel may express his dissenting opinion separately from the decision of the Court'.[202] This may prove an important reform for the future.

The stronger participatory democracy envisioned in the Lisbon Treaty arguably requires – perhaps even demands – heightened trust in the judiciary, if for no other reason than to keep the EU as a whole trustworthy. It may not be an exaggeration to say that since the ratification of the Lisbon Treaty, trust in the judiciary is a key component of EU citizenship. This may require a review of the relationship between EU citizens and their judicial officials, their courts and EU judicial decision-making.

As the CJEU becomes more visible to the EU public, developing means to this end may ultimately prove beneficial – 'respect for the judiciary can only be enhanced if public opinion is able to see that judges are not treated as if they lived in an ivory tower'.[203] The judiciary is the last branch of government precisely because it is the first defence of the citizen. '[In] a democracy, the people should be able to look to the judiciary as "their" judges, not some alien aristocracy set to rule over them.'[204] Judges are citizens, like everyone else[205] and 'live in the real world just like the rest of us'.[206]

---

[202]See Article 51(2) Draft Agreement on the European and Community Patents Court and Draft Statute Brussels, 23 March 2009, 7928/09/PI 23 COUR 29. The CJ found it incompatible in Opinion 1/09 of the Court (Full Court) on the creation of a European and Community Patents Court, 8 March 2011. Changes were made and this has now been given the go-ahead. For commentary see Thorsten Bausch and Hoffmann Eitle, 'European Court of Justice Trashes Planned Unified Patent Litigation System, Kluwer Patent Blog, 8 March 2011, http://kluwerpatentblog.com/2011/03/08/european-court-of-justice-trashes-planned-unified-patent-litigation-system/; 'Unitary Patent on track!', 11 March 2011, http://blog.epo.org/politics/unitary-patent-on-track/

[203]Council of Europe, 'Judicial Power and public liability for judicial acts', Proceedings of 15th Colloquy on European Law, Bordeaux, 17–19 June 1985

[204]Baroness Hale of Richmond, 'A minority Opinion?', Maccabaen Lecture in Jurisprudence, Proceedings of the British Academy 154, 2008, pp. 319–336 at 330

[205]Day O' Connor 2004, 74

[206]Lord MacDonald, Interview, Today Programme BBC Radio 4, 18 August 2011

Further reading

On the role of judges and courts:

Rene Barents, 'The Court of Justice After the Treaty of Lisbon', *CMLR* 47, 2010, pp. 709–728

Marc L. Busch and Krzysztof J. Pelc, 'The Politics of Judicial Economy at the World Trade Organisation', *International Organisation* 64, Spring 2010, pp. 257–279

I. Solanke, 'Diversity and Independence in the European Court of Justice', *Columbia Journal of European Law* 15(1), 2009, p. 89

Eric Stein, 'Lawyers, Judges and the Making of a Transnational Constitution', *American Journal of International Law* 75(1), 1981

Jack B. Weinstein, 'The Role Of Judges In A Government Of, By, And For The People: Notes For the 58th Cardozo Lecture', *Cardozo Law Review* 30(1), 2008

B. de Witte, 'Democratic Adjudication in Europe. Is the European Court of Justice Responsive to the Citizens?', in Michael Dougan, Niamh Nic Shuibhne and Eleanor Spaventa (eds), *Empowerment and Disempowerment of the European Citizen*, Hart Publishing, 2012

On the Civil Service Tribunal:

N. Lavranos, 'The New Specialised Courts within the European Judicial System', *European Law Review* 30, 2005, p. 261

On direct access under Article 263 TFEU:

Anthony Arnull, 'April Shower for Jego Quere', *European Law Review* 29(3), 2004, pp. 287–288

C. Harlow, 'Towards A Theory of Access for the European Court of Justice', *YBEL* 12, 1992, p. 213

Filip Ragolle, 'Access To Justice For Private Applicants In The Community Legal Order: Recent (R) Evolutions', *European Law Review* 28(1), 2003, pp. 90–101

On Article 267 TFEU:

Catherine Barnard, 'The PPU: is it worth the candle? An early assessment', *European Law Review* 34(2), 2009, pp. 281–297

5 Addressing infringements of EU law – who enforces EU law?

Setting the scene

B was a Swedish national living in Hungary. Despite being a migrant worker, his Colombian partner Stella – also the mother of his child – had been refused residency. The authorities refused to recognise him as a migrant EU worker and threatened to deport her. He was sure that there was a mistake but felt helpless – what could he do to challenge the decision of the national immigration authorities?

1. **Introduction**

2. **The Treaty rules**

i. Articles 258 and 259 TFEU: centralised enforcement

ii. Article 260 TFEU: centralised Treaty-based sanctions

3. **Non-Treaty, non-judicial decentralised enforcement**

i. EU Pilot: vertical co-administration

ii. SOLVIT: horizontal co-administration

4. **Assessing administrative accountability and the right to good administration**

5. **Conclusion**

1. Introduction

The scope of EU law is not to be underestimated: in 2010, the *acquis* consisted of around 8,400 regulations and nearly 2,000 directives in addition to the primary law in the Treaties.[1] These measures are no longer limited to economic issues but now also include instruments regulating health and safety, discrimination, criminal justice, as well as migration and asylum. Since 1992, Justice and Home Affairs matters have been coordinated in the EU and the Lisbon Treaty fully incorporated all issues related to these themes – policing[2] is thus now an EU competence, although these matters remain beyond the scope of the CJEU.[3]

This chapter will explore the methods to oversee the application and enforcement of EU law. Who can B turn to for help? There is now no single answer to this question – a key theme is complexity. In 1957, enforcement was predominantly the responsibility of the Commission as 'guardian' of the Treaties, supported by the threat of litigation before the CJEU. Under Article 17 TEU:

> *The Commission shall promote the general interest of the Union and take appropriate initiatives to that end. It shall ensure the application of the Treaties, and of measures adopted by the institutions pursuant to them. It shall oversee the application of Union law under the control of the Court of Justice of the European Union.*

Now, however, there exists a range of means – Treaty and non-Treaty, judicial and non-judicial – to seek enforcement of EU law.

New routes to justice were required for two main reasons, one political and the second practical. First, administrative scandals in the late 1990s led to reform of the Commission[4] to improve responsibility and accountability. The Commission embraced a new culture and control philosophy.[5] Second, the nature of the problem has changed: non-implementation is less prevalent and poor application to everyday situations is increasingly more significant.[6] It is this gap between court decisions and their everyday impact – a familiar problem in federal jurisdictions[7] that needs to be addressed. Lengthy centralised procedures are not necessarily efficient to address misapplication, although it is still needed in relation to serious non-compliance. The time taken to resolve issues is also a concern driving reforms.

However, the evolution of enforcement mechanisms in the EU also reflects a general change in attitudes towards dispute resolution and the delivery of justice – this is a

---

[1] 28th Annual Report on Application of EU Law, COM(2011) 588 final, p. 3

[2] Articles 87 and 88 TFEU. In March 2013, the Commission proposed a new Europol Package.

[3] Article 275 TFEU

[4] COM(2000) 200 of 1 March 2000 – *Reforming the Commission:A White Paper*

[5] European Commission, 'A gap assessment between the internal control framework in the Commission Services and the control principles set out in the Court of Auditors "proposal for a Community internal control framework" opinion No 2/2004', Budget Staff Working Paper 2005, p. 5

[6] *AB (2) MVC v Home Office* [2012] EWHC 226 (QB). See also Esther Versluis, 'Even Rules, Uneven Practices: Opening the "Black Box" of EU Law in Action', *West European Politics* 30(1), 2007, pp. 50–67 on implementation of the Safety Data Sheets Directive of 5 March 1991 (91/155/EEC) which sought to regulate safe handling of dangerous substances and preparations.

[7] Martin J. Sweet, *Merely Judgment: Ignoring, Evading and Trumping the Supreme Court,* University of Virginia Press, 2010

second theme. Most national legal systems encourage use of alternative means such as mediation or negotiation to resolve disputes in place of litigation. Likewise, after 60 years of integration in the EU, there is a trend towards less litigation in the enforcement of single market and competition law. The strategy of command and control is now seen as expensive, inefficient, cumbersome and damaging to EU–member state relationships. The Commission has been encouraged by the member states to undertake action over the years to iron out difficulties arising from the design of legal instruments[8] and of remedies. Emphasis has moved to simplification of legislation, shared responsibility, co-administration and inclusion. The 'governance cycle' envisaged in the Single Market Act 2011[9] stresses resolution through informal cooperation rather than formal litigation.[10]

In the new ecology of enforcement, the Commission has retained the central role given to it in 1957 but now discharges this responsibility using a range of 'management modes'[11] at the EU and national level, each involving a different degree of control by the Commission. This chapter will focus on just two of these management modes: [12] direct centralised and indirect centralised. *Direct centralised* tasks are undertaken directly by the Commission via, for example, Articles 258–260 TFEU. Financial sanctions have been introduced to strengthen these tools. *Indirect centralised* tasks are delegated by the Commission to a variety of bodies (e.g. EU agencies, national public sector bodies or bodies governed by private law with a public service mission) that remain under the control of the Commission. These bodies may work as a network across the member states.

These networks have different characteristics, ranging from those with a statutory basis and formal legal powers which are exercised in parallel to EU rules and indirectly overseen by the Commission[13] to those which are voluntary in nature, devoid of sanctions and predominantly supervise themselves at the national level.[14] SOLVIT and EU Pilot are the newest enforcement networks to tackle problems arising from the misapplication of EU law. Created by the Commission to deflect cases from Article 258, these are electronic procedures that require 'co-administration' – interaction between responsible national bodies. The Commission maintains these networks and plays a background role in both, although it is more prominent in EU Pilot. In 2011, the Commission decided that this procedure will be a formal precursor to the activation of Article 258. These networks raise a final theme: accountability – how is it affected by complexity? These matters will now be discussed, beginning with a review of the Treaty rules.

---

[8]Better Regulation/Smarter Regulation. It has, for example, introduced preventive measures such as inclusion of application of EU law in its impact assessments for new initiatives and promoting implementation plans to support the transposition process for new directives. See COM(2011) 588 final, 28th Annual Report on Application of EU Law, para 3.4. For comment on the use of new tools such as impact assessments and consultation procedures see Alberto Alemanno, 'The Bettter Regulation Initiative at the Judicial gate: A Trojan Horse within the Commission Walls or the Way Forward?', *European law Journal* 15(3), May 2009, p. 382

[9]Communication From The Commission To The European Parliament, The Council, The European Economic And Social Committee And The Committee Of The Regions, 'Single Market Act II – Together for new growth', COM(2012) 573 final

[10]See Commission memo at http://europa.eu/rapid/press-release_MEMO-12-136_en.htm

[11]Article 53 of the Financial Regulation

[12]See Staff Working Paper 2005 for full discussion of the management modes. The EU's decentralised agencies employ more than 7,000 people and received a contribution from the EU budget of 727.5 million euros in 2012.

[13]Council Regulation (EC) No 1/2003 of 16 December 2002 on the implementation of the rules on competition laid down in Articles 81 and 82 of the Treaty, OJ L1/1–25 2003

[14]SOLVIT

2. The treaty rules

From its inception, enforcement of EU law faced many of the same problems encountered in enforcement of international law in general – paradoxically, national acceptance of norms and values set out in international law guarantees state sovereignty – only sovereign states can sign international treaties. Having established their sovereignty, states remain autonomous to determine if and how they implement and enforce international law. Thus by underwriting their sovereignty, international law simultaneously deprives itself of enforcement authority – that is it empowers nation states at its own expense. Compliance with EU law is therefore from one perspective a traditional problem of enforcing international agreements.

In 1957, the Treaty addressed this by incorporating a multi-stage 'pyramid'[15] process into Article 258 TFEU which prioritised the traditional international enforcement mode of elite regulatory bargaining. As the 'Guardian of the Treaty' the Commission bore responsibility for enforcement using dialogue, negotiation and an ultimate threat of judicial sanction. Administrative accountability[16] was low: the Treaty allowed the Commission to forsake the interests of the citizens in pursuit of good relations with the member states. Enforcement was predominantly discretionary, open-ended and cooperative with a minority of cases coming before the Court of Justice.

The Commission infringement database reveals three types of cases: complaints from individuals, Commission own-initiative cases, and non-communication cases. Discovery of infringement is largely due to complaints from the citizen – of the 2,100 infringement proceedings in 2010, just over 40 per cent arose from complaints.[17] The second largest source of work is own-initiative cases where the Commission has itself identified such infringements – these amounted to 35 per cent in 2010. Finally, non-communication cases – cases where the member state has failed to notify the Commission of its measures to transpose a directive – represented 22 per cent.[18]

The infringement procedure deals with different types of problems, including failure to comply with the Treaty, and faulty or incorrect transposition of a directive. Late transposition of directives is also a common problem. This is a specific problem in relation to environment directives – only four member states met the deadline to transpose Directive 2004/35/EC on environmental liability with regard to the prevention and remedying of environmental damage[19] – and the CJEU had to deliver judgments against seven member states. A total of 16 member states failed to fully implement the Better Regulation Directive and the Citizens' Rights Directive[20] by its deadline in May 2011. Only seven member states (including the UK) managed full implementation.

Stella's problems stem from non-compliance with a directive. Research findings suggest that the majority of member states do comply with their obligations under EU law: at the end of 1982, 640 directives were in force with an average transposition rate of 89.58 per cent.

---

[15]Rick Rawlings, 'Engaged Elites, Citizen Action', *European Law Journal*, March 2000
[16]The extent to which administrative authorities are beholden to address and rectify situations which conflict with rights provided in EU law to citizens.
[17]51 per cent in 2006
[18]28th Annual Report
[19]OJ L143/56 2004
[20]This requires an amendment to five existing directives to improve consumer rights in relation to personal data online and privacy.

In 2002, 2,240 directives were in force with an average transposition rate of 98.87 per cent. Transposition rates are therefore high,[21] although this may depend upon the specific sector.[22] However, whenever a member state does not comply with their Treaty obligations, it creates holes in the fabric of EU law and legal uncertainty. Enforcement is therefore not just a matter of securing the dominance of EU law for its own sake: rules need to be followed to ensure that rights are uniform and equally enjoyed by all citizens and residents in all member states.

i.   Articles 258 and 259 TFEU: centralised enforcement

Article 258 TFEU sets out the traditional infringement procedure. It states that:

> *(1) If the Commission considers that a Member State has failed to fulfil an obligation under the Treaties, it shall deliver a reasoned opinion on the matter after giving the State concerned the opportunity to submit its observations.*
>
> *(2) If the State concerned does not comply with the opinion within the period laid down by the Commission, the latter may bring the matter before the Court of Justice of the European Union.*

B could trigger Article 258 TFEU with a complaint directly to the Commission. Any individual can file a complaint, using a standard online form after providing basic personal details including name, address and member state of origin. The procedure is free of charge and there is no test of standing. The grievance must, however, focus on EU – not national – law and thus be within the scope of EU law. After filing her report, she would then have to wait. Making a complaint does not give rise to a right to an infringement proceeding: the Commission will decide if action is appropriate. Just three policy areas – environment, internal market and taxation – account for 52 per cent of all infringement cases.[23]

The start of this process is slow. During the initial period, the Commission enters into dialogue with the member state. The purpose of this exchange is for the Commission to outline its concerns, and gather further information by providing the member state with an opportunity to respond, explaining its actions. Ideally, the member state will take corrective action at this point without need for further intervention. This does indeed happen: in 2010 almost 50 per cent (431 out of 987) of matters were addressed at this stage of bilateral discussions. Where matters are not resolved, a letter of formal notice is sent wherein the Commission requests that the member state provides observations on the matter. Many cases can be disposed of at this initial formal stage (312 out of 987) or after the Commission reasoned opinion (130 out of 987).

The reasoned opinion can be the first stage of the litigation procedure – it becomes the basis of the complaint brought against the member state by the Commission. The reasoned opinion takes the form of a request for full implementation and lists the action

---

[21]Robert Thomson, René Torenvlied and Javier Arregui, 'The Paradox of Compliance: Infringements and Delays in Transposing European Union Directives', *British Journal of Political Science* 37(4), 2007, pp. 685–709. See also Gerda Falkner, Oliver Treib, Miriam Hartlapp and Simone Leiber, *Complying with Europe: EU Harmonisation and Soft Law in the Member States*, Cambridge University Press, 2005; and Tanja A. Börzel, 'Non-compliance in the European Union: Pathology or Statistical Artefact', *Journal of European Public Policy* 8, 2001, pp. 803–824

[22]Markus Haverland, Bernard Steunenberg and Frans Van Waarden, 'Sectors at Different Speeds: Analysing Transposition Deficits in the European Union', *JCMS* 49(2), 2011, pp. 265–291

[23]In 2013, the fewest new infringement proceedings were opened against HR (2), LV (20) and Malta (21); and the most against Italy (104) and Spain (90), 31st Annual Report, p11

required to achieve this. For example, in November 2011, the Commission issued a reasoned opinion to 16 member states that had failed to fully implement new EU telecoms rules into law.[24] Only the failed obligations noted in the reasoned opinion can be brought to the CJEU.[25] It is subsequent to the reasoned opinion that a timeframe emerges: any delayed response by the member state *may* lead to action before the CJEU – even at this stage the Commission retains its discretion on whether to pursue litigation.[26] Having brought the case before the CJEU, it can still then withdraw it.

Only a minority of cases are referred to the CJEU (151out of 987). In 2010, a high percentage (88 per cent) of infringements did not reach the CJEU because corrective action was taken by member states without the need for litigation.[27] The avoidance of litigation is preferable for the Commission and the member state. They are under no pressure of time – there are no time limits prior to submission of the reasoned opinion – this process can continue at the discretion of the Commission. However, while this bilateral, multi-level dialogue may be good for the relationship between the Commission and the member state, it is questionable how it protects the interests of individuals like B, who during this time may be unable to enjoy EU rights, pursue family life or a commercial activity. Faster litigation may be in the best interests of the individual.

Any member state may intervene in an Article 258 TFEU procedure before the CJEU. The CJEU will come to an independent assessment of the behaviour of the member state and will not always agree with the Commission. In *Commission v Portugal*, it did not – it held that a situation of uncertainty existed due to events during the legislative procedure resulting in an insufficiently clear obligation in the directive. A proceeding before the Court is therefore no guarantee of success for the Commission and may explain its preference for pre-judicial action. In addition, a court finding of infringement is no guarantee that a situation would be corrected by the member state. State liability and the financial sanction were created to address this.

VIEWPOINT

Is it in the interests of citizens for the Commission to negotiate with or litigate against the member states?

---

a) Article 259 TFEU

It is worth pointing out briefly here that the Treaty also invites member states to police each other. Under Article 259 TFEU:

> *A Member State which considers that another Member State has failed to fulfil an obligation under the Treaties may bring the matter before the Court of Justice of the European Union. Before a Member State brings an action against another Member State for an alleged infringement of an obligation under the Treaties, it shall bring the matter before the Commission.*

---

[24]'Digital Agenda: Commission presses 16 Member States to implement new EU telecoms rules', European Commission IP/11/1429, 24 November 2011
[25]C-52/08 *Commission v Portugal* [2011] ECR I-4275
[26]See T-54/99 *Max Mobil*
[27]28th Annual Report, p. 4

However, this provision is rarely used[28] – member states avoid holding each other to account. It was invoked by Hungary when the Slovak Republic refused to allow the Hungarian President to enter the country. He had been invited to participate in a ceremonial unveiling of a statue of the founder of Hungary, Saint Stephen, on the day that Warsaw Pact troops invaded Czechoslovakia, supported by Hungarian troops. The action was dismissed because it sought a declaration concerning future action:

> [67] In order to rule on these two heads of complaint, it must be noted that the procedure established under Article 259 TFEU is designed to obtain a declaration that the conduct of a Member State is in breach of EU law and to terminate that conduct 68. Thus, as the aim of the Treaty is to achieve the practical elimination of infringements by Member States and the consequences thereof (Case 70/72 *Commission* v *Germany* [1973] ECR 813, paragraph 13), an action under Article 259 TFEU concerning future possible infringements or limited to seeking an interpretation of EU law is inadmissible.

The procedure described below applies to both Articles 258 and 259 TFEU but there is a key difference: under Article 259, if the Commission does not provide a reasoned opinion within three months, the member state concerned may proceed before the CJEU.

VIEWPOINT

Why do you think that member states avoid the use of Article 259 TFEU?

ii. Article 260 TFEU – centralised Treaty-based sanctions

In 1992 a sanction was added that imposes a penalty payment or lump sum for breach of a CJEU ruling. Financial sanctions were introduced as an additional tool to encourage compliance. There are now two circumstances when fines can be imposed: in non-compliance cases under Article 260(2) and under Article 260(3)[29] in late transposition infringements (LTI's).

a) Non-compliance under Article 260(2)

The financial sanctions under Article 260(2) are a 'special judicial procedure' that can only be used to secure compliance with an Article 258 ruling. They may only be used to enforce CJEU rulings and thus the procedure can only be triggered by 'a failure of a Member State to fulfil its obligations under the Treaty which the Court has held, on the basis of Article 258 TFEU, to be well founded'.[30] In 2013, five Court judgments were delivered under Article 260(2) TFEU. The Court imposed penalty payments against

---

[28]Joined Cases C-15/76 and 16/76 *France* v *Commission* [1979] ECR 321 [27]; C-456/05 *Commission* v *Germany* [2007] ECR I-10517 [25]; and Joined Cases C-514/07 P, C-528/07 P and C-532/07 P *Sweden and Others* v *API and Commission* [2010] ECR I-8533 [119]
[29]Article 260(3) TFEU. See OJ C12, 15 January 2011 for the Commission policy on the application of this paragraph.
[30]C-95/12 *Commission* v *Germany* (Grand Chamber) [23]

Belgium, the Czech Republic, Luxembourg and Sweden but dismissed the claim of the Commission against Germany.[31] The Article 260(2) procedure is as follows:

> *If the Commission considers that the Member State concerned has not taken the necessary measures to comply with the judgment of the Court, it may bring the case before the Court after giving that State the opportunity to submit its observations. It shall specify the amount of the lump sum or penalty payment to be paid by the Member State concerned which it considers appropriate in the circumstances. If the Court finds that the Member State concerned has not complied with its judgment it may impose a lump sum or penalty payment on it. This procedure shall be without prejudice to Article 259.*

There has been a significant change to the original wording of this provision in the Lisbon Treaty. Previously, before bringing the member state before the Court the Commission had to issue another reasoned opinion identifying where the member state concerned had not complied with the judgment of the Court of Justice. This required significant additional work on the part of the Commission and it then had to give the member state additional time to comply. The Lisbon Treaty removed the need for a second reasoned opinion – the Commission must now only give the member state time to establish its position. The procedure is more efficient as the Commission has to conduct just one pre-litigation procedural step – the sending of a letter of formal notice requesting the member state to submit its observations. If the member state fails to reply or satisfy the Commission with its reply, the matter can now be referred directly to the Court. The Commission estimates that the removal of the reasoned opinion will reduce the average Article 260(2) procedure to between 8 and 18 months.[32] The changes should thus enable the Commission to be more effective in its enforcement duties, especially concerning transposition delays.

Notwithstanding this simplification, the Commission cannot overlook this pre-litigation step by determining of its own volition whether a member state has taken the necessary action to comply with an Article 258(2) ruling. It is made unequivocally clear in *Commission* v *Portugal*[33] that it must bring the matter back before the court.

In 2008, the CJ declared that Portugal had failed to comply with its 2004 ruling regarding the repeal of a national law which made the award of financial compensation to persons injured by a breach of European Union law in the area of public contracts conditional on proof of fault or fraud. The faulty national law was replaced in 2008 but there was disagreement over the date of compliance and thus the number of days for which the penalty payment applied: Portugal argued it was 10 days while the Commission argued it was almost 5 months. Portugal appealed the Commission Decision to the General Court.

This is a novelty of the case – this is the first time in which a decision establishing the level of sanctions is the subject of an annulment action under Article 263 TFEU. The CJ confirmed that member states may use Article 263 TFEU to challenge sanction decisions:

> [53] It is true that an action for annulment may be brought, as is the case here, against such a decision before the General Court, the judgment of which may be the subject of an appeal to the Court of Justice.

---

[31]*Commission* v *Belgium*, C-533/11 (lump sum payment: € 10,000,000; penalty: € 859,404 for each six-month period of non-compliance with the judgement under Article 258 TFEU) 31 *Commission* v *the Czech Republic*, C-241/11 (lump sum payment: € 250,000; no daily penalty) 32 *Commission* v *Luxembourg*, C-576/11 (lump sum payment: € 2,000,000; penalty: € 2,800 for each day of non-compliance with the judgment under Article 258 TFEU) 33 *Commission* v *Sweden*, C-270/11 (lump sum payment: € 3,000,000; no daily penalty) 34 *Commission* v *Germany*, C-95/12 (no penalties)
[32]Communication from the Commission – Implementation of Article 260(3) of the Treaty, SEC(2010) 1371 final, p. 2
[33]C-292/ 11 P *Commission* v *Portugal*

The phrase 'such a decision' suggests that such actions will be limited to cases where questions about the Commission jurisdiction are raised. It is unlikely that the Court wishes to encourage these challenges. It may have been reluctant to admit this one but did so due to the need to reassert its authority *vis-à-vis* the Commission under infringement proceedings. Having expanded its jurisdiction under Article 260(2) to review of sanction decisions, it now protected it.

The General Court had found procedural irregularities – the Commission had abrogated the role of the CJ by identifying non-compliance itself[34] – and annulled the decision. The Commission then – overconfidently – appealed the GC ruling to the CJ, arguing that the GC had limited its powers. It is not clear why the Commission expected the Court to hand over its powers. Agreeing that the Commission had erroneously relied 'specifically on its own interpretation' of the effects of the new Portuguese law, the CJ declared its 'exclusive jurisdiction' over infringement proceedings:

> [49] According to the system established by Articles 258 TFEU to 260 TFEU, the rights and duties of Member States may be determined and their conduct appraised only by a judgment of the Court of Justice.

> [50] The Court of Justice thus enjoys, in this regard, exclusive jurisdiction which is directly and expressly conferred on it by the Treaty and on which the Commission cannot encroach when checking whether there has been compliance with a judgment delivered by the Court of Justice pursuant to Article 260(2) TFEU.

Any assessment by the GC would also 'encroach' on that exclusive jurisdiction.[35]

The CJ wanted to put the Commission back in its place but it may have overstated its position: clearly the Commission can also appraise the conduct of the member states and does so on most occasions – the majority of infringement matters do not reach the Court. Nonetheless, the CJ does have a monopoly once the matter has entered its jurisdiction. The Commission cannot 'reclaim' issues from the purview of the Court by independent assessment of whether a measure complies with a judgment delivered under Article 260(2). This would undermine the CJ and, as the CJ pointed out, also constitute a breach of the procedural rights of defence available to the member states in infringement proceedings.[36] The pre-litigation stage under Article 260(2) may be shortened but must be respected.

b) Late transposition infringements (LTI's) under Article 260(3)

Article 260(3) has a truncated pre-litigation stage for failures to comply with notification obligations. This new provision dealing specifically with non-communication of transposed directives creates a new tool whereby the Commission may, at the first stage of referral to the CJEU under Article 258 TFEU, simultaneously suggest that the Court impose a lump sum or penalty payment in the same judgment that finds a member state has failed to fulfil its obligation to notify measures transposing a directive. This applies to cases of total and partial failure, except where this arises through unintentional error:[37]

Article 260(3) When the Commission brings a case before the Court pursuant to Article 258 on the grounds that the Member State concerned has failed to fulfil its

---

[34] [22]
[35] [65]
[36] [55]
[37] Communication from the Commission – Implementation of Article 260(3) of the Treaty, SEC(2010) 1371 final, p. 5

> *obligation to notify measures transposing a directive adopted under a legislative procedure, it may, when it deems appropriate, specify the amount of the lump sum or penalty payment to be paid by the Member State concerned which it considers appropriate in the circumstances. If the Court finds that there is an infringement it may impose a lump sum or penalty payment on the Member State concerned not exceeding the amount specified by the Commission. The payment obligation shall take effect on the date set by the Court in its judgment.*

In *Commission* v *Portugal* the CJ emphasised that the pre-litigation phase was essential to give member states additional time to comply with their obligations or to present their case against the complaints set out by the Commission as regards the continued failure to fulfil their obligations.[38]

In 2013, 74 directives were adopted, compared to 56 in 2012. The greater the use of directives, the more important an effective sanction for non-communication: in 2013, the Commission commenced 478 LTIs a small increase from the 447 in 2012 (the 855 LTIs in 2010 were over 300 more than in 2009).[39] Article 260(3) now creates a one-stop fining procedure for failure to notify – there is no need to await a first judgment fom the CJEU.. Unlike fines/penalty payments under Article 260(2), the sanction applied by the CJ cannot exceed that requested by the Commission. Also, it only applies to *legislative* directives – in relation to *non-legislative* directives under Article 290 and 291 TFEU, the two-step procedure applies: the Commission must first refer the matter to the Court under Article 258 and, in the event of failure to comply with a judgment, back to the Court pursuant to Article 260(2).

ANALYSING THE LAW

Why is failure to notify transposition of a directive so serious?

The Commission hopes that this change will give deadlines some bite and be a strong incentive for timely compliance:

> Prompt transposition of directives by Member States . . . is not only a matter of safeguarding the general interests pursued by Union legislation, where delays are unacceptable, but also and above all of protecting European citizens who enjoy individual rights under such legislation. Ultimately, it is the credibility of Union law as a whole which is undermined when acts take full legal effect in the Member States years later than they should.[40]

c) Application of the financial sanctions

The financial sanctions must be initiated by a request of the Commission but the CJEU decides on their imposition. Although the Treaty presents the lump sum and penalty payment as alternatives, the Commission can request one or other or both: in *Commission* v *France* it asked for both;[41] in *Commission* v *Italy*[42] it only asked for a lump sum to be

---

[38]*Commission* v *Portugal* [56]
[39]28th Annual Report, p. 5
[40]Communication from the Commission – Implementation of Article 260(3) of the Treaty, SEC(2010) 1371 final, p. 3
[41]C-304/02 *Commission* v *France* [2005] ECR I-6263. See also Pål Wennerås, 'Sanctions against Member States under Article 260 TFEU: alive, but not Kicking?', *Common Market Law Review* 49, 2012, pp. 145–176
[42]C-119/ 04 *Commission* v *Italy:* no penalty payment or lump sum was awarded.

imposed. In the former case the court agreed: as a result of its 'general and persistent' breach, France was subjected to a penalty payment of EUR 57,761,250 *and* a lump sum of EUR 20,000,000. In the latter case, the CJ disagreed – the court did not think that the lump sum requested was appropriate and denied the request. In *Commission* v *Germany*, [43] the Court refused to impose either a daily penalty of around EUR 283,000 or the lump sum requested – the Commission failed to make a case for this and was left carrying the costs. When imposed, the daily penalty payment runs from the day on which the judgment is handed down. Rarely has the Court set the first deadline for the penalty payment on a date subsequent to its judgment. [44]

The lump sum has come to be used as a sanction for transgression prior to the CJ ruling; the penalty payment as a prospective sanction to deter continued transgression and encourage speedy compliance. The intention is to adopt the same approach in relation to Article 260(3). This is defended given the objective of the sanction, namely to ensure full and timely compliance. In cases where the Commission proposes a penalty payment alone, it will 'withdraw its action if the Member State notifies the transposition measures required to put an end to the infringement. In contrast, in cases pending in which the Commission has also proposed a lump sum, it will not withdraw its action simply because the required notification has been made'. [45] Decisions will be made on a case by case basis. Article 260(3) [46] will not be used automatically – its use may be determined according to the track record of a member state [47] and its conduct. It is recognised that there may be specific circumstances when penalties will not be appropriate.

The Commission has established guidelines on the application of financial sanctions. In general, usage will follow three broad principles: deterrence, predictability and appropriateness. The ultimate objective of the sanction is to ensure timely transposition; thus the Commission will consider the seriousness of the infringement, its duration and its power to deter. Second, so that member states are clear of the financial consequences, calculation of the sanction will be fixed according to a formula that respects proportionality and can be justified before the Court. [48] Third, the penalties will be substantive rather than symbolic in order to ensure that they are taken seriously and thus effective. [49] Non-transposition creates significant problems for citizens, like B, trying to enjoy the rights set out in EU law.

However, what happens if the state cannot pay? There is no guarantee that member states will comply – sometimes they simply cannot afford to pay. This was the problem in *Commission* v *Greece* (toxic waste in Chania (2000)) where a penalty payment of EUR 20,000 for each day of delay in complying with a 1992 judgment was set. It was also the situation in *Commission* v *Spain* (bathing waters (2003)) where a penalty payment of EUR 624,150 per year until full compliance with a 1998 judgment was set. The fines may create an incentive to pay but cannot guarantee payment or compliance. Thus even these sanctions may not help Stella to access her rights in the Citizenship Directive.

It is perhaps simplistic to think of compliance purely in terms of fear of sanction and deterrence. A far more complex and varied series of factors may influence compliance,

---

[43]C-95/12
[44]See cases C-278/01 *Commission* v *Spain* [2003] ECR I-14141, C-304/02 *Commission* v *France* [2005] ECR I-6263 and C-369/07 *Commission* v *Hellenic Republic* ECR [2009] I-05703
[45]Communication from the Commission – Implementation of Article 260(3) of the Treaty, SEC(2010) 1371 final, p. 6
[46]Wennerås 2012
[47]Communication from the Commission – Implementation of Article 260(3) of the Treaty, SEC(2010) 1371 final, p. 4
[48]In the wake of the euro crisis, the national finances of member states will be taken into account when calculating financial sanctions.
[49]Wennerås 2012

many of which derive from matters other than the actions of the regulated community. Non-compliance and late transposition can arise for a variety of reasons, such as lack of sufficient expertise and resources or complex internal decision-making processes in the member states. Member states have requested more support from the Commission in the period between entry into force of a directive and the deadline for transposition.[50]

APPLYING THE LAW

If Hungary has incorrectly transposed the directive, what should the Commission do? How would this help B?

3. Non-Treaty, non-judicial decentralised enforcement

What can Stella otherwise do to address the misapplication of EU law? The Article 258 procedure is beyond her control – it prioritises the relationship between the Commission and the member states. In the past, treatment of complainants was poor: the individual complainant 'fed' the procedure but had no right to an infringement proceeding or standing before the CJEU: of the 3000 complaints in 2013, bilateral discussions with Member States were opened in relation to just 487. Complainants were not given a clear rationale for Commission decisions to apply or not apply Article 258.[51] The Commission was initially hostile to any suggestion that it had a duty to individual complainants, despite their centrality to enforcement – in response to complaints of its high-handed behaviour raised via the European Ombudsman, it reasserted its discretion[52] to pursue any complaint at its own pace, and the marginal role of the individual complainant.[53] However, given the importance of complaints for compliance, it is in the interests of enforcement to consider how to better protect the interests of the individual. It would be to the detriment of EU law if individuals became disillusioned and cease to inform the Commission of potential breaches.

The Commission has taken action to improve communication with complainants. It will inform them, in advance of the collective decision of the College of Commissioners, if it will open or end an investigation. It also provides updates on the progress of complaints (either in writing or via a notice in the *Official Journal*). In general, the goal is to inform complainants within one year from the date of registration of the complaint. The European Ombudsman remains competent to help individuals who are dissatisfied with the behaviour of the Commission.[54] In addition, the Commission has created electronic resources which empower the individual by providing guidance on the information required to address their needs.[55] The system has become more mechanised: this has introduced speed and accountability to the actions of the Commission as an enforcer, while enabling it to focus on dealing with potential infringements. A new electronic

---

[50]26th Annual Report, p.7
[51]Rawlings 2000. T-104/95 *World Wildlife Fund*
[52]*T-54/99 Max Mobil*; C-141/02 P *Commission v T-Mobile*, e.g. 1,800 complaints re Citizenship Directive; 115 registered, 5 infringement cases opened
[53]Commission Communication to EP and EO on relations with complainant COM(2002)141 final, OJ C244 2002. Updated in Communication from the Commission to the Council and the European Parliament on updating the handling of relations with the complainant in respect of the application of Union law, COM (2012)154 final
[54]As laid out in COM(2007)502
[55]'Your Europe' web portal, http://europa.eu/youreurope/

system (CHAP) was introduced in September 2009 for the registration and management of complaints and enquiries by European citizens on the application of EU law. CHAP was designed to fulfil the undertakings given in 2002 – ensure timely assignment of complaints to the competent Commission department, and provide feedback to the complainants. In 2010, 4,035 cases were created in CHAP (83 per cent were complaints and 17 per cent enquiries).

Further ideas arose from the Single Market Plan, such as the objective to develop non-judicial tools of dispute resolution. This goal has also been enhanced by the citizen-centric logic of the Lisbon Treaty. New indirect centralised measures have been introduced to encourage co-administration; resources for independent action were planned to strengthen citizen confidence in the enforcement system. Since 2002, two new electronic procedures have been introduced: EU Pilot and SOLVIT. These alternative systems for dispute resolution were both designed to delegate responsibility for problem solving to the national level but they allow the Commission to retain oversight as well as some control.

EU Pilot focuses on non-compliance problems that would normally be dealt with under Article 258 TFEU. Initially an informal pre-infringement procedure, the Commission has now announced its intention to incorporate EU Pilot formally into the Treaty procedure. SOLVIT was created to tackle cross-border issues arising from the misapplication of internal market rules. It has a second version – 'SOLVIT+' – which is activated if resolution requires a change to national law. The two initiatives are not linked although the difference between them is slight. As will be explained below, EU Pilot and SOLVIT handle different issues in different ways: the former focuses on non-conformity of national law with EU legislation via communication between the member state and the Commission while the latter deals with poor application via cooperation between national authorities.

i.   EU Pilot: vertical co-administration[56]

The idea for the EU Pilot project was launched in the Commission communication in 2007 on 'A Europe of results'.[57] The Commission suggested the creation of a project to enable it to work more closely with the member states so as to respond faster to questions and find better solutions. The aim was to create an 'early warning mechanism' which would prevent use of infringement proceedings. EU Pilot began life in 2008 as an experiment involving just 15 member states (Austria, Czech Republic, Denmark, Germany, Finland, Hungary, Ireland, Italy, Lithuania, the Netherlands, Portugal, Slovenia, Sweden, Spain and the UK). In 2010 Bulgaria, Estonia and Slovenia signed up and by 2011, 25 member states were involved. In 2012 Luxembourg and Malta joined.

It is no longer experimental: the Commission is so pleased with the results that it is exploring the possibility of extending EU Pilot as an instrument for problem solving and prevention to all member states, including those not yet using EU Pilot.[58] It is now a fully integrated 'governance' tool which will be used to assess the 'performance' of the member states.[59]

---

[56]EU Pilot and CHAP http://ec.europa.eu/eu_law/docs/docs_infringements/annual_report_28/com_2011_588_en.pdf 3.2
[57]COM(2007)502
[58]European Commission, 'Second Evaluation Report on EU Pilot', SEC(2011)1629/2, Brussels, 2011, p. 7
[59]http://ec.europa.eu/internal_market/scoreboard/performance_by_governance_tool/eu_pilot/index_en.htm

The objective of EU Pilot is to ensure conformity with EU law by avoiding the Article 258 procedures and improving the speed of the process.[60] It addresses issues of non-compliance under oversight of the Commission Secretariat General which monitors its functioning, develops it application and irons out operational problems. EU Pilot is a more robust tool than SOLVIT in at least two ways: first, complaints go to the relevant DG in the Commission, rather than the member state and second, rules protecting the identity of complainants in the treatment of correspondence and complaints apply.[61] Access to Commission documents on EU Pilot is governed by Regulation 1049/2001.[62]

EU Pilot is activated when the Commission requires national input to address an enquiry or complaint. It works via a confidential electronic database which facilitates communication between the Commission DGs and national authorities. A network of national Central Contact Points (CCPs) was set up to operate the system by directing files to the correct DG, monitor progress and promote use of the system. The Commission retains responsibility for all issues dealt with under EU Pilot. The DG receives and records the complaint, and assesses suitability to be dealt with under EU Pilot (this will no longer be necessary as all complaints will pass through EU Pilot). The DG then returns the complaint to a CCP in the member state.

The CCP can reject the file as inappropriate for this procedure (2 per cent of files); if it accepts it has a 10-week deadline to respond to a complainant – 67 per cent of cases were dealt with in an average of 73 days, but some 40 per cent took on average 109 days. Responses – explanations and solutions including remedial actions – can be sent by the CCP to the complainant where appropriate or by the Commission, but the Commission will also send its own evaluation of the national response to the complainant and keep the complainant informed on the progress of the issue. Under EU Pilot the Commission works with the member state to find an answer. If necessary, the Commission may launch the Article 258 TFEU procedure – it has done so in 20 per cent of cases since 2008. In 2012, 334 cases went on to the Article 258 procedure and slightly more than this (396) in 2013. The Commission retains oversight and control.

Over 700 cases passed through EU Pilot by early 2010, mainly in the areas of the Environment (36 per cent); Internal market (21 per cent); Tax (8 per cent); Labour law, social security and employment (7 per cent); and Justice, freedom and security (6 per cent). For example, the Commission was able to ensure that Germany's construction of a flood water retention reservoir did not have a negative impact on the protected fauna, flora and wildlife, especially birds, in the construction zone. The Commission also used EU Pilot to ensure that Czech broadcasters respected EU rules protecting the physical, mental and moral development of minors in connection with television programmes and advertising when broadcasting programmes across the border to Romania. Most of these issues were raised by citizens (43 per cent), businesses and civil society (36 per cent).

An issue arose when own-initiative files raised by the Commission (20 per cent) were also included in EU Pilot. This appeared to be a merging of EU Pilot with the Article 258 pre-infringement procedure so that it became a mechanism for complaints (around 60 per cent), enquiries (around 20 per cent) and Commission investigations. The MS

---

[60]https://webgate.ec.europa.eu/pilotms/index.cfm?method=login.show&logged_out=true
[61]Regulation 45/2001 of the European Parliament and of the Council of 18 December 2000 on the protection of individuals with regard to the processing of personal data by the EU institutions and bodies and on the free movement of such data and Commission Communication on relations with the complainant in respect of infringements of EU law [COM final (2002) 0141]
[62]See 2011 'Second Evaluation Report on EU Pilot', p. 13

TABLE 5.1   Characteristics of EU Pilot and SOLVIT

Which procedure?	Scope	Who may use?	Against who m?	Internal market rules?	Legal proceedings?	Transposition problem?	Non-conformity problem?
EU Pilot	No cross-border issue	Natural or legal persons, NGOs	Public body	Yes	May be subject to legal proceedings	Yes	Yes
SOLVIT	Cross-border issues	Natural or legal persons	Public body	Yes (incorrect application)	Not subject to legal proceedings	No	No

Source: Adapted from Centre for Strategy and Evaluation Services (CSES), 'Framework Contract for projects relating to Evaluation and Impact Assessment activities of Directorate General for Internal Market and Services – Evaluation of SOLVIT', 2011, p. 9

reacted negatively to the use of EU Pilot for general communication between the Commission and the member state authorities. However, it seems to have been accepted that there are advantages to this, although it was agreed to use expert meetings for more complex cases. In future, member states will not receive a separate formal letter launching Article 258, but will receive a form sent via EU Pilot.[63] In 2013, 1502 new forms were sent.

VIEWPOINT

Is EU Pilot a better alternative to Article 258 TFEU? Why? If you were B, which procedure would you prefer?

---

ii.   SOLVIT: horizontal co-administration

SOLVIT[64] is an electronic mechanism which operates through a network of SOLVIT centres in the member states. It does *not* deal with problems between commercial actors or between consumers and commercial actors, nor with complaints about EU institutions. It deals only with cross-border problems arising due to poor application of EU law by public authorities in the member states. It will therefore accept complaints from individuals, but also organisations and even MEPs. In 2009, it dealt with 1,550 new cases using a budget of EUR 800,000. Its main areas of use include residency rights (38 per cent); social security (23 per cent); qualifications (15 per cent); tax (4 per cent); employment rights (2 per cent); and customs (1 per cent).

SOLVIT tends to be successful in addressing problems where the law is correct but needs clarification for proper application. The maximum timeframe for resolution is 14 weeks, thus the issues must be straightforward and capable of being resolved quickly. For example, it took two days to help an Austrian company which was prevented from

---

[63]See 2011 'Second Evaluation Report on EU Pilot', p. 4
[64]http://ec.europa.eu/solvit/ Commission Recommendation of 7 December 2001 on principles for using SOLVI' – the Internal Market Problem Solving Network, OJ L331 2001

marketing wood preservative in Hungary because it had no representative in that country but the local authorities insisted that this was a requirement. It took two weeks to secure a VAT refund for a Portuguese company supplying retail goods to shops in Poland and nine weeks for benefits to be reinstated to a Hungarian woman in Belgium, who had been told that she was no longer eligible after giving birth to two children in Belgium.

The SOLVIT procedure has two sites: a SOLVIT centre in the home member state and one in the problem member state. These are usually located with the relevant national administration. Problems are not registered directly but online in a database managed by the Commission.[65] The 'home SOLVIT centre' (normally the centre in the applicant's country of origin) receives the complaint and contacts the client. It liaises with the complainant to collect all necessary documents, prepare a legal analysis of the case and translate it into English. This procedure appears to take on average four weeks. It then sends the case to the 'lead SOLVIT centre' in the host member state through the SOLVIT database. This lead centre can accept or reject the case, but must do so within seven days. If the case is accepted, a solution has to be found within 10 weeks. If the case is particularly complicated, the deadline can be extended by four weeks. All proposed solutions must be in full conformity with EU law – the Commission reserves the right to take action against member states whenever it considers that this may not be the case.

On occasions, a case can be kept open for longer than 14 weeks. These are then dealt with using SOLVIT+. For example it took six months to address the issue of discriminatory pension rules for part-time frontier workers in Liechtenstein. The rule in Liechtenstein did not fully take into account the insurance periods of an Austrian citizen's part-time employment in Liechtenstein because she had kept her residence in Austria. This resulted in a lower level of retirement pension. The mode of calculation therefore discriminated in favour of persons with residence in Liechtenstein, whose insurance periods of part-time employment were fully taken into account. After the intervention of SOLVIT, Liechtenstein adapted its legislation in order to avoid discrimination against frontier workers. In another case it took 14 months to change the provisions of a Hungarian rule which banned the marketing of wine in bottles larger than 2 litres. Because of this rule, a UK company was not allowed to market its beverage in 50-litre kegs. The competent Ministry admitted that the ban contravened EU law and Court of Justice rulings – the Hungarian measure was changed.

Success under SOLVIT appears to be in decline after just 10 years: the caseload has increased tenfold and case handling times are getting longer although case numbers are no longer on the increase. An evaluation conducted in 2011 highlighted that there is still limited knowledge of this procedure and what it is for – 50 per cent of users stumbled upon SOLVIT via an internet search. Another issue is disagreements between the 'home' and 'lead' SOLVIT centre: when this occurs, cases can remain unresolved and abandoned.[66] SOLVIT centres also lack authority when dealing with some national authorities, perhaps due to poorly trained legal staff in some centres. Centres are also underresourced – more than 50 per cent lack the staff required to deal with their caseload.

---

[65]https://webgate.ec.europa.eu/solvit/application/index.cfm?method=webform.homeform&language=en
[66]The most difficult cases to solve include recognition of qualifications (20.8 per cent), motor vehicle registration (17 per cent) and social security cases (17 per cent) – Centre for Strategy and Evaluation Services (CSES), 'Framework Contract for projects relating to Evaluation and Impact Assessment activities of Directorate General for Internal Market and Services – Evaluation of SOLVIT', 2011, p. 35

More fundamentally, it is not clear that businesses prefer an informal approach – this may resolve the immediate issue but may not change the long-term position of the national authority concerned. A significant minority of users (33 per cent) expressed dissatisfaction with the outcome of their case (only 32 per cent were satisfied). SOLVIT is therefore not always meeting expectations.[67]

The Commission has presented proposals to address these matters. These include closer integration between SOLVIT and the central Commission complaints system (CHAPS); ensuring sufficient staff and legal expertise at SOLVIT centres; improvement of quality; and raising awareness.[68] A plan for interoperability of the complaints systems has been produced[69] – SOLVIT may become more centralised when this happens.

VIEWPOINT

Will the inclusion of more actors improve a) enforcement of EU law and b) compliance with EU law?

---

4. Assessing administrative accountability and the right to good administration

Effective enforcement of rules is also about responsible administration. Increased attention is being paid to good administration and administrative accountability. 'Good administration' has been described as a 'polysense principle'[70] that includes a duty to act or refrain from acting in a certain way, such as the prohibition of maladministration.[71] This notion has now been entrenched in EU human rights law: Article 41 of the Charter of Fundamental Rights (CFR) lays out a new fundamental right to good administration. It is the first time that such a right has appeared in a human rights document. Prior to its inclusion, the concept of good administration existed as a principle; as a fundamental right it can form a separate basis for a claim. It creates expectations of a certain standard of behaviour from public powers, establishing forms and procedures that must be respected by the public institutions.[72] Individuals like Stella therefore have the right to have their affairs handled impartially, fairly and within a reasonable time by the institutions and bodies of the Union (to be heard, access to file, given reasons); the right to have the Union make good any damage caused by its institutions or servants in the performance of their duties; and the right to communicate with EU institutions in one of the languages of the Treaties and have an answer in the same language.

---

[67]CSES 2011, pp. 56–57

[68]http://europa.eu/rapid/press-release_MEMO-12-136_en.htm

[69]Cross-sector SOLVIT http://ec.europa.eu/isa/actions/documents/isa-1.14_cross_sector_solvit_en.pdf

[70]Elisabetta Lanza, 'The right to good administration in the European Union. Roots, *rationes* and enforcement in antitrust case-law', Social Science Research Network paper, 2008, p. 485

[71]Under Article 228 TFEU, the European Ombudsman is mandated to examine and report upon 'complaints from any citizen of the Union or any natural or legal person residing or having its registered office in a Member State concerning instances of maladministration in the activities of the Union institutions, bodies, offices or agencies, with the exception of the Court of Justice of the European Union acting in its judicial role'.

[72]Lanza 2008, p. 483

networked administration with agencies in the member states. From the EU perspective, the new management modes each involve a different degree of control by the Commission. These innovations have not replaced Article 258: the various management modes operate alongside each other with different levels of control by the Commission. None are totally beyond the reach of the Commission – it remains the overall 'Guardian of the Treaties'. Centralised control has enhanced application of financial sanctions but the indirect tools work through influence: the exertion of peer pressure through networked action. The most innovation can be seen in relation to consumer policy[78] and competition law[79] where the Commission has developed networks of national authorities which it indirectly oversees.

Articles 258 and 260 TFEU remain the strongest tools; SOLVIT is the weakest. There is very little escape from Article 260: in *Commission v Italy* (state aid),[80] the Court of Justice confirmed that the only defence for a member state is to show conclusively the impossibility of implementing a Commission decision. Internal difficulties would not be accepted as a justification. A member state can refuse to participate in a SOLVIT or EU Pilot procedure yet these are speedy and have proven to be effective, despite high levels of dissatisfaction. They have not removed misapplication, but their introduction has improved the resolution of misapplication for individual complainants. However, such resolutions are faster but narrower as they have no effect in other member states. They also avoid the long delay associated with the Treaty infringement procedure – as long as they are successful. If these procedures do not iron out the difficulties, then they will prolong the infringement. A number of factors can affect their success such as the size of member state; migration trends into and out of that member state; the complexity of the cases; cooperation of member state authorities and the level of political backing for member state centres by national administrations. While they push litigation to the background, they magnify the potential impact of domestic politics. Some member states might therefore still suffer from an 'enforcement deficit'[81] that is difficult to address.

How effectively does this combination of management modes work to secure justice for individuals like Stella, who have to rely on the actions of national authorities? The creation of non-judicial tools has arguably improved access to justice in the EU without increasing access to law.[82] These non-Treaty, non-judicial procedures were devised by the Commission in response to the twin problems of empowerment of the individual and efficiency. Networked negotiation and co-administration have allowed the Commission to be more responsive to citizens – this is a positive development: 'The way in which an institution reacts to complaints and to criticism and suggestions is a key indication of how citizen-centred it is . . . [the] culture of service to citizens is not a culture of blame'.[83] They not only allow the Commission to retreat but also encourage member states to talk to each other about the application of EU law. The Commission, however, remains informed via its database of complaints.

---

[78]Such as ECC-Net http://ec.europa.eu/consumers/ecc/index_en.htm and FIN-NET http://ec.europa.eu/internal_market/fin-net/members_en.htm
[79]http://ec.europa.eu/competition/ecn/competition_authorities.html
[80]C-496/09 *Commission v Italy*
[81]Wennerås 2012
[82]Jerold S. Auerbach, *Justice Without Law: Resolving Disputes Without Lawyers,* Oxford University Press, 1983
[83]Responses to European Ombudsman 2008

The introduction of these mechanisms may signal a more service-oriented administrative culture in the Commission that is centred on the citizen. A new communication from the Commission has introduced safeguards and guarantees to improve the treatment of the individual complainant under the infringement procedure.[84] The new ecology has improved efficiency – the maximum[85] timeframe for matters dealt with under EU Pilot and SOLVIT is 14 weeks; infringement proceedings under Article 258 TFEU can take up to two years. Yet, the prioritisation of informal means of dispute resolution such as advice and cooperation may have a negative impact on uniformity – resolution under SOLVIT and EU Pilot may not result in change to a faulty national law. They also raise the question of accountability – under the more complex system of enforcement, who is ultimately responsible when things go wrong?

---

[84]Communication from the Commission to the Council and European Parliament 'Updating the handling of relations in respect of the application of Union law', COM(2012)154 final, 2 April 2012
[85]Extensions are allowed.

Further reading

On non-compliance with EU law:

Tanja A. Börzel, 'Non-compliance in the European Union: Pathology or Statistical Artefact', *Journal of European Public Policy*, 8, 2001, pp. 803–824

Tanja A. Börzel, Tobias Hoffman, Diana Panke and Carina Sprungk, 'Obstinate and Inefficient: Why Member States do not comply with European law', *Comparative Political Studies* 39(1), 2011, pp. 128–152

Robert Thomson, René Torenvlied and Javier Arregui, 'The Paradox of Compliance: Infringements and Delays in Transposing European Union Directives', *British Journal of Political Science* 37, 2004, pp. 685–709

On Article 260 TFEU:

Pål Wennerås 'Sanctions against Member States under Article 260 TFEU: alive, but not kicking?', *Common Market Law Review* 49, 2012, pp. 145–176

On good administration:

Edoard Chiti, 'An Important Part of the EU's Institutional Machinery: Features, Problems and Perspectives of European Agencies', *CMLR* 46, 2009, p. 1395

Elisabetta Lanza, 'The right to good administration in the European Union. Roots, *rationes* and enforcement in antitrust case-law', Social Science Research Network paper, 2008

Joana Mendes, 'Good Administration in EU Law', EUI Working Paper 2009/09

Part II

EU Law: Principles and Values

6 The supremacy of EU law

Setting the scene

Sir, Your readers may be interested to learn that the German constitutional court has no authority to decide that the Greek bail-out violates the European Union treaties, without first referring that issue to the European Court of Justice under the so-called preliminary rulings procedure. Article 267 of the Treaty on the functioning of the EU provides that any highest court in a member state faced with a question of EU law interpretation is to send the case to the ECJ, because that court has ultimate authority to interpret EU law. The German constitutional court has, sadly, never made use of the preliminary rulings procedure, but neither has it ever decided, on its own, that EU law was violated. It is well aware of the limits on its powers when it comes to questions of EU law, and it is pretty inconceivable that it should transgress these limits. Of course, it can always rule on the constitutionality under German law of the bail-out, but it cannot rule on the no bail-out clause in the EU treaties. For quite some time I have been annoyed that the German court is portrayed as the ultimate authority on whether Germany complies with EU law. As a matter of law, that is simply incorrect.[1]

---

[1] Piet Eeckhout, Professor of European Law and Director, Centre of European Law, King's College London, UK, 7 July 2011 in 'German court is not the ultimate authority on EU' at http://www.ft.com/cms/s/0/8d5f4e9e-a828-11e0-9f50-00144feabdc0.html\#axzz1STIwSeBg. *Source*: German court is not the ultimate authority on EU, Financial Times, 07/07/2011 (Eeckhout, P.), © Piet Eeckhout.

1. Introduction

Where is ultimate authority on EU law? Who takes the final decision on the legality or illegality of EU law – the Court of Justice of the European Union (CJEU)[2] or the highest courts in the member states? The idea at the core of this question on the ultimate authority of EU law is *supremacy*. The purpose of this idea is to qualify the authority of EU law in relation to other sources of law operating within the state system, such as national constitutional law or international law.[3] This idea was introduced as long ago as 1962 by the CJEU but remains controversial, because of how it was introduced and by whom. It has many facets, all of which stem from the assertion by the CJEU that the newly created European Economic Community (EEC) possesses features that differentiate it from all previous organisations created under international law. Four specific assertions will be highlighted as key themes for this chapter. The first is novelty – how new was the EEC? What did it possess that traditional international organisations did not? Second, in what ways was the EEC an independent system of political and legal institutions? To what extent were they self-sufficient and able to act alone? Third, what was the nature of the autonomy of the EEC? How did it derive power to act alone? And fourth, and perhaps most controversially of all, primacy – how did the law of the EEC possess the power to displace any national rule (whether constitutional or ordinary) that conflicted with it? In answering these questions, it will become clear that supremacy has judicial and legislative dimensions with far-reaching implications for legal and political authority in the EU.

In exploring supremacy, this chapter aims to explain how the EEC became a new form of international organisation,[4] or a supranational organisation, the only one of its kind in the world. It will discuss the development of a supranational polity with strong independent powers and the establishment of founding principles which are key to the autonomy of the EU as we know it today. It will also highlight the attitudes of the member states. For while the EU confidently asserts the absolute authority of the CJEU, there are political leaders in many member states – both old and new – who would qualify this.

The chapter begins with a summary of the seminal case, *van Gend en Loos*.[5] This case is often discussed as a revolution in EU law but recent research suggests that this decision was in fact the culmination of a gradual change in the opinion of legal scholars on how EU law should operate.[6] The case will serve as a launch pad into discussion of the controversies that continue to give rise to lively debate on EU law and European integration. While exploring the facets of the concept, I will intertwine debates about the a) legislative and b) judicial dimensions. I will also consider the theoretical and practical legal and political challenges to which it has given rise. The chapter will end with consideration of why supremacy was accepted.

---

[2] The CJEU, formerly the European Court of Justice (ECJ), comprises the Court of Justice (CJ), General Court (GC) and Civil Service Tribunal (CST). Reference will be made to the 'CJEU' or 'the Court' as the collective institution and the CJ and GC as distinct judicial forums within the CJEU.

[3] Neil MacCormick, *Questioning Sovereignty: Law, State, and Nation in the European Commonwealth,* Oxford University Press, 1999

[4] Bruno de Witte, 'The European Union as an International Legal Experiment', in Grainne de Burca and Joseph H.H. Weiler (eds), *The Worlds of European Constitutionalism,* Cambridge University Press, 2012, pp. 19–56

[5] C-26/62 Van Gend en Loos v Nederlandse Administratie der Belastinge (Case 26/62) [1963] ECR 1.

[6] Antoine Vauchez, 'The transnational politics of judicialisation. Van Gend en Loos and the making of EU polity', *European Law Journal,* 16(1), January 2010, pp. 1–28

2. The claims of supremacy

The idea of supremacy first emerged in the 1962 case called *van Gend en Loos*. This case has been described as a 'constitutional juggernaut'.[7] The facts of this case revolve around an everyday trade issue – categorisation of goods for the purpose of levying import duties. The provision at the centre of the dispute was Article 25 TFEU [ex Article 12 EC], which states that 'customs duties on imports and exports and charges having equivalent effect shall be prohibited between Member States. This prohibition shall also apply to customs duties of a fiscal nature.' The case focused on questions sent from a Dutch court to the CJ, enquiring whether this provision was capable of having 'direct effect'. The phrasing of the questions by the national court illustrates that the idea of direct effect was known in some legal systems: it was not a concept created by the CJ but incorporated into EU law by it. The CJEU answered in the affirmative that:

> Article 12 EC [Article 25 TFEU] of the Treaty establishing the European Economic Community produces direct effects and creates individual rights which national courts must protect.

In coming to this conclusion, the CJ made a number of statements pertaining to the character of the EEC, its political and legal relationship with the member states. These comments on the nature of the EEC and EU law (then Community law) were of long-term and constitutional significance. The CJ declared that the legal order created by the Treaty of Rome was an entirely new system, under which constitutional powers had been transferred via a voluntary limitation of sovereign rights by the founding member states, who had chosen to do so in order to create new political institutions endowed with sovereign rights. Consequently, the law arising from the Treaty was a new type of tie that binds: the EEC legal order was not just a loose framework of norms, like other organisations created by international law, but a self-standing (i.e. independent) system of new political and legal institutions, working together to achieve a common goal, for the purpose of which the member states have, albeit in limited spheres, shared thus restricted their sovereign rights.

Against this background, it was therefore possible for EU law to impose obligations and rights upon individuals which become part of their legal heritage, independently of national traditions and legislation:

> The community constitutes a new legal order of international law for the benefit of which the states have limited their sovereign rights, albeit within limited fields, and the subjects of which comprise not only member states but also their nationals. Independently of the legislation of member states, community law therefore not only imposes obligations on individuals but is also intended to confer upon them rights which become part of their legal heritage. These rights arise not only where they are expressly granted by the Treaty, but also by reason of obligations which the Treaty imposes in a clearly defined way upon individuals as well as upon the member states and upon the institutions of the community.

---

[7] Michael Wilkinson, 'Political Constitutionalism and the European Union', *MLR* 76(2), 2013, p. 201

There is a lot to unpack here. Four facets of *novelty, independence, autonomy* and *primacy* will now be discussed in turn.

i.   Novelty – 'a new legal order of international law'

As discussed in Chapter 1, regional cooperation did not begin with the EEC. What then did the CJ mean by claiming that a 'new legal order' had been created by the Treaty of Rome? What was the 'old' order and how did the EEC differ from it? In what way was the EEC 'new'? In order to answer these questions, a basic understanding of the traditional system of international relations is required.

Since the Treaty of Westphalia in the mid-seventeenth century, the basic unit of global interaction has been the independent nation state. These vary in age from 7,000 years[8] to just a few years old.[9] The system of interaction and rules of cooperation between these states is laid out in international law. International law covers a broad range of activities ranging from behaviour during war (e.g. treatment of those wounded in war and war crimes) to treatment of citizens and residents in times of peace (e.g. non-discrimination and human rights). Treaties, conventions and covenants are documents by which states formally agree to avoid certain practices and actions, maintain a standard of behaviour or pursue a common goal. If under any Treaty an enforcement body or an organisation is created, it is the states who agree its aims and set out the tasks to be conducted to achieve those aims. A state must be 'sovereign' in order to agree such objectives. Despite being 'too vague and general to be a helpful decision-making tool',[10] the 'man-made concept' of sovereignty – the idea that a state is autonomous and may exercise its powers internally without interference by any other state – underpins international law.

Under international law, such agreements are voluntary – states agree to observe international norms rather than being obliged to do so. This means that each rule is only as binding as the individual state itself decides, except where this obligation is expressly stated. Joint action traditionally requires unanimity – the agreement of all contracting parties. However, a mark of full membership in the world society of nations is submission to international norms and codes – since the end of the Second World War, state sovereignty has been expressed through the voluntary limitation of sovereignty via membership in international organisations – sovereignty is asserted by its negation.[11] South Sudan will be expected to sign the major international treaties and instruments and in so doing will assert the legitimacy of its sovereignty via membership of the international community.

Furthermore as the signatories of agreements under international law are states, states are the subjects of international law, not the citizens within these states. Traditionally international law does not create rights which citizens can directly rely upon in their national courts. The relationship between national and international law is set out by the national legal system of the signatory state. In a *monist* system of law, national and international law form a single legal system; in a *dualist* system, international law remains separate to national law until incorporated by a domestic act.[12] Thus in monist

---

[8]Ethiopia

[9]South Sudan created 8 July 2011

[10]Sir Konrad Schiemann, 'Sovereignty: a concept creating confusion', paper delivered at the Matrix/ UKAEL seminar '40 Years On – the Sovereignty Debate', 7 March 2013

[11]John Rawls, *The Law of Peoples,* Harvard University Press, 1999

[12]John H. Jackson 'Status of Treaties in Domestic Legal Systems: a policy analysis', *American Journal of International Law* 86, 1992, pp. 310–340

states such as the Netherlands, citizens enjoy direct access to the rights contained in international agreements which that country has signed. In such monist systems, many international rules are directly applicable[13] before national courts. However, numerous other states are dualist – it is only via the creation of a separate national legal instrument that citizens may enjoy the rights provided in instruments of international law. Britain provides a good example of dualism in action. Britain was one of the first signatories of the European Convention on Human Rights (ECHR) agreed in 1950 yet British nationals had to wait until 1998 to enjoy the protection of this Convention. This is because the rights in the Convention could not be enjoyed until a statute created a 'bridge' for them to flow into the national legal system. This 'bridge' was the Human Rights Act of 1998 (HRA 1998). Likewise, the European Communities Act 1972 (ECA 1972) was the bridge for the enactment of EU law in the UK. In *van Gend,* the CJ claimed that law of the EEC could be monist, subject to conditions, because although a creation of international law, the Treaty creating it was more than a voluntary agreement establishing mutual obligations between sovereign states. This was its novelty.

Four justifications were given for this conclusion:

The first focused on the objective of the EEC – the ambition to create a common market suggested that the Rome Treaty was more than an 'old' international Treaty. This justification was clearly not strong enough – the WHO and NATO were also Treaty-based organisations with common objectives. A second justification therefore focused on the subjects of the agreement – in contrast to other international instruments, the Rome Treaty mentioned not only governments but also referred to the 'peoples' of Europe. Third, the Court argued that the EEC Treaty was different because it established 'institutions endowed with sovereign rights' that when exercised would affect both the state signatories and their citizens. This was a reference to, for example, the European Commission which had (and still has) exclusive responsibility for EU policy in areas such as competition law. Finally the Court noted that nationals of the member states are brought together in 'intermediary' bodies such as the European Parliament and the Economic and Social Committee (ECOSOC). These grounds are of varying tenacity, with perhaps the final one being the most questionable – the EP and ECOSOC were at that stage very limited in their role as intermediaries between the EEC and the member state nationals. It is appropriate that the court did not describe these as 'representative' bodies – members were appointed rather than elected.

VIEWPOINT

Find these four justifications in the case *van Gend en Loos* – which is the strongest argument for supremacy?

---

[13]Alicia Hinarejos, 'On the Legal Effects of Framework Decisions and Decisions: Directly Applicable, Directly Effective, Self-executing, Supreme?', *European Law Journal* 14(5), September 2008, pp. 620–634

These elements brought the CJ to the conclusion that the 'Community constitutes a new legal order of international law for the benefit of which the states have limited their sovereign rights'. Crucially the Court added a caveat – sovereign rights were reduced 'within limited fields' only. The subjects of this 'new legal order' were not just the state signatories, but also the nationals of the member states, and beyond this the institutions of the Community – all three levels bore obligations under the Treaty and enjoyed rights provided by it. This multi-level organisation is one of a kind.

This claim has had to be defended repeatedly. In 1991, in its opinion on the authority of the court of the European Economic Area (EEA) to rule on actions of the Community, the CJ re-asserted its argument that the EEC was not a traditional organisation under international law. It defended its position, claiming that an '. . . international Treaty is to be interpreted not only on the basis of its wording, but also in the light of its objectives'. This was the crux of its finding that the EEC and EEA were very different types of agreements and so very different types of organisations: the EEA agreement focused on proper application of rules on free trade and commercial competition between the state signatories whereas the EEC went beyond this. Its bold objective was to promote economic integration to establish an internal market, economic and monetary union and concrete steps towards unity in Europe.

Furthermore, the context of the two agreements differed:

> The European Economic Area is to be established on the basis of an international Treaty which merely creates rights and obligations as between the Contracting Parties and provides for no transfer of sovereign rights to the inter-governmental institutions which it sets up. In contrast, the EEC Treaty, albeit concluded in the form of an international agreement, none the less constitutes the constitutional charter of a Community based on the rule of law.

Thus identical wording does not result in identical organisations – the EEA is a traditional international organisation but the limitation of sovereign rights, the primacy of its law and direct effect means that the EEC was not.[14]

When considering the proposal for a unified Patents Court some 20 years later in 2011, the same reasoning was used:

> [65] It is apparent from the Court's settled case-law that the founding treaties of the European Union, unlike ordinary international treaties, established a new legal order, possessing its own institutions, for the benefit of which the States have limited their sovereign rights, in ever wider fields, and the subjects of which comprise not only Member States but also their nationals (see, inter alia, Case 26/62 *van Gend & Loos* [1963] ECR 1, 12 and Case 6/64 *Costa* [1964] ECR 585, 593). The essential characteristics of the European Union legal order thus constituted are in particular its primacy over the laws of the Member States and the direct effect of a whole series of provisions which are applicable to their nationals and to the Member States themselves (see Opinion 1/91 [1991] ECR I-6079, paragraph 21).[15]

---

[14]Opinion 1/91, 14 December 1991
[15]Draft Agreement on the European and Community Patents Court and Draft Statute Brussels, 23 March 2009, 7928/09/ PI 23 COUR 29. The CJ found it incompatible in Opinion 1/09 of the Court (Full Court) on the creation of a European and Community Patents Court, 8 March 2011.

ANALYSING THE LAW

Read Opinion 1/91 and summarise the ways in which the EEA differs from the EEC according to the CJEU.

The consequences of this 'novelty' were not explored. The CJ did not explain how this 'new' form of international law in the EU related to traditional international law. In subsequent case law, the CJ asserted that the EU was not bound by international law. In *Commission* v *Luxembourg and Belgium*[16] it ruled that member states are obliged to fulfil their obligations under international law even if the EU institutions did not. In *Germany* v *Council*,[17] it ruled that a Union regulation cannot be declared invalid simply because it is contrary to an international Treaty which is binding on the EU: the Treaty must be directly effective in EU law before the Court will take account of it. Thus in relation to 'old' forms of international law, EU law is strictly dualist.

The relationship between these 'new' and 'old' international legal orders came to the fore in *Kadi and Al Barakaat*[18] which has been described as the 'most important judgment ever delivered by the ECJ on the relationship between Community and international law'.[19] It concerned the application of United Nations Security Council (UNSC) counter-terrorism measures, in particular 'smart' sanctions used to freeze the assets of states and persons suspected of involvement in terrorist activities.

Before the collapse of the Taliban in Afghanistan, the UNSC adopted two resolutions requiring all UN member states to freeze the funds and other financial resources owned or controlled by the Taliban and its associates. The Security Council also set up a Sanctions Committee which compiled a list of persons and entities whose funds would be frozen pursuant to the UN resolutions. In order to implement these resolutions, the Council of Ministers of the EU adopted two common positions under what was then the intergovernmental Pillar Two of the TEU (CFSP). These positions, because they were adopted as intergovernmental not Community measures, were implemented by two regulations. The legal basis for these regulations was Articles 60 and 301 EC [Articles 75 and 215 TFEU]. These are special provisions which enabled action to achieve the objectives of the Union (rather than the Community). Article 60 EC [Article 75 TFEU] conferred competence for urgent action on capital movements concerning third countries, and Article 301 EC [Article 215 TFEU] set out the use of qualified majority voting in Community action on foreign and security matters that concerned economic relations with third countries (i.e. state entities)

After the collapse of the Taliban regime, the Security Council adopted two further resolutions which also provided for the freezing of funds but, this time, they were directed against bin Laden, members of the Al-Qaeda network, and the Taliban (i.e. non-state entities).

---

[16]C-90,91/63 *Commission* v *Luxembourg and Belgium* [1964] ECR 625.
[17]C-280/93 *Germany* v *Council* [1994] ECR I-4973.
[18]C-402/05P and C-415/05P Kadi and Al Barakaat v Council and Commission (Kadi I) [2008] ECR I-6351
[19]Takis Tridimas, 'Terrorism and the ECJ: empowerment and democracy in the EC legal order', *ELR* 34(1), 2009, p. 103; Jorge Godhino, 'When Worlds Collide: Enforcing United Nations Security Council Asset Freezes in the EU Legal Order', *European Law Journal* 16(1), January 2010, pp. 67–93

As they no longer controlled the government of Afghanistan, these resolutions therefore targeted solely non-state actors, in other words, private parties. Thus when these resolutions were implemented at EU level an additional legal basis had to be identified to accommodate the fact that these measures targeted individuals. Article 308 EC [Article 352 TFEU], the residual clause, was used to fill the competence gap. These three Treaty provisions – Articles 60, 301 and 308 EC – were used as the legal basis upon which the Council of Ministers adopted two new CFSP common positions and regulations.[20]

In *Kadi and Al Barakaat*, the applicants were, respectively, a Saudi Arabian national and a Swedish national who had been included in the lists drawn up by the UN Sanctions Committee and in the lists incorporated in implementing Community regulations. They brought proceedings before the General Court (GC) seeking the annulment of those regulations, alleging breach of their fundamental rights, namely, the right to a fair hearing, the right to respect for property, and the right for effective judicial review. They challenged the application of the regulations, and whether the EU had authority to apply 'smart' sanctions which imposed punitive economic measures upon individuals as opposed to states.

Authority, or competence, was therefore the first issue that the CJEU had to grapple with. Advocate General Maduro identified sufficient legal authority in Articles 215 and 75 TFEU [ex 301 and 60 EC]. However, the General Court and the CJ found that the contested sanctions could only be adopted on the combined legal basis of what are now Articles 215, 75 and 352 TFEU. They reached this conclusion on the basis of different reasoning. The General Court reasoned that since the sanctions targeted individuals who were neither associated with the incumbent government nor had links with a particular territory, there was no sufficient link between the targeted individuals and a third country and, therefore, Articles 215 and 75 TFEU could not by themselves empower the Community to impose sanctions. It considered, nevertheless, that Community competence could be established with the assistance of Article 352 TFEU [ex 308 EC] as a joint legal basis. For the CJ, however, this would be an incorrect application: this provision was not designed to expand the competences of the EU but only to attain its objectives. Articles 75 and 215 TFEU established the objectives, and it was for the purpose of attaining these objectives that Article 352 TFEU was adduced to the reasoning.

APPLYING THE LAW

Read Article 352 TFEU – summarise the way in which it should be used.

Upon reflection, there is little that is pluralist[21] in this decision. Kelsen would describe it as 'solipsistic and imperialistic': the former that because it sees only the EU legal system and the latter because it views the world from its perspective alone.[22] All of the reasoning has been criticised as, among other things, an unconvincing leap of faith:

---

[20]Implemented respectively by Regulations 881/2002/12 and 561/2003/13.
[21]Giorgi and Triart, 'National Judges, Community Judges: Invitation to a Journey through the Looking-glass', *European Law Journal* 14(6), 2008, p. 693
[22]Kunoy and Dawes, 'Plate Tectonics in Luxembourg', *CMLR* 46(1), 2009, p. 73

The judgment aptly illustrates that, given the integration potential of the EC Treaty, the division of powers between the Community and the Member States remains inherently unstable. As in many previous occasions, the ECJ errs on the side of Community competence on the basis of an instrumental rationale which, in terms of formal reasoning, remains somewhat unconvincing.[23]

Godhino condemns the sanctions as an 'ad hoc (para-)criminal procedure measure, a form of crime prevention and repression, against non-state actors'[24] enacted by political bodies rather than courts, and without judicial oversight. *Kadi* highlights the fundamental dilemma within this facet of novelty: the EU is a new order of international law but does it have the 'original power' or 'ultimate authority'[25] to determine its relationship to international law. Novelty is limited by the fact that the EU can only act within the framework of conferred powers.

ii.   Independence

According to the CJ in *van Gend,* the rights and obligations enjoyed in the Community by nationals, states and EU institutions not only existed, but existed 'independently of the legislation of MS'. The CJ gave clear indication of the relevance of this when it introduced a new *version* of 'direct effect'. Direct effect was itself not new – monist member states acknowledged that international law could have direct effect in national law, while dualist states did not. However, the existence of such direct effects was usually a decision for the national legal system rather than the international organisation. In adopting this characteristic for EU law, the CJ reversed this relationship and then asserted that the 'new legal order' was self-sufficient and self-sustaining: it did not need to rely on national law to give it effect but could *of itself* 'produce direct effects'. This self-determination of direct effect was an exercise of the independent power claimed by the CJ for EU law.

The principle of the possibility of direct effect was the key question put to the CJ in *van Gend* by the *Tariefcommissie* (the Tariff Commission in the Dutch legal system). It asked whether Article 25 TFEU 'has direct application in national law in the sense that nationals of member states may on the basis of this Article lay claim to rights which the national court must protect'.

Various arguments were presented by the intervening states and the European Commission: on the one hand, the Belgian government argued that *van Gend* presented a typical problem of constitutional law relating to a conflict between two international treaties that fell to be determined under Dutch national law according to its constitutional principles and jurisprudence – the question of direct effect did not even arise. On the other hand, the Commission and the company van Gend argued that the question of the effect of Community law on national law in the member states could not be determined according to the national law of each but had to be settled by the Treaty itself.

---

[23]Tridimas 2009, p. 14. See also C. Eckes, *EU Counter-terrorism Policies and Fundamental Rights: The Case of Individual Sanctions,* Oxford University Press, 2009; Stein and Halberstam, 'The United Nations, the European Union, and the King of Sweden: Economic Sanctions and Individual Rights in a Plural World Order', *Common Market Law Review* 46(1), 2009

[24]Godhino 2010, p. 77

[25]Jo Murkens, 'The Future of Staatsrecht: Dominance, Demise or Demystification?', *MLR* 70(5), 2007, pp. 731–758

The CJ replied that, under certain conditions, provisions of EU law could of their own volition be powerful enough to provide rights that individuals could claim before their national courts. This applied to Article 25 which contained a 'clear and unconditional prohibition which is not a positive but a negative obligation' and moreover was not dependent for implementation upon a national legal measure. Consequently, it held that 'the very nature of this prohibition makes it ideally adapted to produce direct effects in the legal relationship between member states and their subjects'.

With this determination, the CJ not only changed the nature of the Treaty of Rome, but also radically altered its relationship with national law: the existence of direct effects became determined by the EU rather than the member states, and furthermore by the judges in the CJ rather than in the national courts or legislatures. The doctrine of direct effect not only impacted upon the prerogatives of national legal codes, but also challenged the decision-making role of national legislatures – dualist nations in particular lost some of their power to determine when and how a provision of EU law would have effect domestically, and with it the ability to 'express the norms in accordance with local usage'.[26] In *van Gend* and subsequently, the Court made a series of decisions whereby all member state legal systems became monist if the conditions for direct effect are fulfilled. For example in the case of *Costa*,[27] the CJ described Article 49 TFEU on freedom of establishment as 'legally complete in itself' and consequently 'capable of producing direct effects on the relations between member states and individuals'. The court again asserted that the Treaty of Rome 'created its own legal system' which upon entry into force became integral to the legal systems of the member states.

The self-determination of direct effect[28] is arguably the clearest sign that EU law is a 'new system of international law' – even before the introduction of EU citizenship in 1992, this transformed the EEC into a new type of international organisation. However, at the same time in the 1960s, elements of the old international norms continued in other parts of the EEC. For example, voting in the Council of Ministers, thanks to General de Gaulle, remained on the basis of unanimity, the traditional method of agreement within international organisations where each state decides for itself and all must agree for action to be adopted. EU law may have asserted its independence, but in EU politics the 'old' system of international law – whereby each member state had a single vote and all heads of government had to agree for any measure to be adopted – continued to prevail.

Examples of the co-existence of old and new forms of international law are visible today. Intergovernmental practices, areas where the member states must all agree for action to be adopted, fall under the former whereas supranational practices organised according to majority decision-making fall under the latter. EU citizenship is a supranational policy area, while Common Foreign and Security Policy (CFSP) remains intergovernmental. The ideas of intergovernmentalism and supranationalism are not, however, fixed categories – areas of policy-making move from one to the other (though predominantly in the direction of intergovernmental to supranational: it is rare to see examples of the reverse). The Schengen Agreement is one example of this.

However, independence is not always absolute and in the case of the EU one needs to consider how this might be constrained. For example, the EU is not self-sufficient in terms

---

[26]Jackson 1992, p. 324
[27]C-6/64 *Costa* v *ENEL* [1964] ECR 585, [1964] CMLR 425
[28]Elise Muir, 'Of Ages in and Edges of EU Law', *Common Market Law Review* 48(1), 2011

of enforcement – secondary legislation and judicial determination under the preliminary ruling or infringement procedures require implementation at the national level. The EU is therefore to a large extent dependent upon national authorities for the practical exercise of its judicial and political authority. This is especially clear to see in the realm of competition law, where the recent modernisation specifically delegated enforcement to national administrative and judicial authorities.[29]

VIEWPOINT

To what extent do you think that the EU legal order can be independent if it depends upon the national institutions for application and enforcement of its norms?[30]

---

iii. Autonomy

In declaring the independence of the EEC legal order, the CJ also claimed that the EEC constituted an autonomous entity. In *van Gend,* the Court held that by signing the Treaty, and 'assigning to the Court of Justice the task of securing uniform interpretation of the Treaty by national courts and tribunals', the signatories not only acknowledged that EU law had an authority of its own, but also one that could be invoked by member state nationals before courts and tribunals in the member states. Thus the founders did not intend to remove the application of EU law from the national courts of law but they did intend to establish an autonomous system of EU law. Autonomy was necessary for that law to be applied effectively and uniformly throughout the EU.

Real power was adduced to this authority in *Costa,*[31] a case which arose in Italy when Mr Flaminio Costa refused to pay his electricity bill to ENEL – he argued that its nationalisation breached EU competition rules on state aids. The Italian authorities viewed this as a matter for national law rather than EU law and held that the preliminary reference made under Article 267 TFEU by the Italian judge to the CJ was inadmissible (see Chapter 4 for discussion of Article 267 TFEU). The Court replied to this overt challenge to its jurisdiction with a declaration that, in voluntarily pooling their resources to create a common market, the signatory member states had permanently limited their sovereign rights:

> By contrast with ordinary international treaties, the EEC Treaty has created its own legal system which, on the entry into force of the Treaty became an integral part of the legal systems of the member states and which their courts are bound to apply. By creating a community of unlimited duration, having its own institutions, its own personality, its own legal capacity and capacity of representation on the international plane and, more particularly, real powers stemming from a limitation of sovereignty or a transfer of powers from the states to the community, the member states have limited their sovereign rights and have thus created a body of law which binds both

---

[29]See Regulation 1/2003
[30]Ines Weyland, 'The Application of Kelsen's Theory of the Legal System to European Community Law: the Supremacy Puzzle Resolved', *Law and Philosophy* 21, 2002, pp. 1–37
[31]C-6/64 *Flaminio Costa v ENEL* [1964] ECR 585

their nationals and themselves . . . The transfer by the states from their domestic legal system to the Community legal system of the rights and obligations arising under the Treaty carries with it a permanent limitation of their sovereign rights.

A fundamental question raised by this assertion of a new legal order was one of political leadership – who were the 'masters of the Treaty'[32] if it were no longer an ordinary international Treaty? How was a non-ordinary Treaty to be understood – as a Constitution, a Convention, a Memorandum of Understanding? If it were a special Treaty, what was the meaning of the conferral of powers in Article 5 TEU which stated – and still states – that the community '. . . shall act only within limits of the powers conferred upon by this Treaty and of the objectives assigned to it therein'? Article 13(2) TEU [ex Article 7 EC] clearly gives each institution authority to act only 'within the limits of the powers conferred upon it by this Treaty'. Clearly, the founder states did not give the Community power to disempower them, thus if final political authority had been transferred as declared, the question which has occupied many scholars is – by what means?

The CJEU seemed to assert that after this conferral a 'big bang' had occurred which released the EEC and its institutions from its founders. Just as an exploding star can create a new planet with its own atmosphere and ecosystem, the EEC changed from a dependent international organisation[33] to an independent self-referential supranational organisation.[34] 'Signatory states' became 'member states' and the rotation reversed: the EEC did not revolve around the member states, but in some spheres the member states revolved around the EEC. This therefore challenged the traditional direction of authority in international law: who were the 'masters' of this new planet? Who had 'competence-competence', that is ultimate power to allocate authority to declare or to determine the limits of the competences of the new Community?[35]

The 'big bang' theory of EU law, whereby it 'emancipated'[36] itself from both international law and national constitutional law, and became supreme over both remains controversial. Is it tenable for EU law to adopt a legal hierarchy that is based on positive constitutional law (rules of validity and recognition), but as seen in *Kadi* rejects subordination of EU law to international law? For many authors the answer is a strong 'no' – this inversion of authority subsequent to its legitimate creation is unsustainable. Such an entity, it is argued, has no source of authority. An international organisation derives its legitimacy from its constituent member states; a nation state derives its legitimacy from its citizens – neither of these sources explain the legitimacy of the EU:

. . . the doctrine in this sense is self-defeating: it cannot be both legally binding and create a new basis for legal validity [. . .] The new legal order cannot be validated by

[32]'Herren der Vertraege'
[33]J.H.H. Weiler and Ulrich R. Haltern, 'The Autonomy of the Community Legal Order –Through the Looking Glass', *Harvard International Law Journal* 37, 1996, p. 411
[34]Jiri Priban, 'The Self-Referential European Polity, its Legal Context and Systemic Differentiation: Theoretical Reflections on the Emergence of the EU's Political and Legal Autopoiesis', *European Law Journal* 15(4), July 2009, pp. 442–461
[35]Weiler and Haltern, 1996, p. 411
[36]Christoph U. Schmid, 'Ways Out of the Acquis Communitaire On Simplification and Consolidation and the Need for a Restatement of European Primary Law', European University Institute, Working Paper RSC No 99/6, May 1999, p. 8

reference to the old, because the new legal order cannot be recognised as it wants to be by the old: the presuppositions in the old order cannot facilitate this . . . It is the very presuppositions and procedures, which we take for granted, of the old order that need to be questioned: it seems then that the only way out of the vicious circle [of sovereignty and constitutionalism] is to begin to consider the legal order . . . from without as an institutional and political artifice.[37]

VIEWPOINT

Read the Eleftheriadis quote again – do you agree that the 'new' EU legal order cannot be recognised by the 'old'?

---

iv. Primacy

A far-reaching consequence of the autonomy of EU law is the idea of primacy. According to this doctrine, EU law takes priority over any conflicting national law. Also when the legality of a Union measure is challenged, the CJEU makes the final determination not the highest courts of the member states. Autonomy is a prerequisite of primacy – in the absence of independent authority, EU law would not be able to displace national law. Prior to the Declaration attached to the Lisbon Treaty, primacy was not found in any EU treaty.

The idea was not explicitly mentioned by the CJ in *van Gend* – it only stressed the duty of the national courts to protect individual rights created by directly effective provisions in the Treaty. Primacy is only mentioned in passing by the Commission, when it noted that 'the national court is bound to ensure that the rules of Community law prevail over conflicting national laws even if they are passed later'.[38] This sentence sowed the seeds of the 'primacy' of EU law.

The CJ first discussed the substance of primacy in *Costa,* when it highlighted the negative consequences that would arise if a national law could take precedence over EU law. It argued that this would undermine the goal of the common market. The reasoning began by situating provisions of EU law in the text and spirit of the Treaty – this source made it impossible for the member states to:

. . . accord precedence to a unilateral and subsequent measure over a legal system accepted by them on a basis of reciprocity . . . the executive force of Community law cannot vary from one state to another in deference to subsequent domestic laws without jeopardising the attainment of the objectives of the Treaty . . .

It would transform the obligations in the Treaty into contingent rather than unconditional undertakings if the member states could avoid or evade them by introducing legislative acts. Although it was originally suggested that primacy applied

---

[37]Pavlos Eleftheriadis, 'Begging the Constitutional Question', *JCMS,* 36(2), June 1998, pp. 255–272
[38]*Van Gend* [7]

only to regulations, primacy in fact attaches to all forms of EU law stemming from the Treaty:

> . . . It follows from all these observations that the law stemming from the Treaty, an independent source of law, could not, because of its special and original nature, be overridden by domestic legal provisions, however framed, without being deprived of its character as community law and without the legal basis of the community itself being called into question . . .

This indicates the potency of primacy: it applies to all national laws, regardless of their longevity or stature in national law (constitutional or otherwise).

ANALYSING THE LAW

Read Article 3 TEU and the preceding extracts from the *Costa* case. How convincing do you find this justification, bearing in mind the objectives of the Treaty laid out in Article 3 TEU?

The total reach of primacy was stated explicitly in *Internationale Handelsgesellschaft*.[39] The case arose due to a dispute over the system of deposits established by an agricultural regulation designed to manage the EU market in cereals, rice and their derivative products. A German trader had lost his deposit payment due to failure to fulfil the obligation to export these products. When the German administrative court was called upon to settle the dispute between two German companies, it decided that the system of deposits was invalid because it was contrary to principles protected in the German constitution, namely freedom of action, economic liberty and proportionality. These principles, the national court argued, had to be 'protected within the framework of community law, with the result that the primacy of supranational law must yield before the principles of the German basic law'. This was not posed as a question, but stated as fact. The CJ robustly retorted that 'in fact' EU law overrides all national, including constitutional, law:

> The validity of measures adopted by the institutions of the community can only be judged in the light of community law. The law stemming from the Treaty, an independent source of law, cannot because of its very nature be overridden by rules of national law, however framed, without being deprived of its character as community law and without the legal basis of the community itself being called in question. Therefore the validity of a community measure or its effect within a member state cannot be affected by allegations that it runs counter to either fundamental rights as formulated by the constitution of that state or the principles of its constitutional structure.

Primacy was justified as necessary to protect the 'uniformity and efficacy of Community law'. In restating this, the Court did not answer any question posed by the German court: it had not asked about primacy but about the legality of the system of deposits. When the CJ did get to this question, it defended the deposit system as proportionate on the

---

[39] C-11/70 Internationale Handelsgesellschaft mbH / Einfuhr- und Vorratsstelle für Getreide und Futtermittel [1970] ECR 1125

basis that it was a necessary and effective management tool, which was activated by the voluntary undertaking of the applicant trader. Alternative tools, such as a system of fines or 'mere declaration' by a trader would not be adequate for the task.

In a more conciliatory mode, however, the Court did introduce a new idea to EU law. In recognition of the legitimate German concern for protection of fundamental rights, it discovered again that 'in fact, respect for fundamental rights forms an integral part of the general principles of law protected by the court of justice' and that the protection of such rights was 'ensured' within the structure and objectives of the EU:

> Respect for fundamental rights forms an integral part of the general principles of law protected by the court of justice. The protection of such rights, while inspired by the constitutional traditions common to the member states, must be ensured within the framework of the structure and objectives of the community.

This passing remark arguably marked the start of a journey which has culminated in the EU Charter of Fundamental Rights and EU accession to the European Convention on Human Rights (ECHR). This may no longer be possible as the CJEU has found accession to the Convention incompatible with Union law. See Opinion 2/13 on EU Accession; commentary available at eutopialaw.com.

The immediate primacy of EU law over all forms of national law was repeated in *Simmenthal*.[40] In 1976 a lower Italian court, the *preture di susa*, sent a question to the CJ asking if national fees levied on meat imports under an Italian law of 1970 were compatible with the Treaty and a directly applicable EU regulation adopted in 1968. The Court had ruled that such fees were incompatible[41] whereupon the concerned Italian finance administration had refused to refund the unlawful fees and appealed the order made by the *preture*. This was therefore a conflict arising due to the application of an older EU law and a subsequent national law.

According to *van Gend*, EU law must be applied in such a situation. The matter was, however, further complicated because under the national judicial hierarchy, the *pretore di susa* could not itself declare the national law inapplicable. It had to refer the case to the Italian constitutional court for it to do so. The *pretore* therefore asked the CJ what it should do: should it follow the national procedure thereby leaving the national law in effect or should it act immediately and disregard the incompatible national law?

Despite the fact that the Italian Constitutional Court had already declared the problematic national legal provisions unconstitutional, the CJ took the opportunity to set out the consequences of a conflict between a directly applicable provision of EU law[42] and subsequent national legislation. In such a situation, the impact was clear: 'rules of Community law must be fully and uniformly applied in all the member states from the date of their entry into force and for so long as they continue in force'. This impact flowed into any case before any court. Further consequences flowed from the principle of primacy and its automatic displacement of conflicting provisions:

> [17] [F]urthermore, in accordance with the principle of the precedence of community law, the relationship between provisions of the Treaty and directly applicable measures of the

---

[40]C-106/77 *Amministrazione delle Finanze dello Stato v Simmenthal SpA* [1978] ECR 629
[41]C-35/76 *Simmenthal SPA v Itlaian Minister for Finance* [1976] ECR 1871
[42]See also Council Regulation 805/68 on the special and general intervention measures for beef

institutions on the one hand and the national law of the member states on the other is such that those provisions and measures not only by their entry into force render automatically inapplicable any conflicting provision of current national law but – in so far as they are an integral part of, and take precedence in, the legal order applicable in the territory of each of the member states – also preclude the valid adoption of new national legislative measures to the extent to which they would be incompatible with community provisions.

The Court equated the legal effect of incompatible national measures with a deliberate flouting of obligations undertaken by the member states. Such action was fatally damaging to the common market:

[18] [I]ndeed any recognition that national legislative measures which encroach upon the field within which the community exercises its legislative power or which are otherwise incompatible with the provisions of community law had any legal effect would amount to a corresponding denial of the effectiveness of obligations undertaken unconditionally and irrevocably by member states pursuant to the Treaty and would thus imperil the very foundations of the community.

It therefore concluded that all national courts were to apply EU law and where necessary set aside any conflicting national law, regardless of any existing national 'legislative, administrative or judicial practice':

[21] It follows from the foregoing that every national court must, in a case within its jurisdiction, apply community law in its entirety and protect rights which the latter confers on individuals and must accordingly set aside any provision of national law which may conflict with it, whether prior or subsequent to the community rule.

[22] Accordingly any provision of a national legal system and any legislative, administrative or judicial practice which might impair the effectiveness of community law by withholding from the national court having jurisdiction to apply such law the power to do everything necessary at the moment of its application to set aside national legislative provisions which might prevent community rules from having full force and effect are incompatible with those requirements which are the very essence of community law.

In cases of conflict, EU law therefore took precedence over all forms of national law. The CJ instructed national courts to ignore national rules which prevented the effectiveness of EU law and the enjoyment of EU rights. National courts are placed under a direct obligation to act on its behalf and give full and immediate effect to EU law, if necessary refusing to apply any conflicting provisions of national law, even if adopted subsequently to the Treaty. Primacy also applies to national procedures: a national court is not to 'request or await the prior setting aside of such provisions by legislative or other constitutional means'.

a) *Factortame*

Primacy reaches deep into national legal cultures. If EU law requires a specific outcome, national law must be changed to achieve this. A good example of this is the case of *Factortame*. In 1989, the British House of Lords (the predecessor to the UK Supreme Court) referred two questions arising in a case brought against the Secretary of State for Transport by a group of predominantly Spanish national appellants that included Factortame Ltd and a number of other companies incorporated in the UK. These companies owned or operated fishing vessels which flew the British flag, as they were listed in the register of British vessels as required by the Merchant Shipping Act 1894. By virtue of this registration, the companies had access to the UK fishing quotas. However, as the vessels were owned or operated by non-nationals without genuine links to the UK, the UK authorities suspected these companies of 'quota hopping' or flying the British flag solely to access UK fish stocks.

In 1988, the UK amended the Merchant Shipping Act to address this problem. The system was radically altered[43] to establish eligibility conditions – only fishing vessels that fulfilled these could register in the UK. The conditions, laid out in section 14 of the 1988 Act, required that the vessel be first, British owned; second, managed, directed and controlled from within the UK; and third, that the manager, operator or user of the vessel be a 'qualified' person (a British citizen resident or domiciled in the UK) or a 'qualified' company (incorporated in the UK and conducting most of its business there, with at least 75 per cent of shares owned by qualified persons and at least 75 per cent of directors being qualified persons). These nationality conditions also applied to those vessels previously entered in the old general register. They were impossible for the appellants to satisfy: as they could not be registered, they would be deprived of fishing rights from 1 April 1989.

The companies challenged the compatibility of Part II of the 1988 Act with EU law and in order to protect their livelihood in the meantime, applied for the grant of interim relief pending judgment on their application. In August 1989, the Commission also brought an infringement action under Article 228 TFEU and likewise applied to the CJ for an interim order to require the UK to suspend the application of the nationality conditions to the nationals of other member states and in respect of fishing vessels that prior to 31 March 1989 conducted a fishing activity under the British flag and fishing licence. The interim order was granted in October 1989[44] and following this the UK amended section 14 of the 1988 Act with effect from 2 November 1989.

Prior to this, there had been significant discussion in the national courts on whether under *national* law British courts possessed power to suspend, by way of interim relief, the application of Acts of Parliament. The Divisional Court of the Queen's Bench Division thought this was possible and suspended the new rules; the Court of Appeal disagreed and overturned this decision. The House of Lords, while recognising that the appellants' claims were well founded, held that the grant of the relief requested was precluded by a common law rule that an interim injunction may not be granted against the government. However, this was the position under national law – the position under EU law might be different.

Thus the House of Lords used Article 267 TFEU to ask the CJ questions on the extent of the power of national courts to grant interim relief where rights claimed under EU law are at issue. Essentially, the highest UK court asked the CJ to ascertain whether a national court must disapply a national rule if in a case concerning EU law that national rule is the sole obstacle preventing it from granting interim relief. The CJ began by repeating its reasoning in *Simmenthal* and then continued that:

[21] It must be added that the full effectiveness of Community law would be just as much impaired if a rule of national law could prevent a court seised of a dispute governed by Community law from granting interim relief in order to ensure the full

---

[43]Part II of the Merchant Shipping Act 1988 and the Merchant Shipping (Registration of Fishing Vessels) Regulations 1988, SI 1988, No 1926
[44]C-246/89 R *Commission v United Kingdom* [1989] ECR 3125

effectiveness of the judgment to be given on the existence of the rights claimed under Community law. It follows that a court which in those circumstances would grant interim relief, if it were not for a rule of national law, is obliged to set aside that rule.

It buttressed this reasoning by invoking the effectiveness of the preliminary reference system, which it claimed would be undermined if a national court having sent a question could not then suspend any legal effects until it had received a reply from the CJ to inform its judgment.[45] Thus the primacy of EU law also requires that a national law be set aside in cases concerning EU law, even where this is not possible under national law.

This reasoning applies equally to situations concerning enforcement of a national measure implementing EU law. In *Zuckerfabrik*, the CJ held that it would compromise the right of individuals to challenge Union acts in the national courts if such disputed acts could not be made inoperative while a decision is awaited. However, in this circumstance additional conditions must be satisfied:

[33] . . . suspension of enforcement of a national measure adopted in implementation of a Community regulation may be granted by a national court only: (i) if that court entertains serious doubts as to the validity of the Community measure and, should the question of the validity of the contested measure not already have been brought before the Court, itself refers that question to the Court; (ii) if there is urgency and a threat of serious and irreparable damage to the applicant; (iii) and if the national court takes due account of the Community's interests.[46]

ANALYSING THE LAW

Why is interim relief necessary to secure the effectiveness of EU law according to the CJ?

---

b) Declarations of invalidity?

Primacy therefore empowers national courts to examine an EU act for validity and immediately disapply national law. They may not conversely declare EU law invalid – this role is reserved for the CJEU alone. The use of EU law to declare national law invalid did not also create a power to declare EU law invalid. The CJEU monopoly on declarations of invalidity is set out in *Foto-Frost*,[47] a case concerning the recovery of duties paid by a firm importing binoculars from former East Germany into West Germany. The case turned upon whether duties had not been levied because of an error on the part of Foto-Frost or of the German authorities: if the latter, no payment would be due according to Council Regulation 1697/79.

The German tax office seized of the dispute decided that it was their mistake and duly requested a fee waiver from the Commission via the Finance Minister. The Commission

---

[45][22]
[46]C-143/88 and C-92/89, *Zuckerfabrik Süderdithmarschen v Hauptzollamt Itzehoe* and *Zuckerfabrik Soest GmbH v Hauptzollamt Paderborn* (1991) ECR I-415 [16, 17 & 33]. See also C-465/93 *Atlanta Fruchthandelsgesellschaft and Others v Bundesamt für Ernährung und Forstwirtschaft* (1995) ECR I-3761; and C-68/95 *T. Port GmbH & Co. KG v Bundesanstalt für Landwirtschaft und Ernährung* (1996) ECR I-6065
[47]C-314/85 Foto-Frost v Hauptzollamt Lübeck-Ost [1987] ECR 1987 4199

refused the fee waiver. When told of this decision, Foto-Frost appealed before the German finance court. The German finance court disagreed with the Commission decision, but was unsure what to do about it. It therefore sent a request for a preliminary ruling to the CJ: its first question was whether a national court can review a Commission decision and declare it invalid. The CJ acknowledged that this had not been answered in the Treaty – while Article 267 TFEU allows for a judicial dialogue between national courts and the CJ, and allows them to consider and decide upon the validity of EU acts, it did not 'settle the question whether those courts themselves may declare that acts of community institutions are invalid'.[48]

Decisions on validity by the national court are permissible because this does not call into question the existence of the measure but the CJ decided that national courts do not have the power to declare acts of the community institutions invalid.[49] The Court argued that this division of powers was necessary to ensure the standardisation of EU law throughout the member states and also to establish a single logic underpinning judicial protection in the EU:

> [15] . . . The main purpose of the powers accorded to the court by Article 177 is to ensure that community law is applied uniformly by national courts. That requirement of uniformity is particularly imperative when the validity of a community act is in question. Divergences between courts in the member states as to the validity of community acts would be liable to place in jeopardy the very unity of the community legal order and detract from the fundamental requirement of legal certainty.
>
> [16] The same conclusion is dictated by consideration of the necessary coherence of the system of judicial protection established by the Treaty. In that regard it must be observed that requests for preliminary rulings, like actions for annulment, constitute means for reviewing the legality of acts of the community institutions . . .
>
> [17] Since Article 173 gives the court exclusive jurisdiction to declare void an act of a community institution, the coherence of the system requires that where the validity of a community act is challenged before a national court the power to declare the act invalid must also be reserved to the court of justice.

The Court also argued that it was in the 'best position' to decide on the validity of Community acts as it collected the information relevant to a decision from both Community institutions and member states. Its answer was therefore wider than the question set: national courts not only had no jurisdiction to declare a Commission decision invalid – they had no authority to declare *any* Community act invalid.

APPLYING THE LAW

Can the German Constitutional Court declare the Greek bail-out invalid?

---

[48][13]
[49][15]

More recently the CJEU confirmed that any dispute concerning the Treaty must be brought before it.[50] Under Article 292 EC [now Article 344 TFEU], Member States 'undertake not to submit a dispute concerning the interpretation or application of this Treaty to any method of settlement other than those provided for therein.' The CJEU has interpreted this provision to assert exclusive jurisdiction in disputes between the member states that involve EU law. An international agreement does not interfere with this. In the *MOX* case, Ireland was found to have violated its obligations under this Article by taking its dispute with the UK before a UN tribunal rather than the CJEU.[51] The claim of exclusive jurisdiction is a continuation of the logic of *Foto-Frost*:

> As the Court of Justice considers itself to be the ultimate guardian of protecting the autonomy of the Community legal order, the protection of its exclusive jurisdiction is of crucial importance. The Court of Justice's strategy to achieve this aim is three-fold. First, extending its jurisdiction regarding mixed agreements and imposing on the Member States a duty of prior information. Secondly, limiting the right of the Member States to choose a dispute settlement system of their choice. Thirdly, pre-empting the exercise of jurisdiction of other international courts and tribunals in cases that potentially involve Community law.

In 2009, primacy was mentioned for the first time in a Declaration attached to the TFEU which simply states that:

> The Conference recalls that, in accordance with well settled case law of the EU Court of Justice, the Treaties and the law adopted by the Union on the basis of the Treaties have primacy over the law of Member States, under the conditions laid down by the said case law.[52]

Primacy is therefore now visible but the further relevance of this Declaration is unclear – is it part of EU law? This would have been the case had it been left in the body of the Treaty, as initially suggested, or if it had been annexed as a protocol.[53] What difference does it make that it is a Declaration? These are in principle non-binding, which makes them easier to negotiate.[54] Indeed, according to the House of Lords, the Declaration makes very little substantive difference: the IGC simply reasserted the primacy of EU law under the conditions laid down by the said case law. Consequently the House of Lords concluded that '. . . the affirmation of this principle in the Declaration does not give it any meaning that it has not previously had: it is a statement of the existing position.'[55] The Declaration changed nothing – it is simply a summary of the idea of the primacy of EU law.

---

[50]C-459/03 Commission v Ireland [2006] ECR I-4635
[51]Nikolaos Lavranos (Case Comment), 'The scope of the exclusive jurisdiction of the Court of Justice', *European Law Review* 32, 2007
[52]Declaration 27 Lisbon Treaty on Primacy of EU Law
[53]Under EU law, protocols have equivalent status to Treaty provisions.
[54]Suzanne Kingston, 'Ireland's options after the Lisbon referendum: strategies, implications and competing visions of Europe', *European Law Review* 34(3), 2009, pp. 455–475
[55]House of Lords Select Committee on European Union, Tenth Report, 2008, Chapter 4, para 4.174

Giorgi and Triart argue that the key to reconciliation of national sovereignty and primacy is for jurists and authorities in the EU and member states to take a fresh look at both – the EU and the national authorities need to move beyond their own perspectives to avoid a sterile stalemate:[56]

> The use by the ECJ of the principle of primacy in relations between the Community legal order and national legal orders provides an illustration of the difficulty in taking account of the validity of perspectives different from one's own. This goes as well for the national jurisdictions which resist the idea of the intrinsic supremacy of Community law, preferring to find the source of this primacy in their own legal order. The national and Community jurisdictions seem, from a theoretical point of view, locked in sterile opposition.

Giorgi and Triart advocate a new way of thinking about legal systems that is heterarchical and pluralist – relationships that are multiple, equal and non-hierarchical, freed from monist viewpoints:

> Now, our objective is to highlight the existence of a plurality of perspectives in intersystemic relations expressing potentially conflicting pretensions, if we understand that each jurisdiction has remained, until now, locked into its monist straitjacket, the push to move beyond the impasse must thus come from the researcher: it is for him, like Alice, to go through the looking-glass. In fact, in *Through the Looking-Glass*, Lewis Carroll up-ends the established order of Alice, in making her penetrate an upside-down world, where she must run to stand still, and is offered a cake when she complains of unquenchable thirst. We thus invite you to penetrate this new world, whether the codes splinter, where monism will no longer be law, where supremacy can be plural and circumstantial. Legal pluralism constitutes a true challenge for the sometimes lethargic imagination of the jurist.

A pluralist, non-hierarchical approach may lead to the idea of 'floating'[57] sovereignty. However, it is hard to see how the CJEU might benefit from such theoretical re-conceptualisation – as the final court of the European Union it requires ultimate rather than shared authority. The next section examines the national responses, which demonstrate that there has been little reimagining in the member states.

VIEWPOINT

How can sovereignty be pluralist?

---

[56]Florence Giorgi and Nicolas Triart, 'National Judges, Community Judges: Invitation to a Journey through the Looking-glass – On the Need for Jurisdictions to Rethink the Inter-systemic Relations beyond the Hierarchical Principle', *European Law Journal* 14(6), November 2008, pp. 693–717

[57]Dora Kostakopolou, 'Floating Sovereignty: A pathology or a necessary means of state evolution?', *OJLS* 22(1), 2002, pp. 135–156

3. The response of the member states to supremacy

The discussion so far shows that from the perspective of EU law, Eeckhout is correct. The question, however, remains – do the national courts agree? Supremacy must be reciprocal - the CJ assertions of supremacy would remain empty if the national judicial and administrative authorities refused to accept it and apply it. As with other aspects of EU law, supremacy is dependent upon member state actions.

In 1962, the Court of Justice effectively staged a judicial version of a *coup d'état* – a *'coup de cour'*. The decision in *van Gend* did not perhaps so much 'beg' the constitutional question[58] as 'best' national legal and political authorities. The member states may have created the EEC in 1957, but it was constituted as a discrete, autonomous entity by the CJEU – the original 'pooling of resources' was transformed into a constitutional moment which laid open to question the ultimate political and judicial authority in the fledgling organisation.

The *coup* was effective because it was premised upon the future of the EEC and thus tapped into the national political will to ensure the success of the European project; it also took advantage of judicial traditions, in particular the culture of deference to the judiciary – this latter guaranteed that while national – including constitutional – courts might dislike and dispute the claims to supremacy of the EU law and the CJEU, self-interest and professional socialisation prevented outright rejection. An outright challenge to the authority of the CJEU would set a precedent for holding any judicial authority to account, and in so doing release an idea that might one day be used against them.[59]

Many national courts, for example in Italy and Germany, have in fact used the supremacy of EU law to weaken the tight constraints of their national judicial hierarchy. Furthermore, even constitutional courts that demonstrate displeasure by refusing to refer any questions to the CJ under the preliminary ruling procedure, such as the German and Italian Constitutional Courts, apply EU law and avoid overt defiance. A provision of EU law has never been found incompatible with the German constitution.

However, the member state response to this *coup de cour,* intended to impose uniform supremacy of EU law, was far from uniform. The national response has varied over time and across member states – there has been much resistance.[60] The member states can be placed upon a spectrum with those national judges that saw EU law as an invasion of national sovereignty and responded with hostility at one end, and those member states that readily accepted the superiority of EU law at the other.

Political commitment to European integration is no indication of the judicial response to supremacy – Germany sits with Britain at one end, where initial hostility ultimately melted into full acceptance and at the other end is Spain, where primacy was no issue at all. All other 28 member states sit in-between these extremes: some of the newer member states sit closer to Germany, others closer to Spain.

---

[58]Eleftheriadis 1998
[59]Karen Alter, *Establishing the Supremacy of European Law*, Oxford University Press, 2001
[60]See Helen Xanthaki and Maria Gaitanidou, 'FIDE 25th Congress, Topic 3: The Area of Freedom, Security and Justice and the Information Society – United Kingdom National Report', http://ukael.org/associates_36_3190942404.pdf

i.   Hostility

From the beginning the German Constitutional Court (GCC) took a differentiated approach to supremacy.[61] It was less protective of national legislation (as seen in *Luetticke*,[62] *Alcan*[63] and *Prantl*[64]), but reacted with hostility when EU law impinged upon constitutional law. In a statement known as *Solange I*,[65] it refuted the claim of political novelty made by the CJEU in *van Gend* by calling the EEC an intergovernmental organisation, and asserted its own autonomy by stating a partial and conditional acceptance of the primacy declared by the CJEU in *Internationale:*

> [2] This Court – in this respect in agreement with the law developed by the European Court of Justice – adheres to its settled view that Community law is neither a component part of the national legal system nor international law, but forms an independent system of law flowing from an autonomous legal source (BVerfGE 22, 293 [296]; 31, 145 [173f.]); for the Community is not a state, in particular not a federal state, but 'a sui generis community in the process of progressive integration', an 'inter-state institution' within the meaning of Article 24 (1) of the Basic Law. It follows from this that, in principle, the two legal spheres stand independent of and side by side one another in their validity, and that, in particular, the competent Community organs, including the European Court of Justice, have to rule on the binding force, construction and observance of Community law, and the competent national organs on the binding force, construction and observance of the constitutional law of the Federal Republic of Germany. The European Court of Justice cannot with binding effect rule on whether a rule of Community law is compatible with the Basic Law, nor can the Federal Constitutional Court rule on whether, and with what implications, a rule of secondary Community law is compatible with primary Community law. This does not lead to any difficulties as long as the two systems of law do not come into conflict with one another in their substance.[66]

The GCC went on to stress that supremacy of EU law was based upon the German constitution. This position was subsequently reversed in a decision in 1987, known as *Solange II,* when the GCC relinquished its right to control the CJEU via review of its respect for fundamental rights. The process of ratification of the Treaty on European Union (TEU) provided an opportunity for the GCC to continue its conciliatory path towards the EU and EU law. In 1993, just before ratification was complete, Mr Brunner[67] lodged a series of complaints based on Article 38 GCC, alleging that ratification of the TEU would breach the German constitution. These included a complaint that the TEU reduced protection of fundamental rights in the Constitution, that the lack of CJ oversight in Pillars Two and Three TEU created a judicial vacuum, and that the citizenship right to vote and stand in local elections infringed German rules on suffrage.

---

[61]Dieter H. Scheuing, 'The Approach to European Law in German Jurisprudence', http://www.germanlawjournal.com/pdfs/Vol05No06/PDF_Vol_05_No_06_703-719_EU_Scheuing.pdf
[62]C-57/65 *Lütticke* 1966 ECR 257
[63]C-24/95 *Alcan II*, 1997 ECR I 1591 [38]
[64]C-16/83 *Prantl* [1984] ECR 1299
[65]*Internationale Handelsgesellschaft von Einfuhr- und Vorratsstelle für Getreide und Futtermittel,* decision of 29 May 1974, BVerfGE 37, 271 [1974] CMLR 540
[66]http://www.ecln.net/documents/Decisions-Germany/summary-solange_i.pdf; ; http://www.utexas.edu/law/academics/centers/transnational/work_new/german/case.php?id=588
[67]*Brunner* [1994] 1 CMLR 57

In a complex judgement, which set out the GCC understanding of the nature of the EU and EU law, all complaints were rejected although the Court stated that:

> with regard to the future, and the present weakness of the Union's own democratic processes, what is decisive, from the viewpoint both of the Treaties and of constitutional law, is that the democratic bases of the Union will be built up in step with the integration process, and a living democracy will also be maintained in the member states as integration progresses.

By 2000, the GCC seemed to refute conclusively any such right for itself, declaring that it would only admit questions of compatibility between EU law and German fundamental rights if the application was accompanied by detailed proof of structural deficits in the EU system. The 'Banana-decision' of 2000 has been described as 'the long-awaited farewell to the inappropriate claim for a German fundamental rights control over Community law'.[68] However, the Lisbon decision of the GCC indicated a relapse. In its evaluation of the Lisbon Treaty, the GCC lay out constitutional limits to integration. This was met with widespread confusion and derision.[69] As in *Brunner* the GCC described the EU as a 'Staatenverbund' (association of states) and established a *domaine reserve* of five broadly described areas wherein significant sovereign power had to remain at the national level:

- criminal law
- basic fiscal decisions,
- monopoly on the use of force,
- the guarantee of a just social order, and
- decisions affecting national culture, such as in relation to education, the family and religion.

VIEWPOINT

Do you agree with the GCC idea of the 'core' of national sovereignty in the twenty-first century?

The UK has also travelled the road from hostility to acceptance. By 1970, before its accession, the CJ had asserted that the Treaty was a non-traditional agreement which created independent (*van Gend*) and autonomous institutions that were permanent (*Costa*), with a legal system that took precedence over national law (*Internationale*). The British response was a robust rejection. In 1971, the House of Lords contradicted these claims with a decision to the effect that the member state signatories had not limited their sovereignty, the Treaty was an ordinary international agreement and thus signing of the Treaty was not irreversible – this was for the UK Parliament to decide at the appropriate

---

[68]Scheuing, http://www.germanlawjournal.com/pdfs/Vol05No06/PDF_Vol_05_No_06_703-719_EU_Scheuing.pdf
[69]Daniel Thym, 'In the name of sovereign statehood', *CMLR* 46, 2009, p. 1795. For further analysis see Gunnar Beck, 'The Lisbon Judgment of the German Constitutional Court, the Primacy of EU Law and the Problem of *Kompetenz-Kompetenz*: A Conflict between Right and Right in Which There is No *Praetor*', *European Law Journal* 17(4), 2011, pp. 470–494

time and until such time the Court would follow the instructions of Parliament not the CJEU.[70] In *Bulmer v Bollinger*,[71] the House of Lords held that the Treaty remains separate to English law and that EU law had equal force to statute. Direct applicability was accepted so that Treaty rights and obligations were immediately effective in the UK but English judges reserved the final word on application. The ECJ (as was) was acknowledged as the 'supreme tribunal' on EU law not due to its own merit but rather because Parliament had decreed this in Section 3 of the European Communities Act 1972.

However, the position began to shift by the end of the 1970s and had reversed by the end of the 1980s. When the CJ held that it had the power to invalidate any national law adopted at any time (*Simmenthal*) and exclusive authority to invalidate EU law (*Foto-Frost*), the House of Lords appeared to agree. In *Macarthys Ltd v Smith*,[72] it held that inconsistent legislation must defer to Community law as it was the duty of the Courts to follow the statute of Parliament. In *Garland v British Rail Engineering*,[73] it stated that statutes passed after the Treaty was signed were to be construed, 'as intended to carry out the obligation and not be inconsistent with it'. In 1989 the ECJ decided the case of *Marleasing*,[74] where it held that EU law possessed power to compel any public authority to act in its favour, and exerted an obligation on national courts to interpret national law in line with Community acts. It was therefore stronger than a national statute. Finally in *Factortame*, the CJ asserted for EU law the power to compel national courts to protect individual rights arising from directly effective Community law, and to disapply any national legal provision which restricts enjoyment of rights guaranteed by Community law. Any vestige of resistance disappeared when the House of Lords agreed: in *Factortame* it held that supremacy of EU law was always inherent in the Treaty, and well established by the time the UK joined the EEC in 1973. It found nothing novel about the fact that in protecting rights given by EC law, national courts must not be inhibited by rules of national law. Since *Factortame*, '. . . Judges have a duty effectively to override legislation when it does not comply with EU law'.[75]

ii. Acceptance

The Spanish have always taken a very positive stance towards European integration: indeed, 77 per cent voted in favour of the Constitutional Treaty (CT). On the eve of its introduction, the constitutional court examined its conformity with the Spanish constitution, in line with its task to 'safeguard the security and stability of any international agreements into which Spain may enter' [25]. The Spanish Constitutional Court (SCC) was asked for its opinion on the compatibility of the Constitution for Europe and the EU Charter for Fundamental Rights, and whether the existing constitutional mechanism (Article 93) was a sufficient and appropriate channel for the incorporation of the CT and a 'transfer to the European Union of the exercise of powers derived from the Constitution'. In particular, the Spanish Council of State sought assurance that the Spanish constitution

---

[70]*Blackburn v Attorney General* [1971] EWCA Civ 7 (10 May 1971)

[71]1974 *HP Bulmer Ltd v J Bollinger* [1974] CA

[72]1979 *Macarthys Ltd v Smith* [1980] IRLR 210 & C129/79 ECJ

[73]C12/81 *Eileen Garland v British Rail Engineering Limited* [1982] ECR 00359

[74]C106/89 *Marleasing SA v La Comercial Internacional de Alimentacion SA* [1990] ECR I-04135

[75]Lord Neuberger Of Abbotsbury, Master Of The Rolls, 'The Supreme Court: Is The House Of Lords "Losing Part Of Itself"?', Lecture, 2 December 2009, para 21 p. 10

remained supreme law in the Spanish legal system. If there was a conflict, the SCC was asked what constitutional reform procedure might be necessary to remove it.

In contrast to such enquiries in other member states[76] the ultimate goal was to facilitate acceptance rather than hinder it. The SCC declared that:

> [35] Once integration has taken place, it should be emphasised that it is no longer the Constitution that is the framework for the validity of Community laws, but the Treaty itself, the signature of which completes the sovereign act of assignment of the exercise of the powers derived from it, although the Constitution requires that the Legal System accepted as a result of the transfer shall be compatible with its basic principles and values.

The SCC found that there was no conflict arising between the CT and the Spanish constitution. It also gave its own interpretation of supremacy and primacy – unlike other constitutional courts, it did not deny EU law supremacy:

> [52] The Constitution has supremacy over or ranks superior to any other law, and more specifically over international treaties, as we stated in Declaration 1/1992 (FJ 1). Now the Declaration of the primacy of Union law by Art.I-6 of the Treaty does not contradict the supremacy of the Constitution.

> [53] Primacy and supremacy are categories that operate in different areas of the law. Primacy operates in the application of valid laws; supremacy in legislative processes. Supremacy is founded on the hierarchical superiority of a law which is, therefore, the source of validity of all lower-ranking laws, with the result that the latter are invalid if they conflict with it. Primacy, on the other hand, is not necessarily based on hierarchy, but rather on the distinction between areas of application of different laws, on valid principles, one of more of which will nevertheless have the capacity to displace others by virtue of their prior or prevalent applicability for various reasons.

There was some disagreement with this understanding of supremacy and conclusion of the SCC – the declaration was not unanimous: three judges gave a dissenting vote, arguing both that there was a conflict and Article 93 of the Spanish constitution was not a sufficient channel for adoption of the CT.[77] Judges Barrio and Arribas argued that Article 93 was not strong enough while Judge García-Calvo y Montiel found the reasoning of the majority weak.[78]

It should not be assumed that the newer member states have fallen meekly into line. A number of constitutional courts in the countries of central and eastern Europe have been criticised for their ready acceptance of supremacy[79] yet others such as Poland, the Czech Republic and Hungary followed the line of resistance originally seen in Germany and Britain. Poland asserted the autonomy of its national constitution and like Britain rejected any idea that the EU was unique. Hungary like Germany warned the EU to respect

---

[76]*Re The Constitutional Treaty and the French* Constitution [2005] 1 CMLR 750

[77]Carmen Plaza, 'The Constitution for Europe and the Spanish Constitutional Court', *European Public Law* 12(3), 2006, p. 361.

[78]For citations and dissenting votes see 'Re the EU Constitutional Treaty and The Spanish Constitution (Declaration 1/2004), (C-6603/2004) Before the Spanish Tribunal Constitucional (Constitutional Court)', 13 December 2004, [2005] 1 CMLR 39

[79]Kyriaki Topidi and Alexander Morawa (eds), *Constitutional Evolution in Central and Eastern Europe*, Ashgate, 2011

Hungarian standards on the rule of law. All three resurrected the conditionality of *Solange*.[80] As Sadurski points out, it is paradoxical that prior to accession, supremacy of the EU was seen to guarantee the sovereignty of the post-Communist satellites, but after accession seen as a threat to the sovereignty of some of these newly independent member states.

Cyprus, however, reacted similarly to Spain with ready cooperation. The Cyprian authorities found that their constitution provided all the power required to accept supremacy, although an amendment was required. Article 169 of the Cyprian constitution (CC) gave the government power to sign international treaties; Article 179 CC stated that the constitution was the supreme law of Cyprus and Article 182 CC established the possibility and procedure for constitutional amendments. This was delayed due to political disagreement but the principle of developing the constitution in order to fulfil obligations arising from the Treaty has not been seen as a form of 'constitutional surrender'.[81]

These interactions with the national courts have created a *de facto* process of constitutionalisation[82] in the EU, whereby the CJEU, national courts and tribunals, politicians and public have argued and reargued the merits and limits of supremacy of EU law, not only with the CJEU but also with each other. This process of constitutionalisation has had two consequences: the creation of a Charter of Rights and the creation of a European Constitution. The former project has to date been more successful than the latter – the political attempt to formally create a European constitution ended abruptly and was abandoned.

4. Explaining the success of supremacy

One may wonder why the CJEU took such a bold and somewhat aggressive step in 1962? It was a small court of just six judges in Europe's smallest state of Luxembourg. The EEC was just six years old and still in its infancy – *van Gend* could have been its death warrant.[83] Why did the CJEU take this risky decision? According to Pescatore, the idea of supremacy was unavoidable:

> The Community legal order is intended to bring about a profound transformation in the conditions of life – economic, social and even political – in the Member States. It is inevitable that it will come into conflict with the established order, that is to say the rules in force in the Member States whether they stem from constitutions, laws, regulations or legal usage . . . Community law holds within itself an existential necessity for supremacy. If it is not capable in all circumstances of taking precedence over

---

[80]Wojciech Sadurski, ' "Solange, chapter 3": Constitutional Courts in Central Europe – Democracy – European Union', *European Law Journal* 14(1), January 2008, pp. 1–35

[81]Christos G. Patsalides, 'Accomodating the principle of supremacy of European Union Law to the Cypriot Legal Order', *European Public Law* 12(3), 2006

[82]Christine Reh, 'The Lisbon Treaty: De-Constitutionalizing the European Union?', *JCMS* 47(3), 2009, p. 625; Matthias Kumm, 'Beyond Golf Clubs and the Judicialisation of Politics: Why Europe has a Constitution Properly So Called', *American Journal of Comparative Law* 54, 2006, p. 505

[83]C.J Carruba, Matthew Gabel and Charles Hankla, 'Judicial Behavior under Political Constraints: Evidence from the European Court of Justice', *American Political Science Review* 102(4), November 2008

national law, it is ineffective and, to that extent, non-existent. The very notion of a common order would thereby be destroyed.[84]

One might also wonder how the entrenchment of supremacy was possible. The answer to this question lies in the power of international law – international law may lack the legitimacy of a 'demos' or legislature and have limited capacity for enforcement but it provides the framework for the cooperation necessary for the survival of the nation state:

Nation states are . . . incompetent. Not one of them, not even the United States as the single remaining super-power, can adequately provide for the needs that its citizens now articulate. The extent of that incompetence has become sharply clearer during this century. The inadequacy of national governments to provide security, prosperity or a decent environment has brought into being a huge array of international rules, conferences and institutions; the only answer to the puzzle of the immortal but incompetent nation state is effective co-operation between those states for all the purposes that lie beyond the reach of any one of them.[85]

Without international law, relations between nation states would be arbitrary and lack any form of accountability. A compelling explanation for national compliance with supremacy is therefore self-interest.[86] From this perspective, the EU is an expression of 'enlightened sovereignty'.

It could also be argued that supremacy was possible because the CJEU was 'tucked away in the duchy of Luxembourg',[87] surrounded by determined legal professionals in Brussels and Luxembourg[88] and supported by tacit agreement from judges in the member states:

The ECJ [CJEU] was emboldened to issue its audacious legal ruling because it had the active and explicit support of a network of jurists who were aiding its endeavours . . . it is quite likely that the ECJ was able to co-opt national judges because the developments the ECJ was promoting mirrored steps being taken simultaneously by national judiciaries. In other words, it was the developments underway within European states – the growth of judicial power, an emerging commitment to asserting and protecting individual's basic rights, and the growth and professionalization of the administrative state in European countries – that provided the ECJ with willing interlocutors that could be mobilized around the ECJ's project of using legal means to force European states to adhere to their European legal commitments.[89]

---

[84]Pescatore, 1973, *L'Ordre Juridique des Communautes Europeennees*, Presses Universitaires de Liege, 2nd edn, 1973, p. 227 in Oppenheimer, *The Relationship between European Community Law and National Law: The cases,* Cambridge University Press, 1994, p. 3
[85]Douglas Hurd, quoted in Tom Bingham, *The Rule of Law,* Penguin, 2010, pp. 113–11 4
[86]Bingham 2010, pp. 110–114
[87]Eric Stein, 'Lawyers, Judges and the Making of a Transnational Constitution', *American Journal of International Law* 75(1), 1981, p. 1
[88]Antoine Vauchez, 'The transnational politics of judicialisation. Van Gend en Loos and the making of EU polity', *European Law Journal* 16(1), January 2010, pp. 1–28
[89]Alter 2001

As Alter explains, there were many reasons why the national authorities were unable to prevent the idea of supremacy from taking hold at the national level: judges in higher courts who opposed the principle could not prevent those in lower courts who did not from sending references to the CJEU, which allowed them to circumvent the national legal hierarchy and the CJEU to hand down expansive interpretations; national judges who followed CJEU rulings revealed the fallacy of the arguments of intransigent judges; finally because of 'national judicial support for ECJ [CJEU] jurisprudence, national governments were forced to frame their response in terms that could persuade a legal audience, and thus they became constrained by the legal rules of the game'.[90] Germany provides an example of this: the German Constitutional Court took a hostile stance towards primacy, judges in lower courts were both sending references to the CJEU and applying EU law themselves.[91] In *Luetticke*,[92] *Alcan*[93] and *Prantl*,[94] they accepted the supremacy of EU law over national legislation, resisting government pressure to not do so.[95] The establishment of supremacy was therefore partly due to the agency of judicial actors in the member states.

VIEWPOINT

Read Antoine Vauchez, 'The transnational politics of judicialisation. *Van Gend en Loos* and the making of EU polity', *European Law Journal* 16(1), January 2010, pp. 1–28. In your view, was the *van Gend* ruling a revolution or an evolution?

Finally, was it worth the controversy? Weiler and Haltern argue that supremacy was indeed necessary: the different national methods of incorporating international law would have resulted in a fragmented Community legal order that was unable to create and support a common market. It is worth considering how the EU might look without supremacy: in relation to the enjoyment of EU rights, there would be less legal certainty if each member states decided independently how it related to EU law; low legal certainty in the EU legal order might undermine international credibility and act as a repellent for international investment and trade, upon which many businesses, jobs and livelihoods rely. The unintended consequences of supremacy should also not be forgotten – without it, there might be no Charter of Fundamental Rights. While the Constitutional text was rejected, it can be argued that the resulting constitutionalisation has led to politicisation[96] that may yet transform EU integration into a project with popular support; it may do this more effectively than the progressive empowerment of the European Parliament. Conversely, however, it can be argued that supremacy has undermined national authority and weakened national democracy without re-creating this at the EU level.[97] There are

---

[90] Alter 2009
[91] Scheuing, http://www.germanlawjournal.com/pdfs/Vol05No06/PDF_Vol_05_No_06_703-719_EU_Scheuing.pdf
[92] C-57/65 *Lütticke* 1966 ECR 257
[93] C-24/95 *Alcan II*, 1997 ECR I 1591 [38]
[94] C-16/83 *Prantl* [1984] ECR 1299
[95] Alter 2001
[96] Reh 2009
[97] Phillipe Schmitter, 'Democracy in Europe and Europe's Democracy', *Journal of Democracy* 14(4), 2003, p. 71

also concerns with the legitimacy of the Court of Justice as a Supreme Court: its jurisdiction remains limited—even with the removal of the Pillar structure, it lacks tools of coercion, its recruitment procedures are opaque and its composition remains unreflective of the peoples of Europe.

5. Conclusion

History is littered with the creation of concepts; the present is dominated by the pretence that these concepts are real. Sovereignty is a good example of this – created in the seventeenth century it no longer means that a state can do what it likes without interference by other states. If declarations of war show states at their worst, signature of international treaties show them at their best. In signing treaties they exercise their sovereignty to limit their sovereignty – whenever a state signs an international agreement, it commits to abide by rules that exist beyond its borders and that will be respected within its borders. Ratification of these instruments signifies acceptance of external accountability, through the force of shared values rather than military force.

The claims of EU law to supremacy continue to challenge the resources of legal and political theory: the traditional concepts of constitutional and international law, and the nation state are not rich enough to describe either what the EU is or the balance in the relationship between it and the member states. This system in which supremacy operates is pluralist and 'non-binary' – it has more than two clear points of reference. As MacCormick argues, 'the best way to conceptualise Community law and member state law at present requires us to acknowledge these co-ordinately valid legal systems'.[98] Giorgi and Triart encourage us to envision a new relationship between multiple, equally legitimate legal orders.

It would be hard to find an alternative for the idea of supremacy – what could replace it? Perhaps this question can only be answered when the specific identity of the EU is pinned down – academics may refer to it as a 'special area of hope' an institutional expression of cosmopolitanism or a special place for civic solidarity'[99] but journalists tend to described it more coldly as a 'bloc'.[100] Supremacy may be peculiar to supranationalism but it exists alongside elements of a traditional international organisation – for example, any member state 'determined to leave the EU would not be held up by legalities – no country can be forced to stay inside'.[101]

---

[98]MacCormick 1999, p. 149
[99]Damian Chalmers, 'Gauging the Cumbersomeness of EU Law', LEQS Paper No. 2, May 2009
[100]Joshua Chaffin, 'Athens faces turmoil if it decides to abandon the euro', *Financial Times*, 18 July 2011
[101]Chaffin 2011

Further reading

On the relationship between the EU and the member states:

Paul Kirchhof, 'The Balance of Powers Between European and National Institutions', *ELJ* 5, 1999, p. 225

Joseph Weiler, The Transformation of Europe, *Yale LJ* 100, 1991, p. 2403

On sovereignty:

Wendy Brown, *Walled States, Waning Sovereignty*, Zone Books, 2010

Dora Kostakopolou, 'Floating Sovereignty: A pathology or a necessary means of state evolution?', *OJLS* 22(1), 2002, pp. 135–156

On a European constitution:

Dieter Grimm, 'Does Europe Need a Constitution?', *European Law Journal* 1, 1995, p. 282

Jürgen Habermas, 'Remarks on Dieter Grimm's "Does Europe Need a Constitution?"', *ELJ* 1, 1995, p. 303

Kiiver, 'The Lisbon Judgment of the German Constitutional Court: A Court-Ordered Strengthening of the National Legislature in the EU', *ELJ* 16, 2010, p. 578

Michael Wilkinson, 'Political Constitutionalism and the European Union', *MLR* 76(2), 2013, p. 191

On pluralism:

Giorgi and Triart, 'National Judges, Community Judges: Invitation to a Journey through the Looking-glass', *European Law Journal* 14(6), 2008, p. 693

Ines Weyland, 'The Application of Kelsen's Theory of the Legal System to European Community Law: the Supremacy Puzzle Resolved', *Law and Philosophy* 21, 2002, pp. 1–37

7 Direct effect, indirect effect and state liability

Setting the scene

Mr Swift owns a removal business. Dr Robertson telephoned him on 27 July 2011 to ask for a quotation for moving his furniture. Mr Swift visited his home the following day to inspect the items to be moved and while he was there the two men agreed a price of £7,595.40. Mr Swift then sent a removal acceptance document by email, which Dr Robertson signed and handed to Mr Swift on his second visit to the house. This document provided for charges in the event of cancellation of the contract less than 10 days before the removal was due to start. Dr Robertson paid a deposit of £1,000. Subsequently, Dr Robertson made enquiries of other removal firms and found one which could undertake the work for £3,490. He telephoned Mr Swift to tell him he wished to cancel the contract, and sent him a letter giving notice of cancellation on 1 August 2011. He refused to pay the cancellation charges on the ground that he had been entitled to cancel the contract by virtue of the Cancellation of Contracts Regulations 2008, introduced to give effect to EU Council Directive 85/577. When Mr Swift issued proceedings, Dr Robertson denied liability and counterclaimed for the return of his deposit.

Robertson v Swift [2014] UKSC 50

1. **Introduction**

2. **Direct effect of EU law**
   i. Treaty provisions
   ii. Regulations
   iii. Decisions
   iv. Directives

3. **Managing the boundaries of direct effect**
   i. Indirect effect
   ii. State liability
   iii. Direct applicability of general principles of EU law

4. **Conclusion**

1. Introduction

Is there any point in a body of law providing rights that cannot be accessed by individuals? If a prohibition needs a procedure to make it effective in practice, this was the job for which direct effect was originally introduced. The idea of direct effect has played a key role in achieving the '*l'effet utile*' or effectiveness of EU law. The empowerment of individuals as enforcers of EU law is part of this ongoing project. The remedy of direct effect is an attempt to bring disobedient member states in line by empowering individuals in proceedings before national courts.[1] Such remedies have evolved to include indirect effect and state liability. The doctrine of direct effect, already present in some national legal systems, made all member states monist *vis-à-vis* EU law when introduced by the CJEU. Pierre Pescatore famously described it as an 'infant disease' of EU law[2] but it is hard to imagine that EU law could have made an impact without direct effect it. On the other hand, although EU law now has more binding force than any other form of international law, direct effect alone is not enough to ensure persons fully enjoy the rights laid out in EU law.

The strategies used to secure the effectiveness of EU law via individual empowerment will be the main themes explored below. It will be seen that there are significant limitations. Direct effect is limited not only by its conditions for application but also the formal characteristics of EU law – it should be noted that the EU *acquis communitaire* consists of more than Treaty law. For example, protection from discrimination is found in many different types of law:

- Treaty on Functioning of the European Union (TFEU) – Article 19 (ex Article 13 TEC)

(1) Without prejudice to the other provisions of the Treaties and within the limits of the powers conferred by them upon the Union, the Council, acting unanimously in accordance with a special legislative procedure and after obtaining the consent of the European Parliament, may take appropriate action to combat discrimination based on sex, racial or ethnic origin, religion or belief, disability, age or sexual orientation.

- Directive 2000/78 establishing a general framework for equal treatment in employment and occupation – Article 1 (OJ 2000 L 303, p. 16)

The purpose of this Directive is to lay down a general framework for combating discrimination on the grounds of religion or belief, disability, age or sexual orientation as regards employment and occupation, with a view to putting into effect in the Member States the principle of equal treatment.

- Charter on Fundamental Rights – Title III (Equality) Article 21 Non-discrimination

Any discrimination based on any ground such as sex, race, colour, ethnic or social origin, genetic features, language, religion or belief, political or any other opinion, membership of a national minority, property, birth, disability, age or sexual orientation shall be prohibited.

---

[1] B. de Witte, 'Direct Effect, Supremacy and the Nature of the Legal Order', in Paul Craig and Gráinne de Búrca (eds), *The Evolution of EU Law*, Oxford University Press, 1999, pp. 177–213
[2] Pierre Pescatore, 'The Doctrine of Direct Effect: An Infant Disease of Community Law', *European Law Review* 8, 1983

Since its introduction the relationship between secondary EU law and direct effect has been questioned – can individuals claim rights found in regulations, decisions, directives, recommendations and opinions before their national courts? What about the provisions of the EU Charter on Fundamental Rights, which now has equal status to the Treaties? As will be seen, despite supremacy, not all forms of EU law are capable of having direct effect. In *van Gend* the CJ was careful to set boundaries to this idea. It did not assert that all Treaty provisions would have direct effect, but set out conditions to determine this.

Subsequent cases have shown that in order to retain the character of the different forms of EU law, direct effect will not apply even where these conditions are otherwise met. The most controversial exception exists in relation to the horizontal direct effect of directives – the rights in a directive cannot be asserted against another individual. For reasons to be explained below, Mr Robertson could not rely on the EU directive in his claim against Mr Swift. However, in order to secure the effectiveness of EU law the CJ has identified alternative doctrines to empower individuals. These include indirect effect, state liability and most recently the direct effect of general principles laid out in the Treaty.

Beyond this, effectiveness remains a challenge especially where EU law is dependent upon national authorities – for example, in *AB*, a home office official in Britain deliberately flouted EU citizenship law and also disobeyed a national court order to provide a residence permit to the long-term partner of a migrant Swedish worker.[3] A further question is the impact of these strategies on legal certainty and the uniformity of EU law – the greater the responsibility upon national judges to apply these remedies, the higher the likelihood of different outcomes and fragmentation of EU law. Lack of uniformity will have a long-term detrimental inpact on effectiveness.

This chapter will consider the application of direct effect to primary and secondary Union law. It will only explore binding EU law – it was clearly stated in *Grimaldi*[4] that recommendations and opinions could not have direct effect as they are not binding. This prevented Mr Grimaldi from relying upon two Commission recommendations[5] which dealt with occupational diseases. The recommendations recognised his particular malady but it was not recognised by the Belgian Occupational Diseases Fund, with the consequence that he was unable to receive compensation. Although the recommendations were deemed to be clear, unconditional and precise, it is clear from the wording in Article 288 TFEU that these are not binding. The CJ therefore decided that the recommendations did not create rights upon which individuals may rely before a national court. However, the CJ stressed that they do have some legal effect:

> [18] . . . national courts are bound to take recommendations into consideration in order to decide disputes submitted to them, in particular where they cast light on the interpretation of national measures adopted in order to implement them or where they are designed to supplement binding Community provisions.

Since the Treaty of Lisbon, the EU Charter on Fundamental rights has equal status to the Treaties – this chapter will therefore also consider the direct effect of Charter provisions.

---

[3] *AB v Home Office* [2012] EWHC 226 (QB)
[4] C-322/88 *Grimaldi v Fonds des maladies professionnelles* [1989] ECR 4407
[5] Commission Recommendation to the Member States of 23 July 1962 concerning the adoption of a European schedule of occupational diseases (OJ 80/2188 1962) and of Commission Recommendation 66/462 of 20 July 1966 on the conditions for granting compensation to persons suffering from occupational diseases (OJ 147/2696 1966)

2. Direct effect of EU law

Direct effect, as a relationship between EU law and its subjects, is distinct from direct applicability, which refers to the relationship between EU law and national law.[6] 'Direct applicability', within the meaning of Article 288 TFEU, means that no national legislation is required to make Union law effective in the national legal system. Direct effects, however, as per the case law of the CJEU, is a question of whether an individual can assert direct rights flowing from EU law, even where there is no national implementing legislation. Only if a provision has 'direct effect' can it be relied upon by a party before a national court. A regulation is always directly applicable but does not always have direct effect.

In order to have direct effect, a provision must contain:

a clear and unconditional prohibition which is not a positive but a negative obligation; the obligation is unconditional; and doesn't require MS legislative intervention.[7]

Using these criteria, in *van Gend* the CJ decided that:

according to the spirit, general scheme and wording of the Treaty, Article 12 [Article 30 TFEU] produces direct effects and creates individual rights directly enforceable in the national courts.

ANALYSING THE LAW

Read the provisions in the introduction. Before going any further consider which you think are clear, precise and unconditional enough to create legal rights that may be invoked before a national court.

i.   Treaty provisions

The *van Gend* test remained the same in relation to traditional international treaties and agreements with non-EU member states. The CJ was called upon to consider whether provisions of the General Agreement on Tariffs and Trade (GATT), signed by all member states, was capable of having direct effect. The question arose during an action by International Fruit Company[8] challenging the compatibility of two Commission Regulations restricting the importation of apples from non-EU countries with the GATT. The question was asked whether those regulations could be valid if they conflicted with a rule of international law. The CJ began by considering whether the Union could be bound by a provision of international law, in other words whether the GATT provision had direct effect:

[7] Before the incompatibility of a community measure with a provision of international law can affect the validity of that measure, the community must first of all be bound by that provision.

---

[6]J.A. Winter, 'Direct Applicability and Direct Effect: Two Distinct and Different Concepts in Community Law', *CMLR* 9(4), 1972
[7]C-26/62 *van Gend en Loos*
[8]C-21-24/72 *International Fruit Company and others* v *Produktschap voor Groenten en Fruit* [1972] ECR 1219

[8] Before invalidity can be relied upon before a national court, that provision of international law must also be capable of conferring rights on citizens of the community which they can invoke before the courts.

The answer was an unequivocal 'no'. As in *van Gend* the CJ considered the purpose, the spirit, the general scheme and the terms of GATT. It concluded that the particular provision in question, Article XI GATT, was not capable of having direct effect. There was no doubt that the GATT provisions were binding on the Union – the Union had participated as a partner in tariff negotiations to the extent that it had assumed the powers previously exercised by the member states. However, the GATT provisions were too flexible and general to create individual rights. Consequently, the validity of the Commission regulations could not be affected by that provision of GATT:

27 . . . when examined in such a context, Article XI of the general agreement is not capable of conferring on citizens of the community rights which they can invoke before the courts.

28 Accordingly, the validity of Regulations Nos 459/70, 565/70 and 686/70 of the Commission cannot be affected by Article XI of the general agreement.

A similar question was addressed in *Demirel*,[9] where the CJ was directly asked whether a provision in an agreement signed with a non-member country was capable of having direct effect. In 1963, the EU signed its first – and thus oldest – Association Agreement with Turkey. The Ankara Agreement provides Turkish citizens with some free movement rights in the EU. When Mrs Demiral, a Turkish national, was threatened with deportation after overstaying on a visa used to visit her husband in Germany, she sought to rely before the German court on a provision of the Ankara Agreement. The German Court asked the CJ if this was possible. The CJ began by stating that:

[14] A provision in an agreement concluded by the community with non-member countries must be regarded as being directly applicable when, regard being had to its wording and the purpose and nature of the agreement itself, the provision contains a clear and precise obligation which is not subject, in its implementation or effects, to the adoption of any subsequent measure.

This could not be said of the provisions under consideration and the CJ found that they:

[23] . . . essentially serve to set out a programme and are not sufficiently precise and unconditional to be capable of governing directly the movement of workers.

The imposition of a general obligation to cooperate in order to achieve specific aims laid out in an agreement cannot confer rights upon individuals: thus the protections in the Ankara Agreement could not constitute rules of EU law that are directly effective in the internal legal order of the member states.

---

[9]C-12/86 *Demirel* v *Stadt Schwäbisch Gmünd* [1987] ECR 3719

However, the test set out in *van Gend*, was amended in cases arising within the EU. In *Costa*[10] the CJ held that if a Treaty provision does not fulfil all requirements, the offending parts can be considered separately. In *Lütticke*,[11] it then stated that absence of implementation was no longer a requirement – Treaty provisions imposing obligations to be met by a specific timeframe became directly effective after the deadline passed. The obligation also no longer had to be negative. This was applied in *Reyners*,[12] where Article 49 TFEU, a positive obligation which required implementation, was given direct effect.

Jean Reyners, a Dutch national was prevented from establishing himself as an advocate in Belgium, despite holding the relevant qualifications to do so, because of his nationality. A Belgian law of 1972 set conditions to the use of the title and exercise of the profession of lawyer by non-nationals. The national court asked itself whether this Treaty provision was 'directly effective' despite the clear need for it to be implemented in further measures. Following *Luetticke*, it was argued that as the transition period had come to an end, Article 49 TFEU should now be directly effective.

The Commission agreed that the provision was at least partially directly effective – the prohibition of discrimination on grounds of nationality in Article 18 TFEU [ex Article 7 EC], which was given further expression in Article 49, set out a clear, precise and unconditional prohibition. The CJ agreed with this:

[24] The rule on equal treatment with nationals is one of the fundamental legal provisions of the community.

[25] As a reference to a set of legislative provisions effectively applied by the country of establishment to its own nationals, this rule is, by its essence, capable of being directly invoked by nationals of all the other member states.

[26] In laying down that freedom of establishment shall be attained at the end of the transitional period, Article 52 thus imposes an obligation to attain a precise result, the fulfilment of which had to be made easier by, but not made dependent on, the implementation of a programme of progressive measures.

The fact that the planned measures had not materialised did not change the nature of the obligation. It remained intact even in the absence of measures required to fully implement the programme set out under Article 49 TFEU and became directly effective after the transitional period.

Defrenne[13] saw the CJ add a new aspect to the idea by giving direct effect to a positive obligation applied against an *individual* not the state. All previous cases had involved vertical direct effect as individuals invoked provisions against the state; in this case, the CJ had to consider whether a Treaty provision could have horizontal direct effects, or be invoked against a private company. In its reply it created a distinction between vertical and horizontal direct effect. Ms Defrenne claimed the right to equal pay contained in Article 157 TFEU. She alleged sex discrimination by her employer, SABENA, because as an 'air hostess' she was paid less than a male 'cabin steward' despite the fact that both posts required the same work.

---

[10]C-6/64 *Costa v E.N.E.L.* [1964] ECR 585
[11]C-57/65 *Lütticke v Hauptzollamt Saarlouis* [1966] ECR 205
[12]C-2/74 *Reyners v Belgium* [1974] ECR 631
[13]C-43/75 *Defrenne v SABENA* [1976] ECR 455

The existence of pay discrimination was not disputed but the member states rose up to reject the first question – whether Article 157 TFEU introduces:

[4] . . . directly into the national law of each member state of the European Community [Union] the principle that men and women should receive equal pay for equal work and does it therefore, independently of any national provision, entitle workers to institute proceedings before national courts in order to ensure its observance?

According to the UK, there were four reasons why Article 157 TFEU was not sufficiently clear or precise to satisfy the conditions for direct effect:

- it contains no comprehensive definition of the principle of equal pay for equal work;
- the concept of pay is itself open to wide interpretation;
- national authorities must work out the details themselves; and
- the provision requires further legislative action.

Ireland likewise argued that national implementation was necessary before it could be enforced. Furthermore, it argued that a provision that pursued a social objective benefitting a particular class of persons (in this case women) rather than the Union as a whole, could not have direct effects. The Commission also argued that the provision was not directly effective due to the need for implementation. However, the Commission suggested that once implementation had occurred, a provision would become directly applicable in relations between member states and individuals.

The members of the Court saw things differently. The Advocate General described Article 157 TFEU as the European response to an obligation laid out in an international Treaty. He regarded the obligation as clear, precise, unconditional and complete. The protection it offered did not depend upon the prior adoption of rules by the Commission or the member states. The judges agreed: the concept of equal pay was as a fundamental principle in the EU, not a vague general declaration. Its specification in Article 157 pursued two objectives: first to prevent competitive advantage based on unfair pay – economic advantage was not to be secured via the exploitation of women workers. Second, it sought to improve the living and working conditions of Europeans, as set out in the Treaty preamble and as clear from the location of Article 157 in the chapter devoted to social policy. The CJ concluded from this dual economic and social aim that 'the principle of equal pay forms part of the foundations of the Community [Union]'.[14]

The use of the word 'principle' could not be used to argue against direct effect – this word was regularly used in the Treaty to stress the fundamental nature of specific provisions .[15] The fact that it was addressed to the member states was also no barrier to individual claims to the rights within it: rights could be simultaneously conferred on any individual with an 'interest in the performance of the duties thus laid down'.[16] In addition, the effectiveness of the provision could not be impaired by dilatory national action. Furthermore, the prohibition was found to extend to all agreements intended

---

[14][12]
[15][28]
[16][31]

to regulate paid labour as well as contracts between individuals.[17] Put together this led to the conclusion that:

> The principle that men and women should receive equal pay, which is laid down by Article 119 [Article 157 TFEU], may be relied on before the national courts. These courts have a duty to ensure the protection of the rights which that provision vests in individuals, in particular in the case of those forms of discrimination which have their origin in legislative provisions or collective labour agreements, as well as where men and women receive unequal pay for equal work which is carried out in the same establishment or service, whether private or public.

Furthermore, the CJ held that this principle was to have been fully secured by the original member states from 1 January 1962 and the newer member states by January 1973. However, given that gender pay discrimination was – and remains – rife throughout the member states, the Court decided to limit the effects of its ruling to future pay claims only. Unfortunately for those whose claims pre-dated the *Defrenne* judgment, Article 157 TFEU could not be used.

APPLYING THE LAW

Explain the difference between vertical and horizontal direct effect. Which would apply to *Grimaldi, International Fruit Company* and *Demirel?*

---

ii. Regulations

Changes to direct effect of Treaty provisions did not necessarily apply to secondary legislation. The question on direct effect of regulations arose together with a request for clarification on direct applicability.[18] The case concerned subsidies given to farmers for slaughtering their milk-producing cows. Two regulations[19] had been adopted introducing a scheme to stabilise the price of milk in the EU by reducing its production. The Italian authorities had made payment of subsidies under the regulations subject to a national condition – the adoption of legislation by the Italian Parliament to allocate the funds. An Italian farmer, despite complying with all conditions in the regulations, was refused the subsidies and complained to the national court. The national court turned to the CJ for guidance on two questions: first, whether the regulations are 'directly applicable in the Italian legal system'; and second, if yes whether 'they create individual rights which national courts must protect.' A single answer was provided:

> [5(2)] The second paragraph of Article 189 [Article 288 TFEU] of the Treaty provides that a regulation shall have 'general application' and 'shall be ... directly applicable in

---

[17][39]
[18]C-93/71 *Leonensio* v *Minstero dell' Agricoltura e Foreste* [1972] ECR 287
[19]Regulation (EEC) No 1975/69 of the Council of 6 October 1969 and of Regulation (EEC) No 2195/69 of the Commission of 4 November 1969 relating principally to the grant of Subsidies to farmers for slaughtering their milk cows

all member states'. Therefore, because of its nature and its purpose within the system of sources of community law it has direct effect and is, as such, capable of creating individual rights which national courts must protect.

As the rights provided concerned financial payments, the only relevant conditions were those set out in the regulation – no further conditions could be imposed by implementing provisions at the national level. It is noticeable that the CJ did not create a clear distinction between direct applicability and direct effect. This was addressed in *Fratelli Variola SpA*[20] where the CJ confirmed that regulations could be both directly applicable and directly effective: as a result of their nature and place in the system of sources of EU law, regulations have immediate effect and confer rights which national courts have a duty to protect. It again stressed that their entry into force is independent of any national measure.

ANALYSING THE LAW

What is the key difference between direct effect and direct applicability?

---

iii. Decisions

The principle of direct effect for decisions was laid out in *Grad*.[21] This case revolved around the harmonisation of rules relating to taxation. A German finance court asked the CJ for an interpretation of two provisions, the first in a decision and the second in a directive. It specifically asked whether these provisions could together produce direct effects in the legal relationships between member states and individuals, i.e. whether the provisions created individual rights which member states must protect. The CJ affirmed that this was possible in principle, despite the wording of Article 288 TFEU:

> [5] ... although it is true that by virtue of Article 189 [now Article 288 TFEU], regulations are directly applicable and therefore by virtue of their nature capable of producing direct effects, it does not follow from this that other categories of legal measures mentioned in that Article can never produce similar effects. ...

Three reasons were given for this finding. First, *'l'effet utile'* (effectiveness) of EU law: it would be incompatible with the binding effect attributed to decisions in Article 288 TFEU if direct effect was excluded in principle. This was especially important where a decision was the means used to ensure all member states acted in a certain way. Direct effect allowed individuals affected to invoke the obligation imposed by a decision thus strengthening its effectiveness by inducing national courts to take it into consideration. Second, a formal argument was used: although the effects of a decision are not identical with those of a provision contained in a regulation, this difference did not per se preclude the result that an individual may enjoy the same right to invoke the measure

---

[20]C-34/73 *Fratelli Variola SpA*. See also C-8/81 *Becker v Finanzamt Muenster-Innenstadt* [1982] ECR 53
[21]C-9/70 *Grad v Finanzamt Traunstein* [1970] ECR 825

before the court. Third, access to justice was invoked: it was argued that as Article 267 TFEU empowers national courts to refer questions regarding the validity and interpretation of all acts of the institutions without distinction, this must also empower individuals to invoke all such acts before the national courts. It required an assessment of each specific case to determine whether the nature, background and wording of the provision is capable of producing direct effects in the legal relationships between the addressee of the act and third parties.

Thus it was held that the provisions in a decision were capable of:

producing direct effects in the legal relationships between the Member States to which the decision is addressed and those subject to their jurisdiction and of creating for the latter the right to invoke these provisions before the courts.

It is noticeable that although the referring court asked about a decision and a directive, the CJ reply mentioned only the decision. This silence on directives was repeated in *Hansa Fleisch*.[22] The case concerned the fees payable by Hansa Fleisch for statutory health inspections of its slaughterhouse, cutting plant and meat-refrigeration unit. The fees were levied according to domestic law rather than the EU decision on charges for health inspections.[23] Hansa Fleisch argued that the demand for fees was unlawful, *inter alia* because the fees invoiced under domestic law exceeded those provided for in the decision. The national court sent two questions to the CJ clearly asking whether the decision, in conjunction with a directive,[24] could have direct effect. The CJ summarised the question as asking first, whether Article 2(1) of Decision 88/408 has direct effect, and second, if it does, whether it can be relied on by an individual as against a member state before the expiry of the implementation period.

It will be remembered that a criterion for direct effect laid out in *van Gend* was an unconditional prohibition. The German authorities argued that Article 2(1) was not an unconditional obligation, because Article 2(2) granted member states a derogation. The CJ disagreed with this and held it to be irrelevant: the possibility of a derogation from clear and precise provisions of a decision did not in itself deprive those provisions of direct effect, especially where – as in this decision – use of the derogation was subject to judicial review.[25]

The question on the impact of the timeframe for implementation on direct effect was also dealt with briefly. Article 11 of Decision 88/408 set out a specific period for implementing the decision. This meant that:

[19] Where a decision addressed to the Member States contains precise and unconditional provisions which must be implemented within a specified period, the provisions may be relied on by individuals as against a Member State only if that State fails to implement the decision before the expiry of the period prescribed or implements it in time, but incorrectly.

---

[22]C-156/91 *Hansa Fleisch v Landrat des Kreises Schleswig-Flensburg* [1992] ECR I-5567
[23]Council Decision 88/408/EEC of 15 June 1988 on the levels of the fees to be charged for health inspections and controls of fresh meat pursuant to Directive 85/73/EEC (OJ L 194/24 1988)
[24]Council Directive 85/73/EEC of 29 January 1985 on the financing of health inspections and controls of fresh meat and poultry meat (OJ L 32/14 1985)
[25]As held in relation to Directives in C- 41/74 *Van Duyn v Home Office* [1974] ECR 1337 [7]

This was because the decision only became binding on addressees after the specific timeframe had expired and thus could also only be relied upon by individuals, or have direct effect, at this point.

In both *Grad* and *Hansa Fleisch,* the CJ responded only in relation to the decision and in both cases it also stressed that decision provisions were directly effective in situations where a private individual relied upon them against a member state (vertical direct effect). Would this also apply to directives?

VIEWPOINT

Which of the three justifications for direct effect of decisions do you find most compelling?

---

iv. Directives

What about directives? Directives must be implemented in a way that secures their effectiveness – in *Commission* v *UK*[26] (cost of judicial proceedings), the CJ held that case law cannot be used to transpose an EU directive. The condition for direct effect that the measure requires no implementation would suggest that directives are per se incapable of direct effects. This is, however, not so.

In *Grad* and *Hansa Fleisch,* the national courts had raised the question of direct effect of directives but the answers given by the CJ had focused on decisions. An answer in relation to directives was first given in *van Duyn.*[27] Ms van Duyn, a Dutch national, sought to enter the UK to take up a post with the Church of Scientology, a lawful organisation considered at that time to be 'socially harmful' by the British authorities – its activities were deemed contrary to public policy and any non-national intending to work for the organisation was refused entry. Ms van Duyn brought an action against the Home Office, claiming that Article 45 TFEU gave her a right to enter and remain in the UK to take up employment. This question, along with others,[28] was referred to the CJ – could (1) Article 45 TFEU and (2) Directive 64/221[29] have direct effects so as to confer on individuals rights enforceable by them in the courts of a member state?

The answer to the first question was yes: Article 45 TFEU was directly effective 'so as to confer on individuals rights enforceable by them in the courts of a member state'. The provision imposed a precise obligation which did not require the adoption of any further measure on the part either of the community institutions or of the member states and which left them, in relation to its implementation, no discretionary power.

The answer in relation to Directive 64/221 was more nuanced. The examination was limited to Article 3(1), as this was the only provision raised in the case. This provision

---

[26]C-530/11 *European Commission* v *UK* on public participation in environmental plans laid out in Directive 2003/05 implementing the obligations arising under the Aarhus Convention on access to information, public participation in decision-making and access to justice in environmental matters
[27]C-41/74 *Yvonne van Duyn* v *Home Office* [1974] ECR 1337
[28]The British judge also asked about the interpretation of 'personal conduct' in Article 3 Directive 64/221
[29]Directive 64/221 of 25 February 1964 on the coordination of special measures concerning the movement and residence of foreign nationals which are justified on grounds of public policy, public security or public health (OJ Series I Volume 1963–1964 pp. 117–119)

stated that 'measures taken on grounds of public policy or public security shall be based exclusively on the personal conduct of the individual concerned'. It was held that it would undermine the binding effect of a directive were the obligations contained therein incapable of direct effects:

[12] ... If, however, by virtue of the provisions of Article 189 [288 TFEU] regulations are directly applicable and, consequently, may by their very nature have direct effects, it does not follow from this that other categories of acts mentioned in that Article can never have similar effects. It would be incompatible with the binding effect attributed to a directive by Article 189 [288 TFEU] to exclude, in principle, the possibility that the obligation which it imposes may be invoked by those concerned ...

In principle, therefore, directives could be directly effective. There was a practical advantage to this: granting direct effects to directives empowered individuals and decentralised enforcement. The effect of directives would be weakened if individuals were prevented from relying on them before their national courts. Beyond this, the CJ argued that Article 267 TFEU implied that directives could be invoked by individuals before the national courts: the preliminary reference procedure empowers national courts to refer questions of validity and interpretation 'of *all* acts of the community institutions, without distinction'. Direct effects could therefore in principle arise from a directive – this would have to be assessed on a case by case basis, taking into consideration 'the nature, general scheme and wording of the provision in question'.[30] Direct effect was therefore to be an exception for directives.

Some were in favour of this development, primarily because it would shift enforcement from the Commission to individuals, thus reducing the burden on the Commission. Direct effect would also encourage individuals to monitor national transposition and could therefore in the long term ensure these were implemented faster. However, there was also dissatisfaction with the reasoning and concern about its consequences: it overlooked the formal distinction in the Treaty between regulations and directives, and intruded upon the discretion given to member states on implementation – in the scheme of the Treaty, individuals were to gain rights from national acts transposing the obligations in a directive, not the directive itself. Introducing this possibility blurred the lines between a regulation and a directive. This, it was argued, would have a negative impact on legal certainty, even more so because directives were not immediately activated but usually had a delay (implementation period) of two years. The legal certainty matter was addressed in *Ratti*[31] and *Becker:*

wherever the provisions of a directive appear, as far as their subject-matter is concerned, to be unconditional and sufficiently precise , those provisions may be relied upon by an individual against the state where that state fails to implement the directive in national law by the end of the period prescribed or where it fails to implement the directive correctly.[32]

---
[30][12]
[31]C-148/78 *Criminal proceedings against Tullio Ratti* [1979] ECR 1629
[32]C-8/81 *Becker* v *Finanzamt Munster-Innenstadt* (1982) ECR 53

Ratti introduced the concept of *estoppel* to EU law: it confirmed that a member state that failed to transpose a directive within the prescribed period could not plead its own wrongdoing against individuals to avoid liability. After the expiration of the implementation period of a directive, national provisions are void regardless of whether the directive was implemented or not.

ANALYSING THE LAW

Summarise the conditions for direct effect of directives. What are the advantages and disadvantages of this?

a) Horizontal direct effect of directives

Beyond this, the question of vertical and horizontal direct effect also had to be answered: against whom could the obligations in a directive be invoked? Who could be held responsible for breach of these rights – only the state, or also a private body? Given the increase in privatisation, a limitation to the former would mean increasing numbers of workers would not be able to enjoy rights in a directive. Inclusion of the latter, however, would potentially hold responsible actors who were in no position to enforce the obligations in a directive.

This question was first broached in *Marshall*.[33] The CJ was asked whether an individual could rely upon the provisions of a directive against an independent health authority that was independent. Ms Marshall was dismissed from her job upon reaching the then pensionable age of 62. The state retirement age for men was 65: she argued this was contrary to Directive 76/207 on equal treatment between women and men. The CJ agreed with her on the substance: the rule constituted sex discrimination. However, there were still two hurdles to cross: first, the right invoked was contained in a directive; and second, the respondent was not a public authority.

The Commission argued that the relevant provision, Article 5(1) of the directive, passed the test: it was sufficiently clear and unconditional to be relied upon before a national court. The health authority and the UK government did not disagree with this but argued that:

> a directive can never impose obligations directly on individuals and that it can only have direct effect against a member state qua public authority and not against a member state qua employer.

The UK argument was that as an employer the state was in the same position as an employer in the private sector. It would also be unfair to private sector employees if only employees in the public sector could rely upon rights in a directive. This was swiftly dismissed – the CJ highlighted that a person may rely on a directive as against the state:

> [49] . . . regardless of the capacity in which the latter is acting, whether employer or public authority. In either case it is necessary to prevent the state from taking advantage of its own failure to comply with Community [Union] law.

---

[33]C-152/84 *M. H. Marshall* v *Southampton and South-West Hampshire Area Health Authority (Teaching)* [1986] ECR 723

However, the scope of direct effect of directives was limited by the fact that under Article 288 TFEU it is only binding upon those to whom it is addressed – member states. The referring court had confirmed that the health authority was a public authority thus the directive could be invoked against it.

The case gave rise to as many questions as it answered: which state organs would be seen as a public authority? Could a police chief,[34] a local authority,[35] a tax authority,[36] a privatised water company,[37] a voluntary aided school[38] or a privatised car manufacturer[39] be held responsible for the transposition of directives? How was the national judge to decide? Guidance was given by the CJ in the case of *Foster*.[40]

The case was a referral sent from the House of Lords, which asked the CJ to give guidance on whether the company British Gas was a body of the kind against which the provisions of the directive could be invoked. The case revolved around the compulsory retirement of women at the age of 60: as in *Marshall* the question was whether this was contrary to the Equal Treatment Directive 76/207. This question had already been answered in the affirmative in *Marshall*: the more crucial question was whether the right to equal treatment in the directive could be invoked against British Gas – was it a public authority?

British Gas was a statutory body created by the Gas Act 1972. It is responsible for developing and maintaining the system of gas supply in Great Britain, and had a monopoly of the supply of gas. Members of British Gas were appointed by the Secretary of State, who had power to direct British Gas in questions relating to the national interest. The company was obliged to submit to the Secretary of State periodic reports on its functions, management and programmes, which were laid before both Houses of Parliament. Under the Gas Act 1972 British Gas also had the right, with the consent of the Secretary of State, to submit proposed legislation to Parliament. However, it was privatised under the Gas Act 1986 – renamed British Gas plc, it inherited the rights and liabilities of its predecessor. Was British Gas plc a body against whom a directive could be invoked?

The CJ replied yes – ' . . . it is necessary to prevent the State from taking advantage of its own failure to comply with Community law' thus:

> [20] It follows from the foregoing that a body, whatever its legal form, which has been made responsible, pursuant to a measure adopted by the State, for providing a public service under the control of the State and has for that purpose special powers beyond those which result from the normal rules applicable in relations between individuals is included in any event among the bodies against which the provisions of a directive capable of having direct effect may be relied upon.

In the case of British Gas plc, the company enjoys, for example, broad powers of entry not given to other private companies.[41] The Foster criteria have not changed: any organisation, whatever its legal form or how it exercises authority, which satisfies them is described as an 'emanation of the state'. If, pursuant to the constitutional structure of the

---

[34]C-222/84 *Johnston* v *Chief Constable of the Royal Ulster Constabulary* [1986] ECR 1651
[35]C-103/88 *Fratelli Costanzo* v *Comune di Milano* [1989] ECR 1839
[36]C-221/88 *ECSC* v *Acciaierie e Ferriere Busseni* [1990] ECR I-495
[37]*Griffin* v *South West Water Services Ltd* [1995] IRLR 15
[38]*NUT & Others* v *Governing Body of St Mary's Church of England (Aided) Junior School* [1997] IRLR 242
[39]*Doughty* v *Rolls Royce plc* [1992] 1 CMLR 1045
[40]C-188/89 *Foster* v *British Gas* [1990] ECR I-3313
[41]Rights of Entry Act 1954

member state, it exercises any authority over individuals then it falls within the EU concept of the 'state'.

Again, as many questions were raised as answered: the scope of this definition was unclear – to what extent could other bodies and institutions be held legally responsible for failure to comply with provisions? Scholars have argued that *Foster* introduced a general test rather than criteria, and did not give conclusive guidance. It was too broad to provide any uniformity. They also argued that *Foster* was short on authoritative guidance – it confirmed that a body with responsibility for providing a public service under the control of the State is *included* within the Community definition, but what beyond this? It was left to the national judge to apply the criteria: in *Eventech*, the Parking Adjudicator was found to be an 'emanation of the state'.[42]

For many, the debate is a distraction – directives should simply be given vertical as well as horizontal direct effect so that they can be invoked against private companies. Arguments in favour of this stress the need to protect the uniform application and effectiveness of EU law: reliance on national authorities undermines compliance with EU law – non-implementation, lack of application and non-compliance damages the economic integration that is crucial for the future of Western Europe.[43] In addition, the continued failure to comply with EU law undermines the credibility of the EU legal system as a whole. Allowing private actions would protect the system.[44] The prohibition of horizontal direct effect is also highly problematic in an economy dominated by private relationships – the majority of workers cannot enjoy rights in EU directives. Finally, the distinction that arises between similarly situated individuals in the public and private sector creates an arbitrary two-tier legal system.[45] Given the increasing preference for use of directives over regulations this exclusion is an ongoing problem.

Arguments against horizontal direct effect of directives focus on the formal aspects of EU law: for AG Slynn, the link between a directive and individuals are too tenuous to create a legal obligation. This would blur the distinction between regulations and directives. The discretion left by directives to individual member states would also damage legal certainty. The CJ highlighted the wording in Article 288 TFEU: a literal interpretation made clear that the binding nature of a directive exists only in relation to:

> each member state to which it is addressed. It follows that a directive may not of itself impose obligations on an individual and that a provision of a directive may not be relied upon as such against such a person.

The CJ ruled against horizontal direct effect of directives in *Faccini Dori*[46] and *Luigi Spano*.[47] Hartley argues that this was due to fear of a negative reaction from the national courts, especially the French *Conseil d'Etat*.[48] This court-created anomaly could of course be addressed by broadening the definition of the 'emanation of the state'. However, this

---

[42]*Eventech Ltd & Parking Adjudicator v LB Camden and Transport for London* [2012] EWHC 1903 (Admin) [6]
[43]Francis Snyder, 'The Effectiveness of European Community Law: Institutions, Processes, Tools And Techniques', *Modern Law Review* 56, 1993, pp. 19–56
[44]Paul Craig, 'The Legal Effect of Directives: Policy, Rules and Exceptions', *European Law Review* 34(3), 2009, p. 349
[45]AG Jacobs
[46]C-91/92 *Faccini Dori v Recreb* [1994] ECR I-3325
[47]C-472/93 *Faccini Dori v Recreb* [1994] ECR I-3325
[48]The French Conseil D'Etat had shown itself ready to flout the rulings of the CJ in the *Cohn-Bendit* case, Conseil d'État judgment of 22 December 1978 [1980] 1 CMLR 543

also has its limits: it ameliorates rather than addresses the problems of effectiveness and leaves the arbitrary nature of the distinction untouched.

APPLYING THE LAW

Why is horizontal direct effect of directives an important issue? How does its absence affect Mr Robertson in his case against Mr Swift?

---

3. Managing the boundaries of direct effect

What remedies exist therefore under EU law when a private company discriminates against one of its employees, or a provision does not satisfy the criteria for direct effect? Since introducing direct effect and excluding horizontal direct effect of directives, the CJEU has identified several doctrines to manage the boundaries of its application. These include a new obligation upon national judges which it hoped would circumvent the concept of 'direct effect' completely. The idea of 'indirect effect' is a departure from *van Gend* as it does not rely upon any intrinsic quality of the provision itself, attaches itself in the same way to Treaty provisions and all secondary legislation, and avoids the dichotomy of vertical and horizontal which plagues direct effect. A further doctrine which is distinct from direct effect is state liability – this allows parties to seek compensation from the state where any of its organs is responsible for a 'sufficiently serious breach'. Finally, in order to circumvent the problem of horizontal direct effect of directives, it has reasserted respect for the general principles of EU law or as some would argue, invented new general principles.

i.   Indirect effect

Indirect effect refers to the requirement that national courts interpret and apply national law in conformity with EU law. It imposes a 'duty of interpretation' upon national judges. The legal basis for this duty is Article 4(3) TEU which calls for 'sincere co-operation' to fulfil obligations arising from the Treaties or acts of the institutions:

---

(3) Pursuant to the principle of sincere co-operation, the Union and the Member States shall, in full mutual respect, assist each other in carrying out tasks which flow from the Treaties. The Member States shall take any appropriate measure, general or particular, to ensure fulfilment of the obligations arising out of the Treaties or resulting from the acts of the institutions of the Union. The Member States shall facilitate the achievement of the Union's tasks and refrain from any measure which could jeopardise the attainment of the Union's objectives.

This principle is not limited to any specific form of EU law but is of most consequence in relation to directives. The interpretive duty requires national provisions to be interpreted in the light of EU directives. National judges are encouraged to read national law in a way that gives effect to the obligations in directives. The duty is activated by the adoption and publication of secondary legislation – in relation to directives, it therefore begins immediately and not after the expiration of the implementation period.

The duty was set out in the case of *von Colson*.[49] The case arose when two women were refused employment in a male-only prison in Germany – two men who were less well qualified were appointed instead. It was agreed that this was contrary to Directive 76/207 on equal treatment. Under German civil law,[50] compensation for such recruitment discrimination required only reimbursement of travel expenses. The national court questioned whether this was adequate to implement Article 6 of Directive 76/207 that called for 'effective sanctions' – in other words, had the obligation in the directive been adequately transposed? It did not specify any form of sanction for unlawful discrimination, only that it be 'effective'.

The CJ began by confirming national discretion but simultaneously stressed that the sanction must nonetheless 'guarantee real and effective judicial protection' and 'have a real deterrent effect on the employer'. In order to do so, compensation must be 'adequate in relation to the damage sustained'. The reimbursement of travel expenses was therefore not 'an effective transposition of the directive'.

Although it was left for the national court to interpret national law, the CJ highlighted the general obligation in EU law on all national authorities, including courts, which required them to interpret national law as if to achieve the aims in a directive:

> [26] . . . however, the member states' obligation arising from a directive to achieve the result envisaged by the directive and their duty under Article 5 of the Treaty to take all appropriate measures, whether general or particular, to ensure the fulfilment of that obligation, is binding on all the authorities of member states including, for matters within their jurisdiction, the courts. It follows that, in applying the national law and in particular the provisions of a national law specifically introduced in order to implement Directive 76/207, national courts are required to interpret their national law in the light of the wording and the purpose of the directive in order to achieve the result referred to in the third paragraph of Article 189.

Von Colson introduced the idea that enforcement of EU law is a duty resting upon all organs of the State. In so doing, it circumvented the problem of the 'disobedient'[51] member state which did not transpose directives, or did so incorrectly. It also avoided the conundrums of direct effect: the wording did not have to be clear or sufficiently precise, and the respondent did not have to be 'an emanation of the state'. It was also more efficient as it did not require a reference to the CJ under Article 267 TFEU or an infringement procedure under Article 228 TFEU. The effectiveness of any measure implementing a directive was to be examined immediately by the national judge for conformity with the requirements of EU law. Where the national judge found lack of conformity, it was to address this. In *von Colson,* this required the introduction of an effective (not only equal) national remedy.

ANALYSING THE LAW

Identify at least two ways in which indirect effect differs from direct effect? Read *Robertson v Swift* [2014] UKSC 50 – how is it relevant in this case?

---

[49]C-14/83 *Sabine von Colson and Elisabeth Kamann v Land Nordrhein-Westfalen* [1984] ECR 1891
[50]Para 611(a)(2) BGB
[51]Carol Harlow, 'Francovich and the Problem of the Disobedient State', *European Law Journal* 2(3), 1996, pp. 199–225

Hartley describes this doctrine as reasonable. However, it was not long before the boundaries of the duty became visible. In *Kolpinghuis*[52] the principle was anchored within general principles of law, especially non-retroactivity of criminal liability. The Dutch public prosecutor sought to rely upon provisions in a directive which had not been implemented by national law at the time the offence was committed. The national court therefore asked the CJ what this meant for the interpretive duty: can a national court interpret existing national provisions in the light of a non-implemented directive (i.e. where no national implementing legislation exists) in criminal proceedings against its own nationals? The CJ replied in the negative – reconfirming the exclusion of horizontal direct effect of directives,[53] it stated that the general principles of law – such as legal certainty and non-retroactivity – limit the obligation on national courts when interpreting directives: 'Thus . . . a directive cannot, of itself and independently of a national law adopted by a member state for its implementation, have the effect of determining or aggravating the liability in criminal law of persons who act in contravention of the provisions of that directive'.[54] In other words, a directive cannot be interpreted to have indirect effect where this would make the accused guilty where s/he otherwise may not be so. This was also stated in *Salo*.[55] Following the rule *nullem crimen sine lege*,[56] the doctrine of indirect effect cannot be used to impose criminal liability or to aggravate punishment.

A national judge cannot be called upon to interpret national law that does not exist. However, where national law does exist, it must be set within the objectives of a directive regardless of whether it was adopted before or after an EU directive. This was set out in the case of *Marleasing*,[57] which brought two private parties before a national court. Their conflict arose from a contractual dispute. Marleasing claimed that the contract founding La Comercial was contrary to the Spanish Civil Code[58] and should be declared void on the ground that its establishment lacked cause, was a sham transaction and was carried out in order to evade its creditors including Marleasing. For its part La Comercial contended that the action should be dismissed in its entirety because Article 11 of Directive 68/151, which lists exhaustively the cases in which the nullity of a company may be ordered, did not include lack of cause among them.

The first problem was that this directive had not been transposed when these events took place – there was no implementing legislation to interpret in the light of the directive, only domestic legislation which pre-dated the directive. The second problem was that this was a horizontal scenario, where the directive was being invoked by an individual against an individual. The question asked of the CJ was whether the interpretation principle is to apply horizontally, that is between two individuals. Adherence to the interpretive duty

---

[52]C-80/86 *Criminal proceedings against Kolpinghuis Nijmegen BV* [1987] ECR 3969
[53][8–10]
[54][13]
[55]C-14/86 *Pretore di Salò* V X [1987] ECR 2545. See Estella Baker, 'The European Union's "Area of Freedom, Security and (Criminal) Justice" ten years on', *Criminal Law Review* 12, 2009, p. 833; Alicia Hinajeros, 'The Lisbon Treaty versus standing still: a view from the third pillar', *European Constitutional Law Review* 5, 2009, p. 99; Maria Fletcher, 'Extending "indirect effect" to the 3rd pillar: the significance of Pupino?' *European Law Review* 30, 2005, p. 862
[56]Protected by Article 7 ECHR
[57]C-106/89 *Marleasing SA v La Comercial Internacional de Alimentacion SA* [1990] ECR I-4135
[58]Articles 1261 and 1275 of the Spanish Civil Code stated that contracts without cause or whose cause is unlawful have no legal effect.

avoided the conundrum and would not penalise either party, but would have a disadvantageous effect on the legal position of one. The interpretive duty took priority:

> [12] . . . As is clear from the preamble to Directive 68/151, its purpose was to limit the cases in which nullity can arise and the retroactive effect of a declaration of nullity in order to ensure 'certainty in the law as regards relations between the company and third parties, and also between members' (sixth recital) . . . It follows, therefore, that each ground of nullity provided for in Article 11 of the directive must be interpreted strictly . . .

> [13] The answer to the question submitted must therefore be that a national court hearing a case which falls within the scope of Directive 68/151 is required to interpret its national law in the light of the wording and the purpose of that directive in order to preclude a declaration of nullity of a public limited company on a ground other than those listed in Article 11 of the directive.

The CJ upheld the prohibition on horizontal direct effect but in applying indirect effect the national court had a duty to ensure the nullification of a company occurred only on those grounds listed in the directive, even where the directive was not implemented. This meant that Marleasing lost, even though it had probably entered into the contract relying on the protection offered under Spanish law. The duty did not, however, require national judges to rewrite national law so that it took on a meaning contrary to its 'ordinary' meaning.[59]

Although it is not mentioned anywhere in the EU Treaty, the CJEU considered indirect effect 'indispensable'.[60] The problem that many commentators have identified with the principle of indirect effect is that judges are asked to 'engage in different legal standards and rules with which they are possibly unfamiliar.'[61]

ANALYSING THE LAW

Are the conditions listed in *van Gend* for direct effect relevant for indirect effect?

---

ii. State liability

As with all CJEU rulings, the decision must be applied in the member state by the national authority. In most cases this will be the same authority that did not respond during the pre-infringement and pre-litigation process. It is therefore not necessarily the case that immediate litigation will result in faster justice or ensure compliance. A stark example of the limits of compliance with infringement proceedings is provided in *Francovich and Bonifaci* v *Republic of Italy*.[62] These cases were joined as they both raised the question of the responsibility of the state for damages arising from breach of EU law. In addressing the questions raised in these cases, the CJ introduced a principle that member states are obliged to make good loss and damage caused to individuals by breaches of Union law for which they can be held responsible, or 'state liability'. State liability was the only 'sanction' prior to 1992.

---

[59]C-334/92 *Wagner-Miret v Fondo de Garantia Salarial* [1993] ECR I-6911. This was also stated in C-176/12 *Association de mediation sociale (AMS) v Union locale des syndicats CGT* (nyr).
[60]C-105/03 *Criminal Proceedings against Maria Pupino* [2005] ECR I-5285 [42]
[61]Dorota Leczykiewicz, 'Constitutional conflicts and the third pillar', *European Law Review* 33, 2008, p. 230
[62]Joined Cases C-6/90 and 9/90 *Andrea Francovich and Danila Bonifaci and others* v *Italian Republic* [1991] ECR I-05357

Mr Francovich was one of many employees at CDN Elettronica SnC in Vicenza not to receive full payment of his wages. After proceedings before the Pretura di Vicenza, CDN was ordered to pay approximately 6 million Italian lira. This was not paid. Mr Bonifaci and 33 other employees also brought proceedings in Italy against their employer, Gaia Confezioni Srl, which was declared bankrupt with an outstanding wage bill of more than 253 million Italian lira. In 1988, five years later, they were told that payment was unlikely. Francovich, Bonifaci and the other employees then claimed the guarantees provided in Directive 80/987, arguing that the Italian Republic should provide compensation for the wage arrears.

In 1980, Directive 80/987 was adopted to provide employees with a minimum level of protection under Union law in the event of the insolvency of their employer (without prejudice to more favourable provisions existing in the member states). In particular it provided specific guarantees of payment of unpaid wage claims. Under Article 11, member states were required to bring into force the laws, regulations and administrative provisions necessary to comply with the directive by 23 October 1983. Italy failed to fulfil that obligation, as held by the CJ in its judgment in *Commission* v *Italy*.[63] When the matter returned to the CJ in 1990, via a reference for a preliminary ruling, the Court decided to create a new remedy which might encourage the member states to comply with its rulings.

The remedy of direct effect was not possible as the provisions of the directive, although sufficiently precise and unconditional in relation to the beneficiaries and the content of the guarantee, did not 'identify the person liable to provide the guarantee and the State cannot be considered liable on the sole ground that it has failed to take transposition measures within the prescribed period.' However:

> The full effectiveness of Community [Union] rules would be impaired and the protection of the rights which they grant would be weakened if individuals were unable to obtain reparation when their rights are infringed by a breach of Community law for which a Member State can be held responsible. Such a possibility of reparation by the Member State is particularly indispensable where the full effectiveness of Community rules is subject to prior action on the part of the State and where, consequently, in the absence of such action, individuals cannot enforce before the national courts the rights conferred upon them by Community law. It follows that the principle whereby a State must be liable for loss and damage caused to individuals by breaches of Community law for which the State can be held responsible is inherent in the system of the Treaty.

A further basis for the obligation of member states to make good such loss and damage was found in Article 4(3) TEU which obliges all member states to 'take any appropriate measure, general or particular, to ensure fulfilment of the obligations arising out of the Treaties or resulting from the acts of the institutions of the Union'.

ANALYSING THE LAW

Which of the justifications for state liability do you find most convincing: the effectiveness of EU law or the obligation undertaken by member states?

---

[63]Case 22/87 *Commission* v *Italy* [1989] ECR 143

Three conditions were laid out in order for state responsibility to arise where damages result from non-transposition of a directive: first, the result prescribed by the directive had to entail the grant of rights to individuals, or be designed for the protection of individuals rather than for the promotion of the general public good; second, it should be possible to identify the content of those rights on the basis of the provisions of the directive; and third, there had to be a causal link between the breach of the State's obligation and the loss and damage suffered by the injured parties.[64] Any damage sustained had to flow directly from the obligation laid out in law.[65]

A further condition that the breach be 'sufficiently serious' is laid out in *Brasserie du Pecheur*.[66] The 'sufficiently serious' concept is not new: under Article 215 TFEU, which sets out non-contractual liability on the part of the Union, the Schoppenstedt formula states that Union bodies would only be liable where the breach was 'sufficiently serious'. It was seen as reasonable to hold the member states to the same level of accountability as the Union institutions themselves 'since the protection of the rights which individuals derive from Community law cannot vary depending on whether a national authority or a Community authority is responsible for the damage'.

A breach is 'sufficiently serious' if it persists despite a finding of an infringement by the CJ (as in *Francovich*), a preliminary ruling or settled case law from which it can be concluded that the conduct constituted an infringement.[67] In *Hedley Lomas*[68] it was held that 'the mere infringement of Community law may be sufficient to establish the existence of a sufficiently serious breach'. This was described as a 'per se breach' in *Dillenkofer*[69] in cases where the original *Francovich* conditions hold. In *Köbler*,[70] non-compliance by a court with its obligation to make a reference for preliminary ruling under Article 267 TFEU was added to this.

The substantive question in *Köbler* was whether length-of-service payments awarded only to university professors working in Austrian universities was in breach of Article 45 TFEU. This question was the subject of an Article 267 reference: the CJ directed the referring court to an earlier judgment[71] and the Austrian Supreme Administration Court duly withdrew its reference (*acte éclairé*). However, it went on to misinterpret the decision[72] as a result of which Köbler lost his case for back payment. The new question before the CJ was therefore whether a government could be held liable for a wrongful decision made by a court of last instance. Could Köbler claim damages from the Austrian state as a result of the misinterpretation of EU law by the Supreme Administration Court and the consequent non-payment to him of the length-of-service increment? If so, under what circumstances and who should adjudicate? Can the civil court award damages based on the decision of a higher court? The CJ replied that the principle of liability is inherent in the Treaty system thus such legal protection of rights must be possible.[73] The same conditions

[64]Joined cases C-6/90 and 9/90 *Andrea Francovich and Danila Bonifaci and others* v *Italian Republic* ECR [1991] I-05357
[65]On this see T-268/06 *Olympiaki Aeroporia Ypiresies AE* v *Commission* ECR [2008] II-01091 and C-508/03, *Commission* v *United Kingdom* [2006] ECR I-3969
[66]Joined cases C-46/93 and C-48/93 *Brasserie du Pêcheur SA* v *Bundesrepublik Deutschland and The Queen* v *Secretary of State for Transport, ex parte: Factortame Ltd and others* [1996] ECR I-01029 [32]
[67]See also *Factortame* [499]; C-424/97 *Haim* v *Kassenzahnarztliche Vereinigung Nordrhein* [2000] ECR I-5123 [36]; C-224/01 *Köbler* v *Austria* [2003] ECR I-10239 [51]
[68]*R* v *Ministry of Agriculture, Fisheries and Food, ex parte Hedley Lomas Ltd* [1997] QB 139 [28]
[69]*Dillenkofer* v *Federal Republic of Germany* [1997] QB 259 [29] and *Rechberger* v *Austria*, [2000] 2 CMLR 1
[70]C-224/01 *Köbler* [55]; restated in C-173/03 *Traghetti del Mediterraneo* [2006] ECR I-5177
[71]C-15/96 *Schöning-Kougebetopoulou* v *Freie und Hansestadt Hamburg* [1998] ECR I-47
[72][63–68]
[73][34]

in *Brasserie* would apply: the rule must confer rights, there must be a direct causal link and it must be a sufficiently serious breach ('manifest infringement').[74] However, Austria was not held liable: although the initial judgement of 1998 infringed EU law, the breach was not manifest in nature and thus not sufficiently serious to incur state liability.

The member state is liable regardless of the organ responsible for breach, even in federal states.[75] State liability applies where the national legislature is responsible for the breaches and whichever State authority whose act or omission is responsible for the breach, regardless of domestic rules on the distribution of powers between the authorities – member states cannot hide behind their national political configuration. It also applies regardless of where blame may fall – the national court is not to make its assessment of reparation of loss or damage conditional upon fault (intentional or negligent) by the organ involved, or pursuit of practices contrary to Union law. Furthermore, the application of the principle cannot be made dependent upon a judgment of the CJ finding an infringement or limited to damage sustained after the delivery of a judgment of the Court finding the infringement in question. Member states may impose a time limit on any action for *Francovich* damages provided that it does not hinder access to a remedy under EU law any more than under national law – the procedural requirement may be 'no less favourable than procedural requirements in respect of similar actions of a domestic nature'.[76]

Guidance was given in *Brasserie* on the calculation of reparations. Under the principle of commensurability, the level of reparation must relate to the loss or damage sustained, in line with national arrangements for settling similar claims based upon domestic law. In arranging domestic access to reparation, the member state must ensure equality: substantive and procedural conditions for seeking reparations for breach of EU law are to be as favourable as those relating to national claims (principal of equality). In particular, they are not to be framed in a way which makes access to reparation virtually impossible or excessively difficult. The CJ also declared that specific damages available under national law for actions based upon domestic law (e.g. exemplary damages under English law) are to be available for claims or actions founded on Union law. However, national limitations under domestic law (e.g. rules limiting damages to specifically protected individual interests not including loss of profit by individuals) are incompatible with Union law.

Cases subsequent to *Brasserie* further refined the meaning of 'sufficiently serious'.[77] A number of caveats were introduced which included the degree of discretion open to the institutions and the clarity or ambiguity of the law which is said to have been breached.[78] In *Haim*[79] the CJ said:

[42] In order to determine whether such an infringement of Community [Union] law constitutes a sufficiently serious breach, a national court hearing a claim for reparation must take account of all the factors which characterise the situation put before it.

---

[74][55]

[75]C-302/97 *Konle v Austria* [1999] ECR I-3099

[76]C-261/95 *Palmisani v INPS* [1997] ECR I-4025 [39–40]

[77]C-178-9/94, C-188-90/94 *Dillenkofer and others v Bundesrepublik Deutschland* [1996] ECR I-4845 (non-transposition of a directive as in Francovich); C-5/94 *The Queen/Ministry of Agriculture, Fisheries and Food, ex parte Hedley Lomas* (Ireland) [1996] ECR I-2553 (lack of discretion left to member state, clarity of the breached Treaty provision, absence of a properly verified ground of justification)

[78]For example in *Brasserie,* the German authorities 'must have known' that the German rules on the designation 'bier' were in breach of EC law given earlier rulings on this.

[79]*Haim v Kassenzahnärztliche* [2002] 1 CMLR 11. See also *R v HM Treasury, ex parte British Telecommunications PLC* [1996] QB 615

[43] Those factors include, in particular, the clarity and precision of the rule infringed, whether the infringement and the damage caused was intentional or involuntary, whether any error of law was excusable or inexcusable, and the fact that the position taken by a Community institution may have contributed towards the adoption or maintenance of national measures or practices contrary to Community law.

This multi-factoral test was used in the case of *Cooper,* the first claim brought in the UK for damages pursuant to the decision in *Köbler.* The claim for damages was based upon the failure of the English courts to correct decisions infringing the EIA Directive.[80] Cooper claimed to have suffered damage in consequence of two judgments of the Court of Appeal refusing judicial review[81] of decisions made by local authorities in relation to a shopping centre in London. Cooper argued that outline planning permission had been given by the Council prior to an environmental impact assessment and this amounted to a procedural irregularity that breached the EIA Directive. This error, he claimed, reached the threshold of 'sufficiently serious'. Plender J disagreed:

> Claims based on the Köbler case are to be reserved for exceptional cases, involving errors that are manifest; and in assessing whether this is the case, account must be taken of the specific characteristics of the judicial function, which entails the application of judgment to the interpretation of provisions capable of bearing more than one meaning.[82]

If the national court decides that the situation is not serious enough, in the absence of a reference under Article 267 TFEU the Court of Justice has no opportunity to assess for itself the presence or seriousness of a breach.[83] State liability is a remedy primarily to be applied by national courts.

This can be problematic, especially if other national judges then refer to these national decisions for guidance. For example in *Negassi and Lutalo,*[84] the Court of Appeal turned to *Cooper* when considering the question of whether state liability arose in a case where the Home Secretary had wrongly transposed Article 11 of the Reception Directive[85] which obliges member states to grant asylum seekers access to the labour market. The claim for state liability arose because the Secretary of State initially applied Article 11 only to a first application for asylum; in *ZO*[86] the Supreme Court made clear that this was erroneous – 'a fresh claim' also fell within the meaning of 'an application for asylum' in Article 11 and 'therefore attracts its protections, whatever, as a matter of construction, they may be'.[87] Prior to the ZO decision, Mr Negassi and Mr Lutalo had been refused permission to work.

---

[80]Council Directive 85/337/EC on the assessment of the effects of certain public and private projects on the environment
[81]See *R* v *London Borough of Hammersmith and Fulham* [2000] 2 CMLR 1021; [2000] ELR 549 and [2000] ELR 532
[82]*Cooper* v *Attorney-General* [2008] EWHC 2178 [91]
[83]See *Aurelio de Brito* v *Secretary of State for the Home Department* [2012] EWCA Civ 709 on the right to permanent residence or *G1* v *Secretary of State for the Home Department* [2012] EWCA Civ 867 on exclusion of a Union citizen from the UK
[84]*Negassi and Anor* v *Home Secretary* [2013] EWCA Civ 151
[85]Council Directive 2003/9/EC, Article 11. This has been recast as Article 15, Directive 2013/33/EU of the European Parliament and of the Council of 26 June 2013 laying down standards for the reception of applicants for international protection.
[86]*ZO* v *Secretary of State for the Home Department* [2010] 1 WLR 1948
[87]*Negassi* [3]

After the ZO ruling, they therefore sought to claim *Francovich* damages due to a serious breach of an obligation arising under EU law.

In considering the seriousness of the breach, the Court of Appeal[88] was influenced by Arden LJ's statement in *Cooper* that 'a breach of EU law "will not be manifest if it represents the answer to which the court has come through undertaking a normal judicial function"'.[89] This idea was used to mitigate the seriousness of the breach by the Home Secretary and led to the conclusion that notwithstanding the strength of his argument, the breach was not sufficiently serious to satisfy this national test:

> [20] It was not deliberate. It was the result of a misunderstanding of new provisions in an area of recent EU concern. It was not a cynical or egregious misunderstanding. It was not confined to the Secretary of State. It was shared, as a matter of first impression, by a number of judges. While now all is clear, I do not think that it can be said to have been self-evidently so before the conclusion of ZO.

The CJ may have come to a different conclusion, particularly given the 'striking'[90] total exclusion of a whole category of asylum seekers. It could be argued that a breach will always be manifest, and thus sufficiently serious, if it entails a breach of the case law of the Court of Justice, or if national measures or practices contrary to EU law have been adopted or retained.

VIEWPOINT

Read *AB* v *Home Office* [2012] EWHC 226 (QB) – to what extent does state liability empower individuals to secure enforcement of EU law?

---

iii. Direct applicability of general principles of EU law

It should be remembered that in *Marshall* the CJ expressly stated that:

> [48] ... according to Article 189 of the EEC Treaty [now 288 TFEU] the binding nature of a directive, which constitutes the basis for the possibility of relying on the directive before a national court, exists only in relation to 'each member state to which it is addressed'. It follows that a directive may not of itself impose obligations on an individual and that a provision of a directive may not be relied upon as such against such a person.

How was the Court therefore to respond when national law, as followed by a private company allowed discrimination on the grounds of age in a way that could not be interpreted to meet the objectives of a directive? This situation arose in *Mangold*[91] and *Seda Kücükdeveci*:[92] both of these cases concerned provisions in German law that seemed to allow discrimination on the grounds of age.

---

[88][19]
[89]Cooper [70]
[90][20]
[91]C–144/04 *Mangold v Helm* [2005] ECR I–9981, 75, 557, 563–86, 710, 728, 740
[92]C–555/07 *Kücükdeveci v Swedex GmbH & Co KG* [2010] ECR I–365, 350, 563–86

Older workers know how difficult it can be to secure permanent employment beyond the age of 45. Firms are reluctant to hire older workers for many reasons, some of which are more realistic than others. If firms are reluctant to hire older persons, does a national law which allows them to conclude a certain type of fixed-term contract with workers over a certain age breach the EU rules prohibiting discrimination on the ground of age? The German legislature had introduced such a rule as part of its labour market policy to encourage the employment of older persons. The German rule allowed employers to conclude fixed-term contracts without restrictions with workers who had already passed the age of 52. Mr Mangold entered into such a contract and subsequently complained that it was incompatible with Article 6(1) of Directive 2000/78 on equal treatment in employment.[93]

The Court and the Commission agreed that the objective of the national law – the vocational integration of unemployed older workers – was a legitimate aim but were the means used to achieve that aim 'appropriate and necessary'? Both the national court and the CJ agreed that they were not: there was no evidence to show that using the single criterion of age was necessary to attain the objective pursued – in fact, the reach of the rule went beyond the objective by depriving all workers – those who were employed as well as those who were unemployed – of stable employment. The impact of the age threshold could not be defended as appropriate and necessary to attain the objective pursued:

> [64] . . . as the national court has pointed out, application of national legislation such as that at issue in the main proceedings leads to a situation in which all workers who have reached the age of 52, without distinction, whether or not they were unemployed before the contract was concluded and whatever the duration of any period of unemployment, may lawfully, until the age at which they may claim their entitlement to a retirement pension, be offered fixed-term contracts of employment which may be renewed an indefinite number of times. This significant body of workers, determined solely on the basis of age, is thus in danger, during a substantial part of its members' working life, of being excluded from the benefit of stable employment which, however, as the Framework Agreement makes clear, constitutes a major element in the protection of workers.

However, the problem was that Mr Mangold worked for a private company and in the absence of horizontal direct effect of directives, could not claim the protection of Directive 2000/78. This was not to be the end of the matter, for the CJ then introduced a new element to direct effect: the direct effect of general principles of EU law. It argued that the directive itself was an expression of the binding principle of non-discrimination set out in Article 19 TFEU. As a Treaty provision, it could be invoked in a national court against an individual:

> [74] . . . above all, Directive 2000/78 does not itself lay down the principle of equal treatment in the field of employment and occupation. Indeed, in accordance with Article 1 thereof, the sole purpose of the directive is 'to lay down a general framework for combating discrimination on the grounds of religion or belief, disability, age or sexual orientation', the source of the actual principle underlying the prohibition of those forms of discrimination being found, as is clear from the third and fourth recitals in the preamble to the directive, in various international instruments and in the constitutional traditions common to the Member States.

---

[93]He also argued that it was incompatible with the EU Framework Agreement on fixed term work concluded between the European trade union bodies – ETUC, UNICE and CEEP – as put into effect by Directive 1999/70/EC of 28 June 1999.

[75] The principle of non-discrimination on grounds of age must thus be regarded as a general principle of Community law . . .

This new status of non-discrimination on the grounds of age made another important difference: it did away with the *Ratti* rule regarding the implementation period. The CJ stated that:

[76] . . . observance of the general principle of equal treatment, in particular in respect of age, cannot as such be conditional upon the expiry of the period allowed the Member States for the transposition of a directive intended to lay down a general framework for combating discrimination on the grounds of age . . .

Thus the principle became directly effective immediately and as per *Simmenthal*,[94] the national court was called upon to set aside any conflicting provision of national law.

The *Mangold* ruling was so controversial that doubts were raised on its longevity. There was no evidence in the Treaties, the common constitutional traditions of the member states or international human rights law of the existence of a general principle of non-discrimination on ground of age. Age was mentioned in the EU Charter on Fundamental Rights but this did not at the time have any binding status. It was therefore hoped by many authors[95] that *Mangold* would be an exception rather than lay down a new rule. These hopes were dashed in the case of *Seda Kücükdeveci,* which consolidated this new jurisprudence.

This case differed from *Mangold* in a number of ways: it arose after the deadline for implementation of the Employment Framework Directive; it concerned the compatibility with it of German law on dismissal; and focused on younger workers. New entrants to the labour market can also find it hard to secure employment, as employers are reluctant to bear the costs of training. Germany had introduced a law to encourage the employment of younger workers – the 'young age exception' in German law allowed periods of employment prior to the 25th birthday of the employee be excluded in calculation of the length of employment. This shortened the notice period the employer had to give and saved the company money by allowing younger workers to be dismissed faster.

Kücükdeveci worked for a German company, Swedex, for 10 years from the age of 18. However, when dismissed in 2006, the company relied upon the 'young age exception' to calculate her notice period as if she had been employed by it for just three years. She contested this, giving rise to a dispute between two individuals. The German court raised a number of concerns to the CJ, in particular whether the matter was to be assessed under Article 19 TFEU or the Framework Directive 2000/78. The CJ gave a lengthy reply:

[19] To answer that question, it must first be ascertained, as the referring court suggests, whether the question should be examined by reference to primary European Union law or to Directive 2000/78.

[20] In the first place, that the Council of the European Union adopted Directive 2000/78 on the basis of Article 13 EC [19 TFEU], and the Court has held that that directive does not itself lay down the principle of equal treatment in the field of employment and occupation, which derives from various international instruments and from the constitutional traditions common to the Member States, but has the sole purpose

---

[94]Case 106/77 *Simmenthal* [1978] ECR 629, [21], and C-347/96 *Solred* [1998] ECR I-937 [30]
[95]Christa Tobler, 'Putting Mangold in perspective', *CMLR* 44, 2007, pp. 1177–1183

of laying down, in that field, a general framework for combating discrimination on various grounds including age (see *Mangold*, paragraph 74).

[21] In that context, the Court has acknowledged the existence of a principle of non-discrimination on grounds of age which must be regarded as a general principle of European Union law (see, to that effect, *Mangold*, paragraph 75). Directive 2000/78 gives specific expression to that principle (see, by analogy, Case 43/75 *Defrenne* [1976] ECR 455, paragraph 54).

[22] It should also be noted that Article 6(1) TEU provides that the Charter of Fundamental Rights of the European Union is to have the same legal value as the Treaties. Under Article 21(1) of the charter, '[a]ny discrimination based on . . . age . . . shall be prohibited'.

[23] For the principle of non-discrimination on grounds of age to apply in a case such as that at issue in the main proceedings, that case must fall within the scope of European Union law.

In contrast to *Bartsch*,[96] as the transposition period had expired by the time the facts of *Kücükdeveci* arose, conditions for dismissal were deemed to fall within the scope of EU law. However, the CJ did not specify whether the ruling was based upon the *Mangold* principle or Directive 2000/78 – it avoided this issue:

[43] It follows from all the above considerations that the answer to Question 1 is that European Union law, more particularly the principle of non-discrimination on grounds of age as given expression by Directive 2000/78, must be interpreted as precluding national legislation, such as that at issue in the main proceedings, which provides that periods of employment completed by an employee before reaching the age of 25 are not taken into account in calculating the notice period for dismissal.

Yet when considering the duty of the national court to achieve the full effectiveness of EU law, it clearly stated that the interpretive duty arises from Article 19 TFEU not the directive:

[51] . . . it for the national court, hearing a dispute involving the principle of non-discrimination on grounds of age as given expression in Directive 2000/78, to provide, within the limits of its jurisdiction, the legal protection which individuals derive from European Union law and to ensure the full effectiveness of that law, disapplying if need be any provision of national legislation contrary to that principle (see, to that effect, *Mangold*, paragraph 77).

There remains significant scope for developing clarity on the relationship between the general principles and direct effect. As these cases are both decisions of the Grand Chamber, Muir asserts that it is at least:

. . . now clear that private parties can rely on the general principle of equality, as given expression in the Framework Equality Directive, in order to set aside conflicting domestic rules in horizontal litigation.[97]

---

[96]C 427/06 *Bartsch* [2008] ECR I-7245
[97]Elise Muir, 'Of ages In – And Edges Of – EU Law', *CMLR* 48, 2011, p. 39 at 40

She describes these cases as setting out new 'edges' in EU law and attempts to identify the precise location of these edges by comparing two models of the relationship between primacy and direct effect. Under the *unitary* model, primacy trumps direct effect: thus if – as in *Mangold* – a provision of EU law takes primacy over national law, there is no need for it to be clear, precise and unconditional. The conditions for direct effect are irrelevant. However, under the *dualist* model, primacy is subject to the conditions of direct effect being satisfied: thus in *Mangold*, Article 19 TFEU would not have direct effect because it fails the test. Under the dualist model, which is more restrictive, the German law would therefore have remained applicable. It is clear that in *Mangold* the Grand Chamber applied the unitary model – nowhere in the case does it discuss the criteria for direct effect. As the dualist approach conducts the test systematically, it arguably contributes more to legal certainty. Yet, the unitary approach may be more effective in the protection of individual rights. While there is lack of certainty, there is at least continuity – the CJ has always argued that EU law should be seen as the 'law of the land' in the member states.[98]

ANALYSING THE LAW

To what extent does the Grand Chamber discuss direct effect in *Mangold* and *Kücükde-vecl*? Do these cases Introduce horizontal direct effect of directives?

AMS[99] has also confirmed the strict rejection of horizontal direct effect of directives. This case, heard before the Grand Chamber, concerned protection of workers' rights. In 2002, the EU adopted Directive 2002/14[100] establishing a general framework for consultation of workers. The French Labour Code implementing the directive introduced exceptions for organisations with low numbers of workers. The Association de Mediation Sociale (AMS), a French community organisation working on the mediation of social disputes and reintegration of workers considered itself to be covered by this exemption and was thus unhappy when the local division of a trade union, the Union Locale des Syndicats CGT, appointed a trade union representative to it. AMS complained to the national courts: in April 2011 the Constitutional Council upheld the disputed provisions of the Labour Code and in July 2011 the Marseille Tribunal found them incompatible with the EU directive. AMS appealed this decision before the French Court of Cassation, which stayed the case to ask the CJ whether the fundamental right of workers to consultation, set out in Article 27 of the Charter in conjunction with Directive 2002/14, could be invoked in a dispute between individuals in order to disapply an incompatible provision of French law?

The Court held that the directive did indeed preclude the incompatible French provisions and furthermore that the relevant Article 3(1) of the directive fulfilled the conditions for direct effect – it was clear, precise and unconditional. However, recalling *Pfeiffer* and *Kücükdeveci* it then stated that 'even a clear, precise and unconditional provision of a directive seeking to confer rights or impose obligations on individuals cannot of itself apply in proceedings exclusively between private parties'[36]. Thus AMS, as a body

---

[98]Sacha Prechal, 'Does Direct Effect Still Matter', *CMLR* 37, 2000, p. 1047
[99]C-176/12 *AMS*
[100]OJ L80/29 2002

governed by private law was unable to rely on the directive. Had it been an 'emanation of the state' it would have been able to do so.

The Court then considered the doctrines developed to ameliorate the lack of horizontal direct effect of directives. It first looked at indirect effect but this was not an option given the contrary wording of the Labour Code provision. It then turned to its newer jurisprudence – as the national provisions were adopted to implement EU law, could Article 27 CFR be directly applicable in the same way that the general principle of non-discrimination on grounds of age in Article 21(1) CFR was found to be directly effective in *Kücükdeveci*? The CJ decided not: unlike Article 21(1), Article 27 is not 'sufficient in itself'[101] to confer on individuals a right that they can invoke in a dispute. Its use of more general wording suggests that in order for it to be fully effective, 'more specific expression in EU or national law' is necessary. It could therefore not be used in isolation as a shield to disapply the effects of incompatible national law in a dispute between two individuals. AMS were instead advised to rely on *Francovich* to seek compensation for any loss sustained.

ANALYSING THE LAW

Read Articles 21(1) and 27 CFR: how does their wording differ? Why did the CJ find that the former is 'sufficient in itself' but the latter not?

Similar advice was given in the earlier case of *Dominguez*,[102] concerning the compatibility of domestic law with Directive 2003/88 on the right to paid annual leave. In this case the CJ summarised the different duties on the national courts to achieve the effectiveness of EU law in proceedings between individuals: first, can indirect effect be used – this is the first step because 'the question whether a national provision must be disapplied in as much as it conflicts with European Union law arises only if no compatible interpretation of that provision proves possible'.[103] Second, is the respondent an 'emanation of the state' such that direct effect can be applied? The question of state liability only arises thereafter:

> [44] . . . it is for the national court to determine, taking the whole body of domestic law into consideration, in particular Article L. 223-4 of the Code du travail, and apply-ing the interpretative methods recognised by domestic law, with a view to ensuring that Article 7 of Directive 2003/88 is fully effective and achieving an outcome consistent with the objective pursued by it, whether it can find an interpretation of that law that allows the absence of the worker due to an accident on the journey to or from work to be treated as being equivalent to one of the situations covered by that Article of the Code du travail. If such an interpretation is not possible, it is for the national court to determine whether, in the light of the legal nature of the respondents in the main proceedings, the direct effect of Article 7(1) of Directive 2003/88 may be relied upon against them. If the national court is unable to achieve the objective laid down in Article

---

[101][49]

[102]C-282/10 *Commission v Ireland* [2011] ECR 2011 I-140

[103][23]

7 of Directive 2003/88, the party injured as a result of domestic law not being in conformity with European Union law can none the less rely on the judgment in *Francovich and Others* in order to obtain, if appropriate, compensation for the loss sustained.

APPLYING THE LAW

Apply the guidance in *Dominguez* to the facts of *AB*. Does this change the outcome?

---

4. Conclusion

Were he alive today, it is hard to know whether Pescatore would think that direct effect has now developed into a mature virus or a valuable tool to secure the effectiveness of EU law. The concept has certainly changed – having been introduced into the Treaty, it was subsequently extended and developed to incorporate different forms of EU law and different situations. It now has vertical and horizontal aspects that apply differentially to the Treaties and the three binding forms of secondary EU law. There has arguably been inconsistency in its development. This was the main theme of section 1. It was shown that the standards shifted subsequent to *van Gend*. The main theme of section 2 was alternative forms of empowerment – as the limits of direct effect became apparent, the CJEU identified alternative doctrines to enable individuals to claim the protection offered by EU law in the national courts.

The identification of its limits – horizontal direct effect of directives – became the starting point for a new doctrine, that of indirect effect. Likewise, the limits of indirect effect launched the doctrine of state liability. The key issue with these alternatives is that they are weakened by reliance on national bodies: national officials can still disobey and prevent enjoyment of rights in EU law; national courts can deny state liability, or avoid the interpretive duty. The introduction of direct effect of a general principle circumvents all tests, implementation timeframes, questions of compatible interpretation and assessment of sufficient seriousness. It can be seen as the completion of a circle, as it takes the court back to reliance on primacy and its original unitary vision of the relationship between EU law and the national legal orders. Could it be that the CJ now agrees with Pescatore and wants to reduce reliance on direct effect in favour of primacy? Such a conclusion is supported by the guidance provided in *Dominguez*, where direct effect is to be considered after indirect effect.

If this is so, it needs to be stated clearly. Despite the controversy of its introduction, this development should be welcomed for its consequences – the decisions in *Mangold* and *Kücükdeveci* make it clear that it is workers, and often those at the edges of the labour market, who suffer by the absence of horizontal direct effect of directives. Having taken this bold step the CJ now needs to clarify the scope of this principle, which will only be credible if it applies to all grounds of discrimination iterated in Article 19 TFEU and as many provisions in the Charter as possible.

Further reading

On direct effect:

Dorota Leczykiewicz, 'Constitutional conflicts and the third pillar', *European Law Review* 33, 2008, p. 230

Pierre Pescatore, 'The Doctrine of Direct Effect: An Infant Disease of Community Law', *European Law Review* 8, 1983

Albertina Albers-Lloren, 'Keeping Up Appearances: The Court of Justice and the Effects of EU Directives', *Cambridge Law Journal* 69, 2011

Elise Muir, 'Of ages In – And Edges Of – EU Law', *CMLR* 48, 2011, p. 39

Sacha Prechal, 'Does Direct Effect Still Matter?', *CMLR* 37, 2000, p. 1047

On state liability:

Carol Harlow, 'Francovich and the Problem of the Disobedient State', *European Law Journal* 2, 1996, pp. 199–225

Tobias Lock, 'Is private enforcement of EU law through state liability a myth? An assessment 20 years after Francovich', *Common Market Law Review* 49, 2012, p. 1675

8 Fundamental rights

Setting the scene

Rosalind Williams Lecraft is an African American woman who gained Spanish citizenship in 1969. At approximately 1 p.m. on 6 December 1992, she arrived at the Valladolid Campo Grande railway station on a train coming from Madrid. She was accompanied by her husband and their son. Moments after she, her husband and son had disembarked from the train, a National Police (Policia Nacional) officer approached her and asked her to provide him with her identity document (the 'Documento Nacional de Identificación' or 'DNI'). The National Police officer did not ask her husband, son, or any other passengers on the platform for their identity documents. She and her husband insisted that the officer explain the reason for the identity check. The National Police officer explained that he had to check the identity of persons who 'looked like her.' When LeCraft's husband asked what the expression 'like her' meant, the police officer answered, 'like her,' while pointing at her, adding that 'many of them are illegal immigrants.' The officer further explained that, in carrying out the identity check, he was obeying an order of the Ministry of the Interior that called on National Police officers to conduct identity checks, in particular, of 'persons of color.' The officer continued to insist that she produce her DNI. Her husband commented to the officer that his request to see her DNI based solely on her skin color constituted racial discrimination. The officer denied this.

Rosalind Williams Lecraft v Spain[1]

1. **Introduction**

2. **A brief history of fundamental human rights**

   i. The UN Declaration of Human Rights (1948)

   ii. The European Convention on Human Rights (1950)

   iii. The EU Charter of Fundamental Rights (2000)

3. **The Court of Justice and the development of fundamental rights as general principles of EU law**

   i. Non-discrimination as a general principle in the Treaty

   ii. The CJEU and fundamental rights as general principles

   iii. Sources of general principles

   iv. Protection of fundamental freedoms and protection of fundamental rights

---

[1]Communication submitted for consideration under the first optional protocol to the International Covenant on Civil and Political Rights (ICCPR), http://www.bayefsky.com/docs.php/area/jurisprudence/Treaty/ccpr/opt/0/state/161/node/4/filename/spain_t5_iccpr_1493_2006

1. Introduction

Human rights are a special class of rights designed to play a special role in a reasonable law of peoples for the present age. Recall that the accepted ideas about international law changed in two basic ways following WWII, and this change in basic moral beliefs is comparable to other profound historical changes. War is no longer an admissible means of state policy. It is only justified in self-defence and a state's internal sovereignty is now limited. One role of human rights is precisely to specify limits to that sovereignty.[2]

Much has changed since human rights were dismissed by Bentham as 'nonsense upon stilts';[3] in the increasingly secular era, Klug describes them as 'values for a godless age.'[4] Human rights refer to a set of values which underpin relationships and actions between individuals and between the state and individuals. Rights are not preferences – rights are considered to have a moral significance which places them above politics. They are values and norms that exist beyond the political process. Human rights have been described as a 'unique form of moral discourse'[5] in at least two ways: first, they promote the idea of a single rationality shared by all educated persons; and second, although they embody normative claims, they are also considered law. Slavery, Colonialism, Apartheid and National Socialism are examples of systems that paid no regard to the values cherished as human rights.

Rights can be placed into four categories of law:

1   Category 1 consists of purely aspirational documents that have no binding effect on states or individuals (such as the Universal Declaration of Human Rights 1948);

2   Category 2 comprises Treaties which bind the signatory states but their effect in national law depends upon whether the state is monist or dualist (such as the European Convention on Human Rights);

---

[2]John Rawls, *The Law of Peoples*, Harvard University Press, 1999
[3]Jeremy Bentham, 'Anarchical Fallacies', Essay of 1843 republished in Philip Schofield, Catherine Pease-Watkin and Cyprian Blamires (eds), *Rights, Representation, and Reform – Nonsense upon Stilts and Other Writings on the French Revolution*, Clarendon Press, 2002
[4]Francesca Klug, *Values for a godless age: the story of the United Kingdom's New Bill of Rights*, Penguin Books, 2000
[5]Clinton Curle, *Humanite: John Humphrey's alternative Account of Human Rights*, University of Toronto Press, 2007, p. 20

3 Category 3 contains statutes and secondary law which empower courts to determine the existence of rights and review compatibility of legislation with them (such as the UK Human Rights Act 1998);

4 represents constitutional Bills of Rights, which give courts the power to strike down legislation incompatible with them (such as the US Constitution or to a more limited extent the EU Charter on Fundamental Rights).[6]

These categories are not mutually exclusive – the UK Human Rights Act 1998 is an example of an aspirational document that can become binding and empower courts to conduct compatibility review.

According to Kennedy, the origin of rights in international law means that they are intrinsically apolitical.[7] A key location for the development of human rights and their practice,[8] as we know them today, was the United Nations. The United Nations was a forum for the post-war reformulation of values in law and politics.[9] It provided a formal space where international norms and beliefs could be debated and re-created at a remove from the national political sphere but not necessarily without the influence of national politics.[10] The UN was also an independent body that could exert pressure on domestic governments to review and perhaps revise practices, policies and laws. This applied to many areas of law[11] beyond human rights.

The essence of a right is that it is afforded immediate protection,[12] even if this protection is not absolute. Rights are 'fundamental' because their existence is not open to dispute, negotiation or compromise, although their substance is subject to interpretation. Rights are anchored in law and they underwrite legal as well as political action – despite their interaction, human rights should not be equated with human rights law.

The four EU 'freedoms' (free movement of goods, workers, services and capital) are like 'rights' – they remain subject to continued debate and negotiation in the national and EU legislatures.[13] The four freedoms pre-date EU rights, which were first mentioned in *Internationale* almost as an afterthought to limit the powers of the EU. Furthermore, a fundamental EU *freedom* can sometimes trump a fundamental *right* such as freedom of expression or association.[14] Fundamental rights are now anchored in the Charter of Fundamental Rights but these have not displaced the single market as the *raison d'etre* of the EU – it is questionable whether they will ever do so.[15]

---

[6]J.D. Heydon, 'Are Bills of Rights Necessary in Common Law Systems?', Lecture delivered at the Oxford Law School on 23 January 2013, pp. 3–4

[7]David Kennedy, 'Receiving the International', *Connecticut Journal of International Law* 10(1), 1994, p. 1

[8]Charles R. Beitz, *The Idea of Human Rights*, Oxford University Press, 2009. For alternative theories of rights see Rawls's *The Law of Peoples* who places rights within the frame of international relations and *realpolitik* and James Griffin, *On Human Rights*, Oxford University Press, 2008 who takes a moral or ethical approach to rights, although rights are not seen as the only source of moral behaviour.

[9]For a critical history of the UN, see Mark Mazower, *No Enchanted Palace: The End of Empire and the Ideological Origins of the United Nations*, Princeton University Press, 2013, or Martti Koskenniemi, *The Politics of International Law*, Hart Publishing, 2011.

[10]John Humphrey gives an insight into the workings of the Commission of Human Rights, see *On the Edge of Greatness: The Diaries of John Humphrey*, McGill-Queen's University Press, 1994–2000.

[11]For example, in 1962 the UN created the United Nations Commission on International Trade Law (UNCITRAL) to harmonise international business transactions.

[12]Armin von Bogdandy, 'The European Union as a Human Rights Organisation?', *CMLR* 37, 2000, pp.1307–1308, 1326 fn 46

[13]Bogdandy 2000, p. 1326 fn 101

[14]C-112/00 *Eugen Schmidberger, Internationale Transporte und Planzüge v Republik Österreich* [2003] ECR I-5659 [59]. Also C-265/95 *Commission v France* [1997] ECR I-6959 and C-36/02 *Omega Spielhalle* [2004] ECR I-9609

[15]Bogdandy 2000

This chapter will explore the appearance and evolution of human rights in EU law, paying particular attention to five themes:

- the history and systematisation of human rights in EU law;
- their initial appearance in EU law via adjudication rather than political deliberation;
- the relationship between general principles, fundamental freedoms and fundamental rights in EU law;
- the use of fundamental rights in EU law, in particular the scope of judicial review by the CJEU; and
- accession to the European Convention on Human Rights.

The use of rights has changed over time. Initially seen primarily as 'negative' entitlements, to be used to provide protection from arbitrary intrusions of government power into the sphere of individual liberty, they have become objective principles which protect against threats by individuals and groups, or basic rights which 'penetrate the whole legal and social order'.[16] Fundamental rights therefore have a dual purpose: to regulate government exercise of authority, but also to inform the way in which individuals behave towards each other. This is summarised in the following table:

Fundamental rights	
Negative entitlements protecting individuals from arbitrary state intrusions	Objective principles to be protected from arbitrary intrusions

The treatment of LeCraft would fall into the first category. As a signatory of the ECHR and other international rights instruments, Spain has a duty to abstain from racial discrimination in the exercise of public powers. I had failed in this obligation by subjecting LeCraft to racial profiling.[17]

2. A brief history of fundamental human rights

Fundamental rights are used to establish behavioural boundaries in the relationship between rulers and the ruled. Prior to 1945, regulation of these relationships was accepted as the exclusive responsibility of sovereign governments. Motivated by the atrocities committed during the Second World War, this deference to state sovereignty changed – 'the doctrine of national sovereignty was morally discredited. It was recognised that states could no longer agree not to interfere in the internal affairs of countries where atrocities were taking place.'[18] Since the end of the Second World War, rights have acted as an entry ticket to the world of international relations – paradoxically, this negation of autonomy now precedes legitimate assertion and recognition of national sovereignty.[19] Acceptance of rights automatically limits how a state may treat those within its borders thus, as

---

[16]Jutta Limbach, 'The Effects of the Jurisdiction of the German Federal Constitutional Court', EUI Working Paper Law No 99/5, p. 12
[17]*Rosalind Williams Lecraft v Spain*; Open Society Institute, *'I Can Stop and Search Whoever I Want' Police Stops of Ethnic Minorities in Bulgaria, Hungary, and Spain*, OSI 2007
[18]F. Klug, K. Starmer and S. Weir, (1996) *The Three Pillars of Liberty*, Routledge, p. 6
[19]C. Chinkin, 'The State that acts alone: bully, good samaritan or iconoclast?', *EJIL* 11(1), 2000, p. 41

Rawls[20] says, respect for fundamental rights goes together with a limitation of state sovereignty – it is impossible to declare respect for rights without ceding some power to an external authority overseeing those rights. Traditional and non-traditional international organisations are the beneficiaries of these powers.

i.   The UN Declaration of Human Rights (1948)

Plans for the transfer of sovereignty via legal entrenchment of rights in international law began on 29 April 1946, when the Economic and Social Council of the United Nations held the first meeting of its Commission on Human Rights (CHR).[21] Mr Henri Laugier, Assistant Secretary General in charge of Social Affairs reminded the meeting in his opening words that:

> . . . it is a new thing and it is a great thing in the history of humanity that the international community organised after a war which destroyed material wealth and spiritual wealth accumulated by human effort during centuries has constituted an international mechanism to defend the human rights in the world . . . We are only at the starting point of a very great enterprise, the volume of which and the action of which will have to grow, day after day.[22]

The objective of the CHR was to discover the basis for a fundamental declaration on human rights which would be acceptable to all current members of the United Nations, and those who might subsequently seek admission into the 'international community'. Its specific task was to 'define the violation of human rights within a nation, which would constitute a menace to the security and peace of the world and the existence of which is sufficient to put in movement the mechanism of the United Nations for the maintenance of peace and security', and beyond this to 'suggest the establishment of machinery of observation which will find and denounce the violations of the rights of man all over the world'.[23]

The CHR drafted the first mainstream declaration on rights, the UN Declaration of Human Rights (UNDHR) proclaimed in 1948[24] to establish basic values to inform human interaction. The preamble of the UN Declaration of 1948 describes recognition of 'rights' as the foundation of freedom, justice and peace in the world; disregard and contempt of them leads to barbarous acts that outrage the conscience of mankind.

> Whereas recognition of the inherent dignity and of the equal and inalienable rights of all members of the human family is the foundation of freedom, justice and peace in the world,

> Whereas disregard and contempt for human rights have resulted in barbarous acts which have outraged the conscience of mankind, and the advent of a world in which human beings shall enjoy freedom of speech and belief and freedom from fear and want has been proclaimed as the highest aspiration of the common people . . .

---

[20]John Rawls, 'The Law of Peoples', in Obrad Savic (ed), *The Politics of Human Rights*, Verso, 1999, pp. 5, 16–45, 33
[21]UN E/HR/6 1 May 1946
[22]UN E/HR/6 pp. 1, 2
[23]UN E/HR/6 p. 3
[24]Signed 10 December 1948

The UN Declaration begins with the acknowledgement of two basic principles: Article 1 states that 'all human beings are born free and equal in dignity and rights. They are endowed with reason and conscience and should act towards one another in a spirit of brotherhood.' Article 2 provided the basis for anti-discrimination law:

> *Everyone is entitled to all the rights and freedoms set forth in this Declaration, without distinction of any kind, such as race, colour, sex, language, religion, political or other opinion, national or social origin, property, birth or other status. Furthermore, no distinction shall be made on the basis of the political, jurisdictional or international status of the country or territory to which a person belongs, whether it be independent, trust, non-self-governing or under any other limitation of sovereignty.*

The sentiments in these Articles may be taken for granted in the twenty-first century but at the time of their drafting, there were many places in the world that did not adhere to them – the Soviet Union had its Gulags, the United States still operated under *de jure* racism, and many European countries still had colonies.[25] Agreement of such principles at the international level therefore brought much hope to many oppressed peoples in the world.

ii.   The European Convention on Human Rights (1950)

The UN Declaration identifies a series of distinct prohibitions and rights as 'inalienable' to every human being.[26] In the years following the UN Declaration, more specific instruments were created which included compliance mechanisms. The first specific UN measure to contain such was the International Convention on the Elimination of All Forms of Racial Discrimination (ICERD), adopted in 1965.[27] The ICERD established a Commission to monitor adherence to the prohibitions it listed. The first regional instrument to do so was the European Convention on Human Rights (ECHR).

The ECHR is a separate rights regime created by the Council of Europe,[28] an organisation that pre-dates the European Union. Created in 1950, two years after the UN Declaration was agreed, the ECHR is the oldest of the regional charters now existing in many parts of the world.[29] It was a pioneering agreement because it included an international court – the European Court of Human Rights (ECtHR) in Strasbourg – to collectively enforce the Convention via individual petition from the signatory state. Nonetheless, there were still ways for states to circumvent enforcement, especially where dualist[30] legal systems require a national statute to implement international law. Thus although the UK was a founder signatory of the ECHR,[31] its dualist system meant that British citizens only

---

[25]Obrad Savic (ed), *The Politics of Human Rights*, Verso, 1999, p. 3

[26]http://www.un.org/en/documents/udhr/

[27]http://treaties.un.org/Pages/ViewDetails.aspx?mtdsg_no=IV-2&chapter=4&lang=en

[28]The Council of Europe is an international organisation created in 1941. It currently has 43 members including Russia and Azerbaijan.

[29]African Charter on International Rights; Inter-American Charter

[30]Fiona de Londras, 'Dualism, Domestic Courts, and the Rule of International Law', Social Science Research Networkpaper, 16 April 16, 2009, http://ssrn.com/abstract=1393293

[31]http://ukhumanrightsblog.com/2013/09/03/why-we-would-be-mad-to-leave-our-european-convention-on-human-rights/#more-19476. See also Ed Bates, *The Evolution of the European Convention on Human Rights, From its Inception to the Creation of a Permanent Court of Human Rights*, Oxford University Press, 2010

became entitled to enjoy the protection of provisions in the ECHR before British courts when the Human Rights Act was introduced by the Labour government in 1998.[32]

The existence of the ECHR is often used to explain why the Treaty of Rome was silent on human rights: all of the founder member states were signatories to the Convention. In addition, the EEC was envisaged as an economic grouping not a political one. However, the situation changed dramatically in the 50 years between 1950 and 2000 when the EU Charter of Fundamental Rights (CFR) was solemnly proclaimed at Nice. Most recently the CFR was given equal status to the Treaties at Lisbon. One may well ask why it took so long – Hartley suggests that this is because rights were recognised to justify supremacy rather than for their own sake – the CJ had no commitment to them per se but sought to further its own institutional agenda.[33] O'Neill and Coppel also argue that the Court has used protection of human rights as no more than a 'slogan' to seize the 'moral high ground'.[34]

iii. The EU Charter of Fundamental Rights (2000)

The contents of these documents were progressive in 1945 but the EU Charter of Fundamental Rights (CFR), agreed in 2000, arguably contains a more 'modern' list of rights – technological developments and social change have given rise to new standards and norms needed to achieve the same ends sought over 50 years ago. There was much scepticism that the EU could create a Bill of Human Rights for around 500 million people – could the member states agree the contents of this? Could they agree on its legal status? Could they endow the CJEU with the necessary power to interpret and apply it?[35] The EU silenced these sceptics in 2000, with a radical change to the appearance of human rights in the EU – at the intergovernmental conference in Nice, the heads of state and government meeting in the European Council agreed a Charter of Fundamental Rights.

This document had a long evolution. An important step was the inclusion in 1992 of Article 6 TEU which for the first time declared that respect for human rights and fundamental freedoms is part of the Union:

---

(1) *The Union is founded on the principles of liberty, democracy, respect for human rights and fundamental freedoms, and the rule of law, principles which are common to the Member States.*

(2) *The Union shall respect fundamental rights, as guaranteed by the European Convention for the Protection of Human Rights and Fundamental Freedoms signed in Rome on 4 November 1950 and as they result from the constitutional traditions common to the Member States, as general principles of Community law.*

---

[32]Lord Bingham, 'The British Legal System and Incorporation of the European Convention on Human Rights: The Opportunity and the Challenge', EUI Working Paper LAW No. 99/5
[33]Trevor Hartley, *The Foundations of European Union Law*, 8th edn, Oxford University Press, 2014
[34]Jason Coppel and Aidan O'Neill, 'The European Court of Justice: Taking Rights Seriously?', *Legal Studies* 12(2), 1992, pp. 227–239, 243 (see also the response by J.H.H. Weiler and Nicolas J.S. Lockhart, ' "Taking Rights Seriously": The European Court and its fundamental rights jurisprudence', *Common Market Law Review* 32, 1995, pp. 61–94 and pp. 579–627
[35]Mauro Cappelletti, Paul J. Kollmer and Joanne M. Olson, *The judicial process in comparative perspective*, Oxford and Clarendon Press, 1999

In 1999 the European Council in Germany decided to draw up a new Charter of Fundamental Rights. The heads of state and government decided that the European Union was at a stage of development where 'the fundamental rights applicable at Union level should be consolidated in a Charter and thereby made more evident'. The purpose of a single Charter was to increase their visibility and thereby their importance and relevance. The Summit also agreed to consider the creation of an Agency for Human Rights.[36] A decision, attached in an Appendix,[37] signified a new and deeper role for human rights and fundamental freedoms in the EU – they were recognised as not just a founding principle of the Union but furthermore an 'indispensable prerequisite for her legitimacy'. However, fundamental rights in the EU were to be all inclusive. The resulting list of rights is long because it encompasses fundamental rights and freedoms, 'basic procedural rights' guaranteed in the ECHR and member state constitutional traditions as general principles of EU law as well as 'economic and social rights' set out in the European Social Charter and the Community Charter of the Fundamental Social Rights of Workers.[38] The Charter design was also to be all inclusive: the idea was to involve a wide variety of actors in the creation of the Charter, presumably so that it would find widespread acceptance and legitimacy.

Despite these goals to stimulate wide social and political discussion and debate, no immediate decision was taken on the status of the Charter when it was completed in 2000, or its relationship to the Treaties. This was deferred until drafting was complete, and then it would be considered not only how but *if* the Charter should be integrated into the Treaties. The European Council commitment extended only to cataloguing rights. Nonetheless, a deadline of December 2000 was set for the preparation of a draft document which the European Council envisaged as the basis of a European Charter of Fundamental Rights.

In September 2000, the European Commission published its first communication on the draft Charter. At the European Council meeting in Biarritz (October 2000), the draft Charter was unanimously approved and forwarded to the European Parliament and the Commission. The European Parliament gave its agreement on 14 November 2000 and the Commission on 6 December 2000. It was signed by the Presidents of the European Parliament, the Council and the Commission, who proclaimed the Charter on behalf of their institutions on 7 December 2000 in Nice. It was incorporated into the Constitution in December 2004.

The Charter contains what can be described as a modern list of fundamental rights (see Table 8.1). Protection under this Charter is far more extensive – it contains 50 Articles in comparison to the 30 of the Convention. Whether more rights make for better protection is debateable – too many rights may reduce the potency of these values. The list could also be described as misguided – can consumer protection really exist as a 'right' alongside freedom from torture? The inclusion of the former is only logical if the EU is viewed as an international trade organisation where the consumer is as important as the citizen. The list of rights in the Charter therefore provides important information on what the EU is and hopes to be. However, more people need to be aware of it: according to a

---

[36]Cologne European Council 3–4 June 1999, Conclusions Of The Presidency, para 44
[37]Cologne European Council 3–4 June 1999, Conclusions Of The Presidency, Annex IV – European Council Decision On The Drawing Up Of A Charter Of Fundamental Rights Of The European Union
[38]Cologne European Council 3–4 June 1999, Conclusions Of The Presidency, Annex IV

TABLE 8.1   List of human and fundamental rights in the UNDHR, the ECHR and the CFR

UN Declaration on Human Rights (1948) 25 Articles: right to life, prohibition of torture, slavery and forced labour, right to liberty and security, fair trial, non-discrimination, remedies, fair hearing, presumption of innocence, right to movement, asylum, nationality, to marry, own property, conscience and religion, freedom of expression, association, democratic participation, social security, to work, rest and leisure, education.
European Convention on Human Rights (ECHR) (1950) 13 Articles: right to life, prohibition of torture, slavery and forced labour, right to liberty and security, fair trial, no punishment without law, respect for family and private life, freedom of thought and religion, freedom of expression, the right of assembly and association, the right to marry, access to a remedy and the prohibition of discrimination.
EU Charter on Fundamental Rights (CFR) (2000) 50 Articles in 6 Chapters: (1) Dignity: inviolability of human dignity; right to life; right to integrity of the person; prohibition of torture and inhuman or degrading treatment and punishment; prohibition of slavery and forced labour. (2) Freedoms: right to liberty and security; respect for private and family life; protection of personal data; right to marry and have a family; freedom of thought, conscience and religion; freedom of expression and information; freedom of assembly and association; freedom of the arts and sciences; right to education; freedom to choose an occupation and a right to engage in work; ability to conduct a business; right to property; right to asylum; protection if expelled or extradited. (3) Equality: non-discrimination (genetic features); cultural, religious and linguistic diversity; equality between men and women; the rights of the child; the rights of the elderly; integration of persons with disabilities. (4) Solidarity: right to information and consultation; right of access to placement services; protection from unjustified dismissal; fair and just working conditions; prohibition of child labour and protection of young people at work; family and professional life; social security and assistance; health care; access to services of general economic interest; environmental protection; consumer protection. (5) Citizens Rights: right to vote and stand in EP elections; right to vote and stand in municipal elections; good administration; access to documents; access to the Ombudsman; right to petition the EP; right to free movement and residence; right to diplomatic and consular protection. (6) Justice: effective remedy and fair trial; presumption of innocence and right of defence; principles of legality and proportionality of criminal offences and penalties; right not to be tried or punished twice in criminal proceedings for the same criminal offence.

Eurobarometer survey[39] few citizens know what the Charter actually is (11 per cent) and when it applies (14 per cent).[40]

The journey from the silence in the Treaty of Rome to the equal status of the Charter of Fundamental Rights in the Treaty of Lisbon travels through international law, national

---

[39]Flash Eurobarometer 340 'The Charter of Fundamental Rights of the European Union', 2012
[40]European Commission, '2011 Report on the application of the EU Charter of Fundamental Rights', COM(2012) 169 final, p. 8

constitutional law, EU case law and secondary EU law. It has not yet come to an end as the Treaty of Lisbon also made provision for the EU to accede to the ECHR. Does this indicate that the CJEU and EU are now taking rights seriously? The recent Opinion 2/13 against accession to the ECHR indicates that the CJEU and EU approach protection of rights very differently.[41] One may well ask why accession to the ECHR is necessary now that the EU has its own Charter? What difference does this make in general and in particular to those like LeCraft who are stopped by police because they are black or belong to a minority ethnic group?

ANALYSING THE LAW

Compare the list of rights in the UNDHR, the ECHR and the CFR – what areas are covered in each? Do you agree that all on the lists are 'rights' – e.g. the right to life, to education or to a holiday? Can disrespect for 'consumer protection' result in 'outrageous acts'? Are any rights contained in all three documents?

---

a) The EU institutional response to the CFR

The Charter was not given a formal legal status but its adoption was taken as a firm political statement. Nicole Fontaine, President of the European Parliament stated that:

> A signature represents a commitment . . . I trust that all the citizens of the Union will understand that from now on . . . the Charter will be the law guiding the actions of the Assembly . . . From now on it will be the point of reference for all the Parliament acts which have a direct or indirect bearing on the lives of citizens throughout the Union.

Likewise Romano Prodi, President of the Commission declared:

> In the eyes of the European Commission, by proclaiming the Charter of Fundamental Rights, the European Union institutions have committed themselves to respecting the Charter in everything they do and in every policy they promote . . . The citizens of Europe can rely on the Commission to ensure that the Charter will be respected . . .

The Council issued no such declaration of support but it did approve the Commission proposal to create a new agency, the Fundamental Rights Agency,[42] to oversee the adherence to fundamental rights in the EU. The Fundamental Rights Agency is responsible for carrying out pre-legislative scrutiny of Commission proposals to verify their compliance with fundamental rights as defined in Article 6 TEU, having regard in particular to the ECHR and the Charter.

The CJEU also began almost immediately to use it as 'soft law' or a guide to public policy, incorporating it in its pronouncements alongside the previous sources of rights. In *Max Mobil*,[43] it highlighted the right to impartial and fair treatment in the Charter:

> . . . it must be emphasized at the outset that the diligent and impartial treatment of a complaint is associated with the right to sound administration which is one of the

---

[41]Coppel and O'Neill 1992, pp. 227–239, 243. Opinion 2/13 of the Full Court, 18 December 2014. See comments at eutopialaw.com
[42]http://fra.europa.eu/en/about-fra
[43]T-54/99 *Max Mobil* [2000] ECR I-1335

general principles that are observed in a State governed by the rule of law and are common to the constitutional traditions of the Member States . . . Article 41(1) of the Charter of Fundamental Rights of the European Union proclaimed at Nice on 7 December 2000 . . . confirms that every person has the right to have his or her affairs handled impartially, fairly and within a reasonable time by the institutions and bodies of the Union.

In *Jego Quere*,[44] it drew upon the right of access to a court:

. . . according to settled case-law, Community law enshrines the right to an effective remedy before a court of competent jurisdiction, a right based on the constitutional traditions common to the Member States and on Articles 6 and 13 of the European Convention on Human Rights, and reaffirmed by Article 47 of the Charter of Fundamental Rights of the European Union proclaimed at Nice on 7 December 2000.

The CJ provided a very clear statement on how it saw and intended to apply the CFR in *Parliament* v *Council*[45] in which it stated that the CFR was integral to a review of the legality of the directive:

The Charter was solemnly proclaimed by the Parliament, the Council and the Commission in Nice on 7 December 2000. While the Charter is not a legally binding instrument, the Community legislature did, however, acknowledge its importance by stating, in the second recital in the preamble to the Directive, that the Directive observes the principles recognised not only by Article 8 of the ECHR but also in the Charter. Furthermore, the principal aim of the Charter, as is apparent from its preamble, is to reaffirm 'rights as they result, in particular, from the constitutional traditions and international obligations common to the Member States, the Treaty on European Union, the Community Treaties, the [ECHR], the Social Charters adopted by the Community and by the Council of Europe and the case-law of the Court . . . and of the European Court of Human Rights'.

The Charter was also cited in cases concerning the protection of human health,[46] the right to asylum[47] and even in relation to the extension of direct effect.[48] The Charter was not used independently but to reaffirm already existing rights. Nonetheless, its use alongside the ECHR raised its contents to the same status in all but name. In addition, it formed part of the rule of law to be reviewed when determining the validity of EU law. It is therefore questionable how important it was that it was not legally binding: this limited, but did not prevent its use.[49] To date it has been cited in more than 30 judgments.[50] The CJ referred to the concept of human dignity in the Charter in *Bruestle*, a case concerning the patentability of human embryos created through therapeutic cloning.[51]

---

[44]C-263/02 *Jego Quere*
[45]*Parliament* v *Council* C-540/03[2006] ECR I-5769 [38]
[46]C-570/07 and C 571/07 *Blanco Pérez and Chao Gómez* [2010] ECR I-4629 (Article 35 CFR)
[47]C-175/ 08 *Abdulla* (Article 18 CFR)
[48]C-555/07 *Kücükdeveci* [2010] ECR I-365
[49]Damian Chalmers, 'European Restatements of Sovereignty', LSE Law, Society and Economy Working Papers 10/2013
[50]Joint Statement on EU Accession to the ECHR issued by the Presidents of the Two European Courts, http://www. echr.coe.int/NR/rdonlyres/02164A4C-0B63-44C3-80C7-FC594EE16297/0/2011Communication_CEDHCJUE_EN.pdf. For a list of cases in 2011 see the Appendix in 'Commission Staff Working Document on the Application of the EU Charter of Fundamental Rights in 2011', SWD(2012) 84 final
[51]C-34/10, *Brüstle* v *Greenpeace* [2011] ECR I-9821

Chalmers questions whether this really was a 'grassroots' document: he argues that the development remained top down with the impetus coming from the European Council rather than the European peoples. The pattern remained the same: rights were entrenched only when elites in the EU decided that they should be. Given the use of the Charter in protecting rights, does this matter? For example, in *NS* the Court issued a landmark ruling[52] on the implementation of EU protection of asylum seekers in the Dublin Regulation determining that:

> [86] If there are substantial grounds for believing that there are systemic flaws in the asylum procedure and reception conditions for asylum applicants in the Member State responsible, resulting in inhuman or degrading treatment, within the meaning of Article 4 of the Charter, of asylum seekers transferred to the territory of that Member State, the transfer would be incompatible with that provision.

Member States are therefore under the obligation to respect the Charter when they establish the responsibility for examining an asylum application. They may not transfer an asylum seeker to another member state if they cannot confirm the absence of systemic deficiencies in the asylum procedure and reception condition. If grounds exist for believing that a person would face a real risk of being subjected to inhuman or degrading treatment, under Article 4 CFR they may not be transferred.[53]

APPLYING THE LAW

Which rights could be used to help LeCraft in her case against Spain?

---

3. The Court of Justice and the development of fundamental rights as general principles of EU law

As can be seen from Table 8.1, 'fundamental rights' in the CFR are called 'human rights' in the UNDHR and ECHR. Non-discrimination was the only fundamental right mentioned in the Rome Treaty in 1957. Fundamental rights were initially only recognised by the CJ as general principles of EU law. The rights protected by the national constitutions in the member states were not directly linked into EU law. The six founder states had all signed up to international rights instruments (such as the UN Declaration) but the rights listed in those documents were also not automatically part of EU law. Also the six founder member states were all ECHR signatories yet its provisions were not part of EU law.[54] The way in which rights in international and national law were incorporated into EU law via case law will be discussed later in the chapter.

---

[52]C-411/10 and C-493/10, *N.S.* v *Secretary of State for the Home Department and M.E. e.a.* v *Refugee Applications Commissioner*. See also *Efrem Medhanye* v *Secretary of State for the Home Department* [2012] EWHC 1799 (Admin)
[53]European Commission, '2011 Report on the Application of the EU Charter of Fundamental Rights', COM(2012) 169 final, p. 6
[54]The EU 's preparations to accede to the ECHR have been stalled by the CJEU Opinion 2/13 of 18 December 2014

i.   Non-discrimination as a general principle in the Treaty

Twentieth century action to protect fundamental human rights initially focused on non-discrimination. The CHR created a sub-commission on the prevention of discrimination and protection of minorities (SPDPM). In 1949, this sub-commission began to systematically study the 'main types of discrimination which impede the equal enjoyment by all of human rights and fundamental freedoms and the causes of such discrimination.'[55]

The idea of non-discrimination incorporated into EC law in 1957 bore little relation to this. As it was linked to economic integration, the scope was much narrower. The Treaty of Rome prohibited non-discrimination on two specific grounds – nationality and sex. Non-discrimination on the basis of nationality, now enshrined in Article 18 TFEU, is the basic principle informing application of the four freedoms in Articles 34, 45, 56 and 59 TFEU. Non-discrimination on the basis of sex was also initially prohibited in relation to equal pay (see Article 157 TFEU).[56]

The broader UN conception of prevention of discrimination was only introduced in 1997, when following political agreement by the European Council in Amsterdam a new Treaty provision (Article 19 TFEU) stated that:

> *acting unanimously on a proposal from the Commission and after consulting the European Parliament, may take appropriate action to combat discrimination based on sex, racial or ethnic origin, religion or belief, disability, age or sexual orientation.*[57]

EU law therefore now prohibits discrimination on grounds other than nationality and sex.[58] Gaps remain[59] – the Framework Directive does not extend to goods and services, for example – but some of these grounds of discrimination, in particular nationality and age,[60] are also protected as general principles of EU law.

ii.   The CJEU and fundamental rights as general principles

The Court of Justice was central to the development of general principles in EU law, including procedural and fundamental rights. The Court made its position on

---

[55]UN E/EN.4/Sub.2/40/Rev.1, 7 June 1949 – United Nations Commission on Human Rights (Sub-commission on preventing discrimination and the protection of minorities), 'The Main Types and Causes of Discrimination', Memorandum submitted by the Secretary General, New York, 1949, p. 1

[56]On EU gender equality law see Ruth Nielsen, *Gender Equality: In European Contract Law*, DPOF Publishing, 2004; Dominique Vos, 'Equality in Law Between Men and Women in the European Community', Kluwer Academic Publishers, 1998; Directorate-General for Employment (Author), Social Affairs and Equal Opportunities (Author), European Commission (Editor),*EU Rules on Gender Equality: How are they Transposed into National Law?* Dictus Publishing, 26 March 2011

[57]Originally Article 13, Treaty of the European Community, as amended by the 1997 Amsterdam Treaty. Now Article 19 TFEU.

[58]Two directives based upon this provision were introduced in 2000: Council Directive 2000/43 (the 'Race Directive') implements the principle of equal treatment between persons irrespective of racial or ethnic origin in the spheres of employment, membership of associations, welfare, social benefits, education and access to goods and services. Council Directive 2000/78 (the 'Framework Directive') establishes a general framework for equal treatment irrespective of religion, belief, disability, age or sexual orientation only in regard to employment and occupation. In accordance with Article 288 TFEU, all member states were immediately obliged to transpose these protections into the national legal orders by December 2003.

[59]The Commission has tried to address this: see 'Proposal for a Council Directive on implementing the principle of equal treatment between persons irrespective of religion or belief, disability, age or sexual orientation', COM(2008) 0426 final. http://eur-lex.europa.eu/LexUriServ/LexUriServ.do?uri=CELEX:52008PC0426:en:NOT

[60]As set out in C-144/04 *Mangold* [2005] ECR I-9981

fundamental rights clear in early cases arising under the ECSC Treaty – in *Stork*[61] wholesalers of coal were told that rights were not protected in EU law, even if these were protected in the national legal systems. The CJ simply refused to accept the argument that a decision of the High Authority breached basic constitutional (economic) rights protected under German law. In *Geitling*[62] the CJ again flatly rejected the idea that a fundamental right in German constitutional law could be relevant to EU law. It also dismissed the suggestion that EU law might itself protect rights. Rights did not exist as obligations in EU law – the judges viewed the EEC as a strictly economic concern. Most notably, in *Sgarlata*[63] it was held that the provisions of the Treaty could not be overridden by an argument based upon other principles of law, even if those principles were common to the legal systems of all the member states.

Beyond the economic argument, the rejection of rights can also be explained from a political perspective: as the CJ stated in *van Gend*, EU law was an independent legal system; the independence and autonomy of this system could potentially be undermined if the CJ recognised the authority of rights protected in alternative systems of law such as the ECHR or the national constitutions. In addition, recognition of the rights in these systems would also require recognition of the courts which oversaw and interpreted them – this could undermine the authority of the CJ itself.

VIEWPOINT

Which do you find more convincing – the economic or political argument explaining the rejection of rights in the original EEC? Read Opinion 2/13 - what is the most relevant argument against accession?

Nonetheless, this unequivocal position had changed by 1969 – rejection was replaced by acknowledgement of certain principles. This was expressed in *Stauder*[64] a case concerning the implementation of a Community scheme to reduce the butter surplus. The Commission had adopted a decision[65] allowing butter to be sold at reduced prices in the member states to recipients of welfare. The implementation of this scheme in Germany required beneficiaries to provide their name and address. Mr Stauder, a welfare recipient in that country, argued that this infringed his right to dignity as protected by the German constitution. The CJ was therefore asked whether this procedure was compatible with the general principles of Community law in force.

Departing from its earlier stance, the CJ did not dismiss outright the suggestion that a right to dignity might be part of EU law. It conducted a linguistic analysis in order to answer the question posed by the national court. By analysing the text of Decision 69/71 EEC in other languages, it concluded that the need for identification was not laid out in the decision itself and ruled that:

> . . . the provision at issue contains nothing capable of prejudicing the fundamental human rights enshrined in the general principles of Community law and protected by the Court.

---

[61]C-1/58 StorkStork & Cie. v ECSC High Authority [1959] ECR 17
[62]C-36,37,38,40/59 Ruhrkohlen-Verkaufsgesellschaft and others v ECSC High Authority [1960] ECR 423
[63]C-40/64 Sgarlata and others v Commission of the EEC [1965] ECR 215
[64]C-29/69 Stauder v Stadt Ulm [1969] ECR 419
[65]Decision of 12 February 1969 (69/71/EEC)

This conclusion therefore recognised the existence of fundamental human rights as a subset of general principles of EU law.[66] No further details were given of general principles. The CJ repeated this position in *Internationale*.[67] *Internationale* saw a challenge to the system of deposits provided for in a Council regulation on the organisation of cereals.[68] The regulation created a system of export licences – non-returnable deposits had to be submitted to secure these. The 'system of deposits' was challenged as 'an excessive intervention in the freedom of disposition in trade' contrary to the principles of freedom of action, economic liberty and proportionality protected in German constitutional law. The German authorities demanded that the 'primacy of supranational law must yield before the principles of the German basic law'.

The CJ rejected any possibility that another court could declare EU law invalid. In *Internationale*, it differentiated fundamental human rights from general principles of law, and identified a source of these – national law. However it made clear that despite this source, the authority and validity of rights rested solely in EU law:

> Respect for fundamental rights forms an integral part of the general principles of law protected by the Court of Justice. Such rights are inspired by member state traditions, ensured by structure and objectives of the Community, but derives its authority and validity solely from Community law.

The presentation of fundamental rights as a subset of general principles of law allowed the Court to assert its authority as a protector of rights as a whole rather than only those relating to the rule of law. In *Internationale*, it told the member states that it shared their values and would defend them. At the same time it found the system at issue in *Internationale* did not infringe any rights: the restriction was proportionate to the interest which the system of deposits sought to advance.

The use of both terms in one sentence suggests a conflation of human rights – such as freedom from torture, the right to life and freedom of expression – with general principles of law, such as legal certainty, non-retroactivity, and due process. However, not every general principle of law equates to a fundamental human right, and not every fundamental human right is a general principle of law: prohibition of torture is the former but not the latter and lawyer-client confidentiality is the latter but not the former whereas the general principle of inviolability of the home is both: it was articulated by the CJ in *Hoechst*[69] and corresponds to Article 12 UNHDR which states that:

No one shall be subjected to arbitrary interference with his privacy, family, home or correspondence, nor to attacks upon his honour and reputation. Everyone has the right to the protection of the law against such interference or attacks.

The difference between the two sets of values becomes clear when their evolution is considered. General principles of law were articulated gradually through case law, notably in cases concerning competition law and economic rights. Thus in developing general principles of law in EU law, the CJ took its inspiration from commercial and contractual relationships. This supports the argument that the language of rights was manipulated

---

[66] Takis Tridimas, *General Principles of EU Law*, 3rd edition, Oxford University Press, 2015
[67] C-11/70 *Internationale Handelsgesellschaft mbH v Einfuhr- und Vorratsstelle für Getreide und Futtermittel* [1970] ECR 1970 1125
[68] Regulation No 120/67/EEC of the Council of 13 June 1967 on the Common Organisation of the Market in Cereals
[69] C-46/87 and 227/88 *Hoechst v Commission* [1989] ECR 2859

to reach essentially market ends. By contrast, fundamental human rights as defined in the UN Declaration of 1948, only appeared with the Charter in 2000. Thus in *Stauder* fundamental human rights were not recognised per se, but only to the extent that they were also general principles of law.

The reliance on case law meant that the development of general principles of law was ad hoc. The right to a due process was highlighted in *Johnston*,[70] where access to a judicial process was described as a general principle of EU law. The idea of proportionality was explained in a number of cases including *Internationale*, *Man Sugar*,[71] *Watson*,[72] *Wijsenbeek*,[73] and *Banana Regime*.[74] Legal certainty and legitimate expectations were addressed in *MAFF*:

> Having regard to the divergent appraisals by the national authorities of the Member States, reflected in the differences between existing national legislation, of the dangers which may result from the use of certain substances having a hormonal action, the Council, in deciding in the exercise of its discretionary power to adopt the solution of prohibiting them, neither infringed the principle of legal certainty nor frustrated the legitimate expectations of traders affected by that measure.[75]

Legitimate expectations encourage the existence of reasonable expectation, reliance upon that expectation and recognises loss resulting from breach of that expectation. These were extended in *Efisol*[76] to those traders who were 'prudent and discriminating'.[77] This meant that in *Adams*,[78] an employee who informed the Commission of the anti-competitive practices of his employer enjoyed a right to expect that his identity would be protected. However, in the so-called 'Banana cases'[79] a trader was not supported in the assertion of a legitimate expectation that an existing Community regime would be maintained. The relationship between general principles and international law was mentioned in *Opel* v *Council*[80] where this principle was described as a corollary of 'good faith' in public international law.

Non-retroactivity precludes a measure from taking effect before its publication. This was allowed only in exceptional circumstances where the measure was accompanied with a statement of reasons justifying the retroactive effect.[81] The impact upon the individual was not decisive: the CJ allowed this both where it disadvantaged[82] or improved an individual's position.[83]

---

[70]C-222/84 *Johnston* v *Chief Constable of the Royal Ulster Constabulary* [1986] ECR 1651. Her employer refused to renew Mrs Johnston's contract due to a decision not to train women in the use of firearms. See also C-222/86 *Unectef* v *Heylens* [1987] ECR 4097

[71]C-181/84 *Man (Sugar)* v *IBAP* [1985] ECR 2889

[72]C-118/75 *Watson and Belmann* [1976] ECR 1185

[73]C-378/97 *Wijsenbeek* [1999] ECR I-6207

[74]C-280/93. [1994] ECR I-4973 These cases (see also C-256/93, C-257/93, C-276/93, C-282/93, C-286/93, C-287/93, C-288/93) arose from Regulation 404/93 on the Common Organisation of the Market in Bananas, OJ L47/1 1993

[75]C-331/88 *The Queen/Ministry of Agriculture, Fisheries and Food, ex parte FEDESA and others* [1990] ECR I-4023

[76]T-336/94 *Efisol* v *Commission* [1996] ECR I-1343

[77]See also C-112/77 *Töpfer* v *Commission* [1978] ECR 1019

[78]C-145/83 *Adams* v *Commission* [1985] ECR 3539

[79]C- 280/93 *Germany* v *Council* (Banana case)

[80]T-115/94 *DEP Opel Austria* v *Council* [1998] ECR II-2739

[81]C-260/91 *Diversinte and Iberlacta* v *Administración Principal de Aduanas e Impuestos Especiales de la Junquera* [1993] ECR I-1885

[82]C-63/83 *R.* v *Kirk* [1984] ECR 2689, but see *Kolpinghuis* or *Arcaro* where EU law is not directly effective

[83]C-310/95 *Road Air* v *Inspecteur der Invoerrechten en Accijnzen* [1997] ECR I-2229

Confidentiality[84] and the right to a hearing arose in a number of competition law cases. *Transocean Marine Paint*[85] nullified a Commission decision on competition in marine paints, which had been adopted without consultation with the affected parties. The CJ held that a person whose interests are perceptibly affected by a decision taken by a public authority must be given the opportunity to make his views known:

> [20] Accordingly, the condition stated in Article 3(1)(d) of the decision was imposed in breach of procedural requirements and the commission must be given the opportunity to reach a fresh decision on this point after hearing the observations or suggestions of the members of the association.

The right to protection against self-incrimination also arose in competition cases, where parties attempted to rely upon it to justify non-cooperation with Commission investigations. However, the principle was held to apply only to persons charged with an offence in criminal proceedings. The CJ held that it does not operate in the economic sphere in order to resist a demand for information during a Commission enquiry.[86] While there was no obligation upon a party subject to a Commission investigation to provide answers which might involve an admission of anti-competitive actions[87] the Commission has the power to request and obtain information:[88] thus parties under investigation were obliged to respond to requests for general information.

ANALYSING THE LAW

Is there a right to silence in EU law? Is this a fundamental human right? Read T-112/98 *Mannesmannrohren*, especially paragraph 63.

---

iii. Sources of general principles

The sources of these general principles varies but often the CJ draws inspiration from the national legal systems. In *Hauer*[89] a complaint was made about the impact of a national law and a Council regulation on the right to an economic activity. Mrs Hauer owned a plot of land and sought authorisation to plant vines. She was refused permission by the state authority of Rheinland Pfalz in Germany.[90] While her complaint on that decision was in progress, the Council adopted a regulation[91] prohibiting any planting of new vines

---

[84]C-155/79 *AM & S v Commission* [1982] ECR 1616
[85]C-17/74 *Transocean Marine Paint Association v Commission* [1974] ECR 1063
[86]C-374/87 *Orkem v Commission* [1989] ECR 3283 [15, 18–35]
[87]T-112/ 98 *Mannesmannroehren*
[88]C-136/79 *National Panasonic v Commission* [1980] ECR 2033
[89]C-44/79 *Hauer v Land Rheinland-Pfalz* [1979] ECR 3727
[90]Under the law relating to the wine industry (Weinwirtschaftsgesetz) of 10 March 1977 the plot of land in question was not considered suitable for wine growing.
[91]Regulation No 1162/76 of 17 May 1976

for three years. A question concerning conflict with a national constitutional right was sent to the CJ. To answer it, the CJ said:

> Fundamental rights form an integral part of the general principles of the law, the observance of which is ensured by the court. In safeguarding those rights, the latter is bound to draw inspiration from constitutional traditions common to the member states, so that measures which are incompatible with the fundamental rights recognized by the constitutions of those states are unacceptable in the community. International treaties for the protection of human rights on which the member states have collaborated or of which they are signatories, can also supply guidelines which should be followed within the framework of community law.

This method of finding 'inspiration' in constitutional traditions common to the member states as well as international treaties was again used in *Nold* to resolve another conflict with economic liberty enshrined in constitutional law. In this case an EU act changing the terms of business meant that Mr Nold lost his status as a wholesaler. He lost his case and was unlikely to have taken any solace from the CJ assurance that 'fundamental rights are an integral part of the general principles of law the observance of which the court ensures'. The repetition of statements made in *Hauer* were unlikely to provide any comfort or confidence in the commitment to fundamental rights.

Nonetheless, such assurances were regularly given, despite it being rare for a right to be common in the sense of being protected in all member states – the CJ identified selective rights rather than those that are truly 'common'.[92] The resort to common constitutional traditions should not be taken to mean that only those traditions present in all member state constitutions could be absorbed into EU law – in *Hauer*, only three out of nine national constitutions were examined by the CJ. A reminder that 'common' does not mean 'universal' is provided in the case of *Mangold*. In this case, a specific form of non-discrimination was raised to a general principle of EU law when the CJ declared that non-discrimination on the grounds of age was a general principle in EU law.[93] Although this declaration mirrored the technique used in the past, it evoked large amounts of harsh criticism from both within and beyond the CJ.[94] This was because in declaring this principle, the CJ appeared to be circumventing the prohibition of horizontal direct effect of directives.

The reference to general human rights instruments as sources of general principles of EU law became more detailed – in *Johnston*,[95] direct mention was made of the ECHR:

> As the European Parliament, Council and Commission recognized in their Joint Declaration of 5 April 1977 and as the court has recognized in its decisions, the principles on

---

[92]Andrew Clapham, 'A Human Rights Policy for the European Community' in *Yearbook of European Law*, Oxford University Press, 1991, pp. 309–366

[93]C-144/04 *Werner Mangold v Rüdiger Helm*[2005] ECR I-9981

[94]See Christa Tobler, 'The Prohibition of Discrimination in the Union's Layered System of Equality Law: From Early Staff Cases to the *Mangold* Approach', in A. Rosas, E. Levits, Y. Bot (eds), *La cour de justice et la construction de l'Europe: Analyses et perspectives de 60 ans de jurisprudence/The Court of Justice and the construction of Europe: Analyses and perspectives on 60 years of case-law*, Den Haag: Asser/Springer, 2013, pp. 443–467; and papers in *Cambridge Yearbook of European Legal Studies 2011–2012, Volume 14*, Hart Publishing, Edited by Catherine Barnard, Marcus Gehring and Iyiola Solanke

[95]See also C-36/75 *Rutili v Ministre de l'intérieur* [1975] ECR 1219 and C-130/75 *Prais v Council* [1976] ECR 1589

which the European Convention for the protection of human rights and fundamental freedoms is based must be taken into consideration in community law.

In *Orkem*,[96] limits to the right to non-self incrimination were determined after examination of the ECHR and the International Covenant on Civil and Political Rights (ICCPR):

> ... in the case of infringements in the economic sphere, in particular of competition law, an undertaking cannot be said to have the right not to give evidence against itself by virtue of a principle common to the laws of the Member States or by virtue of the rights guaranteed by the European Convention for the Protection of Human Rights and Fundamental Freedoms or by the International Covenant on Civil and Political Rights. The Commission may not compel an undertaking to provide it with answers which might involve an admission on its part of the existence of an infringement which it is incumbent upon the Commission to prove ...

In *Elliniki*, the CJ used the right to freedom of expression in the ECHR to evaluate national rules on broadcasting, which prescribed a period between the release of a film in cinemas and its screening elsewhere. The national rules were challenged under Article 56 TFEU on free movement of services – the question was whether they fell under the exceptions provided in Article 66 TFEU:

> ... the national rules in question can fall under the exceptions provided for in those provisions only if they are compatible with the fundamental rights the observance of which is ensured by the Court. As regards rules relating to television, this means that they must be appraised in the light of freedom of expression, as embodied in Article 10 of the European Convention on Human Rights, as a general principle of law the observance of which is ensured by the Court.[97]

The CJ repeated its approach to the ECHR in *Grogan*:

> [31] According to, inter alia, the judgment of 18 June 1991 in *Elliniki Radiophonia Tileorasi*,[98] where national legislation falls within the field of application of Community law the Court, when requested to give a preliminary ruling, must provide the national court with all the elements of interpretation which are necessary in order to enable it to assess the compatibility of that legislation with the fundamental rights – as laid down in particular in the European Convention on Human Rights – the observance of which the Court ensures.[99]

It is worth considering why the ECHR has been so popular before the CJ. This question is answered by the following paragraph in *Prais*:

> Since the European Convention has been ratified by all the member states the rights enshrined in it are, according to the plaintiff, to be regarded as included in the fundamental rights to be protected by community law ...[100]

---

[96]C-374/87 *Orkem v Commission* [1989] ECR 3283)
[97]C-260/89 *Elliniki Radiophonia Tileorasi v Dimotiki Etairia Pliroforissis* [1991] ECR I-2951 [42]
[98]C-260/89
[99]C-159/90 Society for the Protection of Unborn Children Ireland (SPUC)/Grogan and others [1991] ECR I-4685
[100]C-130/75 *Prais*

The 'special significance' of the ECHR was expressed in *Omega Spielhallen*.[101] The ECHR represented a ready-made catalogue of rights upon which the member states agreed. Its contents were therefore safe for the CJ to adopt for its own purposes. Yet in having recourse to this long-established rights instrument, the CJ endangered its own autonomy – the European Court of Human Rights (ECtHR) in Strasbourg oversees the interpretation of the Convention. This fact also partly explains why the CJEU – then as now – opposes accession to the ECHR. In the 1990s many, including some Advocates General, were in favour of this: AG Trabbuchi argued that the ECHR was a ready-made system of principles on which all member states agreed giving the CJ a strong indication of the Community's general principles and human rights. It was also seen as anomalous that the member states were subject to the Convention organs but bodies and measures of the EU were not. Accession to the ECHR was seriously considered in the early 1990s but the CJ wrote two strong opinions[102] against this. It was argued that the standard of protection in the ECHR was too low – it focused on the protection of minimal human rights as understood in the mid-twentieth century.

The CJ therefore positioned itself as a reviewer of the respect for fundamental rights in the member states, assuming the role of judicial protector of human rights in the EU. It stated that it would conduct a compatibility review of national legislation falling within EU competence and fundamental rights as laid out in the ECHR and elsewhere. By declaring itself responsible for compatibility of national and EU law with the ECHR, the CJ pre-empted oversight by the ECtHR of national law that fell within the scope of EU law. This was important if the supremacy of EU law was to be maintained, as well as the independence and autonomy of the CJEU. The CJ therefore created an interactive human rights regime in the EU.

Article 6(3) TEU formalises this interactive rights regime:

Fundamental rights, as guaranteed by the European Convention for the Protection of Human Rights and Fundamental Freedoms and as they result from the constitutional traditions common to the Member States, shall constitute general principles of the Union's law.

In 2015, the ECHR and fundamental rights now constitute general principles of law rather than being integral to them. It is clear that this development of rights in EU law has been ad hoc and not informed by any kind of public debate. It is questionable how far it was informed by moral rather than market values, and thus the extent to which it promoted a social consciousness in the EU rather than a common commercial identity.

ANALYSING THE LAW

List the sources of the general principles in EU law.

---

[101]C-36/02 *Omega Spielhallen- und Automatenaufstellungs- GmbH* v *Oberbürgermeisterin der Bundesstadt Bonn*. See also C-274/99 P *Connolly* v *Commission* [2001] ECR I-1611 [37]; Case C-94/00 *Roquette Frères* [2002] ECR I-9011 [25]; Case C-112/00 *Schmidberger* [2003] ECR I-5659 [71]

[102]Opinion 1/91 of 14 December 1991 [1991] ECR I-6079 and Opinion 2/94 of 28 March 1996 [1996] ECR I-1759

iv. Protection of fundamental freedoms and protection of fundamental rights

Just as there is a difference between general principles and fundamental rights, there is a difference between fundamental rights and the four fundamental freedoms in the Treaty. The difference and the hierarchy between them is illustrated in two specific cases: *Schmidberger*[103] and *Omega Spielhallen*.[104] These cases brought human rights (freedom of expression and assembly, and the right to human dignity) into conflict with the free movement of goods (Article 34 TFEU) and services (Article 56 TFEU). They not only show that these rights belong to different spheres, but also that – perhaps worryingly – the CJEU places some human rights on the same level as the four freedoms. Even if this applies only to those rights that are subject to limitations in human rights law,[105] it is debatable whether the Rome Treaty principles of free movement are of the same social and political importance and weight as, for example, freedom of association or expression.

The conflict in *Schmidberger* arose when an environmental non-governmental organisation, Transitforum Austria Tirol, was authorised to stage a demonstration on the Brenner motorway, a key highway in Austria. The authorities were well organised – a press conference was held to disseminate the information in advance to the media and motorway organisations that the motorway would be closed; local authorities met to ensure that the demonstration would be trouble-free. The demonstration closed the motorway for 30 hours. This closure affected the business of Mr Schmidberger, whose transport firm used it to carry goods (timber and steel) from Italy and Germany – the motorway was the sole transit route for his large lorries. Mr Schmidberger sought damages from Austria for financial loss incurred as a result of being unable to use the motorway. He argued that the authorities should have banned the demonstration, and that failure to prevent the closure amounted to a restriction of free movement of goods that could not be justified by freedom of expression or the freedom of assembly.

The national court rejected his claims for liability but asked the CJ directly whether the closure breached Article 34 TFEU and also whether the principle of the free movement of goods takes precedence over fundamental rights, in particular the freedom of expression and the freedom of assembly guaranteed by Articles 10 and 11 of the ECHR. The answer to the first question was yes: failure to prevent the closure could amount to an unlawful restriction under Article 34 TFEU:[106]

[57] . . . as an indispensable instrument for the realisation of a market without internal frontiers, Article 30 [now Article 34 TFEU] does not prohibit only measures emanating from the State which, in themselves, create restrictions on trade between Member States . . .

[58] The fact that a Member State abstains from taking action or, as the case may be, fails to adopt adequate measures to prevent obstacles to the free movement of goods that are created, in particular, by actions by private individuals on its territory aimed at products originating in other Member States is just as likely to obstruct intra-Community trade as is a positive act.

---

[103]C-112/00 *Eugen Schmidberger, Internationale Transporte und Planzüge v Republik Österreich*
[104]C-36/02 *Omega*. See also C-399/11 *Stefano Melloni* nyr concerning the EU Arrest Warrant.
[105]Such as Article 9(2) on the manifestation of religion, or Article 10 on freedom of expression.
[106]See C-265/95 *Commission v France* [1997] ECR I-6959 [29–31]

The question was therefore whether the Austrian authorities had taken 'necessary and appropriate measures to ensure that that fundamental freedom is respected on their territory'.[107] They had not done so and consequently a key transit route was closed for almost 30 hours, inevitably restricting intra-EU trade.

The failure to take adequate measures was regarded as incompatible with Article 34 TFEU unless it could be justified.[108] Fortunately, the ban could indeed be objectively justified: it was not motivated by discrimination – the Austrian authorities were 'inspired by considerations linked to respect of the fundamental rights of the demonstrators to freedom of expression and freedom of assembly, which are enshrined in and guaranteed by the ECHR and the Austrian Constitution'.[109]

However, this was not the end of the reasoning. Under the ECHR freedom of expression and assembly are not absolute rights:

> [79] . . . whilst the fundamental rights at issue in the main proceedings are expressly recognised by the ECHR and constitute the fundamental pillars of a democratic society, it nevertheless follows from the express wording of paragraph 2 of Articles 10 and 11 of the Convention that freedom of expression and freedom of assembly are also subject to certain limitations justified by objectives in the public interest . . .

As these human rights are limited under the ECHR, justification required a careful balancing act to be conducted:

> [80] Thus, unlike other fundamental rights enshrined in that Convention, such as the right to life or the prohibition of torture and inhuman or degrading treatment or punishment, which admit of no restriction, neither the freedom of expression nor the freedom of assembly guaranteed by the ECHR appears to be absolute but must be viewed in relation to its social purpose. Consequently, the exercise of those rights may be restricted, provided that the restrictions in fact correspond to objectives of general interest and do not, taking account of the aim of the restrictions, constitute disproportionate and unacceptable interference, impairing the very substance of the rights guaranteed.[110]

> [81] In those circumstances, the interests involved must be weighed having regard to all the circumstances of the case in order to determine whether a fair balance was struck between those interests.

The fact that some human rights are limited broadens the scope of the CJ to examine their interaction with the four fundamental freedoms.

It is perhaps worrying, given their very different origins, that the CJ saw free movement of goods and freedom of expression as equally limited and so of equal status. It saw its task in *Schmidberger* to find a balance between the interests affected – the freedom of expression of the environmental organisation, the freedom to move his goods by Mr Schmidberger, and the protection of rights of the Austrian government. While

---

[107][50]
[108]*Schmidberger* [64]
[109][69]
[110]C-62/90 *Commission* v *Germany* [1992] ECR I-2575 [23], and C-404/92 P *X* v *Commission* [1994] ECR I-4737 [18]

recognising the wide discretion of the national authorities, it remained '. . . necessary to determine whether the restrictions placed upon intra-Community trade are proportionate in the light of the legitimate objective pursued, namely, in the present case, the protection of fundamental rights'.[111]

Fortunately in this case, the action was deemed proportionate. As the preparatory action by the Austrian authorities differed significantly from the inaction of the authorities in *Commission* v *France*,[112] respect for human rights triumphed:

[93] . . . the national authorities were reasonably entitled, having regard to the wide discretion which must be accorded to them in the matter, to consider that the legitimate aim of that demonstration could not be achieved in the present case by measures less restrictive of intra-Community trade.

[94] In the light of those considerations . . . the fact that the authorities of a Member State did not ban a demonstration in circumstances such as those of the main case is not incompatible with Articles 30 and 34 of the Treaty, read together with Article 5 thereof.

ANALYSING THE LAW

In *Schmidberger* is freedom of expression more important than free movement of goods?

Measures incompatible with respect for human rights are per se rejected under EU law,[113] but if human rights are limited under the ECHR they will be subject to a balancing test under EU law.

Omega also illustrates the role of a balancing test. The case concerned laser-sports, in particular those simulating homicide. Laserdromes have become popular places of entertainment. Omega, a company specialising in laser-sports, were forbidden to operate their laserdrome in Bonn. The police order stated that 'the games which took place in Omega's establishment constituted a danger to public order, since the acts of simulated homicide and the trivialisation of violence thereby engendered were contrary to fundamental values prevailing in public opinion'.[114]

Omega appealed against this decision to the state and federal courts. The federal administrative court decided to ask the CJ if the prohibition was compatible with the fundamental freedoms in the Treaty – free movement of services and goods. The German court took the position that the constitutional principle of human dignity was being infringed by the ' . . . awakening or strengthening in the player of an attitude denying the fundamental right of each person to be acknowledged and respected, such as the representation, as in this case, of fictitious acts of violence for the purposes of a game'. It was impossible to waive this 'cardinal constitutional principle' of human dignity to accommodate the fundamental freedoms invoked by Omega.

---

[111][82]
[112]Where the French authorities took no action to prevent the blockade organised by French farmers.
[113]See C-299/95 *Kremzow* [1997] ECR I-2629 [14]
[114][7]

The CJ found the prohibition to be a breach of freedom to provide services and free movement of goods, but decided to assess the matter under the former. It therefore considered whether this breach could be justified by the derogation in Article 55 TFEU. Respect for human dignity was recognised as a general principle of law rather than a fundamental right – it was something that EU law 'strived' to respect – but its specific status in German constitutional law was also acknowledged:

[34] As the Advocate General argues in paragraphs 82 to 91 of her Opinion, the Community legal order undeniably strives to ensure respect for human dignity as a general principle of law. There can therefore be no doubt that the objective of protecting human dignity is compatible with Community law, it being immaterial in that respect that, in Germany, the principle of respect for human dignity has a particular status as an independent fundamental right.

[35] Since both the Community and its Member States are required to respect fundamental rights, the protection of those rights is a legitimate interest which, in principle, justifies a restriction of the obligations imposed by Community law, even under a fundamental freedom guaranteed by the Treaty such as the freedom to provide services.

However, was the restriction proportionate – was it necessary for the protection of the interests articulated and appropriate to protect those interests? It did not have to be a 'common conception' mirrored in all the member states in order to be proportionate – member states could adopt different systems of protection and still satisfy this test.[115] Thus the CJ concluded that the German prohibition of games simulating acts of homicide on grounds of public policy – specifically an affront to human dignity – was lawful under EU law:

[39] . . . the prohibition on the commercial exploitation of games involving the simulation of acts of violence against persons, in particular the representation of acts of homicide, corresponds to the level of protection of human dignity which the national constitution seeks to guarantee in the territory of the Federal Republic of Germany. It should also be noted that, by prohibiting only the variant of the laser game the object of which is to fire on human targets and thus 'play at killing' people, the contested order did not go beyond what is necessary in order to attain the objective pursued by the competent national authorities.

[40] In those circumstances, the order of 14 September 1994 cannot be regarded as a measure unjustifiably undermining the freedom to provide services.

The reasoning suggests that the decision may have been different if the national legal system did not contain a fundamental right protecting human dignity.

ANALYSING THE LAW

Identify and list a) the fundamental freedoms in EU law, b) fundamental rights in EU law, and c) general principles of EU law.

---

[115]See C-124/97 *Läärä and others* [1999] ECR I-6067 [36]; C-67/98 *Zenatti* [1999] ECR I-7289 [34]; C-6/01 *Anomar and Others* [2003] ECR I-0000 [80]

4. The scope of Judicial protection of fundamental rights in the Union

In *Internationale*, the CJ stressed that it shared the member state respect for human rights. The Court took it upon itself to provide national courts with guidance to help them determine the compatibility of national legislation with the fundamental rights that the Court ensured. It has conducted a fundamental rights review of national law in cases from *Cinetheque* in 1985 to *Vinkov* in 2012.[116] The Court will consider whether actions of the member states are compatible with obligations entered into, especially those laid out in the ECHR.

However, the Court set limits to its own duty to ensure national observance of fundamental rights. These must fall within the field of Union law as in *Demirel*[117] it stressed that:

[28] . . . it has no power to examine the compatibility with the European Convention on Human Rights of national legislation lying outside the scope of community law.

In this case the absence in EU law of rules on family reunification for lawfully established Turkish workers meant national rules had no connection to EU law – the CJEU therefore had no jurisdiction to determine whether the German rules were compatible with the principles enshrined in Article 8 ECHR.

The scope of judicial review has not been extended by the Charter of Fundamental Rights (CFR). Title VII CFR contains Article 51, laying out the sphere and method of application:

(1) The provisions of this Charter are addressed to the institutions, bodies, offices and agencies of the Union with due regard for the principle of subsidiarity and to the Member States only when they are implementing Union law. They shall therefore respect the rights, observe the principles and promote the application thereof in accordance with their respective powers and respecting the limits of the powers of the Union as conferred on it in the Treaties.

The use of the Charter is therefore circumscribed: as in the past it constrains action by the Union and the member states when implementing Union rules. It does not develop the Union competence to act. It applies to all actions of the EU institutions, agencies and other bodies – this includes not only the institutions listed in Article 3 TEU but also the European Ombudsman and the European Data Protection Supervisor: 'agencies' include the Fundamental Rights Agency as well as those coordinating Common Foreign and Security Policy, EU Internal Security Policy[118] or judicial cooperation in criminal matters;

---

[116]Joined Cases 60 and 61/84 *Cinetheque v Federation nationale des cinemas francais* (1985) ECR 2605; C-260/89 *ERT* [1991] I-2925 [42]; C-299/95 *Kremzow* [1997] ECR I-2629 [15]; C-309/96 *Annibaldi* [2007] ECR I-7493 [13]; C-94/00 *Roquette Frères* [2002] ECR I-9011 [25]; C-349/07 *Sopropé* [2008] ECR I-10369 [34]; C-256/11 *Dereci and Others* [2011] ECR I-11315 [72[; and C-27/11 *Vinkov* [2012] ECR [58]

[117]C-12/86 *Demirel v Stadt Schwäbisch Gmünd* [1987] ECR 3719

[118]The EU Draft Internal Security states 'PRINCIPLES: People in Europe expect to live in security and to enjoy their freedoms: security is in itself a basic right. The values and principles established in the Treaties of the Union and set out in the Charter of Fundamental Rights have inspired the EU's Internal Security Strategy.' (Council, Brussels, 23 February 2010, p. 9)

while 'bodies' covers the European Central Bank, the European Investment Bank, as well as the Economic and Social Committee (ECOSOC) and the Committee of the Regions (COMREG). All such EU institutions and bodies must observe and conform to Charter rights and principles in all of their activities.

The CJ will conduct a compatibility review of the acts of these institutions. In *Schwarz*[119] the CJ was asked to decide on the compatibility of fingerprinting with Articles 7 (respect for family and private life) and 8 (protection of personal data) of the Charter. Article 1(2) of the regulation[120] on security features in passports obliges national authorities to take fingerprints of persons applying for passports. Schwarz declined to give these when he applied for a German passport – he argued the regulation was invalid because Article 1(2) was a breach to private life and the right to protection of personal data, as protected in the Charter. The Court found no breach – it acknowledged that fingerprinting involved the processing of personal data and could potentially undermine these rights. However, the storing of fingerprints was found to be proportionate to the aim of preventing passport falsification and fraud.

By contrast, in deference to subsidiarity, the EU member states are obliged to uphold the Charter only in the circumstances where they are implementing EU law. This means that if a member state is passing a law about internal policing practices or nationality rules, the Charter would not apply. If, however, a member state were passing a law about trade regulation, the Charter would apply. For example, member state airports that plan to use security scanners must comply with minimum conditions set by the EU rules on fundamental rights. The same applies to data harvesting activities.[121]

Article 51(2) states that the Charter can be used only in accordance with Treaty competences:[122] it does not provide any new freestanding rights, even if it covers areas, such as the right to property, not mentioned in the Treaty.

51(2) The Charter does not extend the field of application of Union law beyond the powers of the Union or establish any new power or task for the Union, or modify powers and tasks as defined in the Treaties.

Thus the Charter continues to be predominantly a means by which to evaluate acts of the EU.[123] In relation to national law, it could be argued that little has changed since *Grogan* where the CJ set out its power to review compatibility:

> . . . the Court has no such jurisdiction with regard to national legislation lying outside the scope of Community [Union] law. In view of the facts of the case and of the conclusions which the Court has reached above . . . that would appear to be true of the prohibition at issue before the national court.[124]

Caution and judicial minimalism is sometimes called for in relation to fundamental rights – where there are no judicial standards by which to judge an issue, the issue should

---

[119]C-291/12 *Schwarz* v *Stadt Bochum* nyr
[120]Regulation 2252/2004 on standards for security features and biometrics in passports and travel documents issued by member states
[121]European Commission, '2011 Report on the Application of the EU Charter of Fundamental Rights', COM(2012) 169 final, p. 3
[122]C-400/10 PPU *J McB* [2010] ECR I-8965 [51] – the CFR cannot be used to override Irish national law
[123]Bogdandy 2000
[124]C-159/90 *Grogan*

perhaps not be judged. However, in avoiding the quagmire of a 'judicial no-man's land' a careful balance must be found to ensure that judicial self-restraint does not facilitate the weakening of human rights protections.[125]

Application of the CFR is summarised in Figure 8.1. Case law indicates that it would be wrong to assume any area of national law is automatically beyond the scope of the CFR – the CJ will conduct a broad enquiry. In *Fransson*,[126] a Swedish national who had committed tax fraud was in danger of being punished twice for the same offence, contrary to Article 50 CFR, due to simultaneous imposition of a tax penalty and a criminal penalty. It was ultimately held that the double jeopardy rule (*ne bis idem*) only applies where there are two criminal penalties but prior to this finding the question of admissibility had to be addressed. The question of admissibility arose because the tax penalties imposed upon Mr Fransson and the criminal proceedings under national law were arguably not connected to EU law – without a connecting legal factor, as per Article 51(1) CFR, Article 50 CFR could not apply.

The Grand Chamber confirmed that the 'applicability of European Union law entails applicability of the fundamental rights guaranteed by the Charter' – where:

> [22] . . . a legal situation does not come within the scope of European Union law, the Court does not have jurisdiction to rule on it and any provisions of the Charter relied upon cannot, of themselves, form the basis for such jurisdiction (see, to this effect, the order in Case C-466/11 *Currà and Others* [2012] ECR, paragraph 26).

However, having affirmed this, the CJ then identified a – perhaps tenuous – link: the tax penalties and criminal proceedings to which Fransson was subject were found to be 'partially connected to breaches of his obligations to declare VAT'. In the past, the EU has adopted various measures on a common system of VAT[127] and Article 4(3) TEU states that every member state is under an obligation to take all legislative and administrative measures appropriate for ensuring collection of all the VAT due on its territory and for preventing evasion.[128] In addition, Article 325 TFEU obliges the member states to counter illegal activities affecting the financial interests of the European Union through effective deterrent measures and, in particular, obliges them to take the same measures to counter fraud affecting the financial interests of the European Union as they take to counter fraud affecting their own interests.[129] Bearing also in mind that the EU's own resources include revenue from national VAT,[130] the CJ identified a direct link between the collection of VAT revenue and the EU budget, and concluded that:

> [27] . . . tax penalties and criminal proceedings for tax evasion, such as those to which the defendant in the main proceedings has been or is subject because the information concerning VAT that was provided was false, constitute implementation of Articles

---

[125]For an example of judicial self-restraint see *Shergill and others* v *Kaira and others* [2012] EWCA Civ 983; [2012] WLR (D) 214

[126]C 617/10 *Åkerberg Fransson* (nyr)

[127]Council Directive 2006/112/EC of 28 November 2006 on the common system of value added tax (OJ L347/1 2006)

[128]C-132/06 *Commission* v *Italy* [2008] ECR I-5457 [37 and 46]

[129]C-367/09 *SGS Belgium and Others* [2010] ECR I-10761 [40 to 42]

[130]Article 2(1) of Council Decision 2007/436/EC, Euratom of 7 June 2007 on the system of the European Communities' own resources (OJ L163/17 2007)

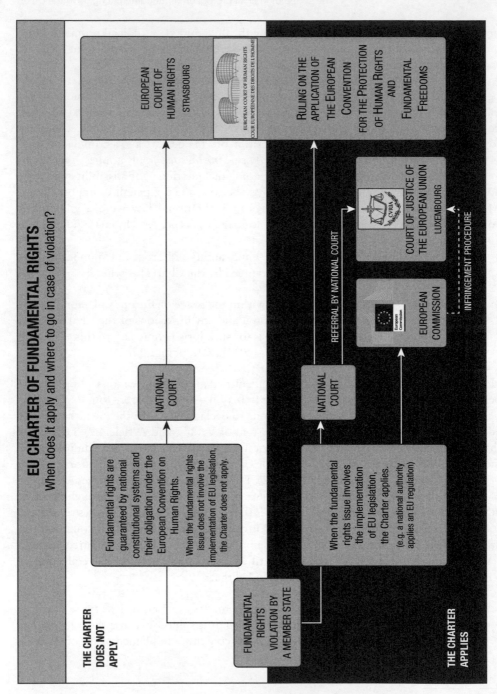

FIGURE 8.1 Overview of the application of the Charter on Fundamental Rights

EU Commission, 'Commission Staff Working Document on the Application of the EU Charter of Fundamental Rights in 2011', SWD (2012) 84 final, p. 3

2, 250(1) and 273 of Directive 2006/112 (previously Articles 2 and 22 of the Sixth Directive) and of Article 325 TFEU and, therefore, of European Union law, for the purposes of Article 51(1) of the Charter.

[28] The fact that the national legislation upon which those tax penalties and criminal proceedings are founded has not been adopted to transpose Directive 2006/112 cannot call that conclusion into question, since its application is designed to penalise an infringement of that directive and is therefore intended to implement the obligation imposed on the Member States by the Treaty to impose effective penalties for conduct prejudicial to the financial interests of the European Union.

Fundamental rights guaranteed in EU law are therefore only applicable in situations governed by EU law but the CJ will take a broad approach to prevent the appearance of zones of law that are effectively exempt from the application of fundamental rights law.

It could be concluded that any link will bring the national act within reach of the Charter. Yet in *Siragusa*,[131] the Court rejected the argument that protection of the landscape was in any way connected to EU law. Siragusa had made modifications to his property in a landscape conservation area without securing the requisite landscape compatibility clearance from the national authority. His retrospective application was rejected under the relevant Italian Decree and he was ordered to restore the site to its former state. Siragusa brought an action contesting that order before the referring court.

The national court asked the CJ whether the Italian order was compatible with Article 17 CFR on the right to property. It suggested that there was a link with EU environmental law as protection of the landscape – the aim of the national Decree – is an aspect of protection of the environment. It referred to various provisions of EU environmental law. In considering this question, the court considered the approach taken in previous cases to determine the scope of Article 51(1). Points to be determined included: first, whether the national legislation is intended to implement a provision of EU law; second, the nature of that legislation; third, whether it pursues objectives other than those covered by EU law; fourth, if it is capable of indirectly affecting EU law; and fifth, whether there are specific rules of EU law on the matter or capable of affecting it.[132]

Bearing this in mind, the 10th Chamber of the CJEU held that an indirect connection with EU environmental law was insufficient:[133]

[27] As the interested parties which have submitted observations have argued, no specific obligations to protect the landscape, akin to those laid down by Italian law, are imposed on the Member States by the TEU and TFEU provisions referred to by the referring court; nor are such obligations imposed by the legislation relating to the Aarhus Convention, nor by Directives 2003/4 and 2011/92 . . .

[30] In that regard, there is nothing to suggest that the provisions of Legislative Decree No 42/04 which are relevant to the case before the referring court fall within the scope

---

[131]C-206/13 *Cruciano Siragusa* (nyr)
[132]*Siragusa* [25]. See also C-40/11 *Iida* [2012] ECR [79]; and C-87/12 *Ymeraga and Others* [2013] ECR [41]
[133]As in C-309/96 *Annibaldi* [1997] ECR I-7493 [21–23]

of EU law. Those provisions do not implement rules of EU law, a fact which distinguishes the case in which the present request for a preliminary ruling has been made from the case which gave rise to the judgment in Case C-416/10 *Križan and Others* [2013] ECR, cited by the referring court.

Križan was an earlier environmental case that concerned urban planning, specifically the location of a new landfill site. Local residents raised a challenge to a national decision based upon national constitutional law and international law. The case also raised the question of whether the decision of a national court restricting the use of property could constitute an unjustified breach of Article 17 CFR. Here there was a direct link as the decision was taken in the context of national proceedings implementing obligations arising from EU law, namely Article 15(a) of Directive 96/61 and Article 9(2) and (4) of the Aarhus Convention. The national judicial decision was not found to be a breach of Article 17 CFR:

[113] . . . the right to property is not an absolute right and must be viewed in relation to its social function. Consequently, its exercise may be restricted, provided that those restrictions in fact correspond to objectives of general interest and do not constitute, in relation to the aim pursued, disproportionate and intolerable interference, impairing the very substance of the right guaranteed.[134]

[114] As regards the objectives of general interest referred to above, established case-law shows that protection of the environment is one of those objectives and is therefore capable of justifying a restriction on the use of the right to property.[135]

APPLYING THE LAW

Would racial profiling by the Spanish police fall within the scope of a) EU law, and b) the CFR? If yes, which Articles would apply?

Title VII CFR also contains Article 52, which lays out the relationship between the Charter, the Treaties, the ECHR and the national constitutions. Under Article 52(2), Charter rights which reflect rights expressly set out in the European Treaties continue to be subject to the conditions and are exercised within the limits defined by those Treaties; as per Article 52(3) those Charter rights which correspond to rights already guaranteed by the ECHR will be given the same meaning, scope and level of protection as provided under

---

[134]Joined Cases C-402/05 P and C-415/05 P *Kadi and Al Barakaat International Foundation* v *Council and Commission* [2008] ECR I-6351 [355], and Joined Cases C-379/08 and C-380/08 *ERG and Others* [2010] ECR I-2007 [80]
[135]See C-240/83 *ADBHU* [1985] ECR 531 [13]; 302/86 *Commission* v *Denmark* [1988] ECR 4607 [8]; C-213/96 *Outokumpu* [1998] ECR I-1777 [32]; and *C379-80/08 ERG and Others* [2010] ECR I-2007[81]

the ECHR.[136] The CJ has already taken steps to clarify the impact of Article 52(3) – the ECHR is to be approached as a minimum rather than maximum standard. This is clear from *McBride*, where it said that:

> [53]. . . it follows from Article 52(3) of the Charter that, in so far as the Charter contains rights which correspond to the rights guaranteed by the ECHR, their meaning and scope are to be the same as those laid down by the ECHR. However, that provision does not preclude the grant of wider protection by European Union law.[137]

Thus there is neither extension nor diminution by the CFR:

> . . . the provisions of the EU Charter should not be understood as allowing for any lowering of the level of protection already afforded to human rights and fundamental freedoms whether under EU law, or under reference to general public international law or to specific international agreements to which the EU or *all* the Member States are party (including, in particular, the ECHR) or under and by the various Member States' national constitutions.[138]

Article 52(4) mandates that Charter rights which parallel fundamental rights recognised within 'the constitutional traditions common to the Member States' should be 'interpreted in harmony with those traditions' and, under Article 52(6), parties are to take 'full account . . . of national laws and practices as specified in this Charter'. In case of any doubt, this is repeated in a Declaration attached to the Lisbon Treaty.[139] Declarations have political force on the participating member states but are not legally binding[140] unless they are formally incorporated into the Treaty by an Annex or a Protocol. They are not classified as Union 'acts'. In *Gestoras*, the CJ confirmed that a Declaration is insufficient to create a legal remedy and cannot be given any legal significance or be used in the interpretation of EU law unless the provision in question makes reference to the content of the Declaration.[141]

What then has been the impact of the Charter? Fundamental rights protection in EU law is a necessary corollary to the Area of Freedom, Justice and Security (AFJS). AFJS includes law-making in areas very close to citizens rights and it is therefore necessary to check on the EU use of power in this area. At present, the Commission prepares annual reports on the implementation of the Charter[142] but an EP report highlights the

---

[136]C-400/10 *J McBride* [53]

[137]Explanation on the provisions of the Charter are provided in OJ C303/17 2007

[138]Guy Harpaz, 'The European Court of Justice and its Relations with the European Court of Human Rights: the Quest for enhanced reliance, coherence and legitimacy', *CMLR* 46, 2009, p. 105

[139]LT Declaration concerning the Charter of Fundamental Rights of the European Union: 'The Charter of Fundamental Rights of the European Union, which has legally binding force, confirms the fundamental rights guaranteed by the European Convention for the Protection of Human Rights and Fundamental Freedoms and as they result from the constitutional traditions common to the Member States. The Charter does not extend the field of application of Union law beyond the powers of the Union or establish any new power or task for the Union, or modify powers and tasks as defined by the Treaties.'

[140]Declaration 17 on the Primacy of EU law is therefore not legally binding. The Treaty contains joint Declarations based on common agreement and unilateral Declarations made by one or more member states such as Declaration 61 by the Republic of Poland on the Charter of Fundamental Rights of the European Union. Declarations can also be attached to Protocols such as the Protocol on the application of the Charter of Fundamental Rights to Poland and to the United Kingdom – Declarations 61 and 62.

[141]See C-354/04P *Gestoras Pro Amnistia and others* v *Council* [60]; also C-292/89 *Antonissen* [1991] ECR I-745 [18]; C-329/95 *VAG Sverige* [1997] ECR I-2675 [23]; and C-49/02 *Heidelberger Bauchemie* [2004] ECR I-6129 [17]

[142]European Commission, '2011 Report on the application of the EU Charter of Fundamental Rights', COM(2012) 169 final

need for in-depth monitoring. The EP study assessed the relevance of the EU Charter in affecting legal competences and working practices of specific EU agencies. It expresses strong concern about the impact on the protection of human rights – multiplicity, overlapping roles, lack of accountability and transparency have undermined the protection of rights:

> The plurality of law enforcement authorities intervening and 'assisting' EU Member States like Italy in border control exempts a proper scrutiny of the activities and inputs of EU agencies like Frontex and Europol. There is a lack of knowledge and public information concerning the actual scope of the EU Home Affairs agencies' actions, which makes it even more difficult to carry out daily monitoring and ex-post evaluation on the compatibility between their activities with fundamental rights envisaged by the EU Charter as well as the procedural guarantees envisaged by EU secondary law, such as the SBC and EU asylum law. The legal vacuums (and extra-legal nature of some of their inputs) and 'the accountability gap' characterising the de jure competences and de facto activities of actors like Frontex and Europol profoundly transform traditional rule of law standards and principles determining and ensuring public authorities' accountability and liability in the case of fundamental rights violations and illiberal practices. They also obscure, and to a certain extent allow, 'power' to evade responsibility and effective legal protection.[143]

Perhaps this is why accession to the ECHR remains necessary. Subsequent to EU accession to the ECHR, protection of fundamental rights may be complete. The following extract from *Frannson* gives an indication of the change that can be expected when the EU signs the ECHR. At present, in the absence of a connection with EU law, *national* law continues to govern the relationship between the member states legal system and the ECHR. Despite the changes in EU law, a conflict between national law and the ECHR is not governed by EU law. This situation will only change when the EU accedes to the Convention – EU law will then influence conclusions to be drawn where there is such a conflict:

> [44] As regards, first, the conclusions to be drawn by a national court from a conflict between national law and the ECHR, it is to be remembered that whilst, as Article 6(3) TEU confirms, fundamental rights recognised by the ECHR constitute general principles of the European Union's law and whilst Article 52(3) of the Charter requires rights contained in the Charter which correspond to rights guaranteed by the ECHR to be given the same meaning and scope as those laid down by the ECHR, the latter does not constitute, as long as the European Union has not acceded to it, a legal instrument which has been formally incorporated into European Union law. Consequently, European Union law does not govern the relations between the ECHR and the legal systems of the Member States, nor does it determine the conclusions to be drawn by a

---

[143]Elspeth Guild, Sergio Carrera, Leonhard den Hertog and Joanna Parkin, 'Implementation of the EU Charter of Fundamental Rights and its Impact on EU Home Affairs Agencies: Frontex, Europol and the European Asylum Support Office', European Parliament Civil Liberties, Justice And Home Affairs, Brussels, 2011, p. 105

national court in the event of conflict between the rights guaranteed by that convention and a rule of national law (see, to this effect, Case C-571/10 *Kamberaj* [2012] ECR, paragraph 62).

VIEWPOINT

In your opinion, what is the impact of the Charter? Does it improve protection for persons 'who look like' Rosalind LeCraft?

---

5. Towards a coherent system for the protection of fundamental rights in EU law

i.   The Lisbon Treaty

Fundamental rights have come a long way in EU law since *Stork* and *Geitling*. They are no longer subject to the whim of the CJEU but are clearly anchored in primary EU law. They are mentioned in numerous places: the preamble of the Lisbon Treaty (LT) sees the member states 'CONFIRMING their attachment to the principles of liberty, democracy and respect for human rights and fundamental freedoms and of the rule of law'; Article 2 LT establishes that 'The Union is founded on the values of respect for human dignity, freedom, democracy, equality, the rule of law and respect for human rights, including the rights of persons belonging to minorities. These values are common to the Member States in a society in which pluralism, non-discrimination, tolerance, justice, solidarity and equality between women and men prevail'; Article 5 LT, again specifies the protection of human rights, in particular the rights of the child.

Most significantly, although its text is not part of it, the Lisbon Treaty provides for recognition of the Charter by giving its provisions binding legal force. This further entrenches rights in EU law. Under Article 6(1) TEU:

The Union recognises the rights, freedoms and principles set out in the Charter of Fundamental Rights of the European Union of 7 December 2000, as adapted at Strasbourg, on 12 December 2007, which shall have the same legal value as the Treaties.

The ability of a document recording existing rights drawn from other sources to itself have legally binding status was described as 'circular'[144] but was nonetheless seen to be valuable:

It may appear somewhat anomalous to give legally binding status to an instrument which self-avowedly records rights deriving from other sources. However, whatever the legal effect of this change—a matter which we consider below – declaring the Charter

---

[144]James Flynn QC, for the Bar Council – House of Lords European Union Committee 10th Report para 5.66

to be legally binding will send a clear message to all institutions and citizens within the Union about the EU's commitment to uphold the rights set out in the Charter.[145]

It is to be hoped that the commitment brings more direct benefits to individuals, but its ability to do this has been curtailed. Article 6 TEU also clearly states the scope of the Charter: it 'shall not extend in any way the competences of the Union as defined in the Treaties': thus the rights, freedoms and principles in the Charter must be interpreted 'in accordance with the general provisions in Title VII of the Charter governing its interpretation and application and with due regard to the explanations referred to in the Charter, that set out the sources of those provisions'.

A new section, added to Article 51 TEU, states that 'The Protocols and Annexes to the Treaties shall form an integral part thereof'. Protocols are ratified as part of the Treaty and their provisions have legal force equal to that of the Treaty text. This is relevant because during negotiations on the Lisbon Treaty, two member states – the UK and Poland – sought and won assurances further limiting the scope of the CFR. These were attached as Protocol 30 to the Lisbon Treaty: Article 1(1) precludes any judicial finding that 'laws, regulations or administrative provisions, practices or action' are inconsistent with the Charter. Article 1(2) confirms that Title IV CFR (Solidarity) which consists of economic and social rights, does not create any justiciable rights. The British position will surprise few, given the longstanding opposition to the Social Charter and the current campaign to limit the role of the ECtHR,[146] but one may have thought Poland with its tradition of '*solidarnosc*'[147] would support this Chapter. In fact Poland did: its concern was that the vision of social and economic rights in the Charter is too liberal. Under Article 2, any Charter reference to national laws and practices applies only to the extent that the rights or principles in the Charter are recognised by the laws and practices of the UK, Poland and the Czech Republic. These two provisions provide legally binding exceptions to the justiciability of the Charter in these three countries.

APPLYING THE LAW

If a member state introduced a new labour law, could this be reviewed for compliance with the EU Charter?

---

ii.   The EU, the CFR and the ECHR

An important Declaration attached to the Lisbon Treaty concerned the relationship between the CFR and the ECHR. The LT Declaration on Article 6(2) TEU states:

> *The Conference agrees that the Union's accession to the European Convention on the Protection of Human Rights and Fundamental Freedoms should be arranged in such a way as to preserve the specific features of Union law. In this connection, the*

---

[145]House of Lords 10th Report para 5.68
[146]Giuseppe Martinico and Oreste Pollicino (eds), *The National Judicial Treatment of the ECHR and EU Laws: A Comparative Perspective*, Europa Law Publishing, 2010
[147]http://www.solidarnosc.org.pl/en/main-page.html

Conference notes the existence of a regular dialogue between the Court of Justice of the European Union and the European Court of Human Rights; such dialogue could be reinforced when the Union accedes to that Convention.

This common political goal has resulted in a political commitment that the EU accede to the ECHR. Article 6(2) TEU itself states that the Union shall accede to the ECHR but that 'such accession shall not affect the Union's competences as defined in the Treaties'. When this happens, the EU will become a formal party to the Convention: like the member states its institutions, including the CJEU, will then be bound by the provisions of the ECHR. The ECHR will thereafter be more than a voluntary source of fundamental rights in the EU.

This is a positive step – on a symbolic level, accession will bring prestige to the EU, raising its profile as a location for the protection of human rights and the legitimacy of its institutions. On a practical level, it will remove the anomaly that the member states are subject to the ECHR but the EU institutions and their acts are not.[148] At present any violation of fundamental rights protected by the ECHR committed by the EU institutions cannot be reviewed by the ECtHR.[149]

Despite current attempts to recalibrate the relationship with the ECtHR, steps to enable the EU to be brought before the Strasbourg court have widespread support in Britain:

We have in the past identified strong reasons for supporting EU accession to the ECHR. The Strasbourg Court would then be recognised as the final authority in the field of human rights. This would assist to avoid any risk of conflict between European Union law and the European Convention on Human Rights as interpreted in Strasbourg, by placing fundamental rights on a single consistent foundation throughout the EU. We continue to be of the view that the Government should encourage Member States to pave the way for accession by the Union to the ECHR at the earliest opportunity.[150]

Conflict has arisen in cases such as *Bosphorous*[151] and *Matthews*,[152] where the CJ and the ECtHR came to different conclusions on the interpretation of the same right. The benefit to the individual was stressed by Layden and Lock.[153]

Overall, it is suggested that EU accession to the Convention will add to the protection of fundamental rights of people in the EU (whether they are EU citizens or not). The main innovation will be that the EU will become directly accountable in Strasbourg. Under the current state of the ECtHR's case law an individual can hold one or more Member States responsible as proxies where she alleges that a violation of her Convention rights can be found either in the EU's Treaties (primary law) or in actions of the Member States required by EU law. This approach will no longer be necessary. But

[148]Christina Eckes 'EU Accession to the ECHR: Between Autonomy and Adaptation', *MLR* 76(2), 2013, p. 254
[149]App No. 73274/01 *Connolly v 15 Member States of the EU*, 9 December 2009
[150]House of Lords EU Committee 10th Report para 5.114
[151]App No. 45036/98, *Bosphorus v Ireland*, 30 June 2005
[152]App No. 24833/94 *Matthews v United Kingdom*, ECtHR 1999-I
[153]Patrick Layden QC and Dr Tobias Lock, 'Protection of Fundamental Rights post-Lisbon: The Interaction between the EU Charter of Fundamental Rights, the European Convention on Human Rights (ECHR) and National Constitutions – United Kingdom National Report', FIDE XXV Congress, 2011, p. 13

what is more important than ironing out this procedural peculiarity, is that accession will close a gap in the ECtHR's jurisdiction to (indirectly) review EU law.

However the peoples of Europe may have to wait for a while until this happens: the incompatibility finding of the CJ is the most significant, but not the only, hurdle. In order for accession to occur the Council must act unanimously after obtaining the consent of the European Parliament.[154] In addition, the agreement can only enter into force after approval by every member state in accordance with their respective constitutional requirements.[155] This will require referendums in some member states.

An immediate issue was that the ECHR was drafted for accession by states – how then could a polity like the EU sign up to it? The Council of Europe acted quickly to agree the changes necessary to facilitate this. The legal basis for EU accession is now provided in Article 59(2) ECHR which states that 'the European Union may accede to this Convention'. This amendment by Protocol No. 14 to the ECHR entered into force on 1 June 2010.[156] When it joins, the EU will send a single judge to the ECtHR, who will sit alongside national judges from the member states and participate with the same status.

Opinion 2/13 undermines years of preparatory work. A formal discussion on accession began on 7 July 2010. Responsibility for agreeing an accession instrument was given to an informal group of 14 persons. Of these 14 individuals, chosen due to their expertise, only seven came from an EU member state. Eight working meetings took place over 11 months with the European Commission and representatives of civil society. By July 2011, a draft accession agreement was ready.[157]

It is worth considering some of the aspects of this agreement, even if its future is uncertain. One of the most sensitive questions addressed is the treatment of complaints brought before the Strasbourg Court against the EU which had not been dealt with by the CJEU. This did not apply to actions for annulment under Article 263 TFEU – applicants seeking direct access will have to bring the matter before the CJEU before it would be admissible by the ECtHR. Under Article 35(1) Convention, applicants must exhaust domestic remedies before turning to the ECtHR. In the context of the EU, this requires the case to go before the CJEU in accordance with EU law – this would fulfil the criterion on 'internal review'. It is unclear what the situation will be if they are unable to prove *locus standi* to have their case heard before the CJEU which may be likely given the restrictive rules applied – even after the Lisbon Treaty changes – to natural and legal persons.

The situation is different in relation to Article 267 TFEU. Under this procedure, the applicant must first go to a national court or tribunal which may or must in turn refer a question of interpretation or validity to the CJEU. If, as is sometimes the case, the national legal authority declines to refer a question to the CJEU, the ECtHR would have to look at the case without the CJEU being able to do so. One suggestion is to introduce a procedure to respect subsidiarity:

In order that the principle of subsidiarity may be respected also in that situation, a procedure should be put in place, in connection with the accession of the EU to the

---

[154]Article 218 (6) TFEU (ex 300 EC)
[155]Article 218(8) TFEU
[156]http://hub.coe.int/what-we-do/human-rights/eu-accession-to-the-convention
[157]Draft legal instruments on the accession of the European Union to the European Convention on Human Rights, CDDH-UE(2011)16

Convention, which is flexible and would ensure that the CJEU may carry out an internal review before the ECHR carries out external review.[158]

Another critical question is what would happen where accountability for the breach of rights is unclear. For example, in *Bosphorous*, Ireland had no discretion as to the action to be taken, as she was implementing EU law. Should the EU therefore have been held responsible? This was not possible at that time because the EU was not a party to the Convention but after EU accession to the ECHR this will become an option for claimants. However, claimants may not know who to hold responsible. In order to avoid difficulties in determining responsibility, the Presidents of both courts agreed that a mechanism should be introduced to allow for participation of the CJEU in proceedings. A 'co-respondent' mechanism was introduced[159] whereby both the member state and the EU could be held responsible for a violation. This was promoted as a way to avoid gaps in accountability. Under this mechanism, neither the member state nor the EU can avoid liability by blaming the other:

> Where an application is directed against one or more member states of the European Union, the European Union may become a co-respondent to the proceedings in respect of an alleged violation notified by the Court if it appears that such an allegation calls into question the compatibility with the Convention right at issue of a provision of European Union law. Where an application is directed against the European Union, the European Union member states may become co-respondents to the proceedings in respect of an alleged violation notified by the Court if it appears that such an allegation calls into question the compatibility with the Convention rights at issue of a provision of the Treaty on European Union, the Treaty on the Functioning of the European Union or any other provision having the same legal value pursuant to those instruments.[160]

This dual liability, like the dual vigilance of direct effect, will benefit individuals. But it leaves unanswered an important question: who are the final protectors of human rights – the member states or the EU?

VIEWPOINT

Are fundamental rights most effectively protected by a) national courts, b) the CJEU in Luxembourg, or c) the ECtHR in Strasbourg?

When the two instruments – the CFR and the ECHR – are both in use, it will not be the case that even where the same rights exist in the text, these will be interpreted in the same way. For example:

> Article 47 CFR (right to an effective remedy and to a fair trial) might be thought, by virtue of Article 52(3) CFR, to correspond to Articles 13 and 6 ECHR. But, according

---

[158]http://www.echr.coe.int/NR/rdonlyres/02164A4C-0B63-44C3-80C7-FC594EE16297/0/2011Communication_CEDHCJUE_EN.pdf
[159]Tobias Lock, 'Walking on a Tightrope: The Draft ECHR Accession Agreement and the Autonomy of the EU legal order', *CMLR* 48, 2011, p. 1025
[160]Lock 2011, p. 1043

to the Explanations, that is not so. In particular, the reference to 'civil rights and obligations' in Article 6 of the Convention is not carried across into Union law, where protection is not so limited. This is an example, according to the Explanations, where the protection afforded to the individual by Union law is more extensive than that envisaged by the Convention. So, although Article 47 CFR *looks* as if it re-states the same principle as is covered by Articles 6 and 13 ECHR, it in fact provides wider protection to the individual.[161]

As seen in *McB*, the difference of a single word will not necessarily make a huge difference – in that case, Article 7 of the Charter and Article 8(1) of the ECHR used identical wording except that one used 'correspondence' and the other 'communications'. The CJ held that the two provisions contained corresponding rights which were to be given the same meaning.[162]

What will accession mean then for those rights that are in the CFR but not in the ECHR? For example, Article 1 of the Charter provides that 'Human dignity is inviolable. It must be respected and protected.' This right in the Charter is based upon EU law[163] and there is no directly equivalent right in the Convention. However, it has been argued that this right is implicit in Article 8 ECHR:

> . . . the ECtHR has developed an extended content for the right to private life set out in Article 8. And there is a provision – Article 7 – in the Charter which also deals with respect for private and family life, and which is almost identical with Article 8 of the Convention. In the absence of any proper consideration of Article 1 CFR by a competent court, its scope must remain uncertain. In particular, it is not clear how far respect for and protection of human dignity can be regarded as a concept separate from the general right to and respect for private life which is enjoined by Article 8 of the Convention. Certainly, in the UK, some courts adopt an approach to Article 8 ECHR which clearly encompasses the concept of dignity.[164]

Whether these changes are good for the autonomy of EU law[165] in the future is another question. Furthermore, a larger question remains: are courts the proper and effective protector of rights?[166]

VIEWPOINT

Why is accession to the ECHR necessary now that the EU has its own Charter?

---

[161]Lock 2011
[162]C-400/10 *McB* [53]
[163]C-377/98, *Netherlands v European Parliament and Council* [70–77]
[164]Layden and Lock 2011, p. 13
[165]Lock 2011
[166]See Heydon 2013

6. Conclusion

This chapter began with a brief explanation of the development of rights in general, starting with the ambitious UNDHR 1948 which proclaimed:

> . . . *THIS UNIVERSAL DECLARATION OF HUMAN RIGHTS as a common standard of achievement for all peoples and all nations, to the end that every individual and every organ of society, keeping this Declaration constantly in mind, shall strive by teaching and education to promote respect for these rights and freedoms and by progressive measures, national and international, to secure their universal and effective recognition and observance, both among the peoples of Member States themselves and among the peoples of territories under their jurisdiction.*

By contrast, ambitions for rights in the EU were more modest. Although fundamental freedoms were entrenched as the pillars of market integration, fundamental rights first appeared in EU law as general principles. These were identified by the CJEU in an ad hoc and non-systematic way. Their application focused on the acts of the EU institutions themselves and the acts of the member states when implementing EU law.

The creation of the Charter on Fundamental Rights has created a more systematic basis for the recognition and protection of fundamental and human rights – they are now more visible and thus more accessible – but their scope of application remains largely the same. There are indeed many more of them: while the ECHR contains less than 20, the CFR contains over 50 substantive rights. It is inevitable that rights change over time – 'the deeply held values of one generation may seem bigoted or wrong-headed to another'.[167] Yet, as impressive as the list in the Charter is, more rights do not remedy gaps in the system of protection.[168] Policing and CFSP remain beyond the CJEU under Article 275 TFEU – only when the CJEU has this jurisdiction will gaps in rights protection be filled.[169]

These rights will co-exist alongside the ECHR if and when the EU finally accedes to this Convention. The EU will become the first non-state signatory. At that point the EU as a whole will become subject to the obligations in the ECHR, like the member states. The CJEU will remain the final arbiter of rights in the Charter, and the European Court of Human Rights in Strasbourg will continue to oversee respect for the Convention. Will the CJEU steer rights in the EU towards an economic interpretation? In *Omega* and *Schmidberger* it made them subject to compliance with the four freedoms. This strongly suggests that it remains focused on the single market.

It can be argued that the CJEU developed a rights profile for the EU but the EP and Commission have gone further to develop a human rights policy that applies in the EU and beyond. However is this enough – does the development of the Charter and accession to the ECHR provide the EU with a human rights profile, or create a human rights policy[170] or even a virtuous community of rights throughout the EU?

---

[167]Heydon 2013, p. 9
[168]Frederic van den Berghe 'The EU and issues of Human Rights protection: same solutions to more acute problems?', *ELJ* 16, 2010, p. 112
[169]Dorota Leczykiewicz, 'Effective judicial protection of human rights after Lisbon: should national courts be empowered to review EU secondary law?', *European Law Review* 35(3), 2010, pp. 326–348
[170]Bogdandy 2000

Further reading

On protection of human rights in the EU in general:

F van den Berghe, 'The EU and issues of Human Rights protection: same solutions to more acute problems?', *ELJ* 16, 2010, p. 112

Joseph H.H. Weiler, 'Eurocracy and Distrust: Some questions concerning the role of the European Court of Justice in the protection of fundamental human rights within the legal order of the European Communities,' *Washington Law Review* 61, 1986, pp.1103–1142

On the EU Charter of Fundamental Rights:

Catherine Barnard, *The EU Charter of Fundamental Rights: Happy 10th Birthday?*, *European Union Studies Association* 24(1), Winter 2011, pp. 5–11

Koen Lenaerts, 'Exploring the Limits of the EU Charter of Fundamental Rights', *European Constitutional Law Review* 8, 2012, pp. 375–403

Steve Peers, Tamara Hervey, Jeff Kenner and Angela Ward (eds), *The EU Charter of Fundamental Rights*, Hart Publishing, 2013

Sybe de Vries et al. (eds) *The Protection of Fundamental Rights in the EU after Lisbon*, Hart Publishing, 2013

On EU accession to the ECHR:

Paul Gragl, *The Accession of the European Union to the European Convention on Human Rights*, Hart Publishing, 2013

Noreen O'Meara, '"A More Secure Europe of Rights?" The European Court of Human Rights, the Court of Justice of the European Union and EU Accession to the ECHR', *German Law Journal* 12(10), 2011, pp. 1813–1832

On the application of the EU Charter:

Leonard F.M. Besselink, *The Protection of Fundamental Rights post-Lisbon, The Interaction between the EU Charter of Fundamental Rights, the European Convention on Human Rights (ECHR) and National Constitutions*, FIDE, 2012

Laurent Pech, 'Between Judicial Minimalism and Avoidance: The Court of Justice's Sidestepping of Fundamental Constitutional Issues in *Römer and Dominguez*', *Common Market Law Review* 49, 2012, pp. 1840–1880

Part III

Rights of Movement and Residence in the EU

9 The Citizenship Directive 2004/38

Setting the scene

Ms C was detained when she arrived at Tegel Airport in Berlin even though her baby daughter was a German citizen and her partner Mr B, with whom she lived in Berlin, was a Swedish national. When she asked the border official for an explanation, she was told it was because first, she was a third country national; and second, she was not married to Mr B. She was told that she would be sent back to Colombia on the next available flight.

1. Introduction

In 2004, five years before the Lisbon Treaty, the Citizenship Directive (CD) 2004/38 was adopted to simplify and strengthen the rights of Union citizens. Despite its name, this important Directive provides rights for both workers and citizens as well as their families. It repealed[1] many of the previous directives that had been adopted to regulate the entry, residence and rights of economically inactive migrants such as students and the elderly. For example, the Student Directive: this set out three conditions when a host member state was to recognise the right of residence for any student accepted to attend a vocational training course for the duration of those studies. The student had first to have access to sufficient financial resources to avoid any reliance upon social assistance during their stay; second, be enrolled on a course at a recognised educational establishment; and third, have comprehensive health coverage in the host member state. The Student Directive annulled the right of residence where these conditions were no longer fulfilled. Similar rules were laid out in the annulled directives for self-employed persons and other economically inactive groups such as pensioners. These rules are now in the Citizenship Directive. In addition, the Citizenship Directive amended Regulation 1612/68 on free movement in the EU for workers – this regulation now exists in a further updated form as Regulation 492/2011.

The Citizenship Directive attempts to be fully comprehensive, providing a single set of rules applicable to all workers, EU citizens and their family members who may be EU nationals or third country nationals. It has been in force since 30 April 2006. Its contents fall into four categories. First, it determines who 'belongs' and who does not by separating those who automatically enjoy citizenship rights from those who can only do so at the discretion of the member states. Second, it sets out the conditions governing the exercise of the rights of EU citizens and their family members to move and reside in the EU. It therefore works with the primary and individual right set out in Article 21 TFEU. It adopts the language used by the CJ in *Gryzelczyk*[2] to describe Union citizenship as 'the fundamental status of nationals of the Member States when they exercise their right of free movement and residence'. Third, it does something new – it creates a right of permanent residence in a host member state for Union citizens and their family members. That there are no territorial exclusions to these EU rights of residence and permanent residence unless similar territorial restrictions apply to the member state's own nationals.[3] Finally, drawing upon case law under free movement of workers, it sets out the limits that can be placed on the rights set out in the first two categories on grounds of public policy, public security or public health.

---

[1]Council Directive 90/364/EEC of 28 June 1990 on the right of residence; Council Directive 90/365/EEC of 28 June 1990 on the right of residence for employees and self-employed persons who have ceased their occupational activity; Council Directive 93/96/EEC of 29 October 1993 on the right of residence for students; Council Directive 68/360/EEC of 15 October 1968 on the abolition of restrictions on movement and residence within the Union for workers of member states and their families; Council Directive 73/148/EEC of 21 May 1973 on the abolition of restrictions on movement and residence within the Union for nationals of member states with regard to establishment and the provision of services; Directives 64/221, 72/194, 75/34 and 75/35
[2]C-184/99 *Grzelczyk* [2001] ECR I-6193
[3]Article 22 CD

2. Determination of belonging

The Citizenship Directive provides direct rights to EU citizens and workers – family members derive rights from these primary holders of rights. Before any derived citizenship rights can be enjoyed, it is necessary to be recognised as a family member. Yet who is family in EU law? This is important because family reunion is integral to the internal labour market – workers are unlikely to seek opportunities to work abroad or commit to this if their loved ones must stay behind – free movement of workers can only be a reality if there is free movement of workers' families. As highlighted in *Dogan*[4] by AG Mengozzi, both the EU legislator and the CJEU recognise a fundamental connection between family life and free movement rights. This connection exists to protect both the freedom and human dignity of migrant workers – family life should not become a casualty of free movement. Thus under EU law the families of workers, and members of their households also enjoy rights to equal treatment – as far as the CJ is concerned, this 'contributes to their integration in the society of the host country, in accordance with the aims of the freedom of movement for workers'.[5] This includes the right to enter and reside, take up jobs and education.

The 'family' was not defined in EU law; thus before harmonising legislation appeared in the form of the CD, the CJ had to grapple with this question. A case arose in the Netherlands, where a residence permit was refused because the authorities disputed that a long-term partner was a 'spouse'.[6] The CJ took a light approach: it did not instruct the national court on who should be recognised as a spouse under national law but held that the principle of non-discrimination demanded that the unmarried partner of a migrant Union worker had to be recognised if recognition would be granted to the unmarried partner of a Dutch worker:

> The possibility for a migrant worker of obtaining permission for his unmarried companion to reside with him, where that companion is not a national of the host member state, can assist his integration in the host state and thus contribute to the achievement of freedom of movement for workers. Consequently, that possibility must be regarded as falling within the concept of a social advantage for the purposes of Article 7 (2) of regulation no 1612/68. It must therefore be concluded that a member state which grants such an advantage to its own nationals cannot refuse to grant it to workers who are nationals of other member states without being guilty of discrimination on grounds of nationality, contrary to Articles 7 and 48 of the Treaty.

The gentle approach did not mean deference to national practices. In *Diatta*[7] it decided, in contrast to the national authority, that separation does not dissolve a marriage; thus a wife who no longer lived with her husband could still rely upon the spousal right to reside – separate living arrangements could not be used to demonstrate breakdown of the marital relationship. The requirement of 'appropriate' accommodation was not also a condition that the family permanently reside together. Spousal rights could be enjoyed until the marriage was formally dissolved.

---

[4]C-138/13 *Naime Dogan v Bundesrepublik Deutschland* (nyr)
[5]C-389-90/87 *Echternach and others v Minister van Onderwijs en Wetenschappen* ([1989] ECR 723)
[6]C-59/85 *Reed* [1985] ECR 1283
[7]C-267/83 *Diatta* [1985] ECR 567

Building upon this, the Citizenship Directive now sets out which family members automatically belong. These include

- the spouse,
- the registered partner (as recognised in domestic law),
- direct descendants (who are either under the age of 21 or dependants of the spouse or partner), and
- dependent direct relatives in the ascending line of the Union citizen or registered partner.[8]

Under Article 3 CD, the directive automatically:

> *shall apply to all Union citizens who move to or reside in a Member State other than that of which they are a national, and to their family members as defined in point 2 of Article 2 who accompany or join them.*

However, anybody not falling under Article 2(2) is designated as 'other family members'. Unmarried partners who co-habit and same-sex partners who are not in a civil partnership fall into Article 3(2) CD, which states:

> *3(2) Without prejudice to any right to free movement and residence the persons concerned may have in their own right, the host Member State shall, in accordance with its national legislation, facilitate entry and residence for the following persons:*
>
> (a) *any other family members, irrespective of their nationality, not falling under the definition in point 2 of Article 2 who, in the country from which they have come, are dependants or members of the household of the Union citizen having the primary right of residence, or where serious health grounds strictly require the personal care of the family member by the Union citizen;*
>
> (b) *the partner with whom the Union citizen has a durable relationship, duly attested.*

Other family members (OFMs) do not enjoy any automatic rights under the Citizenship Directive. OFMs must have their right of residence affirmed by the member state. Such persons may only enjoy rights when the member state recognises them as a 'family member', subject to the production of evidence. In order to be recognised as a family member, they must demonstrate one of three links to the EU citizen:

- dependency (persons who in the home country were provided for by the Union citizen);
- health needs (those who have to be cared for by the Union citizen); and
- intimacy (those who are in an enduring relationship with a Union citizen).

In *Reyes,* the CJEU stressed that these grounds are exhaustive and that employability does not preclude dependency.[9]

It is important to note that OFMs are not mentioned anywhere else in the Citizenship Directive. They are not relevant to EU citizenship law unless and until they are recognised

---

[8] Article 2 Citizenship Directive (CD)
[9] C-423/12 *Flora May Reyes* v *Migrationswet* (nyr)

as 'family members'. This recognition is therefore crucial, as without it there is no access to the rights of residence and free movement. Yet Article 3(2) CD gives little guidance on how OFMs must be treated by the national authorities – it says only that:

> The host Member State shall undertake an extensive examination of the personal circumstances and shall justify any denial of entry or residence to these people.

The Treaty is silent on the scope of this examination or safeguards that must be applied in relation to justification. In the absence of a pan-EU system to determine who belongs under Article 3(2) CD, couples like Ms C and Mr B are left to the discretion of the national authorities. Such broad discretion creates problems, as evident in *Rahman*[10] – this case gave the court an important opportunity to clarify the obligations upon a member state before confirmation of the status of 'family member', in particular the scope and level of discretion left to the member states and the condition of its exercise.

In *Rahman,* the OFMs were the brother, half-brother and nephew of Mr Rahman, a Bangladeshi man who married a migrant EU worker (in his case an Irish woman working in Northern Ireland). The entry clearance given to the three relatives was challenged by the Home Secretary on the basis of unsatisfactory evidence of dependency in Bangladesh upon Mrs Rahman. The Home Secretary disputed first, that they had been dependent upon Mrs Rahman in Ireland before she moved to the UK; second, that they continued to be dependent upon her; and third, that they were members of her household in the UK. The Upper Tribunal sent six questions to the CJEU for a preliminary ruling.

The Grand Chamber considered the breadth of the obligation in Article 3(2) CD and the conditions surrounding the exercise of discretion in that provision. It highlighted that the facilitation of entry and residence extended to OFMs was nonetheless an obligation upon member states to 'confer a certain advantage' that would place dependants in a different category to 'other nationals of third states'.[11] The wide discretion was not to be abused:

> [26] It is incumbent upon member states to ensure that their legislation contains criteria which enable those persons to obtain a decision on their application for entry and residence that is founded on an extensive examination of their personal circumstances and, in the event of refusal, is justified by reasons.

In relation to the exercise of discretion, the Grand Chamber stressed that the relevant authorities must at least have in place a transparent procedure that is amenable to judicial review. OFMs must not be subject to ad hoc decision-making. When member states select criteria, these must be 'consistent with the normal meaning of the term "facilitate" and not be so restrictive as to deprive the provision of its effectiveness'. Furthermore, both national legislation and its application were to be subject to judicial review.[12] The examination could investigate the nature of the dependence claimed, in particular to ensure that 'close and stable family ties' did exist, at the very least at the time when the OFM applies to join the Union citizen upon whom s/he is dependent. The Grand Chamber agreed with the AG that member states could impose particular requirements on the nature and duration of dependence so as to ensure that the situation was 'genuine and stable and has not

---

[10]C-83/11 *Rahman* v *Secretary of State for the Home Office*
[11][21]
[12][26]

been brought about with the sole objective of obtaining entry into and residence in the host member state'.[13]

The sufficiency of this guidance remains to be seen. It has been argued that the EU legislator should do more to prevent divergent treatment of OFMs across the EU:

> It may be correct for the member states to have a monopoly on conferral of nationality but given its importance for enjoyment of EU citizenship rights, should the decision on who is a family member under EU law be left to national discretion? Even after *Rahman*, there is likely to be divergence in the mode of recognition in each MS leading to significant fragmentation in the enjoyment of what should be a coherent EU citizenship right – the right to family life.[14]

OFMs do not therefore enjoy the easy rights of entry provided in Article 5 CD for Union citizens and their families or the rights of residence in Articles 6 and 7 CD. As Weiler argues, solidarity with strangers is limited in EU law.[15]

APPLYING THE LAW

What is Ms C's status under the Citizenship Directive?

The definition of the family in EU law has been criticised as being too narrow, failing to correspond to modern family formations and being premised upon the outdated model of the 'white male bread-winner'. Stalford[16] also argues that it is in conflict with the more substantive approach taken by the European Court of Human Rights under Article 8 ECHR.

VIEWPOINT

Find and read the Article by Helen Stalford. Do you do you agree with her?

---

3. Rights to move and reside

Article 6 CD provides citizens and their family members with residence for up to three months without any conditions or formalities other than possession of a passport or ID card. Article 7 CD sets out the conditions attached to a right of residence for more than

---

[13][38]

[14]Iyiola Solanke, 'Another type of "Other" in EU Law? AB (2) MVC v Home Office and Rahman v Secretary of State for the Home Office', *Modern Law Review* 76(2), 2013, pp. 370–400

[15]Joseph Weiler, 'Thou Shalt not oppress a stranger: on the judicial protection of the human rights of non-EC nationals – a critique', *EJIL* 3, 1992 p. 65

[16]Helen Stalford, 'Mixed Messages: Parental Responsibilities, Public Opinion and the Reforms of Family Law', *International Journal of Law, Policy and the Family* 20(2), 2006, p. 225

three months. Those who wish to remain for more than three months are placed into three categories – these were initially seen as discrete but case law has shown an individual can fall into one or more.[17]

The first category comprises those who are workers or self-employed persons in the host member state. Those in this category also benefit from specific workers' rights provided under Article 45 TFEU and in related secondary legislation such as Regulation 492/2011 on migrant workers and their families. If they are not economically active, they can fall into the second category for those who are self-sufficient. Such persons must have adequate resources for themselves and their family members to prevent them becoming a burden on the social assistance system of the host member state during their period of residence. They must also have comprehensive sickness insurance in the host member state. The final category deals with those in education or training – this longer right of residence can be enjoyed by students and trainees who are enrolled for study at a recognised educational institution and also have comprehensive sickness insurance cover in the host Member State and sufficient resources so that neither they nor their family members become a burden on the social assistance system of the host member state during their period of residence.[18] Member states may not set a fixed amount that they regard as 'sufficient resources' – this must be determined according to the personal situation of the person concerned. As a guide, it must correspond to the eligibility threshold for social assistance or the minimum social security pension paid by the host member state.[19] These provisions incorporate many aspects of the repealed directives.

Family members – including those who are third country nationals[20] – accompanying or joining a Union citizen may reside for more than three months as long as they are also employed/self-employed, self-sufficient through other means or formally enrolled on a course of study.[21] However, rights of family reunion can be limited depending upon the status used to gain residence: member states may restrict rights of residence for family members seeking to join a migrant Union citizen residing in a host member state as a registered student – by way of derogation, only the spouse, registered partner and dependent children shall have the right of residence as family members.[22] The basis of residence is therefore important for family reunion.

The CD protects employed migrant Union citizens in Category 1 from also losing their residence rights if they lose their job. The status as a worker is retained in three circumstances:

- if the inability to work is temporary, caused by illness or accident;
- if unemployment is involuntary after more than 12 months of employment and the person is a registered job-seeker; or
- if the job was a fixed-term contract that ended before 12 months and the person is a registered job-seeker – such persons are seen as workers for at least six months.[23]

---

[17]C-46/12 *LN* v *Styrelsen for Videregaende Uddannelser og Uddannelsesstotte* (nyr)
[18]Article 7(1)(a), (b), (c) CD
[19]Article 8(4) CD
[20]Family rights of non-Union nationals under the CD are to be differentiated from those arising from freedom of establishment – see C-1/05 *Yunying Jia* v *Migrationsverket* [2007] ECR I-1
[21]Articles 7(1)(d) and (2) CD
[22]Article 7(4) CD
[23]As set out in C-292/89 *The Queen/Immigration Appeal Tribunal, ex parte Antonissen* [1991] ECR I-745

Finally a person may retain the status of worker and residence rights if they embark upon vocational training – if, however, a job is left voluntarily to return to study, 'retention of the status of worker shall require the training to be related to the previous employment'.[24]

Administrative formalities to confirm the right to reside are set out in Article 8 CD. The host member state may require Union citizens to register with the relevant authorities within three months of arrival and may also impose sanctions for non-compliance with registration requirements. Union citizens must furnish the authorities with evidence supporting their status as a worker, student or self-sufficient person but the proof required may not be onerous. For example, students may not be required to make a declaration specifying a particular level of resources.[25] This Article also includes details on the administrative formalities for family members who are Union citizens: they may be asked to present a variety of documents in order to be issued a registration certificate: passport or ID card, proof of the existence of a family relationship or a registered partnership, such as a birth or marriage certificate.[26] OFMs pursuing recognition via dependency or ill health are to present to member states:

. . . a document issued by the relevant authority in the country of origin or the country from which they are arriving certifying that they are dependants or members of the household of the Union citizen, or proof of the existence of serious health grounds which strictly require the personal care of the family member by the Union citizen.[27]

Those, on the other hand, in a durable relationship are to present evidence of this.

A separate provision, Article 9 CD, sets out the few administrative formalities for family members who are not nationals of a member state. These persons must apply for and shall be issued a residence card if the planned period of residence is for more than three months. Failure to comply with the requirement to apply for a residence card may again result in 'proportionate and non-discriminatory sanctions'. Under Article 10 CD, member states have six months within which to issue a 'residence card' as evidence of the right of residence; however, a certificate facilitating application for this residence card is to be provided immediately. This did not happen in the case of *AB*.[28]

This case mirrors the setting the scene feature at the start of this chapter. *AB* concerned a young woman who left Bolivia to study and remained in the EU having started a family with a migrant EU worker. The pair did not marry, therefore despite being the parent of a baby EU citizen the lack of formality meant that she fell into the category of 'other family member'. She entered the UK as a student in 2006. Soon after arriving she met Mr B, a Swedish citizen who had lived in the UK since about 1996. Their daughter was born in London in May 2007: as the baby girl was given Swedish citizenship, she was – like her father – a migrant Union citizen. Ms C's student visa expired in January 2008: in March 2008 she applied to the Home Office for an EEA residence card. The ground cited was the existence of a durable relationship with Mr B, a Union citizen and at that time a migrant EU worker. By 2010 she was still waiting.

---

[24]Article 7(3)(d) CD
[25]Article 8(3) CD
[26]Article 8(5)(a) and (b) CD
[27]Article 8(5)(e) and (f) CD
[28]*AB (2) MVC v Home Office* [2012] EWHC 226 (QB)

The case illustrates the (sometimes misplaced) determination of the national authorities to prevent abuse of the EU citizenship rules. Both the preamble[29] and Article 35 CD address this. Article 35 allows Member States to:

> *... adopt the necessary measures to refuse, terminate or withdraw any right conferred by this Directive in the case of abuse of rights or fraud, such as marriages of convenience ...*

Thus where doubts arise, member states may investigate to determine whether the rights granted by the directive are being abused to circumvent national rules on immigration, and can refuse or withdraw the rights of entry or residence if abuse is proven. The directive requires the respect of the principle of proportionality and of the procedural safeguards laid down in Articles 30 and 31 CD. However, Article 35 was not transposed by all member states[30] and the provision has never been cited, even in cases where abuse is suspected.[31]

ANALYSING THE LAW

Read the case *AB (2) MVC* v *Home Office* [2012] EWHC 226 (QB). How did the residency status of the EU citizen change and what difference did this make?

Article 12 CD provides adult spouses with independent rights to reside where the migrant Union worker is no longer in the member state due to departure or has died – 'The worker's death transforms his family members' right of residence into a right of their own.'[32] However non-EU nationals must live in the member state for at least one year before the Union citizen's death. This is a reduction of the two-year qualifying residency period set out in the now repealed Regulation 1251/70.[33] The qualifying timeframe must be continuous. This was confirmed in *Givane*,[34] a case where the Indian family members of a deceased Portuguese worker tried to rely upon these rights to secure indefinite leave to remain in the UK.

Mr Givane, began to work in the UK as a chef in 1992. In 1995 he went to live in India for 10 months, returning in 1996 with a wife and three children, all of Indian nationality. In 1997, Mr Givane died. The request for residency was refused – there was no question

---

[29]Preamble (28) 'To guard against abuse of rights or fraud, notably marriages of convenience or any other form of relationships contracted for the sole purpose of enjoying the right of free movement and residence, Member States should have the possibility to adopt the necessary measures.'

[30]European Commission, 'Report From The Commission To The European Parliament And The Council on the application of Directive 2004/38/EC on the right of citizens of the Union and their family members to move and reside freely within the territory of the Member States', COM(2008) 840/03, p. 9

[31]For example C-86/12 *Adzo Domenyo Alopka, Jarel Moudoulou, Eja Moudoulou* v *Ministre du Travail, de l'Emploi et de l'Immigration*

[32]C-257/00 *Nani Givane and Others and Secretary of State for the Home Department* [2003] ECR I-345 [31]

[33]Article 17 of the CD 2004/38 now includes the main elements of Regulation (EEC) No 1251/70 of 29 June 1970 on the right of workers to remain in the territory of a member state after having been employed in that state (OJ L142/24 1970), and furthermore amends them by granting beneficiaries the more privileged status of permanent residence. Regulation No 1251/70 was repealed with effect from 30 April 2006 by Commission Regulation (EC) No 635/2006 of 25 April 2006 (OJ L112,25/9 2006). Regulation No 635/2006 is directly applicable in the member states and binding in its entirety.

[34]C-257/00 Givane

regarding Mr Givane's status as a worker or of the family unit but it was argued that Mr Givane had not satisfied the requirement of two years' residency in the host state: according to the Home Secretary this had to immediately precede the death of the worker. The Commission and the German government agreed with this, and ultimately so did the CJ. After a fruitless comparison of the phrase 'for at least two years' in the different language versions, it concluded[35] that the period of two years had to be calculated from the time just before the worker's death. This was seen as compatible with Article 45 TFEU and defended as necessary because the two-year condition acts as a twofold guarantee: it establishes a significant connection between the member state, and the worker and his family, and also ensures a certain level of their integration in the society of that state.[36] That connection between the host member state and the worker could not be ensured if the right of residence could be based upon a period of two years at any stage in the worker's life.

However, this qualification residency period does not apply if the third country national is the responsible parent of a child who is enrolled in full-time education,[37] irrespective of the nationality of parent and child, and the age of the child. All that matters is the need for the carer to be present in order for the child to pursue education: in *Alarape*, it was stated that:

> The parent of a child who had attained the age of majority and who had obtained access to education on the basis of Article 12 of Council Regulation (EEC) No 1612/68 (as amended by Parliament and Council Directive 2004/38/EC) could continue to have a derived right of residence under that Article if the child remained in need of the presence and care of that parent in order to be able to continue and to complete his or her education.[38]

It should be noted that Article 12 CD residency rights are not part of the continuum to permanent residency discussed below: third country national parents cannot use the period of residency based on this Article to acquire permanent residence under Article 16 CD. Periods of residence in a host member state completed by third country family members of a Union citizen solely on the basis of Article 12 of Regulation 1612/68 are discrete and cannot 'be taken into consideration for the purposes of acquisition by those family members of a right of permanent residence'.[39]

Any parent wishing to rely upon these rights must be in the same member state as the child. Mr Iida,[40] a Japanese national, shared custody for his daughter with his German wife. The family moved from the United States to Germany in 2005. In 2007, his wife and daughter moved to Austria and he remained at his place of work in Germany. When his wife informed the German authorities that they were living apart, he was refused a residence permit, as he was no longer seen as the spouse of a German national. He tried to acquire residency as the family member of a Union citizen, relying *inter alia* on Article 12(3). This was also unsuccessful: the right applies to those left behind when the migrant Union worker leaves the host state to go elsewhere not to those left behind when the Union citizen leaves – as put by AG Trstenjak:

[35]C-296/95 *EMU Tabac and Others* [1998] ECR I-1605 [36]
[36][46]
[37]Article 12(3)
[38]C-529/11 *Alarape and another* v *Secretary of State for the Home Department* [2013] WLR (D) 168
[39]C-529/11 Alarape
[40]C 40/11 *Yoshikazu Iida* v *Stadt Ulm*

[35] Although Article 12(3) of Directive 2004/38 confers on the 'parent who has actual custody', irrespective of his nationality, a right of residence until the child completes his studies, this provision is, in view of its unambiguous wording, applicable only in the case where the Union citizen moves away from his host Member State and not, as in the case at issue here, where he moves away from his Member State of origin. Therefore, this provision likewise cannot establish a right of residence in Germany for the Japanese father of the German national who has moved to Austria.

Article 13 CD provides spouses with rights to remain where the relationship has broken down,[41] but Mr Iida would have had the same problem – these rights are to be exercised in the *host* state when the Union citizen leaves. They are also highly conditional – residency will be granted where the relationship existed for at least three years in the host state; or the non-EU spouse has custody rights of the children; or the spouse was a victim of domestic violence; or a court has given the spouse a right of access to a minor child in the host state.

Enjoyment of these rights in Articles 12 and 13 is however predicated upon financial self-sufficiency: in order to stay, the spouse must have sufficient resources at their disposal. These conditions must be satisfied before the right of permanent residence is given. This also applies under Directive 2003/109 providing rights of long-term residence to third country nationals.[42] As a long-term resident, Mr Iida would enjoy equal treatment to German nationals[43] – he had in fact made an application for residency under this directive, but withdrew it before his case was heard by the CJ.

4. Rights of permanent residence

Article 7 CD introduces a gradual system of residence rights which culminates in the right of permanent residence after five years. The conditions associated with each stage become more demanding. These stages are summarised in Table 9.1.

The right to permanent residence for workers, Union citizens, their family members who are EU nationals and those who are from beyond the EU is set out in Articles 16–21 CD. The general rule is set out in Article 16 CD:

(1) *Union citizens who have resided legally for a continuous period of five years in the host Member State shall have the right of permanent residence there. This right shall not be subject to the conditions provided for in Chapter III.*

(2) *Paragraph 1 shall apply also to family members who are not nationals of a Member State and have legally resided with the Union citizen in the host Member State for a continuous period of five years.*

It is possible to be a permanent resident in one member state and spend long periods in the home member state: absence of up to six months per year does not jeopardise the status. Longer-term absence due to military service or other 'important reasons such as

---

[41]Article 13 CD

[42]Directive 2003/109 lays out rights of long-term residence for third country nationals such as Mr Iida.

[43]For example in C-571/10 *Kamberaj v IPES* the CJ upheld a claim of equal treatment to housing benefit for a third country national under Article 11(10(d)) of Directive 2003/109.

TABLE 9.1   Residence rights under Article 7 of the Citizenship Directive

Time frame	Who	Conditions	Entry formalities/visa	Loss of rights
Up to 3 months (Art. 6 CD)	All EU citizens and their families	None but no automatic access to social assistance system	Valid ID card/ passport. Non-EU nationals require visa (5.2)	Public policy, health, security
Beyond 3 months (Art. 7.1 CD)	Workers or self-employed; financially self-sufficient; have health insurance; funded students and trainees; family members of the above (EU and non-EU nationals)	No 'unreasonable burden' on social assistance system	Registration with authorities upon production of valid passport and confirmation of employment or enrolment and funding if a student/ trainee	If no longer economically active BUT deportation may not be automatic consequence of request for social assistance
Beyond 5 years	Union citizens with continuous residence of 5 years and non-EU family members	Not subject to any conditions – genuine vehicle for integration into society of member state (*Ziolkowski*)[44]	NA	Upon absence from the member state for a period of 2 consecutive years

pregnancy and childbirth, serious illness, study or vocational training, or a posting in another Member State or a third country' is also accommodated. Once acquired, the right of permanent residence can only be lost through absence from the host member state for more than two consecutive years. Under Article 21 CD, member states may determine independently how continuity of residence may be attested.

Under Article 17(3) CD, the family members of a worker or a self-employed person who live with his/her in the territory of the host member state also have the right of permanent residence in that member state, if the worker or self-employed person has acquired permanent residence there. Article 23 CD also entitles them to take up employment or self-employment there. This applies irrespective of nationality, and under conditions even if the worker or self-employed person dies while still working but before acquiring permanent residence status. There are three conditions for this:

● the worker or self-employed person must have resided continuously in the host member state for two years at the time of death;
● alternatively, the cause of death was an occupational accident or disease; or
● the status can be acquired if the surviving spouse became stateless following marriage to the deceased worker or self-employed person.[45]

---

[44]C-424/10 and 425/10 *Ziolkowski and Szeja* [2011] ECR 2011 I-14035 [41]
[45]Article 17(4)(a)-(c)

In *RM (Zimbabwe)*[46] – RM, a Zimbabwean, had married a Spanish national who had acquired the right to permanent residency six years previously. He died seven months after their marriage and she was able to rely on Article 17 CD: upon marriage, she immediately acquired a permanent right of residence in the UK. Notwithstanding this, under Article 18 CD, the family members of a Union citizen who come from beyond the EU can also acquire the right of permanent residence after 'residing legally' for a period of five consecutive years in the host member state.

A reference from Germany, *Ziolkowski* and *Szeja*,[47] asked the CJ to interpret the phrase 'resided legally'. The question arose because the German authorities had refused the right to permanent residence to two Polish nationals: Mr Ziolkowski, resident in Germany since 1989, and Mrs Szeja, resident in Germany since 1988. Both had been granted residence in Germany on humanitarian grounds based in national law prior to the Polish accession to the EU. Did this constitute 'legal residence' for the purpose of Article 16 CD? The CJ answered this question by stressing that the period of residence had to comply with the conditions set out in Article 7(1) CD:

[46] It follows that the concept of legal residence implied by the terms 'have resided legally' in Article 16(1) of Directive 2004/38 should be construed as meaning a period of residence which complies with the conditions laid down in the directive, in particular those set out in Article 7(1).

[47] Consequently, a period of residence which complies with the law of a Member State but does not satisfy the conditions laid down in Article 7(1) of Directive 2004/38 cannot be regarded as a 'legal' period of residence within the meaning of Article 16(1).

This suggests that receipt of benefits per se does not preclude entitlement to permanent residence. The test is a positive rather than a negative one. Also entry must not be based solely upon Article 7(1) for the right in Article 16 CD to be secured, but the *conditions* laid down in Article 7(1) must be satisfied during that timeframe:

[62] . . . provided the person concerned can demonstrate that such periods were completed in compliance with the conditions laid down in Article 7(1) of Directive 2004/38, the taking into account of such periods from the date of accession of the Member State concerned to the European Union does not give retroactive effect to Article 16 of Directive 2004/38, but simply gives present effect to situations which arose before the date of transposition of that directive.[48]

The case is important because it clarifies that the legal basis for the qualification period of five years prior to permanent residence is EU law and not national law. Importantly, for the many nationals of the countries joining the EU in 2004, the five-year timeframe does not begin only after formal accession to the EU.[49] The case also explains the relationship between the different stages of residence.

The five-year timeframe is relaxed in three circumstances. It is reduced to three years for persons aged at least 60 who have retired or otherwise stopped working in the host

---

[46]*RM (Zimbabwe)* v *Home Secretary* [2013] EWCA Civ 775
[47]C-424/10 and 425/10 *Ziolkowski and Szeja*
[48]C-162/09 *Lassal* [2010] ECR I-9217 [38]
[49][57–60]

member state, provided that they worked in the host member state for at least the preceding 12 months. It is reduced further to two years for workers or self-employed persons who for more than two years resided continuously in the host member state and had to stop working there due to permanent incapacity. However, the residence criterion is removed completely if the incapacity is due to an accident at work or an occupational disease entitling the person concerned to any welfare benefit payable in the host member state. Finally, workers or self-employed persons who reside in the host member state but work in another member state shall gain the status after three years of continuous employment.[50]

Minimal administrative formalities are set out in Articles 19 and 20 CD: Union citizens and their family members must apply for permanent residence, and member states are to issue them with a residence card certifying this status. Family members who are not nationals of a member state should be able to automatically renew their residence card every 10 years.

APPLYING THE LAW

What provisions in the Citizenship Directive can be used in favour of a right to enter and reside for third country nationals? Which help Ms C?

---

5. Derogations in the Citizenship Directive

Under EU law, deportation of a Union citizen, EU migrant worker or family member is an exception not the norm. Deportation is a derogation from the free movement rules and as such is both narrowly defined and interpreted by the CJEU. The same derogations apply to citizens and workers. The national regulatory authority is set out in Chapter VI of the Citizenship Directive, which begins with a reminder that any restriction on the freedom of movement and residence of Union citizens and their family members may not be used for economic goals.

> *Article 27(1) Subject to the provisions of this Chapter, member states may restrict the freedom of movement and residence of Union citizens and their family members, irrespective of nationality, on grounds of public policy, public security or public health. These grounds shall not be invoked to serve economic ends.*

Article 29 CD deals with public health. It restricts derogations on this ground to only those diseases 'with epidemic potential as defined by the relevant instruments of the World Health Organisation and other infectious diseases or contagious parasitic diseases if they are the subject of protection provisions applying to nationals of the host Member State'. If there are 'serious indications' that it is necessary, member states may within three months of arrival insist that migrant Union citizens undergo a medical examination. This must be provided free of charge.

---

[50]Article 17(1)(a)–(c)

Public policy and public security are harder to define. The CJ has not attempted to do so but has stressed that these ideas are to be interpreted restrictively, while respecting member state autonomy:

> [23] . . . the Court has always pointed out that, while Member States essentially retain the freedom to determine the requirements of public policy and public security in accordance with their national needs, which can vary from one Member State to another and from one era to another, the fact still remains that, in the Community [Union] context and particularly as justification for a derogation from the fundamental principle of free movement of persons, those requirements must be interpreted strictly, so that their scope cannot be determined unilaterally by each Member State without any control by the Community [Union] institutions.[51]

The Court's case law has clarified that the concept of public policy assumes not only disruption of the social order but also the existence of a 'genuine, present and sufficiently serious threat to one of the fundamental interests of society'.[52]

Exclusions must be based on one of these three grounds, which are exhaustive. In *Byankov*[53] Bulgarian authorities sought to use the derogation to justify a law stating that a person owing a financial debt to a company may not leave the country. In accordance with Bulgarian law, Mr Byankov was refused travel documents because of a large debt he could not repay. There was no mention of public policy, public safety or public health and it could not be ruled out that the prohibition imposed on him pursued an exclusively economic objective. Accordingly, this was precluded: the court ruled that a national provision which imposed a restriction on the freedom of movement of a member state national solely because he owed a company money was contrary to Article 27 CD.

The CD added further conditions to increase protection against expulsion according to the length of residence: a permanent resident can only be expelled on 'serious grounds'[54] of public policy and public security. A higher tier exists for children and residents of more than 10 years – persons in these groups can only be expelled on 'imperative grounds'[55] of public security alone.[56] In *PI*,[57] recognising the danger in unilateral interpretations by each member state, the Grand Chamber set out clear guidance on the meaning of this phrase. Using information from the Treaty, secondary legislation and the EU Charter, it concluded that violent and repeated rape of an under-age child constituted 'a particularly serious threat to one of the fundamental interests of society, which might pose a direct threat to the calm and physical security of the population'[58] and was thus covered by this concept. Nonetheless, automatic expulsion remains prohibited – expulsion is conditional upon the personal conduct of the individual concerned. Considerations such as age, length of residence, state of health, family and economic situation, social and cultural integration and the extent of his/her links with the country of origin also remain relevant.[59]

---

[51]See C-36/75 *Rutili* [1975] ECR 1219 [26 and 27]; C-30/77 *Bouchereau* [1977] ECR 1999 [33 and 34]; C-54/99 *Église de scientologie* [2000] ECR I-1335 [17]; and C-36/02 *Omega* [2004] ECR I-9609 [30 and 31]
[52]See *Rutili* [28]; *Bouchereau* [35]; and Joined Cases C-482/01 and C-493/01 *Orfanopoulos and Oliveri* [2004] ECR I-5257 [66]
[53]C-249/11 *Byankov v Glaven sekretar na Ministerstvo na vatreshnite raboti* [2012] WLR (D) 269
[54]Article 28(2) CD
[55]Article 28(3) CD
[56]These were incorporated into UK law by the EEA Regulations 2006 (Regulations 19–21). For the UK interpretation of these provisions see *LG (Italy) v SS Home Dept* [2008] EWCA Civ 190 and *LG & CC (Italy) v SS Home Department* [2009] UKAIT 00024
[57]C-348/09 *P.I. v Oberbürgermeisterin der Stadt Remscheid*
[58][28]
[59][32]

Recent case law has developed the concern for rehabilitation and re-socialisation, in particular where the expulsion decision is linked to a criminal sanction. In *Tsakouridis*,[60] the German authorities sought to expel a convicted drug trafficker, although he had been born in Germany and lived there for more than 10 years. The CJ worried about the impact of that decision on his rehabilitation, and on the interests of the Union:

> [50] In the application of Directive 2004/38, a balance must be struck more particularly between the exceptional nature of the threat to public security as a result of the personal conduct of the person concerned, assessed if necessary at the time when the expulsion decision is to be made,[61] by reference in particular to the possible penalties and the sentences imposed, the degree of involvement in the criminal activity, and, if appropriate, the risk of reoffending,[62] on the one hand, and, on the other hand, the risk of compromising the social rehabilitation of the Union citizen in the State in which he has become genuinely integrated, which, as the Advocate General observes in point 95 of his Opinion, is not only in his interest but also in that of the European Union in general.

> [51] The sentence passed must be taken into account as one element in that complex of factors. A sentence of five years' imprisonment cannot lead to an expulsion decision, as provided for in national law, without the factors described in the preceding paragraph being taken into account, which is for the national court to verify.

The balance between rehabilitation and security was applied domestically in the cases of *Batista*[63] and *Essa*.[64] In *Batista*, the existence of a relationship in Britain was seen as a crucial source of support which would be missing if the defendant was deported back to Portugal. In *Essa*, however, the immigration authorities decided to expel a 23-year-old Dutch national who had resided in the UK for 11 years. Since leaving school in 2005, Essa had collected criminal convictions, culminating in a custodial sentence in 2007 for the violent robbery of a passenger on a train. The court decided that upon his release he should be deported back to the Netherlands: this was held to be in accordance with the CD as the rehabilitation planned in the UK could just as easily be carried out in the Netherlands.

In addition, exclusion measures 'taken on grounds of public policy or public security shall comply with the principle of proportionality' – this means that they must serve a legitimate aim. In addition, any decision must 'remain within the limits of what is appropriate and necessary in order to achieve the aim in view and that the principle of equal treatment be reconciled as far as possible with the requirements of the aim thus pursued'.[65] A glance at the cases on age discrimination shows how closely the CJEU now conducts this test. Thus in order to be justified, any measure taken on grounds of public policy or public security must first be based exclusively on the personal conduct of the individual concerned and second be proportionate – justifications isolated from

---

[60]*Land Baden-Wurrtemberg v Tsakouridis* [2011] 2 CMLR 11
[61]See C-482/01 and C-493/01 *Orfanopoulos and Oliveri* [2004] ECR I-5257 [77 to 79]
[62]See C-30/77 *Bouchereau* [1977] ECR 1999 [29]
[63]*Batista v SS Home Dept* [2010] EWCA Civ 896 [27]
[64]*Essa v SS Home Dept* [2012] EWHC 1533 (QB)
[65]C-319/03 *Briheche* [2004] ECR I-8807 [24]

the particulars of the case or that pursue general aims of prevention or deterrence are unacceptable.[66]

Finally, safeguards are provided in Articles 30–33 CD, which call for notification, procedural rights, review, and prohibit automatic exclusion. National authorities may not adopt a blanket position: any expulsion decision must be preceded by careful consideration of individual circumstances. Case law has shown that the CJEU carefully reviews these provisions and ensures that where deportation is sought, the decision-making procedures and the possibility for appeal are clear and transparent. Clear and comprehensive written notification must be provided of any decision taken under Article 27(1), stating the specific ground upon which the decision is based, unless as per Article 30(2), this is 'contrary to the interests of State security'. The notification must also state clearly where and the conditions under which an appeal may be lodged. Unless it is a case of urgency, persons must be given at least one month to leave the territory.

Procedural safeguards set out in Article 31 CD stress that expelled persons must have access to judicial and administrative redress procedures in the host member state in order to appeal against or seek review of any decision taken against them on the grounds of public policy, public security or public health. Removal must normally be suspended in the presence of an application for an interim order until a decision is taken on it, unless the expulsion decision enacts a previous judicial decision; or there has already been access to judicial review; or the expulsion decision is based on imperative grounds of public security under Article 28(3). Individuals may only be prevented from submitting a defence in person if this may give rise to 'serious troubles to public policy or public security' or if they have been denied entry to the territory.

Furthermore, under Article 32 CD expulsion orders may not be permanent – there must be possibility of review after a maximum of three years from the exclusion order. Persons must establish presence of a 'material change' in the circumstances which led to the exclusion decision. A decision must be reached within six months – during this time the applicant has no right of entry to the member state. Finally Article 33 CD confirms that expulsion orders may also not be automatically imposed as a penalty or legal consequence of a custodial sentence. If a member state delays enforcement of an expulsion order for more than two years, it must confirm that the individual concerned is currently and genuinely a threat to public policy or public security. If there has been any material change, the expulsion order may not be enforced.

The CD seeks to balance the interests of the EU as a whole against the freedom of an individual member state to expel a Union worker and citizen. To summarise, five key principles guide a decision taken on the grounds of public security and public policy:

a proportionality;
b the personal conduct of the person concerned;
c whether the personal conduct represents a genuine, present and sufficiently serious threat affecting one of the fundamental interests of society;
d prohibition of expulsion for purposes of general deterrence;
e irrelevance of a person's previous criminal convictions.

Factors such as age, health, family and economic circumstances, length of residence, social and cultural integration as well as links with the country of origin must also be considered.

---

[66]C-33/07 *Ministerul Administraliei I Internelor v Jipa* [2008] 3 CMLR 23; *Bouchereau* [2008] 1 QB 732

There is an emphasis on avoiding the exportation of a problem from one member state to the other unless there is a very serious issue.[67]

APPLYING THE LAW

Summarise the derogations in the Citizenship Directive from the right to enter and reside. Can any be applied to Ms C?

---

6. Conclusion

The Citizenship Directive catalogues the most important rights for EU workers and citizens. Its contents have been influenced by CJ case law and since 2006, its provisions have been further developed and fleshed out by case law. The definition of 'family member' can be broadened to reflect twenty-first-century family formations. In particular, there remains room for improvement in the treatment of 'other family members' – too much discretion is left to the member states, allowing widely divergent treatment of this group across the 28 member states. If citizenship freedoms are indeed 'fundamental', they should be so to the same extent in all member states.

However, harmonisation in law does not guarantee uniform application at the national level. In the first 30 months after activation of the Citizenship Directive, the Commission received 1,800 individual complaints, 40 questions from the European Parliament and 33 petitions on its application. It registered 115 complaints and opened 5 infringement cases. A Commission report in 2008 highlighted that transposition of the Citizenship Directive had been incorrect and incomplete in all member states. There were problems securing the rights of family members as laid out in Article 3; Article 7(3) on the retention of worker status was incorrectly transposed in 17 member states – most provided for retention of right of residence but not status of worker which is much broader and confers protection against expulsion, more favourable basis for permanent residence and unrestricted right of equal treatment.[68] Thirteen member states attempted to deport those who sought to access social assistance under Article 14(3) and refused to grant the right of permanent residence. The rules concerning expulsion in Chapter VI were also subject to insufficient and incomplete transposition – in Italy and Finland expulsion was automatic if the crime was of a certain gravity. The material safeguards were found to be incorrectly transposed and the procedural safeguards inaccurately transposed; for example, in the UK not all were informed of the right to redress. The Commission found – perhaps unsurprisingly given the range and sensitivity of rights involved – that no member state had transposed any Article effectively and correctly, although it did note that some had adopted more favourable measures. The situation continues to require close attention. As judges seem less keen to

---

[67]See *Essa* [56]

[68]European Commission, 'Report From The Commission To The European Parliament And The Council on the application of Directive 2004/38/EC on the right of citizens of the Union and their family members to move and reside freely within the territory of the Member States', COM(2008) 840 final

refer cases in this area to the CJ, the onus is on the Commission to enforce these rights. As the CJ noted in *Carpenter*,[69] the family life of migrant EU nationals must be ensured by enabling family members to join and remain with them.[70]

The CD not only collated the rights scattered in various secondary legislation but also updated and extended them in important ways – the strengthening of the right to remain after the death or departure of the source of rights and the higher protections against deportation are important developments. Yet areas remain for attention – as *AB* shows, the discretion enjoyed by the member state to regulate the extended family allows for arbitrary behaviour by national authorities. *Rahman* was an important start to laying down parameters for the exercise of national discretion.[71]

Further reading

On the EU Citizenship Directive:

Elspeth Guild, Steve Peers and Jonathan Tomkin, *The EU Citizenship Directive: A Commentary,* Oxford University Press, 2014

On EU citizenship and welfare rights:

Koen Lenaerts, 'European Union Citizenship, National Welfare Systems and Social Solidarity', *Jurisprudence* 18(2), 2011, pp. 397, 401

On the human rights of EU citizens:

Joseph Weiler, 'Thou Shalt not oppress a stranger: on the judicial protection of the human rights of non-EC nationals – a critique', *EJIL* 3, 1992, p. 65

On the family rights of EU citizens:

Helen Stalford, 'Mixed Messages: Parental Responsibilities, Public Opinion and the Reforms of Family Law', *International Journal of Law, Policy and the Family* 20(2), 2006, p. 225

---

[69]C-60/00 *Carpenter* [2002] ECR I-6279 [38]
[70]The CJ was criticised for this and the subsequent decision in *Jia* – see Alina Tryfonidou, 'Jia or "Carpenter II": the edge of reason', *European Law Review* 32(6), 2007, pp. 908–918
[71]Iyiola Solanke, 'Another Type of "Other": AB v Home Office & Rahman v Home Office', *Modern Law Review*, 76(2), 2013, pp. 383–400

10 European Union citizenship

Setting the scene

Ms C, a Bolivian national, entered the UK as a student in 2006. Soon after arriving she met Mr B, a Swedish citizen who had lived in the UK since about 1996. Their daughter was born in London in May 2007: as the baby girl was given Swedish citizenship, she was like her father a migrant Union citizen. Ms C's student visa expired in January 2008: in March 2008 she applied to the Home Office for an EEA residence card. The ground cited was the existence of a durable relationship with Mr B, a Union citizen and at that time a migrant EU worker. She did not receive the certificate as requested and the request was subsequently refused on the ground that Mr B was not a migrant worker.

AB v Home Office [2012] EWHC 226 QB

1. Introduction

If a nation can be described as an 'imagined community',[1] citizenship is the glue linking the members of the nation. Almost everybody is a citizen of a country yet most individuals think little about what citizenship means – it is a status that is taken for granted. Those most likely to appreciate its value are those who are stateless or not citizens of the country in which they have settled and so do not enjoy the privileges associated with belonging, such as free healthcare, housing, and education. War and unrest have increased the number of persons, especially children, who are stateless.[2]

Citizenship, or belonging, can be described as a 'status bestowed on those who are full members of a community'.[3] All those with this status are equal in relation to duties and rights within that community. As well as binding together those eligible for this equality, citizenship also creates a boundary between them and persons who are not eligible. Citizenship therefore demarcates the 'political community' of the nation and binds citizens to a particular mode and expectations of rule and rights. It is less important for its own sake than for the protection it affords – for example, citizens cannot be deported. This status also acts as a welfare status – it secures inclusion in the 'right to regard' guaranteeing access to various rights, including residency rights and social benefits provided by the state.

For Marshall,[4] a civilised society was obliged to recognise the debt it owed to its citizens, who bore the insecurity and inequality created by free market capitalism. Social services were a form of compensation for continued economic disparity and inequality. These were, he stressed, social rights, 'the social and political debt of a civilised society to all its citizens' that corrected the wrongs arising from industrialisation. Citizens are therefore protected when they cannot work and thus cannot provide for themselves due to age, illness or lack of jobs. Esping Andersen[5] takes this further – he argues that these social rights bestowed upon citizens are in fact 'inviolable' – they should have the same status as fundamental rights, such as the right to life or property. He argues if social rights are indeed.

> 'given the legal and practical status of property rights, if they are inviolable, and if they are granted on the basis of citizenship, they will entail a decommodification of the status of individuals vis a vis the market'

Decommodification refers to the idea that social welfare – income support, healthcare, education, housing benefit for example – will be accessible to a citizen regardless of any individual contribution. In other words, decommodification insists upon 'a standard of civilisation which is conditional only on the discharge of the general duties of citizenship' and enjoyment of social rights does not 'depend upon the economic value of the individual claimant.' Social rights can be enjoyed by all equally irrespective of earnings.

This chapter will explore the character of EU citizenship and the substance of the rights associated with it. The key question is whether it has enough substance to act as a 'glue' and bind the nationals in the 28 EU member states. Furthermore, what is its value – is it

---

[1] Benedict Anderson, *Imagined Communities: Reflections on the Origins and Spread of Nationalism,* Verso, 1991
[2] http://statelessuk.info/about/
[3] T.H. Marshall, *Citizenship and Social Class,* Cambridge University Press, 1950
[4] Marshall 1950, p. 28. See also p. 8
[5] Esping Andersen, *The Three Worlds of Welfare Capitalism,* Princeton University Press, 1990

an 'inviolable' status, giving rise to rights that exist regardless of any economic activity? An answer can be found by examining the extent to which citizenship binds EU nationals to each other. One way of exploring this is to consider how equally EU citizens are treated when they move from their home member state to a host member state – are they protected from discrimination? The right to equal treatment will be the first theme explored below. The value of citizenship will be illustrated by considering what citizens must do to access social rights – what conditions exist? The second theme of this chapter will be exploration of the extent to which Union citizens are *decommodified*. Investigation of concepts such as 'social integration', 'genuine link' and 'genuine enjoyment' will shed light on this. Citizenship provides an opportunity to observe the impact of the Advocate General opinion on EU law; thus some of the following cases will be discussed in detail. However, before looking at these themes, the chapter will summarise the rules on EU citizenship.

2. The rules on EU citizenship

There are three main routes to citizenship and its privileges. It is acquired either by virtue of being born in a country (*ius soli*), or to parents of that country (*ius sanguinis*). Alternatively, people can become citizens of a country by application (naturalised citizens). In some countries, such as the United States, all persons born in that country will automatically become citizens (14th Amendment), however this principle of *ius soli* is becoming rare. Much more common is the principle of *ius sanguinis*, according to which persons born in the country will only be citizens if their parents are citizens. The European Union introduced a fourth route to citizenship when it created 'European Union citizenship' in 1992. European Union citizens hold a citizenship that is linked to national citizenship. EU citizenship is the only form of citizenship in the world that is acquired automatically by those who are nationals of a member state. These principles are just a starting point: in reality the application of the rules is complex and varied – some countries allow dual citizenship while others do not; individuals can change their citizenship or renounce it but states may not arbitrarily deprive a citizen of this status.[6] As the EU is not a nation state, EU citizenship does not give Union citizens dual nationality.

i.   TFEU: Articles 20–24

Only those who are member state nationals can become Union citizens: this status is part of the heritage of all those who are nationals of a member state. It cannot be held or acquired independent of national citizenship. Union citizenship cannot be bought or applied for. Article 20(1) TFEU declares that:

> *Citizenship of the Union is hereby established. Every person holding the nationality of a Member State shall be a citizen of the Union. Citizenship of the Union shall be additional to and not replace national citizenship.*

---
[6]http://eudo-citizenship.eu/docs/policy_brief_loss.pdf

Union citizenship is therefore additional to national citizenship and confers extra rights without replacing national citizenship. A Protocol attached to the Treaty on European Union contains a 'Declaration on nationality of a member state' – this establishes that the question of whether an individual possesses the nationality of a member state is to be settled solely by reference to the national law of the member state concerned. EU law can only confer Union citizenship not national citizenship. Member states may lodge a declaration with the Council Presidency establishing who is to be considered their nationals for the purpose of EU law. When a member state decides who is or is not a citizen all other member states must accept this unconditionally. This was clarified in *Micheletti*.[7] Mr Micheletti held dual Argentinian and Italian nationality. When he tried to establish himself as a dentist in Spain, the authorities there refused him permission, arguing that because his habitual place of residence was Argentina, his effective nationality was Argentinian. The CJ refused to allow this, saying:

[10] Under international law, it is for each Member State, having due regard to Community law, to lay down the conditions for the acquisition and loss of nationality. However, it is not permissible for the legislation of a Member State to restrict the effects of the grant of the nationality of another Member State by imposing an additional condition for recognition of that nationality with a view to the exercise of the fundamental freedoms provided for in the Treaty.

Habitual residence cannot be considered in determining citizenship of a member state.

This unique mode of acquisition has a distinct disadvantage. It means that there are thousands of people resident in the EU who are locked out of the privileges of Union citizenship because they do not hold the citizenship of the country in which they reside. This can be for a number of reasons – they may be unable to fulfil the strict eligibility criteria or dual nationality may be prohibited, or they may even hold the 'wrong' type of citizenship. This latter problem befell Mrs Kaur, a Ugandan Asian who was a 'citizen of the United Kingdom and Colonies' until that category was abolished by the British Nationality Act 1981. She then became a 'British Overseas Citizen', a status which gave her no right to enter or remain in the United Kingdom. As such, she was also not a person to whom Union citizenship was extended.

As EU citizenship law has only one mode of acquisition, Mrs Kaur and others like her who are nationals of non-member states are described as 'third country nationals' (TCNs) in EU law. According to the EU fund for the 'Integration of Third Country Nationals' (INTI) a 'third-country national' is 'any person who is not a citizen of the EU within the meaning of Article 17(1) of the Treaty'[8] [Article 20(1) TFEU]. When nationals from non-EU member states do become EU citizens, this can be overlooked by national judges.[9]

Citizenship has been described as the 'right to have rights'. Titmuss wrote that the way in which society organises and structures its social institutions can foster integration or alienation.[10] By making EU citizenship dependent upon member state nationality millions

---

[7]C-369/90 *Mario Vicente Micheletti and others v Delegacion del Gobierno en Cantabria* [1992] ECR I-4239
[8]Commission Report on the results achieved and on qualitative and quantitative aspects of implementation of the European Fund for the Integration of third-country nationals for the period 2007–2009 (report submitted in accordance with Article 48(3)(b) of Council Decision 2007/435/EC of 25 June 2007), COM(2011) 847 final, 5 December 2011, p. 3
[9]In *A, B, C v Home Secretary* [2013] EWHC 1272 (Admin) a German national of Ghanaian origin was mistakenly treated as a non-EU citizen [40]
[10]Richard Titmuss, *The Gift Relationship: From Human Blood to Social Policy,* George, Allen and Unwin, 1970, p. 225

of EU residents are locked out of this status. It has created two classes of people, namely those who:

> '*really* enjoy and experience full inclusion, participation and membership and those who do not; those who have sufficient enabling resources to allow them to be included as full members of society and those who have insufficient; those who enjoy the *power* to be *real citizens* and those who do not [italics in original].'[11]

EU nationals possess the right to live and work anywhere in any of the 28 member states, being guaranteed all the social benefits of the host country; non-EU nationals have little or no freedom of movement within the EU and no access to associated rights, entitlements and benefits (employment rights, family reunion, access to housing and welfare, freedom from discrimination).[12] Those in the latter group thus have limited rights. Their status does not only establish a political relationship between the individual and the state, but also establishes relationships of rights, authority and power between individuals.

It is difficult to justify why third country nationals who live, work and contribute to a national economy should be denied full access to Union citizenship rights and have no way to become a Union citizen. The majority are lawful residents who contribute financially and yet have no rights to move freely within the territory of the member states.[13] At present the EU is a 'two-tier society' to which millions of workers, like Mr Zambrano,[14] contribute economically but are refused many privileges. Union citizenship provides gains to the majority at the expense of large groups of minorities, particularly racial and ethnic minorities, who are locked out of the educational and career opportunities their taxes help to make available to Union citizens. A simple way to address this would be to make residency the basis of Union citizenship.

ANALYSING THE LAW

What rules apply to the acquisition of EU citizenship? Are there too many or too few?

Third country nationals may derive rights from a family member who is a Union citizen. EU law also recognises and extends some rights directly to third country nationals. Article 17(3) of Directive 2004/38 offers the status of 'long-term resident'[15] irrespective of nationality and other directives, such as Directive 2003/109,[16] have been passed specifically to extend some equal rights to legal residents holding this status.[17] For example, in *Kamberaj* it was used to secure equal treatment for a long-term resident in Italy in relation to

---

[11]P. Close, *Citizenship, Europe and Change*, Macmillan, 1995, p. 52
[12]Johal and Winstone, *At The Border – Black People in Europe*, NAREA, 1992, p. 15
[13]The Runnymede Trust, 'The Intergovernmental Conference and the Future of Multi-Ethnic Britain', Wiston House Working Paper, 28/29 June 1996
[14]see C-34/09 *Ruiz Zambrano*
[15]Directive 2004/38 is also known as the 'Citizenship Directive'.
[16]C-502/10 *State Secretary van Justitie* v *Mangat Singh*; C-40/11, *Yoshikazu Iida* v *Stadt Ulm*
[17]D. Acosta Arcarazo, *The Long Term Residence Status as a subsidiary form of citizenship – an analysis of Directive 2003/109*, Martinuss Nijhoff, 2010

housing benefit.[18] Also Directive 2004/114[19] provides third country nationals with rights of entry – in *Alaya*,[20] the CJ confirmed that the conditions for and exceptions to residence laid out in that directive are exhaustive. Member states cannot add to these in a way that makes admission more difficult for third country nationals.

The INTI Fund is designed to promote the European agenda for legally resident third country nationals, as laid out in the Europe 2020 Strategy and the Stockholm Programme.[21] The premise underlying this agenda is, however, slightly misleading as it suggests that third country nationals are migrants new to the EU: the largest group of TCNs resident in the EU are the Turkish nationals and their descendants who began to settle in Germany after the Second World War. They are TCNs because Germany prohibits dual citizenship. Thus thousands of persons who speak German as a first language, have been educated and socialised in Germany and plan to retire there, carry Turkish citizenship. Recent case law also highlights that TCNs are not per se foreign, new to the EU or asylum seekers: an applicant in the *Dereci* case, Mr Kokollari, had spent 27 of his 29 years living in Austria.[22]

APPLYING THE LAW

What status do Mr B and Ms C have under EU citizenship law?

Citizenship rights were categorised by the sociologist T. H. Marshall,[23] who identified three elements: a civil element, a political element and a social element. The civil element includes the rights necessary for individual freedoms such as liberty of the person, freedom of speech, the right to own property and to conclude valid contracts, and the right to justice. This right to justice is an umbrella right: it includes the right to equal protection under law, and to defend and assert all other rights on terms of equality with others. The most important institution in relation to civil rights is therefore the CJEU. The political element consists of the right to participate in the exercise of political power both as a member of a body invested with political authority or as an elector. The relevant institutions for the enjoyment of political citizenship are parliaments and local government. The social element covers the right to economic welfare and security, the 'right to share in the full social heritage and to live the life of a civilised being according to the standards prevailing in society'. The institutions most associated with this right are the educational system and social services.[24]

---

[18]C-571/10 *Servet Kamberaj v istituto per l'Edilizia sociale della Provincia autonoma di Bolzano (IPES)*
[19]Council Directive 2004/114/EC of 13 December 2004 on the conditions of admission of third country nationals for the purposes of studies, pupil exchange, unremunerated training or voluntary service (OJ L375/12 2004)
[20]C-491/13 *Ben Alaya v Bundesrepublik Deutschland*
[21]European Commission, 'European Agenda for the Integration of Third-Country Nationals', SEC(2011) 957 final
[22]C-256/11 *Murat Dereci and Others v Bundesministerium für Inneres* [2011] ECR I-11315
[23]Marshall 1950
[24]Marshall 1950, pp. 10–11

Union citizenship brings with it just four distinct rights. These privileges may be limited in range but offer important protection to those who enjoy them:

Article 20 TFEU (ex Article 17 TEC)

(2) Citizens of the Union shall enjoy the rights and be subject to the duties provided for in the Treaties. They shall have, inter alia:

(a) *the right to move and reside freely within the territory of the Member States [Art. 21 TFEU];*

(b) *the right to vote and to stand as candidates in elections to the European Parliament and in municipal elections in their Member State of residence, under the same conditions as nationals of that State [Art. 22 TFEU];*

(c) *the right to enjoy, in the territory of a third country in which the Member State of which they are nationals is not represented, the protection of the diplomatic and consular authorities of any Member State on the same conditions as the nationals of that State [Art. 23 TFEU];*

(d) *the right to petition the European Parliament, to apply to the European Ombudsman, and to address the institutions and advisory bodies of the Union in any of the Treaty languages and to obtain a reply in the same language [Art. 24 TFEU].*

Articles 21–24 TFEU expand upon these rights. They are described as 'inherent in EU citizenship'[25] but none of them are absolute – they are to be exercised in accordance with the conditions and limits defined by the Treaties and by the measures adopted by the institutions. Many of these conditions and limitations are found in secondary legislation.

Most case law has considered the implications and consequences of the right to move and reside freely: it is the exercise of this right that has given rise to numerous cases on access to social rights – especially welfare benefits – in a host member state. There has been little activity under the others. Article 22 voting rights were considered in 2004, when the CJ was asked to deal with two issues concerning access to European Parliament elections. In the first case, Spain accused the UK of breaching EU law by allowing inhabitants of Gibraltar to vote in the EP elections;[26] in the second case, Dutch inhabitants of a Dutch overseas territory, Aruba, argued that they had been deprived of their right to vote in EP elections.[27] The right to consular protection was the subject of Decision 95/553/EC. This

---

ANALYSING THE LAW

How do the rights in Article 20 TFEU fit into Marshall's categories? Which do you think is most important for Mr B and Ms C?

---

[25]European Commission, EU Citizenship Report 2010 'Dismantling the obstacles to EU citizens' rights', Brussels, COM(2010) 603 final, p. 2
[26]Spain used the power in Article 227 TFEU by which a member state can accuse another member state of infringing the Treaty. The UK has recently used this power in the recent disagreement over Gibraltar
[27]C-145/04 *Spain* v *UK* [2006] ECR I-7917 and C-300/04 *Sevinger* v *College van Burgemeester en wethouders van den Haag* [2006] ECR I-8055

decision outlines examples of occasions where consular support might be required. These include cases such as arrest or detention; accident or serious illness; an act of violence against a citizen; death; and help for a distressed citizen or repatriation.[28]

ii.   Mainstreaming of Union citizenship

The range of citizenship rights has not increased since 1992. What has changed quite dramatically is the position of Union citizenship in EU policy-making: from its original marginal position, the Commission has declared its objective to build 'a citizen's Europe' that is centred on the citizen and works towards removing obstacles faced in enjoying citizenship rights. In 2010, it stated that its political objective is that 'EU citizenship progresses to become a tangible reality in their daily lives'.[29] The Stockholm Programme, outlining the work programme of the EU in the field of Freedom, Security and Justice also puts the citizen at the heart of European policies in this field. The preamble of the EU Charter of Fundamental Rights, states that the Union 'places the individual at the heart of its activities, by establishing a citizenship of the Union and by creating an area of freedom, security and justice'.

The upgraded status of citizens in EU law and policy is underpinned by new citizenship values set out in the Lisbon Treaty. Citizens are now mentioned early in the TEU, first appearing in a new Treaty chapter on democratic principles. This chapter lays out the principles underlying citizenship. Article 9 TEU positions the citizen at the heart of the Union, making her the focus of all activities while stressing the complementary relationship between Union and national citizenship:

> *In all its activities, the Union shall observe the principle of the equality of its citizens, who shall receive equal attention from its institutions, bodies, offices and agencies. Every national of a Member State shall be a citizen of the Union. Citizenship of the Union shall be additional to and not replace national citizenship.*

Article 10 stresses the participation of citizens in the EU democracy – citizens are directly represented within the EU in the European Parliament and every citizen has the right to participate in the democratic life of the EU. Article 10(3) links transparency and subsidiarity to citizenship – decisions must be taken as openly and closely as possible to the citizen. Article 11(4) introduces a new procedure for direct participation, allowing citizens to directly influence the legislative agenda of the EU without going through their MEPs: under the 'European Citizens Initiative', a minimum of one million citizens across at least seven member states 'may take the initiative of inviting the European Commission, within the framework of its powers, to submit any appropriate proposal on matters where citizens consider that a legal act of the Union is required for the purpose of implementing the Treaties'.[30] This new procedure has already given rise to an impressive number of cross-border collaborations between citizens.[31] As a result of its

---

[28]European Commission, 'Diplomatic and consular protection of Union citizens in third countries', Green Paper, Brussels, COM(2006) 712 final
[29]European Commission, EU Citizenship Report 2010 'Dismantling the obstacles to EU citizens' rights', Brussels, COM(2010) 603 final, p. 2
[30]European Commission, 'Proposal for a Regulation of the European Parliament and of the Council on the citizens' initiative', Brussels, SEC(2010) 370 COM(2010) 119 final
[31]List of open initiatives available at http://ec.europa.eu/citizens-initiative/public/initiatives/ongoing

introduction, there has arguably been more interaction between Union citizens across the member states in the last two years than ever in the history of European integration. It should, however, be remembered that as Union citizens are centred, citizens from outside of the Union resident in the EU are marginalised, regardless of how settled they may be.

Cases such as *Wijsenbeek*[32] and *Oulane*[33] also underline the continuing power of the state to check the identity of those within or entering their territories. In *Wisjenbeek*, a Dutch national, was subjected to criminal proceedings because he refused to show his passport at Rotterdam Airport after disembarking a flight from Strasbourg – he claimed that this identity check was contrary to the EU citizenship provisions. The court sided with the national authorities:

> [45] . . . as Community law stood at the time of the events in question, neither Article 7a nor Article 8a of the Treaty precluded a Member State from requiring a person, whether or not a citizen of the European Union, under threat of criminal penalties, to establish his nationality upon his entry into the territory of that Member State by an internal frontier of the Community, provided that the penalties applicable are comparable to those which apply to similar national infringements and are not disproportionate, thus creating an obstacle to the free movement of persons.

Internal checks also continue to be permissible. Mr Oulane, a French national, was detained in the Netherlands and threatened with deportation for failing to present an identity card or passport to establish his status as an EU national. The Court supported such identity checks:

> [56] . . . it is for nationals of a Member State residing in another Member State in their capacity as recipients of services, to provide evidence establishing that their residence is lawful. If no such evidence is provided, the host Member State may undertake deportation, subject to the limits imposed by Community law.

External border controls have formally disappeared in much of the EU due to the Schengen Convention (CISA), which provided for the gradual abolition of border controls between the contracting states. It contains provisions for the free movement of people, including third country nationals with corollary ('flanking') measures relating to external border controls, asylum and immigration.[34] CISA was initially an intergovernmental agreement, 'developed secretively by unaccountable interior ministry officials without proper parliamentary or judicial constraints'[35] and signed by a small group of member states to create a travel zone free of passport controls. The provisions of the CISA are only lawful insofar as they are compatible with EU law, including the derogations on the grounds of public policy and public security in the Citizenship Directive. The Schengen Information System (SIS) operates alongside the CISA as a database containing names of individuals considered to be security threats.[36]

At Amsterdam, ministers agreed to incorporate the Schengen Convention from the third pillar into the framework of the Community. Although not all member states have

---

[32]C-378/97 *Florus Ariël Wijsenbeek* [1999] ECR I-6207
[33]C-215/03 *Oulane* [2005] ECR I-1215
[34]European Commission, *The Week in Europe*, W/E 24/97
[35]Damian Chalmers, 'Cut off from Europe – the fog surrounding Luxembourg', *European Law Review* 33(2), 2008, pp. 135–136
[36]The use of this database was considered in C-503/03 *Commission v Spain* [2006] ECR I-1097.

signed this Convention – the UK is not a member – case law and Treaty amendments have since elevated these norms to the full status of the *acquis communitaire*. MEP Martin Bangemann proposed that all border controls should be removed on 1 January 1993 and travellers should simply be able to 'wave' their passport at border officials. However, passport controls remain rigorous when travelling into or out of the Schengen zone, and for black and ethnic minority people travelling both inside and outside the Schengen zone, racial profiling is a regular occurrence in many member states.

3. The right to equal treatment of EU citizens

Non-discrimination could not be taken for granted: although this central concept in Article 18 TFEU underpins the four freedoms, it was not automatically applied to EU citizenship. The Treaty said nothing about non-discriminatory treatment of Union citizens. Non-discrimination on the grounds of nationality was only clearly linked to free movement of workers, goods, capital and services. Yet the idea of citizenship requires that all who belong to the polity are treated in the same way in similar circumstances. If EU citizenship has any meaning, it must at least mean that all citizens will be treated in the same way as citizens of the member state to which they have moved. This was first discussed in relation to citizenship by the Advocates General (AsG). In order to add substance to the content of Union citizenship, the AsG had included in their opinions arguments that the right to non-discrimination on the grounds of nationality was also a citizenship right.

i.   Application of the principle of non-discrimination to EU citizenship

AG Lenz first tackled this in *Faccini Dori*,[37] a case concerning consumer protection in door-to-door sales. The EU had adopted a directive[38] strengthening consumers rights, but Italy had failed to transpose this. The CJ did not allow Ms Dori to rely on the directive directly, as this would have been horizontal direct effect. In his attempt to persuade the Court to accept horizontal direct effect of directives, Lenz invoked Union citizenship. He argued for the removal of this disparity because the 'introduction of citizenship of the Union raises the expectation that citizens of the Union will enjoy equality, at least before Community law'.[39] The Court was not convinced. It was silent on citizenship and stressed the obligation of the national court to interpret Italian law as far as possible in light of the objectives of the Directive.[40]

In an opinion the following year, AG Léger mentioned equal treatment of Union citizens in *Boukhalfa*.[41] This case was set within the employment context and concerned pay differences between staff hired locally and those hired in the EU. Léger argued strongly

---

[37] C-91/92 *Paola Faccini Dori* v *Recreb Srl* [1994] ECR I-3325
[38] Directive 85/577 EEC
[39] [53]
[40] [25–26]
[41] C-214/94 *Boukhalfa* v *Bundesrepublik* Deutschland [1996] ECR I-2253

against this pay discrimination. His final argument encouraged the Court to apply 'the 'new' concept of European citizenship':

> [63] . . . The recognition of European citizenship . . . is of considerable symbolic value and is probably one of the advances in the construction of Europe which has received most public attention . . . If all the conclusions inherent in that concept are drawn, every citizen of the Union must, whatever his nationality, enjoy exactly the same rights and be subject to the same obligations. Taken to its ultimate conclusion, the concept should lead to citizens of the Union being treated absolutely equally, irrespective of their nationality.

This would mean employees be treated the same regardless of place of hire. The Court agreed with Léger's conclusion but was silent on the content of his reasoning.

AG La Pergola made another attempt to promote this link between non-discrimination and Union citizenship in the joined cases of *Stoeber and Piosa Pereira*[42] in which both parties had spent time working abroad and had children living abroad. The legal dispute arose in the question of whether they should receive family allowance in respect of the child living abroad. In helping the Court answer the question, La Pergola argued that legislation providing for different treatment between a worker whose children are resident in Germany and one whose children are resident in other member states – constitutes covert discrimination.[43] Just before closing his opinion, La Pergola reminded the Court that it had not yet ruled on the citizenship provisions and encouraged the court to consider them. He stated:

> [50] . . . Those provisions, on which the Court has not yet had occasion to rule, represent, as Advocate General Léger noted in his recent opinion in *Boukhalfa*, progress of major significance in the construction of Europe. Their ultimate purpose is, after all, to bring about increasing equality between citizens of the Union, irrespective of their nationality.

Again the Court agreed with his conclusion, but remained silent on citizenship. That silence was only broken in Martinez Sala[44] when the Grand Chamber finally declared that:

> Article 8(2) [20 TFEU] of the Treaty attaches to the status of citizen of the Union the rights and duties laid down by the Treaty, including the right, laid down in Article 6 of the Treaty, not to suffer discrimination on grounds of nationality within the scope of application *ratione materiae* of the Treaty.

This meant that as a Union citizen lawfully resident in Germany, Ms Sala – a Spanish national – had to be treated in the same way as a German woman in her position, that is, expecting a baby. The child raising allowance could not be withheld from her simply because she did not have a formal residence permit. This case confirmed that equal treatment was a right for *citizens* as well as *workers*.

---

[42]C-4/95 and 5/95 *Piosa Pereira* [1997] ECR I-511
[43][46]
[44]C-85/96 *Martínez Sala v Freistaat Bayern* [1998] ECR I-2691

The equality of Union citizens meant that in *Trojani*[45] an economically inactive French national resident in Belgium, living in a Salvation Army Hostel, could rely on Article 20 TFEU to be granted social assistance benefits – as he was lawfully resident in Belgium, the refusal to grant him social assistance benefit constituted discrimination on the grounds of nationality:

> A citizen of the European Union who does not enjoy a right of residence in the host Member State under Articles 39 EC, 43 EC or 49 EC [45, 49 or 56 TFEU] may, simply as a citizen of the Union, enjoy a right of residence there by direct application of Article 18(1) EC [21 TFEU] . . . Once it is ascertained that a person in a situation such as that of the claimant in the main proceedings is in possession of a residence permit, he may rely on Article 12 EC [18 TFEU] in order to be granted a social assistance benefit such as the minimex.

The Court stressed that this right is *'subject to the limitations and conditions'* referred to in that provision, but also that the authorities must apply those limitations and conditions in compliance with general principles of Union law, especially proportionality. In general, the proportionality examination requires consideration of the aim – is it legitimate and important enough to justify limitation of a fundamental right? It must then be shown that the measure is connected to that objective and that no less intrusive option could have been used. Finally, it must be confirmed that, considering the aim and its consequences, a balance has been struck between the rights and interests of all concerned parties.

Proportionality is illustrated in the case of *de Cuyper*.[46] Mr De Cuyper, a Belgian national, became unemployed in Belgium, was granted unemployment allowances, and a further dispensation relieved him from having to sign on every week. However, he had to declare that he was living in Belgium. A routine inquiry into his case in April 2000 revealed that he had been resident in France since January 1999. His unemployment allowance was immediately stopped and repayment of over 12,000 euros demanded on the ground that as of January 1999 he no longer satisfied the requirement of actual residence laid down in Belgian law.

De Cuyper contested that decision before the labour court in Belgium, which asked the CJ whether Article 20 and 21 TFEU Article prohibit national provisions making entitlement to an allowance conditional on actual residence in the member state, especially this particular allowance granted to unemployed persons aged over 50 who are exempt from the requirement to register as job seekers. The CJ recognised that the rule may restrict free movement but held that it was proportionate and thus did not breach Article 21 TFEU:

> [39] It is established that national legislation such as that in this case which places at a disadvantage certain of its nationals simply because they have exercised their freedom to move and to reside in another Member State is a restriction on the freedoms conferred by Article 18 EC on every citizen of the Union.[47]

---

[45] C-456/02 *Trojani* [2004] ECR I-7573
[46] C-406/04 *De Cuyper* [2006] ECR I-6947
[47] See, to that effect, C-224/98 *D'Hoop* [2002] ECR I-6191 [31], and C-224/02 *Pusa* [2004] ECR I-5763 [19]

[40] Such a restriction can be justified . . . if it is based on objective considerations of public interest independent of the nationality of the persons concerned and proportionate to the legitimate objective of the national provisions.

The objective of the residency rule was to enable the Belgian authorities to monitor compliance with the statutory rules associated with unemployment benefit – it satisfied the proportionality requirement because it was the least intrusive way to achieve this legitimate aim.[48]

VIEWPOINT

In your view, what role does the principle of proportionality play in EU citizenship law?

ii.   Restrictions on the right to equal treatment – Article 24 Citizenship Directive

The application of the principle of non-discrimination must be regarded alongside a derogation in Article 24 CD. This provision, like Article 35 CD, seeks to address potential abuse of free movement rights by individuals. It allows member states to delay enjoyment of equal treatment – it may only be immediately enjoyed by those who are economically active.

Article 24(1) affirms equal treatment for Union citizens and their families:

> *Subject to such specific provisions as are expressly provided for in the Treaty and secondary law, all Union citizens residing on the basis of this Directive in the territory of the host Member State shall enjoy equal treatment with the nationals of that Member State within the scope of the Treaty. The benefit of this right shall be extended to family members who are not nationals of a Member State and who have the right of residence or permanent residence.*

This is then limited by Article 24(2) which contains a derogation whereby the host member state may refuse, prior to acquisition of the right of permanent residence, to provide grants and loans for studies and vocational training to persons who are not workers, self-employed persons, or members of their families:

> *By way of derogation from paragraph 1, the host Member State shall not be obliged to confer entitlement to social assistance during the first three months of residence or, where appropriate, the longer period provided for in Article 14(4)(b), nor shall it be obliged, prior to acquisition of the right of permanent residence, to grant maintenance aid for studies, including vocational training, consisting in student grants or student loans to persons other than workers, self-employed persons, persons who retain such status and members of their families.*

[48][47]

This derogation has rarely been used,[49] but appeared in two cases concerning education finance, *Commission v Austria*[50] and *LN*.[51] These two cases saw the CJ rule on it for the first time. Although it was intended as a shelter for the member states from 'benefit shopping', the CJ has approached it in the same way as other derogations – its use must be narrowly circumscribed. Also, the derogations apply in the same way to decisions concerning non-EU nationals, as held in *Commission v Spain*.[52]

In *Commission v Austria,* Austria was accused of breaching EU law by its system for granting reduced bus fares to students. In order to be eligible for this subsidy, the parents of the student had to be in receipt of Austrian family allowances. Clearly, such a requirement would be harder to fulfil by non-Austrian Union citizens who studied in that country. It was therefore potentially indirectly discriminatory and unlawful unless it could be justified.

The Austrian government argued that the transport subsidy was a family benefit. The Court did not accept this and held that it was national aid granted to students to cover their maintenance costs.[53] Such a rule, which made it harder for non-Austrian Union citizens to access this social benefit, was precluded by the Treaty unless it could be justified and found proportionate. It was held to be neither. The Court based its reasoning on the principle of equal treatment inherent in the autonomous and fundamental nature of Union citizenship[54] which meant that the inequality of treatment arising from the system of eligibility for reduced fares was contrary to the principles of Union citizenship.

> [50] In the present case, making the reduced transport fares subject to the grant of Austrian family allowances, as provided for by certain Länder, gives rise to unequal treatment as between Austrian students pursuing their studies in Austria and students from other Member States pursuing their studies there as well, since such a condition is more easily fulfilled by Austrian students because their parents as a rule receive those allowances.

> [51] Such inequality of treatment is contrary to the principles which underpin the status of citizen of the Union, referred to in paragraph 38 of this judgment, that is, the guarantee of the same treatment in law in the exercise of the citizen's freedom of movement.

The Austrian scheme could not be saved by the Article 24 CD derogation. In the first ruling on the use of this provision, the CJ stressed that as:

> [54] Article 24(2) is a derogation from the principle of equal treatment provided for in Art 18 TFEU, of which Art 24 (1) of Directive 2004/38 is merely a specific expression, it must be interpreted narrowly.

---

[49] Article 24(1) was mentioned in *Förster* [55] and *Bressol* [34]

[50] C-75/11 *Commission v Austria*

[51] C-46/12 *LN*

[52] C-503/03 *Commission v Spain* [2006] ECR I-1097. This was the first case requiring the Court to rule on the relationship between the Schengen agreement and the Treaty provisions on free movement of persons. The German government had entered alerts against the names of two Algerian nationals in the Schengen Information System. Relying on the fact that there were alerts on the SIS, without investigating the matter further Spain refused to grant them entry visas to join their Spanish wives. The CJ found Spain to be in breach of its Treaty obligations – the authorities had failed to verify whether the presence of Mr Farid and Mr Bouchair would constitute a genuine, present and sufficiently serious threat affecting one of the fundamental interests of society, as laid out in the CD. The Court also ruled that aspects of the CISA were incompatible with Union law, in particular with regard to the concept of public policy.

[53] [42–44]

[54] [38–39]

The first consequence of this narrow interpretation was the scope of the derogation – not all forms of maintenance aid fell within it – 'only maintenance aid for studies consisting in student grants or student loans' were covered; subsidised bus fares were not.[55]

The Danish government also invoked Article 24(2) in the case of *LN*. A young man of no specified nationality – the case notes only that he is a Union citizen – had applied for and secured a job in Copenhagen, Denmark which he began in June 2009. However, in March 2009 he had enrolled at Copenhagen Business School (CBS) for a full-time course beginning in September 2009. When his full-time studies began, he resigned from his full-time job and continued with part-time work. In August 2009, when still a full-time worker, he applied to the Danish Students Grants and Loans Scheme. This scheme provides education assistance to 'applicants for courses of study' in Denmark or abroad 'under the conditions laid down in EU law and the EEA Agreement'.

The rules implementing this decision state that 'an EU citizen who is a worker or self-employed person in Denmark under EU law may be granted assistance for education in Denmark or abroad on the same terms as a Danish citizen'. This also applied to EU citizens who could show 'a substantive and temporal connection between the education and the previous work in Denmark' or an involuntarily unemployed person who required retraining. EU and EEA citizens who are not workers or self-employed persons in Denmark become entitled to this education assistance only after five years' continuous residence in Denmark (by which time they will also be eligible for permanent residence under Article 16 of the Citizenship Directive 2004/38).

His application was refused in October 2009 and subsequently in 2010 his status was officially changed from that of worker to student. As he had applied to the CBS in March 2009, before gaining employment, he had entered Denmark primarily for the purpose of pursuing a course of study. This, it was argued, placed him outside Article 45 TFEU and within Article 7 CD. According to the responsible Danish authorities, as a *student* he therefore did not fulfil the requirements for access to education finance.

Furthermore, it was argued that the derogation in Article 24(2) applied to his situation. As a non-worker enrolled at a place of education for the purposes of study, Mr N was a person from whom member states could withhold access to student grants and loans during the first three months of residence. Denmark and Norway argued that:

> [22] Articles 7(1)(c) and 24(2) of Directive 2004/38, read together, must be interpreted as meaning that a citizen of the Union who studies full-time in a host Member State and who entered the territory of that Member State for that purpose may be refused maintenance aid for studies for the first five years he is resident in the country, even if he is in part-time employment alongside his studies.

These arguments were unsuccessful – the CJ refused to preclude the possibility that LN might be a worker under Article 45 TFEU. As in previous cases, this was an objective test not determined by the level of remuneration or hours worked and the intention or motive of the individual played no part in it:

> [46] . . . in order to assess whether employment is capable of conferring the status of worker within the meaning of Article 45 TFEU, factors relating to the conduct of the person concerned before and after the period of employment are not relevant in

---

[55]C-75/11 *Commission v Austria* [53–55]

establishing the status of worker within the meaning of that Article. Such factors are not in any way related to the objective criteria referred to in the case-law.

As in settled case law, the only test allowed by the national authorities is to establish that the work activities are 'effective and genuine' and not 'on such a small scale as to be regarded as purely marginal and ancillary', as stressed in *Levin*.[56] Once that condition is satisfied, the motives which may have prompted a person of a member state to seek employment in another member state are of no account and must not be taken into consideration. Intention is not part of the test to determine the status of a worker. This status may not be made contingent upon the various objectives pursued by a national of a member state applying to enter the territory of a host member state. The derogation was therefore not relevant to the situation, as on the facts, it appeared that LN would indeed be a worker.

The derogation in Article 24 CD illustrates that social rights of economically inactive Union citizens are not inviolable. However, it cannot be used to impinge arbitrarily upon the equal treatment of Union citizens and it is not all encompassing – only specific forms of maintenance fall within its scope. Furthermore, the CJ appears in *LN* to have widened the category of a worker to remove more situations from its ambit. This short judgment may therefore have far reaching consequences if its line of reasoning is developed. It will be welcome to the increasing number of students across the EU who work to support themselves during their studies: if they can show that the pursuit of effective and genuine employment activities is one objective among many, such students will satisfy the test as a worker and thereby gain access to workers' rights under EU law. Crucially, enrolment at an educational institution does not automatically lock them out of the status of a 'worker'. It is for the national court to determine if the test is satisfied.

Finally, it is clear that the CJ will now examine the use of derogations by the member states to ensure that they are not being used to protect national social advantages to an excessive degree. Just as Union citizens are not to abuse the privileges of EU law, Union member states are not to abuse the derogations from it.

ANALYSING THE LAW

To what extent does the ruling in *LN* blur the line between the different categories of residence in Article 7 CD? Is the applicant a student, a worker or both?

---

4. Decommodification of Union citizenship

EU citizenship was a new concept in the Treaty – its substance therefore had to be developed.[57] In particular, if the Union citizen was to be decommodified, this status had to be distinguished from the migrant 'worker.' A major decision was taken in the case of

---

[56]C-53/81 *Levin* v *Staatssecretaris van Justitie* [1982] ECR 1035
[57]For a discussion of this development see N. Reich and S. Harbacevica, 'Citizenship and Family on trial: a fairly optimistic overview of recent court practice with regard to free movement of persons', *Common Market Law Review* 40, 2003, pp. 615–638; C. Jacqueson, 'Union Citizenship and the Court of Justice: something new under the sun? Towards social citizenship', *European Law Review* 27, June 2002, pp. 260–281

Grzelczyk[58] – a key ruling that raised the value of EU citizenship by describing it as a 'fundamental status', thereby endowing it with substance of its own. The status was, however, then restricted with the requirement that citizens wishing to access social rights be 'socially integrated'. Further concepts were also developed to provide rights for minor EU citizens but likewise subsequently limited. Thus this new 'fundamental status' has not made social rights inviolable – on the contrary it has develop alongside further conditions and limitations on the enjoyment of EU citizenship rights.

i.   Grzelczyk *and the declaration of Union citizenship as a 'fundamental status'*

Rudy Grzelczyk, a French national, went to Belgium to undertake university studies at the Catholic University of Louvain. For the first three years of his study, he survived by taking various jobs and obtaining credit. However, due to the increased study load at the beginning of his fourth and final year, he could not work. He applied for, and was initially granted assistance from a non-contributory social benefit (the 'minimex') which was available to students of Belgian nationality. However, this decision was subsequently repealed – due to the refusal by the Belgian ministry to reimburse the authorising agency – and the assistance was withdrawn. The Belgian ministry concluded that Grzelczyk was neither a Belgian national nor an EU migrant worker but a student; as such, because he had had recourse to social assistance[59] he no longer satisfied the conditions of residency. Rudy challenged this decision, arguing that it was nationality discrimination contrary to the EU Treaty.

In order to confirm its interpretation, the Belgian Labour Court used Article 267 TFEU to ask the CJ whether Article 18 TFEU prohibited the restriction of the minimex to workers only. A second question raised the relevance of the financial conditions in the former Student Directive for EU citizens studying abroad: what would be the correct response where such a student ran out of money before the study period expired?

The answers to these questions were clear from the perspective of the member states. Rudy was a student according to the Belgian, Danish and British governments – social advantages were to be enjoyed by migrant workers rather than migrant students; as Grzelczyk lacked sufficient resources, the rights contained within the directive lapsed. However, the Commission argued that Grzelczyk should be treated as a worker because he had supported himself for three years. If he were a Belgian worker, he would be granted the minimex. The refusal to grant this to him therefore constituted discrimination on the grounds of nationality.

AG Alber dismissed the binary worker/student discussion and opined that there was nothing to prevent Rudy from being both. Grzelczyk fulfilled the decisive criteria given in *Lawrie Blum,* thus was a worker, regardless of the student status of his jobs.[60] Notwithstanding his status as a worker, he was simultaneously enrolled at an educational institution so was also a student. A pragmatic approach was taken to the question of which status took precedence: 'the interests of free movement dictate that the consequences more favourable to the holder of the right of residence should apply'.[61] EU law,

---

[58]C-184/99
[59]Contrary to the provisions of the now repealed Directive 93/96.
[60][67]
[61][92]

he argued, did not 'trap' an individual within a status, but acknowledged that this might change after entry to a host member state.[62] This flexible and pragmatic approach was repeated in *LN*. It is more suited to the realities of student life in the twenty-first century.

AG Alber also noted that Grzelczyk pursued occupational activity and study *simultaneously*. In such circumstances, he argued, 'a connection between occupational activity and study results, on the one hand, from the time factor itself and, on the other, from the fact that the occupational activity was pursued for the purpose of completing the study'. His employment was clearly not marginal as these funds maintained him. Where, as in his case, work is pursued for the purpose of completing a period of study, this 'cannot call into question the status of a worker', in so far as the pursuit of the occupational activity is not 'totally marginal and ancilliary'.[63] In contrast to past case law which had highlighted a thematic connection, Alber introduced the idea of a 'connection of purpose'[64] as a guarantee of the status of worker. This line of reasoning brought Grzelczyk within the scope of Article 45 TFEU on free movement of workers.

However, could Grzelczyk also rely directly on Article 20 TFEU? Alber argued that European citizenship was an 'individual legal status'[65] with autonomous legal content which, as it falls within the scope of the Treaty, was also subject to the general prohibition of discrimination on the grounds of nationality. As such, a citizen of the Union with an unrestricted right to reside could in principle claim equal treatment with nationals in relation to social benefits. Thus he concluded that it is in principle incompatible with the provisions on equal treatment and citizenship for the minimex, a non-contributory social benefit, to be unavailable to all citizens of the Union.[66] He reasoned that in the absence of clear guidance as to when public funds are 'unreasonably' burdened, this provision was to be seen as a limitation rather than a total prohibition on access to welfare.[67] Although the member states had discretion to decide when an unreasonable burden arose, this discretion was to be applied flexibly.

AG Alber's ideas found their way into the CJ judgment. The Court dealt swiftly with the debate as to whether Grzelczyk was a worker or student. It went beyond both of these categories to introduce a new status which overrode them – Union citizenship. This, it declared:

> [31–32] . . . is destined to be the fundamental status of nationals of the member states, enabling those who find themselves in the same situation to enjoy the same treatment in law irrespective of their nationality, subject to such exceptions as are expressly provided for . . . A citizen of the European Union, lawfully resident in the territory of a host Member State, can rely on Article 6 of the Treaty in all situations which fall within the scope ratione materiae of Community law.

In this one sentence, citizenship became the trump status in the Union. This had been suggested by La Pergola in the *Sala* case where he stated that 'citizenship of the Union . . . is the fundamental legal status guaranteed to the citizen of every member state by the legal

---

[62][92]
[63][93]
[64][100]
[65][120]
[66][126]
[67][122]

order of the Community and now of the Union'. The Court now continued to say that migrant students are also citizens:

> [36] There is nothing in the amended text of the Treaty to suggest that students who are citizens of the Union, when they move to another member state to study there, lose the rights which the Treaty confers on citizens of the Union. The fact that a Union citizen pursues university studies in a member state other than the state of which he is a national cannot, of itself, deprive him of the possibility of relying on the prohibition of all discrimination on grounds of nationality laid down in Article 6 of the Treaty.

Changes to the Treaty on European Union which added to Title VIII a new chapter devoted to education and vocational training indicated that this area now fell within the material scope of the Treaty and was a context in which all Union citizens could expect equal treatment. The idea of *financial solidarity* in Directive 93/96 was used to build a bond between EU citizens that encountered temporary difficulties.[68] It concluded that Articles 18 and 21 TFEU [then 12 and 18 EC] protected legally resident non-nationals from being made to satisfy conditions not applied to nationals of the host MS. EU citizen-students were therefore to be treated equally to students who were nationals of the host state.

Grzelczyk was a major decision – it was the first time that the CJ recognised Union citizenship as an independent and fundamental legal status, decoupled from economic activity.[69] AG Geelhoed tried to develop this decoupling in *Ninni Orasche*.[70] Franca Ninni-Orasche left her native Italy in order to join her Austrian husband in his home country. The reason for her migration was therefore neither work nor study but reunion with her husband, who was himself not a migrant worker under EU law. Between 1993 and 1999 she held a residence permit which also gave her permission to work. She did not, however, work very much: in 1995, she worked for two and half months as a waitress. In October 1995, she received her diploma from Italy which enabled her to undertake university studies in Austria. She began to study languages in 1996, and applied for a grant to finance this study. This was refused on the basis that she did not satisfy the conditions to warrant equal treatment with an Austrian national, that is she could not be construed as a migrant EU worker. Ninni-Orasche appealed this decision, claiming infringement of her right to equal treatment before the law and infringement of EU law.

The Austrian Administrative Court sent two questions to the CJ concerned with her status as a worker: first, whether the short period of two and a half months in employment brought an EU national under the scope of Article 45 TFEU; and second, whether a migrant worker who accepts a fixed-term contract is to be viewed as giving up employment voluntarily or involuntarily. AG Geelhoed concluded that Mrs Ninni-Orasche could in principle be a worker despite the conditions of her employment.[71] As is the prerogative of Advocates General, he then considered the situation under citizenship law despite the fact that the national court did not raise this issue. In so doing, he pre-empted a question which was yet to come before the CJEU: the consequences of economic inactivity in relation to Union citizenship. Could a lawfully resident Union citizen who had never worked access welfare benefits in a host member state?[72]

---

[68][44]
[69]M. Dougan and E. Spaventa, 'Educating Rudy and the Non English Patient: A Double Bill on the Residency Rights Under Article 18 EC', *European Law Review* 28, 2003, p. 699
[70]C-413/01 *Ninni-Orasche* [2003] ECR I-13187
[71][35]
[72]This has recently been answered by the Grand Chamber in C-333/13 *Elisabeta Dano* v *Jobcenter Leipzig*. See comment at eutopialaw.com

He started from the fact that Mrs Ninni-Orasche was in Austria neither to study nor to work. Unlike Grzelczyk, who had migrated to Belgium in order to study, Mrs Ninni-Orasche had migrated for family reunion. Although her right of residence in Austria derived from Austrian rather than EU law, this did not preclude her from relying upon her status as a Union citizen: as AG Alber pointed out in *Grzelczyk*, Union citizens have a right to depend upon the most favourable set of rules where an overlap occurs.[73] Neither did this preclude her case being considered according to the 'tenor' of *Grzelczyk*. AG Geelhoed called upon the principle of financial solidarity. This principle could, he argued, 'in specific, objectively verifiable circumstances, create a right to equal treatment'. Such objective circumstances, such as nationality and residency status, existed in the situation of Ninni-Orasche. In the absence of harmonisation of social security, long-term legally resident EU nationals such as Mrs Ninni-Orasche who can satisfy such objective criteria should also enjoy 'financial solidarity'. Given her link to the society of the host state, such an 'EU national acquires the right to equal treatment in law'.[74] From this perspective, the refusal of the Austrian ministry made solely on the grounds of nationality, constituted 'blatant discrimination' contrary to Article 18 TFEU. However, the CJ did not take up the invitation to comment on these aspects of citizenship – it merely confirmed that the concept of a worker did not exclude those on short fixed-term contracts. The question returned, however, in *Bidar*.

VIEWPOINT

Why do you think the CJ declared citizenship a 'fundamental status' instead of an 'alternative' status in EU law?

ii. Bidar *and the principle of social integration*

The idea of financial solidarity introduced in *Grzelczyk* goes to the heart of the welfare state and decommodification. Social rights clearly cost but those costs are borne collectively by the polity to support individuals during their time of need. Can this idea of solidarity underpinning the national welfare state be transposed upwards to undergird EU citizenship? Can it support a nascent transnational 'welfare state' in the EU? Somek argues that whereas:

> . . . national solidarity is, legally speaking, based upon birth in the country, descent from other nationals, acquisition as a consequence of residence and enculturation (see literacy tests), the ground for the enjoyment of transnational solidarity remains strangely indeterminate.[75]

---

[73]C-184/99 [83]
[74]C-413/01 [92]
[75]Alexander Somek, 'Solidarity decomposed: being and time in European citizenship', *ELR* 32(6), 2007, pp. 787–818. See also Catherine Barnard, 'EU Citizenship and the Principle of Solidarity', in E. Spaventa and M. Dougan (eds), *Social Welfare and EU Law*, Hart Publishing, 2005, p. 157, at pp. 157–160; 'Solidarity and New Governance in Social Policy', in G. de Búrca and J. Scott (eds), *Law and New Governance in the EU and the US*, Hart Publishing, 2006, p. 153

This 'indeterminate' nature of this idea of transnational financial solidarity was soon to be addressed. It was strengthened by being embedded in a condition of social integration – thus under EU law, social rights could be enjoyed only by those showing a genuine link to the host member state by being settled there. Ironically, to enjoy the fullest social rights as a migrant Union citizen, it is therefore necessary to become stationary.

The idea of a genuine link to society first made its appearance in a case concerning equal treatment of students, *D'Hoop*.[76] A Belgian student, D'Hoop, was refused a social benefit in Belgium solely because she had completed her secondary education in France – secondary education in Belgium was a condition of eligibility for the 'tideover allowance'. The CJ held that although it was 'legitimate for the national legislature to wish to ensure that there is a real link between the applicant for that allowance and the geographic employment market concerned'[77] the rule was 'too general and exclusive in nature' – it was arbitrary as it prioritised a factor that was 'not necessarily representative of the real and effective degree of connection between the applicant for the tideover allowance and the geographic employment market'.[78] Consequently, Belgium was precluded from 'refusing to grant the tideover allowance to one of its nationals, a student seeking her first employment, on the sole ground that that student completed her secondary education in another Member State'.[79]

Union citizens are therefore not automatically entitled to social benefits. Member states have significant discretion but the rules used to demonstrate a 'link' cannot be arbitrary nor ad hoc. The quality of the link to and integration in society rather than the labour market was developed in *Bidar*.[80] A French national, Bidar, arrived in the UK in August 1998 to live with his grandmother because his mother was ill. Following the death of his mother in 1999, his grandmother in the UK became his legal guardian. He completed secondary school in the UK and then secured a place at university. His problems began when he applied for funding to finance these studies. His local authority granted him assistance with tuition fees, but refused to give him a student loan for maintenance costs on the grounds that he did not fulfil the requirement of four years' 'settlement' in the UK.[81] Bidar challenged this decision on the grounds that it constituted discrimination contrary to Articles 18 and 21 TFEU.

The question facing the CJ was whether a lawfully resident Union citizen who had never been economically active in his home or host state, had migrated neither for work nor study, but for family reasons and had begun to study at high school rather than university level in another member state could be granted education finance. Would such a person be sufficiently integrated to make refusal of a maintenance grant contrary to EU law? This was rejected by the member states. The UK, Germany and other intervening member states argued that there was no distinction between the situation of Bidar and Grzelczyk: both were students and fell under the Student Directive. Thus by applying for maintenance assistance, Bidar had taken himself out of the scope of the directive.

AG Geelhoed took a different stance. He put Bidar and Grzelczyk in two distinct groups of economically inactive Union citizens – 'Group A' comprised those who, like

---

[76]C-224/98
[77][38]
[78][39]
[79][40]
[80]C. Barnard, 'Case note on Case C-209/03 *Bidar*', *Common Market Law Review* 42, 2005, p. 1465
[81]In order to qualify for a student loan a person must be 'ordinarily resident' in the UK or EEA (periods of study do not count).

Grzelczyk, move to another EU member state in order to study there; 'Group B' consisted of those who, like Bidar and Ninni-Orasche, exercise the Article 21 TFEU right to move to another member state and subsequently decide to pursue studies there. The question of entitlement to educational finance for students who are already resident in a member state as EU citizens was 'uncharted territory'[82] but he argued the logic adopted in *Grzelczyk* should nonetheless apply. The principle of financial solidarity was highlighted:

> [45] In such exceptional situations the principle of financial solidarity between the nationals of the Member States entails that once a student has commenced a course of studies in another Member State and has progressed to a certain stage of these studies, that State should enable him to complete these studies by providing the financial assistance which is available to its nationals.

Bidar, as a lawfully resident Union citizen exercising a Treaty right, was to be able to enjoy equal treatment in respect of all circumstances falling under EU law, which given provisions on education included maintenance payments. As the condition of 'being settled' was not applied to British nationals (who needed only to have been 'ordinarily resident' within the United Kingdom for the three years prior to commencing study), AG Geelhoed found it 'quite clear that this amounts to an indirect discrimination on grounds of nationality'. There was no justification for this.

Did the CJ agree with this? For the most part, the ideas in the AG opinion were adopted. The CJ used AG Geelhoed's distinction between students abroad who are EU citizens and EU citizens living abroad who wish to study. The latter are residents in the first instance and students in the second. Thus, if lawfully resident, they are protected by the principle of equal treatment.[83] Agreeing with the AG, the settlement rule was found to be disproportionate. The CJ held that it was overly exclusive as it made it almost impossible for any national of another member state to obtain settled status as a student, regardless of the actual degree of integration into the host society, and hence to enjoy the right to assistance to cover maintenance costs. This treatment could not be justified 'by the legitimate objective which those rules seek to secure'.[84]

Notwithstanding the principle of financial solidarity with nationals of other member states, the CJ did concede some regulatory autonomy to the member states – they could continue to ensure that such study finance did not become an 'unreasonable burden which could have consequences for the overall level of assistance which may be granted by the State'.[85] The Court did not give any clear guidance on the idea of 'unreasonable'. In conclusion, the CJ decided that Article 18:

> [63] . . . must be interpreted as precluding national legislation which grants students the right to assistance covering their maintenance costs only if they are settled in the host Member State, while precluding a national of another Member State from obtaining the status of settled person as a student even if that national is lawfully resident and has received a substantial part of his secondary education in the host Member State and has consequently established a genuine link with the society of that state.

---

[82][20]
[83][46]
[84][61]
[85][56]

By stressing the existence of a 'link' to society, the CJ obliged member states to treat integrated migrant Union citizens as if they 'belonged' to the host nation. Regardless of the reason for migration, if they are socially integrated then Union citizens can expect equal access to welfare advantages in another member state.

ANALYSING THE LAW

Explain the concept of 'social integration' – how can this be demonstrated?

---

iii. Förster *and the contours of a 'genuine link'*

AG Geelhoed stressed the importance of a structural link regulating eligibility for social advantages. The link to the labour market was de-emphasised: market citizens must demonstrate 'effective and genuine' employment; social citizens need to show a 'genuine link' to society or social systems such as education. In Bidar's case the link to be established was twofold: the 'degree of affinity' with the educational system and the degree of integration into society – where:

> [60] . . . an EU citizen has followed his secondary education in a Member State other than that of which he is a national, which is more adapted to preparing him for entry to an establishment of higher or tertiary education in that Member State than elsewhere.

Geelhoed suggested that in assessing the degree of integration, member states should focus on subjective factors, such as the age of the Union citizen migrating, and objective criteria (the need for ensuring continuity in the education of the applicant, the likelihood that he will enter the national employment market and the possibility that he may not be eligible for maintenance assistance from other sources).[86] He concluded that a requirement that excluded a person demonstrating a 'genuine link with the national education system or society' from maintenance assistance is disproportionate.[87] In a clear promotion of decommodification, AG Geelhoed suggested that the general principles of liberty and dignity applied to the economically active could be transferred to the economically inactive to create the best possible conditions for integration.[88]

The CJ agreed with Geelhoed that it would be 'legitimate for a Member State to grant such assistance only to students who have demonstrated a certain degree of integration into the society of that state'.[89] This was partially accepted: the UK, Germany, Austria, the Netherlands and Finland all agreed that member states should have a right to ensure the presence of a 'real link' between the student and the member state or its employment market, or alternatively, evidence of a sufficient degree of integration in society.[90] The CJ also agreed that the existence of a certain degree of integration could be regarded as established where the student has resided in the host member state for a 'certain length

---

[86] Such as the member state of which he is a national as he no longer fulfils the eligibility criteria in that member state [62]
[87] *Bidar* [61]
[88] [63]
[89] [57]
[90] [56]

of time'. What would be an appropriate length of time? Subsequent case law has touched upon this.

Förster[91] considered the type of rules which could be used to demonstrate social integration, in particular the length of time that might be imposed. This case concerned a German student who had settled in the Netherlands in 2000, where she pursued training as a primary school teacher and subsequently a first degree. She undertook casual work during her studies, including one year in a work placement in a school for children with behavioural difficulties. She did not work during 2003 but in 2004 found a job as a social worker.

From 2000 she had received a maintenance grant from the Dutch authorities, the IB-Groep, on the basis that she was a 'worker' under Article 45 TFEU and thus should be treated in the same way as Dutch students. When IB-Groep discovered that she had been unemployed during 2003, it requested repayment of the funds given. The matter revolved around whether she could be considered as 'integrated' into Dutch society prior to her degree or did the rule requiring five years of continuous residence, adopted following *Bidar*, apply? As such a restriction did not apply to Dutch students, was it compatible with EU law? Was five years an appropriate timespan to achieve social integration or would this be considered discriminatory and prohibited by Article 18 TFEU?

A condition of five years' uninterrupted residence was held appropriate to demonstrate integration into the society of the host Member State'.[92] This was held not to be excessive primarily because five years is also the timeframe used in Article 16 of the Citizenship Directive to acquire the status of long-term resident.[93] However, the requirement also had to be proportionate.[94] The fact that this policy was laid out clearly in a rule meant that it satisfied the criteria of clarity and proportionality:

> [57] By enabling those concerned to know, without any ambiguity, what their rights and obligations are, the residence requirement laid down by the Policy rule of 9 May 2005 is, by its very existence, such as to guarantee a significant level of legal certainty and transparency in the context of the award of maintenance grants to students.

Thus the Court concluded that although a student who is a national of one member state and travels to another to study there can rely on Article 18 TFEU to obtain a maintenance grant after a certain time of residency, that Article 'does not preclude the application to nationals of other Member States of a requirement of five years' prior residence'.[95]

O'Leary argues that this decision is incoherent with previous case law:

> From the point of view of the coherence of the Court's legal reasoning, however, this conclusion is not without its difficulties. The right of Member State nationals to reside in another Member State is conferred directly by Art.18 EC [21 TFEU]. The Baumbast ruling made that clear. Their right to equal treatment based on lawful residence for a certain period of time in the host Member State derives from Art.12 EC [18 TFEU]. A Directive, particularly one whose legal basis includes Arts 12 and 18 EC, should not

---

[91]C-158/07 *Jacqueline Förster v Hoofddirectie van de Informatie Beheer Groep* [2008] ECR I-8507
[92][52]
[93][55]
[94][53]
[95][71]

detract from the requirements flowing from those provisions of the EC Treaty. In *Förster*, the Court used the Directive [CD 2004/38] to confirm that the Dutch residence requirement was not disproportionate when it could have been expected to question whether the Dutch residence requirement and, consequently, the Directive itself were compatible with its interpretation of Arts 12 and 18 EC. As previously indicated, this contrasts starkly with the Court's previous requirement of a case by case assessment of the circumstances of the benefit claimant and his or her demonstration of a real or effective link with the host Member State, and its rejection of the imposition of blanket requirements 'which might favour an element which is not necessarily representative of a such a degree of connection to the exclusion of other representative elements.[96]

Later cases have clarified that the idea of social integration cannot be used to exclude migrant citizen students from access to welfare per se. *Bressol*[97] brought to consideration a Belgian rule which gave preferential access to certain medical courses to resident students – non-residents were selected by drawing lots. This was clearly indirect discrimination on the basis of nationality but could it be justified? The answer was affirmative – '. . . a difference in treatment based indirectly on nationality may be justified by the objective of maintaining a balanced high-quality medical service open to all, in so far as it contributes to achieving a high level of protection of health'[98] – but the national court had to be convinced that the preventive measures were proportionate bearing in mind the actual level of risk.

The Court then set out a series of investigatory steps that the national authorities and courts were to undertake in order to establish a genuine risk of a shortage of public health expertise. The derogation had to be supported by evidence including detailed specific data and figures demonstrating this. In this case, it would require the competent national authorities to conduct an analysis to assess – for *each* of the nine courses concerned – 'the maximum number of students who can be trained at a level which complies with the desired training quality standards' as well as 'the number of graduates who must establish themselves within the French Community to carry out a medical or paramedical occupa-tion there in order to be able to ensure adequate public health services'. The analysis furthermore had to consider the impact of non-resident students on the objective of ensur-ing the availability of professionals within the French Community. The authorities also had to take into account the possibility that resident students may decide to leave Belgium to exercise their profession in another country. Finally, they had to assess the impact of doctors trained elsewhere practising in Belgium.[99]

If the national court considered the risks to public health to be genuine after this pre-liminary examination, it then had to assess whether existing legislation was appropriate to protect public health, and in particular whether a simple restriction of the number of non-resident students 'can really bring about an increase in the number of graduates ready to ensure the future availability of public health services within the French Community'.[100] It then had to conduct a proportionality test, considering in particular whether less restrictive measures could be as effective in protecting the public interest.

---

[96]Siofra O'Leary, 'Equal treatment and EU citizens: A new chapter on cross-border educational mobility and access to student financial assistance', *European Law Review* 34(4), 2009, pp. 612–627
[97]C-73/08 *Bressol and others* [2010] ECR I-2735
[98][62], also C-169/07 *Hartlauer* [2009] ECR I-0000 [47]
[99]C-127/08 *Blaise Baheten Metock and Others* v *Minister for Justice, Equality and Law Reform* [2008] ECR I-6241 [71 and 72]
[100]C-34/09 *Gerardo Ruiz Zambrano* v *Office national de l'emploi (ONEm)* [2011] ECR I-1177 [76]

The nature of this guidance suggests concerns at the Luxembourg court that member states are trying to abuse the derogations. Signs of concern are also visible in *Commission v Austria* where the CJ stressed that the proof required to demonstrate a genuine link with the host society must not be 'too exclusive in nature' or arbitrary.[101] Potential factors for use to ascertain this were given:

> [63] ... as the Advocate General has noted in point 76 of her Opinion, the genuine link required between the student claiming a benefit and the host Member State need not be fixed in a uniform manner for all benefits, but should be established according to the constitutive elements of the benefit in question, including its nature and purpose or purposes. The objective of the benefit must be analysed according to its results and not according to its formal structure.[102]

In relation to a transport subsidy for students, a genuine link between the student and the host member state could be evidenced, for example, enrolment of the person in question is at a private or public establishment that is either accredited or financed by the host Member State in accordance with Article 7(1)(c) Citizenship Directive.

APPLYING THE LAW

Consider whether the Dutch residence requirement in *Förster* is proportionate. Would you describe Mr B and Ms C as 'socially integrated'?

---

iv. Zambrano *and genuine enjoyment of citizenship rights*

The CJ emphasises a genuine link for older Union citizens; it uses the idea of 'genuine enjoyment' for minors. EU law protects the rights of migrant Union citizens who are students and also minor Union citizens who may or may not be migrants. This has been a controversial development because these questions have arisen in families where the parents are themselves not Union citizens. The CJEU has struggled to decide how to treat non-EU parents of Union citizens in EU law – do they have a right to reside or can they be deported, in line with the preference of most member states? The problem with deportation is that it also deprives the baby of the enjoyment of the rights and privileges associated with their Union citizenship.

The question first arose in *Chen:*[103] a Chinese couple avoided the strict one-child policy of China by ensuring that their second child was an Irish citizen – Ireland at that time used the policy of *ius soli*: thus when the child was born there it automatically became Irish. As an Irish national, baby Catherine was also a Union citizen and in exercise of her right to free movement, she settled with her Chinese mother in Wales, thereby becoming a migrant Union citizen. The CJ held that neither the child nor the mother could be deported: Article 21 TFEU and the CD conferred a right to residence for an indefinite period – as long as the minor is a national of a member state, is covered by appropriate

---

[101]*Commission v Austria* [62]
[102]C-22 and 23/08 *Vatsouras and Koupatantze* [2009] ECR I-4585) [41 and 42]
[103]C-200/02 *Kunqian Catherine Zhu and Man Lavette Chen v Secretary of State for the Home Department* [2004] ECR I-9925

sickness insurance and is in the care of a parent who has sufficient resources for that minor not to become a burden on the public finances of the host member state. Those same provisions also provided for the parent who is that minor's primary carer to reside with the child in the host member state.

Baumbast[104] raised similar questions, but the situation involved different social circumstances of the migrant family. It many ways it is a case about migrant workers but the ruling included important comments on Article 21 TFEU, therefore it will be discussed here. The case concerned the right for migrant workers to remain in the UK following a change of status. The key applicant was a German national, Mr Baumbast, who had migrated with his Columbian wife and their two children (one with Colombian, the other with dual Colombian and German nationality) to work in the UK. Between 1990 and 1995, when he was a migrant Union worker, he and the family were granted a residence permit. The application for an extension was, however, refused as after 1995 most of Baumbast's work was in China and Lesotho. He therefore no longer fell within the scope of Article 45 TFEU or satisfied the legal conditions to secure a right of residence under former Directive 90/364: he was no longer working nor seeking work in the UK. However, as in *Chen,* deportation would affect the minor Union citizen.

This case is important because it raised a key question before the CJ: was Article 21 TFEU directly effective, so that Mr Baumbast could rely on it as he no longer fell within the scope of Article 45 TFEU? Luckily for him, the answer was affirmative:

> [94] A citizen of the European Union who no longer enjoys a right of residence as a migrant worker in the host Member State can, as a citizen of the Union, enjoy there a right of residence by direct application of Article 18(1) EC [21 TFEU].

As always, the exercise of this right remained subject to limitations and conditions applied in compliance with general principles of Community law and proportionality. Nonetheless, the CJ identified a detriment to the Union citizen child: if the key carer had to leave, then the child would also have to leave and consequently would be deprived of its heritage as a Union citizen. The children were also recognised as having a right to remain under Article 12 of Regulation 492/2011 and by virtue of this Mrs Baumbast could also stay – as the primary carer of a Union citizen, Mrs Baumbast enjoyed a right to reside. All three were eventually granted indefinite leave to remain – ironically only Mr Baumbast did not have permission to reside in the UK.

The residence rights granted to the Chen and Baumbast families under EU law would fall into the second category in the Citizenship Directive residence to a migrant – albeit minor – EU citizen who was self-sufficient. The parents derived rights from the Union citizen – Mrs Chen and Mrs Baumbast were allowed to stay only because of their role in ensuring the enjoyment of the rights granted to the Union citizen. They also had sufficient resources for themselves and their children. What would happen if the parents did not – would they be deported? Were EU citizenship rights only for children of high income families?

This was answered in *Zambrano,*[105] a case which developed the right to parenting of baby Union citizens. In *Zambrano,* a Colombian couple had started a family in Belgium.

---

[104]C-413/99 *Baumbast and R v Secretary of State for the Home Department* [2002] ECR I-7091

[105]Iyiola Solanke, 'Using the Citizen to Bring the Refugee In: Case C-34/09 Gerardo Ruiz Zambrano v Office national de l'emploi (ONEM)', *Modern Law Review* 75(1), 2012, pp.101–111; also see Alina Tryfonidou, 'Redefining the Outer Boundaries of EU Law: The Zambrano, McCarthy and Dereci trilogy', *European Public Law* 18(3), September 2012, p. 493

The parents, asylum seekers fleeing political persecution at home, did not register their two children with the Colombian Embassy. The babies would therefore have been stateless were it not for a provision in Belgian nationality law that babies who could not adopt the nationality of their parents automatically received Belgian citizenship. As Belgian nationals, the babies were also Union citizens, like Catherine Chen. Unlike baby Catherine, the Zambrano babies remained in their home state. The parents were refused a right to reside in Belgium but were not forced to leave. Despite this, Mr Zambrano was able to work and paid all necessary taxes. It was only when he sought to access unemployment benefit that the authorities sought to deport him. This decision was challenged as incompatible with EU citizenship law.

The CJ decision continued the reasoning seen in *Chen*: refusal of a right of residence and right to work for the non-EU parent would 'have the effect of depriving the baby Union citizens of the genuine enjoyment of the substance of the rights conferred by virtue of their status as citizens of the Union'. This effect was likely for two reasons: first, refusal of a right of residence to Mr Zambrano would result in a situation where the infant EU-citizen would be forced to leave with their parents. Second, refusal of a work permit would have the same impact: 'if a work permit were not granted to such a person, he would risk not having sufficient resources to provide for himself and his family, which would also result in the children, citizens of the Union, having to leave the territory of the Union'. Thus refusal would deny the infants of any enjoyment of the 'substance of the rights conferred on them by virtue of their status as citizens of the Union'[106] and was incompatible. The Grand Chamber concluded that Article 20 TFEU:

[49] . . . precludes national measures which have the effect of depriving citizens of the Union of the genuine enjoyment of the substance of the rights conferred by virtue of their status as citizens of the Union. A refusal to grant a right of residence to a third country national with dependent minor children in the Member State where those children are nationals and reside, and also a refusal to grant such a person a work permit, has such an effect.

The absence of migration did not affect this finding. It should be remembered that Article 20 TFEU creates a right to 'move and reside' – these two rights have been read as cumulative since their introduction: the right to reside only arose after the right to move had been exercised. In the absence of this, the situation was wholly internal. *Akrich*[107] also stressed that entry into the member state must be lawful to enjoy citizenship rights:

[50] . . . in order to benefit from [Article 10, Regulation 1612/68] . . . a national of a non-Member State married to a citizen of the Union must be lawfully resident in a Member State when he moves to another Member State to which the citizen of the Union is migrating or has migrated.

---

[106]*Zambrano* [42–45]
[107]C-109/01 *Akrich* [2003] ECR I-9607

This latter point was specifically reversed in *Metock*,[108] a case where the Irish government sought to deport third country national spouses of Union citizens because prior to marriage they were unlawfully resident in Ireland:

> [58] It is true that the Court held in paragraphs 50 and 51 of *Akrich* that, in order to benefit from the rights provided for in Article 10 of Regulation No 1612/68, the national of a non-member country who is the spouse of a Union citizen must be lawfully resident in a Member State when he moves to another Member State to which the citizen of the Union is migrating or has migrated. However, that conclusion must be reconsidered. The benefit of such rights cannot depend on the prior lawful residence of such a spouse in another Member State.[109]

Two reasons were given for this reversal: first, it would fragment the free movement of Union citizens if national immigration law were the basis of family reunification under EU law – there would be a variance across the EU according to the provisions of national law concerning immigration, with some member states permitting entry and residence of family members of a Union citizen and other member states refusing them. This would not be compatible with the vision of the internal market. Second, the ruling in *Akrich* conflicted with the provisions of the Family Reunification Directive[110] which obliged member states to authorise entry and residence to the spouse of a lawfully resident national of a non-member country lawfully resident in its territory where the spouse is not already lawfully resident in another member state. Consequently, it decided that:

> [70] Directive 2004/38 confers on all nationals of non-member countries who are family members of a Union citizen within the meaning of point 2 of Article 2 of that directive, and accompany or join the Union citizen in a Member State other than that of which he is a national, rights of entry into and residence in the host Member State, regardless of whether the national of a non-member country has already been lawfully resident in another Member State.

Yet *Metock* retained the role of migration – the CJ decided that movement remained a prerequisite to the right to reside:

> [77] the Treaty rules governing freedom of movement for persons and the measures adopted to implement them cannot be applied to activities which have no factor linking them with any of the situations governed by Community law and which are confined in all relevant aspects within a single member state.

However, in *Zambrano* AG Sharpston questioned this and considered whether the citizenship right to reside could be enjoyed in the home member state. She argued that despite being in the home state this was not a purely internal situation:

> [95–96] . . . the *children's situation* falls, by reason of its nature and its consequences, within the ambit of EU law. Moreover, like Catherine Zhu, Diego and Jessica cannot

---

[108]C-127/08 *Blaise Baheten Metock and Others v Minister for Justice, Equality and Law Reform* ECR I-06241. Discussed in C. Costello, 'Metock: Free Movement and "Normal Family Life" in the Union', *CMLR* 46, 2009, p. 587; N. Cambien, 'Blaise Baheten Metock and Others v Minister for Justice, Equality and Law Reform', *Columbia Journal of European Law* 15, 2009, p. 321

[109]See C-459/99 *MRAX* [59] and C-157/03 *Commission v Spain* [28]

[110]Council Directive 2003/86/EC of 22 September 2003 on the right to family reunification (OJ L251/12 2003)

exercise their rights as Union citizens (specifically, their rights to move and to reside in any Member State) fully and effectively without the presence and support of their parents. Through operation of the same link that the Court accepted in *Zhu and Chen* (enabling a young child to exercise its citizenship rights effectively) it follows that Mr Ruiz Zambrano's situation is likewise not one that is 'purely internal' to the Member State. It too falls within the ambit of EU law.

The Grand Chamber decision did not discuss this. Indeed, drawing upon *Grzelczyk,* it stated only that as citizenship is the fundamental status of nationals of the member states, Article 20 TFEU itself contains power to shield stationary EU citizens from any national decisions which would entail a denial of the genuine enjoyment EU citizenship rights. Even if it agreed with AG Sharpston's conclusion, it was silent on her reasoning – it neither agreed nor replaced it with reasoning of its own, a fact for which it has been sharply criticised. For example, it has been argued that in *Zambrano* the CJ explicitly 'embraced'[111] purely internal situations without extensive explanation as to the reason why. The CJ has also been accused of avoiding an important issue:

> In a very short judgment, the Court found yet a third way to allow the Ruiz Zambrano family to rely on EU law. The Court decided not to use Article 18 TFEU, leaving that particular Pandora's box unopened. Neither did the Court rely on a combination of Article 20 and a wider reading of Article 21 TFEU. Instead, the decision rests solely on Article 20 TFEU, which establishes citizenship of the Union. The Court found that this provision 'precludes national measures which have the effect of depriving citizens of the Union of the genuine enjoyment of the substance of the rights conferred by virtue of their status as citizens of the Union' [para 42]. Thus the children fell within the scope of EU law, and Mr. Ruiz Zambrano derived from this not only a right of residence (as in Chen) but also the right to work in order to provide the necessary, sufficient resources. This decision extends the scope of EU law; the only question is how far.[112]

APPLYING THE LAW

Consider how the *Zambrano* case can be applied to help Ms C when the authorities threatened to deport her?

The immediate fear was that floodgates had been opened. For example, in Germany, *Der Spiegel* declared that the *Zambrano* ruling allowed that 'illegal immigrants living in the Union may stay if their child is an EU citizen'.[113] However subsequent decisions by the CJ and national courts have demonstrated that the right is limited.[114] This idea of 'genuine

---

[111]Kay Hailbronner and Daniel Thym, 'Case Note on Zambrano', *CMLR* 48, 2011, p. 1253

[112]Alicia Hinarejos, 'Extending Citizenship And The Scope Of EU Law', *Cambridge Law Journal,* 2011, p. 310

[113]http://www.lto.de/de/html/nachrichten/2731/bleiberecht-fuer-auslaendische-eltern-wenn-luxemburg-keine-ausnahmen-zulaesst-waeren-die-konsequenzen-enorm/

[114]See C-356/11 and C-357/11 *O and another v Maahanmuuttovirasto & Maahanmuuttovirasto v L* [2012] WLR (D) 371; also comment on HC and *Sanneh* at http://eutopialaw.com

enjoyment' does not create an easy way for non-EU citizens to evade national immigration laws. *Zambrano* established a high test for the derivation of residence rights by so-called 'Zambrano carers' from stationary Union citizens. This test calls for a risk analysis: will refusal of residence or social rights by the member state force the EU citizen to quit the EU?

In *McCarthy*[115] and *Dereci*[116] the Grand Chamber made it clear that the mere desire of a stationary Union citizen to live with family for financial or emotional reasons is by itself too weak an argument to 'support the view that the Union citizen will be *forced* to leave Union territory if such a right is not granted'.[117] The central question, as laid out in *Zambrano,* is whether the decision of the member state leads, for the Union citizen concerned, to the denial of genuine enjoyment of the substance of the rights conferred by virtue of his status as a citizen of the Union The key criterion determining the answer to this question is whether the EU citizen must leave not only the member state of which she is a national but also the 'territory of the Union as a whole'.[118] This was not so in either of these cases – in order to enjoy the same rights as migrant Union citizens, stationary Union citizens have to show that for them family reunion is essential, not just desirable.

In *McCarthy,* the rupture of strong emotional and psychological ties within the family did not demonstrate compulsion to leave – diminution of the enjoyment of family life does not engage *Zambrano* rights. Mrs McCarthy, held dual British and Irish nationality. She was born and lived in the United Kingdom where she looked after her disabled child. In 2002 she married a Jamaican national and in 2004, she and her husband applied for a residence permit and residence document under EU law as, respectively, a Union citizen and the spouse of a Union citizen. The Home Secretary rejected the applications, meaning that Mr McCarthy would be deported. The CJ also rejected a request to apply the *Zambrano* approach as:

> [49] No element of the situation of Mrs McCarthy, as described by the national court, indicates that the national measure at issue in the main proceedings has the effect of depriving her of the genuine enjoyment of the substance of the rights associated with her status as a Union citizen, or of impeding the exercise of her right to move and reside freely within the territory of the Member States, in accordance with Article 21 TFEU. Indeed, the failure by the authorities of the United Kingdom to take into account the Irish nationality of Mrs McCarthy for the purposes of granting her a right of residence in the United Kingdom in no way affects her in her right to move and reside freely within the territory of the Member States, or any other right conferred on her by virtue of her status as a Union citizen.

> [50] In that regard, by contrast with the case of *Ruiz Zambrano,* the national measure at issue in the main proceedings in the present case does not have the effect of obliging Mrs McCarthy to leave the territory of the European Union. Indeed, as is clear from paragraph 29 of the present judgment, Mrs McCarthy enjoys, under a principle of international law, an unconditional right of residence in the United Kingdom since she is a national of the United Kingdom.

---

[115]C. Taroni, 'Union Citizenship as a Source of Rights? Case C-434/09, Shirley McCarthy v Secretary of State for the Home Department, Judgment of the Court (Third Chamber) 5 May 2011, nyr', *Journal of Contemporary European Research* 8(1), 2012, p. 145

[116]C-256/11 *Murat Dereci and others v Bundesministerium fuer Inneres.* For comment see Niamh Nic Shuibhne, '(Some Of) The Kids Are All Right: Comment on McCarthy and Dereci', *Common Market Law Review* (2012) 49(1), 2012, p. 349

[117]*Dereci* [68]

[118][66]

In *Dereci* the CJ was again of the opinion that none of the Union citizens were 'forced' to leave the Union. They could apparently live well enough without their spouse or child. The applicants in this case were all third country nationals. None had exercised a right to free movement: Mr Dereci, a Turkish national, entered Austria illegally and married an Austrian national by whom he had three small children bearing Austrian nationality; Mr Maduike, a Nigerian national, also entered Austria illegally and married an Austrian national with whom he lived in Austria; Mrs Heiml, a Sri Lankan national, married an Austrian national before entering Austria legally but her residence permit had expired; Mr Kokollari entered Austria legally at the age of two with his parents holding Yugoslav nationality – at 29 he lived in Austria maintained by his mother, an Austrian national; and Mrs Stevic, a 52-year-old Serbian national seeking family reunification in Austria with her father, an Austrian national since 2007. The further question of whether the refusal undermined the right to family life was to be answered by reference to human rights law: Article 7 Charter on Fundamental Rights and Article 8 ECHR.

Dereci and *McCarthy* clarify that compulsion relates solely to factual consequences – the test is on the *practical impact* of national measures. Likewise, in *Alokpa*[119] the CJ held that as the Togolese mother could enjoy a right to reside in France, the state of which the children were nationals and where their father lived, the refusal by the Luxembourg authorities to grant her a right of residence there did not result in her children being obliged to leave the territory of the European Union.

Residence and welfare rights will only be granted to the non-migrant Union citizen if it can be shown that these are essential for continued residence in the EU. In order to be successful, the stationary EU citizen must produce compelling evidence – beyond consideration of economic and emotional well-being – that remaining in the EU is only possible with the presence of the TCN family member. These judgments have been criticised as incoherent and leading to uncertainty.[120] The functional view of family life also seems to contradict the emerging concern in the EU with children's rights[121] and the international agenda on the importance of parenting.[122] The strict approach taken to this test by national courts is also contrary to this: British judges have come to their own conclusion on the meaning of 'compulsion' – in *Sanneh* the judge decided that if a 'Zambrano carer' is tenacious enough to find ways to survive destitution, she is not *compelled* to leave and thus may be refused access to benefits.[123]

In *O v M*[124] the CJ limited *Zambrano* rights to biological relatives with clear parenting responsibilities for minor EU citizens. In that case, two women from beyond the EU had married and divorced EU citizens. Each wife had one child who became an EU citizen. The women subsequently remarried non-EU citizens and each bore another child, who

---

[119]C-86/12 *Alokpa and Moudoulou v Ministre du Travail, de l'Emploi et de l'Immigration*

[120]Shuibhne 2012

[121]'Towards An EU Strategy on the Rights of the Child' at http://ec.europa.eu/justice/policies/children/policies_children_intro_en.htm

[122]On cases in the United States concerning termination of parental rights as a result of deportation see C.E. Hall, 'Where Are My Children . . . and My Rights? Parental Rights Termination as a Consequence of Deportation', *Duke Law Journal* 60, 2011, p. 1459

[123]*Sanneh v Home Secretary* [2013] EWHC 793 (Admin). See also http://eutopialaw.com/2014/05/28/zambrano-unwritten/\#more-2458

[124]Joined cases C-356/11 and 357/11 *O and another v Maahnmuuttovirasto and Maahnmuuttovirasto v L* . See also *Temilola Opeyemi Aladeselu, Felix Adelekan Anthony and Paschal Tobechukwu Ashiegbu v Home Secretary* [2013] EWCA Civ 144

was not an EU citizen. The Finnish court asked the CJ if they could in those circumstances refuse residence permits to the non-EU citizen husbands who had no custody rights over the child EU citizen. In other words, could the 'Zambrano citizen' shield a non-biological family member from expulsion? This was in principle allowed – the permit could be refused so long as this would not deny 'genuine enjoyment' and guaranteed the best interests of the child and the promotion of family life, as required by the directive on family reunification[125] and the EU Charter on Fundamental Rights. This decision paves the way for family fragmentation – it is unlikely that national authorities will decide in favour of the parent from beyond the EU. These cases seem to confirm that even if migration may no longer be essential, at present it is harder for stationary Union citizens to access social rights.

VIEWPOINT

To what extent does the CJ decision in the *Zambrano* case leave EU citizenship law vulnerable to abuse?

---

5. Conclusion

Although Marshall's trilogy focuses on England, most agree with his tripartite categorisation of the key components of citizenship. His three elements are often used to evaluate the substance of citizenship in different parts of the world[126] and were used here to explore Union citizenship. EU citizenship challenges Marshall's basic assumption that citizenship, nationality and the nation state were congruous terms, fitting into each other like Russian dolls. As the Commission Citizenship report highlights, a state is home to more than its own citizens – there are migrant and temporary workers, foreign residents and denizens as well as asylum seekers and undocumented migrants[127] all of whom have different rights and are in no way not all equal.[128]

EU citizenship rights do not map neatly onto Marshall's three categories and are at present far from inviolable. The substance of these rights is a work in progress. The development has been incremental – the Union citizen first had to be removed from the shadow of the 'worker' to become an autonomous concept, freed from the assumptions associated with migrant Union workers. As shown, the opinions of the Advocates General in the CJ were central to this conceptual shift. Examination of key cases and concepts leads to the conclusion that decommodification remains an ideal – the rights are subject to conditions and limitations and may also be derogated from in circumstances. National authorities may limit provision to those who can demonstrate a genuine connection with the society of the member state concerned. It is now relatively accepted that in relation

---

[125]Directive 2003/86 on the right to family reunification
[126]http://www.intrac.org/data/files/resources/121/Briefing-Paper-20-Social-movements-and-citizenship.pdf
[127]William Rogers Brubaker, 'Membership without Citizenship: the economic and social rights of non-citizens', in *Immigration and the Politics of Citizenship in Europe and North America,* University Press of America, 1989
[128]See Baubock, 'Temporary Migrants, Partial Citizenship and Hypermigration', *Critical Review of International Social and Political Philosophy* 14, 2011, p. 665

to access to these rights '. . . the notion of a "structural link" plays a dual pivotal role . . . first, some degree of a structural link is required to trigger the right to equal treatment. Second, the degree of the structural link informs the degree of solidarity owed to the migrant citizen.'[129] Transnational solidarity thus remains constrained.

However, Union citizenship rights are at least no longer residual – as this is the 'fundamental status', they can arise in all cases and be used alongside more specific rights given to workers and the self-employed. The idea put forward in *Skanavi and Chryssanthakopoulos*[130] that Article 21 TFEU could only be used if the case did not fall within the scope of a more specific free movement provision now seems increasingly irrelevant. In *LN*, the Court also seemed to depart from this. The decision differentiated between the 'fundamental freedom' guaranteed in Article 45 and the 'exercise of freedom' conferred by Article 21 TFEU but seemed to conflate these into a single right enshrined in Articles 18, 21 and 45 TFEU to move and reside freely in a host member state without being subjected to direct or indirect discrimination.

The question arises as to whether the CJEU is moving towards a single approach to free movement in the EU The Commission has argued that citizenship separates freedom of movement from 'its functional or instrumental elements (the link with an economic activity or attainment of the internal market) and raises it to the level of a genuinely independent right inherent in the political status of the citizens of the Union'.[131] However Prebil points out that cases such as *de Cuyper* show that Article 21 TFEU is as easily triggered as the other free movement provisions and should, therefore, be constructed analogously to them.[132] Is this conflation a good idea – can things (products and capital) be regulated in the same way as people (workers and citizens)? As Zeliker asks, can human beings with basic needs, feelings and families be treated 'in the same impersonal, economizing manner used for less sacred commercial products'?[133]

---

[129]Yuri Borgmann-Prebil, 'The Rule of reason In European Citizenship', *European Law Journal* 14(3), May 2008, pp. 328–350

[130]C-193/94 *Skanavi and Chryssanthakopoulos* [1996] ECR I-929. See also C-348/96 *Calfa*, C-255/99 *Anna Humer*, C-92/01 *Stylianakis*, C-470/04 *N v kantoor Almelo*

[131]AG Ruiz-Jarabo Colomer in joined cases C-65/95 and C-111/95 *The Queen v Secretary of State for the Home Department, ex parte Mann Singh Shingara and ex parte Abbas Radiom* [1997] ECR I-3343 [34]

[132]Prebil 2008, p. 348

[133]Vivianne Zeliker, *Economic Lives: How Culture Shapes the Economy*, Princeton University Press, 2011, p. 67

Further reading

On EU citizenship law in general:

Alicia Hinarejos, 'Extending Citizenship And The Scope Of EU Law', *Cambridge Law Journal*, 2011, p. 310

N. Reich and S. Harbacevica, 'Citizenship and Family on trial: a fairly optimistic overview of recent court practice with regard to free movement of persons', *Common Market Law Review* 40, 2003 pp. 615–638

Alexander Somek, 'Solidarity decomposed: being and time in European citizenship', *European Law Review* 32(6), 2007, pp. 787–818

On EU citizens and education:

Siofra O'Leary, 'Equal treatment and EU citizens: A new chapter on cross-border educational mobility and access to student financial assistance', *European Law Review* 34(4), 2009, pp. 612–627

On EU citizenship law and children:

C. E. Hall, 'Where Are My Children . . . and My Rights? Parental Rights Termination as a Consequence of Deportation', *Duke Law Journal* 60, 2011, p. 1459

Niamh Nic Shuibhne, '(Some Of) The Kids Are All Right: Comment on McCarthy and Dereci', *Common Market Law Review* 49(1), 2012, p. 349

On third country nationals and EU citizenship law:

Rainer Baubock, 'Temporary Migrants, Partial Citizenship and Hypermigration', *Critical Review of International Social and Political Philosophy* 14, 2011, p. 665

11 Migrant workers

Setting the scene

'On average EU migrants are more likely to be in employment than nationals living in the same country (despite the fact that unemployment rates tend to be relatively higher amongst EU migrants) . . . The overall rate of inactivity among EU migrants has declined between 2005 and 2012 – from 47% to 33%. This happened despite an increase in the rate of unemployment among intra-EU migrants during the economic crisis. Pensioners, students and jobseekers accounted for more than two-thirds of the non-active EU migrant population (71%) in 2012 – although significant differences can be found between countries. Other non-active intra-EU migrants e.g., homemakers fulfilling domestic tasks and other non-active family members of EU nationality account for 25% of the entire non-active EU migrant population. Persons who cannot work due to permanent disabilities represent a relatively small group of migrants (3%). The vast majority of non-active EU migrants (79%) live in economically active households, with only a minority of them living with other household members out of work. The majority of currently non-active migrants have worked before in the current country of residence (64%). Non-active intra-EU migrants do not form a static group. A third of EU migrant jobseekers (32%) were employed one year before. Evidence shows that the vast majority of migrants move to find (or take up) employment.'

Source: Executive Summary, European Commission Study on 'benefit tourism'[1]

1. **Introduction**

2. **Article 45 TFEU**

i. Secondary legislation

3. **The Definition of a 'worker' in EU law**

i. Non-discrimination on grounds of nationality – Article 45(2)

4. **The reach of transnational solidarity in the EU**

5. **Beyond the scope of free movement of workers**

i. Restrictions justified by 'public policy, public security or public health' – Article 45(3)

ii. Employment in the 'public service' – Article 45(4)

iii. Non-migrant workers

6. **Conclusion**

---

[1]http://ec.europa.eu/employment_social/empl_portal/facebook/20131014%20GHK%20study%20web_EU%20migration.pdf

1. Introduction

How does EU law support those who want to work in another member state? People have moved abroad to work for centuries. Labour migration was central to the post-Second World War economic reconstruction of Europe. According to Titmuss,[2] the 'borrowing of human capital' supplemented the 'borrowing of finance' to pay for the provision of welfare – it is cheaper to import expertise rather than invest in education and training. Skilled labour from many parts of the world, including former colonies and Eastern Europe, makes a significant contribution to sustaining the standard of living in Western Europe.

The Treaty of Rome elevated migration to a freedom: free movement of workers is one of the four fundamental freedoms of the internal market. A central goal of the European Union is the creation of a European labour force that is fully mobile, where workers can move from one member state to another with few obstacles in relation to their departure, arrival, residence, settlement and integration. The vision is inspired by the American labour market, where a single social security number facilitates movement of individuals across the 52 states to take up training, work and residency. Such mobility is crucial for achievement of 'ever closer union of peoples'. Free movement is therefore a 'fundamental right for workers and their families'[3]. Inn comparison the Treaty only confers on EU citizens a 'primary and individual right to move and reside freely'[4] in the EU. Working life is fundamental to the organisation of the EU, and the further removed an individual is from this, the weaker the freedom.

Creating an internal labour market of 500 million people is a complicated business, conceptually and practically. Conceptually, it requires the shifting of boundaries around 28 nation states to a single boundary encircling the EU as a whole – 'freedom, as free movement of persons, depends on the boundary that closes off the internal market from an external market'.[5] The internal labour market was initially seen to have advantages for the workers of Europe: the free movement of labour would allow workers to go to the places where their labour was needed and could be put to best use. The larger the EU, the wider – in theory – the options to find work beyond the home country from Portugal to Poland and Ireland to Latvia. Free movement of labour would not only provide opportunities for individuals to live and work abroad, but would reduce unemployment in their places of origin and ensure the optimal allocation of resources.

In practical terms, it requires making provision for workers, and their families, when they are employed or may be jobless. Workers have significant needs that move with them: they need living wages,[6] adequate housing, training and welfare support when they are unable to work or temporarily unemployed. Workers also often have partners,

---

[2]Richard Titmuss, *Commitment to Welfare,* George, Allen & Unwin, 1968, p. 126. For example, by 1986 the US had saved around $4,000 million as a result of not having to fully train medical personnel. Foreign doctors as human capital to the US exceeded the total of US aid to foreign countries.
[3]Regulation 492/2011, Recital (4)
[4]Directive 2004/38, Recital (1)
[5]Hans Lindahl, 'Finding a Place for Freedom, Security and Justice: The European Unity and its Claim to Territorial Unity', *European Law Review* 29, 2004, pp. 461–484, 468
[6]http://www.livingwage.org.uk/

spouses and dependants that must travel with them and have a similar set of needs. They also need to be guaranteed certain rights in order to make migration attractive – the right to equal treatment being perhaps the most fundamental. Thus a corollary to the internal labour market is the internal welfare state which provides social benefits and support for workers and their families: even those able to pursue an international career in the EU[7] may need support if their circumstances change. In order, therefore, to create an internal labour market, workers need not only the relevant skills[8] but also secure rights to enter a country, stay and thrive there.

Yet transnational social support is limited. The member states have remained protective of their welfare systems, and resist facilitating access for migrant workers arguing the existence of rampant 'benefit tourism'. This resistance acts as a hindrance and deterrent.

In contrast to previous periods, migrants are not seen as an 'at risk' group in need of protection but are a risk: migration – or the migration of some – is seen as a security threat.[9] In 2004 the Commission announced that 'the Union must guarantee a high level of security so that freedoms can be exercised to the full'.[10] Securitisation no longer refers solely to defence policy but also to internal freedoms and movement, taking account of people's everyday feelings of security. This link has been criticised by Kostakopoulou because 'when the agenda is dominated by security concerns, the range of policy options becomes narrow'. It also creates a backdrop for anti-immigrant public sentiment and the introduction of policies designed to create a hostile environment.[11]

EU law provisions to create the internal labour market are therefore tied up with a number of flanking issues that focus on welfare and the EU internal security agenda. The task of the provisions in EU law providing free movement to workers is to tackle national rules that hinder movement. Rules obstructing entry and settlement of migrant workers and their families have to be removed or disapplied. As seen from the opening extract, the European Commission study found no evidence of benefit tourism.

This chapter explores three specific themes in relation to the full exercise of free movement of EU workers. First, it will explore the definition of a worker – who gets to enjoy the privilege of an international career in the EU? Is the movement from one state to another a EU norm as it is in the United States? Second, what is the level of transnational solidarity for the economically active, and how does national action help or hinder this? Finally, what situations do not attract the protection of Article 45 TFEU – when can member states undermine the creation of an internal labour market? However, before looking at these themes in detail, the Treaty provision and related secondary law providing rights to the employed will be fully set out.

---

[7]Eures.com is a platform for the exchange of information of job vacancies across the EU.
[8]Patterns of migration in the EU are to some extent determined by the type of jobs predominant in a member state – maritime and fishing skills are useful only in other coastal countries: for example, see for a historical and comparative account of jobs in Europe, Colin Crouch 'Change in European Societies since the 1970s', *West European Politics* 31(1–2), January–March 2008, pp. 14–39
[9]Dora Kostakopoulou, 'The Area of Freedom, Security and Justice and the Political Morality of Migration and Integration', in Hans Lindahl (ed), *A Right to Inclusion and Exclusion? Normative Fault Lines of the EU's Area of Freedom, Security and Justice*, Hart Publishing, 2009, pp.185–207
[10]Communication From The Commission To The Council And The European Parliament, 'Area of Freedom, Security and Justice: Assessment of the Tampere programme and future orientations', Brussels COM(2004) 4002 final, p. 4
[11]Decca Aitkenhead, 'Sarah Teather: "I'm angry there are no alternative voices on immigration"', *Guardian*, 12 July 2013, http://www.theguardian.com/theguardian/2013/jul/12/sarah-teather-angry-voices-immigration

2. Article 45 TFEU

The range of tools provided to create the EU labour force is not extensive. Despite the importance of a mobile labour force to EU integration, this aspiration rests upon Article 45 TFEU, which states that:

---

(1) *Freedom of movement for workers shall be secured within the Union.*

(2) *Such freedom of movement shall entail the abolition of any discrimination based on nationality between workers of the Member States as regards employment, remuneration and other conditions of work and employment.*

(3) *It shall entail the right, subject to limitations justified on grounds of public policy, public security or public health:*

> (a) *to accept offers of employment actually made;*
> (b) *to move freely within the territory of Member States for this purpose;*
> (c) *to stay in a Member State for the purpose of employment in accordance with the provisions governing the employment of nationals of that State laid down by law, regulation or administrative action;*
> (d) *to remain in the territory of a Member State after having been employed in that State, subject to conditions which shall be embodied in regulations to be drawn up by the Commission.*

(4) *The provisions of this Article shall not apply to employment in the public service.*

Article 45 is vertically and horizontally directly effective.[12] This provision is also 'directly applicable in the legal system of every member state'[13] and has a wide reach. It applies to all legal relationships that, due either to the place where they are entered into or where they take effect, can be located within the territory of the Union.[14] It covers different phases of the employment relationship – the pre-employment phase as well as the period of employment and post-employment. It applies to employers in the private and – subject to Article 45(3) – in the public sector.

In addition, it extends to all rules aimed at regulating employment, even those concerning employment agencies. Private organisations and employers can make use of Article 45 in the same way as individual workers. In *ITC*,[15] a private sector recruitment agency, complained that a provision in the German social code breached Article 45 TFEU. It had been contracted to find work for unemployed persons and received a fee of 1,000 euros for each successful placement that was a minimum of three months long, provided at least 15 hours of work per week and was subject to social security contributions in Germany. When ITC found a job for a client in the Netherlands, the authorities refused to pay the fee because the job was not in Germany, thus not subject to German social security contributions.

---

[12]C-36/74 *Walrave and Koch* v *Association Union Cycliste Internationale and others* [1974] ECR 1405
[13]C-167/73 *Commission* v *France* [1974] ECR 359
[14]C-214/94 *Ingrid Boukhalfa* v *Bundesrepublik Deutschland* [1996] ECR I-2253
[15]C-208/05 *ITC Innovative Technology Centre GmbH* v *Bundesagentur für Arbeit*. See also C-379/11 *Caves Krier Frères* [2012] ECR I-0000 [28] and C-202/11 *Anton Las* v *PSA Antwerp NV*

The *Sozialgericht Berlin* (Social Court of Berlin) referred the case to the CJ asking whether the provisions of the national Social Law Code infringed Article 45, and whether ITC could rely on this provision as opposed to Mr Halacz. The CJ, citing *Clear Car Autoservice*[16] replied that:

> Whilst it is established that the right to freedom of movement detailed in Article 39 TEC [45 TFEU] benefits workers, there is nothing that indicates that those rights cannot be relied upon by others . . . In stating that the voucher only applies to jobs found within Germany, the German authorities are deterring (or preventing) agencies and job seekers from finding employment in another Member State. The EC Treaty provides citizens the right to move from their Member State of origin to another in order to work . . . and any national legislation that would deter someone from leaving their State of origin therefore constitutes an obstacle to that freedom.

The CJ described the German legislation as 'tantamount to an outright negation of the freedom of movement' and also held it as an infringement of the freedom to provide services. Although the Agency was not prevented from carrying out its activity, it was less likely to seek opportunities outside of Germany for fear of not getting paid. Therefore, EU law prohibited the German rule.

Even tax rules can be prohibited under Article 45 TFEU if they hinder mobility. In *Commission v Sweden*[17] the CJ held that a Swedish tax rule was incompatible with Article 45. Under Swedish law the deferral of capital gains tax arising from the sale of private property was made dependent upon the purchase of a new property on Swedish soil. The Commission alleged that this was a breach of the free movement of persons and capital and thus infringed *inter alia* Article 45 TFEU. The CJ agreed:

> It is clear that someone who sells their property in Sweden in order to take up the right to freedom of movement enshrined in Articles 39 and 43 TEC [45 and 49 TFEU] and move to another Member State is at a disadvantage compared to a person who chooses not to move country. As this legislation will affect the assets of such a person, it is likely to deter him from moving from Sweden . . .

Likewise social security rules which require recipients to remain resident in the member state can breach Article 45.[18]

Access to the labour market of another member state is meaningless without permission to live in that member state. Residency rules are a significant challenge for non-nationals, thus the right to reside is crucial for EU workers. Residency rights in turn become the basis of equal treatment in access to basic welfare services, such as housing. Article 45 secures for migrant Union workers both a personal right of residence and the right to have their family join them in the host member state. National authorities may not deny workers who are lawfully present the right to stay in their territory. This was seen not only in *Kempf*[19] and *Collins*,[20] but also in *Trojani*[21] and *Ioannidis*.[22] These rights

---

[16] C-350/96 *Clear Car Autoservice v Landeshauptmann von Wien* [1998] ECR I-2521
[17] C-104/06 *Commission v Sweden* [2007] ECR I-671
[18] C-224/02 *Pusa* [2004] ECR I-5763
[19] C-139/85 *Kempf v Staatssecretaris van Justitie* [1986] ECR 1741
[20] C-138/02 *Collins* [2004] ECR I-2703)
[21] C-456/02 *Michel Trojani v Centre public d'aide sociale de Bruxelles (CPAS)* [2004] ECR I-7573
[22] C-258/04 *Ioannidis* (minimex in Belgium) [2005] ECR I-8275

to enter and remain are granted directly by EU law – the national residence permit merely reflects the exercise of those rights:

> The right of nationals of a Member State to enter the territory of another Member State and reside there for the purpose of seeking or pursuing an occupation or rejoining their spouses or families is a right conferred directly by the Treaty or by the provisions adopted for its implementation. The issue of a residence permit does not create the rights guaranteed by Community [Union] law and the lack of a permit cannot affect the exercise of those rights. Therefore, the enjoyment of the rights which a member of the family of a worker of a Member State derives from the provisions of Community [Union] law may not be made subject to the grant of a residence permit which meets certain conditions.[23]

Migrant workers and their family will therefore enjoy a right of residence in another member state for longer than three months if seeking or pursuing employment – in other words, if a worker. It should be noted that this unequivocal residence right can, however, only be directly enjoyed by nationals of the member states – non-EU nationals can derive rights from a family member who is an EU national or from the less generous secondary legislation that has been adopted specifically to regulate their free movement.[24]

i.   Secondary legislation

Article 46 TFEU also gives the European Parliament and the Council of Ministers competence to adopt secondary legislation to bring about free movement of Union workers. Article 47 TFEU highlights migration opportunities for younger workers and Article 48 TFEU makes provision for the introduction of measures to coordinate social security benefit systems for these workers and the self-employed. Self-employed persons are covered in Article 56 TFEU (see Chapter XII).

It is under Article 46 that secondary legislation laying out the conditions for free movement of both workers and citizens has been adopted. Rights had developed in a piecemeal fashion since 1964, resulting in the existence of a variety of regulations and directives dealing with different aspects of free movement.[25] The legal framework is now less cluttered and there are two main pieces of legislation to bear in mind. In 2004, the Citizenship Directive[26] was adopted which amended Regulation 1612/68 and repealed Directives 90/364, 90/365 and 93/96 as well as Directives 64/221, 68/360, 72/194, 73/148, 75/34 and 75/35. Regulation 1612/68 subsequently went through reform and has now been recast as Regulation 492/2011.[27] The core rules that must be implemented into national law are therefore laid out in Regulation 492/2011 and Directive 2004/38.

The Citizenship Directive 2004/38 provides rights for both workers and citizens and their families – the CD describes free movement as a 'fundamental right for workers and

[23]Joined cases C-389/87 and 390/87 *G.B.C. Echternach and A. Moritz v Minister van Onderwijs en Wetenschappe* [1989] ECR 723
[24]Directive 2003/109 – see C-571/10 *Kamberaj*, C-40/11 *Iida*
[25]Directive 64/221 – outlines derogations from free movement; Directive 68/360 – conditions of entry and residence of workers and self-employed; Regulation No 1612/68 – substantive rights and entitlements of workers and their families; Regulation No 1250/70 – protects rights of the worker and family to remain in territory of member state (in event of retirement, incapacity, etc.) under conditions; Directives 90/364, 90/365 and 93/96
[26]Directive 2004/38/EC of the EP and Council of 29 April 2004 on the right of citizens of the Union and their family members to move and reside freely within the territory of the member states, OJ L158/77 2004
[27]Regulation No 492/2011 of the EP and CM of 5 April 2011 on the freedom of movement of workers within the Union, OJ L141/1 2011

their families'. Family reunion is integral to the internal labour market – workers are unlikely to seek opportunities to work abroad or commit to this if families must stay behind. Free movement of workers can only be a reality if there is free movement of workers families. Thus under EU law the families of workers, and members of their households also enjoy rights to equal treatment – as far as the CJ is concerned, this 'contributes to their integration in the society of the host country, in accordance with the aims of the freedom of movement for workers'.[28] This includes the right to enter and reside, take up jobs and education.

Further rights are laid out in Regulation 492/2011.[29] The sole purpose of Regulation 492/2011 is to secure free movement of workers within the EU. It clearly lays out a right for member state nationals to take up and pursue an activity as an employed person in another member state.[30] They are eligible for employment on the same terms as nationals and to any assistance that would be offered to nationals to find employment.[31] A migrant EU worker enjoys equality in relation to pay, dismissal and re-employment,[32] as well as the same social and tax advantages as national workers,[33] access to vocational training,[34] trade union membership[35] and perhaps most importantly, housing.[36] Children enjoy equal access to education at all levels on the same basis as children of that member state.[37] As long as an EU migrant has the status of a worker.

VIEWPOINT

To what extent can the EU emulate a US labour market model? What drives people to move to another country? If you did so, what would be your major concerns?

3. The definition of a 'worker' in Article EU law

An EU national is the migrant worker upon whom the Treaty bestows rights.[38] A third country national can derive rights from the EU national or secure them directly via secondary legislation on third country nationals.[39] Children enjoy independent citizenship rights. In order to enjoy any of the rights provided in Article 45(1), Regulation 492/2011 and Directive 2004/38, the EU national must simply show that s/he is a worker – it is this status that regulates access to free movement as a fundamental right.

Given the centrality of this concept to the creation of a single labour market, it is perhaps surprising that neither Article 45 TFEU nor the secondary instruments define it. It was the CJ that held this to be a Union rather than a national concept and imposed a

---

[28]*Echternach and Moritz*
[29]Updated Regulation No 1612/68
[30]Article 1
[31]Article 5
[32]Article 7(1)
[33]Article 7(2)
[34]Article 7(3)
[35]Article 8
[36]Article 9
[37]Article 10
[38]See C-83/11 *Rahman*.
[39]These are limited – see C-571/10 *Kamberaj*.

single meaning. It is likely that left to the member states, there would now be 28 different definitions adopted according to the specificities of each labour market and welfare system. As the CJ said in *Hoekstra*:

> If the definition of this term were a matter within the competence of national law, it would therefore be possible for each member state to modify the meaning of the concept of' migrant worker' and to eliminate at will the protection afforded by the Treaty to certain categories of person.[40]

This was reconfirmed in *Allonby*[41] where the CJ emphasised that: 'the term worker . . . cannot be defined by reference to the legislation of the Member States but has a Community meaning. Moreover, it cannot be interpreted restrictively.' According to AG Wahl, it is a matter of primary EU law that cannot be 'meaningfully limited by a provision of secondary law'.[42]

VIEWPOINT

Do you agree with this? Should legislation have been used?

From 1963, the CJ has introduced a broad interpretation which encompasses full- and part-time workers in the public and private sectors on any type of contract, whether permanent, temporary, fixed or atypical. The open approach adopted by the Court may not have been the preference of member states concerned with benefit shopping but it has allowed the European labour market to respond to new types of working arrangements – such as 'zero-hours' contracts – emerging in the ever-changing global economy. The recognition of low paid, ad hoc, unskilled work also enables women and minority workers to access the rights in the Treaty – these groups are more flexible, will accept lower pay, less privileged working conditions, part-time contracts and shift work. However, while it is a EU concept, there is no single definition of a worker in EU law: as the CJ has said, 'it varies according to the area in which the definition is to be applied'.[43]

In *Levin*[44] income was eliminated as a factor in the determination of who is a worker. Mrs Levin, a British national married to a non-EU national, applied for a permit to reside in the Netherlands. The permit was refused on the basis of Dutch legislation, on the ground that she was not engaged in a gainful occupation in the Netherlands – she had only a minimal income to support herself. As a result she was not a 'favoured EEC citizen'

---

[40]C-75/63 *Hoekstra v Bestuur der Bedrijfsvereniging voor Detailhandel en Ambachten* (BBDA) [1964] ECR 177
[41]*Allonby v Accrington & Rossendale College and Others* [2004] ICR 1328
[42]AG opinion in C-507/12 *Jessy St. Prix v Secretary of State for Work and Pensions* [30]
[43]C-393/10 *Dermod Patrick O'Brien v Ministry of Justice, formerly Department for Constitutional Affairs* [30] (on whether a judicial office-holder was a 'worker' – it decided in the affirmative [42] but in *The President of the Methodist Conference v Percy* [2013] UKSC. The Supreme Court held that priests are not 'employees' and thus not workers (see also *Percy v Board of National Mission of the Church of Scotland* [2005] UKHL 73, [2006] 2 AC 28)); C-85/96 *Martínez Sala* [1998] ECR I-2691 [31] and C-256/01 *Allonby* [2004] ECR I-873 [63]
[44]C-53/81 *Levin*

within the meaning of that legislation. The CJ overruled the Dutch authorities: the key factors were whether the person concerned pursued an activity that is:

> effective and genuine activity as an employed person. Once this condition is satisfied, the motives which may have prompted the worker to seek employment in the member state concerned are of no account and must not be taken into consideration.

The remuneration does not have to be in the form of wages: in *Steymann*[45] the claimant lived in a religious community where he was entitled to lodging and pocket money, but not to formal wages, in return for services as a handyman. In this case the Court recognised that the work constituted an effective and genuine activity as Steymann undertook jobs that had an economic relevance for the community – if he did not do them, somebody would have to be hired to do these tasks. The fact that the employment relationship is unconventional does not mean that it is not an effective economic activity. The number of hours worked is also irrelevant to the definition of a worker.[46] In *Wippel*,[47] an Austrian part-time worker whose contract stipulated that she was not entitled to be offered any minimum amount of work, nor was she bound to accept work if it was offered, was held to be a worker. Those on zero-hour contracts are therefore workers under EU law.

The meaning of an 'employed person' was clarified in *Lawrie Blum*.[48] Blum, a British national, trained as a teacher in Germany. She was, however, refused admission to the preparatory training required to pass the subsequent state examination. Without this, she could not complete her professional training as a teacher in a state school or qualify for appointment in a private school. The issue was that trainee teachers in Germany become civil servants and enjoy advantages associated with that status. According to the applicable national law, admission was restricted therefore to German nationals, unless a specific derogation had been made.

The German court argued that Lawrie-Blum was not a worker under Article 45. The CJ reminded the German court that this was a 'Community concept' that was to be interpreted broadly and in accordance with:

> [17] . . . objective criteria which distinguish the employment relationship by reference to the rights and duties of the persons concerned. The essential feature of an employment relationship, however, is that for a certain period of time a person performs services for and under the direction of another person in return for which he receives remuneration

As these criteria were satisfied – as a trainee teacher, Lawrie Blum was under the supervision of the school; her work and working hours were determined by the school; the provision of lessons were of economic value to the school; and remuneration was provided–so in line with *Levin* and *Kempf*, the hours worked and low pay were irrelevant considerations, provided that the activities performed were effective and genuine. Consequently:

> [22] . . . The reply to the first part of the question must be that a trainee teacher who, under the direction and supervision of the school authorities, is undergoing a period of service in preparation for the teaching profession during which he provides services

---

[45] C-196/87 *Steymann v Staatssecretaris van Justitie* [1988] ECR 6159
[46] C-139/85 *Kempf v Staatssecretaris van Justitie* [1986] ECR 1741; C357/89 *Raulin v Minister van Onderwijs en Wetenschappen* [1992] ECR I-1027
[47] C-313/02 *Wippel v Peek & Cloppenburg GmbH & Co KG* [2005] ICR 1604
[48] C-66/85 *Lawrie Blum v Land Baden-Württemberg* [1986] ECR 2121

by giving lessons and receives remuneration must be regarded as a worker within the meaning of Article 48(1) of the EEC Treaty, irrespective of the legal nature of the employment relationship.

This tripartite test of an employment relationship – if a) services performed are of an economic value; b) the services are supervised; and c) remuneration (of any level) is provided for the services received – was confirmed in the case of *Collins* and *van Delft:*[49]

> the concept of 'worker', within the meaning of Article 48 [now 45] of the Treaty and of Regulation No 1612/68, has a specific Community meaning and must not be interpreted narrowly. Any person who pursues activities which are real and genuine, to the exclusion of activities on such a small scale as to be regarded as purely marginal and ancillary, must be regarded as a 'worker'. The essential feature of an employment relationship is, according to that case-law, that for a certain period of time a person performs services for and under the direction of another person in return for which he receives remuneration.

Workers benefit from this inclusive approach, but there is a downside to it: it validates and entrenches flexible employment relationships that are beneficial to business in terms of both costs and profits but may disadvantage workers. – Flexible working arrangements allow employers to structure their labour requirements around peak trading times and pass the cost of business instability on to the workforce: part time and short-term contracts release employers from the burden of health and insurance contributions, which boosts profits by reducing wage related costs. The definition is therefore a double-edged sword: it enables more workers to access the privileges of living and working in one of the wealthiest regions of the world but in doing so consigns them to work that is both highly casual and repetitive, provides no long-term security, and may be under- or unprotected by legislation.

Flexi-jobs have a long-term impact upon benefit status and consequences for family life, especially family reunification, and life during retirement from the workforce. The low-income status as a worker will result in low income during a number of crucial stages in the life cycle such as pregnancy, motherhood and old age. Osberg *et al.* point out that:

> the people who are forced to rely on low paid, insecure and part time work are also often forced to rely on transfer payments through unemployment insurance or social assistance; indeed whole industries are becoming dependent on the idea that transfer payments are there to finance their work force during the times when they are not needed by firms.[50]

In addition, the emphasis on 'the receipt of remuneration'[51] is exclusive. For all its breadth, the centrality of income per se to the definition excludes a group who have never been recognised for their labour – carers, who are unpaid, do not enjoy rights under Article 45 TFEU.[52] Neither do workers who have jobs created by sheltered employment, such as those with disabilities. It was decided in *Bettray*[53] that a person undertaking

---

[49]C-138/02 *Collins;* C-345/09 *van Delft and Others* [2010] ECR I-0000 [89]. See also *Kurz v Land Baden-Württemberg* [2002] ECR I-10691 para 32; *Allonby v Accrington & Rossendale College and Others* [2004] ICR 1328
[50]L. Osberg, F. Wien and J. Grude, *Vanishing Jobs – Canada's Changing Workplace,* James Lorimer and Co., 1990, p. 96
[51]Advocate General in *Wippel v Peek and Cloppenburg GmbH & Co KG* [2005] ICR 1604
[52]See Nicole Busby, *A Right to Care? Unpaid Work in European Employment Law,* Oxford University Press, 2011
[53]C-344/87 *Bettray v Staatssecretaris van Justitie* [1989] ECR 1621

rehabilitation work under a Social Emploment Programme does not count as a worker. The CJ held that where the employment relationship is merely ancilliary to wider social objectives, it is outside the scope of Article 45. Thus work under a rehabilitation programme is not a genuine and effective economic activity as its primary purpose is preparation for reintegration into the labour market. This can exclude millions of workers with a disability.[54] Unlike in *Steymann,* the work conducted by *Bettray* did not have an economic purpose. Thus the definition bridges the traditional public/private divide between the state and non-state sector, but perpetuates the divide between the public arena of paid work from the private arena of unpaid labour in the home home and excludes those whose labour is under-valued.[55]

ANALYSIS OF THE LAW

Who is included and who is excluded in the definition of a worker? How can it be improved?

The Citizenship Directive clarifies that under conditions jobseekers[56] who are temporarily unavailable for work enjoy this status. Article 7 CD places the case law under Article 45 TFEU on a statutory basis but does not confine the definition of a 'worker' to its contents. Retention of the status of worker is therefore not limited to the situations listed in Article 7(3)(d), such as illness or accident. In *Jessy St Prix,*[57] the CJ held that a pregnant worker temporarily unable to be economically active due to pregnancy-related incapacity also retained the status of a worker and thus remained eligible for income support. The UK authorities had refused income support to Ms St Prix because she voluntarily left her job due to pregnancy complications, using the literal argument that as she was not a 'worker' she therefore had no right to reside.

a) Trainees and students

In accordance with Regulation 492/2011, workers and their families gain not only valuable rights of entry and residence but also become eligible for equal treatment in relation to access to employment and training, welfare assistance and social benefits. The definition of a 'worker' includes those undertaking vocational training and even – under some circumstances – students. Both higher education and university education constitute vocational training.[58] The central question is whether the training constitutes an effective and genuine activity? Training for rehabilitation does not but training in relation to a specific trade or profession does. In *Gravier*[59] the CJ held that:

> Any form of education which prepares for a qualification for a particular profession, trade or employment or which provides the necessary skills for such a profession, trade

---

[54]10 million people in the UK have a disability – see Debbie Andalo, 'Tapping into the talent pool', *The Guardian*, 13 July 2013
[55]S. Okin, 'Gender, the public and the private', in D. Held (ed), *Political Theory Today*, Polity, 1991. However, carers can find some enjoyment of free movement under the citizenship provisions.
[56]C-292/89 *Antonissen*
[57]C-507/12 *Jessy St Prix v Secretary of State for Work and Pensions*
[58]C-24/86 *Blaizot v Université de Liège and others* [1988] ECR 379 [15–20]; C-42/87 *Commission v Belgium* [1988] ECR 5445 [7–8]; and C-147/03 *Commission v Austria* [2005] ECR I-5969 [33]
[59]C-293/83 *Gravier v City of Liege* [1985] ECR 593

or employment is vocational training, whatever the age and the level of training of the pupils or students, even if the training programme includes an element of general education. The term 'vocational training' therefore includes courses in strip cartoon art provided by an institution of higher art education.

Thus it is not necessary to actually be in employment to qualify as an EU worker – training in the context of an occupation, such as sandwich courses, also falls within this concept. As now stated in the Citizenship Directive,[60] there must be a clear link between the training and occupation for the full range of workers' rights to be enjoyed. This provision was influenced by judicial decisions. In *Brown*[61] a migrant Union worker from Scotland left casual employment in France to pursue full-time studies that were not in any way linked to his former employment. As a result he forfeited some of the rights associated with the status of a worker. In this case the employment was held to be ancilliary, that is not formally linked to subsequent study as preparation for employment. In *Bernini*,[62] a worker who left employment to take up full-time studies, retained the status of a worker because there was a link between the previous employment and the studies undertaken. Cases such as LN suggest that the national court may no longer require evidence to prove that the trainee has worked long enough.

As persons on vocational training courses are also under certain conditions workers, they enjoy the right to equal treatment with nationals undergoing the same training. This can have financial implications: in *Gravier,* it meant that the claimant did not have to pay a registration fee imposed only upon non-nationals – this was discrimination contrary to the Treaty:

> The imposition on students who are nationals of other member states of a charge, a registration fee or the so-called 'minerval' as a condition of access to vocational training , where the same fee is not imposed on students who are nationals of the host member state, constitutes discrimination on grounds of nationality contrary to Article 7 of the Treaty.

In *Lair,*[63] retention of the status of a worker gave the claimant access to a maintenance grant usually reserved for nationals. The CJ defined this as a social advantage within the meaning of Article 7(2) Regulation 1612/68 – as such it could not be withheld from a worker:

> A grant awarded for maintenance and training with a view to the pursuit of university studies leading to a professional qualification constitutes a social advantage within the meaning of Article 7(2) of Regulation No 1612/68. A national of another Member State who undertakes university studies in the host State leading to a professional qualification, after having engaged in occupational activity in that State, must be regarded as having retained his status as a worker and is entitled as such to the benefit of Article 7 (2) of Regulation No 1612/68, provided that there is a link between the previous occupational activity and the studies in question. The host Member State cannot make the right to social advantages provided for in Article 7 (2) of Regulation

---

[60]The conditions for retention of the status are now set out in CD Article 7(3) (d).
[61]C-197/86 *Brown v Secretary of State for Scotland* [1988] ECR 3205
[62]C-3/90 *Bernini v Minister van Onderwijs en Wetenschappen* [1992] ECR I-1071
[63]C-39/86 *Lair* [1988] ECR 3161

No 1612/68 conditional upon a minimum period of prior occupational activity within the territory of that State.

The situation is less clear for students. A person who migrates for the purpose of study but satisfies the *Lawrie Blum* criteria cannot automatically be deemed a non-worker – in *LN*[64] the CJ ruled that enrolment at an establishment of study did not *automatically* preclude a Union citizen from having the status of 'worker' within the meaning of Article 45 TFEU and consequently from being entitled to the social advantages linked to that status. This case arose when a student applied for education assistance granted to 'workers' under Danish law. The national court could not exclude the student immediately but was required to investigate the nature of the employment undertaken to ascertain whether the status of worker was appropriate.

As was held in *Ninni Orasche*,[65] 'factors relating to the conduct of the person concerned before and after the period of employment are not relevant in establishing the status of worker' within the meaning of Article 45 TFEU. The status is not contingent upon any kind of original intent. It was stressed that the fact that the

> 'person had entered the territory of the host member state with the principal intention of pursuing a course of study was not relevant for determining whether he was a "worker" within the meaning of Article 45 TFEU and, accordingly, whether he was entitled to that aid under the same terms as a national of the host member state pursuant to Article 7(2) of Regulation No 492/2011'.

This means that students who simultaneously pursue effective and genuine employment activities can enjoy the status of 'worker' under Article 45 TFEU and the benefits associated with that status, such as maintenance aid for studies which is granted to the nationals of that member state.

Thus to summarise – the definition of a worker centres on genuine and paid economic activity, which excludes volunteers, carers and other persons, predominantly women, whose work can be described as a labour of love. Nonetheless, the definition is broad, even allowing different categories of persons to retain their status as a worker or self-employed person when they are jobless.

APPLYING THE LAW

Is it possible for an Erasmus student to be a worker under EU law?

---

ii.   Non-discrimination on grounds of nationality – Article 45(2)

The status of worker protects the holder from discrimination on grounds of nationality – this is the key privilege afforded to migrant EU workers. This is a specific application of the principle in Article 18 TFEU. It is the single most important right enjoyed by workers and their families, guaranteeing equal treatment in relation to 'employment, remuneration

---

[64]C-46/12 *LN v Styrelsen for Videregående Uddannelser og Uddannelsesstøtt* [2013] WLR (D) 77
[65]C-413/01 [28]

and other conditions of work and employment, as well as the right to move freely within the Union to pursue activities as employed persons'.[66] It applies to 'direct' and 'indirect' discrimination.

Direct discrimination refers to less favourable treatment on the grounds of nationality that is overt. An example of this is a provision in the French Maritime Code requiring a proportion of ship crew to be French.[67] Another example is a rule stating that members of a cycling team must be of the same nationality.[68] In *Walrave & Koch* Article 45 TFEU was used to challenge rules of cycling organisations, the Union Cycliste Internationale and the Dutch and Spanish cycling federations. The rules in question mandated that in certain medium-distance races, the two members of the cycling team (pacemaker and stayer) had to be of the same nationality. A challenge to this rule was brought by two Dutch nationals who normally took part in such races as pacemakers. The rule was found to be discriminatory, opening the way for cyclists to be employed in multinational teams. Rules refusing benefits to non-nationals, when national workers in similar situations would receive them, are also direct discrimination contrary to Article 45[69] as are national rules that only compensate recruitment agencies for placing unemployed persons in a job in Germany but not elsewhere.[70]

Indirect discrimination arises from rules which are neutral, as they apply to nationals and non-nationals, but in fact place non-nationals at a disadvantage. In order for a measure to be indirectly discriminatory, 'it is not necessary for it to have the effect of placing all the nationals of the Member State in question at an advantage or of placing at a disadvantage only nationals of other Member States, but not nationals of the State in question'.[71] An example of such covert discrimination was found in *Ugliola*,[72] where the neutral criterion for benefits (military service in Bundeswehr) could be more easily fulfilled by nationals. It was clear that few non-Germans would be able to satisfy this. Another example was found in *Sotgiu*,[73] where those employed in Germany received a higher separation allowance than those located abroad at the time of their initial employment. Again, fewer non-nationals would qualify for the higher allowance under this rule.

Indirect discrimination can be justified where it satisfies the proportionality test – pursuit of a legitimate aim using means best suited to achieve the declared ends. In *Lyyski*,[74] the Swedish authorities refused a Swedish teacher access to a vocational training course because he taught at a Swedish school in Finland. Under the STT Regulation, a requirement of access to the training was employment in a school in Sweden. It did not take the CJ long to determine that this placed those exercising the right to free movement at a disadvantage.[75] However, although the application of such legislation was liable to restrict the freedom of movement for workers, the CJ continued that 'it could avoid the prohibition under Article 39 EC [45 TFEU] if it pursued a legitimate aim compatible with the Treaty and were justified by pressing reasons of public interest' and beyond that if

---

[66]Regulation 492/2011, Recital (2)
[67]C-167/73 *Commission v France* [1974] ECR 359
[68]C-36/74 *Walrave and Koch v Association Union Cycliste Internationale and others* [1974] ECR 1405
[69]C-85/96 *Martínez Sala v Freistaat Bayern* [1998] ECR I-2691 (pregnancy benefits); C-184/99 *Grzelczyk* (non-contributory allowance)
[70]C-208/05 *ITC Innovative Technology Centre GmbH v Bundesagentur für Arbeit*
[71]See, to that effect, C-388/01 *Commission v Italy* [2003] ECR I 721 [14]
[72]C-15/69 *Ugliola* [1969] ECR 363
[73]C-152/73 *Sotgiu v Deutsche Bundespost* [1974] ECR 153
[74]C-40/05 *Lyyski* [2007] ECR I-99
[75][37]

the 'application of that measure would still have to be such as to ensure achievement of the aim in question and not go beyond what is necessary for that purpose'.[76]

The national authorities claimed the aim of the rule was preservation or improvement of the education system. This was held to be legitimate – the STT Regulation addressed a national shortage of teachers – but was the measure proportionate? The information before the CJ did not clarify whether the practical element of the training was essential but the conclusion was that if, as a matter of principle, the application made by *Lyyski* was rejected solely because he was not employed in a Swedish school, this might:

[46] . . . in fact prove to be contrary to the objectives pursued and disproportionate, particularly if, when all equivalent applications from teachers employed in Swedish schools have been able to be fulfilled, the obstacles to completion of the practical part of the training course can be removed without difficulty. In such circumstances, it cannot be excluded that the manner in which the STT Regulation is applied goes beyond what is necessary to attain the objective of preserving and improving the Swedish education system.

It was left to the national court to decide if application of the STT Regulation was proportionate to the objective pursued.

In contrast, a language requirement for teachers in Ireland was held proportionate by the CJ as it was a part of state policy to promote the Irish language. In *Groener,*[77] the employer imposed – in line with government policy – a language requirement upon teachers which precluded non-Irish teachers from gaining employment in Irish schools. As the rule was not overtly discriminatory, the CJ undertook an examination of the role of teachers in the educational process, and their role in implementing this policy. It found the aim legitimate and the means proportionate. Where the discrimination is unintentional, states have a wider scope to defend national rules. Indirect discrimination was also proportionate where discrimination is necessary to maintain coherence of a financial system.[78] A residence requirement for studying finance in the Netherlands was, however, seen as disproportionate.[79] Yet more recently, AG Mengozzi has suggested that such a requirement should be seen as proportionate in the context of Luxembourg, where up to 44 per cent of workers are non-nationals.[80]

It should, however, be noted that the concept of discrimination is not essential for a national rule to contravene the Treaties – rules which are deemed a hindrance or obstacle to the internal labour market will also breach Article 45. It was a football case that highlighted this broader application of Article 45 TFEU. The transfer rules regulating international football stipulated that a player had to be released from one club before he could play for another. Release is dependent upon payment of a transfer fee. Non-payment of a transfer fee would therefore jeopardise a footballer's career. This was the case for national and non-national players, thus the rule was neutral in law and in fact. Despite this, the non-origin specific rule was held to be an excessive hindrance/obstruction to free

---

[76]See, *inter alia*, C-19/92 *Kraus* [1993] ECR I-1663 [32]; C-415/93 *Bosman and others* [1995] ECR I-4921 [104]; C-224/01 *Köbler* [2003] ECR I-10239 [77]; and C-109/04 *Kranemann* [2005] ECR I-2421 [33]
[77]C-379/87 *Groener v Minister for Education and City of Dublin Vocational Education Committee* [1989] ECR 3967
[78]C-300/90 *Commission v Belgium* [1992] ECR I-305
[79]C-542/09 *Commission v Netherlands*
[80]C-20/12 *Elodie Giersch*

movement and thus contrary to the Treaty.[81] The issues in this case did not stop with the transfer arrangements. The '3+2 rule' also breached free movement law. This rule regulated the players fielded by any individual team – for any match only three foreign and two acclimatised players were to be fielded. The existence of a quota based upon nationality was found to be directly discriminatory. There may have been a legitimate reason for these sporting rules and had they been formulated differently, the decision may have changed. The type of organisation is less important than the nature of the rule. The CJ takes a gentler approach where rules are not designed to be discriminatory, and if they are indirectly discriminatory they can be justified.

4. The reach of transnational solidarity in the EU

In a nation state, welfare provision would be the corollary to the labour market. The purpose of the welfare state is to provide for workers when they are unable to work due to illness, injury or temporary joblessness. States traditionally extend this protection to nationals by virtue of the fact that they are workers, or simply because, due to their citizenship they are seen to 'belong' to the national territory. Neither the Treaty nor secondary legislation establish a common scheme of social security or welfare: different national social security schemes continue to exist but EU law requires these schemes to be coordinated[82] when, for example, benefits are being calculated. Thus in *Salgado Gonzalez*[83] the Spanish authorities were precluded from excluding periods of working life spent in another member state when calculating the retirement pension of a Spainard who had exercised free movement rights to work in Portugal. Even though the tax contributions were paid in Portugal, Regulation No 1408/71[84] requires the pension be calculated as if she had carried out her entire working life in Spain:

> . . . according to settled case law, member states retained the power to organise their social security schemes. Therefore, in the absence of harmonisation at EU level, it was for the legislation of each member state to determine, in particular, the conditions for entitlement to benefits. In exercising those powers, member states had none the less to comply with the law of the European Union and, in particular, with the provisions of the FEU Treaty giving every citizen of the Union the right to move and reside within the territory of the member states. In the instant case, contrary to the requirements of Article 46(2) of the Regulation, the theoretical amount of the applicant's retirement pension was not calculated as it she had carried out the entirety of her professional life in Spain. If the national legislation had set out adjustment mechanisms for the method of calculation of the theoretical amount of the pension in order to take account of the exercise by the worker of his right to freedom of movement, the situation would have been different.

This undermines the traditional philosophy of welfare as it decouples tax contributions from eligibility for income related benefits such as a retirement pension. However, any

---

[81]C-415/93 *Bosman*
[82]C-212/06 *Government of the French Community and Walloon Government* [2008] ECR I-1683 [43], and C-503/09 *Stewart* [2011] ECR I-0000 [75]
[83]C-282/11 *Salgado González v Instituto Nacional de la Seguridad Social (INSS) and another* [2013] WLR (D) 80
[84]Article 45(1)

other decision would severely undermine free movement and make the creation of an internal labour market impossible.

Beyond this fundamental non-discrimination, for migrant EU workers, gainful employment alone regulates access to welfare and benefits – it provides evidence of a link to the member state:

> [65] As regards migrant workers and frontier workers, the fact that they have participated in the employment market of a Member State establishes, in principle, a sufficient link of integration with the society of that Member State, allowing them to benefit from the principle of equal treatment, as compared with national workers, as regards social advantages. That principle is applicable not only to all employment and working conditions, but also to all the advantages which, whether or not linked to a contract of employment, are generally granted to national workers primarily because of their objective status as workers or by virtue of the mere fact of their residence on the national territory.[85]

> [66] The link of integration arises from, inter alia, the fact that, through the taxes which he pays in the host Member State by virtue of his employment, the migrant worker also contributes to the financing of the social policies of that State and should profit from them under the same conditions as national workers. 67 That conclusion is borne out by the third recital in the preamble to Regulation No 1612/68, according to which the mobility of labour within the Community must be one of the means by which the worker is guaranteed the possibility of improving his living and working conditions and promoting his social advancement, while helping to satisfy the requirements of the economies of the Member States.[86]

There is no 'European Welfare State' or EU system of social security as such but the extension of social advantages and welfare benefits to migrant Union workers creates a rudimentary internal welfare state, which provides equal treatment in relation to, for example, employment allowances and unemployment benefits, pregnancy and healthcare benefits, housing and education.

What level of social assistance can workers expect from the national welfare system in their time of need? These must at least be equal to those received by national workers. Thus in *Sotgui* it was deemed indirectly discriminatory to pay a lower separation allowance to those workers situated abroad at the time of their initial employment – clearly more Germans than non-Germans would be able to satisfy this condition. Similarly in *Ugliola* – a national rule providing employment security to conscripted members of the German army must provide the same security to conscripts of other armies.

In *Martinez Sala*[87] it was found contrary to EU law to require a resident non-national to produce a formal residence permit in order to receive a child-raising allowance, whereas a national was only required to be permanently or ordinarily resident in that Member State. Ms Martinez Sala had lived in Germany for over 20 years, and had been in employment for much of that time but had also experienced spells of unemployment. Despite the length of her stay in Germany, the basis of her residency was a series of residence permits the last of which was due to expire in April 1995. She had applied for a

---

[85]See C-85/96 *Martínez Sala* [1998] ECR I 2691 [25] and *Commission v Germany* [39]
[86]C-542/09 *Commission v the Netherlands*
[87]C-85/96 Martinez Sala

child benefit during a period when she did not have a permit but was lawfully in Germany. Her application was refused on the ground that she did not have German nationality, a residence entitlement or a residence permit.

The lawfully resident family members of migrant Union workers also enjoy access to social benefits in the host member state. Access to benefits, such as education, is possible even after the migrant worker has left. In *Echternach and Moritz*[88] the son of an employee at the European Space Agency, a worker within the meaning of Article 45, won a right to complete his education when his father returned home. The child was unable to transfer back into the educational system in the home member state – he therefore had to stay without his family but were the national authorities obliged to allow this? The CJ said yes:

> When, after his father's return to the Member State of origin, the child of such a worker cannot continue his studies there because of the non-coordination of school diplomas and has no choice but to return to the country where he attended school in order to continue studying, he retains the status of member of a worker's family within the meaning of Regulation No 1612/68.

Integration would be thwarted if children did not have the possibility of successfully pursuing and completing their education in another member state, when this is interrupted by labour migration.

Echternach and Moritz clarifies that assistance for maintenance and education provided to migrant workers and their families constitutes a social advantage. This applies to migrant workers residing in a host member state and frontier workers employed in that member state while residing in another member state.[89] Under Regulation 492/2011, a member state must also provide migrant Union workers with the opportunity to pursue education and training in another member state if its own nationals enjoy this option.[90] Member states may not install rules that make it harder for migrant workers to satisfy eligibility citeria than national workers.

In 2007, a complaint was made to the Commission that the Dutch government had done this. A provision of Dutch law stipulated a residence requirement which made student eligibility for financial support for programmes outside of the Netherlands ('portable funding') subject to lawful residence in the Netherlands for at least three of the six years preceding the enrolment for higher education.[91] It was clearly easier for nationals to fulfil this criterion than non-nationals. The Commission brought this issue before the CJ, which declared it indirect discrimination incompatible with Article 45(2) TFEU and Article 7(2) of Regulation No 1612/68:

> [37] . . . it should be noted that the equal treatment rule laid down both in Article 45 TFEU and in Article 7 of Regulation No 1612/68 prohibits not only overt discrimination on grounds of nationality but also all covert forms of discrimination which,

---

[88] C-389/87 *Echternach & Moritz* [1989] ECR 723
[89] C-213/05 *Geven* [2007] ECR I-16347[15]
[90] Case 235/87 *Matteucci* [1988] ECR 5589 [16], and C-308/89 *di Leo* [1990] ECR I-4185 [14]
[91] C-542/09 *Commission v The Netherlands*. See F. De Witte, 'Who funds the mobile student? Shedding some light on the normative assumptions underlying EU free movement law: Commission v Netherlands', *Common Market Law Review* 50, 2013, pp. 203–216

through the application of other criteria of differentiation, lead in fact to the same result.[92]

[38] That is the position, in particular, in the case of a measure – such as that at issue in the present case – which requires a specified period of residence, in that it primarily operates to the detriment of migrant workers and frontier workers who are nationals of other Member States, in so far as non-residents are usually non-nationals.[93]

It was deemed irrelevant that the same rule might also operate to the detriment of some nationals.

The CJ noted the different logic informing access to study finance for workers and economically inactive citizens, as was the case in *Bidar*[94] and *Förster*.[95] In such cases, the Court stresses the need for the applicant to demonstrate a certain degree of social rather than economic integration into the host member state in order to receive a maintenance grant. Workers already do this by virtue of their employment, in particular the taxes that they pay to contribute to the social policies of the host state – thus in *Elodie Giersch*[96] the children of frontier workers could not be treated differently to other workers.

This distinction between workers and citizens is also expressed in Article 24 CD – Article 24(1) provides that all EU citizens residing on the basis of the CD in the territory of the host member state are to enjoy equal treatment 'within the scope of the Treaty' but Article 24(2) provides that a member state may withhold specific forms of study finance and benefits to those who are not recognised as workers or self-employed and their families.

Yet there are limits to transnational solidarity – *Samin and Dano*[97] emphasise that the worker must be *available* to work. Mr Samin, born in Iraq but arrived in England in 2005 bearing Austrian nationality. He worked for no more than 10 months in total, until he lost his job in 2006. He was diagnosed with longstanding clinical depression, arising from traumatic experiences during his time in the Iraqi army. In 2007 he attempted suicide and in 2010 was diagnosed as being a high risk of self-harm. In addition, he suffered from diabetes, high blood pressure and gall stones. Samin had received treatment under the National Health Service, housing benefit to pay his rent as well as jobseeker's allowance and incapacity benefit. It was against this background of despair that he sought to avail himself of social housing under the Housing Act 1996: a homeless person who is a migrant worker also has a right to housing provision on the same basis as a national worker.

The first matter considered by the national judge was whether he was eligible to receive this support as a non-national: the test depended upon whether Mr Samin was a 'qualified person' as defined by the UK Immigration Regulations 2006. This Regulation transposes aspects of the CD 2004/38 into national law, including the range of persons who can gain access to a variety of state benefits including council tax benefit, employment support

[92]See C-57/96 *Meints* [1997] ECR I-6689 [44] and C-269/07 *Commission v Germany* [2009] ECR I-7811 [53]
[93]See C-224/97 *Ciola* [1999] ECR I-2517 [14] and C-382/08 *Neukirchinger* [2011] ECR I-0000 [34]
[94]C-209/03 *Bidar* [2005] ECR I-2119
[95]C-158/07 *Förster* [2008] ECR I-8507
[96]C-20/12 *Elodie Giersch and others* v *Luxembourg*
[97]*Samin* v *City of Westminster* [2012] EWCA Civ 1468 (21 November 2012)

allowance and housing benefit. As in the CD, beneficiaries are students, jobseekers, workers, self-employed persons and those who are self-sufficient as well as those who are unable to work as set out in Article 7(3)(a). Regulation 6(2)(a) repeats this verbatim. It provides that those who are temporarily unavailable to work due to illness, accident or involuntary unemployment retain the status of a worker. Mr Samin hoped to bring himself under this section: he therefore had to demonstrate that his inability to work was temporary – did he have any chance of a return to work or was his departure from the labour market permanent?

The court applied the objective test used by the Court of Appeal in *SSHD v FMB*,[98] *Konodbya*[99] and *de Brito*[100] – the central question was whether there were 'realistic prospects of a return to work'. Mr Samin was found to be unfit for employment beyond an 'incidental interruption' and thus beyond the scope of the CD and the benefits available under it. The decision of the court perhaps summarises the state of the internal welfare state at the present time:

> [21] There is no difficulty in accepting that it is an underlying principle of European law that the self-sufficient should be entitled to move freely, with their families, between member States. But as the recitals also show, this is not an unqualified principle. The qualification is that States are not obliged to make their separate and disparate social benefits schemes available to those who have come from other States unless it is incidental to their right to free movement for the purpose of supporting themselves and their families by work or otherwise. Recitals (1)–(3) cannot be read without reading also (10) & (16). The Directive does not give unlimited right of residence in State A to the citizens of State B. It insists on the right being given where, in essence, the citizen is self-supporting.

Was this a correct interpretation of the directive? Samin argued that the correct test would be whether there was 'any chance' of a return to work, as used by the CJEU in cases such as *Bozkurt*,[101] *Nazli*[102] and *Dogan*.[103] This suggestion was dismissed because these cases did not raise questions under the CD.[104] The CJ would not necessarily agree with this but the answer will remain unknown until the interpretation of this issue arises in another court before another judge – in this instance the request to refer the matter to the CJEU was declined.[105] It may have been that the CJ would have suggested this situation be considered under the citizenship provisions.[106] White concludes that:

> levels of social solidarity among the Member States are still relatively undeveloped. Member States still tend to see themselves as having a higher responsibility to look after their own nationals than nationals of other Member States who fall on hard times while resident in the host Member State.[107]

---

[98]*SSHD v FMB* [2010] UKUT 447
[99]*Konodbya v RB Kensington and Chelsea* [2012] EWCA Civ 982
[100]*De Brito v SSH* [2012] EWCA Civ 709
[101]C-434/93 *Bozkurt v Staatssecretris van Justitie* [1995] ECR I-1475
[102]C-340/97 *Nazli v Stadt Nurnberg* [1995] ECR I-1475
[103]C-383/03 *Dogan v Sihcerheitsdirektion fuer das Bundesland Vorarlberg* [1995] ECR I-1475
[104]These cases were based on provisions of Decision 1/80 on free movement of Turkish workers in the EU.
[105]*Samin* [20]
[106]In *Iida v Stadt Ulm*, the AG focused her analysis on CD 2004/38 but the CJ based its reasoning on Directive 2003/109 (paras 36ff).
[107]Robin C. A. White, 'Revisiting Free Movement of Workers', *Fordham International Law Journal* 33(5), 2011

VIEWPOINT

Do you agree with White?

5. Beyond the scope of free movement of workers

Not every rule will be caught by Article 45: in *Graf*[108] the CJ held that a rule requiring three years of service for compensation for unfair dismissal was 'too uncertain and indirect' a link to the hindrance of free movement for workers. There was no hindrance to market access and thus no breach was found. The sections below outline other circumstances when rules fall outside of Article 45 TFEU.

i.   Restrictions justified by 'public policy, public security or public health' – Article 45(3)

Under Article 45(3), free movement of workers is subject only to specific limitations that must be justified on one of three grounds – public policy, public security or public health. These grounds are also listed in the Citizenship Directive 2004/38.[109] Generally, member states seek to use these to prevent entry and/or secure deportation of an EU migrant worker or citizen. In many cases, a member state will try to use them to justify the deportation of a person trying to claim benefits. Initial guidance on when this would be acceptable arose from case law; the rules are now found in Chapter VI of the Citizenship Directive (CD).

Labour exchange is such a fundamental element in the construction of the internal market that national rules are allowed to prevent it in very narrow circumstances. However, public policy and public security are difficult to define. The CJ has not attempted to do so but has stressed that these ideas are to be interpreted restrictively, while respecting member state autonomy:

> [23] . . . the Court has always pointed out that, while Member States essentially retain the freedom to determine the requirements of public policy and public security in accordance with their national needs, which can vary from one Member State to another and from one era to another, the fact still remains that, in the Community context and particularly as justification for a derogation from the fundamental principle of free movement of persons, those requirements must be interpreted strictly, so that their scope cannot be determined unilaterally by each Member State without any control by the Community institutions.[110]

The Court's case law has clarified that the concept of public policy assumes not only disruption of the social order but also the existence of a 'genuine, present and sufficiently

---

[108]C-190/98

[109]Article 27, Chapter VI

[110]See C-36/75 *Rutili* [1975] ECR 1219 [26 and 27]; C-30/77 *Bouchereau* [1977] ECR 1999 [33 and 34]; C-54/99 *Église de scientologie* [2000] ECR I-1335 [17]; and C-36/02 *Omega* [2004] ECR I-9609 [30 and 31]

serious threat to one of the fundamental interests of society'.[111] In order to be justified, any measure taken on grounds of public policy or public security must first be based exclusively on the personal conduct of the individual concerned and second be specific to the case. Justifications isolated from the particulars of the case or that pursue general aims of prevention and deterrence are unacceptable.[112] This has since been entrenched in Article 27 of Directive 2004/38.

Prior to 2004, the CJ used case law to stress that exclusion must be based exclusively on personal conduct which is a genuine, present and serious threat.[113] In *Van Duyn*,[114] the British authorities tried to prevent a Dutch national entering the UK to take up a job with the Church of Scientology. This was not a banned organisation, although it was regarded with some suspicion by the authorities. The CJ stressed that the notion of 'personal conduct' referred to present actions of the individual rather than past actions of those a person may be associated with. This was highlighted again in *Bonsignore*:[115] the threat to public security must arise from the individuals own actions. A threat had to be both genuine and serious[116] in order for the derogation to apply. A member state cannot punish non-nationals for engaging in activities tolerated of nationals – in *Jany* the Dutch authorities failed to justify the decision to deport sex workers as it took no measures against Dutch women offering these services.[117]

The case law on the derogation in Article 45(3) was summed up in the decision of *Orfanopoulos and Olivieri*.[118] German authorities sought to expel two non-nationals who were long-term residents but had been sentenced respectively to a term of youth custody of at least two years and to a custodial sentence for a drug-related offences. However, deportation was not possible under EU law because:

> [68] Community law precludes the deportation of a national of a Member State based on reasons of a general preventive nature, that is one which has been ordered for the purpose of deterring other aliens (see, in particular, *Bonsignore*, paragraph 7), in particular where such measure automatically follows a criminal conviction, without any account being taken of the personal conduct of the offender or of the danger which that person represents for the requirements of public policy (see *Calfa*, paragraph 27, and *Nazli*, paragraph 59).

As with any derogation, the use of Article 45(3) must be proportionate – any decision must 'remain within the limits of what is appropriate and necessary in order to achieve the aim in view and that the principle of equal treatment be reconciled as far as possible with the requirements of the aim thus pursued'.[119] Additional rights are provided in the Citizenship Directive 2004/38.

---

[111]See *Rutili* [28]; *Bouchereau* [35]; and joined cases C-482/01 and C-493/01 *Orfanopoulos and Oliveri* [2004] ECR I-5257 [66]

[112]C-33/07 *Ministerul Administraliei I Internelor v Jipa* [23] [2008] 3 CMLR 23; *Bouchereau* [2008] 1 QB 732

[113]This also applies to restrictions on nationals leaving their own state – see C-430/10 *Gaydarov v Direktor na Glavna direktsia'Ohranitelna politsia' pri Ministerstvo na vatreshnite raboti* – a convicted criminal can only be prevented from leaving his state provided that there is a genuine threat affecting the fundamental interests of society.

[114]C-41/74 *Van Duyn v Home Office* [1975] [1974] ECR 1337

[115]C-67/74 *Bonsignore v Oberstadtdirektor Koeln* [1975] ECR 297

[116]C-30/77 *Bouchereau* [1977] ECR 1999

[117]C-115 and 116/ 81 *Adoui and Cornaille v Belgium*; [1982] ECR 1665 C-268/99 *Jany v Staatssecretaris van Justitie* [2001] ECR I-8615

[118]C-482 and 493/ 01 *Orfanopoulos and Olivieri v Land Baden-Wurttemberg* [2004] ECR I-5257

[119]C-319/03 *Briheche* [1977] ECR 1999 [24]

ANALYSING THE LAW

Do these derogations help or hinder the creation of an internal labour market?

---

ii.   Employment in the 'public service' – Article 45(4)

Article 45(4) adds another limitation – free movement rights may be withheld in relation to jobs that fall within the 'public service'. This is the only sphere of activity explicitly excluded from these rules. It relates to but is not synonymous with the 'public sector'. The public sector comprises those services – from defence to healthcare – that are conducted to secure the efficient functioning of the State. The range of jobs which fall within this sector vary from one member state to another. For example, in Germany lawyers and trainee teachers are civil servants employed by the State; in Britain they are not. Hence the size of the public sector varies from member state to member state: it is significantly smaller in Britain than Germany, and ever decreasing as public services are increasingly delivered by private firms. Public sector jobs are traditionally held to be especially important to State security and stability; as such the holders are required to have a certain sense of loyalty to the State. Consequently, they are usually preserved for nationals. Article 45(4) allows member states to exclude these jobs from the free movement provisions and discriminate in relation to who they are offered to.

The scope of this sector has been a site of conflict and tension between the EU and national authorities. The broader the scope, the higher the number of jobs beyond the reach of the internal labour market. While the national authorities have favoured a broad interpretation, the EU has favoured the opposite. Ultimately, the CJ gave this phrase a Union meaning, determined by the functions of a job rather than the institution within which it is located.

In *Sotgui* the CJ was asked to decide whether a national rule which based the calculation of separation allowance on the place of original employment was contrary to Article 45. Those hired in Germany received a higher allowance than those hired elsewhere which placed non-nationals at a disadvantage. Germany attempted to justify this policy using Article 45(4). This was rejected by the CJ – first, the definition of the public service must be a Union concept and cannot be determined by the name given to a post or by the fact that it is governed by public law. Second, the use of the derogation is confined to admission not treatment. It therefore could not be used to justify discrimination in relation to remuneration or any condition of employment once they have been admitted to the public service.

The Court has therefore contained the potential breadth of the 'public service' by confining its reach only to those posts which regularly require the exercise of public authority.[120] The provision has been used not only to create the internal labour market, but also to change the reach of the State. There is actually no single concept of the 'state' in EU law: the state under Article 45 is narrower than the notion used in relation to direct effect'.[121] A series of cases brought by the Commission, as part of its campaign to

---

[120]D. O'Keefe, 'Union Citizenship', in D. O'Keefe and P. Twomey (eds), *Legal Issues of the Maastricht Treaty*, Wiley Chancery Law, 1994
[121]C-188/89 *Foster* [1990] ECR I-3313

harmonise the understanding of the State and prise open the public services in the member states, led to a string of important decisions against Belgium, France and Luxembourg.

In *Commission* v *Belgium*[122], infringement proceedings under Article 258 TFEU were used to challenge rules stipulating Belgian nationality as a requirement for a range of posts including gardeners, security guards, nurses, and railway workers in local authorities and public organisations. Before the CJ, Belgium, France, Germany and the UK argued that these fell within Article 45(4) – this was an institutional concept which related to the form of the job not its content. It was easy for the CJ to counter this argument by changing the priorities from the form of the job to its content. It introduced a test stressing the latter:

> [1] By providing that the provisions of this Article shall not apply to employment in the public service, Article 48(4) of the EEC Treaty removes from the ambit of Article 48(1) to (3) a series of posts which involve direct or indirect participation in the exercise of powers conferred by public law and duties designed to safeguard the general interests of the state or of other public authorities. Such posts in fact presume on the part of those occupying them the existence of a special relationship of allegiance to the state and reciprocity of rights and duties which form the foundation of the bond of nationality. On the other hand the exception contained in Article 48(4) does not apply to posts which, whilst coming under the state or other organisations governed by public law, still do not involve any association with duties belonging to the public service properly so called.

Thus the rule specifying Belgian nationality for certain jobs was contrary to Article 45. The two criteria laid out were cumulative: to fall within the provision the post had to include both 'direct or indirect participation in the exercise of powers conferred by public law' and 'duties designed to safeguard the general interests of the State'. Only such posts could contain the range of tasks that might require the holder to care deeply about the well-being of the State.

This understanding of public office can be compared with that provided by LJ Leveson in a recent case concerning prison officers who were convicted of misconduct in public office – one had had a sexual relationship with a prisoner and her colleagues knew yet failed to report this. Leveson stated that:

> The test for identifying a public office turned on the nature of the duty undertaken and, in particular, whether it was a public duty in the sense that it represented the fulfilment of one of the responsibilities of government such that the public had a significant interest in its discharge extending beyond an interest in anyone who might be directly affected by a serious failure in the performance of the duty.[123]

The defendants fell within this definition because they were civil servants and employees of HM Prison Service under the umbrella of the National Offenders Management Service. They had also signed a declaration to acknowledge that they were subject to the Official Secrets Act and they had been vetted for security clearance. As part of their job they had been issued with prison keys and individual cell keys and had unaccompanied access to prisoners. It was also argued that inherent in the nature of a public office was a level of trust concerning the public.

---

[122]C-149/79 *Commission* v *Belgium* [1982] ECR 1845
[123]*Regina* v *Cosford and others* [2013] EWCA Crim 466; [2013] WLR (D) 147

VIEWPOINT

Why do prison officers fall under Article 45(4)?

In *Commission* v *France*,[124] the CJ added some detail to the type of duties that might be concerned with the general interests of the State. The case revolved around a rule in France that non-nationals could only be employed as a nurse in public hospitals on fixed contracts. As contract workers, they enjoyed fewer advantages and safeguards than those – predominantly nationals – not on fixed contracts. According to the Commission, this rule therefore acted as a deterrent – fewer than 5 per cent of those employed under contract were foreigners. It was argued that these jobs satisfied the two-part test but this was not accepted by the CJ. A high hurdle was set around Article 45(4):

> 'in order to be made inaccessible to nationals of another MS, it is not sufficient for the duties inherent in the post at issue to be directed specifically towards public objectives . . . Those who occupy the post must don full battle dress: . . . the duties must involve acts of will which affect private individuals by requiring their obedience.'

Likewise, Article 45(4) does not allow a member state to reserve for its own nationals employment as master of vessels flying the national flag. The preservation of national identity could only be a priority if this was a major part of the job:

> Article 39(4) EC [45(4) TFEU] must be construed as allowing a Member State to reserve for its nationals the post of master of vessels flying its flag and engaged in small-scale maritime shipping (Kleine Seeschifffahrt) only if the rights under powers conferred by public law granted to masters of such vessels are in fact exercised on a regular basis and do not represent a very minor part of their activities.[125]

In *Commission* v *Luxembourg*[126] the CJ did, however, accept an argument that the demographic situation of a member state may require specific changes to be made when implementing free movement of workers. However, the existence of such a right did not permit the unilateral exclusion of non-national workers from entire areas of occupational activity.[127]

It is impossible to make a list of all the jobs which might fall into Article 45(4). They could include jobs related to banking, policing, penal institutions, defence, the judiciary and taxation but none of these areas are per se excluded from the free movement rules:[128] it depends upon the specific role in question. It is questionable whether a private company paid by the state to perform public functions could use the exception under Article 45(4) – although this might be possible depending upon the nature of the duties. It is ironic that in interpreting this provision, the CJ called upon a very traditional notion of loyalty to the State, which sits uncomfortably with the idea of Union citizenship.[129] The exception is also limited to access, not treatment.

---

[124]C-307/84 *Commission* v *France* [1986] ECR 1725
[125]C-47/02 *Anker and others* [2003] ECR I-10447. See also C-405/01 *Spanish Merchant Navy* (*Colegio de Oficiales de la Marina Mercante Española*) [2003] ECR 2003 I-10391
[126]C-473/93 *Commission* v *Luxembourg* [1996] ECR I-3207
[127][45], C-20/12 *Elodie Giersch*
[128]Communication From The Commission 'Free movement of workers – achieving the full benefits and potential', COM(2002) 694 final
[129]O'Keefe 1994

> ### ANALYSING THE LAW
>
> Explain the difference between a functional and an institutional understanding of the 'public service'.

iii. Non-migrant workers

Only workers enjoy rights of free movement under Article 45 TFEU, and only those workers who move across a border. The internal labour market is designed to protect migrant Union workers from discrimination – Article 45 does not apply to sedentary workers who have not left their home member state. This can give rise to the situation described as 'reverse discrimination'[130] where those who have not migrated – and therefore do not fall within the scope of EU law – are placed at a disadvantage compared to those who have.

An example can be seen in the case of *Morson and Jhanjan*[131] – two residents of Surinam, a former Dutch colony, travelled to the Netherlands to visit their children who were Dutch citizens. While there, they requested permission to reside relying upon Article 10 of Regulation 492/2011 which gives parents of migrant workers the right to family reunion. However, the children were Dutch nationals employed in the Netherlands and had never been employed in another member state. As they had not exercised the Treaty right to free movement, they could not benefit from it.

A key condition of access to rights is employment in another member state thus migration is a necessary trigger for the application of Article 45. Their situation would have been very different if they were in another member state *or* if they were not Dutch themselves. Likewise, in *Uecker and Jacquet*[132] two spouses of Russian and Norwegian nationality, married to German men who lived and worked in Germany, could not invoke Article 45 to secure permanent job contracts. As their husbands were not migrant Union workers, their situation fell under national law. EU law does not determine how member states treat their own nationals, just as in relation to goods it does not determine the alcohol content of cassis made in Germany.

This issue has been tackled before the CJ many times.[133] Since the creation of EU citizenship in 1992, reverse discrimination has not been addressed:

> While reverse discrimination might be justified in the context of a Community pursuing purely economic aims, where the only purpose is to ensure that goods and economic operators can move freely between Member States, the maintenance of such situations seems difficult to sustain in the light of the creation of a Union citizenship. Indeed, this new concept demonstrates that the objectives of European integration are not restricted anymore to economic interpenetration – and thus free movement – but include, in addition, the construction of an integrated Community of citizens sharing a common sense of identity *vis-à-vis* the Union and of solidarity between nationals of different Member States. Reverse discrimination, more than constituting a problem of

---

[130]Camille Dautricourt and Sebastien Thomas, 'Reverse discrimination and free movement of persons under Community law: all for Ulysses, nothing for Penelope?', *European Law Review* 34(3), 2009, pp. 433–454
[131]C-35 and 36/82 *Morson and Jhanjan* v *Staat der Nederlanden* [1982] ECR 3723
[132]C-64 and 65/96 *Uecker and Jacquet* v *Land Nordrhein-Westfalen* [1997] ECR I-3171
[133]See Dautricourt and Thomas 2009, pp. 433–454

movement of economic operators, appears therefore as a form of unequal treatment among Union citizens which is highly counterproductive when one considers the aim of horizontal integration.[134]

Spouses who have a right to reside also have a right to work, but only in the host member state. In *Mattern and Cikotic*[135] Ms Mattern, a national of Luxembourg, lived and worked in Belgium with her husband, a third country national. He found work in Luxembourg but the authorities refused to provide him with a work permit. He argued that he did not need a work permit, because as the spouse of a migrant Union worker he was eligible to take up paid employment in Luxembourg. He was wrong: family rights only exist in the member state hosting the source of the rights, which in this case was Belgium.

[24] . . . it follows from the actual wording of Article 11 of the Regulation that the right of a national of a third country married to a Community national to have access to the labour market may be relied on only in the Member State where that Community national pursues an activity as an employed or self-employed person.

[26] It is common ground that at the time of the facts in the main proceedings Ms Mattern was not pursuing any activity as an employed or self-employed person in a Member State other than Belgium.

[27] Accordingly, Mr Cikotic, could rely on Article 11 of the Regulation only in Belgium in order to have access in that Member State to the labour market under the same conditions as those prescribed for nationals of that State.

[28] In the light of the foregoing, the reply to the question referred must be that Article 11 of the Regulation does not confer on a national of a third country the right to take up an activity as an employed person in a Member State other than the one in which his spouse, a Community national, pursues or has pursued an activity as an employed person in exercise of her right to free movement.

The case underlines the role of migration in securing free movement rights as a Union worker. As repeated in *Lyyski*,[136]

With regard to the freedom of movement for workers within the meaning of Article 39(1) EC [45 (1) TFEU], the Court has held that any Community national who, irrespective of his place of residence and his nationality, has exercised that right and who has been employed in a Member State other than that of residence falls within the scope of that Article (see, inter alia, Case C-18/95 *Terhoeve* [1999] ECR I-345, paragraph 27).

VIEWPOINT

Should migration continue to be the trigger for workers' rights under EU law?

---

[134]Dautricourt and Thomas 2009, p. 436
[135]C-10/05 *Mattern and Cikotic* [2006] ECR I-3145
[136]C-40/05 *Kaj Lyyski* v *Umeå universitet* [2007] ECR I-99

6. Conclusion

The rules on free movement of workers are designed to ensure that Union workers can go where their labour is needed without facing discrimination on the basis of nationality. Given the ambition of this goal, the Treaty contains few tools to achieve it. Incorrect transposition is an easy way to undermine labour market integration.

Increased migration has occurred against the background of the changing structure of the labour market. The shift from manufacturing to service sector jobs may make free movement of services and freedom of establishment more important. In addition, it is questionable how necessary movement of employed workers will be in the long term – in the digital age it is surely cheaper and more efficient for work and services to move electronically rather than people?

'Flexible' employment has brought new opportunities but it should be remembered that the 'flexible' economy has a less attractive side: the creation of a deregulated labour force capable of relocating and adapting much faster to the needs of the European market has a particularly negative impact on employees who are un- and underprotected by legislation.[137] Thus changes fall differentially upon groups of workers depending upon generation, gender and race:

> The young and the old are both likely to concentrate in precarious jobs, an extreme case being the concentration of the young in temporary contracts in Spain. Ethnic minorities and recently arrived immigrants are likely to be heavily concentrated in insecure locations, including the black economy. In central and southern Europe women are also often in insecure jobs; in northern Europe they are more likely to be in fairly secure but part time posts.[138]

Case law remains important to ensure the definition of a worker also includes the millions of people across the EU in these groups as well as those – mainly women – performing caring and mothering tasks for no pay.

Workers enjoy more freedom to move than citizens – they are protected by Article 45 TFEU as long as they migrate. Although it should be noted that, despite its importance to the project of European integration, the free movement of workers was withheld from some member states. One novelty of the enlargement process which culminated in 2004 was the ability of the existing member states to temporarily opt out of this.[139] Some of the older member states, including the UK, adopted a transitional period during which time, free movement rights for workers in some of the 10 new countries were suspended until 2011. A similar transitional period was adopted in 2007 with the accession of

---

[137]Valerie Amos, 'The Effects of 1992 and the Single European Market on black and migrant women', paper delivered at Runnymede Trust seminar, February 1991
[138]Colin Crouch, 'Change in European Societies since the 1970s', *West European Politics* 31(1–2), January–March 2008, pp. 14–39, 26
[139]The Accession (Immigration and Worker Registration) Regulations 2004 (SI 2004/1219, 'the 2004 Regulations') came into force on 1 May 2004. They governed the terms upon which nationals of the A8 states (8 of the 10 states which acceded to the European Union in 2004 following the Treaty on Accession signed in Athens on 16 April 2003) were admitted as workers to the United Kingdom labour market following accession. On the exercise of free movement rights under them see *Mariusz Szpak v SS Work and Pensions and SS Home Department* [2013] EWCA Civ 46.

Romania and Bulgaria. In 2009, the Coalition government decided to remove the restrictions.[140] Paradoxically, however, free movement of workers is enjoyed by nationals of a country that has not joined the EU: as a result of the Association Agreement signed in 1964, Turkish nationals can work and reside in all EU member states.[141]

Further reading

On free movement in general:

Robin C. A. White, 'Revisiting Free Movement of Workers', *Fordham International Law Journal* 33(5), 2011

John Sides and Jack Citrin, (2007) 'European Opinion About Immigration: The Role of Identities, Interests and Information', *British Journal of Political Science* 37, 2007, pp. 477–504

On EU labour market law:

Colin Crouch, 'Change in European Societies since the 1970s', *West European Politics*, 31(1–2), January–March 2008, pp. 14–39

Jeff Kenner, *EU Employment Law*, Hart Publishing, 2013

On free movement rights of third country nationals:

Richard Ball, *The Legitimacy of The European Union through Legal Rationality – Free Movement of Third Country Nationals*, Routledge, 2012

On free movement rights of students:

F. De Witte, 'Who funds the mobile student? Shedding some light on the normative assumptions underlying EU free movement law: *Commission* v *Netherlands*', *Common Market Law Review* 50, 2013, pp. 203–216

On reverse discrimination:

Camille Dautricourt and Sebastien Thomas, 'Reverse discrimination and free movement of persons under Community law: all for Ulysses, nothing for Penelope?', *European Law Review* 34(3), 2009, pp. 433–454

---

[140]See the Migration Advisory Committee 'Review of the UK's transitional measures for nationals of member states that acceded to the European Union in 2004', April 2009
[141]C-485/07 *Raad van bestuur van het Uitvoeringsinstituut werknemersverzekeringen* v *Akdas and others* [2011] WLR (D) 209

Part IV

EU Internal Market and Competition Law

12 Free movement of goods

Setting the scene

In February 2013, the UK authorities notified the Commission that Findus, one of the largest manufacturers of processed foods, had been using horsemeat instead of beef in a ready-made meal. Findus bought the products from a French supplier, Comingel. Comingel bought the raw meat from a meats trader in France, Spanghero. The meat apparently originated in Romania but was bought through middlemen based in Cyprus and the Netherlands. Several other member states also reported discovery of horsemeat in the human food chain: the UK, Ireland, Luxembourg, Sweden, Poland, Romania, Italy and France as well as Germany, Greece, the Netherlands, Belgium, Austria, Lithuania, the Czech Republic, Slovenia and Denmark. The issue was put down to fraudulent labelling rather than weak food safety regulation.[1] In response to recommendations following the Elliott Review,[2] the UK government announced it would create a Food Crime Agency alongside plans to introduce country of origin labelling from April 2015.

---

[1] http://ec.europa.eu/food/food/horsemeat/plan_en.htm

[2] HM Government, 'The Elliott Review into the Integrity and Assurance of Food Supply Networks – Final Report – A National Food Crime Prevention Framework', July 2104, https://www.gov.uk/government/uploads/system/uploads/attachment_data/file/350726/elliot-review-final-report-july2014.pdf

1. Introduction

Although the new growth strategy for the EU, 'Europe 2020', includes the goal to remove 20 million people from poverty,[3] the Treaty of Rome was not an anti-poverty manifesto. Part One of the Treaty of Rome laid out the principles of the Community – it was designed to deliver 'a harmonious development of economic activities, a continuous and balanced expansion, an increase in stability, an accelerated raising of the standard of living, and closer relations between the States belonging to it'.[4] The goal was to create a common market, a single trading area, not a European welfare state. The expectation was that the creation of a common market would have two major benefits for the peoples of Europe as consumers and producers. First, it would enhance the purchasing choices of consumers as the best products would be available everywhere. Second, it would promote wealth for producers (and thus economic growth for nations) by reducing transaction costs and producing 'economies of scale' – in a larger market more products can be made which lower both production costs and potentially the price of purchase. Profitability is easier in larger markets, because higher production numbers reduce average production costs and raise profits – the hope was for European industry to operate within a market the size of the United States as this could in theory increase both productivity and income levels.[5] However, realisation of economies of scale relies upon the desire of producers to achieve profitability via economies of scale rather than by other means, such as mergers and acquisitions.[6] This latter method removes rather than creates jobs, and thus reduces the number of workers and of consumers.

The 'common market' was to be created in phases. These phases included the removal of customs duties and the creation of a common customs tariff; the abolition of obstacles to free movement of goods, persons, services and capital; the adoption of a common agricultural and transport policy; the institution of a competition policy; coordination of economic policies; approximation of national laws; the raising of living and working conditions; the establishment of a European Investment Bank; and increase in trade with overseas countries and territories.[7] Given the focus on transnational trade, discrimination on the basis of nationality was specifically prohibited in Article 7. A transitional period of 12 years, divided into 3 stages of 4 years, was given to establish the common market.

These phases of integration can be seen as incremental levels of commitment: the creation of a free trade area (removal of customs duties/quotas on mutual trade) can develop into a full customs union (a common tariff on goods from outside the free trade area) which in turn evolves into a common market (free movement within the customs union) and finally into an economic union (creation of a common currency controlled by a central authority and a single monetary and fiscal policy). Neither model incorporates per se currency and monetary policy or the creation of a single government (federal state).

---

[3]See http://ec.europa.eu/europe2020/index_en.htm and B. Nolan and C.T. Whelan *Poverty and Deprivation in Europe,* Oxford University Press, 2011
[4]Article 2 TEC (now repealed)
[5]Alan Milward, *The European Rescue of the Nation State London,* 2nd edn, Routledge, 2000, p. 124
[6]European Commission, 'The Single Market and Tomorrow's Europe: A Progress Report from the European Commission', OOPEC, 1996, p. 101
[7]Article 3 TEC (Article 8 TFEU)

a) Levels of integration

Levels of integration

	Joint action (e.g. information gathering/ sharing)	Free trade of goods (removal of quotas and tariffs)	Common commercial policy (common external tariff)	Mobility for factors of production (finance, goods, services, labour)
Free Trade Area (e.g. EFTA, 1960)	YES	YES	NO	NO
Common Market (e.g. EEC, 1957)	YES	YES	YES	YES

FIGURE 12.1   Levels of integration in the EU

Adapted from Ali M. El Agraa (ed), *The European Union: History, Institutions, Economics and Policies*, 5th edn, Prentice Hall Europe, 1998

There is also large scope for determining the reach of economic integration: should this be limited to primary products (such as agricultural produce) or also include manufactured products (such as toys, cars, mobile phones and computers)? Finally the meaning of integration has to be determined – does this mean that the border will be removed so that there is a single trading space, or that the border will be ignored at mutually agreed moments so that products can be treated in a particular way? The Rome Treaty envisaged a single trading space, hence the name the 'common market'.

'Common' meant uniform – the initial vision was to remove all borders to achieve free movement of primary and manufactured goods. By opting for the goal of removal of borders, the EEC set itself a significant challenge. The Treaty lay out an ambitious blueprint to create a common market of six separate countries each with its own languages and values, as well as different habits of production and consumption, spending and saving. It gave little guidance on key questions such as how are such differences to be addressed in order to create a single economic area where goods, persons, capital and services can move without hindrance? When are national preferences to be accepted as valuable cultural norms rather than rejected as hidden economic protectionism? Creation of a common market via the removal of borders requires removal of national product standards,[8] registration rules[9] and rules on product usage.[10] Even rules relating to minimum prices can become an issue – in *LIBRO*[11] the CJEU ruled against a national provision prohibiting book importers from selling their books below the recommended retail price in the state

---

[8]C-261/81 *Walter Rau* [1982] ECR 3961; C-166/03 *Commission v France* (Gold Alloy) [2004] ECR I-6535
[9]C-88/07 *Commission v Spain* [2009] ECR I-519
[10]C-110/05 *Commission v Italy* [2009] ECR I-519
[11]C-531/07 *Fachverband der Buch- und Medienwirtschaft v LIBRO* [2009] ECR I-3717

of publication. However, it is clear that the removal of borders requires more than this – it calls for a radical shift in values, attitudes, behaviour and expectations. As the case law shows, the Belgians have specific expectations on how to package butter, the Italians their preferences for the ingredients of spaghetti, and Germans for additives of beer.

Removal of national rules does not mean that a common market is devoid of regulation – on the contrary it is a highly regulated space. It was to be created by the move towards a new common sense, manifested in new harmonised legislation prioritising EU-wide trade interests rather than national ones. Achieving the Treaty vision has required both deregulation and subsequent – or simultaneous[12] – harmonisation and reregulation with the introduction of a single EU rule. The process is long and involves numerous actors requiring: a) complaint by consumers or producers in the member states; b) judicial review by national and the EU courts; and c) creation of legislation by national and EU legislators.

Harmonisation brings costs to some as well as advantages to others: for example, in *Gonzalez Sanchez,* a patient infected with Hepatitis C during a blood transfusion lost her claim against the provider of medical services because the national Spanish law was incompatible with the harmonised EU instrument – the Product Liability Directive.[13]

The creation of the Single European Act (SEA) in 1986 was a response to the limited success in realising a common market in the first 30 years of the EEC. The SEA proposed a total of 280 measures and set the deadline of 1992 for the achievement of free movement. It took a more pragmatic approach – the emphasis was on the agreement of minimum standards and mutual recognition rather than full harmonisation and a single rule. More recently harmonisation has been approached using voluntary methods, such as the Open Method of Coordination (OMC).[14] This focuses on soft law – benchmarking, guidelines, best practice in areas such as pensions and social policy. Its flexibility is both an advantage and disadvantage – under the OMC there are no fixed objectives, the agreements are non-binding and thus non-reviewable.[15]

It is no longer assumed that a common market requires common rules.[16] The legislative goal has moved from the creation of harmonised rules to minimum guidelines and best practice. The judicial approach has also evolved, especially in relation to non-fiscal rules. The single market is created by disapplying two types of national rules: fiscal rules (taxes and customs fees) applied at the border or internally and non-fiscal rules that treat non-national products differently. The type of national rules targeted have shifted as the goal of market access has replaced the prevention of discrimination. This goal of market access has arguably created a right to trade under Article 34 TFEU, thus neutral product rules that obstruct market access, either via the arrangements by which products can be sold or consumer dissuasion, will be incompatible with Article 34.

---

[12]Fernanda G. Nicola, 'Transatlanticisms: Constitutional asymmetry and selective reception of US law and economics in the formation of European private law', *Cardozo Journal of International and Comparative Law* 16, 2008, p. 111
[13]Case C-183-00 *Gonzalez Sanchez* v *Medcina ASturiana SA* [2002] ECR I-03901 on Council Directive 85/374, OJ L210/29 1985. Discussed in Nicola 2008. The directive was very controversial – France took more than a decade to implement it – see Case C-52/00 *Commission* v *France* [2002] ECR I-3827 and Case C-177/04 *Commission* v *France* [2006] ECR I-2461.
[14]European Commission 'A renewed commitment to social Europe: Reinforcing the Open Method of Coordination for social protection and social inclusion', COM(2008) 418 final
[15]Martin Lodge, 'Comparing Non-Hierarchical Governance in Action: the Open Method of Co-ordination in Pensions and Information Society', JCMS 45(2), June 2007, pp. 343–365
[16]Weatherill, 'The proceedings of the W.G. Hart Workshop held in London in 2003', in Tridimas and Nebbia (eds), *European Union Law for the Twenty-First Century,* Hart Publishing, 2004

2. Fiscal rules: customs duties and CEEs

All nations prefer to promote domestically produced goods. Consumption of domestic goods protects jobs and can create new ones. A simple way to make goods made abroad less attractive to domestic consumers is to make them more expensive by, for example, applying costs at their point of entry. Such taxes are a common tool to protect a domestic market. Their imposition increases costs: producers are likely to increase the price that consumers must pay to protect their profit margins. Thus imported products are more expensive and less attractive to the average consumer than domestic goods. For the internal market to have a chance of success, as a first step such fiscal barriers had to be removed. The founder member states laid out in the Treaty a limited range of deregulatory tools to remove this protectionism and secure the free movement of goods. The fiscal rules address customs duties or charges having an equivalent effect that are applied when a good crosses a border. These are laid out in Articles 28–30 TFEU (ex 23–25 TEC). In addition, internal taxes which treat domestic products more favourably than imports are addressed by Articles 110–113 TFEU (ex 90–93 TEC).

i.   Discriminatory border taxes – Articles 28–30 TFEU

Taxes levied at the border are the most common measure used to protect trade in national goods. The removal of these fiscal barriers to free movement of goods begins in Article 28 TFEU which provides that:

The Union shall comprise a customs union which shall cover all trade in goods and which shall involve the prohibition between Member States of customs duties on imports and exports and of all charges having equivalent effect, and the adoption of a common customs tariff in their relations with third countries.

This also applies to goods from outside the EU in free circulation between the member states. Although the Treaty covers 'all trade in goods', it does not define what these are. In *Commission v Italy (Arts Treasures)*[17] the CJ decided that a good would be any tangible product 'which can be valued in money and which are capable . . . of forming part of commercial transactions'. This definition is broad enough to include objects of artistic and historic value; hence Italy's imposition of a tax on items of archaeological and ethnographic interest when these were exported to other member states fell within its scope.

Article 30 TFEU contains an unequivocal prohibition on customs duties and charges having an equivalent effect. It states:

'Customs duties on imports and exports and charges having equivalent effect (CEE) shall be prohibited between the member states. This prohibition shall also apply to customs duties of a fiscal nature.'

---

[17] C-7/68 *Commission v Italy* (Arts Treasures) [1968] ECR 423; [1969] CMLR 1

A CEE is a customs duty in all but name. The key elements of this were laid out in *Commission* v *Italy*:[18]

> any pecuniary charge, however small and whatever designation and mode of applica-tion, which is imposed unilaterally on domestic or foreign goods when they cross a frontier, and which is not a customs duty in the strict sense, constitutes a charge hav-ing equivalent effect . . . even if it is not imposed for the benefit of the state, is not discriminatory or protective in effect or if the product on which the charge is imposed is not in competition with any domestic product.

A regional tax, applied when goods cross an internal border within a member state,[19] falls under this test, as does a charge for an import licence at the external border.[20]

This is one of the clearest prohibitions in the Treaty and perhaps for this reason, was the basis of the doctrine of direct effect.[21] Its clear purpose is to protect the free movement of goods and prevent any fragmentation by national border tariffs. Its application is absolute: it applies regardless of the objective of the charge,[22] the level of the fee,[23] whether it is administered by a public or private body[24] and irrespective of what it is called, who benefits or whether monies are refunded[25] or where it is levied.[26] Neutral fees can be classed a CEE if they relate to inspections conducted under different regimes.[27] This strict prohibition can only be lifted if three circumstances arise whereby:

> [1] the charges relating to a general system of internal dues applied . . . to domestic products and imported products alike . . .

> [2] they are payment for a service in fact rendered to the economic operator . . . if it attaches to inspections carried out to fulfil obligations imposed by Community law, and provided that . . . the fees do not exceed the real costs of the inspection . . .

> [3] the inspections in question are obligatory and uniform for all the products con-cerned in the Community, that they are prescribed by Community law in the general interest of the Community and that they promote the free movement of goods.[28]

In order to be accepted, it must be clear that the fee provides a genuine and specific benefit to traders.[29] In *Commission* v *Belgium* it was not clear that the fee for internal clearance provided any kind of benefit. The benefit must be specific – the argument that a fee might enhance general competitiveness was rejected in *Cadsky*.[30] It might be argued that there should be broader exceptions or at least a *de minimis* rule attached to Article 30. For example there may

---

[18]C-2 and 3/69 *Social Fonds voor Diamantarbeiders* [1969] ECR 211, [1969] CMLR 335. See also C-24/68 *Commission v Italy* (Statistical Levy) [1969] ECR 199; [1971] CMLR 611
[19]C-363, 407, 409 and 411/93 *René Lancry SA v Direction Générale des Douanes* [1994] ECR I-3957
[20]C-10/65 *Deutschmann v Bundesrepublik Deutschland* [1965] ECR 46 9hw
[21]See C-26/62 *Van Gend en Loos*
[22]C-2 and 3/69 *Social Fonds voor Diamantarbeiders v Brachfeld and others* [1969] ECR 211; C-441 and 2/98 *Kapniki Mikhailidis* [2000] ECR I-7145
[23]C-24/68 *Commission v Italy* (Statistical Levy) [1969] ECR 193
[24]C-16/94 *Dubois & General Cargo* [1995] ECR I-2421
[25]C-77/76*Fratelli Cucchi v Avez* [1977] ECR 987
[26]C-78/76 *Firma Steinike and Weinlig* [1977] ECR 595
[27]C-29/72 *Marimex SpA v Amministrazione delle finanze dello Stato* [1972] ECR 1309
[28]C-46/76 *Bauhuis v Netherlands* [1077] ECR 14. See also C-132/82 *Commission v Belgium* [1983] ECR 1049; [1983] CMLR 600; C-18/87 *Commission v Germany* [1988] ECR 5427
[29]C-132/82 *Commission v Belgium* [1983] ECR 1649
[30]C-63/74 *Cadsky S.p.a. v Istituto Nazionale per il Commercio Estero* [1975] ECR 281

be a significant public interest in the government conducting veterinary and health and safety inspections but these are incompatible with Article 30[31] unless payable for inspections carried out in accordance with a Union directive.[32] Where such inspections are conducted, the level of the fee must be proportionate[33] and relate to the actual cost of the inspection.[34]

APPLYING THE LAW

Under what conditions could the UK authorities impose a custom duty on meat from France a) before the horsemeat scandal, or b) after the 2013 horse-meat scandal?

---

ii.   Taxes on goods in general circulation – Article 110 TFEU

Taxes do not only have to be applied at the border – they can be applied once goods are in general circulation within a member state, designed in a way that protects domestic goods. Article 110 TFEU has two strands: Article 110(1) deals with taxes applied to *similar* goods, while Article 110(2) focuses on taxes applied to *competing* goods. Both prohibit governments from using taxation policy to protect domestic producers from competition by non-national producers. This Article is directly effective[35] and as clarified in *Co-Frutta*,[36] covers all products coming from the member states, including products originating in non-EU countries which are in free circulation in the EU.

Article 110(1) No Member State shall impose, directly or indirectly, on the products of other Member States any internal taxation of any kind in excess of that imposed directly or indirectly on similar domestic products.

Article 110(1) is designed to target the situation where different taxation regimes apply to similar or comparable products solely because of origin, that is discriminatory internal systems of taxation. As stated by the CJ in *Siilin*,[37] 'Article 95 of the Treaty [110 TFEU] seeks to guarantee the complete neutrality of internal charges as regards competition between products already on the domestic market and imported products.' The purpose, as stated in *Commission* v *Italy* 'is to eliminate all forms of direct or indirect discrimination'.[38] It does not lay out a per se prohibition as in Article 30 TFEU – member states may impose taxes on producers and have autonomy over the content of those taxes as long as the taxation policy makes no distinction according to the origin of the goods. The Court looks to see *how* not if taxes are levied. They will be compatible with Article 110(1) as long as they contain neither protectionist nor discriminatory intent.

---

[31]C-46/76 *Bauhuis* [1977] ECR 5
[32]C-18/87 *Commission v Germany* [1988] ECR 5427
[33]C-170/88 *Ford Espana v Spain* [1989] ECR 2305
[34]C-111/89 where charges for the inspection of plants to be exported were calculated by weight; C-18/87 *Commission v Germany*
[35]C-57/65 *Lütticke v Hauptzollamt Saarlouis* [1966] ECR 205
[36]C-193/85 *Cooperativa Co-Frutta Srl v Amministrazione delle finanze dello Stato* [1987] ECR 2085
[37]C-101/00 *Tulliasiamies and Siilin* [2002] ECR I-7487
[38]C-277/83 *Commission v Italy* [1985] ECR 2049

Two different tests are applied:

1 The **formal** test investigates categorisation – it asks whether the items occupy the same fiscal or customs category? In other words are Converse and Adidas trainers both 'footwear'? Are apples and avocados both 'fruits'?
2 The **substantive** test considers how the products are used: do Converse/Nike shoes or apples/avocados meet similar consumer needs?

In order to determine this, attention is paid to four aspects:

- the raw product,
- the method of production,
- product and
- consumer niche.

In *Commission v Denmark*[39] the court found it 'clear from a comparison of wine made from grapes and wine made from other fruit . . . that they are similar products'. A tax policy will therefore be found directly discriminatory if the goods are similar but the tax treatment of the foreign good is different. This was also found in *Lütticke*,[40] as only imported powdered milk was subjected to tax. Likewise in *Commission v Italy*[41] imported regenerated oil was taxed higher than domestic regenerated oil although both were similar goods serving similar needs.

APPLYING THE LAW

Conduct the formal and substantive tests on Converse/Nike shoes and apples/avocados. Consider whether they fall into the same category and serve similar needs?

Article 110(1) also tackles indirect discrimination: in *Humblot*,[42] a higher tax on cars over 16cv had a disparate impact on foreign cars – most domestically produced vehicles were below this so the impact of the tax was to reduce competition for domestic cars. Likewise in *Commission v France (tobacco)*[43] it was found that the higher tax on light tobacco had a disparate impact on importers as dark tobacco was primarily domestically produced.

It is important to note that unlike rules which are directly discriminatory, disparate impact rules can be objectively justified. If justified they are held not to be in breach of Article 110(1). Unlike Article 30 TFEU, under Article 110(1), legitimate economic and social interests are recognised. In *Weigel*[44] the CJ confirmed that:

Community law does not as yet restrict the freedom of each Member State to establish a tax system which differentiates between certain products, even products which are similar within the meaning of the first paragraph of Article 90 EC [110 TFEU],

---

[39]C-106/84 *Commission v Denmark* [1986] ECR 833
[40]C-57/65 *Lütticke v Hauptzollamt Saarlouis* [1966] ECR 205
[41]C-277/83 *Commission v Italy* [1985] ECR 2049
[42]C-112/84 *Humblot v Directeur des services fiscaux* [1985]ECR 1367
[43]C-302/00 *Commission v France* [2002] ECR I-2055
[44]C-387/01 *Weigel* [2004] ECR I-4981

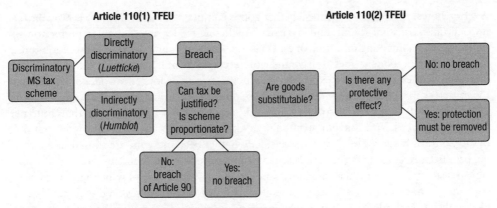

FIGURE 12.2 Application of Articles 110(1) and 110(2) TFEU

on the basis of objective criteria. Such differentiation is compatible with Community law . . . if it pursues objectives of economic policy which are themselves compatible with the requirements of the Treaty and secondary legislation, and if the detailed rules are such as to avoid any form of discrimination, direct or indirect, against imports from other Member States or any form of protection of competing domestic products.

A member state can save its rule if it demonstrates the existence of a legitimate national interest that is not based on origin or designed as a protectionist measure. This can include the poor state of national roads,[45] social objectives[46] or the preservation of petrol.[47] However, justification will not be successful if the majority of heavily taxed products are imports.[48]

Where the taxation policy is found to be justified the member state is called upon to remedy the situation by an equalisation of taxes (levelling up or down); the offending portion of tax must be removed to equalise taxation. This can sometimes result in reverse discrimination: in *Peureux*,[49] a French law imposing a tax on distillers could be enforced on domestic producers but not importers. This was tolerated as a 'special feature' of national law.

By contrast Article 110(2) targets *competing* products:

. . . no Member State shall impose on the products of other Member States any internal taxation of such a nature as to afford indirect protection to other products.

In *Cooperativa Co-Frutta*[50] the CJ explained that it 'precludes the charging of a consumer tax on certain imported fruit where it may protect domestic fruit production'. It is

intended to cover all forms of indirect tax protection in the case of products which, without being similar within the meaning of the first paragraph of Article 95, are nevertheless in competition, even partial, indirect or potential competition, with each other.

---

[45]C-132/88 *Commission v Greece* (taxation of cars) [1990] ECR I-1567
[46]C-252/86 *Bergandi* [1988] ECR 1343 – regional tax policy to discourage certain types of games machines; C-196/85 *Commission v France*: [1988] ECR 1343 preferential tax treatment for certain type of sweet wine to boost regional economy
[47]C-140/79 Chemial Farmaceutici [1981] ECR 1: taxation policy to promote agriculture and limit use of petroleum
[48]C-106/84 *Commission v Denmark* [1986] ECR 833
[49]C-86/78 *Peureux* [1979] ECR 897
[50]C-193/85 *Co-Frutta v Amministrazione delle finanze dello Stato* [1987] ECR 2085

A different test is used to determine whether goods compete – the key question is how the tax impacts upon consumer habits and in particular whether it encourages them to prefer domestic goods over competing imported ones. Does the taxation policy corrode consumer interest in non-national goods – does it drive their preferences? A policy may, for example, make imported leather gloves more expensive than domestically produced woollen mittens. Can the mittens can be substituted for gloves? If so, does the taxation policy make gloves more expensive? If gloves were not so expensive would they be as or more popular than mittens?

Commission v *UK*[51] brought the different taxation of cheap wine and beer to the attention of the Court of Justice. The CJ had to consider whether beer and wine are similar or competing products. According to the CJ, these beverages served the same function and it was possible that the taxation, rather than individual tastes, raised the cost of wine thereby skewing consumer behaviour to prefer beer. It therefore decided that the taxes on these items had to be equalised. A similar conclusion was made in *Commission* v *Italy:*[52] imported bananas which were more expensive, had to compete with other domestically produced lower priced fruits despite the fact that both satisfied similar consumer needs. The different taxation therefore had a protective effect. The remedy required the removal of the protective effect.

Often of course, national measures can impose both import restrictions and customs controls on the same items – in *Denkavit*[53] there was both a charge (a potential CEE under Article 110) and an inspection to be addressed under Article 34 TFEU. Where this is the case both infringements must be dealt with and assessed separately.[54]

ANALYSING THE LAW

Explain the difference between Article 110(1) and (2). How do they differ from Article 30 TFEU?

3. Non-fiscal rules: quantitative restrictions and MEQRs

Tax policy may be the easiest way for a government to encourage its citizens to prefer domestic goods but it is not the only method. There is a plethora of discriminatory and neutral rules relating to products themselves or where and how they are sold that can also affect opportunities for traders and influence consumer behaviour. These can include national product standards, rules for certificates and prior authorisation, additional technical requirements for imports, registration rules affecting market access, rules on minimum prices and product usage.

In the Treaty, these *non-fiscal* rules which deter imports fall into two categories: rules that lay out quantitative restrictions on imports, or rules which have an 'equivalent effect' to a quantitative restriction. Article 34 TFEU contains a clear prohibition:

Quantitative restrictions on imports and all measures having equivalent effect shall be prohibited between Member States.

---

[51]*Commission* v *UK* (Wine and Beer taxes) [1983] ECR 2265
[52]C-184/85 *Commission* v *Italy* (Bananas) [1987] ECR I-2055
[53]C-251/78 *Denkavit Futtermittel* [1979] ECR
[54]See also C-29/72 *Marimex:* [1972] ECR 1309 lawfulness of fee must be assessed separately to the physical inspection

It works on two types of national rules:

- those which lay out numerical limits (quantitative restrictions or QRs) on imports, and
- those which have the effect of curtailing trade even if they do not set out quotas (measures having the equivalent effect to a quantitative restriction, or MEQRs).

Its application and interpretation will be the focus of the rest of this chapter.

In *Geddo*,[55] a QR was defined as 'measures amounting to a total or partial restraint of imports, exports or goods in transit' – this can be seen in quotas or full bans. An MEQR can take on a variety of forms – it can be a physical check at borders, a requirement for import licences, technical rules, promotional campaigns or even national inaction in the face of private individuals engaging in protective activity.[56] If they prevent or hinder the free movement of goods, they are a measure with a similar effect to a quantitative restriction. Given the ambitious goal of a common market, no exhaustive list was created of an MEQR – this is an open concept. It has been the focus of much litigation before the CJEU, which has adopted a wide interpretation to this idea. This is directly effective and thus can be used before national courts. Where national judges require an interpretation of EU law to make a ruling, questions can be referred via Article 267 TFEU.

This provision was initially activated when national rules breached the fundamental principle of non-discrimination on the basis of nationality:[57] goods are to be treated the same under non-fiscal rules, regardless of origin. Directive 70/50 set out guidelines showing the two types of discriminatory measures falling within its scope.

Distinctly applicable rules are overtly discriminatory measures that impede trade by applying less favourable and more onerous conditions to imported goods, solely because of the national origin of a product, as seen for example in *Dassonville*.[58] Such rules (e.g. subsidies for domestic goods, minimum and maximum prices for imports) overtly encourage consumers to purchase domestic products. By contrast *indistinctly applicable* rules apply equally to all products regardless of origin. However, such measures are indirectly discriminatory because in practice they have the effect of impeding or restricting the sale of goods made in other member states: they have a discriminatory *impact*. The neutral non-origin specific rule on the alcohol content of cassis in *Cassis de Dijon*,[59] for example, appears to place an equal burden on domestic and foreign producers of cassis – as it applies to every producer of cassis; but if cassis is made with a different level of alcohol in another member state then this rule is actually more burdensome on foreign producers. They must either make two different batches of cassis – one for the home and one for the foreign market – or only sell their cassis at home. These indistinctly applicable rules hinder the creation of a common market as they prevent the sale of goods made to different specifications. Even if this standard applies to everybody, it therefore disrupts economic integration.

---

[55] C-2/73 *Geddo v Ente Nazionale Risi* [1973] ECR 865
[56] C265/95 *Commission v France (Spanish strawberries)* [1997] ECR I-6959
[57] The idea of discrimination has since 1997 extended to apply beyond nationality (see Article 19 TFEU).
[58] C-8/74 *Dassonville* [1974] ECR 837
[59] C-120/78 *Rewe-Zentral AG v Bundesmonopolverwaltung für Branntwein (Cassis de Dijon)* [1979] ECR 649; [1979] CMLR 494

Directive 70/50 set out 19 different directly discriminatory or distinctly applicable practices.[60] However, it was soon overtaken by case law – the CJ set out its own interpretation of an MEQR in *Dassonville*. This case concerned Belgian legislation requiring a certificate of authentication for imports of Scotch whisky. Only direct importers could verify the origin of their whisky and obtain the certificate. Mr Dassonville sold whisky in a shop in Belgium that he imported from Scotland via France. There were no certification laws in France as required under Belgian law. As Dassonville had not imported his whisky directly (it was a parallel import) he could not acquire a certificate and he was prosecuted under Belgian law. The CJ held that this rule undermined parallel imports – the outcome was a restrictive effect on free trade. In giving its decision, the CJ provided a standard definition (the 'Dassonville formula') of an MEQR which went far beyond the concepts in Directive 70/50:

[5] . . . all trading rules enacted by member states which are capable of hindering, directly or indirectly, actually or potentially, intra-community trade are to be considered as measures having an effect equivalent to quantitative restrictions.

True to the goal of cross-border economic interpenetration, Article 34 was given a reach encompassing rules that *could* hinder cross-border trade, whether they actually did or not. It did not matter whether the rule was distinctly or indistinctly applicable – even if it does not discriminate at all and places an equal burden, in law and in fact, on domestic and imported goods. Any rule with a negative effect on cross-border trade acts as a significant impediment to market access.[61] Their existence obstructs creation of a level economic playing field. However, such rules may be justified by legitimate and proportionate social goals – the available derogations may be determined by whether the measure is distinctly (as in *Dassonville*) or indistinctly (as in *Cassis*) applicable.

a) The 'economic constitution'

The decision in *Dassonville* appeared to create an absolute right to trade (economic due process) going beyond the more limited prevention of discrimination (anti-protectionism). Economic due process prioritises access to the market – it promotes open competition and unfettered pursuit of commercial activity; anti-discrimination on the other hand has a more limited goal – it seeks fair competition between traders in all member states and the removal of protectionism via discriminatory rules.[62]

It has been argued that *Dassonville*, in taking the focus of Article 34 TFEU beyond discrimination, transformed the Treaty into an 'economic constitution.' An economic constitution protects rights of economic exchange – the right to pursue a trade, own property – and guarantees individuals entry into relationships of exchange. The role of the economic constitution is to:

provide a minimal regulatory framework to avoid monopolies, ensure the private ownership of the means of production and protect individual freedom.[63]

---

[60]Article 2 D70/50. See for example the distinctly applicable provisions in C-249/81 *Commission v Ireland* (Buy Irish) [1982] ECR 4005; C-207/83 *Commission v UK (Origin marking)* [1985] ECR 1201. But see C-12/74 *Commission v Germany* [1975] ECR 181: origin marking acceptable where indicative of quality, materials and manufacturing methods.
[61]C-405/98 *Gourmet International Products* [2001] ECR I-1795
[62]Miguel Maduro, 'Reforming the Market or the State? Article 30 and the European Constitution: Economic Freedom and Political Rights', *European Law Journal* 1, 1997, pp. 55–80
[63]Nicola 2008, p. 135

These rights are accompanied by social responsibilities – the economic constitution does not focus solely on trade. Instead, it raises individual economic rights to the same level as individual social rights. Market and social rights are tethered together, making them interdependent. The economic constitution creates a 'social-market economy' also known as 'ordoliberalism'.[64] In the social-market economy, law is used to protect economic rights not for the sake of the market but for the sake of stability in society. A major concern under the economic constitution is the relationship between the state and the market and the place of collective goods (public health, public morality, the environment, social cohesion).

Thus in *Dassonville* the CJ made a strong statement on the future it envisaged for economic integration in the EU. It subsequently expanded enjoyment of this absolute right to trade in two ways – by enhancing the focus of Article 34 on the consequences of decisions and by including omission to act within its scope. However, it also limited enjoyment of this right by first, introducing additional grounds for exceptions to protect national interests, and second, re-focusing Article 34 so that 'selling arrangements' fall per se beyond its scope.

4. The shifting target of Article 34 TFEU

i.   Scope of application

Initially, Article 34 TFEU only applied to acts of public authorities. However, it was clarified that it is the consequence of a decision rather than the nature of the decision-making body that determines the application of this Article. Local authority actions can violate Article 34 – authorities cannot favour domestic over imported producers in public procurement procedures.[65] Private entities whose activities are linked to public power also fall within its scope. In 'Buy Irish', the organisation whose rule was under challenge was closely linked to the government:

> . . . the Irish Government appoints the members of the management committee of the Irish Goods Council, grants it public subsidies which cover the greater part of its expenses and, finally, defines the aims and the broad outline of the campaign conducted by that institution to promote the sale and purchase of Irish products. In the circumstances the Irish Government cannot rely on the fact that the campaign was conducted by a private company in order to escape any liability it may have under the provisions of the Treaty.[66]

In *Apple and Pear Council*,[67] a body set up under statute and funded by mandatory levies paid by individuals was held to be subject to Article 34, and in *R* v *The Pharmaceutical Society*[68] it was held that if functions are conferred by a member state, a body responsible for the regulation and disciplinary standards of a trade or profession is also bound by Article 34. Likewise a body responsible for national standardisation and certification of

---

[64]Daniel Yergin and Joseph Stanislaw, *Commanding Heights,* Simon & Schuster, 1998
[65]C-45/87 *Commission* v *Ireland (Dundalk Water Supply)* [1988] ECR 4929
[66]C-249/81 *Commission* v *Ireland (Buy Irish)* [1982] ECR 4005
[67]C-222/82 *Apple and Pear Council* v *Lewis* [1983] ECR 4083
[68]C-266/87 *R* v *The Pharmaceutical Society* [1989] ECR 1295

products, even if not-for-profit, comes within its scope. In *Fra.bo SpA*,[69] the CJ held that the decisions of the Deutsche Vereinigung des Gas- und Wasserfaches eV (DVGW), an organisation classed in Germany as a 'public benefit' body was subject to Article 34. DVGW must approve any product used in the supply of drinking water before it is considered compliant with national legislation. DVGW refused to certify the copper fittings produced by Fra.bo, an Italian company whose goods were approved for use in Italy. Fra. bo brought an action against DVGW arguing that its decision was contrary to Article 34 as it restricted access to the German market. The CJ agreed – even though DGGW is a private body under German law, the decisions of DVGW affected the market access:

> [30] . . . in practice, the lack of certification by the DVGW places a considerable restriction on the marketing of the products concerned on the German market . . . almost all German consumers purchase copper fittings certified by the DVGW.

> [31] In such circumstances, it is clear that a body such as the DVGW, by virtue of its authority to certify the products, in reality holds the power to regulate the entry into the German market of products such as the copper fittings at issue in the main proceedings.

> [32] Accordingly, the answer to the first question is that Article 28 EC [Article 34 TFEU] must be interpreted as meaning that it applies to standardisation and certification activities of a private-law body, where the national legislation considers the products certified by that body to be compliant with national law and that has the effect of restricting the marketing of products which are not certified by that body.

For the purposes of Article 34, the formal structure of the body is not determinative – it is necessary to examine the effects of its activities and decisions. The CJ will look beyond the nature of the body to the authority of its rules. It will also look at the purpose of the acts, regardless of whether these are binding or merely seek to exert influence. Regardless of the means used to implement it, the campaign in 'Buy Irish' was deemed to be a:

> [23] . . . a reflection of the Irish government's considered intention to substitute domestic products for imported products on the Irish market and thereby to check the flow of imports from other member states.

Likewise, in *Commission* v *UK*[70] a scheme which required all goods to be clearly marked with the country of origin was found to be a MEQR. The rule was non-discriminatory in form only – it hampered the sale of goods made in other countries. Again the CJ looked at the purpose of the rule and assessed its impact on economic integration:

> [17] . . . secondly, it has to be recognized that the purpose of indications of origin or origin-marking is to enable consumers to distinguish between domestic and imported products and that this enables them to assert any prejudices which they may have

---

[69]C-171/11 *Fra.bo SpA v Deutsche Vereinigung des Gas- und Wasserfaches eV (DVGW)*. For comment see Rob Van Gestel and Hans-W. Micklitz, 'European Integration Through Standardization: How Judicial Review Is Breaking Down the Clubhouse of Private Standardization Bodies', *Common Market Law Review* 50, 2013, pp. 145–182. Particularly interesting is their comment that standardisation bodies are also undertakings under Article 101 TFEU.
[70]C-207/83 *Buy Irish* [1985] ECR 1201

against foreign products. As the court has had occasion to emphasize in various contexts, the Treaty, by establishing a common market and progressively approximating the economic policies of the member states seeks to unite national markets in a single market having the characteristics of a domestic market. Within such a market the origin-marking requirement not only makes the marketing in a member state of goods produced in other member states in the sectors in question more difficult; it also has the effect of slowing down economic interpenetration in the community by handicapping the sale of goods produced as the result of a division of labour between member states.

Bearing this in mind, the CJ decided that the origin-marking was liable to increase the production costs of imported goods and make them more difficult to sell in the United Kingdom market. Such campaigns are far from rare:

> Campaigns that encourage the purchase of national products as opposed to imported products have a long history around the globe. This is especially true of the food sector, where the quality of goods cannot always be easily recognized and where one must also take into consideration that food is closely related to the land, nation's survival, prosperity and public security. In recent years, as we are facing three coinciding crises (economic, food and environmental), these campaigns are particularly wide-spread. However, within the EU such intentional boosting of consumer ethnocentrism contravenes the central idea of the single market.[71]

Country of origin labelling (COOL) is permissible in line with EU regulations.[72] It will apply to meat products when the new 'Food Information to Consumers' (FIC) Regulation 1169/2011 becomes applicable on 13 December 2014.

APPLYING THE LAW

Consider whether the planned UK introduction of country of origin labelling is an example of 'ethnocentric consumerism' contrary to Article 34 TFEU? Read Article 26 FIC – when is COOL mandatory?

---

ii. Omission to act

Article 34 applies to acts as well as omissions to act. The scope of *Dassonville* includes failure to act by a member state. This was made clear in *Commission v France*.[73] French farmers decided to demonstrate their dissatisfaction with the predominance of imports by violently attacking lorry drivers transporting agricultural products from other member states – including Spain, Denmark and Belgium – in France. Lorries were intercepted and loads destroyed by groups of French farmers. Threats were also made against French

---

[71]Janja Hojnik, 'Free Movement of Goods in a Labyrinth: can *Buy Irish* survive the crises?', *CMLR* 49, 2012, p. 291
[72]COOL is mandatory for honey (Directive 2011/100/EC), fruit and vegetables (Regulation No 543/2011), olive oil (Regulation No 1019/2002), fishery and aquaculture products (Regulation No 1379/2013) and beef (Regulation No 1760/2000 and Regulation 1825/2000).
[73]C-265/95 *Commission v France* [1997] ECR I-6959 [29]

supermarkets selling agricultural products originating in other member states, and such goods were damaged when displayed in shops in France. The official response to this action was permissive. After 10 years of receiving complaints of vandalism, the Commission decided to act by issuing an Article 258 TFEU infringement proceeding against France for failure to act. The complaint was upheld:

[30] As an indispensable instrument for the realization of a market without internal frontiers, Article 30 [34 TFEU] therefore does not prohibit solely measures emanating from the State which, in themselves, create restrictions on trade between Member States. It also applies where a Member State abstains from adopting the measures required in order to deal with obstacles to the free movement of goods which are not caused by the State . . .

[32] Article 30 [34 TFEU] therefore requires the Member States not merely themselves to abstain from adopting measures or engaging in conduct liable to constitute an obstacle to trade but also, when read with Article 5 of the Treaty, to take all necessary and appropriate measures to ensure that that fundamental freedom is respected on their territory.

In *Commission* v *France* the CJ argued that omission to act is therefore just as likely to obstruct cross-border trade as is a positive act. A different decision was reached in *Schmidberger*[74] which also involved individuals taking private action.

Schmidberger arose when the Austrian authorities failed to take action to prevent demonstrators forming a blockade across a major trade route, the Brenner motorway. As a result, traffic was disrupted for nearly 30 hours. However, the circumstances were very dissimilar to those in *Commission* v *France*: the CJ distinguished the two cases from the outset. In *Schmidberger*:

- the demonstration had been authorised by the competent authorities;[75]
- the obstacle to free movement was confined to a single route, on a single occasion – the 'geographic scale and the intrinsic seriousness of the disruption' was limited in comparison with *Commission* v *France*;[76]
- the demonstration was an expression of a fundamental right by citizens 'manifesting in public an opinion which they considered to be of importance to society' – their goal was not to restrict trade in goods of a particular type or from a particular source or destroy goods in transit or on display;[77]
- the authorities had taken steps to limit and minimise the disruption caused by the demonstration – there had been an extensive media campaign in Austria and neighbouring countries to inform economic operators of the traffic restrictions and security was in place;[78]

In addition, it was:

[88] not in dispute that the isolated incident in question did not give rise to a general climate of insecurity such as to have a dissuasive effect on intra-Community trade flows

---

[74]C-112/00 *Eugen Schmidberger, Internationale Transporte und Planzüge* v *Republik Österreich* [59] [2003] ECR I-5659. Also *Commission* v *France*.
[75][84]
[76][85]
[77][86]
[78][87]

as a whole, in contrast to the serious and repeated disruptions to public order at issue in the case giving rise to the judgment in *Commission* v *France*, cited above.

In the light of these circumstances, Austria was found not to have breached Article 34 TFEU.

ANALYSING THE LAW

Summarise the key distinguishing features between these two cases. Which do you find most convincing? Why is it important that omissions to act breach Article 34 TFEU?

---

5. Derogations

Every economic activity inherently has 'harmful effects':[79] for every economic advantage, there is a disadvantage which can be benign, local or global. A farmer who allows his cattle or chickens to stray can damage crops in a neighbouring field; smoke from a factory which provides jobs to a community damages the homes over which it falls and sometimes the health of those living in them.[80] This concept of harmful effects can be applied to economic integration under Article 34 – licence rules or product requirements damage the economic potential of other actors. In most cases these harmful effects are tolerated for the goal of economic integration. Under certain conditions, the Treaty recognises that such effects can be excessive, and in such circumstances the goal of economic due process is deprioritised. Market fragmentation is then tolerated for the sake of collective goods.

i. Article 36 TFEU

Infringement of economic due process is allowed in the form of derogations laid out in the Treaty. Article 36 TFEU provides grounds by which the member states can retain distinctly applicable national rules by derogating from Articles 34 and 35 TFEU. These include: public policy, public health and public morality; the protection of health and life of humans, animals or plants;[81] protection of national treasures of artistic, historic or archaeological value; and protection of industrial and commercial property.[82] These Treaty derogations are exhaustive – that is they cannot be added to.

It is for the member state to make the case that the harmful effects go beyond what is acceptable. A key condition for successful use of a derogation is that of 'proportionality'. This requires 'that there be a reasonable relationship between a particular objective and the administrative or legislative means used to achieve that objective'.[83] The idea is that the

---

[79]R.H. Coase, 'The Problem of Social Cost', *Journal of Law and Economics* 3, 1960 reprinted in R.H. Coase, *The Firm, the Market and the Law*, University of Chicago Press, 1990

[80]Dan Danielson, 'Local Rules and a Global Economy: An Economic Policy Perspective', *Transnational Legal Theory* 1(1), 2010, p. 70

[81]See for example C-67/97 *Bluhme* [1988] ECR I-8033 on protecting biodiversity

[82]C-190/87 *Oberkreisdirektor für das Land Nordrhein-Westfalen* v *Moormann BV* [1988] ECR 4689: pre-harmonisation only

[83]De Burca, 'The Principle of Proportionality and its Application in EC Law', *Yearbook of European Law* 13(1), 1993, pp. 105–150

CJ searches for a 'fit' or match between objective and its measure, bearing in mind the affected rights and the interests. AG van Gerven put forward a structure to the proportionality review in *SPUC* v *Grogan*:[84] it begins with clarification of the national aim, asking in particular whether the aim is *legitimate?* The second step is a review of the measure: is the measure a *necessary* and *appropriate/effective* means of achieving the aim? Attention then shifts to the affected interest – is the applicant's interest valid? Finally a balancing test is conducted to evaluate the effect and consider whether there is a means of achieving the aim which would be less restrictive of the applicants interest – is it *proportionate?* The national measure, in order to be justified, must both effectively protect the public good it purports to protect[85] and take the measure which is the least restrictive of trade possible.[86]

Some differences have been noted in the application of the proportionality test. Public policy is such a nebulous concept that it is subject to close scrutiny:

> The concept of public policy . . . must be interpreted strictly, so that its scope cannot be determined unilaterally by each member state without being subject to control by the institutions of the community . . . the particular circumstances justifying recourse to the concept of public policy may vary from one country to another and from one period to another, and it is therefore necessary in this matter to allow the competent national authorities an area of discretion within the limits imposed by the Treaty.[87]

Public health is more open to objective review. In *APESA*,[88] the CJ upheld a prohibition on advertising of beverages with more than 23 degrees alcoholic content as justified as part of a public health strategy. The court does recognise scientific studies, such as those produced by the World Health Organisation (WHO), used by member states to justify their restrictions on certain goods. The case of *Red Bull*[89] shows that a single study can suffice. Red Bull is marketed as the drink that 'gives you wings' – it contains taurine, caffeine, vitamins and sugar which, the company claims, kick-starts the body's metabolism and keeps people alert. One can of Red Bull contains 80mg of caffeine – equivalent to one cup of coffee.[90] The French Food Safety Agency concluded that excessive consumption of taurine causes behavioural problems and France refused to authorise sale of Red Bull, along with other vitamin-fortified foods such as Danone yoghurt and Kellogg's cereals. The European Commission challenged the French ban after manufacturers complained it was inhibiting imports.

The CJ supported France: although some toxicology experts had concluded that the caffeine levels in Red Bull are safe, France had a right to ban the drink on the advice of its own experts. The CJ applied what is known as the 'precautionary principle':[91] it recognised the limits of scientific evidence and because this was inconclusive allowed the French ban. However, as scientific knowledge develops the derogation is less accepted – in 2008 France allowed Red Bull to be sold using the original recipe. It is still banned in Denmark and Norway.

---

[84] C-159/90 *Society for the Protection of Unborn Children Ireland* v *Grogan and others* [1991] ECR I-4685
[85] C-104/75 *De Peijper* [1976] ECR 2; [1978] CMLR 271
[86] C-309/02 *Radlberger Getränkegesellschaft and S. Spitz* [2004] ECR I-11763 (transposition time)
[87] C-41/74 *Van Duyn* [1974] ECR 1337
[88] C-176/90 *APESA* [1991] 1 ECR 4151
[89] C-24/00 *Commission of the European Communities* v *French Republic* [2004] ECR I-1277
[90] Three years ago, Ross Cooney, 18, from Ireland, died after he shared four cans of Red Bull and played in a basketball match. An inquest into his death ruled that he died from Sudden Adult Death Syndrome.
[91] See cases T-74/00, T-76/00, T-83–85/00, T-132/00, T-137/00 and T-141/00 *Artedogan GmbH and Others* v *Commission* [2002] ECR II-4945

It is questionable how strictly proportionality is applied in cases involving public health. How protective can member states be when it comes to smoking and fertility, deodorants, alcohol, BSE or fortified foods such as vitamin bars and energy boosting drinks that are lawfully manufactured and marketed in other MS? In relation to public health there is a strong EU interest which demands strong member state justification. In *Sandoz*[92] a Dutch rule required foods fortified with vitamins to have prior authorisation before sale. The CJ recognised a legitimate concern but found the means disproportionate – labelling was a reasonable alternative.

The CJ appears to rely on labelling as an alternative to many forms of state measures.[93] As the horsemeat scandal shows, labelling is not always an effective solution: it can provide cover for fraud.[94] It can also be meaningless without context and misleading. A further disadvantage is that labels are of no use to the illiterate, and are often not read by the literate. The reliance on science is also worrying – scientific risk can be wrongly assessed: in 1995 the Commission argued that BSE posed no threat to public health.[95] Science contains its own limitations – certainty is limited to what has been tested[96] and the context of those tests may not account for varieties or different levels of exposure to chemicals or vitamins in fortified foods.[97] Scientific certainty also does not shift consumer uncertainty, as seen in the public reaction to GMO in foods.[98] Finally, research can be buried and scientists can be silenced by powerful pharmaceutical companies – the fact that a drug is on the market does not mean that it is not dangerous.[99] Proportionality may be a limited tool to address these complex issues.

Public morality is more subjective. These values are less malleable by scientific standards than public health. In cases concerning public morality, the CJ will recognise yet scrutinise national reasons.[100] The CJ has shown reluctance to scrutinise the justification for national measures in this area too closely but it has not automatically accepted 'public morality'. This is especially so where the forbidden imports are lawfully sold in the member states, as was the situation in *Conegate*.[101] This case concerned the importation of inflatable dolls 'of a sexual nature'. The CJ questioned not only whether the measure was necessary, but also whether it was the real reason for the national action. It held that a member state may not invoke grounds of public morality 'in order to prohibit the

[92]C-174/82 *Sandoz* [1983] ECR 2445; C-178/ 84 *Commission v Germany* [1987] ECR 1227; C-420/01 *Commission v Italy (Red Bull)* [2003] ECR I-6445; C-322/01 *Doc Morris v Deutscher Apothekerverband* [2003] ECR I-14887
[93]Case 27/80 *Criminal Proceedings Against Fietje* [1980] ECR 3839
[94]European Commission, 'Medical devices: European Commission asks for further scientific study and draws first lessons from the recent fraud on breast implants', press release, 2 February 2012
[95]Three independent non-food Scientific Committees made up of external experts provide the Commission with the scientific advice it needs when preparing policy and proposals relating to consumer safety, public health and the environment. The Committees also draw the Commission's attention to the new or emerging problems which may pose an actual or potential threat. They are: the Scientific Committee on Consumer Safety (SCCS), the Scientific Committee on Health and Environmental Risks (SCHER) and the Scientific Committee on Emerging and Newly Identified Health Risks (SCENIHR).
[96]The scandal in early 2012 on PIP breast implants led, for example, to a reassessment of the use of silicone. See 'The Safety of PIP Silicone Breast Implants', Scientific Committee on Emerging and Newly Identified Health Risks (SCENIHR), 1 February 2012, http://ec.europa.eu/health/scientific_committees/emerging/docs/scenihr_o_034.pdf. For details of the issue see http://www.guardian.co.uk/world/2012/mar/15/pip-breast-implant-scandal-7000-more.
[97]In C-54/85 *Mirepoix* the CJ did take account of different levels of activity.
[98]Enzo Loner, 'The Importance of Having a Different Opinion – Europeans and GM Foods', *European Journal of Sociology* (1)31, 2008
[99]Ben Goldacre, 'Bad Science – our collective medical incompetence', *Guardian,* July 17 2010
[100]C-41/74; C-34/79 *Henn and Darby* [1979] ECR 3795; C-121/85 *Conegate* [1986] ECR 1007
[101]C-121/85 *Conegate* 1986 ECR 1007

importation of certain goods on the grounds that they are indecent or obscene where the same goods may be manufactured freely on its territory and marketed on its territory'. However, in *Henn and Darby*[102] the CJ supported the British ban on the importation of pornographic films into the UK despite the fact that the UK treatment of domestic and imported porn was arbitrarily different. The UK successfully relied upon Article 36 – the CJ held that the UK was entitled to ban imports even if a different standard was applied.

VIEWPOINT

Read the Article 'Thalidomide victims get apology from makers after half a century'.[103] How reliable is scientific evidence? To what extent should the Court defer to it?

---

ii.   The mandatory requirements

As a Treaty provision, Article 36 TFEU can only be expanded by the member states via a Treaty amendment. The CJ has, however, used case law to further restrict the right to trade, creating greater sensitivity to the harmful effects of economic integration in EU law.

In *Dassonville,* it suggested a 'rule of reason' which allowed measures which hinder trade within 'reason' to escape the reach of Article 34:

> [6] in the absence of a community system guaranteeing for consumers the authenticity of a product's designation of origin, if a member state takes measures to prevent unfair practices in this connection, it is however subject to the condition that these measures should be reasonable and that the means of proof required should not act as a hindrance to trade between member states and should, in consequence, be accessible to all community nationals.

It expanded upon this in *Cassis*[104] and added substance to the idea by giving some examples.

Germany had a rule mandating that cassis must contain a minimum alcohol content of 25 per cent. This rule applied to all fruit liqueurs marketed in Germany regardless of where they were made – it was an indistinctly applicable technical standard. Cassis made in countries such as France, where there was no such rule, could therefore not be marketed in Germany unless a separate batch was made according to German specifications. Thus this ostensibly neutral rule actually hindered intra-Union trade by creating a dual burden for non-German producers of cassis. It undermined economic interpenetration. The German rule was deemed to obstruct consumer choice and impede trade:

> The concept of 'measures having an effect equivalent to quantitative restrictions on imports' contained in Article 30 of the EEC TreatyTreaty [34 TFEU], is to be understood to mean that the fixing of a minimum alcohol content for alcoholic beverages

---

[102]C-34/79 *Henn and Darby* 1979 ECR 3795
[103]http://www.guardian.co.uk/society/2012/sep/01/thalidomide-victims-get-apology-from-grunenthal
[104]C-120/78 *Rewe-Zentral AG v Bundesmonopolverwaltung für Branntwein (Cassis de Dijon)* [1979] ECR 649; [1979] CMLR 494

intended for human consumption by the legislation of a member state also falls within the prohibition laid down in that provision where the importation of alcoholic beverages lawfully produced and marketed in another member state is concerned.

Thus there was no justification for spirits lawfully produced in one member state to be prevented from being sold in another.

The CJ considered whether there was any good reason for the German law – was it in any way 'necessary to satisfy a mandatory requirement'? According to the German government the answer was yes: the rule protected public interest by providing consumers with consistency and regulating alcohol intake. This was robustly rejected by the CJ as significant enough to displace the priority of economic due process:

[14] . . . it is clear from the foregoing that the requirements relating to the minimum alcohol content of alcoholic beverages do not serve a purpose which is in the general interest and such as to take precedence over the requirements of the free movement of goods, which constitutes one of the fundamental rules of the community.

The practical effect of the rule was rather to promote national beverages by excluding foreign ones – unilateral rules of a minimum alcohol content imposed by a member state constituted an incompatible obstacle to trade. New mandatory requirements were introduced:

[8] Obstacles to movement within the community resulting from disparities between the national laws relating to the marketing of the products in question must be accepted in so far as those provisions may be recognized as being necessary in order to satisfy mandatory requirements relating in particular to the effectiveness of fiscal supervision, the protection of public health, the fairness of commercial transactions and the defence of the consumer.[105]

These grounds are non-exhaustive, potentially limitless as long as the national rule does not discriminate according to nationality. Since this case, they have been extended to include: prevention of tax evasion and unfair competition; environmental protection;[106] improvement of working conditions; press diversity; fundamental rights; and road safety.[107]

These additional derogations could initially only be used to defend *indistinctly* applicable rules, but since *de Agostini*,[108] mandatory requirements can be used to justify *distinctly* applicable measures. As with Article 36 derogations, they must be proportionate: in *Commission v France*[109] a double description was 'not proportional to the aim of ensuring fair trade and consumer protection – the CJ held that the aim was achievable using measures less restrictive to intra-EU trade. It is, however, noticeable that in *Commission v Italy*,[110] the CJ did not impose an exhaustive burden of proof upon Italy to demonstrate the non-availability of a less burdensome national measure to secure road safety.

---

[105]On consumer protection see also: C-407/85 *Drei Glocken v USL Centro Sud* [1988] ECR 4233; C-27/80 *Anton Fietje* [1980] ECR 3839; [1981] CMLR 722; C-448/98 *Guimont* [2000] ECR I-10663
[106]C-302/86 *Commission v Denmark* [1988] ECR 4607, [1989] 1 CMLR 619; C-2/90 *Commission v Belgium* [1992] ECR I-4431, [1993] 1 CMLR 706
[107]C-110/05 *Commission v Italy* [2009] ECR I-519
[108]C-34-36/95 *de Agostini* [1997] ECR I-3843
[109]C-166/03 *Commission v France* (2004) [2004] ECR I-6535
[110]C-110/05 *Commission v Italy*

APPLYING THE LAW

Under what conditions can Article 36 TFEU or the mandatory requirements be used to support a ban on meat from France or other parts of the EU?

6. Market access

EU trade law challenges prevailing common sense. It has been used to remove national regulations that may have been in existence for many years. It could be argued that EU law is undermining important national traditions and eroding culture. On the other hand, one could assert that EU law served a useful purpose in forcing the administration to reflect anew upon the value of norms entrenched out of habit rather than for objective reasons. Article 34 TFEU imposes an obligation to review norms held as common sense and where necessary justify or revise them.

Dassonville increased the scope of this review, both horizontally and vertically. It changed the relationship between the CJ and the EU legislature: national rules were struck down by judicial edict rather than removed via democratic negotiation. Craig and De Burca[111] question whether this establishes a balanced relationship between the CJ and the EU legislature – has the CJ usurped the role of the Commission by extending Article 34 TFEU rather than allowing the legislature to find common cause using Article 114 TFEU for harmonisation? However it can be argued that no more efficient method existed given the challenges of pursuing re-regulation – it is very time consuming. There are also advantages of deregulation – for example, it reduces the creation of static 'Euro-products'[112] and thus keeps product diversity alive. Arguably, the Court acts because the legislature cannot or should not act. However re-regulation/positive integration is unavoidable, as where national market rules are upheld by the CJ,[113] the internal market remains fragmented until new legislation puts a common rule in place. *Cassis* also affected the relationship between the CJ and the national legislature. It introduced the concept of 'mutual recognition' which secures market access by obliging national authorities to accept standards of control conducted by the home state. National legislatures lose some autonomy as a result.

Dassonville was also a gift to wily industrialists. The phrase 'all trading rules' created a powerful tool to be wielded by traders who could afford to challenge any national measure that they judged a hindrance to their interests. They could attempt to redraft the national statute book using Article 34 as part of a commercial strategy.[114] The provision was easy to misuse as any national rule that could be linked to an effect on trade would be caught by it and therefore potentially unlawful unless shielded by Article 36 TFEU or a mandatory requirement.[115] It could be used to challenge rules from the location of

---

[111]Paul Craig and Gráinne de Búrca, *EU Law, Text Cases and Materials,* Oxford University Press, 2011
[112]Damian Chalmers, Gareth Davies and Giorgio Monti, *European Union Law, Cases and Materials,* Cambridge University Press, 2010
[113]As, for example in C-176/90 *APESA* v *DSSC* [1991] ECR I-04151 the CJ upheld a prohibition on advertising of beverages with more than 23 degrees alcoholic content as justified as part of a public health strategy.
[114]This was recognised by the CJ in joined cases C-267 and 268/91 *Keck* and was the reason for the re-examination in that case: '[14] In view of the increasing tendency of traders to invoke Article 30 of the Treaty as a means of challenging any rules whose effect is to limit their commercial freedom even where such rules are not aimed at products from other Member States, the Court considers it necessary to re-examine and clarify its case-law on this matter.'
[115]National judges often deflect attempts to misuse Article 34 TFEU: see Stephen Weatherill 'The Road to Ruin: "Restrictions on Use" and the Circular Lifecycle of Article 34 TFEU', *European Journal of Consumer Law* 2, 2012

aquariums to building regulations and opening hours. As will be seen below, opening hours did indeed become the focus of a campaign by a powerful DIY-business in Britain.

i.   Mutual recognition

Many national trade rules refer to product content. These product requirements are regularly found to be disguised protectionism. In *Walter Rau*[116] the CJ found an indistinctly applicable Belgian rule stipulating that margarine must be sold in cubes contrary to Article 34. Despite being non-origin specific, the rule had a protective effect as it hindered trade by undermining economies of scale. The Belgian government argued that this was in the interests of the consumer, but the CJ determined that, despite the justifiable goal, the interests of the consumer could be protected by a less onerous method – clear labelling.

In the German 'beer purity' case[117] the CJ also overruled the German tradition prohibiting the use of additives in beverages described as 'beer'. The beer purity laws in Germany stipulated that only beer made from barley, hops, yeast and water could be sold as beer. This was justified by the German government as necessary to protect public health and the consumer: it was concerned to prevent overexposure to certain additives.

The derogation was strictly scrutinised due to the strong interest in securing free movement. The CJ acknowledged a legitimate goal but found the rule disproportionate to secure this aim – labelling could meet these objectives. The measure was too disruptive of free movement of goods – it effectively sealed off the German market to beers lawfully produced and marketed in other member states. It was held to be overly paternalistic as it allowed the government to remove choice from the German consumer. In addition, however, the CJ was not convinced of the genuineness of the public health arguments – beer containing the additives in question was lawful in other member states, which was used to conclude that there was no danger to public health.

Product requirements were undermined by the introduction of a single concept. The CJ used *Cassis* to introduce the pivotal concept of 'mutual recognition' to promote economic integration. The principle of mutual recognition promotes 'national treatment'. Instead of member states deciding whether a product could be lawfully marketed in their territory, this concept requires them to recognise the manufacturing rules and traditions of other member states. The Court stated in *Cassis* that it found:

> [14] . . . no valid reason why, provided that they have been lawfully produced and marketed in one of the member states, alcoholic beverages should not be introduced into any other member state.

Thus a product lawfully produced and marketed in any part of the Union is not to be prevented from circulation to consumers in any other member state. Lawfulness in one member state provides a stamp of approval, or passport, for any product throughout the single market. Recognition of the exporting member state traditions does not prohibit the importing state from conducting *different* types of checks – they simply may not repeat those already conducted prior to export. It only applies in sectors where there is no harmonisation.

---

[116]C-261/81 *Walter Rau* v *Lebensmittelwerke* v *De Smedt PVBA* [1982] ECR 3961
[117]C-178/84 *Commission* v *Germany* [1987] ECR 1227

Paradoxically, alongside mutual recognition the ruling created 'reverse discrimination': the German government could not force non-national producers to put less alcohol in their cassis, but the CJ did not go so far as to compel the German authorities to disapply the rule in relation to national producers. The CJ ruling went only so far as to remove the potential protective effect of the German rule; it did not remove the rule itself. Non-German producers and German consumers were empowered as they could enjoy a wider choice of goods, but not German producers – they still had to adhere to the German norm.[118] In addition, the retention of the national rule meant that the market remained fragmented. Mutual recognition therefore secures market access but did not promote economic integration.

Nonetheless, it has been argued that governments prefer mutual recognition to harmonisation:

> . . . mutual recognition of national standards fosters product differentiation and thereby increases market power and profits for all firms including the producers of lower-quality products. Provided that the increase in profits more than offsets potential losses in consumer surplus, mutual recognition will be preferred by most governments to harmonization.[119]

ANALYSING THE LAW

How does the concept of mutual recognition help traders? Why do governments also prefer it?

---

ii. Selling arrangements

The *Dassonville* formula provided little clear guidance as to what type of rules would not fall foul of Article 34 TFEU: the formula was so wide, potentially any rule could be found to be a breach whether it concerned cross-border trade or not, even rules on shop opening times. There was a time when the high streets of Britain were empty on a Sunday – the Shops Act 1980, prohibited trading on Sunday. It was argued, however, by a home improvement company that the ban on Sunday trading breached Article 34 TFEU. Could such a rule be an MEQR? Could it, as stated in *Dassonville*, hinder cross-border trade? The national court was unsure and so asked the CJ for a preliminary ruling on whether the concept of 'measures having an effect equivalent to quantitative restrictions' covers national law prohibiting retailers from opening on Sunday if as a consequence fewer goods were sold in those premises, including goods imported from other member states.

The answer was yes: the existence of the Shops Act was found to fall within the scope of Article 34 but ultimately the traders were disappointed as the rule was found to be justifiable:

> [11] The first point which must be made is that national rules prohibiting retailers from opening their premises on Sunday apply to imported and domestic products alike.

---

[118]This situation differs from the application of Article 34 to purely internal situations as arose in C-321-24/94 *Pistre* and C-448/98 *Guimont* (Emmenthal).
[119]Stefan Lutz and Mario Pezzino 'International Strategic Choice of Minimum Quality Standards and Welfare', *JCMS* 50(4), 2012, pp. 594–613

In principle, the marketing of products imported from other Member States is not therefore made more difficult than the marketing of domestic products . . .

[17] The reply to the first question must therefore be that Article 30 of the Treaty [34 TFEU] must be interpreted as meaning that the prohibition which it lays down does not apply to national rules prohibiting retailers from opening their premises on Sunday where the restrictive effects on Community trade which may result there from do not exceed the effects intrinsic to rules of that kind.[120]

Another example of the broad reach of Article 34 is provided by *Cinéthèque*.[121] This case concerned the tradition of delaying release of DVDs of films until the end of their run in cinemas. It was argued that this enforced delay was contrary to the Treaty. AG Slynn suggested that Article 34 should not apply: the Cinéthèque rules fell outside the Article as they did not impose *additional* measures upon the importers. The CJ disagreed: the rules fell within Article 34 but again, they were justifiable because they were designed to support the film industry, applied irrespective of origin and were proportionate. Thus it was:

. . . conceded that a national system which, in order to encourage the creation of cinematographic works irrespective of their origin, gives priority for a limited initial period to the distribution of such works through the cinema, is so justified . . . provided that the prohibition applies to domestically produced and imported cassettes alike and any barriers to intra-Community trade to which its implementation may give rise do not exceed what is necessary for ensuring that the exploitation in cinemas of cinematographic works of all origins retains priority over other means of distribution.

A further case, *Keck*,[122] illustrated that the lack of outer limits to Article 34 brought it too close to Article 101 TFEU on competition law. Two traders, Mr Keck and Mr Mithouard, had offered goods for sale at a price lower than that which they paid for them. This reselling of products in an unaltered state at prices lower than their actual purchase price ('resale at a loss') was contrary to French law[123] and they were subjected to criminal prosecution. They argued that a general prohibition on resale at a loss was incompatible with Article 34 TFEU.

The CJ used this case as an opportunity to tackle the limitless reach of Article 34. It repeated the *Dassonville* formula but then honed in on the aspect of 'intra-Community trade' and the objective of the rule – the prohibition of resale at a loss was clearly not designed to regulate trade in goods between member states[124] even if it could restrict the volume of sale of products from other member states. The key question was 'whether such a possibility is sufficient to characterize the legislation in question as a measure having equivalent effect to a quantitative restriction on imports'.[125]

The answer to this question produced a distinction between 'product requirements' and 'selling arrangements' – the former were the focus of Article 34, the latter not. This

---

[120]C-145/88 *Torfaen Borough Council v B & Q plc* [1989] ECR 3851 (*Sunday Trading*). See also C-69 & 258/93 *Punto Case SpA* on Sunday trading in Italy.
[121]C-60, 61/84 *Cinéthèque SA and others v Fédération nationale des cinémas français* [1985] ECR 2605
[122]C-267, 268/91 *Keck & Mithouard* [1993] ECR I-6097
[123]Article 1 of French Law No 63-628 of 2 July 1963
[124][12]
[125][13]

long extract should be read carefully. It is easy to assume that the CJ excluded all 'selling arrangements' from the reach of Article 34 TFEU – it did not:

[15] It is established by the case-law beginning with 'Cassis de Dijon' that, in the absence of harmonization of legislation, obstacles to free movement of goods which are the consequence of applying, to goods coming from other Member States where they are lawfully manufactured and marketed, rules that lay down requirements to be met by such goods (such as those relating to designation, form, size, weight, composition, presentation, labelling, packaging) constitute measures of equivalent effect prohibited by Article 30 [34 TFEU]. This is so even if those rules apply without distinction to all products unless their application can be justified by a public-interest objective taking precedence over the free movement of goods.

[16] By contrast, contrary to what has previously been decided, the application to products from other Member States of national provisions restricting or prohibiting certain selling arrangements is not such as to hinder directly or indirectly, actually or potentially, trade between Member States within the meaning of the Dassonville judgment (Case 8/74 [1974] [ECR 837), so long as those provisions apply to all relevant traders operating within the national territory and so long as they affect in the same manner, in law and in fact, the marketing of domestic products and of those from other Member States.

[17] Provided that those conditions are fulfilled, the application of such rules to the sale of products from another Member State meeting the requirements laid down by that State is not by nature such as to prevent their access to the market or to impede access any more than it impedes the access of domestic products. Such rules therefore fall outside the scope of Article 30 of the Treaty [Article 34 TFEU].

[18] Accordingly, the reply to be given to the national court is that Article 30 of the EEC Treaty [34 TFEU] is to be interpreted as not applying to legislation of a Member State imposing a general prohibition on resale at a loss.

The ruling sought to refocus the application of Article 34 TFEU on items that fell into three categories:

a. lawfully marketed goods that were
b. obstructed in their passage across borders by
c. rules relating to their 'designation, form, size, weight, composition, presentation, labelling, packaging'.

A distinction was made between such 'product requirements' that hindered economic due process and other rules relating to the commercial environment, described as 'certain selling arrangements', that did not 'hinder directly or indirectly, actually or potentially, trade between Member States' but could obstruct *market access*. Both types of rules would attract Article 34: as put by Barnard[126] the former would fall per se within Article 34 while the latter would fall per se beyond its reach. The determining factor was their impact on access to the market by traders and products: were the rules universal in their application, and do they have the same impact in law and fact on all products?

---

[126]Catherine Barnard, *The Substantive Law of the EU: The Four Freedoms,* Oxford University Press, 2013

A 'selling arrangement' was not defined in *Keck*. It refers to the conditions affecting the *sale* of a product or the methods by which products can reach the consumer in the host market, for example whether medical products be sold online. It differs from mutual recognition, which is a product-based principle that addresses the entry of goods into foreign markets. Selling arrangements focus on market conditions rather than the product itself: a selling arrangement it asks whether a host state tolerates conditions that exert any punitive effect on foreign traders and their goods.

The principle of 'market access' shifts attention from the product per se to its ability to be purchased in the host trading environment. Market access goes beyond mutual recognition. It is no longer enough for member states to passively accept foreign goods; they are now also required to be proactive in securing equal market access for them, that is ensuring that they are as available for purchase as similar domestic goods. The key question is: how 'welcoming' is the commercial space to foreign products – are there any state-imposed disruptions making their sale more difficult in comparison to national products? As long as the same burden falls on all traders, the national rule prescribing selling arrangements will not even fall under Article 34; however, if it did and was proportionate, the rule could survive a challenge under Article 34.

APPLYING THE LAW

Re-read paragraphs 15 and 16 of *Keck*: when does Article 34 TFEU apply to selling arrangements? Is country of origin labelling a product requirement or selling arrangement?

---

iii. Operationalising 'selling arrangements'

Selling arrangements can be put into two categories: static and dynamic. Static selling arrangements includes retail networks, licensing regimes, opening hours, staffing levels; dynamic ones would include advertising and marketing. Subsequent case law demonstrated that the distinction between selling arrangements and product rules was not as straightforward as initially thought, and also that even selling arrangements can impose an unfair burden that negatively affects market access. Thus although Keck 'de-centralised'[127] selling arrangements, it did not remove them totally from Article 34.

The difficulty of separating selling arrangements from product rules became apparent in *Familiapress*.[128] This case raised the question of when a selling arrangement is integral to a product. An Austrian newspaper publisher, Vereinigte Familiapress Zeitungsverlags- und vertriebs GmbH ('Familiapress'), brought proceedings against Heinrich Bauer Verlag, a newspaper publisher established in Germany responsible for a weekly magazine *Laura* sold in Germany and Austria. *Laura* contained crossword puzzles: readers sending in the correct solution were entitled to be entered in a draw for two prizes of DM500. There were two other puzzles in the same issue, for prizes of DM1,000 and DM5,000 respectively, which were also to be awarded by drawing lots among the persons sending in the correct answers. Familiapress sought an order that Heinrich Bauer Verlag should

---

[127]Nicola 2008, p. 119
[128]C-368/95 *Vereinigte Familiapress Zeitungsverlags- und vertriebs GmbH v Heinrich Bauer Verlag* [1997] ECR 3689

cease to sell in Austria such publications offering readers the chance to take part in games for prizes. This, it argued, breached the Austrian Law on Unfair Competition.[129]

Was the Austrian rule prohibiting competitions in magazines a product requirement or a selling arrangement? The CJ found that it was both and that it furthermore affected market access of non-national traders:

[11] The Court finds that, even though the relevant national legislation is directed against a method of sales promotion, in this case it bears on the actual content of the products, in so far as the competitions in question form an integral part of the magazine in which they appear. As a result, the national legislation in question as applied to the facts of the case is not concerned with a selling arrangement within the meaning of the judgment in Keck and Mithouard.

[12] Moreover, since it requires traders established in other Member States to alter the contents of the periodical, the prohibition at issue impairs access of the product concerned to the market of the Member State of importation and consequently hinders free movement of goods. It therefore constitutes in principle a measure having equivalent effect within the meaning of Article 30 of the Treaty [34 TFEU].

Because it reduced economies of scale, the Austrian law created a burdensome sales environment for non-national traders and was an MEQR. In the absence of this effect, it would have fallen outside of Article 34 TFEU. The definition of an MEQR is thus determined by the *effect* of a rule as well as its character.

However, even selling arrangements can have this effect. An indication of when selling arrangements affect market access was provided in *Franzén*[130] and *Mars*.[131] Criminal proceedings were brought against Harry Franzén for infringement of the Alcohol Law (Alkohollag)[132] which regulates production and sale in alcoholic beverages (drinks exceeding 2.25 per cent alcohol) in Sweden. The Alkohollag limits trade in such beverages to three groups of licence holders:

a   a 'beverage retail licence' is required to sell wine, strong beer and spirit drinks over the counter;
b   a 'production licence' is required to produce alcoholic beverages;
c   a 'wholesale licence' is required to engage in wholesale trade in spirits, wine and strong beer.

Persons holding a production licence may engage in wholesale trade in the products covered by the licence. Holders of either of these licences may also import wine, strong beer or spirit drinks into Sweden. Holders of production or wholesale licences may sell beverages only to the company responsible for their retail, to other holders of production or wholesale licences or to holders of beverage retail licences. The retail company itself may apply for licences in order to effect wholesale sales of alcoholic beverages to holders of beverage retail licences. Under the Alkohollag a statutory body, wholly owned by the Swedish State, Systembolaget Aktiebolag,[133] was created to be responsible for the retail of wine, strong beer and spirits.

---

[129]Gesetz über unlauteren Wettbewerb 1992 (the UWG)
[130]C-189/95 *Harry Franzén* [1997] ECR I-5909
[131]C-470/93 *Verein gegen Unwesen in Handel und Gewerbe Köln e.V. v Mars GmbH* [1995] ECR I-1923
[132]Swedish Law on Alcohol of 16 December 1994
[133]Its activities, operation and inspection procedures are laid down in an agreement made with the State.

Only 223 licences were given up to 1996. They cost SKR25,000 (non-refundable). Each year the holder of a licence also had to pay a charge for the monitoring of his premises, at rates set by the State. At the time of the case, the basic rate was between SKR10,000 and SKR323,750, depending on the kind of beverages and the quantities produced or marketed. The intentional or inadvertent sale of alcoholic beverages without a licence was subject to criminal penalties. Mr Franzén was prosecuted before a Swedish court for intentionally selling without a licence wine purchased from Systembolaget or imported from Denmark. He claimed that he could not be convicted of any offence because the Alkohollag was contrary to Article 34 TFEU. The Swedish court therefore asked the CJ whether a statutory monopoly such as that of Systembolaget was compatible with EU law.

Franzén's arguments were strong: the maintenance of the Swedish retail monopoly impeded the import of alcoholic beverages into Sweden and enabled Systembolaget to promote the marketing of domestic products. Alcoholic beverages produced in other member states could only be sold in Sweden if imported by a production or wholesale licence-holder and if selected on the basis of restrictive and arbitrary criteria set by Systembolaget. Such beverages could be marketed only through a restricted sales network and they could only be promoted by Systembolaget. The CJ was convinced of the negative economic effects of this retail network on non-national traders.

However, could negative effects be justified? The Swedish government argued that the purpose of the Alkohollag was to limit consumption of alcoholic beverages, in particular those of high alcoholic strength, in order to reduce their harmful effects on human health. However, the harmful effects of the licensing system were not assuaged by either Article 36 or the mandatory requirements – despite applying to all products equally, it created a selling arrangement which operated to the disadvantage of non-national traders in alcoholic drinks. Thus the CJ decided that:

> Articles 30 and 36 of the EC Treaty [34 and 36 TFEU] preclude domestic provisions allowing only traders holding a production licence or a wholesale licence to import alcoholic beverages on conditions such as those laid down by Swedish legislation.

ANALYSING THE LAW

Why did Franzén fall under Article 34 and not Article 101 TFEU?

A similar logic was used in *Deutscher Apothekenverband*,[134] in relation to a German law which allowed medicinal products to be sold only through pharmacies located in Germany: while this was acknowledged as a selling arrangement, it was deemed an impediment to market access for non-national pharmacies who could otherwise reach customers in Germany via orders over the internet. However in *Commission v Greece*,[135] a Greek rule restricting the distribution of pharmaceutical products to pharmacists was deemed a selling arrangement and beyond Article 34.

---

[134]C-322/01 *Deutscher Apothekerverband* [2003] ECR I-14887
[135]C-391/92 *Commission v Greece* [1995] ECR I-1621

In *TK-Heimdienst*,[136] an Austrian trading rule[137] which allowed only those traders with a permanent establishment in the same or adjacent district to conduct door-to-door sales of bread, meat, fruit and vegetables was also deemed an impediment to market access. Only bakers, butchers and grocers licensed to sell goods in a permanent shop were permitted to sell these same goods door-to-door in the same or a neighbouring district. Infringements of this rule was a breach of competition law and contrary to public policy.[138]

TK-Heimdienst, a retail trader, sold and delivered deep-frozen goods to regular customers at regular intervals. Goods were either ordered in advance at the registered office or with the drivers direct, or bought on the spot. However, it breached the law by selling groceries door-to-door in the district of Bludenz which did not lie adjacent to Haiming, Völs or Wolfurt where TK-Heimdienst traded from permanent establishments. The Schutzverband, an association for the protection of the economic interests of undertakings, one of whose main purposes is to combat unfair competition, brought an action under Article 53a of the Austrian code seeking, *inter alia,* an order restraining TK-Heimdienst from selling groceries door-to-door in Bludenz.

TK-Heimdienst argued that the rule breached Article 34. The Schutzverband and the Austrian government argued that the national law was a selling arrangement that merely controlled the pool of persons authorised to make sales on rounds. It applied to all the relevant economic operators who conducted business in Austria and thus fell outside of Article 34. The CJ disagreed:

[26] Such legislation imposes an obligation on bakers, butchers and grocers who already have a permanent establishment in another Member State and who wish to sell their goods on rounds in a particular administrative district such as an Austrian Verwaltungsbezirk to set up or purchase another permanent establishment in that administrative district or in an adjacent municipality, whilst local economic operators already meet the requirement as to a permanent establishment. Consequently, in order for goods from other Member States to enjoy the same access to the market of the Member State of importation as domestic goods, they have to bear additional costs ...

Despite being a selling arrangement, the rule had a heavier impact on the market access for non-national traders. It therefore fell within Article 34 as the rules imposed a dual burden.

VIEWPOINT

Do you agree with this decision? Why?

Advertising has been a slippery issue under Article 34: is it a product requirement or a selling arrangement? It was found to be a selling arrangement in proceedings brought by a French import company Édouard Leclerc-Siplec[139] against TF1 Publicité and M6 Publicité. The latter companies refused to broadcast an advertisement on the distribution of fuel in

---

[136]C-254/98 *Schutzverband gegen unlauteren Wettbewerb and TK-Heimdienst Sass GmbH* [2000] ECR I-151
[137]Article 53a(1) of the Gewerbeordnung 1994 (Austrian Code of Business and Industry 1994)
[138]Article 1 of the Gesetz gegen den unlauteren Wettbewerb (Law against unfair competition)
[139]C-412/93 *Société d'Importation Edouard Leclerc-Siplec v TF1 Publicité SA and M6 Publicité SA* [1995] ECR I-179

E.Leclerc supermarkets on the ground that French law[140] excluded the distribution sector from televised advertising. The CJ placed this rule beyond the scope of Article 34:

[22–23] A provision such as that at issue . . . concerns selling arrangements since it prohibits a particular form of promotion (televised advertising) of a particular method of marketing products (distribution) . . . those provisions, which apply regardless of the type of product to all traders in the distribution sector, even if they are both producers and distributors, affect the marketing of products from other Member States and that of domestic products in the same manner . . .

24 The reply should accordingly be that on a proper construction Article 30 of the Treaty [34 TFEU] does not apply where a Member State, by statute or by regulation, prohibits the broadcasting of televised advertisements for the distribution sector.

Yet the CJ held that a total ban on advertising of alcohol on radio, television and in non-trade literature falls within Article 34. The question arose in the *KO* cases.[141] As seen in the *Franzén* case, Sweden regulates closely the sale of alcohol of more than 2.25 per cent alcoholic content; it totally bans public advertisement of these products in all media other than the alcoholic beverage trade press. Gourmet International Products AB breached this rule when they allowed three pages of adverts to appear in their non-trade subscription magazine *Gourmet*, even though only 10 per cent of the readership were private individuals. The Swedish Consumer Ombudsman brought a complaint before the Swedish court, which in turn asked the CJ whether the absolute ban on advertising fell within Article 34 TFEU. The Swedish court, the Consumer Ombudsman and the intervening governments claimed that if it did, the derogation provided for in Article 36 TFEU of the Treaty covered the national prohibition.

They emphasised in particular that the prohibition was not absolute and did not prevent members of the public from obtaining information in restaurants, on the Internet, in an 'editorial context' or by asking the producer or importer to send advertising material. Furthermore, the Swedish government reminded the Court of its acknowledgment that, at that stage of Community law, member states are at liberty, within the limits set by the Treaty, to decide on the degree of protection which they wish to afford to public health and on the way in which that protection is to be achieved.[142] Moreover, the Swedish government maintained that the legislation constituted an essential component of its alcohol policy.

Gourmet International claimed that the outright prohibition on advertising was disproportionate, since the protection sought could be obtained by a more limited prohibition focusing on public places or press aimed at children and adolescents. It reminded the Court that the Swedish policy on alcoholism already included a monopoly on retail sales, the prohibition on sales to persons under the age of 20 and information campaigns. The total ban on advertising was therefore perhaps overkill.

The CJ observed that:

A prohibition on advertising . . . must therefore be regarded as affecting the marketing of products from other Member States more heavily than the marketing of domestic

---

[140]Article 8 of Decree No 92-280 of 27 March 1992, implementing Article 27(1) of the Law of 30 September 1986 on freedom of communication and setting general principles for advertising and sponsorship, JORF of 28 March 1992, p. 4313
[141]C-34-36/95 *Konsumentombudsmannen (KO)* v *De Agostini (Svenska) Förlag AB* and C-405/98 *Konsumentombudsmannen (KO)* v *Gourmet International Products* [2001] ECR I-1795
[142]Joined Cases C-1 and 176/90 *Aragonesa de Publicidad Exterior and Publivía* [1991] ECR I-4151

products and as therefore constituting an obstacle to trade between Member States caught by Article 30 of the Treaty [34 TFEU].

It did acknowledge the genuine objective of the Swedish government to protect public health, and recognised that this obstacle may be justified by the protection of public health as long as the measures are proportionate:

> Articles 30 and 36 of the Treaty do not preclude a prohibition on the advertising of alcoholic beverages such as that laid down in Article 2 of the Alkoholreklamlagen, unless it is apparent that, in the circumstances of law and of fact which characterise the situation in the Member State concerned, the protection of public health against the harmful effects of alcohol can be ensured by measures having less effect on intra-Community trade.[143]

Prohibitions on advertising were also in conflict with Article 34 where they prevented economies of scale. Thus in *Mars*[144] the CJ held that:

> Although it applies to all products without distinction, a prohibition such as that in question . . . which relates to the marketing in a Member State of products bearing the same publicity markings as those lawfully used in other Member States, is by nature such to hinder intra-Community trade. It may compel the importer to adjust the presentation of his products according to the place where they are to be marketed and consequently to incur additional packaging and advertising costs.

APPLYING THE LAW

Is the rule in *Walter Rau* a selling arrangement or a product requirement?

iv. Consumer dissuasion

A different set of issues arise when the CJ is asked to consider whether national rules stipulating how certain goods can be *used* falls within the scope of Article 34 TFEU. This question has so far appeared in relation to the use of jet-skis,[145] tinted windows[146] and motorcycle trailers.[147] Opinions among the Advocates General diverged: AsG Leger, Bot and Kokott argue that such issues were beyond Article 34 but AG Maduro[148] argues the contrary. The CJ has thus far sided with Maduro but found in some cases that the rules were justifiable.

Portuguese law prohibited the affixation of tinted film to the windows of passenger seats in motor vehicles. This was defended as necessary to combat crime and guarantee road safety – tinted windows made it impossible to see inside vehicles and thus enforce

[143] C-405/98 *Gourmet International Products* [2001] ECR I-1795
[144] C-470/93 *Verein gegen Unwesen in Handel und Gewerbe Köln v Mars* [1995] ECR I-1923
[145] C-142/05 *Mickelsson and Roos* [2009] ECR I-4273
[146] C-265/06 *Commission v Portugal* [2008] ECR I-2245
[147] C-110/05 *Commission v Italy* (Leger and Bot)
[148] C-158/04 and C-159/04 *Alfa Vita Vassilopoulos and Carrefour-Marinopoulos* [2006] ECR I-8135

rules such as the wearing of seat belts. Although the ban simply limited use, it was found to be a product requirement that undermined the marketing of lawfully marketed tinted film:

> A Member State whose legislation prohibits the affixing of tinted film to the windscreens and the windows alongside the passenger seats in motor vehicles fails to fulfil its obligations under Articles 28 EC and 30 EC [34 and 36 TFEU] and Articles 11 and 13 of the Agreement on the European Economic Area. That prohibition affects the marketing of almost all coloured film, lawfully manufactured and marketed in other Member States or in States party to the EEA Agreement intended to be affixed to the windows of motor vehicles and is excessive and disproportionate with respect to the objectives of combating crime and ensuring road safety which it seeks to guarantee.

The CJ acknowledged the importance of being able to observe passengers in motor vehicles, but did not think the ban was necessary to achieve this aim – it found the complete ban disproportionate and argued that films which were thinner should be permitted:

> Therefore, although it may be capable of facilitating the inspection of the passenger compartment of motor vehicles by means of simple observation from outside the vehicles, it does not follow that it is necessary to attain those objectives. In that connection, a visual inspection is only one means among others in order to fight crime and prevent offences relating to the obligation to wear seat belts, and at least some films, namely those with a sufficient degree of transparency, permit the desired visual inspection of the interior of motor vehicles.

A more lenient approach was taken towards an Italian rule[149] which prohibited the use of trailers designed for use with motorcycles. These were used in many member states, but forbidden in Italy in order to promote road safety.

> [57–8] Article 56 of the Highway Code prevents a demand from existing in the market at issue for such trailers and therefore hinders their importation . . . its effect is to hinder access to the Italian market for trailers which are specially designed for motorcycles and are lawfully produced and marketed in Member States other than the Italian Republic, constitutes a measure having equivalent effect to quantitative restrictions on imports within the meaning of Article 28 EC [34 TFEU], unless it can be justified objectively.

However, given the imperative requirement of road safety it held that:

> . . . Member States cannot be denied the possibility of attaining an objective such as road safety by the introduction of general and simple rules which will be easily understood and applied by drivers and easily managed and supervised by the competent authorities.

This decision was reaffirmed in *Mickelsson and Roos*.[150] A Swedish rule[151] set out that jet-skis could only be used on 'general navigable waterways' and such other waterways

---

[149]C-110/05 *Commission v Italy*

[150]C-142/05 [2009] ECR I-4273

[151]Regulation No 1993/1053 on the use of jet-skis (personal watercraft) (förordning (1993/1053) om användning av vattenskoter), as amended by Regulation No 2004/607 (förordning (2004/607)

as expressly permitted by local rules. As a matter of fact, no such local rules had been passed and consequently jet-skis could only be used on 'general navigable waterways'. But 'general navigable waterways' are relatively few in Sweden and very busy with commercial traffic. In practice, therefore, the actual use of jet-skis in Sweden is marginal. Mickelsson and Roos were prosecuted by the Åklagaren (Public Prosecutor's Office) for failure to comply with this prohibition. They argued that the rule was contrary to Article 34. As in the cases above, the Court of Justice held that this Swedish rule on the use of jet-skis was an MEQR but it could be justified under Article 36 TFEU.

A different type of prohibition on usage was examined in *Commission v Austria:*[152] an Austrian rule prohibited lorries of over 7.5 tons carrying goods as diverse as waste material, ferrous ore and cereal from using a section of motorway on a main transport route between southern Germany and northern Italy. The rule was adopted in order to protect the ambient air quality in accordance with EU law.[153] It applied to any goods transporter regardless of nationality. The court held that it nonetheless breached Articles 34 and 35 TFEU because:

> [116] . . . By forcing the undertakings concerned to seek viable alternative solutions for the transport of the goods covered by the contested regulation, the sectoral traffic prohibition is liable to have a substantial effect on the transit of goods between northern Europe and northern Italy (see, to that effect, Case C-320/03 *Commission v Austria,* paragraphs 66 and 68).

The rule was an obstacle to cross-border trade, especially market access. It could not be justified under Article 36 TFEU, as less restrictive measures had not been considered.

It is not immediately clear how restrictions on the use of products breaches Article 34. The CJ explained this in *Commission v Italy:*[154] Article 34 contains three key principles which member states are obliged to respect: non-discrimination, mutual recognition and unhindered access to national markets. These principles create three categories of MEQRs:

1 national rules which have the 'object or effect' of less favourable treatment of imports;
2 rules laying down general requirements applicable to all products but which act as an obstacle to lawfully manufactured and marketed goods from other member states;
3 the final group was left wide open – 'any other measure which hinders access of products originating in other Member States to the market of a Member State' is an MEQR.[155]

Rules concerning product usage do not fall into category 1, but can fall into category 3:

> [57] Even if the national regulations at issue do not have the aim or effect of treating goods coming from other member States less favourably, which is for the national court to ascertain, the restriction which they impose on the use of a product in the territory

---

[152]C-28/09 *Commission v Austria* [2011] ECR I-13525

[153]Directive 96/62 on ambient air quality and management OJ L 296/55 1996

[154]C-110/05 *Commission v Italy*

[155]The failure of the French authorities to act against French farmers intercepting and destroying imported goods in C-265/95 *Commission v France* might fall into this category. But see also C-112/00 *Schmidberger* where the Austrian government's respect for the right to demonstrate was upheld.

of a member State may, depending on its scope, have a considerable influence on the behaviour of consumers, which may, in turn, affect the access of that product to the market of that member State. Consumers, knowing that the use permitted by such regulations is very limited, have only a limited interest in buying that product.

Finally, there is no *de minimis* rule in Article 34 – the level of impact makes no difference to finding of an MEQR.[156]

ANALYSING THE LAW

Explain why consumer dissuasion is incompatible with Article 34 TFEU.

---

7. Conclusion

Trade is not a benign activity: as seen by the unregulated trade in financial services markets, too much free trade and open markets can have serious negative consequences for real people and real lives. Thus trade regulation is a necessity. The rules that fragment the EU single market may reflect a strong cultural preference of nationals in a member state – why should Swedes have to accept the advertising of alcohol so that a Maltese beverage company can make them aware of its wines and spirits? Yet if access to the 28 national markets in the EU remains difficult for non-national traders, how can the single market ever become a reality?

The rules explored perform different functions. Articles 28–30 TFEU are triggered by duties and other charges arising when a good crosses an external or internal border, whether it be a duty or a charge for a service. It is an absolute prohibition with very limited scope for member states to justify such charges. These fiscal provisions spare producers taxes which make their wares less attractive to the consumer in other member states; consumers consequently benefit from a wider choice of goods – from shoes to cars to breads – from a wider variety of places. In order to create a fast and efficient EU customs administration, a measure was adopted on the use of electronic means to deal with customs and trade.[157] In addition steps have been taken to tackle international fraud and enhance customs co-operation.[158]

Article 110 TFEU focuses on taxes applied to products once within the member state: under Article 110(1) products made of and used for similar ends may not be treated differently by national taxation policy. An exception exists in relation to indirect discrimination. No such exception exists where tax schedules discriminate between competing goods: if sales of a domestic product are likely to increase if the price of an imported product goes up, the member state is called upon to remove the potential adverse impact

---

[156]C-166/03 *Commission v France* [2004] ECR I-6535

[157]Decision No 70/2008/EC of the European Parliament and of the Council of 15 January 2008 on a paperless environment for customs and trade (OJ L23 2008)

[158]Communication from the Commission to the European Parliament and the Council, 'Enhancing police and customs co-operation in the European Union', COM(2004) 376 final

of different taxation – taxation policy may not be used to 'crystallise' consumer habits and thereby protect national products.[159]

Article 34 TFEU targets rules which include product checks, product requirements, selling arrangements, distribution requirements and product usage. The focus of this provision has evolved from *Dassonville* to *Cassis,* through *Keck* to *Mickelson and Roos.* However, the CJ appears to still be searching for the correct balance that encompasses the broadest range of rules possible but prevents misuse by powerful interests. It is still not entirely clear whether the priority for Article 34 is anti-protectionism (non-discrimination) or economic due process (a right to trade). In *Alfa Vita,* AG Maduro raised this question again. For him the priority of the economic constitution should be to ensure that non-national interests are considered. Rules should therefore be designed without discrimination.

It seems that the product is at the heart of the logic of Article 34. The role of the CJ is to guarantee that selfish policies do not hinder cross-border trade.[160] The CJ tries to identify what the 'good' needs to move freely – what is good for the good? So far it has stated clearly that the good needs entry to the territory (mutual recognition) and an unfettered pathway to consumers (market access). In developing jurisprudence on national rules relating to product usage, the CJ has left a door open to identify other 'needs' for goods.

It relies on the idea of proportionality to determine the degree of discretion left to member states. The structure of the proportionality review assumes a clear set of goals for legislation which can be assessed. A review of legislative papers will, however, reveal that it is difficult to say any legislation has a unitary set of goals – most legislation tries to accommodate a plurality of interests. Greater use of proportionality also increases discretionary power and may permit incursion into legislative prerogatives thereby potentially undermining subsidiarity.

Does there need to be more formality and less flexibility? The obstacles to the internal market are moving targets – less malleability might undermine the potency of Article 34 to tackle them and move trade law in the EU to a new common sense. Indeed, in the age of electronic commerce, free movement of payments will become as important as free movement of goods. It remains to be seen whether consumers are sufficiently protected when they purchase goods across borders.[161]

Is the development of the meaning of an MEQR under Article 34 TFEU good for the peoples of Europe, as traders, as consumers and in their non-economic capacity as citizens? Traders do indeed have more opportunity to benefit from economies of scale – access to larger markets reduces unit costs. This in theory can be good for the consumer, as long as those reduced unit costs are translated into lower prices rather than higher profit margins. The increased choice of products available to consumers is also a clear benefit. Economic integration is also positive for residents and citizens, even if in the short term, there is conflict as norms and values collide: the collision will always result in debate, which can only be healthy in a democracy.

A number of challenges concerning normative and institutional choices remain. What should be the role of the court compared to a legislature?[162] Is a court the correct institution

---

[159]Communication from the Commission to the European Parliament and the Council, 'Promoting Good Governance in Tax Matters', COM(2009) 201 final

[160]C-158/04 and C-159/04 *Alfa Vita Vassilopoulos and Carrefour-Marinopoulos*

[161]Regulation on ODR. See Study Group on Social Justice in European Private Law, 'Social Justice in European Contract Law: A Manifesto', *ELJ* 10, 2004, pp. 653, 672 (in Nicola 2008, p. 144)

[162]James E. Fleming, *Securing Constitutional Democracy – the case of autonomy,* University of Chicago Press, 2006

to host these debates? The answer perhaps depends upon the role of the CJEU in the EU democracy. Also, is it perhaps too distant to sit in judgment on rules that have been debated and agreed by democratically elected law-makers within a state. To some extent, the CJEU has been thrust into this role as the legislative institutions have become mired in conflict. However, judges are not experts and judicial procedures are expensive; furthermore they are ad hoc events reaching decisions focused on the specifics of the case. The concern remains whether the CJEU is being asked to do too much – is it the correct institutional authority to regulate the EU single market and determine the legitimacy of social goals?

Further reading

On trade and economic theory:

R.H. Coase, 'The Problem of Social Cost', *Journal of Law and Economics* 3, 1960, reprinted in R.H. Coase, *The Firm, the Market and the Law*, University of Chicago Press, 1990

Dan Danielson, 'Local Rules and a Global Economy: An Economic Policy Perspective', *Transnational Legal Theory* 1(1), 2010, p. 70

Fernanda G. Nicola, 'Transatlanticisms: Constitutional asymmetry and selective reception of US law and economics in the formation of European private law', *Cardozo Journal of International and Comparative Law* 16, 2008, p. 87

On country of origin labelling:

Janja Hojnik, 'Free Movement Of Goods In a Labyrinth: Can *Buy Irish* Survive The Crises?', *CMLR* 49, 2012, p. 291

On the precautionary principle:

Fisher, Jones and vom Schomberg, *Implementing the Precautionary Principle: Perspectives and Prospects*, Edward Elgar, 2006

De Sadeleer, 'The Precautionary Principle in EU Environmental and Health Law', *European Law Journal* 12, 2006, p. 139

Anna Szajkowska, 'The Impact of the definition of the precautionary principle in EU food law', *CMLR* 47, 2010, p. 173

On mutual recognition:

Stefan Lutz and Mario Pezzino, 'International Strategic Choice of Minimum Quality Standards and Welfare', *JCMS* 50(4), 2012, pp. 594–613

On public opinion and food law:

Enzo Loner, 'The Importance of Having a Different Opinion – Europeans and GM Foods', *European Journal of Sociology* 49(1), 2008, p. 31

13 Freedom of establishment and free movement of services in the EU

Setting the scene

Dozens fell ill and five were hospitalised after eating the 'Cronut Burger' at the Food Festival in Croatia. The vendor that produced this 'doughnut burger' was traced to a small firm established in Vienna, Austria. The Austrian authorities immediately shut it down and the Croatian authorities declared new Festival rules: all vendors, in order to secure a spot, now had to provide a full menu and full list of all ingredients used. A fee is payable for an authorisation certificate and licence to attend. The information has to be provided in the national language meaning overseas operators must pay for a translation. Only licences from the national authority are recognised – no other body can be used. Additionally, only applications from vendors with a permanent establishment will be considered.[1]

---

[1]Please note that while the place names are real, these events are entirely fictitious.

1. Introduction

In order to enable the self-employed to conduct cross-border economic activities, the Treaty also guarantees freedom of movement in two areas beyond goods: establishment and services. This chapter will consider how this branch of EU internal market law supports persons – self-employed as well as legal persons (companies) lawfully conducting business in one member state – to:

1 carry on an economic activity in a stable and continuous way in another member state (freedom of establishment: Article 49 TFEU); or
2 offer and provide their services in other member states on a temporary basis while remaining in their country of origin (freedom to provide services: Article 56 TFEU)

under the same conditions as nationals of the other member state.

They benefit from the protection offered by Article 18 TFEU of non-discrimination on the grounds of nationality. However, as in other free movement areas, protection has been extended to those rules which also hinder or deter the effective enjoyment of these freedoms. These free movement rules help independent traders to operate in other countries, but with some limitations.

Before looking at the rules and their interpretation, it will help to clarify what a 'service' is. Many activities fall under this heading – this word covers a large category of economic activities. The World Trade Organisation Council of Services covers activities as diverse as accounting, aviation and air transport, architecture, engineering, energy, the environment, banking and finance, legal, logistics, maritime, postal, education, telecommunications and tourism.[2] Services can be classified as distributive (wholesale and retail, transportation and communications), producer (advisory, legal services, banking and finance), personal (hotels and catering) and social (health and education). Each type of service has specific characteristics requiring a specific regulatory style. They evolve over time in line with consumer demands: in nineteenth-century Britain, the service sector was dominated by domestic service; in the twenty-first century, retail is the dominant sector along with health and social services. This diversity and dynamism may be why the regulation of service activities has been described as 'chaotic'.[3]

Services are distinct from goods but can be provided during the assembly of a good and after its purchase to facilitate use of a good. Services can be provided as an 'intermediary' phase in the production process of items such as phones and televisions – for example when a Korean firm assembles a product such as the iPad for the creator, Apple. As the CJ said in *Saachi*, a television signal must 'by reason of its nature, be regarded as provision of services' but 'trade in material, sound recordings, film apparatus and other products used for the diffusion of television signals are subject to the rules relating to freedom of movement for goods'.[4]

A service is therefore an input acquired to achieve a particular end. Sometimes that end is a specific product, but often it is also something more intangible – for example, the

---

[2] See the Report by the Chairman of the Council on Trade in Services at http://www.wto.org/english/tratop_e/serv_e/dom_reg_negs_e.htm
[3] Richard Snape, 'Regulating Services Trade: Matching Policies to Objectives', in Takatoshi Ito and Anne O. Krueger (eds) *Trade in Services in the Asia Pacific Region,* NBER East Asia Seminar on Economics (EASE), Volume 11, University of Chicago Press, 2003 p. 96
[4] C-155/73 *Giuseppe Sacchi* [1974] ECR 409 6–7

services of a financial advisor are bought to secure financial well-being. Services do not always result in a 'product' per se: we often purchase a service with a goal in mind rather than a material object. The goal itself is likely to be unique, tailored to the needs of the recipient. The service provider helps to achieve that goal by providing expert input, which is also unique and tailored to the specific needs, but also intangible and non-storable. An example is the broadband and mobile phone packages that are purchased to suit individual communication needs and budgets.

Services can be provided by a person who is self-employed – many plumbers, electricians, carpenters in the construction industry and building trade work for themselves. In contrast to an employed worker,[5] they determine their own hours of work, set their own fees and organise their own tax payments. However, services can also be provided by persons working for established companies: KPMG, a large global consultancy, employs experts to provide financial, management and accountancy services to businesses and governments around the world. EU rules cover service provision by those operating as sole traders – such as small caterers – as well as larger establishments that provide services in the EU.

Services are of increasing importance: barely existent in 1957, they have for the last 30 years been the largest growing sector of the global economy, accounting for two-thirds of global output, one-third of global employment and almost 20 per cent of global trade. The pace of growth has differed from place to place: in Britain, 9 per cent worked in manufacturing in 2011 and 81 per cent worked in services. The sector is predominantly female – 92 per cent of women in work are employed in the services sector, although men are not far behind with 71 per cent.[6] Services now represent 70 per cent of employment in the EU GDP; 9 out of every 10 new jobs are in the service sector.[7] In short, services are important: Hatzopoulos calls them 'the driving force of the EU economy.'[8]

It should be noted that some – but not all – social services provided by the state such as health, education and care services, are in EU law designated 'services of general economic interest' (SGEI) and 'social services of general interest' (SSGI). This includes activities such as childcare or postal services, debt advisory or drug rehabilitation services as well as social security schemes.[9] They are not covered by the internal market rules on free movement of services and establishment – the internal market focuses on what can be described as 'commercial' rather than 'social' services although there is a fine line between the two. The Treaty does not specify which services may be provided or businesses established hence these rules apply to an ever-expanding range of commercial activities. As well as rules relating to qualifications and authorisation, in *Mobistar*,[10] a national tax measure was found capable of being a restriction on the freedom to provide services.

---

[5]C-66/85 *Lawrie Blum* v *Land Baden-Württemberg* [1986] ECR 2121
[6]Office of National Statistics, 'After 170 years of labour market change, now only 1 per cent of workers are in agriculture' at http://www.ons.gov.uk/ons/rel/census/2011-census-analysis/170-years-of-industry/170-years-of-industrial-changeponent.html. See also Rosemary Bennett 'How British Workers left the land to sow careers in service sector', *The Times*, 6 June, 2013, p. 4
[7]Preambular Para 4, Services Directive
[8]Vassilis Hatzopoulos, 'The Courts Approach to services (2006–2012): from case law to case load?', *CMLR* 50, 2013, pp. 459–512; see also Enchelmaier, 'Always at your service (within limits): The ECJ's case law on Article 56 TFEU (2006–11)', *European Law Review* 36(5), 2011, pp. 615–650
[9]European Commission Staff Working Document, 'Guide to the application of the European Union rules on state aid, public procurement and the internal market to services of general economic interest, and in particular to social services of general interest', SWD(2013) 53 final, p. 22
[10]Joined cases C-544/03 and C-545/03 *Mobistar and Belgacom Mobile* [2005] ECR I-7723 [28]

The regulation of services pursues both economic (market failure, protection and promotion of competition) and non-economic objectives:

> Services are regulated to pursue a variety of objectives, economic and noneconomic. Among the former are problems associated with asymmetric information (including consumer protection and prudential requirements), monopoly (including natural monopolies), public goods and externalities, protection of intellectual property, and the improvement of the terms of foreign trade and investment. There are also technical matters (e.g., the scarcity of the radio frequency spectrum) that are of economic importance. Among the noneconomic objectives are distributional matters including universal availability, cultural and social objectives, and national ownership. Of course, there are also straight-out industry protection objectives for many governments.[11]

The regulation has to accommodate different 'modes' – the World Trade Organisation (WTO) identifies four 'modes' of trade in commercial services:

1 'cross-border supply', such as international phone calls, where services are supplied from one country to another – (the service travels);
2 'consumption abroad' where recipients consume a service in another country, as tourists do when they go abroad – (the recipient travels);
3 'commercial presence' where a non-national entrepreneur or company seeks to establish subsidiaries or branches to provide services in another country (e.g. foreign banks setting up operations in a country) – (pursuit of an economic activity);
4 'presence of natural persons' where individuals travel from their own country in order to supply services in another (e.g. fashion models, medics or consultants) – (the service provider travels).[12]

National rules can regulate the service provider, the service itself (how and where it is provided, for example) or the recipient of the service. These rules can be imposed by the

TABLE 13.1   Illustrative cases by mode and sector

Mode	Distributer	Producer	Personal	Social
1. 'cross-border supply' (Article 56 TFEU)	Bond; Debauve; Gambelli	Van Binsbergen; Alpine Investments	Carpenter	Commission v France ('doctors')
2. 'consumption abroad' (Article 56 TFEU)			Luisi & Carbone	Cowan; Muller Faure; Watts
3. 'commercial presence' (Article 49 TFEU)	Viking; SEPLA	Thieffrey; Vlassopoulou		van Wesemael
4. 'presence of natural' (Article 49 or 56 TFEU)		Haim; Bouchoucha		'Tourist Guide' cases

---

[11]Snape 2003, p. 83
[12]http://www.wto.org/english/thewto_e/whatis_e/tif_e/agrm6_e.htm

home state or the host/importing state. They can be discriminatory or non-discriminatory, subjecting non-national services and providers to different rules or rules which are neutral but act as a deterrent. Unless justified, they will breach the free movement rules. EU rules on free movement of services therefore cover the *service* itself as well as the *service provider*. In some instances these rules guarantee rights of the *recipient* of the service: needless to say, just like the service provider, the service recipient can be an individual or a firm. EU law covers all of these modes of movement and will apply as long as one of the trio – the service, the recipient or the provider – is located in another member state. Thus the situation in *van Binsbergen*,[13] where a Dutch lawyer used Article 56 to challenge Dutch rules, was not a wholly internal affair because the recipient of the planned services was in a different member state. Likewise in *Carpenter,* a British national in England could use Article 56 to challenge British immigration rules that would prevent him providing services abroad.[14] Under these provisions, the emphasis falls strictly on cross-border activities. The Court clarified in the 'Tourist Guide' cases that Article 56 applies

> 'in all cases where a person providing services offers those services in a Member State other than that in which he is established, wherever the recipients of those services may be established'.[15]

Where all the relevant elements of the activity under question fall wholly within a single member state, these provisions will not apply.[16] In *Debauve*,[17] where the situation appeared to be confined to a single member state, the CJ held that:

> [9] . . . the provisions of the Treaty on freedom to provide services cannot apply to activities whose relevant elements are confined within a single member state. Whether that is the case depends on findings of fact which are for the national court to establish.

The modes will be used as themes to explore the concepts used by the Court to create a single internal market in services. Cases arising from broadcasting rules and gambling will demonstrate the deference to national autonomy in issues of 'cross-border supply'. However, cases concerning 'consumption abroad', in particular of healthcare services, demonstrate a less deferential approach. The strongest defence of free movement of services and establishment appears in cases dealing with 'commercial presence' and 'presence of natural persons' – it will be seen that the CJ tries to defend the rights of natural and legal persons under these provisions. Before plunging into the case law, the primary and secondary rules will be laid out.

2. The EU rules

The Treaty law tackling national restrictions on freedom of establishment and free movement of services are found in Articles 49 and 56 TFEU respectively. These two provisions must address different types of national rules. National rules can be adopted which affect the recipient, the service provider or the service itself. Rules can restrict the provision of

---

[13]C-33/74 *Van Binsbergen v Bedrijfsvereniging voor de Metaalnijverheid* [1974] ECR 1299
[14]C-60/00 *Mary Carpenter* [2002] ECR I-6279
[15]C-154/89 [*Commission v France* [1991] ECR I-659 10]
[16]See also C-60/91 *Criminal proceedings against José António Batista Morais* [1992] ECR I-2085 [8]; C-134/95 *USSI N. 47 di Bella Biella v INAIL* [1997] ECR I-195; C-108/98 *RI. SAN* [1999] ECR I-5219
[17]C-52/79 *Procureur du Roi v Marc J.V.C. Debauve and others* [1980] ECR 833

a service per se, but predominantly they regulate who may provide a service and how a service may be provided – a service may be banned (such as abortion services in Ireland),[18] or restricted to certain statutory bodies and mode of delivery (as in gambling in Italy). Such rules can take the form of a total or partial prohibition, qualification requirements and procedures, authorisation and licensing requirements and technical standards. These rules affect market access as well as the exercise of an economic activity. Market access restrictions can include quantitative restrictions such as caps on the number of service suppliers (e.g. doctors) in an area or the number of employees; or rules requiring specific types of legal entity for certain activities. A national rule may impose differential taxes or additional charges, licensing or residency requirements on non-nationals that national providers are spared.

As with goods and workers, such rules can be directly discriminatory, indirectly discriminatory or non-discriminatory – any rule which acts as a deterrent will attract Articles 49 and 56 TFEU, even if they constitute an equal obstacle to both foreign and national providers.[19] The obligation of equal treatment prohibits this discriminatory treatment of non-national services and service providers when compared to national services and service providers. Non-discriminatory practices include governance rules that stipulate national residency or lay out long, complex and confusing procedures which hinder or discourage non-national service providers to seek access to the market of another member state.

i.   Article 49 TFEU

The right of establishment is set out in Article 49 TFEU. It prohibits:

> *restrictions on the freedom of establishment of nationals of a Member State in the territory of another Member State.*

The prohibition is therefore only triggered by transnational situations. Freedom of establishment covers primary and secondary establishment: it includes 'the right to take up and pursue activities' either as a self-employed person (natural person) or a company (legal person). Article 49 also creates a right to set up and manage undertakings, in particular companies or firms.[20] There is no distinction in the treatment of natural and legal persons: lawfully formed companies and firms that have their registered office, central administration or principal place of business within the Union shall 'be treated in the same way as natural persons who are nationals of Member States'.[21] It is clear from the *Viking*[22] case and the other three cases in the 'Laval-quartet' that this Article confers rights upon a private undertaking which can be asserted against public bodies such as trade unions.

---

[18]C-159/90 *SPUC* v *Grogan* [1991] ECR I-4685

[19]C-76/90 *Manfred Säger* v *Dennemeyer & Co. Ltd* [[1991] ECR I-4221 12]

[20]Defined in Article 54(2) as companies or firms constituted under civil or commercial law, including cooperative societies, and other legal persons governed by public or private law, save for those which are non-profit-making. Article 54 also applies to free movement of services.

[21]Article 54(1)

[22]*ITF and Finnish Seamen's Union* v *Viking Line ABP and OU Viking Line Eesti* [2007] ECR 1-10779. The 'Laval-quartet' cases are C-341/05, *Laval un Partneri Ltd* v *Svenska Byggnadsarbetareförbundet and Others,* C-346/06 *Rüffert* [2008] ECR I-1989 and C-319/06 *Commission* v *Luxembourg* [2008] ECR I-4323.

Discriminatory regulation can be subtle. Italian legislation on social housing lay down a nationality requirement: only Italian nationals were eligible to buy or lease housing built or renovated using public funds. Reduced rate mortgage loans were also only available to Italian nationals. A Belgian national who sought to pursue activities as a self-employed person in Italy complained to the Commission about this rule when his loan application was refused as a result of it. Could access to social housing fall under the freedom of establishment? There was no doubt that this could be the case:

[15] for a natural person the pursuit of an occupation does not presuppose solely the possibility of access to premises from which the occupation can be pursued, if necessary by borrowing the amount needed to purchase them, but also the possibility of obtaining housing. It follows that restrictions contained in the housing legislation applicable to the place where the occupation is pursued are liable to constitute an obstacle to that pursuit.[23]

'Equality of competition' requires that non-nationals operate under the same conditions as nationals: any restrictions placed on housing or facilities to gain housing undermined that equilibrium, even if the housing were required on a temporary basis. Consequently 'housing legislation, even where it concerns social housing, must be regarded as part of the legislation that is subject to the principle of national treatment which results from the provisions of the Treaty concerning activities as self-employed persons.'[24] These restrictions in Italian housing law therefore breached both Article 49 and 56 TFEU.

In order to comply with Article 49, national authorities must ensure that non-national natural and legal persons are able to engage in these activities 'under the conditions laid down for its own nationals by the law of the country where such establishment is effected' subject only to the provisions of free movement of capital. The prohibition also applies to restrictions on secondary establishment – the setting-up of agencies, branches or subsidiaries by nationals of any member state who are already established in the territory of another member state. Articles 54 and 55 TFEU (ex Articles 293 and 294 TEC) oblige member states to treat non-nationals in the same way as their own nationals as regards participation in the financing of companies or firms.

The transfer of undertakings is perhaps the most fundamental expression of enjoyment of this freedom. Companies exist only by virtue of national legislation that grants them this status, and governs their incorporation and their everyday functioning.[25] Thus if national rules exist to prevent a company from leaving or entering a territory, there will be no freedom of establishment. Such rules can withdraw recognition as well as, limit or set residential conditions upon recognition. They can frustrate company transfers, cross-border company mergers as well as cross-border company conversion.

In the absence of a uniform EU definition of companies, the initial approach to such national rules was cautious: in *Daily Mail*[26] the widely varying national rules on companies

---

[23]C-63/86 *Commission of the European Communities v Italian Republic* 1988 [ECR] 29
[24][17]
[25]C-81/87 *Daily Mail and General Trust* [1988] ECR 5483 [19]; C-210/06 *Cartesio* [2008] ECR I-9641 [104]
[26]C-81/87

was the basis for deciding that Article 49 did not confer a directly effective right upon a company to transfer its principal place of business to another member state without restrictions. However in cases such as *Centros*,[27] *Uberseering BV*[28] and *Inspire Article Ltd*[29] the pendulum appeared to swing in the opposite direction – in these cases Article 49 was used to protect freedom of establishment rights even though it was clear that the objective of overseas incorporation was to avoid more stringent national rules. However, this approach has been modified.

In *SEVIC*[30] and *Vale Construzioni:*[31] in Vale Construzioni remained supportive of national legislation on companies, especially given 'the absence of a uniform definition in EU law of the companies which may enjoy the right of establishment on the basis of a single connecting factor'.[32] Yet it held that the fact that national law alone defines the 'connecting factor' required of a company to be incorporated in its territory and sets out the rules governing incorporation, functioning and retention of status as a company, does not remove it from the purview of Article 49. Thus national legislation enabling national companies to convert, but not companies governed by the law of another member state to do so, is within the scope of Articles 49 TFEU and 54 TFEU.[33] The Hungarian rules were discriminatory – they clearly treated non-national companies less favourably and acted as a deterrent[34] that could not be justified. Notwithstanding the specific challenges of cross-border conversions, the rule was too general to be either legitimate or proportionate:

> [39] In so far as concerns justification on the basis of overriding reasons in the public interest, such as protection of the interests of creditors, minority shareholders and employees, the preservation of the effectiveness of fiscal supervision and the fairness of commercial transactions, it is established that such reasons may justify a measure restricting the freedom of establishment on the condition that such a restrictive measure is appropriate for ensuring the attainment of the objectives pursued and does not go beyond what is necessary to attain them.[35]

> [40] However, such justification is lacking in the present case.

VIEWPOINT

Does the Croatian law fall under Article 49 TFEU? Is it discriminatory or non-discriminatory?

---

[27] C-212/97 *Centros Ltd v Erhvervs-og Selskabsstyrelsen* [1999] ECR I-1459
[28] C-208/00 *Uberseering BV v Nordic Construction Company* [2002] ECR I-9919
[29] C-167/01 *Kamer van Koophandel en Fabrieken voor Amsterdam v Inspire Article Ltd* [2003] ECR I-10155. For comment on economic integration and regulatory arbitrage in these cases see P. Schammo, 'Arbitrage and abuse of rights in the EC legal system', *European Law Journal* 14(3), 2008, pp. 351–376
[30] C-411/03 *SEVIC Systems* [2005] ECR I-10805 [19]
[31] C-378/10 Vale *Construzioni* [2012]
[32] C-371/10 *National Grid Indus* [2011] ECR I-0000 [26]
[33] [32–33]
[34] [36]
[35] *SEVIC Systems* [28 and 29]

ii. Article 56 TFEU

Under this Article:

. . . restrictions on freedom to provide services within the Union shall be prohibited in respect of nationals of Member States who are established in a Member State other than that of the person for whom the services are intended.

It prohibits overt and covert discrimination[36] and as it is directly effective[37] may be used by individuals before national courts. Nationals of countries beyond the EU are explicitly excluded from this freedom by Article 56(1) but the Treaty gives the European Parliament and the Council discretion to use the ordinary legislative procedure (OLP) to extend this freedom to 'nationals of a third country who provide services and who are established within the Union'.

The Treaty allows any person providing a service to 'temporarily pursue his activity in the Member State where the service is provided, under the same conditions as are imposed by that State on its own nationals'. This gives rise to three basic questions:

1 Who is a service provider?
2 What is a service for the purposes of the Treaty?
3 When is it temporary?

The 'what' question may be the easiest to answer even if this is an amorphous sector. The Treaty drafters did not attempt a fixed definition – Article 57 TFEU specifies four types of activities:

• activities of an industrial character,
• of a commercial character,
• of craftsmen, and
• of the professions.

Services in transport, banking and insurance are explicitly excluded by Article 58 TFEU. The only 'definition' of a service offers limited guidance – services are identified negatively, as those activities not governed by the Treaty provisions on goods, capital and persons and using an economic rationale, as activities 'normally provided for remuneration'.

The role of remuneration can be seen in the case of *Grogan* in which the Irish applicants were students voluntarily providing information on abortion services in England. As abortion is contrary to the Irish Constitution,[38] this was an unlawful activity. However, as the students were not acting on behalf of any particular clinic they could not rely upon Article 56 TFEU – because the material was distributed voluntarily, there was no economic activity thus they were not providing a service under EU law. This emphasis on financial gain also places private education[39] within the reach of EU law on services but not education that is state financed or provided as a not-for-profit activity.[40] Contributions to operating expenses do not count as remuneration.

---

[36]Joined cases 62 and 63/81 *Société anonyme de droit français seco and société anonyme de droit français desquenne & giral* v *Etablissement d'assurance contre la vieillesse et l'invalidité* [1982] ECR 223 8
[37]C-33/74 *Van Binsbergen* v *Bedrijfsvereniging voor de Metaalnijverheid* [1974] ECR 1299 [24] '. . . the provisions of Article 59, the application of which was to be prepared by directives issued during the transitional period, therefore became unconditional on the expiry of that period.'
[38]http://www.guardian.co.uk/world/2013/apr/08/abortion-refusal-death-ireland-hindu-woman
[39]C-109/92 *Stephan Max Wirth* v *Landeshauptstadt Hannover* [1993] ECR I-6447
[40]C-263/86 *Belgian State* v *René Humbel and Marie-Thérèse Edel* [1988] ECR 5365 17–18; Wirth [15]

APPLYING THE LAW

Read paragraphs 17–22 of *Grogan:* how does the CJEU decide that abortion is a service?

According to the CJEU, a service must therefore involve payment or exchange of money. However, the financial aspect need not be guaranteed – in *Schindler*,[41] gambling was held to be a service despite the chance nature of the return. Sporting or leisure activities can also fall under the scope of Article 56 TFEU.[42] However, a service is not a service when a provider is trying to circumvent national professional rules:

[13] . . . a member state cannot be denied the right to take measures to prevent the exercise by a person providing services whose activity is entirely or principally directed towards its territory of the freedom guaranteed by Article 59 [56 TFEU] for the purpose of avoiding the professional rules of conduct which would be applicable to him if he were established within that state; such a situation may be subject to judicial control under the provisions of the chapter relating to the right of establishment and not of that on the provision of services.[43]

What is the difference between services and establishment? Establishment under Article 56 was defined in *Factortame*[44] as 'the actual pursuit of an economic activity through a fixed establishment in another member state for an indefinite period'. In order to be distinguished from services, the activity in another member state must be pursued on a 'stable and continuous basis'[45] as distinct from a temporary service provision. The key determining factors are the 'duration, regularity, periodicity and continuity of the provision of the services'.[46] However, the precise dividing line is unclear as according to *Gebhard*[47] a service provider may also have an office or administrative infrastructure required to provide repeated temporary services in the host member state. *Gebhard* also stated that the provisions on free movement of workers, services and freedom of establishment were 'mutually exclusive'[48] and that according to the wording of the Treaty, freedom of establishment took priority over services.

This has more recently been revised, to the extent that services are now given priority unless there is evidence that the rules on establishment apply. Hatzopoulous[49] identifies three elements – 'factual', 'intentional' and 'activity': it must be demonstrated that the service providers have been established in the host state for a long time (factual); that they intend to remain established there (intentional); in order to reach the customers of the host state (activity). All three elements must be evident for the rules on establishment to apply.

---

[41]C-275/92 H.M. *Customs and Excise* v *Schindler* [1994] ECR I-1039
[42]C-36/74 *Walrave and Koch* v *Association Union Cycliste Internationale and others* [1974] ECR 1405
[43]C-33/74 *Van Binsbergen*
[44]C-221/89 *Factortame* [1991] ECR I-3905, [1991] CMLR 589 [200]
[45]C-55/94 *Gebhard* v *Consiglio Dell'Ordine Degli Avvocati e Procuratori di Milano* [1995] ECR I-4165
[46]In Cases C-316, 358, 359, 360, 409 and 410/07, *Markus Stoß ea* v *Land Baden-Württemberg* [2010] ECR I-8069. Article 49 was used in relation to a self-employed person running an office providing permanent services to an undertaking in another member state. See also C-148/10 *DHL,* judgment 13 October 2011, pp. 54–55
[47]C-55/94 *Gebhard* v *Consiglio dell'Ordine degli Avvocati e Procuratori di Milano* [1995] ECR I-4165
[48][20]
[49]Hatzopoulos, *Regulating Services in the EU*, Oxford University Press, 2012

As with free movement of goods, failure to act can also breach Article 56 TFEU. Italy was found to have failed by taking no action to transpose measures designed to enable non-nationals to access occupations in the media. Italy argued that to transpose the measures into national law would be 'pointless and burdensome' as the Treaty provisions upon which they were based were directly effective.[50] The Commission and the CJ agreed that integration may not be pursued by inaction: member states must actively repeal measures which conflict with free movement.

[13] . . . that argument is ill-founded. The incompatibility of national legislation with provisions of the Treaty, even provisions which are directly applicable, can be finally remedied only by means of national provisions of a binding nature which have the same legal force as those which must be amended. As the court has consistently held with regard to the implementation of directives by the member states, mere administrative practices, which by their nature are alterable at will by the authorities and are not given the appropriate publicity, cannot be regarded as constituting the proper fulfilment of obligations under the Treaty.

Article 56 does not require service provision in the member state of establishment[51] to be activated – the firm in *Carmen Media*[52] was limited to 'offshore bookmaking' and thus unable to provide such services in the member state in which it was established. It nonetheless fell within the Article, as it was established in a member state other than that of the recipient, and could use Article 56 to defend its gambling services in Germany.

APPLYING THE LAW

Does the Croation rule fall under Article 56 TFEU? Is it discriminatory or non-discriminatory?

---

iii. The derogations[53]

National rules can act as a cloak for protectionism, but regulation of services is rarely for this purpose alone. As Snape[54] mentions, regulation addresses a number of issues including consumer protection – one reason for the pervasive regulation of services is the informational inequality between service providers and recipients. National rules may be introduced not to protect traders but to protect the public interest or public goods such as health and safety or the environment. Regulation of gambling may be pursued in the consumer interest or tight broadcasting rules may seek to limit access to pornography in order to avoid long term social costs in terms of addiction, individual and family debt or sexual exploitation of women and girls.

---

[50]C-168/85 *Commission of the European Communities v Italian Republic* [1986] ECR 2945 [7–9]
[51]See C-56/96 VT4 [1997] ECR I-3143 [22]
[52]C-46/08 *Carmen Media Group* [2010] ECR I-8149
[53]J. Snell, 'Freedom to provide services in the case law and in the Services Directive: Problems, solutions and institutions', in U. Neergaard, R. Nielsen and L. Roseberry (eds), *The Services Directive: Consequences for the Welfare State and the European Social Model*, DJOF, 2008, p. 171
[54]Snape 2003

The 'liberalisation' resulting from the removal of national regulation restricting cross-border services may therefore have deleterious social effects and conflict with social values. As with goods, national authorities can defend their rules by using a derogation, either that in the Treaty or the Court-created 'rule of reason'. Separate derogations exist for Articles 49 and 56 TFEU.

a) Article 51 TFEU

Freedom of establishment is limited first, by Article 51 (ex Article 45 TEC) which excludes 'activities which in that State are connected, even occasionally, with the exercise of official authority'. The European Parliament and the Council may exercise their discretion to include other activities to which freedom of establishment should not apply. The meaning of Article 51 was clarified in *Reyners*,[55] when Belgium asserted that professional activities involving contact with the courts fell within its scope. This was rejected:

> [51] professional activities involving contacts, even regular and organic, with the courts, including even compulsory cooperation in their functioning, do not constitute, as such, connexion with the exercise of official authority.

> [52] the most typical activities of the profession of advocate . . . cannot be considered as connected with the exercise of official authority.

> [54] it is therefore right to reply to the question raised that the exception to freedom of establishment provided for by the first paragraph of Article 55 [49 TFEU] must be restricted to those of the activities referred to in Article 52 [56 TFEU] which in themselves involve a direct and specific connexion with the exercise of official authority.

In *Thijssen* it was confirmed that the office of approved commissioner in relation to insurance undertakings did not satisfy those criteria.[56] The need for activities to have a direct and specific connection to the exercise of official authority was repeated in two infringement cases brought by the Commission in relation to private inspection bodies and organic farm products in Germany and Austria.[57] In both countries this activity was restricted to those who had an establishment in the member state, restricting the freedom to those already established elsewhere. As a whole professional activity could not be covered by the derogation, this was rejected. In both cases the private bodies were under the supervision of a higher public body and exercised devolved authority that was auxiliary and preparatory.[58] Bodies conducting vehicle inspections are also not considered to be exercising official authority.[59]

b) Article 52 TFEU

Second, Article 52 provides a derogation on grounds of public policy, public security and public health – this provision can be used to justify discriminatory rules and is to be interpreted strictly.[60] Thus in *ERT*, an objective to 'avoid disturbances due to the restricted

---

[55]C-2/74 *Jean Reyners v Belgian State* [1974] ECR 631
[56]C-42/92 *Adrianus Thijssen v Controledienst voor de verzekeringen* [1993] ECR I-4047
[57]C-404/05 *Commission v Germany*; C-393/05 *Commission v Austria* [2007] ECR I-10195
[58]*Commission v Austria* [42]
[59]C-438/08 *Commission v Portugal* [2009] ECR I-10219
[60]C-260/89 *Elliniki Radiophonia Tiléorassi* (ERT) [1991] ECR I-2925 [24]

number of channels available' could not justify a discriminatory monopoly on broadcast rights. A further exception has been developed by the Court for rules which are an 'over-riding reason in the general interest' – this has mostly been used in relation to healthcare.

The Dutch authorities attempted to use the Article 52 public policy derogation in *Bond:*[61] they argued that the prohibition in the 'Kabelregeling' on advertising and subtitles in programmes transmitted from abroad was necessary in order to protect non-commercial undertakings and thus maintain diversity in the national broadcasting system. While the aim legitimate, the means were disproportionate:

> Even where they are presented as being justified on grounds of public policy, namely the maintenance of the non-commercial and, hence, pluralistic nature of the national broadcasting system, such discriminatory restrictions cannot fall within the deroga-tions authorized by Article 56 of the Treaty [52 TFEU] since they are not proportionate to the intended objective.

Public health was invoked in *Consiglio dei ministri:* the region of Sardinia attempted to defend a regional tax on airflight stopovers as justified by environmental protection to be regarded as 'public health' grounds. The tax, it claimed, was designed to protect the envi-ronment and countryside of Sardinia by, first, discouraging squandering of the environ-mental and coastal landscape heritage, and second, by financing the expensive restoration of coastal areas. The tax was an expression of the 'polluter pays' principle as it was indi-rectly imposed on the operators of a mode of transport seen as a key source.[62] Even such well-intentioned derogations must be proportionate:

> [42] In that regard, it should be borne in mind that, according to settled case-law, irrespective of the existence of a legitimate objective which serves overriding reasons relating to the public interest, a restriction on the fundamental freedoms guaranteed by the EC Treaty may be justified only if the relevant measure is appropriate to ensur-ing the attainment of the objective in question and does not go beyond what is neces-sary to attain that objective.[63] Furthermore, national legislation is appropriate to ensuring attainment of the objective pursued only if it genuinely reflects a concern to attain it in a consistent and systematic manner.[64]

The attempt was unsuccessful: even if the tax was justified, its implementation was dis-criminatory as only those domiciled outside of the region were liable to pay it.[65]

As stated in Article 61

As long as restrictions on freedom to provide services have not been abolished, each Member State shall apply such restrictions without distinction on grounds of nationality or residence to all persons providing services within the meaning of the first paragraph of Article 56.

---

[61]C-352/85 *Bond van Adverteerders* v *Netherlands State* [1988] ECR 2085
[62][41]
[63]As stated in C-150/04 *Commission* v *Denmark* [2007] ECR I-1163 [46]; *Government of the French Community and Walloon Government* [55]; and C-222/07 *UTECA* [2009] ECR I-0000 [25]
[64]C-169/07 *Hartlauer* [2009] ECR I-0000 [55]
[65][43]

c) The 'rule of reason'

The CJEU has developed a further range of reasons which can be used to defend non-discriminatory national rules restricting free movement of services or establishment of any person. In the absence of harmonisation, these stand available for use if a protectionist objective is absent. They were first introduced in *van Binsbergen* where a Dutch rule stating that legal services could only be provided by those established in the Netherlands was challenged as contrary to the Treaty. The ruling discussed the conditions under which a non-discriminatory restriction could be objectively justified in the public interest. The aim of the restriction must be compatible with Union aims – the rules must relate to a profession, be equally applicable to nationals and non-nationals; and be proportionate – the most appropriate means to achieve the stated aims:

> [12] . . . however, taking into account the particular nature of the services to be provided, specific requirements imposed on the person providing the service cannot be considered incompatible with the Treaty where they have as their purpose the application of professional rules justified by the general good – in particular rules relating to organisation, qualifications, professional ethics, supervision and liability – which are binding upon any person established in the state in which the service is provided, where the person providing the service would escape from the ambit of those rules being established in another member state . . .

> [14] . . . in accordance with these principles, the requirement that persons whose functions are to assist the administration of justice must be permanently established for professional purposes within the jurisdiction of certain courts or tribunals cannot be considered incompatible with the provisions of Articles 59 and 60 [56 and 57 TFEU], where such requirement is objectively justified by the need to ensure observance of professional rules of conduct connected, in particular, with the administration of justice and with respect for professional ethics.

This wording was subsequently refined and in *Gouda and others*[66] the Court summarised the range of 'overriding reasons relating to the public interest' that it would accept:

> [14] . . . the overriding reasons relating to the public interest which the Court has already recognized include professional rules intended to protect recipients of the service;[67] protection of intellectual property;[68] the protection of workers;[69] consumer protection;[70] the conservation of the national historic and artistic heritage;[71] turning to

---

[66] C-288/89 *Stichting Collectieve Antennevoorziening Gouda and others v Commissariaat voor de Media* [1991] ECR I-4007
[67] Joined cases 110/78 and 111/78 *Van Wesemael* [1979] ECR 35 [28]
[68] C-62/79 *Coditel* [1980] ECR 881
[69] C-279/80 *Webb* [1981] ECR 3305 [19]; Joined cases 62/81 and 63/81 *Seco v EVI* [1982] ECR 223 [14]; C-113/89 Rush Portuguesa [1990] ECR I-1417 [18]
[70] Case 220/83 *Commission v France* [1986] ECR 3663; Case 252/83 *Commission v Denmark* [1986] ECR 3713; Case 205/84 *Commission v Germany* [1986] ECR 3755; Case 206/84 *Commission v Ireland* [1986] ECR 3817; *Commission v Italy*; and *Commission v Greece*
[71] *Commission v Italy*

account the archaeological, historical and artistic heritage of a country and the widest possible dissemination of knowledge of the artistic and cultural heritage of a country.[72]

To this list can be added the financial balance and stability of national healthcare systems.

APPLYING THE LAW

Can the Croatian authorities use any of these derogations?

iv. Secondary legislation

As with other areas of harmonisation in EU law, secondary legislation is required to set new standards where a gap has been created by the removal of national rules. Competence to create secondary legislation to attain freedom of establishment is set out in Article 50 TFEU: the European Parliament and the Council are to adopt directives using the OLP and in consultation with the Economic and Social Committee. A priority area mentioned for secondary legislation concerns services which impact upon production costs or those which act as a restraint on trade in goods. Article 60 goes further by obliging member states to pursue deregulation of services beyond any adopted directives if the general and sector-specific economic situation allow for this.

An indication of the importance of freedom of establishment and free movement of services to the Union economy is given in Article 51, where a long list of tasks is laid out for these two institutions. Together with the Commission they must:

a. adopt directives in areas where freedom of establishment makes a 'valuable' contribution to the development of production and trade;
b. ensure close cooperation between the competent national authorities and coordination of national rules to safeguard the interests of members;
c. remove administrative procedures and practices, as well as state aids, that may distort freedom of establishment;
d. adopt rules allowing workers of one member state employed in the territory of another member state to stay in that territory in order to take up activities there as self-employed persons, as if they had arrived intending to do such; and
e. secure the abolition of restrictions on freedom of establishment in every branch of activity in relation to the conditions:
   i) for setting up agencies, branches or subsidiaries in the territory of a member state;
   ii) for running those subsidiaries in the territory of a member state; and
   iii) governing the entry of personnel belonging to the main establishment into managerial or supervisory posts in such agencies, branches or subsidiaries.

---

[72]*Commission v France* and *Commission v Greece*

Article 52 (ex Article 46 TEC) allows member states to retain legal or administrative rules providing for special treatment of foreign nationals on grounds of public policy, public security or public health. Indeed, such measures are to be coordinated using directives and the procedure OLP. The Treaty specifically mentions the adoption of directives for the mutual recognition of qualifications in Article 53 (ex Article 47 TEC): a different approach is taken for different fields – the European Parliament and Council of Ministers are to use the OLP to adopt directives for the 'mutual recognition' of formal qualifications such as diplomas and certificates and to coordinate national standards in relation to the taking up and pursuit of activities by the self-employed. However, in the case of medical and pharmaceutical professions, a slower pace was adopted – progressive abolition of restrictions was to be dependent upon coordination of the exercise of these professions in the various member states.

Recognition of qualifications has been a challenge to free movement of services in the internal market. Given the variety of standards across the diverse number of professions, member states have been unwilling to accept other standards in the absence of safeguards. Not all professions are pursued in all member states, and not all professions are regulated: member state A may have strict qualifications controlling a particular service, while member state B has none. This disparity in regulation can thwart free movement of services if left unchecked. However, consumers need and expect certainty of the quality of services they procure.

In 1985 the Commission published a White Paper on completing the internal market.[73] It focused on the removal of physical and technical barriers. The Commission announced a new approach to harmonisation based on the creation of European standards. Different standards would no longer be a ground for obstructing free movement. Equivalent or additional testing was to be prevented. Judgments of the Court introduced the principles of mutual recognition of qualifications[74] and 'home country control'[75] in relation to credit institutions. This principle plays the same role in services as in goods: the major responsibility for regulation and supervision lies with home state. Further (complementary) regulation by the host state can only be justified if it serves the public interest in a manner that does not duplicate the home state regulation.

The adoption of secondary legislation limits the use of the derogations. Mutual recognition of qualifications was important in case law concerning cross-border medical services: this was used to undermine arguments based on quality. For example in *Stamatelaki*[76] the CJ rejected the argument of the Greek government relating to the quality of treatment in other member states on the basis that since the adoption and implementation of Council Directive 93/16/EEC of 5 April 1993[77] to facilitate the free movement of doctors and the mutual recognition of formal qualifications, private hospitals in other member states are subject to quality controls and that doctors established in those member states who operate in those establishments provide professional guarantees equivalent to those of doctors established in Greece.[78]

---

[73]European Commission, 'Completing the Internal Market', White Paper, COM(85) 310 final, http://europa.eu/documents/comm/white_papers/pdf/com1985_0310_f_en.pdf
[74]COM(85) p. 28
[75]COM(85) p. 28
[76]C-444/05
[77]OJ L165/1 1993
[78][37]

An attempt was made to harmonise standards in Directive 2005/36 on the recognition of professional qualifications.[79] This directive provided for the mutual recognition of qualifications limited, however, to the pursuit in the host member state of the same profession for which the beneficiary is qualified in the home member state.[80] It replaced the 15 separate directives adopted between 1977 and 2003 that had previously addressed the issue of qualifications for distinctive regulated professions such as a doctor or a vet, nurse or lawyer, pharmacist or architect. Article 3 defines a 'regulated profession' as 'a professional activity or group of professional activities, access to which, the pursuit of which, or one of the modes of pursuit of which is subject, directly or indirectly, by virtue of legislative, regulatory or administrative provisions to the possession of specific professional qualifications'. The ability to use a professional title constitutes a 'mode of pursuit'.

Mutual recognition has made progress towards harmonisation in areas with fewer educational and professional qualifications (such as healthcare); it has been less successful in areas like law, where each member state has its unique system. The Directive on Professional Qualifications was a useful consolidation and simplification of the 15 directives which preceded it. In 2011, the Commission proposed a Green Paper on the modernisation of this directive.[81]

More recently, a controversial directive has been adopted. Directive 2006/123[82] on Services,[83] also known as the Bolkestein Directive or more pejoratively the 'Frankenstein' Directive gave rise to huge demonstrations in Germany and France: 40,000 people in Berlin and 15,000 in Strasbourg took to the streets in protest at the potential for the directive to further depress wage levels and undermine job security. The objective of the directive – to create a real internal market in services – was seen by protesters as the precursor to job losses, welfare cuts and ultimately poverty.

It can be argued that the Services Directive goes no further than the Treaty: it applies only in the specific contexts covered by Articles 49 and 56 TFEU – first, where an entrepreneur or undertaking wishes to establish a permanent presence in a different member state; and second, during cross-border service provision, especially where The directive obliges member states to guarantee this freedom of access to service provision and the freedom of establishment.

However, the consequences of these freedoms are significant: as with free movement of goods, the creation of a real internal market in services will provide consumers with increased and perhaps improved choices; but it may also reduce work opportunities for domestic service providers and entrepreneurs. Thus in guaranteeing access to non-national service providers, member states may simultaneously be undermining wages, losing jobs, reducing tax receipts and thus necessitating welfare cuts. These fears drove protesters onto the streets in 2006.

---

[79]OJ L255/22 2005
[80]Article 4(1)
[81]European Commission, 'Modernising the Professional Qualifications Directive', Green Paper, COM(2011) 367 final
[82]Directive 2006/123/EC of the European Parliament and of the Council of 12 December 2006 on services in the internal market
[83]Barnard, 'Unravelling the Services Directive', *CMLR* 45, 2008, pp. 323–394; Hatzopoulos, 'Assessing the Services Directive 2006/123/EC', *Cambridge Yearbook of European Law* 10, 2008, pp. 215–261

The protesters won some concessions but the directive was adopted in 2006, with an implementation deadline of 2009. It applies to a wide range of services including business, construction, education, retail and regulated professions such as accountancy and engineering. As per case law, it only applies to those services provided for payment so, for example, covers only private and not state-supported education. In addition, some sectors are explicitly excluded – one of the most important concessions won by the protesters was the removal of social services, such as childcare and care for the elderly. Other excluded sectors include healthcare, gambling activities, financial services, communications and transport. The preamble sets the tone of the directive – much of it concerns what is not included. For example, it clarifies that the directive does 'not oblige Member States either to liberalise services of general economic interest or to privatise public entities which provide such services or to abolish existing monopolies for other activities or certain distribution services', while preambular paragraph 35 excludes sporting activities pursuing wholly social or recreational objectives.

The substantive elements of the directive cover the principles of non-discrimination and proportionality, administrative simplifications and authorisations, and quality of services. In relation to service and establishment in the covered sectors, the directive prohibits any discrimination based on nationality or the residence of the service beneficiary. It also calls upon member states to ease administrative burdens by removing the need for prior authorisation and fulfilment of formal requirements such as the translation and certification of original documents. All authorisation activities must be non-discriminatory and proportionate. Legal requirements on who can provide a service that cannot be justified must be repealed. In general, the country to which the service provider moves to become established may only enforce its own standards where these are non-discriminatory, proportionate and justified for reasons of public order, public safety, public health or environmental protection.[84] This wording was a reworking of one of the most controversial principles in the draft directive, the 'country of origin' principle. However, in order to avoid a decline in standards, the directive promotes voluntary cooperation in drawing up 'quality charters' or European 'codes of conduct' by sectoral and professional bodies and associations. Such voluntary codes are regularly used at the national level. The problem is that they can be rejected.

VIEWPOINT

Read the Article at: http://www.independent.co.uk/news/uk/home-news/plans-for-new-food-labelling-to-combat-uk-obesity-are-dealt-blow-as-cadbury-and-cocacola-reject-traffic-light-system-8664362.html. Are voluntary codes strong enough to protect the consumer interest and ensure consumers of quality?

---

[84]Article 16

3. The hindrance of cross-border supply

This section focuses on national rules regulating gambling and communications in the form of broad casting, both distributive services that have proven to be controversial before the Court. The CJ has responded with deference to content rules and rules creating a state monopoly on gambling activities. In relation to broadcasting, it has been deferential to national social and cultural policy, such as the promotion of media plurality. It also initially responded very sympathetically to member state concerns of addiction and crime in cases of gambling and gaming but this has waned slightly, giving rise to closer examination of member state behaviour.

i.   Broadcasting and content regulation

In order to control information and images disseminated via television, national rules regulate the content of programmes and the use of advertising. This has become more difficult with the spread of cable and satellite television – most programmes now streamed into living rooms do not originate in the home member state. One of the earliest cases raised questions on whether a broadcaster may use Article 56 to challenge national rules regulating cable television transmitted from abroad.

In *Debauve*[85] criminal charges were brought against three Belgians for breaching Belgian law.[86] The law forbade national radio and television broadcasting organisations, which had a legal monopoly on broadcasting, from transmitting commercial advertising. The same prohibition applied to cable television and foreign programmes. However, given the practical difficulty of monitoring this, the rule was rarely enforced – the government had never imposed any penalties or withdrawn a licence on this basis. The cable providers had therefore ignored this prohibition and upon being sued argued that the law was contrary to free movement of services.

There was no doubt that cable transmissions fell within the scope of Article 56 TFEU.[87] The court conducted a comparative review of the treatment of commercial advertising in the various member states and found a myriad of schemes that were equally or less restrictive. The Belgian prohibition was ultimately sanctioned because it applied equally to both cable and television broadcasts; thus there was no discrimination on the basis of the national origin of the advertisements. The CJ decided that the Article did not:

[16] . . . preclude national rules prohibiting the transmission of advertisements by cable television – as they prohibit the broadcasting of advertisements by television – if those rules are applied without distinction as regards the origin, whether national or foreign, of those advertisements, the nationality of the person providing the service, or the place where he is established.

Content restrictions would be compatible as long as they fell equally on national and non-national operators. A different conclusion was reached in *Bond*[88] precisely because

---

[85]C-52/79 *Procureur du Roi* v *Marc J.V.C. Debauve and others*
[86]Article 21 of the Arrêté Royal of 24 December 1966
[87]It was decided in C-155/73 *Giuseppe Sacchi* v *Tribunale civile e penale di biella* (1974) ECR 490 that television signals fell within Article 56; cable signals are treated in the same way.
[88]C-352/85 *Bond van Adverteerders and others* v *The Netherlands State*.

national television broadcasters were not subject to the prohibition of advertisements endured by cable broadcasters established in a different member state. The Dutch 'Kabelregeling' laid out certain prohibitions on the content of broadcast transmissions. In particular, it forbade the transmission of commercial advertising targeting the Dutch public or containing Dutch subtitles in cable radio and television programmes sent from abroad. A group comprising advertisers and a cable network challenged this prohibition of advertising and subtitling in television programmes transmitted from abroad as contrary to the free movement of services.

APPLYING THE LAW

Is the new Croatian rule applied without distinction to national and non-national caterers?

Consideration of Dutch media rules arose again in the *Mediawet* cases.[89] Both cases concerned conditions imposed on the retransmission of advertisements contained in radio and television programmes broadcast from other member states. In these cases, 10 operators of cable networks in the Netherlands were fined for transmitting programmes of foreign broadcasters that contained advertising entirely or partly in Dutch. This was contrary to Dutch law (Article 66 of the Mediawet) which prohibited such in order to secure media plurality. The network operators argued in response that the Mediawet provision was contrary to Article 56 TFEU. As in *Bond,* the Court agreed in *Mediawet I* with the network operatore. The conditions in the Mediawet imposed a dual restriction:

[17] . . . First, they prevent operators of cable networks established in a Member State from transmitting radio or television programmes supplied by broadcasters established in other Member States which do not satisfy those conditions. Secondly, they restrict the opportunities afforded to those broadcasting bodies to include in their programmes for the benefit in particular of advertisers established in the State in which the programmes are received advertising intended specifically for the public in that State.

The next question was whether those restrictions could be justified – could media plurality be added to the list of overriding reasons relating to the general interest? The first answer was yes: such restrictions could be imposed in order to protect consumers against excessive advertising or, as an objective of cultural policy, in order to maintain a certain level of programme quality.[90] However, behind the cultural policy lay an economic consequence: the financial outcome of such a restriction was that it protected the national broadcasting authority, the STER, from competition. Having identified this discriminatory and protectionist consequence, the Court fell back upon the narrower derogation of public policy in Article 56 rather than the broader exceptions of 'general interest'. It had

---

[89]C-288/89 *Gouda (Mediawet I)* and C-353/89 *Commission of the European Communities* v *Kingdom of the Netherlands (Mediawet II). Mediawet II* also challenged the legal obligation to use the services of a national undertaking for the production of radio and television programmes.
[90][27]

already held in *Bond* that 'economic aims cannot constitute grounds of public policy within the meaning of Article 56 of the Treaty'[91] thus these restrictions in the Mediawet could not be justified. In *Mediawet II*, protectionist rules were also found incompatible with the Treaty. The conclusion was the same in both cases:

> [48] It must therefore be held that, by prohibiting operators of cable networks established in its territory from transmitting radio or television programmes containing advertisements intended specifically for the Dutch public which are broadcast by broadcasting bodies established in the territory of another Member State if certain conditions relating to the structure of those bodies or advertising contained in their programmes which is intended for the Dutch public are not fulfilled, the Kingdom of the Netherlands has failed to fulfil its obligations under Article 59 of the Treaty [56 TFEU].

The maintenance of cultural policy objectives was also of no use to Belgium in infringement proceedings by the Commission.[92] A range of laws applicable in the Flemish community discriminated against non-national broadcasters – for example, prior authorisation was needed to transmit commercial programmes from other member states. Upon investigation of the claimed cultural objectives, the Court found that the purpose of the measure was to restrict genuine competition with the national broadcasting stations in order to maintain their advertising revenue.[93] As discriminatory rules, the measures could only be justified by the limited grounds in Article 52 was which do not include cultural policy. Accordingly, Belgium had failed to fulfil its obligations under the Treaty.

ANALYSING THE LAW

Is there an economic consequence to the new Croatian rule? Who wins, who loses?

---

ii.   Gambling and state monopolies

Content regulation in broadcasting will be tolerated as long as it does not discriminate and is not disguised protectionism. The following cases show that the CJ is even more lenient towards state regulation of gambling and gaming activities. These are also activities where services can move without either the service provider or recipient leaving their home: gambling can now be conducted online or even on the telephone. This has made their regulation more complex, especially with the onset of e-gambling. Gambling, betting and games of chance such as lotteries and scratch cards offering financial riches have been discussed many times in Luxembourg. They are to be differentiated from electrical, electromechanical and electronic games, which are not played with the hope of winning large sums of money.[94] These games with high winnings can ruin lives as gamblers beg, borrow or steal to participate or pay their debts. Gambling addiction can place emotional and mental as

---

[91][34]
[92]C-211/91 *Commission v Belgium* [1992] ECR I-6757
[93][9]
[94]C-65/05 *Commission v Greece* [2006] ECR I-10341

well as financial strain on individuals. Rates of depression and suicide are high – almost double the national average – among gamblers. Addicts are known to turn to theft and fraud to fuel their habit.[95] Yet gambling per se is not a criminal activity. It has been highly restricted in most member states because of its social consequences and it is these restrictions that have been challenged. The restrictions have taken the form of monopolies on who can provide these services and how. Their existence and compatibility is complicated by the fact that although restricted, such activities are sometimes promoted by the state.[96] The CJ initially responded sympathetically but increasingly firmly as it came to suspect the national authorities of protectionism. *Schindler* was the starting point for the CJ jurisprudence in this area. This case confirmed that games of chance are a service – the three legitimate justifications in that case have been replaced with the 10-part test in *Stoss*.[97]

a) The tri-partite 'overriding public interest' justification in *Schindler*

Two organisers of a national lottery (the SKL) in Germany (which they organised on behalf of four German states) invited British nationals to participate in it. The invitations were sent by mail from the Netherlands. The letters were intercepted and confiscated by customs officers at Dover on the ground that they breached UK law regulating lotteries. The German organisers argued that this was contrary to free movement of goods and services.

The first question was which freedom applied: is a lottery a good under Article 34 TFEU – does the need to buy tickets make it such? The answer of the Court was no: the tickets were objects but their purchase was not an end in itself – the end was participation in a lottery thus the issue was one for Article 56 TFEU. Some of the intervening member states argued that a lottery was not an economic activity but one organised for recreation or amusement. Traditionally, lotteries were run either directly by a public authority or at least under the control of a public authority making them a not-for-profit activity. These arguments were not accepted – the chance nature of the return in a lottery did not prevent them being an 'economic activity'.

The fact that it was also played for recreation and entertainment, like amateur sport, did not remove it from the realm of services – it always yielded a gain for the organiser and potentially a win for the player. In addition, all participants engaged for profit – the use of profits for charitable acts did not alter the economic nature of the activity.[98]

As a service, did the British law therefore breach the Treaty? The law applied to any operator and agent running a large-scale lottery and in particular to the advertising and distribution of tickets for such lotteries, irrespective of the nationality and whatever the member state or states of establishment. It was not therefore discriminatory on the basis of the nationality of the economic agents concerned or of the member state in which they are established. The Commission argued, however, that the legislation was in fact discriminatory because it permitted a single person to operate several small lotteries, which was equivalent to one large lottery. It also permitted similar games of chance such as football pools or bingo. This was not accepted:

[51] . . . even though the amounts at stake in the games so permitted in the United Kingdom may be comparable to those in large-scale lotteries and even though those games

[95]http://www.nhs.uk/Livewell/addiction/Pages/gamblingaddiction.aspx
[96]See, for example http://www.diabetes.org.uk/Get_involved/Your-chance-to-win/Weekly_lottery/
[97]C-316/07, C-358/07, C-359/07, C-360/07, C-409/07 and C-410/07 *Stoß* [2010] ECR I-8069
[98]*Schindler* [34–35]

involve a significant element of chance they differ in their object, rules and methods of organisation from those large-scale lotteries which were established in Member States other than the United Kingdom before the enactment of the National Lottery Act 1993. They are therefore not in a comparable situation to the lotteries prohibited by the United Kingdom legislation and, contrary to the arguments of the Commission and the defendants in the main proceedings, cannot be assimilated to them.

[52] In those circumstances legislation such as the United Kingdom legislation cannot be considered to be discriminatory.

Yet, even though non-discriminatory, the law was held to be an obstacle.

The next relevant question was whether it could be justified? The CJ had already stated in previous cases that the protection of the recipients of the service, of consumers more generally, as well as the maintenance of order in society would be recognised as 'overriding reasons relating to the public interest'.[99] Now, moral, religious and cultural considerations came to the fore to defend a certain amount of 'latitude' for the national authorities. The CJ acknowledged three grounds of objective justification: first, it deferred to the 'moral, religious or cultural aspects of lotteries' which lead member states to in general restrict and prohibit gambling so as to prevent it from being a source of private profit. Second, it noted the high risk of crime or fraud associated with lotteries necessitated careful regulation; and finally, it recognised the individual and social consequences of gambling addiction. A further ground supporting the national law, although not an objective justification, was the significant contribution of lotteries to the financing of benevolent or public interest activities such as social works, charitable works, sport or culture.[100] Taking these concerns of social policy and fraud prevention into consideration, the national law was held to be compatible with free movement of services.

VIEWPOINT

Which of the three justifications cited by the CJ in *Schindler* do you find the most important? Rank them.

Schindler set the tone for CJ reasoning in cases in this area – the case was subsequently referred to on a regular basis. *Läärä*[101] concerned national legislation in Finland that gave a single public body, the RAY, exclusive right to run the operation of slot machines. The RAY carried out this activity under the control of the State and paid its proceeds to the State. These funds were then used by the State to fund charities and other public activities. Slot machines were seen as analogous to lotteries. Unlike, the law in *Schindler,* the Finnish law did not prohibit the use of slot machines totally but restricted access to them. The rule did not involve discrimination on grounds of nationality – it applied without

---

[99]See Joined cases 110/78 and 111/78 *Ministère Public* v *Van Wesemael* [1979] ECR 35 [28]; Case 220/83 *Commission* v *France* [1986] ECR 3663 [20]; and Case 15/78 *Société Générale Alsacienne de Banque* v *Koestler* [1978] ECR 1971 [5]
[100]*Schindler* [60]
[101]C-124/97 *Läärä and others* [1999] ECR I-6067

distinction to any operator interested in this activity, whether established in Finland or in another member state. However, there was no disagreement that it impeded freedom to provide services, as it directly or indirectly prevented operators in other member states from making slot machines available to the public. The key question was therefore whether it could be justified, either by the Treaty derogations or by overriding reasons relating to the public interest.

The government called upon the second and third justifications in *Schindler*. It argued its law was a response to concerns with addiction to gambling and the risk of crime and fraud by those who became so addicted. It also argued that the legislation ensured that the funds collected from slot machines were only used for charitable or other benevolent purposes. The Court returned to *Schindler* in its reasoning, affording the national authorities a margin of autonomy to determine both how to protect the players and general public order. These were held to be legitimate aims – yet – were they necessary and appropriate? Could other less onerous means, such as a code of conduct or tax on the licensed bodies, be as effective? The answer was no:

> [41] . . . the obligation imposed on the licensed public body, requiring it to pay over the proceeds of its operations, constitutes a measure which, given the risk of crime and fraud, is certainly more effective in ensuring that strict limits are set to the lucrative nature of such activities.

> [42] In those circumstances, in conferring exclusive rights on a single public body, the provisions of the Finnish legislation on the operation of slot machines do not appear to be disproportionate, in so far as they affect freedom to provide services, to the objectives they pursue.

As in *Schindler*, the rule was therefore found compatible with Article 56 by virtue of the public interest objectives underlying it. The CJ deferred to the national moral stance against gambling.

A subsequent case, *Anomar*, dealt with Portuguese legislation that likewise restricted the operation and playing of games of chance to specific locations and bodies.[102] The rules applied to both Portuguese and non-Portuguese nationals and restricted activities to casinos in permanent or temporary gaming areas created by decrees. Under Portuguese law these decrees were public policy rules justified in the public interest: they were highly symbolic and designed to attain objectives of legitimate social purposes such as fair play and produce advantages to the public sector. However they acted to stifle the market in sale of gaming machines. Did they breach Article 56 TFEU? The challenge by a group of eight Portuguese companies involved in the marketing and operation of gaming machines failed – all intervening governments supported the compatibility of the decrees with EU law, such being 'justified by overriding reasons relating to the public interest such as the protection of consumers, prevention of fraud and crime, protection of public morality and the financing of public-interest activities'.[103] Given the similarity of these exclusivity decrees to the Finnish legislation, they were found to be proportionate to their objectives.[104] It was irrelevant that some member states had less restrictive legislation – member

---

[102]C-6/01 *Anomar and others v Estado português* [2003] ECR I-8621
[103][70]
[104]C-124/97 *Läärä and Others* [42]. See also C-67/98 *Zenatti* [1999] ECR I-7289 [35]

states enjoyed a wide margin of discretion to define methods. Once legislation was found compatible with the Treaty:

[88] . . . the choice of methods for organising and controlling the operation and playing of games of chance or gambling, such as the conclusion with the State of an administrative licensing contract or the restriction of the operation and playing of certain games to places duly licensed for that purpose, falls within the margin of discretion which the national authorities enjoy.

Thus national rules constituting a barrier to the freedom to provide services could be justified by 'overriding' concerns of social policy and the prevention of fraud. The only victory won by the eight companies was a clear statement that gambling and similar activities were defined as 'economic activities' under Article 2.[105]

VIEWPOINT

Do you think that the CJ has given too much deference to the member states in these cases?

---

b) From 'overriding' to 'imperative'

Like slot machines, betting is also considered analogous to lotteries: while not 'pure chance', participants engage with an expectation of cash winnings. Furthermore, they involve the same risks of crime and fraud and may have the same damaging individual and social consequences.[106] Betting can also be conducted online – persons can enjoy this service in the comfort and privacy of their own home. Consumers do not have to visit a casino or betting shop, buy scratch cards, or find a machine to throw coins into. It is therefore more invisible, easier to become addicted to and harder to regulate. Consumers also do not have to be in the same member state as the service provider.

Like the *Sunday Trading Cases*,[107] the betting cases have an air of strategic litigation about them. A series of cases concerning online betting began when Mr Zenatti[108] was prosecuted because he acted as an agent for Italians to place bets with a UK betting company. This was contrary to Italian legislation on betting, which permitted just two specific national bodies to conduct this activity – the Comitato Olimpico Nazionale Italiano (National Olympic Committee, 'CONI') and the Unione Nazionale Incremento Razze Equine (National Union for the Betterment of Horse Breeds, 'UNIRE') – or persons and bodies entrusted by them. As in *Läärä*, the state regulated the use of the funds collected and used for charitable purposes, such as the promotion of sporting activities, to those living in poverty. Nonetheless, the non-discriminatory exclusivity rule prevented other operators in Italy and elsewhere from providing this service and thus constituted an obstacle to the freedom to provide services.

---

[105][47, 48]
[106]*Zenatti* [18–19]
[107]See for example C-145/88 *Torfaen Borough Council v B & Q PLC* [1989] ECR 3851
[108]*Zenatti*

As in *Läärä*, betting was partially prohibited rather than totally banned: the activity could be undertaken but only by specific bodies. The restriction to specific authorities was justified as a means to prevent betting from 'being a source of private profit, to avoid risks of crime and fraud and the damaging individual and social consequences of the incitement to spend which it represents', and as previous cases in Italy allowed it only to the extent to which it could be socially useful to the promotion of competitive sports.[109] The CJ found this restriction of betting to certain bodies in principle justifiable, as long as this was to pursue the objectives claimed.

The state monopoly was challenged again in *Gambelli*[110] but this time by a network of licensed agencies in the UK and Italy linked by the internet to a bookmaker, Stanley International Betting Ltd (Stanley), registered in England. Stanley belonged to Stanley Leisure, the fourth largest bookmaker and largest casino operator in the UK, licensed to conduct betting activity in the UK and abroad. Mr Gambelli and his co-defendants were registered data transmission centres (DTCs), authorised to transmit data. Stanley used these DTCs to offer bets on national, European and world sporting events; individuals placed bets at home via, for example, the internet, fax or telephone. The DTCs operated as independent intermediaries contracted to collect bets, register intentions to bet and forward them to Stanley. Given the CONI monopoly on bets for sporting events, Gambelli and 137 other defendants were accused of fraud against the State.

Gambelli differed in two ways from *Zenatti*: first, the Italian legislation had been amended, and second, these rules were now also hindering freedom of establishment – Stanley was unable to pursue its lawful activity of bookkeeping. The decision began with a brief consideration of whether the Italian legislation was also a restriction on the freedom of establishment, and concluded that it was – where an established company such as Stanley was working with established agencies to pursue the same activity 'any restrictions on the activities of those agencies constitute obstacles to the freedom of establishment'.[111]

Free movement of services was also restricted. Although the rules had been amended after *Zenatti* to enable non-state bodies to tender for a licence to pursue betting activities, in practice it was difficult for any non-national body to satisfy them – the remaining prerequisites were indirectly discriminatory:

[47] . . . the Italian Government acknowledged that the Italian legislation on invitations to tender for betting activities in Italy contains restrictions. According to that Government, the fact that no entity has been licensed for such activities apart from the monopoly-holder is explained by the fact that the way in which the Italian legislation is conceived means that the licence can only be awarded to certain persons.

Given that the restriction on service provision now affected an established company and explicitly involved e-commerce, reasoning was borrowed from *Alpine Investments*, a case likewise concerning an established organisation prohibited from providing its service in another member state via electronic communications. In *Alpine Investments* the Court held that Article 56 TFEU 'covers services which the provider offers by telephone to

---

[109][30]
[110]C-243/01 *Criminal proceedings against Piergiorgio Gambelli and Others* [2003] ECR I-13031
[111][46]

potential recipients established in other Member States and provides without moving from the Member State in which he is established'.[112] It followed therefore that Article 56 TFEU applied to services which an established provider such as Stanley offers 'via the internet — and so without moving — to recipients in another Member State, in this case Italy, with the result that any restriction of those activities constitutes a restriction on the freedom of such a provider to provide services'.[113]

As the rules now breached Article 49 as well as Article 56, were the previous justifications applicable? Was there a reason of overriding general interest that could be invoked? The Greek and Portuguese governments proposed a new reason: tax revenue. This was rejected[114] – as in *Zenatti,* financial considerations could at most be 'an incidental beneficial consequence and not the real justification for the restrictive policy adopted.'[115] The restrictions had to reflect a concern to bring about a genuine reduction of gambling opportunities. The Court repeated its words from *Schindler, Läärä* and *Zenatti* that:

> [63] . . . moral, religious and cultural factors, and the morally and financially harmful consequences for the individual and society associated with gaming and betting, could serve to justify the existence on the part of the national authorities of a margin of appreciation sufficient to enable them to determine what consumer protection and the preservation of public order require.

To this, however, it now added that the restrictions on an established company must be justified by *imperative* requirements in the general interest[116] in addition to non-discrimination and proportionality.

The idea of 'imperative requirements in the general interest'[117] in *Gambelli* seems stronger than the previous 'overriding': 'imperative' leans towards unavoidable reasons rather than those that might be preferential. Three specific lines of guidance were given to the national court to help it decide on the restrictions instituted by the Italian legislation. Henceforth, public order concerns could not be invoked if:

1 betting is encouraged for the 'financial benefit of the public purse';
2 the rules applied with distinction to national and non-national operators;
3 the rules were disproportionate in light of the Court's broader case law[118] – was incarceration really necessary to prevent fraud?[119]

Behind this guidance lurked a suspicion, hinted at in *Zenatti,* that the public interest defence was disguised protectionism – the national court had pointed out that Italy was in fact pursuing a policy of substantially expanding the consumption of betting and gaming in order to raise funds for the State but was also protecting the State monopoly, CONI. Thus while continuing to support national regulatory autonomy for the fulfilment of public order objectives in a consistent and systematic manner, even where these

---

[112]C-384/93 *Alpine Investments* [1995] ECR I-1141 [22]
[113][54]
[114]C-264/96 *ICI* [1998] ECR I-4695 [28], and C-136/00 *Danner* [2002] ECR I-8147 [56]
[115][62]
[116][65]
[117][67]
[118]The CJ specifically cited C-193/94 *Skanavi and Chryssanthakopoulos* [1996] ECR I-929 [34 to 39] and C-459/99 *MRAX* [2002] ECR I-6591 [89 to 91]
[119][69–72]

obstructed freedom of establishment and services, those objectives would not be accepted if their main purpose was something else. The CJ therefore concluded that the Italian legislation was incompatible but could be justified. This more detailed enquiry was left to the national court to determine, taking into account whether ' . . . the detailed rules for its application, actually serves the aims which might justify it, and whether the restrictions it imposes are disproportionate in the light of those aims'.[120]

APPLYING THE LAW

Could the new Croatian law be disguised protectionism?

---

c) 'Controlled expansion'

The matter did not end there: *Placanica*[121] picked up where *Gambelli* left off. Mr Placanica and his co-applicants were also part of the Stanley network, sued for fraud because they did not possess the requisite police authorisation. The matter was referred back to Luxembourg whereas in *Gambelli,* the measures were held to be contrary to Articles 49 and 56.[122] The CJ took up the question of justification and itself conducted the work it had hoped the Italian courts would conduct – a detailed assessment on the legitimacy and proportionality of each aspect of the Italian legislation. It dismissed as disguised protectionism the idea that the licensing requirement was a means to reduce gambling but gave more credence to the licensing as a method to curb criminality and fraudulent betting by limiting them to controllable channels – in other words, if people were prone to gamble, better for them to use state controlled operators than the mafia! The Italian government and national court claimed this 'controlled expansion' was the true goal of the Italian legislation.

This objective of 'controlled expansion' is counter-intuitive but does indeed explain what appears to be an inconsistent policy, especially perhaps in relation to e-gambling:

> [55] . . . Viewed from that perspective, it is possible that a policy of controlled expansion in the betting and gaming sector may be entirely consistent with the objective of drawing players away from clandestine betting and gaming – and, as such, activities which are prohibited – to activities which are authorised and regulated. As the Belgian and French Governments, in particular, have pointed out, in order to achieve that objective, authorised operators must represent a reliable, but at the same time attractive, alternative to a prohibited activity. This may as such necessitate the offer of an extensive range of games, advertising on a certain scale and the use of new distribution techniques.

It was therefore acknowledged that the Italian licensing system could constitute an efficient means to control operators in the betting and gaming sector so as to prevent the

---

[120][76]

[121]Joined cases C-338/04 *Criminal proceedings against Massimiliano Placanica,* C-359/04 *Christian Palazzese* and C-360/04 *Angelo Sorricchio* [2007] ECR I-1891

[122][43, 44]

exploitation of these activities for criminal or fraudulent ends.[123] As before, it was left to the national court to determine whether the rules restricting the number of active operators *genuinely* contributed to the stated objective: to prevent the exploitation of gambling for criminal or fraudulent purposes and whether they were proportionate.[124]

The tender procedure remained problematic – it was held incompatible with Articles 49 and 56 TFEU. This also applied to any rule connected with this procedure, such as the requirement that those holding a licence must then obtain police authorisation or face criminal penalties: a member state could not 'apply a criminal penalty for failure to complete an administrative formality where such completion has been refused or rendered impossible by the member state concerned, in infringement of Community [Union] law'.[125]

A similar Austrian restriction was considered in *Englemann,* where only public limited companies were allowed to operate gambling activities. This was not ruled out per se but it was left for the national court to decide whether any justification was proportionate.[126] In *Biasci and Others*[127] need for prior police authorisation and a licence were held to be compatible with Articles 49 and 56 TFEU.

d) 'Consistency'

As the CJ gained familiarity with the gambling cases, it stiffened its stance towards 'controlled expansion', introducing the need for the national authorities to show consistency in their aims and objectives. The idea of 'consistency' has been used by the CJ to prevent protectionism in national regulation of gambling. It was first visible in a case on online gambling from the Netherlands, where a second British bookmaker, Ladbrokes, was prosecuted for pursuing its betting activities there.[128]

As in Italy, Dutch gambling legislation is based on a system of exclusive licences – organisers and promoters of gambling require an administrative licence and only one licence is granted by the national authorities per gambling activity. Gambling could not be offered via the internet. A non-profit-making foundation governed by private law called De Lotto held the Dutch licence for sports-related prize competitions, the lottery and numbers games. It began a court proceeding when Ladbrokes infringed its monopoly by offering sports-related bets on their internet site and via freephone to Dutch residents. Ladbrokes were ordered by a Dutch court to block access to its internet site and freephone games to Dutch consumers. Ladbrokes appealed and a reference was made to the CJEU.

The decision began with clarification of the scope of activities that would be caught under Article 56 TFEU when the party was an *established* service provider in a member state wishing to pursue the *same* activity in another member state:

[15] Article 49 EC [56 TFEU] requires the abolition of all restrictions on the freedom to provide services, even if those restrictions apply without distinction to national

---

[123][57]

[124][58]

[125][69]; see C-5/83 *Rienks* [1983] ECR 4233 [10 and 11]

[126]C-64/08 *Criminal proceedings against Ernst Engelmann* [2010] ECR I-8219 [31]. In this case, the obligation on persons holding concessions to operate gaming establishments to have their seat in Austria also constituted a restriction on freedom of establishment – it discriminated against companies established in another member state and prevented them from operating gaming establishments in Austria by way of an agency, branch or subsidiary. The categorical exclusion of such operators was disproportionate, going beyond what is necessary to combat crime. Other measures were available to achieve this aim [37].

[127]C-660/11 *Biasci and Others* v *Ministero dell'Interno and Questura di Livorno* and C-8/12 *Cristian Rainone and Others* v *Ministero dell'Interno and Others* [29]

[128]C-258/08 *Ladbrokes Betting & Gaming Ltd and Ladbrokes International Ltd* v *Stichting de Nationale Sporttotalisator* [2010] ECR I-4757

providers of services and to those from other Member states, when they are liable to prohibit, impede or render less advantageous the activities of a service provider established in another Member State where it lawfully provides similar services. The freedom to provide services is for the benefit of both providers and recipients of services.[129]

Exclusivity rules that discourage providers or recipients of services fall within its scope. This was also confirmed in *Sporting Exchange* and *Liga Portuguesa* – legislation granting exclusive gaming rights to a single operator, prohibiting any non-national operator from offering such services via the internet services constitutes a restriction on the freedom to provide services.[130]

As in Italy, the behaviour of the Dutch authorities was contradictory – the monopoly was defended as a means to curb addiction to gambling yet new gambling activities were planned. This was seen in *Placanica:* could it be argued that in order for the state to successfully control gambling desires, it had to continually offer gambling activities that were novel and appealing? The initial answer was conditional – it depended upon the extent of unlawful gambling:

> [30] Since the objective of protecting consumers from gambling addiction is, in principle, difficult to reconcile with a policy of expanding games of chance characterised, inter alia, by the creation of new games and by the advertising of such games, such a policy cannot be regarded as being consistent *unless* the scale of unlawful activity is significant and the measures adopted are aimed at channelling consumers' propensity to gamble into activities that are lawful.

Thus there had to be evidence of increased unlawful gambling: the introduction of new games would then clearly be justified as an attempt to draw people towards lawful gambling. There was some evidence that Dutch consumers were resorting to secret gambling, thus there was a rationale to the behaviour: to remove the allure of secret gambling and reduce addiction to gambling it had to offer attractive alternatives. It was also relevant that the funds de Lotto collected were distributed among institutions working in the public interest, particularly in the fields of sport, physical education, general welfare, public health and culture. The final decision was left to the national court but the CJ agreed that the Dutch rules to curb gambling addiction could:

> [38] . . . be regarded as limiting betting activities in a consistent and systematic manner even where the holder(s) of an exclusive licence are entitled to make what they are offering on the market attractive by introducing new games and by means of advertising. It is for the national court to determine whether unlawful gaming activities constitute a problem in the Member State concerned which might be solved by the expansion of authorised and regulated activities, and whether that expansion is on such a scale as to make it impossible to reconcile with the objective of curbing such addiction.

However, even given this, why did this apply to an established entity such as Ladbrokes that was fully licensed and regulated to offer its activities in the UK? Why was it not allowed to pursue these same activities in the Netherlands? What happened to home state control?

---

[129]C-42/07 *Liga Portuguesa de Futebol Profissional and Bwin International* [2009] ECR I-7633 [51]
[130]C-42/07 *Liga Portuguesa* [52] and C-203/08 *Sporting Exchange* [2010] I-4695 [24]

This question was addressed in the later case of *Sporting Exchange*[131] where another UK-based betting company, Betfair in offering bets solely via phone and the internet again challenged De Lotto's monopoly in the Netherlands. In its answer, the CJ now focused on the difficulty of tackling internet crime:

[33] . . . the internet gaming industry has not been the subject of harmonisation within the European Union. A Member State is therefore entitled to take the view that the mere fact that an operator such as Betfair lawfully offers services in that sector via the internet in another Member State, in which it is established and where it is in principle already subject to statutory conditions and controls on the part of the competent authorities in that State, cannot be regarded as amounting to a sufficient assurance that national consumers will be protected against the risks of fraud and crime, in the light of the difficulties liable to be encountered in such a context by the authorities of the Member State of establishment in assessing the professional qualities and integrity of operators.[132]

[34] In addition, because of the lack of direct contact between consumer and operator, games of chance accessible via the internet involve different and more substantial risks of fraud by operators against consumers compared with the traditional markets for such games.[133]

The higher risk and danger of online fraud allows the use of exclusivity clauses even in relation to established operators. Home state control is not sufficient to address this. Exclusivity clauses in relation to online gambling are justified by the objective of combating fraud and crime.[134]

VIEWPOINT

Why might the principle of 'home state control' be too weak to control online gambling?

Nonetheless penalties for unauthorised online gambling must be proportionate. This matter arose in a case from Sweden,[135] whereas in Italy and the Netherlands a licence was necessary to pursue gambling activities. A licence could be obtained by *any* Swedish legal person that was

a non-profit-making;
b pursued socially beneficial objectives in Sweden; and
c engaged in activities to advance that objective.

Organisation of gambling without a licence in Sweden was a criminal offence. Illegal promotion of gambling organised abroad to Swedish consumers was punishable by a

---

[131]C-203/08 *Sporting Exchange Ltd v Minister van Justitie*
[132]*Liga Portuguesa* [69]
[133]*Liga Portuguesa* [70]
[134]C-203/08 *Sporting Exchange* [57]; *Liga Portuguesa* [72]
[135]Joined cases C-447 and 448/08 *Criminal proceedings against Otto Sjöberg and Anders Gerdin* [2010] ECR I-6921

fine or six months' imprisonment. The two applicants ran national newspapers which carried adverts for four for-profit gambling organisations established outside of Sweden. The adverts offered internet poker and sports betting to Swedish consumers. They were fined for doing so without the correct authorisation.

Given the broad reach of Article 56, there was little chance that the rules would not constitute a restriction: they undermined both the freedom of Swedish residents to receive, on the internet, services offered in other member states and also a restriction on the freedom of gambling operators established in other member states to provide services in Sweden.[136] The key question was whether these could be justified. The majority of the reasoning was taken from *Liga Portuguesa*.[137] However, part of the reasoning referred back to *Schindler:* the restrictive rules were justified because the companies placing the adverts were *for-profit* – a fundamental principle in the Swedish legislation was the exclusion of such companies.[138] The CJ recognised this and in doing so repeated its premise from Schindler that:

> [43] Considerations of a cultural, moral or religious nature can justify restrictions on the freedom of gambling operators to provide services.

This was particularly so in relation to allowing social profit to arise from 'the exploitation of a social evil or the weakness of players and their misfortune'. Thus a member state was allowed to restrict the operation of internet gambling by entrusting it to public or charitable bodies. The gaming operators which placed the advertisements were private undertakings run for profit, which could never have obtained licences for the operation of gambling under Swedish legislation.[139] The prohibition on the promotion of their services to Swedish consumers reflected 'the objective of the exclusion of private profit-making interests from the gambling sector and may moreover be regarded as necessary in order to meet such an objective'.[140] The main answer was therefore that Article 56 TFEU did not prevent member states applying legislation prohibiting the advertisement to residents of gambling organised for profit by private operators in other member states. Had they been not-for-profit organisations of the type allowed to pursue these economic activities under Swedish law, the decision may have been different. Article 56 did, however, call for any punishment to be the same regardless of whether the adverts promoted online gambling in the same or another member state.[141]

Consistency was used to challenge exclusivity in online gaming in Germany. Carmen Media, a betting agency established in Gibraltar and authorised to conduct 'offshore bookmaking' (marketing of bets abroad) claimed infringement of Article 56 TFEU when it was refused permission to offer bets via the internet to consumers in Schleswig-Holstein in Germany.[142] In order to prise open the highly lucrative national market, it argued that the public monopoly on sporting bets was contrary to the *Gambelli* requirements of consistency and systematic action against gambling addiction. Drawing upon *Ladbrokes*, Carmen Media also argued that other forms of gambling and betting were being expanded

---

[136][34]
[137][56–61]
[138][41]
[139][44]
[140][45]
[141][57]
[142]C-46/08 *Carmen Media Group*

even though these forms of gambling entailed a higher risk of addiction than bets on sporting competitions and lotteries.

As in previous questions, the devil was in the detail of the national regulation rather than its existence per se. National authorities enjoyed a 'margin of discretion' in determining methods. However, the German system was neither consistent nor systematic: first, control was split between the federal and regional governments; and second, some gambling activities were subject to a public monopoly while others were controlled via a system of private authorisations. On the face of it, this seemed neither systematic nor consistent but given the margin of discretion, a blanket approach was inappropriate – as in *Placanica,* it was necessary to conduct a separate examination for each of the restrictions imposed by national law to determine whether, in particular, it is suitable for achieving the goals asserted by the member state concerned (legitimate) and whether it does not go beyond what is necessary in order to achieve those objectives.[143]

A differentiated system of control ranging from very to less restrictive does not indicate a lack of legitimacy: divergence does not automatically undermine a consistent and systematic approach[144] and is not per se proof that a regulatory monopoly is disguised protectionism. However, it was contradictory that the stated federal policy included plans to increase the number of casinos in Germany (from 66 to 81 between 2000 and 2006)! In such circumstances, the CJ politely informed the referring court, it may legitimately be concluded that the scheme falls outside of Article 56. If the authorities pursue policies seeking to *encourage* participation in gambling rather than to reduce or limit such opportunities, this:

> [68] . . . has the effect that the aim of preventing incitement to squander money on gambling and of combating addiction to the latter, which was at the root of the establishment of the said monopoly, can no longer be effectively pursued by means of the monopoly, with the result that the latter can no longer be justified having regard to Article 49 EC [56 TFEU].

Article 56 therefore allows for differential regulation of gambling activities: a member state can prohibit the organisation and promotion of internet gambling and betting in pursuit of public policy objectives (squandering of money on gambling, combating addiction and protecting young persons) even if similar gambling activities remain authorised through more traditional channels. However, it is incongruous to simultaneously pursue a long-term policy to expand gambling. Expansion may have been more acceptable if evidence demonstrated that consumers were increasingly using unlawful channels.

ANALYSING THE LAW

Why was expansion acceptable in *Placanica* but not *Carmen Media*?

---

[143][60]
[144][64]

e) The 10-point test

Stoss[145] represents a watershed in the freedom to provide internet gambling services. In contrast to *Läärä,* 13 member states intervened in this case. It mirrored the situation arising in *Gambelli* where independent operators were prevented by national law from acting as intermediaries for betting operators located in other member states. The rule in this case was German; the applicants were bookmakers who handled bets for authorised operators established in Austria and the UK, Malta and Gibraltar. All complained to the courts when they were threatened with fines for these activities. The state monopoly was held to be a restriction – the important question was whether it could be justified and in particular how proportionality was to be demonstrated.

On the basis of the judgment in *Lindman,*[146] the CJ clarified that a study was not necessary to justify a public monopoly. However, a measure as restrictive as a public monopoly had to demonstrate the need for a particularly high level of consumer protection and had to be set within a legislative framework suitable for 'ensuring that the holder of the said monopoly will in fact be able to pursue, in a consistent and systematic manner, the objective thus determined'.[147] As stated in *Placanica* and *Carmen Media,* suitability could only be addressed after a detailed separate examination of each of the restrictions imposed by the national legislation: was it suitable to achieve the objective claimed and was it the least onerous way to achieve those objectives?[148]

Aspects of the enquiry were now laid out: the nature of each game had to be taken into account. At least 10 elements were to be considered including the method of organisation, mode of play, the levels of stake and winnings, the numbers of players involved, the presentation, frequency of play, length of play, repetition, and the reactions of players. The Advocate General suggested it was also important to consider whether they require the physical presence of the player to differentiate between games offered in casinos and slot machines in casinos or other establishments.[149] Given these different characteristics, divergence in methods of control did not per se deprive of legitimacy a public monopoly designed to achieve '. . . the objective of preventing citizens from being incited to squander money on gambling and of combating addiction to the latter . . .'.[150] However, the legitimacy of a divergent regulatory system would be undermined by public and aggressive promotion of gambling.

It was the national court that highlighted two glaring incongruities: first, the holder of the public monopoly on sporting bets was engaged in intensive advertising campaigns of lottery games, to which its monopoly extended. This was suspect because the adverts promoted the raising of finance for the social, cultural or sporting activities to which the profits were put. This suggested that the monopoly was less aimed at discouragement of

---

[145]C-316/07, C-358/07, C-359/07, C-360/07, C-409/07 and C-410/07 *Markus Stoß and others*
[146]In C-42/02 *Lindman* [2003] ECR I-13519 held that differential taxation of money won through an overseas lottery was incompatible. Attempts to justify this by overriding reasons in the public interest included considerations such as the prevention of wrongdoing and fraud, the reduction of social damage caused by gaming, the financing of activities in the public interest and ensuring legal certainty, or the need to combat the damaging consequences of gambling.
[147][83]
[148][49]
[149][95]
[150][96]

gambling and that '. . . maximisation of the profits destined for such activities was an end in itself of the monopoly'.[151] As the Advocate General pointed out, advertising was in danger of trivialising gambling or giving it a positive image by enticing messages – it had to remain '. . . measured and strictly limited to what is necessary in order thus to channel consumers towards authorised gaming networks'.[152] Second, restrictions on casino and other automated games, which had higher potential risk of addiction than sporting bets, were being relaxed and supply expanded by the public authorities, especially on the internet but also in restaurants, cafes and other places.[153]

The final decision was for the national courts but, as in *Carmen Media,* the fact that the authorities conducted and tolerated:

> [106] . . . policies aimed at encouraging participation in those other games rather than reducing opportunities for gambling and limiting activities in that area in a consistent and systematic manner, has the effect that the objective of preventing incitement to squander money on gambling and combating addiction to the latter, which was at the root of the establishment of the said monopoly, can no longer be effectively pursued by means of the latter, so that the latter can no longer be justified having regard to Articles 43 EC [49 TFEU] and 49 EC [56 TFEU].

Stoss gave a clear answer to the question of home state control. The proportionality test does not include a duty to recognise authorisation given by another member state – unlike in relation to producer services, there is no duty of mutual recognition-absent harmonisation.[154] In determining, according to their own scale of values, the level of protection sought, each member state retained autonomy to require any gambling operator offering bets to consumers in its territory '. . . to hold an authorisation issued by its competent authorities, without the fact that a particular operator already holds an authorisation issued in another Member State being capable of constituting an obstacle'.[155] The only constraint was that the authorisation procedure must be non-discriminatory and proportionate, as stated in *Placanica.*[156] As in that case, it was however incompatible with EU law for a member state to apply a criminal penalty for failure to satisfy an administrative formality where such had been refused or rendered impossible by the member state concerned.[157]

Divergent regulation of gambling, betting and gaming remains compatible, as long as it is not accompanied by an *incongruous* policy of expansion. As the CJ ultimately is in favour of national regulation and a wide margin of national discretion, strategic litigation may in fact have made matters worse for private operators. Further guidance on the role of evidence and advertising in justification of state monopolies on gambling was given in *Dickinger and Ömer.* The CJ stressed that in order to be consistent with the objective of reducing addiction and crime, national measures promoting state gambling activities had to be:

a. based on a finding that gambling addiction and crime can be remedied by promoting authorised gaming activities, and

---

[151][100]
[152][103]
[153][100]
[154]See also Joined cases C-660/11 *Daniele Biasci and Others v Ministero dell'Interno and Questura di Livorno* and C-8/12 *Cristian Rainone and Others v Ministero dell'Interno and Others* [43].
[155][113]
[156][48&49]
[157][115]

b. allow only moderate advertising, strictly limited to that necessary to channel consumers to these regulated routes.[158]

The rules on free movement of services and freedom of establishment cannot be manipulated by private parties to undermine national regulatory systems that address complex and sensitive national problems but they also cannot be used by public authorities to protect state monopolies. As stated in Pfleger, In order to be compatible with Article 56 TFEU, national legislation must 'genuinely' seek to limit gambling or fight fraud 'in a consistent and systematic manner.'[159]

APPLYING THE LAW

Can non-Croatian caterers rely upon the principle of home state control?

Online gambling is a fast-growing service activity in the EU: annual growth rates are almost 15 per cent and annual revenues in 2015 are expected to be in the region of 13 billion euros, up from 9.3 billion euros in 2011. Regulation is a challenge:

> The nature of the online environment means that gambling sites may operate in the EU, outside any form of control carried out by regulators within the EU. Consumers in Europe also search across borders for online gambling services which, if not properly regulated, may expose them to significant risks. The extensive range of offers and the rising level of demand for online gambling services pose a number of challenges when it comes to ensuring the proper implementation of public policy objectives at the national, EU and international level.[160]

The Commission has undertaken a consultation on the increasing prevalence of online gambling with a view to developing a harmonised approach in the EU. In 2012 it issued a communication for cooperation in the regulation of online gambling.[161] The key objective is to improve protection of all European consumers, including minors and vulnerable groups. It accepts that the development of an attractive range of legal gambling opportunities is vital to effective prevention of consumer use of unregulated sites. It plans to establish an expert group on gambling, composed of representatives of member states, to exchange experiences and good practices as well as to provide advice and expertise on the preparation of EU initiatives. Proposed actions will seek to address the risks emanating from unregulated markets and organised crime, such as fraud and rigging of events.

VIEWPOINT

Given the risks to society, is the CJ's approach to online gambling robust enough?

---

[158]C-347/09 *Dickinger and Ömer* [2011] ECR I-8185 [96 and 99]
[159]C-390/12 *Robert Pfleger and Others*
[160]European Commission, 'Towards a comprehensive European framework for online gambling', COM(2012) *596* final, p. 3
[161]COM(2012) *596* final

4. The hindrance of consumption abroad

To what extent can private persons use these rules to challenges restrictions on the receipt of services abroad? A wide variety of services can be consumed abroad – as shown in *Grogan*, as long as the criteria of remuneration is satisfied, and the cross-border element is present, it will be recognised as a service. Articles 49 and 56 TFEU have been used to challenge financial norms, provisions of national criminal law as well as healthcare practices. The last in particular has given rise to controversial debates, as persons unable to receive treatment in their home member state have travelled across a border to receive treatment elsewhere. The court has taken a more sympathetic to approach complaints concerning national barriers to consumption of healthcare abroad. This has forced discussion of the territorial assumptions underpinning the financing of national healthcare systems, which have remained largely unchanged since the immediate post-war period. These cases on consumption of medical services abroad therefore raise important questions on the future of public healthcare.

i.   Tourism and the receipt of services

A tourist is a person abroad who receives a variety of services for a limited period of time: accommodation, entertainment, catering, shopping, etc. Article 56 TFEU did not mention freedom to receive services but this was incorporated by the decision in *Luisi and Carbone*,[162] a case concerning Italian legislation limiting the amount of foreign currency that could be taken abroad. For many years, before the introduction of the euro, tourists were prohibited by law from exporting large amounts of cash. Movement of cash was regulated in order to maintain stability.

The CJ decided that such rules limited free movement of services. The reasoning behind this decision was not extensive but presented as a corollary of the situation laid out in the Treaty:

> [10] By virtue of Article 59 of the Treaty [Article 56 TFEU], restrictions on freedom to provide such services are to be abolished in respect of nationals of member states who are established in a member state other than that of the person for whom the service is intended. In order to enable services to be provided, the person providing the service may go to the member state where the person for whom it is provided is established or else the latter may go to the state in which the person providing the service is established. Whilst the former case is expressly mentioned in the third paragraph of Article 60, which permits the person providing the service to pursue his activity temporarily in the member state where the service is provided, the latter case is the necessary corollary thereof, which fulfils the objective of liberalizing all gainful activity not covered by the free movement of goods, persons and capital.

It followed from this that restrictions on those travelling abroad to be the recipients of services were not compatible with Article 56. Tourists, persons travelling to receive medical treatment, or for education or business were all to be regarded as 'recipients of services'.[163] This applied to those who left their home to receive services as well as those who

---

[162]Joined cases 286/82 and 26/83 *Luisi and Carbone* v *Ministero dello Tesoro* [1984] ECR 377
[163][16]

stayed at home to receive them, as in *Gambelli* the gambling case discussed above Gambelli and agents like him were prevented by a provision of Italian criminal law from using a service which moved via the internet to them. A criminal prohibition on a natural or legal person using the internet at home to place a bet via the internet with a bookmaker established in another member state also infringed this freedom to receive services:

> [55] In addition, the freedom to provide services involves not only the freedom of the provider to offer and supply services to recipients in a Member State other than that in which the supplier is located but also the freedom to receive or to benefit as recipient from the services offered by a supplier established in another Member State without being hampered by restrictions.[164]

> 5[7] Such a prohibition, enforced by criminal penalties, on participating in betting games organised in Member States other than in the country where the bettor is established constitutes a restriction on the freedom to provide services.

Article 56 therefore protected *Gambelli* and his co-defendants operating as DTCs in Italy for Stanley in the UK – the Italian prohibition was a restriction on the right of the bookmaker freely to provide services, even if Gambelli was established in the same member state as the recipients of the services. The freedom to *receive* services is therefore protected for organisations as well as individuals.

ANALYSING THE LAW

Explain the difference between the receipt of services in *Luisi and Carbone* and *Gambelli*.

The approach towards receipt of services was repeated in *Cowan*.[165] Mr Cowan, a British citizen, was a tourist in France when he was attacked at the exit of a Paris Metro station. Mr Cowan sought a compensation benefit provided in the French criminal code to victims of an assault causing serious physical injury who could not obtain 'effective and adequate' compensation for the harm from any other source. However, Cowan was denied the benefit because he was not a French national or a foreign national resident in France. This was clearly discrimination but did the situation come within the scope of EU law? If Mr Cowan was seen as a recipient of services the principle of non-discrimination would apply.

The French government argued that it did not. It put forward three arguments. First, the rule at issue did not restrict free movement; second, it linked the compensation to national solidarity – receipt, it argued presupposed a 'bond with the State' which a tourist receiving services does not possess; and third, it argued that the compensation rule fell

---

[164]See Joined cases 286/82 and 26/83 *Luisi and Carbone* [1984] ECR 377 [16], and C-294/97 *Eurowings Luftverkehr* [1999] ECR I-7447 [33 and 34]
[165]C-186/87 *Ian William Cowan v Trésor public* [1989] ECR 195

under the law of criminal procedure, which at that time was beyond the scope of EU law.[166] None of these arguments were accepted:

> [17] That reasoning cannot be accepted. When Community law guarantees a natural person the freedom to go to another Member State the protection of that person from harm in the Member State in question, on the same basis as that of nationals and persons residing there, is a corollary of that freedom of movement. It follows that the prohibition of discrimination is applicable to recipients of services within the meaning of the Treaty as regards protection against the risk of assault and the right to obtain financial compensation provided for by national law when that risk materializes. The fact that the compensation at issue is financed by the public treasury cannot alter the rules regarding the protection of the rights guaranteed by the Treaty.

VIEWPOINT

How does the new Croatian law affect the receipt of services?

---

ii. Receipt of healthcare services

As stated in *Luisi and Carbone*, in addition to tourists, persons travelling to receive medical treatment, or for education or business were all to be regarded as 'recipients of services'.[167] Fewer cases have concerned education. This is because education that is not provided for profit falls outside of Article 56 TFEU – it is not seen as an economic activity. The emphasis on financial gain places private education[168] within the reach of EU law on services but not education that is state financed or provided as a not-for-profit activity.[169] Contributions to operating expenses do not count as remuneration. A large amount of case law has developed under Articles 49 and 56 TFEU around freedom to provide and receive medical services in another member state. It can be argued that this case law is creating the basis for a minimal European welfare state.[170]

The application of Article 56 TFEU to the field of public health has not been without controversy – public health is a derogation mentioned in Article 52 TFEU. However, the derogation does not exclude the public health sector as a sector of economic activity per se from freedom to provide services.[171] *Webb* confirmed that the special nature of certain services does not remove them from the reach of the fundamental principle of freedom

---

[166]Even where member states retain competence, 'Community law sets certain limits to their power' such that legislation may not discriminate against those guaranteed equal treatment and fundamental freedoms. Case 203/80 *Casati* [1981] ECR 2595

[167][16]

[168]C-109/92 *Stephan Max Wirth v Landeshauptstadt Hannover*

[169]C-263/86 *Belgian State v René Humbel and Marie-Thérèse Edel* [17–18]; C-109/92 *Stephan Max Wirth v Landeshauptstadt Hannover* [15]. See also C-76/05 *Herbert Schwarz and Marga Gootjes-Schwarz v Finanzamt Bergisch Gladbach*; C-318/05 *Commission of the European Communities v Federal Republic of Germany* (non-tax deductibility of fees paid for private education in another member state)

[170]M. Dougan, 'Expanding the frontiers of EU citizenship by dismantling the territorial boundaries of the national welfare States?', in C. Barnard and O. Odudu (eds), *The Outer Limits of EU Law*, Hart Publishing, 2009, p. 119

[171]See also Case 131/85 *Gül v Regierungspräsident Düsseldorf* [1986] ECR 1573 [17], C-158/96 *Kohll v Union des caisses de maladie* [1998] ECR I-1931 [45 and 6]

of movement.[172] *Müller Faure and van Riet* also clarified that this derogation only applies under certain circumstances:

> [67] It is apparent from the Court's case-law that the objective of maintaining a high-quality, balanced medical and hospital service open to all, may fall within one of the derogations provided for in Article 56 of the EC Treaty [Article 52 TFEU], in so far as it contributes to the attainment of a high level of health protection.[173] In particular, that Treaty provision permits Member States to restrict the freedom to provide medical and hospital services in so far as the maintenance of treatment capacity or medical competence on national territory is essential for public health, and even the survival of the population.[174]

Later cases confirm that in the absence of a European welfare state or harmonisation of healthcare services, it is for the member states to organise their individual social security systems,[175] to determine the conditions covering the right or duty to be insured with a social security scheme[176] and the conditions for entitlement to benefits.[177] However, notwithstanding this deference to national autonomy, achievement of the fundamental freedoms requires member states to make adjustments to their systems.[178]

A much repeated question before the Court has been whether the rules on free movement of services prohibit national territorial exclusivity laws. This is not a straightforward matter; ethical questions can also arise during consideration of these exclusivity laws. For example, in *Commission v France*,[179] Article 49 TFEU was used to challenge a French law obliging medical practitioners established in their home member state to cancel their professional registration before being eligible to practice in France. This rule applied to doctors, midwives and dental nurses. The rule existed to ensure a high level of patient care: the formal end of activities in the home member state was designed to ensure that the medic was always available to their patients in the host member state, so as to provide continuous and reliable care. The French government therefore sought to justify it before the CJ on the ground of public health. The CJ, however, found the rule 'too absolute and general in nature' to satisfy such a justification. Upon investigation, it was found to be differentially applied and unduly restrictive: first, it was applied more strictly upon non-national practitioners and even doctors close to the border were not allowed to open a second practice in France with the result that a 'dental practitioner established in another member state can never be authorized to open a second practice in France'.[180] Second, not all illnesses required the doctor to be in close proximity to the patient. The restrictions therefore discriminated against non-national practitioners and the Court agreed that France had failed to fulfil its obligations. However, many people – especially the elderly – might feel safer knowing that their medical advisor is nearby. Should realisation of the internal market ignore this?

---

[172]C-279/80 *Webb* [1981] ECR 3305 [10]
[173]*Kohll* [50], and *Smits and Peerbooms* [73]
[174]*Kohll* [51], and *Smits and Peerbooms* [74]
[175]Case 238/82 *Duphar and Others v Netherlands* [1984] ECR 523 [16] and C-70/95 *Sodemare and Others v Regione Lombardia* [1997] ECR I-3395 [27]
[176]C-110/79 *Coonan v Insurance Officer* [1980] ECR 1445 [12] and C-349/87 *Paraschi v Landesversicherungsanstalt Württemberg* [1991] ECR I-4501 [15]
[177]Joined cases C-4/95 and C-5/95 *Stöber and Piosa Pereira v Bundesanstalt für Arbeit* [1997] ECR I-511 [36]
[178]See *Müller-Fauré and van Riet* [100 and 102]
[179]C-96/85
[180][12]

Territorial exclusivity rules requiring patients who want reimbursement to acquire prior authorisation before receiving medical treatment abroad have also been challenged. The answer has been differentiated, depending upon whether the care required hospitalisation, or the treatment was scheduled. These cases will be the focus of this section. In addressing these rules, the CJ has given much consideration to their role in the maintenance of financial balance and stability of national public health systems. These systems form part of the national welfare state and each member state has developed its own method of organisation to provide cost-effective, quality and reliable medical care to those in need. As a public benefit, these services are free at point of use – individuals pay in advance, prior to a medical need or hospitalisation arising. In some countries payment is made into a compulsory public medical fund – subscribers must contribute irrespective of desire or need. Payment can also be organised via direct taxation (as in the case of the National Health Service (NHS) in the UK) or in other systems individuals pay into a public insurance fund of their choice (such as in Germany). These schemes also provide healthcare for those with low or no income: in the Netherlands, workers on a low annual income, persons in receipt of social benefits and dependent members of their families living with them in the same household are compulsorily and automatically insured in a specific scheme.

Territorial exclusivity is a means to secure the stability of these healthcare systems by balancing payments in and treatments provided. Subscribers who require medical attention must seek this within their home member state except in an emergency or if they have received prior authorisation to receive care elsewhere. The objective of such exclusivity rules is to secure the financial stability of these schemes as well as to retain a balanced budget through control of overall expenditure. Where authorisation has been given, persons are eligible to claim reimbursement for the costs incurred. In the absence of authorisation, reimbursement is unlikely. Authorisation can be difficult to obtain, especially in relation to non-emergency operations. This prior authorisation requirement has been the focus of many challenges to the receipt of medical – hospital and non-hospital – care abroad. The broad restrictions imposed by these rules have been effectively challenged under Article 56 TFEU. Where a rule has survived scrutiny under Article 56 TFEU, it is due to overriding reasons related to the general public interest – the derogation also used in the gambling cases.

a) 'Overriding reason in the general interest'

This court-made derogation has helped patients access medical professionals across borders. Its meaning was clarified in *Kohll*.[181] A Luxembourg national, Mr Kohll, wanted his daughter to receive dental treatment in Trier, a city in neighbouring Germany. An issue arose when his medical insurer and the sector tribunal refused to authorise this treatment on the grounds that the proposed treatment was not urgent and could be provided in Luxembourg. Mr Kohll appealed, arguing that the national rules were incompatible with Regulation 1408/71 and free movement of services. The CJ therefore had to determine whether Article 56 TFEU precluded application of the national social security rules: were they a barrier to the freedom to provide services? If so, could they be justified either by the Treaty derogations or by overriding reasons relating to the general interest?

Citing *Webb*, the rules were brought under Article 56 TFEU: the dispute concerned non-hospital treatment – a service, provided for remuneration – by an orthodontist

---

[181]C-158/96 *Raymond Kohll v Union des caisses de maladie*

established in another member state and the national rule had the 'effect of making the provision of services between Member States more difficult than the provision of services purely within one Member State'.[182] This was so, because prior authorisation was not required for any medical costs incurred within the home member state:

[34] While the national rules at issue in the main proceedings do not deprive insured persons of the possibility of approaching a provider of services established in another Member State, they do nevertheless make reimbursement of the costs incurred in that Member State subject to prior authorisation, and deny such reimbursement to insured persons who have not obtained that authorisation. Costs incurred in the State of insurance are not, however, subject to that authorisation.

[35] Consequently, such rules deter insured persons from approaching providers of medical services established in another Member State and constitute, for them and their patients, a barrier to freedom to provide services.[183]

The rule discouraged free movement but could it be justified? Was there a legitimate need to control health expenditure and balance the social security budget, and was prior authorisation the only effective and least restrictive means of so doing? Kohll's insurer, the Luxembourg government and the Commission argued that 'the risk of upsetting the financial balance of the social security scheme, which aims to ensure a balanced medical and hospital service available to all its insured persons, constitutes an overriding reason in the general interest capable of justifying restrictions on freedom to provide services'.[184] However, this failed because treatment cost the same in both states – as there was no cost difference, there was no serious risk of undermining the financial balance of the system. In the absence of such a risk the rule could not be justified as an overriding reason in the general interest.

The rule could also not be justified as necessary to 'guarantee the quality of medical services' to all insured persons – mutual recognition of qualifications of doctors and dentists presupposes any difference in quality of treatment from one member state to another. The prior authorisation rule could therefore not be justified on grounds of public health in order to protect the quality of medical services provided in other member states.[185] It had to go:

[52] However, neither UCM nor the Governments of the Member States which have submitted observations have shown that the rules at issue were necessary to provide a balanced medical and hospital service accessible to all. None of those who have submitted observations has argued that the rules were indispensable for the maintenance of an essential treatment facility or medical service on national territory.

[53] The conclusion must therefore be drawn that the rules at issue in the main proceedings are not justified on grounds of public health.

[182]*Kohll* [33]; C-381/93 *Commission* v *France* [1994] ECR I-5145 [17]
[183]Joined cases 286/82 and 26/83 *Luisi and Carbone* v *Ministero del Tesoro* [1984] ECR 377 [16] and C-204/90 *Bachmann* v *Belgium* [1992] ECR I-249 [31]
[184][38]
[185][48/9]

Reimbursement of the cost of dental treatment provided abroad could not be made conditional upon prior authorisation by the social security institution in the home states. Territorial exclusivity in this circumstance was not justified.

This justification also failed in *Stamatelaki*.[186] Under national law, treatment was free if a patient insured under the Greek social system was treated in a private Greek hospital but not if the private hospital were in another member state. Emergency treatment was only reimbursed if provided at a private hospital in Greece, but not if provided at a private hospital in another member state.[187] The law was found to act as a deterrent for patients and providers of healthcare. It was 'immaterial' that the hospital was private – previous rulings applied and the Greek rule was examined to assess whether it introduced or maintained unjustified restrictions free provision of services in the healthcare sector.[188] The rule was found to be legitimate as an 'overriding reason in the general interest' – the Greek government argued that 'the balance of the national social security system could be upset if insured persons had the option of recourse to private hospitals in other Member States without an agreement having been entered into with those hospitals, given the high cost of hospital treatment of this type'.[189] Although the objective was deemed legitimate, the method was disproportionate: the same objective could be achieved using a prior authorisation scheme arranged to comply with the requirements set out in the cases of *Müller-Fauré and van Riet*.[190]

APPLYING THE LAW

Can the Croatian law be justified as an 'overriding reason in the public interest'?

---

b) Reimbursement of hospital costs

There were some unique elements to *Kohll*: the treatment was recognised in both member states, costs were equal in both member states and the most expensive element of medical care – hospitalisation – was not required. The question of reimbursement for hospitalisation for treatment not recognised in the home state arose in *Smits and Peerbooms*.[191] It engaged legal teams from 11 of the then EU15 and 2 from EFTA. In this joined case, two Dutch nationals had applied to their healthcare funds – Stichting VGZ and Stichting CZ – for the reimbursement of hospital treatment costs incurred in Germany and Austria respectively. Mrs Geraets-Smits, who suffered from Parkinson's disease, had travelled to Germany for specialist treatment: Stichting VGZ refused reimbursement of the costs of the treatment as there was no medical necessity (the same treatment for Parkinson's was available in the Netherlands). Mr Peerbooms fell into a coma following a road accident in December 1996. He was taken to hospital in the Netherlands and then transferred in

---

[186]C-444/05 Stamatelaki [2007] ECR I-3185
[187][26]
[188]See, in particular, C-157/99 *B.S.M. Geraets-Smits v Stichting Ziekenfonds VGZ and H.T.M. Peerbooms v Stichting CZ Groep Zorgverzekeringen* [2001] ECR I 5473 [44 to 46] and C-372/04 *Watts* [92]
[189][33]
[190][81 and 85]
[191]C-157/99 *Smits and Peerbooms*

a vegetative state to the University Clinic in Innsbruck in Austria in February 1997 where he received special intensive therapy using neuro-stimulation, a treatment not widely used in the Netherlands and specifically prohibited for patients of Mr Peerboom's age. Sticht-ing CZ refused to pay the costs of the treatment at the University Clinic in Innsbruck on the basis that adequate treatment was available in the Netherlands. By June 1997 Mr Peerbooms came out of his coma and by the end of that month was transferred to a clinic in the Netherlands for further treatment.

Neither treatments would have been received in the Netherlands and neither party had received prior authorisation as required. Given this, did Article 56 preclude these rules mak-ing the reimbursement of costs for hospital care in another member state conditional upon prior authorisation by a medical insurer, authorisation being granted only if a) the proposed treatment was recognised by the individual's insurance scheme (rule of recognition) and b) the treatment abroad was necessary and could not be given by a care provider with whom the home sickness insurance fund had a prior arrangement (medical necessity). These two conditions of recognition and medical necessity in Dutch law did not deprive nationals from seeking medical treatment abroad but made reimbursement much more difficult and refusal more likely. They represented a significant hurdle. Also, they did not apply to hospitalisa-tion costs incurred in the Netherlands. Thus as in *Kohll*, it was the case that:

> [69] . . . rules such as those at issue in the main proceedings deter, or even prevent, insured persons from applying to providers of medical services established in another Member State and constitute, both for insured persons and service providers, a barrier to freedom to provide services.[192]

Could such rules be objectively justified? The strongest justification would be that this rule was necessary to avoid risk of seriously undermining the financial balance in the social security system. The attempt to invoke this as an overriding reason in the general interest capable of justifying a barrier to the principle of freedom to provide services was unsuccessful in *Kohll*[193] but it fared better here, given hospitalisation:

> [77] As may be seen, in particular, from the contracting system involved in the main proceedings, this kind of planning therefore broadly meets a variety of concerns.

> [78] For one thing, it seeks to achieve the aim of ensuring that there is sufficient and permanent access to a balanced range of high-quality hospital treatment in the State concerned.

> [79] For another thing, it assists in meeting a desire to control costs and to prevent, as far as possible, any wastage of financial, technical and human resources. Such wastage is all the more damaging because it is generally recognised that the hospital care sec-tor generates considerable costs and must satisfy increasing needs, while the financial resources which may be made available for health care are not unlimited, whatever the mode of funding applied.

New technologies are expensive – for example, the installation of positron emission tomography, used in the detection and treatment of cancer, represents an investment of

---

[192]See also *Luisi and Carbone* [16], C-204/90 *Bachmann* [1992] ECR I-249 [31] and *Kohll* [35]
[193][41]

hundreds of thousands, even millions, of pounds, in its purchase, installation and use. If persons insured could seek treatment involving the use of major medical equipment in other member states freely, this investment would be wasted and the long-term supply of up-to-date treatment would also be jeopardised, undermining the planning and management by the national authorities and putting the financial balance in question.[194] Considering this, the CJ decided that prior authorisation was a measure 'both necessary and reasonable' – it would 'jeopardise [the planning required to maintain a] rationalised, stable, balanced and accessible supply of hospital services'[195] if insured persons could freely use services in any hospital they wished.

Yet while prior authorisation was now found in principle to be compatible with Article 56 TFEU, were the two conditions of recognition and medical necessity proportionate? The answer was yes, as long as in practice recognition was determined according to the norms prevailing in international medical science rather than just in the Netherlands; and that authorisation was refused on the ground of lack of medical necessity only if the same or equally effective treatment was available without 'undue delay' at an establishment having a contractual arrangement with the insured person's sickness insurance fund. The Dutch law promoting territorial exclusivity was therefore found compatible with Article 56 as long as these caveats applied. Freedom to receive health services could be limited – patients were not free to receive certain expensive medical services in another member state.

VIEWPOINT

Are these caveats valid – should financial stability be enough to justify territorial exclusivity rules?

---

c) 'Undue delay' in hospital care

What, however, comprises 'undue delay' in treatment – one month, three months, one year? This concept was used without definition in many cases. It was used by clever patients who were impatient with long waiting lists for treatment in the home member state. Ms van Riet suffered terrible wrist pain and was told she would have to wait about six months for treatment in the Netherlands. Before receiving authorisation, she went to Belgium for treatment at a hospital with whom her insurer had no prior agreement. Determining an absence of 'medical necessity', the insurer rejected her claim for reimbursement. The case coincided with that of Mrs Müller Faure,[196] who had received dental treatment while on holiday in Germany. In the absence of prior authorisation and 'medical necessity', her claim for reimbursement was also partly rejected – only part of the treatment was paid for and none of the related costs. Given the similarity of the questions raised by these circumstances, the reasoning was for the most part drawn from *Smits-Peerboom*. It was irrelevant that the issue here was based on a system of benefits-in-kind (free treatment at partner organisations) rather than reimbursement – the matter nonetheless fell under Article 56 TFEU.

---

[194]C-512/08 *Commission v France* [2010] ECR I-8833 [39–41]. See also V.R. Fuchs, 'Economics, values and health care reform', *American Economic Review* 86, 1996, pp. 1–24
[195][81]
[196]C-385/99 *Müller-Fauré and van Riet*

The novel element in this case was the justification: could the specific feature of the system – benefits in kind and agreements-based treatment rather than reimbursement of costs – justify refusal to provide cash reimbursement? The CJ was also asked to consider the relevance of more expensive hospital treatment and the existence of national waiting lists. The waiting list could be interpreted in two ways: a waiting list indicates both need and capacity to supply – could this justify a restriction of patients going abroad when they could have the treatment at home? Or alternatively, did the existence of a waiting list indicate 'undue delay' and relieve patients from waiting to receive treatment at home?

Waiting lists are only relevant to hospital services so it was dealt with separately to non-hospital services. The issues of quality, stability and wastage, as highlighted in *Smits and Peerbooms*,[197] were significant. Three key justificatory arguments were considered:

1 the quality of public health – to what extent did the system of agreements ensure a high-quality, balanced medical and hospital service open to all;
2 the financial stability of the social security system – did this system enable the authorities to control expenditure by adjusting it to projected requirements, according to pre-established priorities; and
3 national values – to what extent was this system an essential characteristic of the sickness insurance scheme in the Netherlands?[198]

The CJ accepted that unconditional free movement of large numbers of hospital patients could undermine the system and would inevitably cause wastage where hospitals had surplus capacity to provide treatment:

[91] . . . were large numbers of insured persons to decide to be treated in other member states even when the hospitals having agreements with their sickness insurance funds offer adequate identical or equivalent treatment, the consequent outflow of patients would be liable to put at risk the very principle of having agreements with hospitals and, consequently, undermine all the planning and rationalisation carried out in this vital sector in an effort to avoid the phenomena of hospital overcapacity, imbalance in the supply of hospital medical care and logistical and financial wastage.

However, the existence of national waiting lists for a specific treatment did not indicate wastage due to surplus supply and could not be an *automatic* reason to refuse prior authorisation – the specific circumstances attaching to the patient's medical condition had to be considered.[199] These considerations did not apply to non-hospital medical services – the use of non-contracted providers in other member states or the removal of the need for prior authorisation would not destabilise the Dutch system to the extent required to justify this barrier to freedom to provide services. Nor would the removal of the requirement to receive prior authorisation for non-hospital health care provided in another member state alter the 'essential characteristics' of the Dutch public healthcare system.

The conclusion therefore differentiated between hospital and non-hospital costs – the former was a risk to be recognised, the latter was not. In relation to hospital care authorisation could be refused if treatment were available without 'undue delay' at a partner organisation. The principle of medical necessity to limit free movement of patients

---

[197][104–6]
[198][66]

[199][92]

helped to maintain 'an adequate, balanced and permanent supply of high-quality hospital treatment' and assured the financial stability of the sickness insurance system. However, legislation making prior authorisation necessary for reimbursement of non-hospital care costs provided in another member state by a non-partner entity was an unjustified restriction on the free movement of patients to receive services.

This approach towards hospital care was confirmed in *Inisan*[200] and *Leichtle*.[201] The idea that medical necessity meant 'absolute necessity' was ruled out in the latter case: a member state could not make reimbursement of associated medical costs (such as board, lodging, travel, visitors' tax) arising from treatment in another member state dependent upon an expert report 'that the proposed cure is absolutely necessary owing to the greatly increased prospects of success in that other Member state'.[202]

However, none of these cases clarified the concept of 'undue delay'. This question arose again when the NHS refused to reimburse the cost of hospital treatment received in France by a British national, Mrs Watts.[203] Mrs Watts had initially been given a waiting time of 12 months for hip-replacement surgery, but this was later reduced to 3–4 months. Her case was considered routine and she was not given permission to travel abroad for a faster operation. Nonetheless, suffering constant pain and severe immobility, she decided to do so. At the same time she sought judicial review of the NHS decision. The British High Court dismissed her application – the waiting time of 3–4 months was not 'undue delay' thus she was not entitled under Article 56 to claim reimbursement of her treatment in France.

The CJ decided that Article 56 TFEU applied as well as Regulation No 1408/71 – the 'fact that national legislation may be in conformity with Regulation No 1408/71 does not have the effect of removing that legislation from the scope of the provisions of the EC Treaty'.[204] The reasoning in the previous cases under Article 56 was largely repeated. As in *Müller-Faure*, the method of operation and financing of the NHS was irrelevant: the situation fell under Article 56 TFEU. Despite the lack of harmonisation at the EU level, Member states still had to comply with EU law on the freedom to provide services:[205] the need to receive prior authorisation from the NHS for treatment abroad, when this was not necessary for treatment under the NHS in the UK, was found to constitute, both for patients and service providers, an obstacle to the freedom to provide services.[206]

As in *Müller-Faure*, this remained open to justification. Repeating *Smits and Peerboom*,[207] prior authorisation of medical costs incurred abroad was deemed 'a measure which is both necessary and reasonable'.[208] This was in principle therefore compatible with Article 56 as long as the system of authorisation satisfied five criteria. The criteria summarise previous case law:[209]

1 it is 'based on objective, non-discriminatory criteria which are known in advance' – this would prevent any arbitrary exercise of national discretion;
2 it is 'easily accessible, efficient, objective and impartial';

[200] C-56/01 *Patricia Inisan v Caisse primaire d'assurance maladie des Hauts-de-Seine* [2003] ECR I-12403
[201] C-08/02 *Ludwig Leichtle v Bundesanstalt für Arbeit* [2004] ECR I-2641
[202] See *Leichtle*
[203] C-372/04 *Watts* [2006] ECR I 4325
[204] [46–47]
[205] *Smits and Peerbooms* [44 to 46], *Müller-Fauré and van Riet* [100] and *Inisan* [17]
[206] *Smits and Peerbooms* [69] *Müller-Fauré and van Riet* [44]
[207] [76 –80]
[208] [110]
[209] *Smits and Peerbooms* [90], *Müller-Fauré and van Riet* [85] and *Inisan* [49]

3 refusals to grant authorisation can be the subject of judicial or quasi-judicial review;[210]
4 refusals to grant authorisation are properly reasoned and refer to the specific provisions;
5 any review of refusals can include use of 'objective and impartial independent experts'.

Applying the above criteria, it was not possible for the NHS to refuse to grant prior authorisation simply because a waiting list existed. The decision had to be based upon:

> an objective medical assessment of the patient's medical condition, the history and probable course of his illness, the degree of pain he is in and/or the nature of his disability at the time when the request for authorisation was made or renewed.[211]

Refusal of authorisation may also not be based on the order of priorities, the fact that the hospital treatment under the national system is free of charge, the availability of specific funds to reimburse the cost of treatment to be provided in another member state, or a comparison between the cost of the same treatment in member states.[212] Costs, including ancillary expenditure associated with the medical treatment, were to be reimbursed but in a revision of the earlier ruling in *Vanbraekel and Others*,[213] the insured person's right to additional reimbursement was limited to the costs actually incurred in the member state of stay.[214]

Mr Elchinov from Bulgaria was in a similar situation to Mrs Watts. He also applied to his national health fund, the NZOK, for permission under Regulation 1408/71 Article 22 to seek specialist treatment abroad but before receiving an answer went abroad anyway. Under the national rules, payment for hospital treatment abroad was totally dependent upon prior authorisation: the rules therefore excluded persons like Mr Elchinov who could not wait for this. The authorisation was also refused on the basis that his treatment – an advanced therapy for cancer unavailable in Bulgaria – was not a benefit covered by the regulation. The case called for an interpretation of Article 56 and the Regulation. The blanket exclusion was described as a disproportionate 'deprivation' that could not be justified by the danger of damage to the financial balance of the system. In the absence of any imperative reason, the Bulgarian legislation was prohibited. Furthermore, authorisation could not be refused if the list of benefits covered was vague and ambiguous, or if

TABLE 13.2 'Undue delay' and hospitalisation – acceptable and unacceptable reasons for refusing authorisation

Acceptable	Individualised and objective medical assessment	History and course of illness	Degree of pain of patient	Nature of the disability
Unacceptable	Existence of a waiting list	General priorities	Availability of free/cheaper treatment	Availability of funds to reimburse cost of treatment

---

[210][116]
[211]See *Watts*
[212][123]
[213][53]
[214]*Watts* [131 and 143]

an alternative and equally effective treatment was unavailable in the home member state. This decision may appear 'patient-friendly' in the short term, but given the cash-strapped situation of many healthcare systems – perhaps especially in eastern Europe – it may lead in the long term to the removal of such operations from insurance packages.[215]

VIEWPOINT

Do you agree that waiting lists should not be considered when deciding whether a person may go abroad for public healthcare?

---

d) Scheduled vs. unscheduled hospital treatment

The relationship between Regulation 1408/71 and free movement of services was further explored in infringement proceedings between the Commission, Spain and France. *Commission v Spain*[216] introduced a distinction between scheduled and unscheduled (or emergency) hospital treatment abroad. The dispute concerned the refusal by a Spanish insurance fund to full reimbursement of medical costs arising from unscheduled treatment undertaken during a trip abroad. In contrast to previous healthcare cases, the individual had not gone abroad specifically for medical treatment. Article 56 nonetheless applied – as per *Luisi and Carbone, Cowan* and *Calfa*,[217] 'persons established in a Member State who travel to another Member State as tourists or on a study trip must be regarded as recipients of services' and:

> [52] . . . the freedom to provide services encompasses the freedom of an insured person established in a Member State to travel – as a tourist or student, for example – to another Member State for a temporary stay and to receive hospital care there from a provider established in the latter Member State, where the need for such care during that stay arises because of his state of health.

However, as the treatment was 'unscheduled'[218] the question of costs was distinguished from *Watts*, which concerned 'scheduled'[219] treatment. This made all the difference to the position under Article 56 TFEU: scheduled treatment obliges the member state to, without 'undue delay', provide the insured person with a level of cover equal to that offered under the home health system within a medically acceptable length of time. This is not so with unscheduled treatment, as referred to in Article 22(1)(a) of Regulation 1408/71 – there is no right to cost-neutral emergency medical assistance abroad:

> [61] With regard to an insured person whose travel to another Member State is for reasons relating to tourism or education, for example, and not to any inadequacy in the

---

[215]Anne Pieter van der Mei, 'Case note', *CMLR* 48, 2011, pp. 1297–1311
[216]C-211/08 *Commission v Spain* [2010] ECR I-5267
[217]Joined cases 286/82 and 26/83 *Luisi and Carbone* [1984] ECR 377 [16]; C-186/87 *Cowan* [1989] ECR 195 [15]; and C-348/96 *Calfa*[1999] ECR I-11 [16]
[218]Article 22(1)(a) of Regulation No 1408/71
[219]Article 22(1)(c)

health service to which he is affiliated, the rules of the Treaty on freedom of movement offer no guarantee that all hospital treatment services which may have to be provided to him unexpectedly in the Member State of stay will be neutral in terms of cost.

In the absence of coordination of national social security laws, emergency hospitalisation in another member state may be to the advantage or disadvantage of an individual.[220] The reasoning focused on the different deterrent effects: limited reimbursement of costs for emergency treatment would not act as a deterrent in the same way as non-reimbursement of costs for scheduled treatment. This is because the financial implications could be pre-determined in relation to scheduled treatment and any possibility for national insurance funds to refuse full reimbursement could deter an insured person from pursing treatment abroad; the deterrent amounts to a restriction on the freedom to provide services. As costs are impossible to predict in relation to emergency/unscheduled treatment, this deterrent effect did not exist [64–65]. Furthermore, the rules on limited reimbursement for unscheduled hospital treatment abroad were necessary to maintain balance in the system:

[78] . . . cases in which unscheduled hospital treatment provided to an insured person during a temporary stay in another Member State bring about – as a consequence of the application of the legislation of the Member State of stay – a heavier financial burden for the Member State of affiliation than if that treatment had been provided in one of its own establishments, are deemed to be counterbalanced overall by cases in which, on the contrary, application of the legislation of the Member State of stay leads the Member State of affiliation to incur lower costs for the hospital treatment in question than those which would have resulted from the application of its own legislation.

An obligation to reimburse higher costs would not only upset the delicate financial balance but would also undermine the system established by Regulation No. 1408/71. Consequently, the Commission lost and the action against Spain was dismissed. The Commission also lost its infringement proceedings against France[221] for the same reason: the restriction on reimbursement costs for unscheduled treatment was justified in light of the dangers to the organisation of public health policy and the financial balance of the social security system; and the procedure complied with the criteria laid out in *Müller-Fauré and van Riet*.

Kaczorowska argues that this case law has brought into existence a new right, a right to healthcare as provided in Article 35 of the Charter of Fundamental Rights:

The outcomes of the creation of the new right to effective and speedy medical treatment by the Court of Justice are twofold. The first is that the judgments of the Court have instilled in the Member States a new impetus to reconsider and define their future health policies at both national and European levels. The second is that the Court of Justice, by establishing the new right, has brought the EU closer to all of its citizens. Now, they are entitled to benefit from high-quality healthcare in their Member State of insurance but, if this cannot be achieved, they can seek medical treatment in another Member State, for which the Member State of their insurance will be liable. . . . it can be said that the Court of Justice has, to a great extent, attained the main objective of

---

[220]Joined cases C-393/99 and C-394/99 *Hervein and Others* [2002] ECR I-2829 [50 to 52]; C-387/01 *Weigel* [2004] ECR I-4981, [55]; and C-392/05 *Alevizos* [2007] ECR I-3505 [76]
[221]C-512/08 *Commission* v *France* [2010] ECR I-8833

Article 35 of the Charter of Fundamental Rights of the European Union. Indeed, it would appear that the Court of Justice has, by creating a new right to effective and speedy medical treatment, accomplished what it was hoped would be achieved by Article 35. There is no doubt that the new right, even in its imperfect form, provides a tangible right for EU citizens. They will neither have to wait indefinitely to obtain medical treatment nor have to accept substandard treatment in their member state of insurance.[222]

VIEWPOINT

Do you agree – has the CJEU used Articles 49 and 56 TFEU to develop EU citizenship and welfare rights?

5. Commercial presence

The freedom of established persons to provide a range of services in other member states is addressed under both Articles 49 and 56 TFEU. The major obstacles here include rules stipulating that a national presence is required in order to provide a service on the territory, even where the non-national service provider is established in their home state. Such rules are often introduced for the protection of the consumer. They tend to be non-discriminatory but can mask protectionist goals. As they make it harder for non-nationals to provide the same service as a national, they breach Articles 49 and 56 TFEU – in most cases, the national rule is found to be disproportionate. Such rules can be found in the finance, insurance and legal sectors. They will be explored below.

Insurance services are sensitive, complex and have been particularly troublesome. The scope for fraud and harm to the consumer is significant. National authorities must ensure that any insurer has the capital available to cover any number of claims at all times. This task is easier and more effective if insurers are resident in the national territory. In contrast to the gambling cases, national rules have sought to protect the consumer by imposing residency requirements rather than creating state run monopolies.

For example, under Dutch law, persons providing insurance services were obliged to reside in the Netherlands as well as have an office there. However, this type of rule, limiting provision of a service to those habitually resident, clearly has the potential to deprive free movement of services of all effectiveness. In *Coenen,* which concerned a Dutch national living in Belgium who had provided insurance services to clients in the Netherlands, this requirement of a permanent private residence was deemed too restrictive to be compatible with Article 56 TFEU.[223] However, the rule was held to be acceptable as an exception where other less restrictive measures were not available to ensure accordance with national professional rules.

---

[222]Alina Kaczorowska, ' Review of the Creation by the European Court of Justice of the Right to Effective and Speedy Medical Treatment and its Outcomes', *European Law Journal* 12(3), May 2006, pp. 345–370
[223]C-39/75 *Coenen v Sociaal Economische Raad* [1975] ECR 1547 [11]

A similar issue arose in *Commission* v *Germany:*[224] in 1983, Germany introduced a new Insurance Supervision Law (the Versicherungsaufsichtsgesetz) which stated that those providing insurance services had to be established and authorised in Germany and also that insurance brokers in Germany could only use insurers established in Germany for their German clients. As in *van Wesemael*[225] and *Webb*,[226] it was recognised that such restrictions were appropriate for certain service sectors. However, the duplications unnecessarily raised costs and were therefore restrictions of freedom to provide services:

[28] . . . the requirements in question in these proceedings, namely that an insurer who is established in another member state, authorized by the supervisory authority of that state and subject to the supervision of that authority, must have a permanent establishment within the territory of the state in which the service is provided and that he must obtain a separate authorisation from the supervisory authority of that state, constitute restrictions on the freedom to provide services inasmuch as they increase the cost of such services in the state in which they are provided, in particular where the insurer conducts business in that state only occasionally.

Consequently, the requirements in the Supervision Law could *only* be compatible with free movement of services if three conditions were met:

1 that 'in the field of activity concerned there are *imperative reasons relating to the public interest* which justify restrictions on the freedom to provide services' (consumer protection);
2 that the *public interest is not already protected* by the rules of 'the state of establishment' ('home state rule'); and
3 that the rules are the *least onerous possible,* or 'the same result cannot be obtained by less restrictive rules' (proportionality).

ANALYSING THE LAW

Which of these conditions do you think is the most important to help non-national establishments?

Many of the intervening member states (Belgium, Denmark, France, Ireland and Italy) had introduced similar legislation in order to protect the consumer from abuse – insurers were subject to mandatory rules concerning their financial base and the conditions of insurance offered to policy-holders. The Court accepted therefore that the first condition was met – there were imperative reasons relating to the public interest, specifically protection of the consumer. Inspection of these national rules demonstrated that they differed widely, leading to the conclusion that the second condition also held – Germany

---

[224]C-205/84 *Commission* v *Germany* [1986] ECR 3755
[225]C-110 and 111/78 *Van Wesemael and Follachio* [1979] ECR 35
[226]C-279/80 *Webb*

was indeed justified in laying down its own rules of authorisation as the rules in the home state did not cover the same aspects of consumer protection.

Only the third condition remained: were these rules proportionate or did they exceed what was necessary?[227] The answer to this was yes and no: in principle, authorisation did provide an effective means to ensure supervision and protect the interests of the consumer[228] but in practice this was not always the case – in some insurance sectors mandatory rules were not needed due to the nature of the risk and the party seeking insurance. The blanket rule requiring establishment in the host state therefore went beyond that necessary and was not compatible with the Treaty. The focus on proportionality stressed that it was a matter of the means used to achieve the objective, rather than the objective itself.

VIEWPOINT

To what extent do you think territorial rules are necessary to protect consumers buying: a) holiday insurance; b) home insurance; and c) life insurance?

A non-discriminatory establishment rule again came to the fore in *Commission* v *Denmark*.[229] A Danish rule that allowed only insurance undertakings established in Denmark to provide co-insurance services in that state as leading insurers. Another rule obliged any insurer located in Denmark or offering insurance services from Denmark to gain prior authorisation before providing these services in other EU member states. The Commission brought similar infringement actions against France,[230] Ireland[231] and Germany.[232] The fact that these rules were common practice across the sector in different member states led it to suspect economic protectionism rather than consumer protection. It saw these rules requiring a permanent establishment to provide co-insurance services as a serious restriction. This was especially so as the norm for insurance undertakings is to conduct business as co-insurers.[233] Such rules could only be justified if they met the three conditions laid out in *Commission* v *Germany*.

This was not the case. As in *Commission* v *Germany*, the first and second conditions were met – the Court recognised that in principle restrictions might be warranted in the insurance sector for the protection of the consumer and that divergence in national laws meant consumer protection was not necessarily guaranteed by the rules of the state of establishment. However, the requirement of an establishment represented the very negation of the freedom to provide services and was too onerous – it exceeded what was necessary to attain the objective pursued and was therefore contrary to free movement of services. A requirement of host state establishment in the specific field of co-insurance where the undertaking already had a permanent establishment in the home state was per

---

[227][41]
[228][46]
[229]C-252/83. See Cases 220/83, 252/83, 205/84 and 206/84, *Commission* v *France, Denmark, Germany and Ireland*, [1987] 2 CMLR 69 et seq
[230]C-220/83 *Commission* v *France* [1986] ECR 3663
[231]C-206/84 *Commission* v *Ireland* [1986] ECR 3817
[232]C-205/84 *Commission* v *Germany* [1986] ECR 3755
[233][18]

se contrary.[234] Like Germany, Denmark also failed to fulfil its obligations. By contrast, however, in *Commission v Belgium*,[235] a Belgian rule making tax deductions dependent upon the use of an insurer established in the member state was not contrary to Article 56 TFEU. In this case, the restriction was held to be indispensable to the public interest objective pursued.

The same approach is taken in the legal sector where territorial rules are also common. This is visible in *Säger* where national legislation prevented lawyers established outside of Germany from monitoring and renewing patents.[236] The Court stressed the application of Article 56 TFEU to rules causing any hindrance, even if national providers were equally affected:

> [12] . . . Article 59 EC [56 TFEU] requires not only the elimination of all discrimination against a person providing services on the ground of his nationality but also the abolition of any restriction, even if it applies without distinction to national providers of services and to those of other Member States, when it is liable to prohibit or otherwise impede the activities of a provider of services established in another Member State where he lawfully provides similar services.

Likewise, in *Commission v France*,[237] a law reserving rights to appear in court to lawyers belonging to the local Bar of the relevant Court was held to be incompatible with free movement of services. The Court refused to accept as proportionate the French action to secure client contact and compliance with procedural and ethical practice:

> [35] In the first place, as the Court stated in its judgment in *Klopp*, at paragraph 21, modern methods of transport and telecommunications enable lawyers to maintain the necessary contacts with clients and the judicial authorities. Furthermore, the expeditious conduct of the proceedings, in compliance with the principle that both sides must be given the opportunity to state their case, can be ensured by imposing on the lawyer providing services obligations which restrict the pursuit of his activities to a lesser extent. That aim could therefore be achieved by requiring the lawyer providing services to have an address for service at the chambers of the lawyer in conjunction with whom he works, where notifications from the judicial authority in question could be duly served.

Thus even where the Court recognises as legitimate a public interest justifying a restriction on the freedom to provide services, it may find the measures adopted disproportionate to the needs asserted.

Perhaps most controversially, the same approach has also been applied to trade union activities. Viking, a Finnish ferry company carrying passengers across to Estonia, was in financial difficulty. Its business was failing and it blamed this on high labour costs set out in a collective agreement with the Finnish Seamans Union (FSU). In a bid to return to profitability, it sought to evade the FSU agreement by re-registering its vessel, the Rosella, in Estonia. This would effectively transfer establishment to Estonia and enable Viking to pay its employees less. To protect the jobs of its members and discourage this 'wage tourism', the FSU contacted the International Transport Federation (ITF), a collective organisation of which it was a member, asking it to encourage all other trade unions to

---

[234][20–21]
[235]C-300/90 *Commission v Belgium* [1992] ECR I-305
[236]C-76/90 *Manfred Säger v Dennemeyer & Co. Ltd*
[237]C-294/89 *Commission v France* [1991] ECR I-3591

refuse to negotiation with Viking. The ITF did so, on the grounds that it sought to combat the use of 'flags of convenience' by unscrupulous employers. Was this behaviour caught by Article 49 TFEU – did it undermine freedom of establishment?

The Court stressed that the principle in Article 49 extends to non-state entities such as Viking, a private company. It also emphasised that Article 49 applied not only to actions of public authorities but also 'rules of any other nature aimed at regulating in a collective manner gainful employment, self-employment and the provision of services'. Thus the promotion by a trade union of collective industrial action against Viking was found to be a restriction of freedom of establishment. The industrial action to combat 'wage tourism' had the effect of 'making less attractive, or even pointless' Viking's exercise of freedom of establishment. The CJEU held that:

> where industrial action infringes an employer's free movement rights under Article 49 (and also Article 56 TFEU), these Treaty provisions can have horizontal direct effect against the unions organizing the action. Unions may defend themselves against these claims by asserting a right to strike (which the Court recognized as a fundamental right within Community law) but only where they are acting proportionately in the exercise of that right.[238]

Recognising that EU law has a social as well as economic purpose and therefore the need to balance free trade principles against social policy objectives, it held that a public interest justification could succeed as long as it were proportionate. If, for example, it were shown that the jobs or working conditions of the workers at Viking were 'not jeopardized or under serious threat' by the reflagging, the public interest justification would however fail. The appropriateness and necessity of the collective action was to be decided by the national court.

Viking and Laval gave rise to intense judicial and political debate.[239] The use of Article 49 to remove the rights of workers has been condemned as a disturbing example of how legal persons (companies) can exploit EU freedoms to the detriment of workers.[240] For others, however, it is a welcome example of the EU responding to globalisation through removal of outdated territorial privileges so that the surplus of capital in western Europe can be harnessed with the surplus of labour in eastern Europe.[241] Inspired by *Viking* and *Laval*, British Airways subsequently attempted to use both Article 49 and 56 TFEU against a Spanish trade union that had called its members out on strike in order to protect their jobs.[242]

VIEWPOINT

Who do you agree with – Barnard or Engle? Should investors be free to move their businesses and capital, even if this is to the detriment of workers?

---

[238]A.C.L. Davies, 'One Step Forward, Two Steps Back? The *Viking* and *Laval* Cases in the ECJ', *ILJ* 37(2), 2008, p. 126
[239]Jonas Malmberg, 'The Impact Of The ECJ Judgments On Viking, Laval, Rüffert And Luxembourg On The Practice Of Collective Bargaining And The Effectiveness Of Social Action', Report Commissioned By European Parliament Directorate General For Internal Policies – Policy Department A: Economic And Scientific Policy – Employment And Social Affairs I P/A/Empl/St/2009-11
[240]C. Barnard, 'Social Dumping or Dumping Socialism', *Cambridge Law Journal* 67, 2008, p. 262
[241]E. Engle, 'A Viking We Will Go! Neo-Corporatism and Social Europe', *German Law Journal* 11(6), 2010, p. 633
[242]*British Airways & Anor v Sindicato Espanol de Pilotas de Lineas Aereas* [2013] EWHC 1657 (Comm). The case was thrown out for lack of jurisdiction.

Finally, protection of the consumer interest and the prevention of fraud have resulted in a high level of regulation of services in the financial sector across the EU. A key case concerned a prohibition of cold calling. In *Alpine Investments*[243] a Dutch law banned firms from calling individuals, without their prior consent, to offer financial services both within the Netherlands and to other member states from the Netherlands. Despite being a non-discriminatory rule, it constituted a restriction on the freedom to provide cross-border services – this situation had extra-territorial effects and so was not analogous with free movement of goods:

[36] Such a prohibition is not analogous to the legislation concerning selling arrangements held in *Keck* and *Mithouard* to fall outside the scope of Article 30 of the Treaty [34 TFEU].

[37] According to that judgment, the application to products from other Member States of national provisions restricting or prohibiting, within the Member State of importation, certain selling arrangements is not such as to hinder trade between Member States so long as, first, those provisions apply to all relevant traders operating within the national territory and, secondly, they affect in the same manner, in law and in fact, the marketing of domestic products and of those from other Member States. The reason is that the application of such provisions is not such as to prevent access by the latter to the market of the Member State of importation or to impede such access more than it impedes access by domestic products.

[38] A prohibition such as that at issue is imposed by the Member State in which the provider of services is established and affects not only offers made by him to addressees who are established in that State or move there in order to receive services but also offers made to potential recipients in another Member State. It therefore directly affects access to the market in services in the other Member States and is thus capable of hindering intra-Community trade in services.

However, the restriction was proportionate – it was legitimate, necessary and appropriate: maintenance of the good reputation of the financial sector was a legitimate interest which could justify the imposition of restrictions on the movement of financial services.

6. Presence of natural persons

i. Recognition of qualifications

A key obstacle to self-employed persons pursuing an economic activity in another member state has been recognition of qualifications. As in other areas, a law reserving provision of certain services to a member state's own nationals will breach Article 56 TFEU. It is forbidden to favour domestic providers of services, and discriminate against a provider on grounds of nationality (natural persons) or place of establishment (legal persons). National providers might be given preferential treatment through obligatory possession of a licence, qualification or permit.

---

[243]C-384/93 *Alpine Investments* [1995] ECR I-1141

A good example is provided in the series of cases concerning tourist guides. In France,[244] Italy,[245] Greece[246] and Spain[247] national rules made the provision of these services by guides from other member states conditional upon possession of an occupational qualification. These rules hampered the freedom to provide services of non-national tour guides and the freedom of choice of the tourist themselves.

In *Commission v France*, the need for a licence was seen as a restriction: it prevented tour companies using their own non-national staff to provide these services, as well as self-employed guides from offering their services to such companies. Furthermore, it restricted the choice of tourists themselves to use the services they desired.[248] Despite being designed to address a legitimate goal – the 'general interest in the proper appreciation of places and things of historical interest and the widest possible dissemination of knowledge of the artistic and cultural heritage of a country'[249] – the licensing rule went 'beyond what is necessary' to safeguard that objective by being protectionist and contrary to the interests of tourists:

> [19] . . . a licence requirement imposed by the Member State of destination has the effect of reducing the number of tourist guides qualified to accompany tourists in a closed group, which may lead a tour operator to have recourse instead to local guides employed or established in the Member State in which the service is to be performed. However, that consequence may have the drawback that tourists who are the recipients of the services in question do not have a guide who is familiar with their language, their interests and their specific expectations.

When dealing with the same question concerning tourist guides in Italy, the Court highlighted conditions similar to those laid out in *Commission v Germany:*[250] home state control was to be the norm and any departure from this had to be objectively justified. An occupational qualification could in principle be compatible with Article 56 only if three conditions were met: first that

> 'with regard to the activity in question there are overriding reasons relating to the public interest which justify restrictions on the freedom to provide services'; second that 'the public interest is not already protected by the rules of the State of establishment'; and third, that 'the same result cannot be obtained by less restrictive rules'.[251]

However, this was not the case: consumer protection and the conservation of the national artistic and historic heritage were acceptable interests to seek to protect but as in *Commission v France*, the requirement of a licence went beyond what was necessary to protect that interest. Thus as in that case, the measure was incompatible not because of the restriction per se, but because of their scale:

> [24] . . . in view of the scale of the restrictions it imposes, the legislation in issue is disproportionate in relation to the objective pursued, namely the conservation of the historical and artistic heritage of the Member State in which the tour is conducted and the protection of consumers.

The diploma demanded under Greek law for tourist guides suffered the same fate.

---

[244]C-154/89 *Commission v France* [1991] ECR I-659
[245]C-180/89 *Commission of the European Communities v Italian Republic.*
[246]C-198/89 *Commission v Greece* [1991] ECR I-727
[247]C-375/92 *Commission v Spain* [1994] ECR I-923
[248][13]
[249][17]
[250]C-205/84 *Commission v Germany* [1986] ECR 3755 [27]
[251][18]

ii. Membership of professional bodies

Non-recognition of qualifications can affect eligibility for membership of professional bodies, without which practice of a regulated may be impossible. Conditions of membership of professional bodies have been the focus of much litigation before, and even after the directive on the recognition of qualifications. National authorities have not been keen to fully accept education and professional certificates gained elsewhere, even if these are accepted by the educational authorities. This conundrum arose in *Thieffry*[252] in which the academic qualifications of a Belgian lawyer were accepted: his Diploma of Doctor of Laws from Belgium was recognised by a French university as equivalent to the French legal degree and he could therefore obtain a qualifying certificate to practice as an advocate after passing the relevant exam in accordance with French law. However, when he applied for admission to the Paris Bar, he was refused on the ground that he did not present a French legal degree: equivalence at the University did not guarantee equivalence at the Paris Bar. He was therefore not treated in the same way as a holder of the French qualification.

Likewise, in *Vlassopoulou*[253] a Greek lawyer who had gained a doctorate in law in Germany and practised as a lawyer in Germany was refused admission as a lawyer to the local and regional courts in Mannhem and Heidelberg because she did not have the statutory qualifications[254] necessary for admission to the profession of lawyer (Rechtsanwalt) – a German law degree, the First State Examination, a completed preparatory training period and the Second State Examination. The impact of this treatment on establishing a commercial presence is clear – persons would be discouraged from exercising their rights under Articles 49 and 56 TFEU. This concern was expressed in *Vlassopoulou*:

> [15] It must be stated in this regard that, even if applied without any discrimination on the basis of nationality, national requirements concerning qualifications may have the effect of hindering nationals of the other Member States in the exercise of their right of establishment guaranteed to them by Article 52 of the EEC Treaty [49 TFEU]. That could be the case if the national rules in question took no account of the knowledge and qualifications already acquired by the person concerned in another Member State.

Such deterrence would thwart the achievement of the internal market in services, consequently none of these national restrictions on access to the exercise of a profession were upheld. Home state rule applied. In *Thieffry* it was held that the restriction was particularly unjustified where it lead to refusal of admission to a profession of an individual whose diploma had in fact been recognised by the competent authority:

> [19] . . . of the country of establishment and who furthermore has fulfilled the specific conditions regarding professional training in force in that country, solely by reason of the fact that the person concerned does not possess the national diploma corresponding to the diploma which he holds and which has been recognized as an equivalent qualification.

---

[252]C-71/76 *Thieffry* v *Conseil de l'ordre des avocats de la Cour de Paris* [1977] ECR 765
[253]C-340/89 *Vlassopoulou* [1991] ECR I-2357
[254]Laid down by Paragraph 4 of the Bundesrechtsanwaltordnung [Federal regulation on the profession of Rechtsanwalt] (Bundesgesezblatt 1959 I, p. 565)

Refusal of recognition could not be justified by the contents of national legislation. In such circumstances recognition of a non-national qualification by the relevant competent national authority overrode national legislation – 'the act of demanding the national diploma prescribed by the legislation of the country of establishment constitutes . . . a restriction incompatible with the freedom of establishment guaranteed by Article 52 of the Treaty [49 TFEU]'.[255] This was expanded into a general principle in relation to qualifications and also refined in *Vlassopoulou* – a more balanced approach was adopted according to which member states could no longer dismiss overseas qualifications but were not obliged to automatically accept these:

> [16] . . . a Member State which receives a request to admit a person to a profession to which access, under national law, depends upon the possession of a diploma or a professional qualification must take into consideration the diplomas, certificates and other evidence of qualifications which the person concerned has acquired in order to exercise the same profession in another Member State by making a comparison between the specialized knowledge and abilities certified by those diplomas and the knowledge and qualifications required by the national rules.

The examination allows the member state to take into consideration objective differences, such as the scope of the profession and the national legal systems. If a comparative examination of diplomas indicate high similarity, the non-national diploma is to be recognised as fulfilling the requirements laid down by its national provisions; but if comparison demonstrates just a partial correspondence between the knowledge and qualifications certified by the foreign diploma and those required by the national provisions, the host member state is 'entitled to require the person concerned to show that he has acquired the knowledge and qualifications which are lacking'.[256] The onus then shifts to the individual to demonstrate to the national authorities that the qualification gap is not a knowledge gap: practical experience or a course of study can be used as evidence of this.

The same principle applies to training periods – national authorities must 'determine whether professional experience acquired in the Member State of origin or in the host Member State may be regarded as satisfying that requirement in full or in part'.[257] In *Colegio de Ingenieros de Caminos* the CJ developed the notion of 'partial access',[258] but while member states must under certain conditions accommodate a partial taking-up of the profession on request of the professional, they may still impose restrictions to protect consumers and recipients of services as long any such measures are both necessary and proportionate.

APPLYING THE LAW

Would a more proportionate response be for the Croatian authorities to examine the qualifications of non-national caterers? Would this address their objective?

---

[255]Thieffrey [27]
[256][19]
[257]*Vlassopoulou* [21]
[258]C-330/03 *Colegio de Ingenieros de Caminos, Canales y Puertos* [2006] ECR I-801

Subsequent to the directive on mutual recognition of qualifications, governments retain the strongest regulatory autonomy in relation to those educated beyond the EU and even here they must act fairly. In *Haim*,[259] an Italian national sought to set himself up as a dentist having gained a Diploma in Dentistry at the University of Istanbul in Turkey in 1946. The diploma had been recognised in Belgium, where he had practised for eight years. The German Association of Dental practitioners of Social Security Schemes (KVN) refused, however, to recognise his qualification thereby preventing him from providing services in Germany as a dental practitioner of a social security scheme. The KVN insisted that it would only do so after Mr Haim had completed a two-year preparatory training period. In the German rules transposing the directive, dental practitioners who had qualified in another EU member state after 1986 were exempt from the two-year training period.

The question arose whether this was contrary to Article 20 of Directive 78/686, which allows member states that required their own nationals to complete a training period to impose the same on non-nationals – but only for a period of six months and only until 1994. Mr Haim was refused in 1988, which meant he was within the timeframe but was the two-year training period compatible with the directive? Mr Haim lost most of his case – the fact that he had completed his training in a non-EU country was very relevant. Article 20 and the directive confers rights only on those holding qualifications gained *in* the member states.[260] Furthermore, as a non-EU qualification, the fact that Belgium had recognised his diploma did not oblige Germany to do the same[261] – there is no obligatory mutual recognition of recognition. However, the German authorities could not refuse his request without examining his work experience: as in *Vlassopoulou*, the fact that he had practised as an authorised person elsewhere in the EU protected him by creating a presumption of competency which the national authorities had to investigate.[262]

The cases above concern persons wishing to pursue an activity abroad that they have conducted at home. The CJ has introduced a presumption of competence – in the absence of harmonisation, member states have more flexibility but limited discretion. Limiting discretion is also important in relation to those taking up a new activity. However, what if a person is trying to evade national professional rules? For example, would it be contrary to refuse to recognise the diploma of a person wishing to pursue an occupation as an osteopath or estate agent? Could Article 49 TFEU be used to deflect criminal charges where an individual is seeking to take up new activities in a host member state? These questions arose in two cases from France and Spain. In both cases, there seemed to be a lingering suspicion of an attempt to evade national rules by gaining qualifications abroad.

In *Bouchoucha*,[263] a French national, gained a Diploma in Osteopathy in the UK (his diploma from another member state was enough to bring the situation under EU law). He returned to France and began to practise osteopathy, a profession restricted in France to those with medical qualifications. He was fined and ordered to pay damages to three civil parties. He argued that his conviction was contrary to Article 49. It was clear that his situation fell under Article 49: as a French national he could not be excluded from freedom of establishment rights at home in France due to non-recognition of his

[259]C-424/97 *Haim* [2000] ECR I-5123
[260]*Haim* [17]
[261]This was first stated in C-154/93 *Tawil-Albertini* [1994] ECR I-0000
[262]*Haim* [29]. See also C-238/98 *Hocsman* [2000] ECR I-6623 [23], and C-31/00 *Dreessen* [2002] ECR I-663
[263]C-61/89 *Criminal proceedings against Marc Gaston Bouchoucha* [1990] ECR I-3551

qualifications – as in *Knoors*,[264] Bouchoucha was ' . . . in a situation which may be regarded as equivalent to that of any other person enjoying the rights and liberties guaranteed by the Treaty'. However, as the French authorities pointed out, his diploma came from the European School of Osteopathy which did not enjoy any mutual recognition within the EU and therefore was not regarded as a professional qualification under EU law. The Court emphasised that as in *Knoors*:

[14] . . . it is not possible to disregard the legitimate interest which a Member State may have in preventing certain of its nationals, by means of facilities created under the Treaty, from attempting to evade the application of their national legislation as regards vocational training (paragraph 25).

[15] That is true in particular where the fact that a national of a Member State has obtained in another Member State a diploma whose scope and value are not recognized by any Community provision might place his Member State of origin under an obligation to allow him to exercise the activities covered by that diploma within its territory even though access to those activities is restricted there to the holders of a higher qualification which enjoys mutual recognition at Community level and there is nothing to indicate that the restriction is arbitrary.

Article 49 did not, therefore, preclude a member state from restricting a medical activity to those with medical qualifications.[265]

A similar question arose in *Borrell and others*.[266] Borell had been subject to criminal proceeding because he had set up as an estate agent in Spain without the correct qualification. After setting out the tests and conditions developed through the case law, the judgment concluded that subject to conditions, the rules on freedom of establishment do not affect the member states' power to impose criminal penalties on non-nationals who may pursue regulated professions without the correct qualifications.[267] In other words, freedom of establishment cannot be relied upon where it is used to evade national regulations and rules.

7. Conclusion

Under EU law, a range of commercial activities can be conducted across national borders under the scope of Articles 49 and 56 TFEU. Article 56 applies where the person providing the service and the recipient are established in different member states;[268] where the services are provided without the provider nor the recipient moving from their different member states;[269] and where consumers themselves move to receive or benefit from services.[270] Services are treated differently under EU law, depending upon the sector and

---

[264] C-115/78 *Knoors v Staatssecretaris van Economische Zaken* [1979] ECR 399
[265] [16]
[266] C-104/91 *Aguirre Borrell and others* [1992] ECR I-3003
[267] [19]
[268] C-55/98 *Vestergaard* [1999] ECR I-7641 [19]
[269] C-384/93 *Alpine Investments* [1995] ECR I-1141 [21 and 22] and C-243/01 *Gambelli and Others* [2003] ECR I-13031 [53]
[270] *Luisi and Carbone, Cowan*

mode – this may be why they are described as chaotic. The approach seems most consistent in relation to commercial presence and presence of natural persons: the same general principles apply – the CJ will consider whether the rule addresses a public concern (such as consumer protection), the level of home state rule and finally, most importantly, proportionality.

Consumption abroad can be challenging, especially as seen in relation to social services such as healthcare. The CJ has recognised the need to manage the public finances of national healthcare services, but has not excluded them from the reach of the freedom of patients to receive these services. Restrictions such as the need to gain prior authorisation have been accepted as compatible with Article 56 TFEU as long as they are clear, objective, non-discriminatory and open to judicial challenge. Differentiations have been made between hospital and non-hospital care, scheduled and emergency/unscheduled treatment.

Cross-border supply is the most challenging mode, especially in relation to distributor services such as online gambling. The legal response to online gambling inevitably lags behind actual developments – online technology is developing faster than the law, providing diverse remote distribution channels that seek to keep these activities beyond the reach of both national and EU law. The CJ response is designed to find a balance which acknowledges national difficulties and respects national social values. A margin of appreciation is allowed but as the 10-part test in *Stoss* demonstrates, the CJ is vigilant to identify disguised protectionism.

The cases considered demonstrate the complexity of regulating services. A key question is the extent to which it is possible to create an internal market in services and protect consumer welfare in the EU. Governments struggle to protect consumers from 'rogue' service providers and other types of fraudsters – removal of national regulation by the CJ can leave consumers vulnerable. An answer would be the creation of harmonised EU rules but progress on standardisation of services has been slow. The Commission proposal for revision of the European standardisation system may improve this.[271]

One of the biggest problems remains the recognition of qualifications. Consider it was in 1986 that Mr Heylens, a qualified professional Belgian football trainer, was prosecuted by a French football trainers' trade union because he was performing this role in France without the French qualification;[272] in 2013, an experienced British ski instructor providing tuition in France was arrested and charged because he lacked the qualification required by the French authorities.[273] That after 30 years such cases still arise indicates that national authorities still seek to protect national workers. It is worth noting that a 2011 report identified around 4,700 regulated professions covering about 800 categories in the then EU-27.[274] These and other cases on freedom of establishment illustrate that despite the General Programme[275] instituted in 1962 and the subsequent directives, these freedoms remain complex and can be difficult to exercise, especially the freedom to transfer the seat of undertakings.

---

[271]Presented 1 June 2011
[272]C-222/86 *Heylens* [1987] ECR 4097
[273]http://news.sky.com/story/1073885/british-ski-coach-arrested-at-french-resort; 'French ski rules are protectionist', *Evening Standard*, 5 April 2013, http://www.bnegroup.org/media/bne-directors-letter-in-the-london-evening-standard/
[274]COM(2011) 367 final, p. 7
[275]General Programme on the abolition of restrictions on freedom of establishment, OJ English Special Edition, Second Series (IX), p. 7

Many issues arising from recognition of qualifications have been addressed via the Professional Qualifications Directive but progress is too slow given the pressing growth needs facing the EU. According to the Commission Green Paper, higher mobility is required to meet the challenges of the future:

Mobility of professionals is still low in the EU. The number of complaints, SOLVIT cases and questions raised with Your Europe Advice and analysis of these cases provide clear evidence of a need to modernise the rules. In addition, intra-EU trade in services (including professional services) represents only about 25 per cent of overall trade within the EU. This share is far too low when considered against the background of the overall importance of the services sector to the EU economy (70 per cent of GDP). More can be achieved. Increased mobility would also respond to the challenge of filling high-skill jobs, as the active population declines. According to the projections of the European Centre for the Development of Vocational Training (Cedefop), 16 million more people will be needed to fill high-skill jobs by 2020, which under current trends will lead to severe shortages of qualified professionals . . . A projected shortage of one million health professionals is of particular concern . . . [276]

One proposal to address this particular issue is the voluntary 'European Professional Card'.[277]

Complex barriers can arise at any stage in the provision or enjoyment of a service, from 'establishment in a new member state, use of inputs necessary for the provision of the service, promotion, distribution and selling of services, to the after-sales phase'.[278] Restrictions include conditions of membership of professional bodies, authorisation rules and procedures[279] or residence or establishment requirements. Many barriers identified by the Commission 2002 still exist and the Services Directive is unlikely to be able to tackle them in its current form, although its 'Points of Single Contact' will help remove general lack of knowledge surrounding enjoyment of this freedom.[280] There is a limit to what can be achieved via litigation, especially if national judges reject the presentation of 'Euro-points'.[281]

---

[276]COM(2011) 367 final, p. 1

[277]See also Commission Staff Working Document, 'Delivering the Single Market Act: State of Play', SWD(2012) 21 final, p. 2

[278]Report from the Commission to the Council and the European Parliament, 'The State of the Internal Market for Services', COM/2002/0441 final

[279]C-51/96 *Deliege* [2000] ECR I-2549 brought an authorisation rule to the attention of the CJ: the Belgian judo federation required all professional or semi-professional athletes or persons aspiring to take part in a professional or semi-professional activity to have been authorised or selected by their federation in order to be able to participate in a high-level international sports competition. Such a rule would be incompatible with Article 56 TFEU if it were not inherently necessary for the purpose of organising competitive sport.

[280]The Services Directive obliges every member state to have a 'Point of Single Contact' (PSC), an e-government portal for entrepreneurs in the service sector. See http://ec.europa.eu/internal_market/eu-go/

[281]*Eventech* v *Parking Adjudicator* [2012] EWHC 1903 (Admin) [55]

Further reading

On the harmonisation of services in the EU:

Ulla Neergaard, Ruth Nielsen and Lynn Roseberry (eds), *The Services Directive: Consequences for the Welfare State and the European Social Model*, DJOF, 2008

On free movement of services in general:

Mads Adenas and Wulf Hennig Roth, *Services and Free Movement in EU Law*, Oxford University Press, 2013

Frank S. Benyon, (ed) *Services and the Citizen*, Hart Publishing, 2013

Vassilis Hatzopoulos, *Regulating Services in the EU*, Oxford University Press, 2012

Kerry A. Chase, 'Moving Hollywood Abroad: Divided Labor Markets and the New Politics of Trade in Services', *International Organisation* 62, Fall 2008, pp. 653–687

Alexander Lehmann, Natalia T. Tamirisa and Jaroslaw Wieczorek, 'International Trade in Services: Implications for the IMF', IMF Policy Discussion Paper PDP/03/6, 2003

On free movement of services and fundamental rights:

Jonas Malmberg, 'The Impact of the ECJ Judgments on Viking, Laval, Rüffert and Luxembourg on the Practice of Collective Bargaining and the Effectiveness of Social Action', European Parliament, IP/A/EMPL/ST/2009-11, 2010, http://www.europarl.europa.eu/document/activities/cont/201107/20110718ATT24274/20110718ATT24274EN.pdf

Christian Joerges and Florian Rödl, 'Informal Politics, Formalised Law and the "Social Deficit" of European Integration: Reflections after the Judgments of the ECJ in *Viking* and *Laval*,' *European Law Journal*, 15(1), January 2009, pp. 1–19

On the regulation of online gambling:

Stefaan Van den Bogaert and Armin Cuyvers, 'Money for nothing: The case law of the EU Court of Justice on the regulation of gambling', *CMLR* 48, 2011, pp. 1175–1213

Julia Hörnle, 'Online gambling in the European Union: A tug of war without a winner?', *YEL* 30, 2011, 255–297

James Banks, Online Gambling and Crime: Causes, Controls and Controversies, *Ashgate*, 2014

14 Competition law

Setting the scene

In 2012 Lance Armstrong, a professional road racing cyclist internationally famous for his successful battle against cancer and winning the gruelling Tour de France seven times, was caught using performance enhancing drugs.[1] He was stripped of his seven victories as well as the bronze medal he won at the Sydney Olympic Games. Armstrong's doping activities only came to light when a fellow cyclist on the US Postal Service Team 'blew the whistle' by reporting Armstrong to the authorities.

---

[1]See http://abcnews.go.com/US/lance-armstrong-opens-living-lie-documentary/story?id=20174492. Armstrong is now the subject of a fraud lawsuit brought by the US Justice Department. Also http://sportslawbulletin.org/2013/09/19/lessons-from-lance-recovering-sponsorship-and-endorsement-monies/

1. Introduction

A whistle-blower is the term used to describe a person who reports unlawful activity within their organisation to the relevant authorities. Whistle-blowers are crucial in competition law – as in sport, anti-competitive practices tend to be conducted covertly. The role of the whistle-blower in EU competition law illustrates three basic aspects of this field of law. First, the commercial market activities that competition law seeks to regulate are hidden. Second, competition law is public interest law – it regulates a public trading space, the 'market', in the public interest. Third, competition law regulates the activities of economic actors or 'undertakings' in the market. These are mostly but not always private bodies.

The chief purpose in regulating covert commercial conduct is to ensure that economic activities remain competitive: that is informed by honest rivalry, management of risk and equal chance of success.[2] However, an additional objective is protection of the competitive process: sport shares this understanding of the fundamental tenets of competition. Every participant should have the same chance of success, free from manipulation, protection or advantage. Perversion of the competitive process can arise in sport from use of performance enhancement drugs and in commercial trading practices from price fixing cartels,[3] exclusive agreements[4] or capacity hoarding.[5]

Competition law is not a new area of activity for the Union – it was listed in the Treaty of Rome as an area of Community competence: under Article 3 TEC, the activities of the EEC included not only the '*elimination*' of customs duties but also the '*adoption*' of common policies including a common agricultural policy (CAP), common transport policy and common competition policy. As in other areas, a common competition policy was deemed necessary to facilitate trade integration and create a stable environment for trade, investment and consumption.[6] In *Continental Can* it described Article 3(1)(g) as a requirement 'so essential that without it numerous provisions of the Treaty would be pointless'.[7] In *Crehan*[8] it reiterated that:

[20] . . . according to Article 3(g) of the EC Treaty (now, after amendment, Article 3(1) (g) EC), Article 85 of the Treaty [101 TFEU] constitutes a fundamental provision which is essential for the accomplishment of the tasks entrusted to the Community and, in particular, for the functioning of the internal market.[9]

It has been used by the Court to 'support an expansive reading of the competition rules as fundamental provisions essential for the accomplishment of the Treaty objectives'.[10]

---

[2] In C-519/04 *Meca Medina* it was argued that anti-doping rules were an unlawful restriction of competition [42].

[3] C-204–5, 211, 213, 217, 219/00 *Aalborg Portland AS and others v Commission* [2004] ECR I-123

[4] T-83/91 *Tetra Pak v Commission* [1994] ECR II-755; C-344/98 *Masterfoods and HB* [2000] ECR I-11369

[5] Energy giant E-ON avoided fines after agreeing to restructure its business to prevent its domination of gas transportation infrastructure. See http://europa.eu/rapid/press-release_MEMO-09-567_en.htm. The Commitments are binding and laid out in a decision – see Commission Decision in Case COMP/39.315, OJ C352/10 2010.

[6] See S. Weatherill, 'Why Harmonise', in T. Tridimas and P. Nebbia (eds) *European Union Law for the Twenty-First Century'*, Hart Publishing, 2004

[7] C-6/72 *Europemballage Corporation and Continental Can Company v Commission* [1973] ECR 215

[8] C-453/99 *Courage and Crehan* [2001] ECR I-6297

[9] See also judgment in C-126/97 *Eco Swiss* [1999] ECR I-3055 [36]

[10] Ben Van Rompuy (2011) '"Thanks Nicolas Sarkozy, but no thanks." CJEU rules on status of Protocol on Internal Market and Competition', *Eutopia Law*, 9 December 2011, http://eutopialaw.com/2011/12/09/thanks-nicolas-sarkozy-but-no-thanks-cjeu-rules-on-status-of-protocol-on-internal-market-and-competition/#more-822 09.12.11

Article 3(1)(g) has now been repealed and replaced by a Protocol[11] but as the CJ confirmed,[12] competition remains a central area of the activities of the EU. Continuing application of different rules in different member states hinders pursuit of trade integration – common rules are necessary to create stability for trade, investment and cross-border consumption. The CJ stressed in *FAPL* that divisions between member state markets prevent the creation of a single market.[13] In *Teliasonera*[14] the CJ also 'affirmed that the requirement of undistorted competition belongs to the fundamental principles of the economic constitutional law of the EU'.[15] The Commission was given full autonomy over this aspect of the EU 'economic constitution' and bears ultimate responsibility for enforcement of EU competition law.

Articles 101 to 108 TFEU regulate competition in the EU. Focus will fall on Chapter I of Title VII, which lays out the common rules on competition that apply to undertakings, as opposed to states.[16] These provisions are used to prevent commercial cheating and ensure that all traders have an equal chance to succeed in economic activities. The aim of EU competition law enforcement under Articles 101 and 102 is 'to ensure that companies compete on their merits rather than engaging in anticompetitive conduct'.[17] Articles 101 and 102 TFEU are directly effective and 'create rights for the individuals concerned which the national courts must safeguard'.[18]

The exploration below will be structured around four themes. First, the realm of competition law – competition law can only exist alongside the idea of the market and the concept of market structure. A lively and interesting debate rages between decision-makers in the Commission, the General Court and the Court of Justice on the role of the market structure in activation of competition law. The second theme is the target of competition law – which bodies fall within its scope? The CJ has taken a broad approach to the idea of the 'undertaking' and this has had specific consequences for public and not-for-profit bodies. The third theme explores the 'special responsibility' of certain undertakings and what this means in relation to abuse of dominance under Article 102 TFEU. Finally, the modernisation of the enforcement architecture will be examined, and in particular the implications of the growing support for private enforcement of EU competition law. The chapter begins, however, with a discussion of the Treaty provisions.

2. The Treaty provisions

For a practice to be unlawful under Articles 101 and 102 TFEU, it must have an 'impact' on cross-border trade. This impact can be direct, indirect, actual or potential: in *STM*, it was held that:

> . . . in order to determine whether an agreement which contains a clause 'granting an exclusive right of sale' comes within the field of application of Article [101 TFEU], it

---

[11]Protocol (No 27) on Internal Market and Competition: 'the internal market as set out in Article 3 of the Treaty on European Union includes a system ensuring that competition is not distorted.'
[12]C-496/09 *Commission v Italian Republic* [2011] ECR I-11483
[13]C-403/08 and 429/08 *Football Association Premier League Ltd & Ors v QC Leisure & Ors (C-403/08) Murphy v Media Protection Services Ltd (C-429/08)* [2011] ECR I-9083 [139]
[14]C-52/09 *TeliaSonera Sverige* [2011] ECR I-527
[15]Van Rompuy 2011
[16]These are dealt with under Section 2 of Chapter I in Title VII dealing with state aids (Articles 107–109). These provisions will not be examined.
[17]European Commission, DG Competition Management Plan 2010, 12 May 2010, p. 19
[18]C-127/73 *BRT and SABAM* [1974] ECR 51 [16] (BRT I) and C-282/95 P *Guérin Automobiles v Commission* [1997] ECR I-1503 [39]

is necessary to consider in particular whether it is capable of bringing about a partition-
ing of the market in certain products between Member States and thus rendering more
difficult the interpenetration of trade which the Treaty is intended to create.[19]

Both Articles are directly effective and create rights for individuals which national courts
must safeguard.[20]

The practices listed in Articles 101 and 102 TFEU are not exhaustive. Antitrust law
is a growing field – as the Competition Commission reaches into more sectors of the
economy, new vocabularies of anti-competitive practices emerge. It would be impossible to list in advance all of the tactics undertaken by firms to gain and secure a market
advantage. Some practices are sector specific: for example, 'capacity hoarding' appears
in energy cases such as that involving the Italian energy company, *ENI*,[21] and its subsidiaries in Austria and Germany.[22] In 2006, the Commission had conducted surprise
inspections at the premises of ENI, its subsidiaries and the companies controlled by
ENI active in the transmission of gas in and into Italy.[23] These gave rise to concerns
that the company was deliberately booking space in the gas transmission pipelines
which it would then not use ('capacity hoarding'). This, it was feared, excluded rival
providers ('network foreclosure') and harmed customers by artificially raising prices.[24]
On the basis of these concerns, the Commission decided to initiate antitrust proceedings
against ENI in 2007.

i.   Article 101 TFEU

Article 101 TFEU states:

---

*The following shall be prohibited as incompatible with the internal market: all
agreements between undertakings, decisions by associations of undertakings and
concerted practices which may affect trade between Member States and which
have as their object or effect the prevention, restriction or distortion of competition
within the internal market . . .*

This includes, but is not limited to, price fixing,[25] limitation of production, market-
sharing[26] and market-allocation[27] and unfair trading terms[28]. Each of these categories can
include myriad activities: price fixing covers linking prices of products; exchanging

---

[19]*C-56/65 Societe Technique Miniere v Machinenebau Ulm GmbH*
[20]*C-127/73 BRT and SABAM* [1974] ECR 51 [16] (BRT I) and *C-282/95 P Guérin Automobiles v Commission* [1997]
ECR I-1503 [39]
[21]*C-352/10 ENI*, Case COMP/B1/39315 – Final Decision
[22]*C-352/10*
[23]*C-352/10*
[24]http://ec.europa.eu/competition/elojade/isef/case_details.cfm?proc_code=1_39315
[25]See the 'Consumer detergents' settlement decisions at http://ec.europa.eu/competition/elojade/isef/case_details.
cfm?proc_code=1_39579; *C-48/69 ICI*
[26]*C-41/69 Chemiefarma*
[27]*C-56 and 58/64 Consten and Grundig; C-403/08 Football Association Premier League Ltd and Others v QC Leisure
and Others FAPL* and *C-429/08 Karen Murphy v Media Protection Services Ltd*
[28]*C-27–76 United Brands, C-95/04 P British Airways*

sensitive price information coordinating prices; or subsidising retailers' expenses. These are all seen as restrictive anti-competitive practices.

This area of EU law is distinct from those spheres regulated under Articles 34–36 TFEU– as the CJ explained in *van de Haar*:

> Article 85 [101 TFEU] of the Treaty belongs to the rules on competition which are addressed to undertakings and associations of undertakings and which are intended to maintain effective competition in the common market . . . that provision only comes into consideration with regard to agreements, decisions or practices restricting competition which appreciably affect intra-Community trade. Article 30 [34 TFEU], on the other hand, belongs to the rules which seek to ensure the free movement of goods and, to that end, to eliminate measures taken by member states which might in any way impede such free movement.[29]

It was also stressed in *van Eycke* that Article 101 TFEU is concerned with the conduct of undertakings and not legislation or regulations adopted by member states.[30] Although EU competition law also governs a public space – the market – it differs from Article 34 TFEU in three specific ways:

1 Article 101 TFEU only affects for-profit economic activities;
2 it has a *de minimis* rule and only applies where the impact is 'appreciable'[31] and 'perceptibly' restricts competition within the common market;[32] and
3 infringements give rise to fines that can cost a firm millions of pounds.

Prevention, restriction or distortions can be 'vertical' (between firms active at different phases of market activity, e.g. manufacture and retail) or 'horizontal' (between competitors undertaking the same economic activity, e.g. mobile phone salespersons). The case of *Consten and Grundig*[33] is an example of a vertical restrictive practice. In this case an exclusive trading agreement was concluded by non-competing undertakings: Grundig, a manufacturer of electronic goods endowed Consten, a retailer in France, with exclusive trading rights of Grundig goods in France. Details of this exclusive vertical agreement only came to light when Consten sought to sue another retailer in France for selling Grundig products. The exclusive agreement was held to be anti-competitive.

Horizontal restrictions arise when rival firms in the same sector cooperate in a way which transforms their competitive relationship into one of cooperation: in *T-Mobile*,[34] for example, sales representatives from various mobile companies in the Netherlands including Vodafone, Orange, O2 and T-Mobile, were found to have colluded by discussing sensitive company information relating to remuneration of sales personnel. Although

---

[29]C-177 and 78/82 *van de Haar and Kaveka de Meern BV* [1984] ECR 1797
[30]C-267/86 *Van Eycke v ASPA* [1988] ECR 4769 [16]
[31]C-5/69 *Völk v Vervaecke* [1969] ECR 295 [7]; C-7/95 P *John Deere v Commission* [1998] ECR I-3111 [77]; Joined cases C-215/96 and C-216/96 *Bagnasco and Others* [1999] ECR I-135 [34]; and C-238/05 *Asnef-Equifax and Administración del Estado* [2006] ECR I-11125 [50]. Consideration must be given to the situation that would prevail in the absence of the agreement.
[32]C-226/11 *Expedia Inc v Autorite de la concurrence and Others* [17]. See also C-70/93 *BMW v ALD* [1995] ECR I-3439 [18]; C-306/96 *Javico* [1998] ECR I-1983 [12]; and C-260/07 *Pedro IV Servicios* [2009] ECR I-2437 [68]
[33]C-56 and 58/64 *Consten and Grundig v Commission of the EEC* [1966] ECR 299
[34]C-8/08 *T-Mobile Netherlands and Others* [2009] ECR I-4529

the CJ accepted that the discussion did not relate to prices,[35] it nonetheless held that such exchange of information could undermine the autonomy of an undertaking.[36] Likewise in *ICI*[37] producers of the same chemical simultaneously raised their prices over a time period. No actual plan was found, but the price alterations seemed to go beyond coincidence. In both cases anti-competitive conduct was found.

Cases such as *T-Mobile,* and *ICI* demonstrate that a formal agreement is unnecessary to breach EU competition law, and a single meeting may suffice.[38] In *ChemieFarma*[39] nothing had been committed to paper: the collusion was based upon a 'gentleman's agreement'. Given these rulings, the Court has had to provide clarification on the meaning of an 'agreement', 'decision' and 'concerted practice'. This has been described in the past as any indication of a 'concurrence of wills'[40] or action demonstrating 'continuance in time'.[41] In *T-Mobile* the CJ clarified that these forms of cooperation exist on a continuum – they represent different levels of intensity of the same conduct – the substitution of competitive risks for practical cooperation:

[23] As a preliminary point, the definitions of 'agreement', 'decisions by associations of undertakings' and 'concerted practice' are intended, from a subjective point of view, to catch forms of collusion having the same nature which are distinguishable from each other only by their intensity and the forms in which they manifest themselves.[42]

[24] It follows, as the Advocate General stated in essence at point 38 of her Opinion, that the criteria laid down in the Court's case-law for the purpose of determining whether conduct has as its object or effect the prevention, restriction or distortion of competition are applicable irrespective of whether the case entails an agreement, a decision or a concerted practice.

[26] With regard to the definition of a concerted practice, the Court has held that such a practice is a form of coordination between undertakings by which, without it having been taken to the stage where an agreement properly so-called has been concluded, practical cooperation between them is knowingly substituted for the risks of competition.[43]

The same test therefore applies to each – the CJ avoided elaborate reasoning with this conflation. In addition, a single case may include all forms of conduct or just elements of each. The precise intensity may however become relevant when the fine is being set.

APPLYING THE LAW

Read C-8/08 *T-Mobile*: how did the parties substitute risk for cooperation?

---

[35][39]

[36]C-40–48, 50, 54–56, 111, 113–114/73 *Suiker Unie and others* v *Commission [1975] ECR 1663*

[37]C-48/69 *ICI* v *Commission* (Dyestuffs) [1972] ECR 619

[38]C-8/08 *T-Mobile* [60] '. . . a single meeting between competitors may constitute a sufficient basis on which to implement the anti-competitive object which the participating undertakings aim to achieve.'

[39]C-41/69 *Chemiefarma* v *Commission* [1970] ECR 661

[40]T-41/96 *Bayer* v *Commission* [2000] ECR II-3383

[41]Polypropelene Decision OJ L230/01

[42]See C-49/92 P *Commission* v *Anic Partecipazioni* [1999] ECR] I-4125 [131]

[43]See Joined cases 40/73 to 48/73, 50/73, 54/73 to 56/73, 111/73, 113/73 and 114/73 *Suiker Unie and Others* v *Commission* [1975] ECR 1663 [26], and Joined cases C-89/85, C-104/85, C-114/85, C-116/85, C-117/85 and C-125/85 to C-129/85 *Ahlström Osakeyhtiö and Others* v *Commission* [1993] ECR I-1307 [63]

Under Article 101 the undertaking does not have to be dominant – any agreement, decision or concerted practice must be shown to have the prevention, restriction or distortion of competition as either its 'object or effect'. The 'object' relates to the purpose of the agreement; the 'effect' to its consequence or impact. The CJ has clarified that these are not cumulative criteria and that they can be activated independently:

> [28] As regards the distinction to be drawn between concerted practices having an anti-competitive object and those with anti-competitive effects . . . an anti-competitive object and anti-competitive effects constitute not cumulative but alternative conditions in determining whether a practice falls within the prohibition in Article 81(1) EC [Article 101(1) TFEU].[44]

They are to be assessed separately as an anti-competitive object may be found in the absence of an anti-competitive effect, or vice versa – a cartel may not achieve its goals. In determining the anti-competitive nature of the object, consideration must be given to the substance of the agreement, its goals and the context in which it should operate:

> [135] . . . In order to assess whether the object of an agreement is anti-competitive, regard must be had *inter alia* to the content of its provisions, the objectives it seeks to attain and the economic and legal context of which it forms a part . . .[45]

Thus in *T-Mobile* it was held that '. . . an exchange of information between competitors is tainted with an anti-competitive object if the exchange is capable of removing uncertainties concerning the intended conduct of the participating undertakings'.[46] However such an examination is not always necessary – the CJ held in *Barry Brothers*[47] that some forms of agreement are per se anti-competitive, that is 'by their very nature . . . injurious to the proper functioning of normal competition' – in such circumstances the intention is irrelevant.

Where the anti-competitive object is established, there is no need to consider the actual effects.[48] This was the finding in *FAPL,* which concerned a contractual obligation to prevent cross-border satellite reception of live football matches. The FAPL organised its distribution of licences to show live Premier League football matches on a national and regional basis. In granting licences, the FAPL obliged licence holders to encrypt their broadcasts so that they could only be accessed by viewers in that member state or region. Although it sought to justify this practice before the CJ, it was unable to do so and its prohibition of parallel broadcasts was held to be anti-competitive by object:

> [140] . . . where a licence agreement is designed to prohibit or limit the cross-border provision of broadcasting services, it is deemed to have as its object the restriction of competition, unless other circumstances falling within its economic and legal context justify the finding that such an agreement is not liable to impair competition.

---

[44]C-8/08 *T-Mobile*
[45]C-403 and 429/08 *FAPL*
[46][43]
[47]C-209/07 *Beef Industry Development* and *Barry Brothers* [2008] ECR I-8637
[48]C-8/08 *T-Mobile* [29–30]

The effect, or impact, must be examined – the CJ has held that where evidence of an anti-competitive object is not forthcoming, examination is necessary to determine the consequence of the practice:

> [135] . . . it is only secondarily, when the analysis of the content of the agreement does not reveal a sufficient degree of impairment of competition, that the consequences of the agreement should be considered . . . and for it to be open to prohibition it is necessary to find that those factors are present which show that competition has in fact been prevented, restricted or distorted to an appreciable extent.[49]

Yet even where an anti-competitive effect is found, interference may be ameliorated if the firms can show that the agreement is necessary for the promotion of growth and innovation. Article 101(3) (discussed in 'Derogations' below) is the only method provided in the Treaty to avoid the grasp of Article 101(1). Neither of these applied in the *FAPL* case.

ANALYSING THE LAW

Why is the anti-competitive *object* as important as the anti-competitive *effect*?

---

ii. Article 102 TFEU

By contrast Article 102 TFEU focuses on abuse of a dominant position:

Any abuse by one or more undertakings of a dominant position within the internal market or in a substantial part of it shall be prohibited as incompatible with the internal market in so far as it may affect trade between Member States.

Abuse covers a broad range of actions: tying and bundling,[50] withholding essential information, offering payments and rebates or imposing exclusivity clauses on contractors. Incentives can also be found anti-competitive, as seen in a number of cases: British Airways were found to have breached Article 102 with their fidelity building scheme of incentives for travel agents.[51] Abuse appears in two broad forms: exploitative and exclusionary. The majority of cases fall into the latter category and include various forms of foreclosure of the market such as predatory pricing, refusal to supply and margin squeeze.

The Commission uses competition law to 'liberalise' important sectors of the economy. One area of focused activity has been the energy sector. Rising energy costs have led to the search for new ways to satisfy consumer demand and stabilise prices. An EU enquiry into this sector concluded that competition remained underdeveloped despite years of liberalisation. Markets remained highly concentrated with few actors, cross-border market integration was low, energy grids and transport pipes were closed to new entrants and investment was low. In addition to capacity hoarding, abuses include capacity degradation and withholding, strategic underinvestment, pre-emptive long-term booking and

---

[49]C-403 and 429/08 *FAPL*. See also T-328/03 O2 *Germany GmbH* v *Commission* [2006] ECR 2006 II-1231
[50]'T-83/91 *TetraPak*; T-167/08 *Microsoft* v *Commission* – see settlement decisions at http://ec.europa.eu/competition/elojade/isef/case_details.cfm?proc_code=1_37792'
[51]C-95/04 P *British Airways* v *Commission* [2007] ECR I-2331

abusive maintenance of pricing zones. For example, ENI, had booked capacity over a long period of time in excess of its actual needs.[52] Proceedings under Article 102 have also been opened in the *CEZ* case.[53]

Dominance is a key concept – a firm engaging in abusive behaviour will not attract Article 102 if it is not dominant. An undertaking must satisfy both of these elements – dominance and abuse – in order for its practices to be a breach. As stated in *Chemistree,*

> [22] It is not a breach of competition law for an undertaking that is not in a dominant position unilaterally to refuse to supply a customer, however long standing that customer may be.[54]

It might seem strange that dominance is at odds with EU competition law: surely the larger the firm, the more independent it can be? This is indeed logical but the danger exists that large firms can become tyrannical. It is this potential for economic tyranny that is the target of Article 102, which is why the provision focuses on the *abuse* of dominance not dominance per se. As the CJ stated in *United Brands:*[55]

> [65] . . . the dominant position referred to in this Article relates to a position of economic strength enjoyed by an undertaking which enables it to prevent effective competition being maintained on the relevant market by giving it the power to behave to an appreciable extent independently of its competitors, customers and ultimately of its consumers.

In *Hoffman la Roche*[56] the CJ further explained that a dominant position does not preclude competition unless it 'enables the undertaking which profits by it, if not to determine, at least to have an appreciable influence on the conditions under which that competition will develop, and in any case to act largely in disregard of it'. Dominance becomes abusive when undertakings use their size to protect and strengthen their market position. Market pre-eminence should be based on merit because firms which secure a foothold by virtue of size alone are likely to squeeze out competition and be oblivious to

[52]For Commission energy decisions see Distrigaz, case COMP/37966 Distrigaz, 11 October 2007 at http://ec.europa. eu/competition/elojade/isef/case_details.cfm?proc_code=1_37966; E.ON, COMP/39.388 German Electricity Wholesale Market, COMP/30389 German Electricity Balancing market, 26 November 2008 at http://ec.europa.eu/competition/ elojade/isef/case_details.cfm?proc_code=1_39388; E.ON, COMP/39.317 – E.ON Gas, 4 May 2010 at: http://ec.europa. eu/competition/elojade/isef/case_details.cfm?proc_code=1_39317; GdF Suez, case COMP 39316 – Gaz de France, 3 December 2009 at http://ec.europa.eu/competition/elojade/isef/case_details.cfm?proc_code=1_39316; RWE, COMP/39.402 – RWE Gas Foreclosure, 18 March 2009 at: http://ec.europa.eu/competition/elojade/isef/case_details. cfm?proc_code=1_39402; EDF, Case COMP/39.386 – Long-term contracts France, 17 March 2010 at http://ec.europa. eu/competition/elojade/isef/case_details.cfm?proc_code=1_39386; ENI, Case COMP/39.315 – ENI, 29 September 2010 at http://ec.europa.eu/competition/elojade/isef/case_details.cfm?proc_code=1_39315; and Svenska kraftnät, Case COMP/39351 – Swedish Interconnectors, 14 April 2010 at http://ec.europa.eu/competition/elojade/isef/case_ details.cfm?proc_code=1_39351. A recent decision with fine see GdF/E.ON (Megal pipeline), Case COMP//39.401 – E.ON/GDF, decision on 16 October 2009 at http://ec.europa.eu/competition/elojade/isef/case_details.cfm?proc_ code=1_39401. A decision based on Article 106 TFEU is the Greek Lignite, Case COMP/38700 – Greek Lignite and electricity markets, decisions on 5 March 2008 and 4 August 2009 at http://ec.europa.eu/competition/elojade/isef/ case_details.cfm?proc_code=1_38700.
[53]CEZ, Case COMP/39727 – CEZ and others, opening of proceedings on 15 July 2011 at http://ec.europa.eu/ competition/elojade/isef/case_details.cfm?proc_code=1_39727
[54]*Chemistree Homecare Limited* v *Abbvie Ltd* [2013] EWHC 264 (Ch); *Chemistree Homecare Ltd* v *Abbvie Ltd* [2013] EWCA Civ 1338
[55]C-27/76 *United Brands* v *Commission* [1976]ECR 425
[56]C-85/76 *United Brands* v *Commission* [1976] ECR 425

consumer preferences. The two key elements of dominance therefore incorporate structural and efficiency concerns: the ability to prevent rivalry and risk in the market, and the ability to undermine consumer welfare.

The legal test for dominance was set out in *United Brands* (UBC). United Brands imported fruits from South America to Europe. It used its own ships to transport bananas to ports in Germany (Bremerhaven) and the Netherlands (Rotterdam). From here the products were distributed to different markets in the EU. Although the transport and unloading costs were the same, the retail price of the bananas differed in each member state where they were sold. United Brands argued that the price was market specific. The Commission was unconvinced by this justification and decided that United Brands had breached Article 102. In order to make this finding, the Commission decided that UBC held a 'dominant market position'.

In assessing dominance, the Commission has tried to clarify its test for determining the relevant market.[57] Key aspects in relation to the product market include:

- evidence of substitution in recent past;
- statistical and economic tests on prices;
- view of customers and competitors;
- consumer preferences as per market studies and surveys;
- barriers and costs associated with switching demand to potential substitutes; and
- different categories of consumer and price discrimination.

Similar questions arise in relation to the geographic market but additional considerations here include:

- the nature of demand for the product (based on language or culture?);
- views of customers and consumers;
- current geographic pattern of purchases;
- trade flows/shipment patterns; and
- barriers to switching.

The identification of the geographic market gives the Commission an idea of which other firms impose a competitive constraint on the undertaking under investigation.

ANALYSING THE LAW

Why is dominance a prerequisite for abuse?

---

iii. Derogations

There are no derogations from Articles 101 or 102 TFEU. The only way in which a practice may escape is by the application of Article 101(3). This provision is limited – it applies

---

[57]The 1997 Notice on the definition of relevant market for the purpose of EU competition law (OJ C372 1997) is a consolidation of case law that formalises the structure of defining the relevant market and identifies key issues, but it is non-binding.

only to restrictive agreements. According to Article 101(3), any agreement, decision or undertaking falling under Article 101(1) may be lawful if it:

(a) contributes to improving the production or distribution of goods or to promoting technical or economic progress, while (b) allowing consumers a fair share of the resulting benefit, and which does not:

(c) impose on the undertakings concerned restrictions which are not indispensable to the attainment of these objectives;

(d) afford such undertakings the possibility of eliminating competition in respect of a substantial part of the products in question.

These conditions are cumulative: in order for an agreement to qualify, all four strands of this provision must be satisfied. A market specific analysis is conducted to ensure that any claimed efficiency gains (in relation for example to cost or scope) are substantiated, that any restrictions are unavoidable and necessary to produce these efficiencies, that these efficiencies do benefit consumers and that in securing these efficiencies competition is not completely eliminated – the agreement must not be a) overly restrictive or b) cushion participants from all competition.

Cooperation agreements between competitors are strictly scrutinised. Firms should be in no doubt that they bear the burden to prove that their agreement fulfils these criteria:

[84] . . . it is settled case-law that, in relation to Article 81(3) [101(3) TFEU], it is for the undertakings concerned to present to the Commission the evidence establishing that the agreement fulfils the conditions imposed by that provision (C-56-8/64 *Consten and Grundig*) . . . a person who relies on that provision must demonstrate, by means of convincing arguments and evidence, that the conditions for obtaining an exemption are satisfied (C-42/84 *Remia* [45]) . . . when dealing with an application for annulment of such a decision, it [the GC] carries out a restricted review of its merits . . .[58]

Article 101(3) can therefore be used to defend restrictive practices which parties enter into voluntarily. It applies to those agreements between individual firms which may be anti-competitive in the short term but pro-competition in the long term. It can only apply to an agreement prohibited under Article 101(1) where the undertaking has met the four cumulative criteria in Article 101(3).[59] In *CECED*,[60] an individual exemption was granted to a manufacturers' association of washing machines that had signed an agreement to improve the energy efficiency of machines. This would have been anti-competitive under Article 101(1) but for the facts that it offered long-term benefits to consumers in the form of cheaper bills; the efficiencies used the least restrictive option possible and competition still existed because consumers could choose between models based upon price and design.

---

[58]C-501/06 P, C-513/06 P, C-515/06 P and C-519/06 P *GlaxoSmithKline Services and others v Commission and others* [2009] ECR I-9291
[59]C-68/12 *Protimonopolný úrad Slovenskej republiky v Slovenská sporiteľňa a.s*
[60]Commission decision 00/475 in case CECED, OJ L187/47 2000

Companies planning to enter into joint ventures can therefore benefit from Article 101(3) if they demonstrate objective advantages which outweigh any disadvantages. British Airways and Iberia were able to demonstrate this when they sought permission for a proposed cooperation in terms of pricing and scheduling. Although the Commission raised concerns about the impact on consumer choice (price increases could arise where the two airlines dominated routes, such as from London to Barcelona, Madrid and Seville), such disadvantages were outweighed by the potential benefits to travel beyond the EU, for example wider choice of routes to the Middle East and Latin America. However, in order to obtain clearance, both companies had to agree to give up some slots to and from Spain to other airlines. In 2010 this venture was extended to include American Airlines: as members of the One World Alliance these three airlines can now cooperate on management of flight schedules, capacity and pricing, and share revenues on their routes between North America and Europe. In order to allay Commission concerns of reduced competition on routes between London and the USA, the parties agreed to make available to competitors a total of 49 slots per week for transatlantic flights at either London-Gatwick or London-Heathrow. Consumers will also potentially gain more choice as competing airlines will be allowed to offer their passengers flight packages which include those of the One World Alliance members.[61] By contrast, the Commission blocked the proposed merger between Irish airlines Ryanair and Aer Lingus – it considered that these would be detrimental to the consumer in a way that could not be ameliorated by any concessions: prices were likely to increase and choice decrease.

Block exemptions are also possible. Creation of such measures reduce the burden on the Commission – where a block exemption exists there is no need to notify the Commission. The original system of block exemptions worked on a very simplistic basis: two lists were created – those on the 'white list' were acceptable and could be inserted into agreements; the 'black list' contained clauses which if used would lead to refusal of exemption. The simplicity was found to be flawed. Thus in 1999, the Commission unveiled a new approach. The new system retains flexibility yet offers greater specificity. Detailed conditions now have to be met for the exemption. For example under Regulation No. 330/2010 on Vertical Agreements, a presumption of compatibility is possible where the agreement satisfies the terms laid out in Article 101(3), involves retailers with less than 50 million euros annual turnover and less than 30 per cent market share, and does not include use of any hardcore restrictions such as price fixing or market allocation. It is hoped that this approach will be easier for businesses to use.

The examples above cover cases where restrictions are entered into voluntarily. However, this is not a factor in the Court's decision-making. Any agreement deemed anti-competitive is automatically void[62] unless Article 101(1) is deemed to be inapplicable because Article 101(3) applies. The Commission has produced guidelines wherein it outlines that economic efficiencies are the priority for these exemptions.[63] There is no equivalent provision under Article 102 – separate guidelines indicate when it will consider efficiencies produced by abuses of dominance.[64]

---

[61]John Kallaugher and Andreas Weitbrecht, 'Developments under articles 101 and 102 TFEU in 2010', *ECLR* 32(7), 2011, p. 335
[62]Article 101(2)
[63]Guidelines on the application of Article 81(3) of the Treaty, OJ C-101/97 2004
[64]Communication from the Commission, 'Guidance on Enforcement Priorities in Application of Article 82', COM(2009)/C-45/02

One question that has been raised is whether the focus on economic goals, in particular consumer welfare, is too narrow – should Article 101(3) also apply to agreements focused on non-economic benefits, such as environmental protection? Kingston argues that it is 'fundamentally wrong to regard EU competition law as a "special" area of EU law insulated from environmental considerations'. She suggests that consumer welfare is a short-sighted goal for Article 101(3) and presents three arguments of principle – legal systematic, governance and economic – to support her view that environmental benefits should be taken into account. For example, from a legal systematic view she argues that:

. . . the Treaty competition rules should, where possible, be interpreted consistently with the Treaty internal market (free movement) rules. As environmental protection is a valid justification for proportionate Member State measures otherwise restrictive of free movement of goods, this implies that it should, in principle, be possible to justify otherwise anti-competitive restrictions on similar grounds.[65]

VIEWPOINT

Read the Article by Suzanne Kingston – should a state monopoly on recycling be exempt from Article 101(1) under Article 101(3)?

---

3. The realm of EU competition law

The idea of economic competition is related to the notion of a 'market'. A 'market' is a forum for exchange – of products, of goods, of services. The market is not a nebulous concept in competition law – as will be seen below it performs a key role and is therefore carefully defined. The market space has a structure which can be more or less protective of competition. A fundamental debate in competition law is whether it should be activated by measures that harm the process or those that undermine the structure? Another way of framing this question is to ask whether the impact of practices should be the target of regulation or whether their existence per se should be enough.

i.   The market as a trading space

As demonstrated by Second Life, e-Bay and Amazon, markets are now also virtual and electronic. A market can be defined by specific products, but also by geography (the territory over which goods are made available) and time (the season(s) in which goods are made available). There is no set product or geographic market. Each must be defined in relation to the specifics of the case. Determination of the product market requires consideration of the 'particular features of the product in question'; the geographic market requires identification of 'a clearly defined geographic area in which it is marketed and

---

[65]Suzanne Kingston, 'Integrating Environmental Protection and EU Competition law', *ELJ* 16(6), November 2010, pp. 780–805, p. 791

where the conditions of competition are sufficiently homogeneous for the effect of the economic power of the undertaking concerned to be able to be evaluated'.[66]

In the Commission investigation into monopolistic advertising practices by Google, the relevant product market was defined as the 'search engine market': despite operating via the 'world-wide web' as search engines are organised by nation, the relevant geographic market was also defined on this basis:

[89] According to recent data, in the US, Google had a market share of 66.2%, Yahoo of 16.4%, and Bing of 11.8%. In the UK, just as in many other European countries, Google had a market share of 90.83%, Yahoo of 3.21, and Bing of 3.12% ... The basic conclusion is that a single firm (Google) is emerging to dominate the market at least in the US and in Europe.

In *British Airways,* the relevant product market was identified as 'air travel agency services':

[90] ... services which airlines purchase from travel agents for the purposes of marketing and distributing their airline tickets ... that practice by airlines has the effect of creating a market for air travel agency services distinct from the air transport markets.

The geographic market was identified as 'the territory of the United Kingdom, given the national dimension of travel agents' business'.[67] The geographic market comes in many shapes and sizes: in *Hilti* v *Commission*[68] it covered the whole of the EU; in *Wood Pulp,*[69] the globe, in *Magill* v *Commission*[70] it was a single member state and in *Corsica Ferries*[71] it was a single port.

Market definition has a practical relevance – it is a core element of the Commission's evaluation on the assessment of dominance.[72] Market definition is a key but intermediate step which helps to structure the economic analysis of competing products[73] by determining the economic power of an entity. Determination of the market share plays a major role: 'market shares provide a useful first indication for the Commission of the market structure and of the relative importance of the various undertakings active on the market'.[74] Market shares will be interpreted in the context of the relevant 'market conditions': this includes consideration of constraints on expansion and entry to actual and potential competitors as well as constraints imposed by the buying power of the undertaking's customers, in particular their bargaining strength. The CJ has stressed that market share is not the only factor but is highly significant:

[133] ... as far as concerns in particular the concept of a dominant position ... although possession of large market shares is not necessarily and in every case the only factor

---

[66]*United Brands* [11]

[67][90]

[68]T-30/89 *Hilti v Commission* [1991] ECR II-1439

[69]Joined cases C-89/85, 104/85, 114/85, 116/85, 117/85, 125 to 129/85 *Ahlström Osakeyhtiö and others v Commission* [1988] ECR 5193

[70]C-241/91 P and C-242/91 P *RTE and ITP v Commission* (Magill) [1995] ECR I-743

[71]C-49/89 *Corsica Ferries France v Direction générale des douanes* [1989] ECR 4441

[72]Commission Notice on Market Definition OJ C372/5

[73]Jonathan Faull and Ali Nikpay, *Faull and Nikpay: The EC Law of Competition,* 2nd edn, Oxford University Press, 2007, para 1.184

[74]Commission Guidance, para 10

establishing the existence of a dominant position, it has however in this connection a considerable significance which must of necessity be taken into consideration in relation to his possible conduct on the market.[75]

The assessment of market power under Article 102 TFEU calls for careful analysis: the larger the market the harder it will be to demonstrate dominance. Definition of the market is therefore highly contested – firms often raise strong challenges to the Commission's assessment. The Commission must be able to defend its definition of the market within which the firm operates: failure to conduct a proper and objective evaluation can lead to the case being overruled by the CJ.

In *United Brands,* the Commission identified a narrow product market – it maintained that bananas form a product market distinct from other fresh fruits; UBC argued that bananas and other fresh fruits formed one integral market. When United Brands appealed the Commission decision before the CJ, the first question dealt with the market power of United Brands – could it undermine competition and ignore consumer preferences? Two indices were used to assess its share of market power – the 'product' market and the 'geographic' market.[76]

An important idea in determining the relevant product market is substitutability: how interchangeable are bananas with other fruits? If bananas are too expensive, do consumers eat strawberries or pineapple instead? This question investigates the impact of a 'Small, Substantial Non-transitory Increase in Price' (SSNIP) – to what extent do consumers have a choice when faced with price increases? The CJ considered that the banana has specific characteristics that distinguish it from other fruits: bananas are arguably a non-seasonal fruit, being readily available all year. Consumers are therefore unlikely to seek a substitute for it, as it is always obtainable in sufficient quantities. It therefore has limited competition from other fresh fruit. In addition it addresses specific consumer needs:

> [31] . . . the banana has certain characteristics, appearance, taste, softness, seedlessness, easy handling, a constant level of production which enable it to satisfy the constant needs of an important section of the population consisting of the very young, the old and the sick. . .

> [33] . . . the conditions of competition are extremely limited and that its price adapts without any serious difficulties to this situation where supplies of fruit are plentiful.

> [34] It follows from all these considerations that a very large number of consumers having a constant need for bananas are not noticeably or even appreciably enticed away from the consumption of this product by the arrival of other fresh fruit on the market and that even the personal peak periods only affect it for a limited period of time and to a very limited extent from the point of view of substitutability.

> [35] Consequently the banana market is a market which is sufficiently distinct from the other fresh fruit markets.

The Commission definition of the geographic market was accepted by the CJ as Germany, Denmark, Ireland and the Netherlands: this was the economic environment in which the

---

[75]C-85/76 *Hoffmann-La Roche* v *Commission* [1979] ECR 461 or *Michelin* v *Commission*
[76]Commission Notice 1997 on the definition of relevant market for the purpose of EU competition law

CJ set consideration of UBC's power to hinder effective competition.[77] The question was therefore whether UBC enjoyed a dominant position in the product market of bananas in this defined geographic market.

The final decision included consideration of several factors, including the specific company structure of UBC.[78] The CJ found that UBC was a company with a high level of vertical integration: it owned plantations and had significant leverage over others which gave it a virtually independent supply of bananas; it owned premises where packaging could be undertaken; it had its own means of transport in South America and across the Atlantic, shipping three consignments per week into Europe; and it had significant research and development technology at its disposal and enjoyed a strong brand name, Chiquita. Chiquita, according to the CJ, had attained a 'privileged position' as the premier brand name in the banana market with the result that any distributor had to offer it to the consumer[79] for whom bananas were synonymous with Chiquita (just as the brand name Hoover is synonymous with the vacuum cleaner).

Beyond this, UBC's share of the relevant market was 'always more than 40% and nearly 45%'.[80] Its dominance arose from an accumulation of advantages that it enjoyed.[81] The CJ found that:

> [121] UBCs economic strength has thus enabled it to adopt a flexible overall strategy directed against new competitors establishing themselves on the whole of the relevant market.

It abused that dominance in three ways: by imposing restrictive conditions (traders were unable to sell bananas while still green); by refusal to supply a firm in Denmark that also sold rival bananas; and by adopting an exploitative pricing policy.

Market share can be either absolute or relative: as seen in UBC, a market share of between 41 per cent and 45 per cent taken in conjunction with other attributes was seen to be dominant, yet in *British Airways* a market share of less than 40 per cent was held to contribute to dominance. British Airways (BA) maintained that it did not 'act with an appreciable degree of independence either in relation to its competitors'[82] but when looked at in relative terms, it was clear that its market share outstripped that of its nearest rivals: of all air tickets sold in 1998, BA accounted for 39.7 per cent; Virgin Airways just 5.5 per cent; with American Airlines even lower at 3.8 per cent. Quantas and KLM together accounted for only 3.3 per cent.[83]

Sometimes it is not possible to take a general approach to this assessment: in *Hoffman la Roche*[84] the Commission had to conduct a separate analysis for each group of vitamins sold by the company. This case concerned the use of 'fidelity rebates' to promote the sale

---

[77]*UBC* [36]
[78]*UBC* [66–67]
[79][93]
[80][108]
[81][129]
[82][176]
[83]T-219/99 *British Airways v Commission* [2003] ECR II-5917 [211]
[84]C-85/76

of vitamin tablets: the CJ found the constituent elements of dominance present in relation to the groups of vitamins A, B2, B6, C, E and H, but not in relation to Vitamin B3.[85] Hoffman la Roche was found to have abused its position of dominance by forcing around 30 retailers to buy all or most of their vitamins exclusively from Roche, or gave them an incentive to do so in the form of a discount. Purchasers were therefore 'tied' to obtaining all or most of their requirements from Roche. This was found to be an abuse:

> [89] . . . an undertaking which is in a dominant position on a market and ties purchsers – even if it does so at their request – by an obligation or promise on their part to obtain all or most of their requirements exclusively from the said undertaking abuses its dominant position within the meaning of Article 86 of the Treaty [102 TFEU], whether the obligation in question is stipulated without further qualification or whether it is undertaken in consideration of the grant of a rebate.

Recently, questions have been raised in relation to the market share as an indication of the market power of online entities – if 'competition is only a click away', how much market power does a search engine like Google really have? Patterson argues that for 'information intermediaries' like Google and Bing, the 'most commonly used measure of monopoly power, market share, is not a valid one'.[86] He argues that it is quality that determines search engine power – the key question is the extent to which it can survive despite providing poor quality information. Does Google remain the preferred search engine even when it doesn't answer our questions? Furthermore, what is the impact of e-commerce on the definition of the geographic market – for solely online undertakings, such as Amazon, e-Bay or an app maker, how is this to be defined?[87]

VIEWPOINT

Can pyjamas be substituted for a track suit? Are the two products interchangeable?

---

ii.   Market structure – maximalist and minimalist approaches

The market share is key to the application of EU competition law; market structure informs its activation. Competition law is concerned with the general trading environment as well as specific trading practices. The two are of course linked: commercial behaviour can change the structure of the market, for example where it prevents a rival firm from becoming established. A monopolistic market structure is arguably bad for the economy and society – it prevents innovation and job creation, causes supply shortages and pushes up prices. Beyond this, monopolies allow elites to transform economic dominance into social and political power. The same applies to monopsonies[88] (where buyers dominate) and oligopolies. In any of these market structures, exchange can be perverted

---

[85][68]

[86]Mark R. Patterson, 'Google and Search-Engine Market power', *Harvard Journal of Law and Technology*, Occasional Paper Series July 2013, p. 4

[87]I am grateful to Iris Dager for bringing this question to my attention.

[88]See T-319/99 *Fenin* v *Commission* [2003]ECR II-357; C-205/03 P *FENIN* v *Commission* [2006] ECR I-6295

because those wielding significant market power not only control availability of goods and thus consumer behaviour but also market entry and thus the existence of independent rivalry.

Competition law can also be used to maintain a market structure that is characterised by plurality, risk, rivalry and equality. It is used to prevent and repair imperfect market structures as well as protect and promote market equilibrium. Equilibrium exists where there is a plurality of traders offering the same product (heterogeneity), where prices are flexible and respond to consumer demand, where traders and entrepreneurs can enter and exit relationships of exchange easily and at low cost, and last but not least, where consumers are fully informed of the variety of prices for any product and can ascertain quality. As put by the OFT in the Roma Mobility Scooter Decision:

> Well-functioning markets depend both on competition working well and on consumers making good choices. Consumers drive competition where they are empowered to shop around through access to readily available and accurate information about the products they are seeking and the various offers available in the market. The provision of price and product information plays an important role in this respect.[89]

There are divergent approaches to the use of competition law to protect the market structure. According to DG Commission, competition per se is of no value – it is relevant only for its promotion of efficiency:

> Competition is not an end in itself. It is an indispensable element of a functioning Single Market guaranteeing a level playing field. It contributes to an efficient use of society's scarce resources, technological development and innovation, a better choice of products and services, lower prices, higher quality and greater productivity in the economy as a whole. Therefore, competition contributes to the wider objectives of boosting strong and sustainable growth, competitiveness, employment creation and tackling climate change. Competition policy therefore contributes directly to the Europe2020 strategy for smart, sustainable and inclusive growth. Historical evidence suggests that the causal link between effective competition and economic growth is particularly important in times of economic crisis.[90]

The first sentence in this mission statement – 'competition is not an end in itself' – contrasts with the approach to competition law taken by the CJ. For the CJ, competition law is not only about efficiency but about the economic environment per se:

> '. . . the Court has held that, like other competition rules laid down in the Treaty, Article 81 EC [101 TFEU] aims to protect not only the interests of competitors or of consumers, but also the structure of the market and, in so doing, competition as such.'[91]

---

[89]OFT decision on Roma-branded mobility scooters: prohibitions on online sales and online price advertising, CE/9578-12, 5 August 2013, para 1.12
[90]European Commission, Mission Statement – DG Competition Management Plan 2010, 12 May 2010
[91]C-501/06 GSK [63] (October 2009), repeated in C-68/12 *Protimonopolný úrad Slovenskej republiky v Slovenská sporiteľňa a.s,* where the CJ ruled that an agreement to exclude an unlawfully operating undertaking breached Article 101 TFEU.

For the Court and its Advocates General,[92] competition is to be valued in and of itself, and thus protected as an end in itself because where competition is compromised, disadvantages to consumers are also likely to arise:

> [86] Accordingly, Article 82 EC [102 TFEU] applies not only to conduct which can directly prejudice consumers, but also to conduct which can prejudice them indirectly in that it is detrimental to a state of effective competition for the purposes of Article 3(1)(g) EC.

Many competition law scholars and lawyers profoundly disagree with this attention to indirect harm to competitions. This broad approach is criticised as damaging to a clear and consistent EU competition law:

> The battle has been to restrict the use of competition law machinery to the task of tackling inefficiency. Modernisation seemed to accept this. Whilst the Court of First Instance took the Union within touching distance of an efficiency orientated competition law, the Court of Justice has put a single objective competition law beyond our grasp . . . whether a multi-goal Union competition law can ever be made to work in anything but an arbitrary manner remains to be seen.[93]

Thus a basic questions surrounding competition law arises from its application: when should law intervene and why – where there is direct or indirect, potential or actual harm to the consumer? Should there be any exceptions? How important are other public policy objectives? These fundamental questions go to the logic that informs the finding of a breach of EU competition law: should this be determined by the nature of the practice alone, the motivation of the parties, the consequences of their action on the market, or all three? In relation to the scope of EU competition law – is it strictly an area of commercial law or does it also perform a social function? In other words should it focus strictly on economic *efficiency* or does it also have a wider economic and social role to perform? These two broad questions are related: application of a competition law that is focused on efficiency alone will prioritise the actual impact of practices while a competition law encompassing broader aims will be triggered by any practice regardless of actual impact.

This debate is encapsulated in two main models of competition law: the minimalist **efficiency** model, represented above by the Commission and Odudu, has been developed by what is known as the 'Chicago school'. This approach, which gained traction during the 1960s, sees competition purely as a means to an end and legal intervention as necessary only where efficiency and consumer well-being is endangered or compromised. The structure of the market is of no inherent importance; what matters is the actual, direct outcomes for consumers. Intervention is strictly informed by economic analysis, and is minimal.

---

[92]See opinion of AG Kokott in *British Airways* [86]: 'As already mentioned, Article 82 EC [102 TFEU] is not designed only or primarily to protect the immediate interests of individual competitors or consumers, but to protect the structure of the market and thus competition as such (as an institution), which has already been weakened by the presence of the dominant undertaking on the market.'

[93]O. Odudu, 'The Last Vestiges of Overambitious EU Competition Law', *Cambridge Law Journal* 69(2), 2010, p. 248

The older maximalist **structural** model of competition law is favoured by the CJ. Promoted by the 'Harvard school', this approach is keenly sensitive to the structure of the market and is triggered predominantly by concerns to protect market plurality and thereby promote rivalry. Due to its concern with concentrations of power, it identifies a breach if a prohibited practice is discovered, regardless of the actual impact on efficiency and well-being. This has been described as per se *illegality* – decisions are based upon general assessments as opposed to specific economic analysis. The result is a broad approach to the protection of competition.

Neither model is perfect: the Chicago model perhaps underestimates harm, while the Harvard model overestimates it – the Harvard model is seen as overactive and the Chicago as underactive. Power is regarded differently: for the Chicago school power is seen as a spur to innovation ('Goliath spurs David to innovate') while for the Harvard school power is corrosive ('Goliath must be tamed so that David's ability to compete is protected').[94] It is ultimately not clear which model best protects the citizen, consumer and entrepreneur.

For this reason a third model has become popular which combines aspects of both approaches. Known simply as 'post-Chicago', this approach tries to avoid the extremes of its predecessors by taking both structure and efficiency into account. Structure is as important as economic analysis; while some practices are prohibited per se this is limited although state intervention is appropriate to promote rivalry. A finding of anti-competitive practices requires fact-based economic analysis.

The different impact of these models can be seen by considering the soap powder price fixing by Henkel, Unilever and Procter & Gamble: under Harvard this would always be per se anti-competitive; for Chicago it would be so if it undermined consumer welfare and efficiency; under post-Chicago it would depend upon the extent of its impact.

APPLYING THE LAW

Re-read *T-Mobile*: which approach was used here – maximalist or minimalist? Which of these approaches to competition law do you support and why?

A further question, less discussed than it perhaps should be by proponents of the Chicago School, is who exactly competition law seeks to protect: who is the 'consumer'? The 'consumer' is not defined anywhere in the Treaties: is this the everyday citizen or the large retailer/entrepreneur sourcing goods to sell? The question is relevant because the 'fragmented'[95] consumer in EU competition law may require different types of treatment to protect her interests in the market – the former will be interested in choice, quality and price whilst the latter is more concerned with market entry and exit.

---

[94]Alberto Pera, 'Changing views of competition, economic analysis and EC Anti-Trust law', *European Competition Journal* 4(1), June 2008, pp. 127–168, 142
[95]Marco Dani, 'Assembling the fractured European consumer', *European Law Review*, 36(3), 2011, pp. 362–338

4. Understanding the undertaking

The 'undertaking' is a key concept, referred to in both Articles 101 and 102. Yet it is not defined anywhere in the Treaty. As with other central concepts, the CJ created an EU definition. The CJ decided in an early case that a broad interpretation would be given to this term. In so doing it established a wide scope of application for EU competition law, bringing myriad types of activities regardless of their commercial or non-commercial nature under the scope of EU competition law – size, income and sector are all irrelevant – an undertaking can be a for-profit or not-for-profit, public sector or private sector. In *Hofner* the CJ was asked whether a state-run recruitment agency fell under Article 101 – it decided that it did:

> [21] It must be observed, in the context of competition law, first that the concept of an undertaking encompasses every entity engaged in an economic activity, regardless of the legal status of the entity and the way in which it is financed and, secondly, that employment procurement is an economic activity.[96]

The fact that employment procurement activities are entrusted to public agencies does not affect the economic nature of such activities. On the contrary, even an agency with a statutory mandate to provide services of general economic interest, remains subject to the competition rules '. . . unless and to the extent to which it is shown that their application is incompatible with the discharge of its duties'.[97]

i.   Commercial entities – parent companies and subsidiaries

The undertaking applies to single as well as group concerns. A parent company will be liable for the actions of its subsidiary if the entities form a single economic entity, even if the parent company did not sanction the actions of the subsidiary.[98] However, a small company that belongs to a larger parent company may avoid liability if it can demonstrate independent decision-making. In order to determine this, the CJ will investigate where decisions on market conduct are made and whether instructions are given to ascertain the nature of links between the entities and crucially, whether the 'parent' company exercise a 'decisive influence' over its subsidiary.[99] The CJ assumes a rebuttable presumption that a parent company exercises a decisive influence over the market conduct of a wholly owned subsidiary and that they therefore constitute a single undertaking within Article 101 TFEU:

> [38] . . . the concept of an undertaking includes an economic unit which may consist of more than one legal or natural person, such as a group of companies. Where, for example, a company does not decide independently on its own conduct on the market, but in all material respects carries out the instructions given to it by its parent company, having regard to the economic, organisational and legal links between them, the unlawful conduct of the subsidiary will be imputed to the parent company. In such a

---

[96]C-41/90 *Höfner and Elser v Macrotron* [1991] ECR I-1979
[97]*Höfner* [24]. See C-155/73 *Sacchi* [1974] ECR 409
[98]C-48–57/69 *ICI v Commission*
[99]C-73/95P *Viho Europe BV v Commission* [1996] ECR I-5457

situation, in the language of EU jurisprudence, the parent exercises a 'decisive influence' over its subsidiary. The subsidiary is not absolved from its own personal responsibility, but its parent company is liable because in that situation they form a single economic entity for the purposes of Article 101. In EU jurisprudence, the (rebuttable) presumption is that a parent company exercises a decisive influence over the market conduct of a wholly owned subsidiary and that they therefore constitute a single undertaking within Article 101.[100]

The actions of one undertaking will not always be attributed to the other in all circumstances: in *Siderurgica Aristrain Madrid SL*[101] the fact that the share capital of two commercial companies was held by the same entity did not establish the existence of a single economic unit under Article 101. There was no link to suggest that the actions of one company were attributable to the other. In *Emerson Electric,* the British Court of Appeal decided that the fact that a European parent company had been found guilty of infringing European competition law did not enable action to be brought against an English subsidiary that had not been an addressee to the Commission decision on infringement.[102]

This *Dassonville*–style all-encompassing approach also includes undertakings that operate in 'cyberspace' such as Google[103] and Facebook.[104] While perhaps necessary for consistency and coherency, the broad definition introduced a problem into Article 101 which remains to be clarified: would restrictive practices by undertakings designed to serve public interest goals be nullified as anti-competitive?

ii.   Public 'undertakings' and the scope of EU competition law

The situation of public sector bodies under EU competition law arose in the case of *Albany International BV,*[105] when a private company objected to the compulsory affiliation and payment into a state run pension scheme for textile workers, the Textile Industry Trade Fund. The pension fund enjoyed an exclusive right to manage the pension scheme for this sector – it was granted exclusive responsibility under public law so as to secure the social goal of pension coverage throughout the population. The Dutch norm was that every worker would receive a pension equal to 70 per cent of their final salary. This exclusive right was described as a monopoly. It could only be a restriction under Article 101 if the pension fund was found to be an undertaking.

The pension fund was clearly fulfilling a social function: it supplemented the statutory pension for textile workers on low wages.[106] However this did not place it per se beyond

---

[100]*KME Yorkshire Ltd v Toshiba Carriers* [2012] EWCA Civ 1190. See also C-97/08P *Akzo Nobel NV & Os v Commission* [2009] ECR I-8247, Advocate General Kokott [39–44], CJ [54–61 and 77]; T-25/06 *Alliance One International Inc v Commission* [2011] [80–85]; T-43/02 *Jungbunzlauer AG v Commission* [2006] ECR II-3435 [129]; C-286/98 P *Stora Kopparbergs Bergslags v Commission* [2008] ECR I-9925 [29]

[101]C-196/99 P *Siderurgica Aristrain Madrid SL v Commission* [2003] ECR I-11005 [99]: see also T-358/06 *Wegenbouwmaatschappij J Heijmans BV v Commission* 4 July 2008 (Second Chamber) [2008] ECR II-110 (Summ. pub.) [30]

[102]*Emerson Electric Co and others v Morgan Crucible Co plc and others* [2012] EWCA Civ 1559; [2012] WLR (D) 354

[103]COMP/C-3/39.740, COMP/C-3/39.775 and COMP/C-3/39.768. On virtual and physical markets see Alexei Alexandrov, George Deltas and Daniel F. Spulber, 'Antitrust And Competition In Two-Sided Markets', *Journal of Competition Law and Economics* 7(4), 2011

[104]Ioannis Lianos and Evgenia Motchenkova, 'Market Dominance and Quality of Search Results in the Search Engine Market', CLES Working Paper Series 2/2012

[105]C-67/96, *Albany International BV v Stichting Bedrijfspensioenfonds Textielindustrie,* ECR [1999] I-5751. See also C-219/97 *Drijvende Bokken* [1999] ECR I-6121

[106]C-67/96 *Albany* [105]

EU competition law: it was found to be an undertaking[107] in spite of its social policy objectives because it engaged in 'an economic activity in competition with insurance companies'.[108] The fact that it was non-profit making and organised to promote social solidarity were 'not sufficient to deprive the sectoral pension fund of its status as an undertaking within the meaning of the competition rules of the Treaty'.[109] However, given 1) the pursuit of a social objective, 2) the goal of solidarity and 3) limitations on investments made by the sectoral pension fund that made it less competitive than comparable services provided by other insurance companies, the CJ did recognise that these constraints might be enough to '. . . justify the exclusive right of such a body to manage a supplementary pension scheme'.[110]

Regulated professions can also be undertakings, as seen in *Wouters:*[111] in order to prevent conflicts of interest, Dutch law regulated the types of professional partnerships that members of the Bar could enter into. Wouters, a member of the Amsterdam Bar, was prohibited from entering into professional partnerships with a firm of tax consultants and accountants. He argued this breached Article 101 TFEU. As in *Albany,* the applicability of Article 101 was refuted by the Dutch authority – it pointed out that the Bar of the Netherlands is a body governed by public law, established by statute in order to guarantee, in the public interest, the independence and loyalty to the client of members of the Bar who provide legal assistance.[112]

The CJ disagreed – as set out in *Hofner,*[113] the legal status and financing of an entity does not preclude it from definition as an undertaking engaged in an economic activity.[114] Any activity consisting of offering goods and services on a given market is an economic activity[115] – this applied to members of the Bar:

> [48] Members of the Bar offer, for a fee, services in the form of legal assistance consisting in the drafting of opinions, contracts and other documents and representation of clients in legal proceedings. In addition, they bear the financial risks attaching to the performance of those activities since, if there should be an imbalance between expenditure and receipts, they must bear the deficit themselves.
>
> [49] That being so, registered members of the Bar in the Netherlands carry on an economic activity and are, therefore, undertakings for the purposes of Articles 85, 86 and 90 of the Treaty. The complexity and technical nature of the services they provide and the fact that the practice of their profession is regulated cannot alter that conclusion.[116]

It should be noted that this applied to members of the Bar not the Bar itself: the Bar did not normally conduct any economic activity so was not an undertaking per se.[117] Yet

---

[107][87]
[108][84]
[109][85]
[110][86]
[111]C-309/99 *J. C. J. Wouters and others* [2002] ECR I-1577
[112]*Wouters* [32]
[113]C-41/90 *Höfner and Elser* [1991] ECR I-1979 [21]
[114][46]. See also C-244/94 *Fédération française des sociétés d'assurances and Others* [1995] ECR I-4013 [14]; and C-55/96 *Job Centre* [1997] ECR I-7119, *Job Centre II* [21]
[115]C-118/85 *Commission v Italy* [1987] ECR 2599 [7]; C-35/96 *Commission v Italy* [1998] ECR I-3851, CNSD [36]
[116]See, with regard to medical practitioners, Joined cases C-180/98 to C-184/98 *Pavlov and Others* [2000] ECR I-6451 [77]
[117]C-180/98 to C-184/98 *Pavlov and others* [112–115]

when the Bar adopted the regulation prohibiting certain forms of economic activity by its members, it stepped into the realm of Article 101:

> [58] When it adopts a regulation such as the 1993 Regulation, a professional body such as the Bar of the Netherlands is neither fulfilling a social function based on the principle of solidarity, unlike certain social security bodies . . . nor exercising powers which are typically those of a public authority . . . It acts as the regulatory body of a profession, the practice of which constitutes an economic activity.

Its statutory role as protector of members' rights and interests or as the professional regulator did not change this finding.[118] The national legal framework within which the rules were created did not limit the scope of EU competition rules.[119] If this were so, it would perhaps be too easy to shield national law from EU law. Thus:

> [71] . . . a regulation concerning partnerships between members of the Bar and other members of liberal professions, such as the 1993 Regulation, adopted by a body such as the Bar of the Netherlands, must be regarded as a decision adopted by an association of undertakings within the meaning of Article 85(1) [101(1) TFEU] of the Treaty.

APPLYING THE LAW

What must be considered to determine whether a firm is an undertaking?

---

iii. Public 'undertakings' and the application of EU competition law

In *Wouters* and *Albany*, the bodies at issue were held to fall within Article 101 TFEU, yet the CJ then found that this Article did not apply. In *Wouters*, while the CJ acknowledged the potential benefits of a multi-disciplinary partnership between lawyers and accountants – such as provision of a wider range of services and economies of scale[120] – it also recognised the specific obligations of professional conduct upon lawyers that did not apply to other professions such as accountants. It therefore used the proportionality test to introduce a caveat to the application of Article 101(1):

> [97] . . . For the purposes of application of that provision to a particular case, account must first of all be taken of the overall context in which the decision of the association of undertakings was taken or produces its effects. More particularly, account must be taken of its objectives, which are here connected with the need to make rules relating to organisation, qualifications, professional ethics, supervision and liability, in order to ensure that the ultimate consumers of legal services and the sound administration of justice are provided with the necessary guarantees in relation to integrity and experience.[121] It has then to be considered whether the consequential effects restrictive of competition are inherent in the pursuit of those objectives.

---

[118]C-180/98 to C-184/98 *Pavlov and others* [59]; see C-1/12 *Ordem dos Técnicos Oficiais de Contas v Autoridade da Concorrência* (Mandatory Training Systems)
[119]C-180/98 to C-184/98 [66]. See also C-123/83 *BNIC v Clair* [1985] ECR 391 [17]
[120]C-180/98 to C-184/98 *Pavlov and others* [87–89]
[121]See C-3/95 *Reisebüro Broede* [1996] ECR I-6511 [38]

The CJ found the 1993 regulation reasonable and necessary to ensure the proper practice of the legal profession in the Netherlands. Although it restricted competition, the effects of the regulation did not 'go beyond what is necessary in order to ensure the proper practice of the legal profession'.[122] The Dutch regulation was a reasonable rule that was also proportionate. Public interest arguments presented by the Dutch authority were used to shield the Dutch rule from the impact of Article 101(1).

The same style of contextual reasoning was used in *Albany*. Having brought the pension fund within the scope of competition law, the CJ then shielded it from an adverse finding. It also brought another anti-competitive provision into play – Article 106(2) on services of a general economic interest (SGEIs). These are generally defined as economic services which operate in a market environment – it is a category that has grown and will continue to expand as the state divests itself of responsibility to provide public services such as care homes for the elderly or vulnerable, job centres, social housing, prisons, transport and pensions. If the textile pension fund fell into this Article, the restriction of competition could be justified 'as a measure necessary for the performance of a particular social task of general interest with which that fund has been charged'.[123]

In order to decide this, the consequences of the lack of exclusivity had to be considered: what would happen if the exclusive right of the fund to manage the supplementary pension scheme for all workers in a given sector were removed? The CJ opined that this would place older employees and those in vulnerable jobs at risk of losing their pensions because:

[108] . . . undertakings with young employees in good health engaged in non-dangerous activities would seek more advantageous insurance terms from private insurers. The progressive departure of 'good' risks would leave the sectoral pension fund with responsibility for an increasing share of 'bad' risks, thereby increasing the cost of pensions for workers, particularly those in small and medium-sized undertakings with older employees engaged in dangerous activities, to which the fund could no longer offer pensions at an acceptable cost.

This was deemed a likely scenario in this case: the supplementary pension scheme managed exclusively by the pension fund was clearly based on the principle of solidarity – contributions paid were low and did not reflect the risk arising from the obligation to accept all workers. This obligation gave the fund a number of novel traits: members did not have to undergo a prior medical examination; members continued to accrue pension rights despite exemption from payment of contributions if they were unable to work; the fund would discharge arrears of contributions due from an employer in the event of insolvency; and the level of pension payments was indexed in order to maintain their value.[124] These traits made the fund less competitive than comparable insurance companies[125] and justified the exclusive right it enjoyed to manage the supplementary pension scheme. The CJ held that the removal of this right 'might make it impossible for it to perform the tasks of general economic interest entrusted to it under economically

---

[122]C-180/98 to C-184/98 *Pavlov and others* [109]. See also C-250/92 *DLG* [1994] ECR I-5641 [35]
[123]C-180/98 to C-184/98 *Pavlov and others* [98]
[124][109]
[125][110]

acceptable conditions and threaten its financial equilibrium'[126] and concluded that Articles 102 and 106 TFEU (then Articles 86 and 90 EC) did not 'preclude the public authorities from conferring on a pension fund the exclusive right to manage a supplementary pension scheme in a given sector'.[127]

ANALYSING THE LAW

Under what circumstances does EU does competition law not apply to undertakings with social objectives?

The judicial reasoning in *Albany* refined the ideas underpinning the decision in *Poucet and Pistre*[128] where the CJ held that competition law would not apply where the activity was engaged in was for the pursuit of a social aim, applied the principle of solidarity and was non-profit making. These cases confirm the **functional** approach: it is the nature of the *activity* that determines whether the body is to be treated as an undertaking when it is held to be such. In these cases, because the activities in question formed part of a social security scheme founded on the principle of national solidarity, they were not economic activities and the bodies performing those activities were not to be treated as undertakings.[129] These decisions were in turn embedded by legislative action – the Council adopted Directive 98/49/EC of 29 June 1998 on safeguarding the supplementary pension rights of employed and self-employed persons moving within the Union.[130] This reasoning – recognition of anti-competitive practice as essential for successful redistribution of social risk – was repeated in the later case of *BUPA*[131] which adopted and refined the systematic criteria for determining a service of a general economic interest laid out in *Altmark*.[132]

The importance of a contextual and functional analysis in determining the application of EU competition law was emphasised in the case of *Meca Medina and Majcen*[133] where anti-doping rules were challenged as restrictive of competition:

[42] . . . the compatibility of rules with the Community rules on competition cannot be assessed in the abstract (see, to this effect, Case C-250/92 DLG [1994] ECR I-5641, paragraph 31) . . .

[43] As regards the overall context in which the rules at issue were adopted, the Commission could rightly take the view that the general objective of the rules was, as none of the parties disputes, to combat doping in order for competitive sport to be conducted fairly and that it included the need to safeguard equal chances for athletes, athletes' health, the integrity and objectivity of competitive sport and ethical values in sport.

---

[126][111]
[127][123]
[128]Joined cases C-159/91 and C-160/91 *Poucet and Pistre* [1993] ECR I-637. See also C-264/01 *AOK-Bundesverband and others* [2004] ECR I-2493 where the CJ decided that associations of sickness funds do not act as undertakings or associations of undertakings in the activity of providing statutory health insurance or in determining the maximum fixed amounts of reimbursement.
[129]*Poucet and Pistre* [18–20]
[130][106] (OJ L209/46 1998)
[131]T-289/03 *BUPA and others v Commission* [2008] ECR II-81
[132]C-280/00 *Altmark Trans and Regierungspräsidium Magdeburg* [2003] ECR I-7747 [88–93]
[133]C-519/04 *David Meca-Medina and Igor Majcen v Commission of the European Communities*. See also T-508/09 and C-269/12P *Cañas v Commission Cañas v Commission*.

[44] In addition, given that penalties are necessary to ensure enforcement of the doping ban, their effect on athletes' freedom of action must be considered to be, in principle, inherent itself in the anti-doping rules.

Thus, the CJ held that even if anti-doping rules can be regarded as a decision of an association of undertakings, they do not constitute a restriction of competition incompatible with Article 101 TFEU. Such limitation is inherent in the organisation and proper conduct of competitive sport, unavoidable for healthy rivalry between athletes. They were held justified by a legitimate objective.

iv. Activities of public undertakings under EU competition law

The CJ clarified the type of activities which would *not* be caught by the Treaty rules on competition: activities which by their nature, aim and regulation do not belong to the sphere of 'economic activity' – this has been held in relation to management of a public social security system,[134] air space control,[135] a database storage system run by a public authority,[136] and action to monitor marine pollution.[137] Activities which fulfil social or solidarity functions remain beyond the reach of Article 101 TFEU.

In January 2012, Hinchingbrooke became the first NHS hospital – delivering NHS services by NHS staff in buildings and assets owned by the NHS – to be fully managed by a private company.[138] It is questionable whether a case involving this for-profit hospital would qualify for the contextual approach laid out in W*outers* or have to satisfy the conditions laid out in Article 101(3) TFEU.[139] An answer to this question might be found in the case of *FENIN*,[140] where the CJ confirmed the refinement of its functional approach by distinguishing between the **purchase** and **use** of goods.

FENIN is an association of undertakings engaged in the sale of medical goods and equipment, particularly medical instruments, used in Spanish hospitals. The members of FENIN sell these goods to 26 bodies that manage the Spanish national health system, collectively known as the 'Sistema Nacional de Salud' (SNS). Sales of medical goods and equipment to SNS bodies represents over 80 per cent of income for the FENIN member undertakings – as the dominant buyer, the SNS enjoys a monopsony. The SNS was an unreliable customer and was consistently late with payment. Annoyed at this, FENIN complained to the Commission that the SNS was abusing a dominant position under Article 102 TFEU.

Applying *Poucet and Pistre,* the Commission dismissed the claim on two grounds: first, the 26 ministries and other organisations in question were not acting as undertakings when they participated in the management of the public health service; and second, that the 'demand' of the organisations could not be dissociated from the subsequent 'supply' which they provide.[141] FENIN challenged this finding: it argued that a different approach was required as the situation did not involve a social body dealing with its members (as

---

[134]C-159/91, C-160/91 *Poucet and Pistre* [1993] ECR I-637 [18 and 19]

[135]C-364/92 *Sat Fluggesellschaft* [1994] ECR I-43 [30]

[136]C-138/11 *Compass-Datenbank GmBH v Republik Oesterreich* [2012] WLR (D) 202

[137]C-343/95 *Diego Calì & Figli* [1997] ECR I-1547 [22 and 23]

[138]See http://www.hinchingbrooke.nhs.uk/

[139]See 'Is the NHS subject to EU competition law?' at http://eutopialaw.com/2013/07/19/is-the-nhs-subject-to-competition-law/

[140]T-319/99 *Federación Española de Empresas de Tecnología Sanitaria (FENIN)*; C-205/03 P *Federación Española de Empresas de Tecnología Sanitaria (FENIN)* v *Commission of the European Communities*

[141]FENIN

in *Albany*); the current question was whether social bodies act as undertakings when purchasing from third parties goods that they need in order to provide services to their members. The SNS was a purchaser and seller of goods: it acted as a middleman, buying from FENIN members and selling to medical organisations (its members).

In defence of its position, FENIN cited two AG opinions. In *Fédération française*[142] Advocate General Tesauro emphasised that the principle of solidarity was not always decisive. Meanwhile, in *Albany*, Advocate General Jacob stated that a non-profit-making character or the pursuit of non-economic objectives was in principle 'immaterial' to whether an entity is to be regarded as an undertaking.[143] The General Court was not persuaded by these arguments. It repeated the functional approach, namely that it is the activity of offering goods and services on a given market that is the characteristic feature of an economic activity[144] not purchasing per se: the use to which the purchased goods will be put must therefore be taken into account. An economic activity therefore has two elements – purchasing and use – which must both be examined: 'The nature of the purchasing activity must therefore be determined according to whether or not the subsequent use of the purchased goods amounts to an economic activity.'[145] Thus an organisation which purchases any amount of goods in order to use them in the context of a purely social activity does not act as an undertaking:

[37] Whilst an entity may wield very considerable economic power, even giving rise to a monopsony, it nevertheless remains the case that, if the activity for which that entity purchases goods is not an economic activity, it is not acting as an undertaking for the purposes of Community competition law and is therefore not subject to the prohibitions laid down in Articles 81(1) EC and 82 EC [Articles 101(1) TFEU and 102 TFEU].[146]

Furthermore it was clear that the principle of solidarity underpinned the SNS: its funds came from social security contributions and other State funding, and its services were provided free of charge to its members on the basis of universal cover. The GC therefore concluded that in managing the SNS, the 26 organisations did not act as undertakings when purchasing from the members of FENIN 'the medical goods and equipment which they require in order to provide free services to SNS members'.[147] Would this apply where an organisation only partially performs a social activity, as at Hinchingbrooke Hospital? In *Ferlini*,[148] AG Cosmas suggested that a public hospital acts as an undertaking where it provides care to patients who are not members of the social security scheme by which it is financed.

APPLYING THE LAW

Consider whether a) the Hinchingbrook, b) the Law Society and c) Universities act as undertakings.

---

[142]C-244/94 *Fédération française des sociétés d' assurance and Others* [1995] ECR I-4013, I-4015 [20]
[143]AG opinion *Albany* [312]
[144]C-35/96 *Commission v Italy* [1998] ECR I-3851 [36];
[145]*FENIN* [36]
[146]*FENIN*
[147]*FENIN* [40]
[148]AG opinion, C-411/98 *Ferlini* [2000] ECR I-8081, I-8184 [110–116]

FENIN appealed to the CJ, arguing that the GC definition of an economic activity was too narrow and would enable many bodies to escape the reach of EU competition law.[149] The two CJEU courts, however, were united:

> [25] . . . In accordance with the case-law of the Court of Justice, the Court of First Instance also stated, in paragraph 36 of the judgment under appeal, that it is the activity consisting in offering goods and services on a given market that is the characteristic feature of an economic activity . . .

> [26] The Court of First Instance rightly deduced, in paragraph 36 of the judgment under appeal, that there is no need to dissociate the activity of purchasing goods from the subsequent use to which they are put in order to determine the nature of that purchasing activity, and that the nature of the purchasing activity must be determined according to whether or not the subsequent use of the purchased goods amounts to an economic activity.

FENIN's plea was dismissed as partly inadmissible and partly unfounded.

To summarise, the idea of an undertaking in EU competition law is broad: as noted by Chalmers, inventors, opera singers, barristers, sporting associations, agricultural cooperatives and multinational corporations can all act as undertakings.[150] Yet while many types of activity may fall under its scope a contextual approach will be applied to determine if the contested decisions are anti-competitive and thus incompatible with Article 101(1). Undertakings performing a public interest function benefit from a purposive test which is not open to strictly commercial entities – these are restricted to justification under Article 101(3).

There has been some debate as to whether the CJ 'necessity' test and 'functional' approach suggest the existence of a rule of reason within Article 101(1) where activities are essential or simply in pursuit of the public interest. These interests may include the promotion of social solidarity by sharing of social risks, the administration of justice by the sound provision of legal services and guarantee integrity of service, or in competitive sport, the protection of rivalry between athletes and the integrity of athletic events. To what extent should competition law recognise and defer to non-economic objectives?[151]

ANALYSING THE LAW

What problems might arise if the definition of an undertaking was narrowed to exclude non-economic activities? Read the Article at http://competitionbulletin.com/2012/09/02/regulating-charges-for-special-police-services/. Should competition law apply here?

---

[149]C-205/03 P *FENIN* v *Commission* [2006] ECR I-6295 [23]
[150]*Reuter/BASF* [1976] OJ L254/40; *RAI/UNITEL* [1978] OJ L157/39; *The distribution of Package Tours during the 1990 World Cup* [1992] OJ L326/31; C-250/92 *Gottrup Kilm* v *DLG* [1994] ECR I-5641
[151]Non-economic justifications are possible under WTO law – see Stefan Zleptnig, *Non-Economic Objectives in WTO Law: Justification Provisions of GATT, GATS, SPS and TBT Agreements,* Martinus Nijhoff Publishers, 2010

5. The 'special responsibility' of dominant commercial undertakings

It might be argued that judgments punishing large firms will ultimately undermine competition as they seem to punish successful innovation. The CJ has, however, decided that firms in a dominant market position, like United Brands, have a 'special responsibility' – while they may take action to protect their market position, they may not refuse to supply goods. *United Brands* fell squarely into this category – it refused to supply its 'Chiquita' banana to a Danish distributor, who promoted a competitive brand of banana: such 'reprisal abuse' for 'disloyal conduct' by a dominant firm is a breach of Article 102.

Refusal to supply in order to remove competition is likewise an abuse of a dominant position. Commercial Solvents[152] used this tactic in order to gain a foothold for its own subsidiary, ICI, in the market of medicines to treat tuberculosis. Commercial Solvents was the only producer in the world of the raw materials from which Ethambutol (the drug to treat tuberculosis) could be made – it was without question dominant in the market. There were only three manufacturers of the drug in the EU – Commercial Solvents refused to supply raw materials to one of them, Zoja. The CJ was clear that this refusal to supply was an abuse under Article 102: it would result in elimination of competition from the downstream market. This idea was fleshed out in the case of *Magill*[153] where the CJ introduced the idea of the doctrine of 'essential facilities' to emphasise the role a dominant player must take in conducting its commercial affairs. This doctrine refers to resources without which a product or service cannot be made or provided. Withholding 'essential facilities' or engaging in practices which strengthen market position results in foreclosure.

VIEWPOINT:

Do you agree with the idea that large firms have a 'special responsibility'?

i.   Foreclosure of the market to strengthen competitive position

Foreclosure of the market can take a number of forms, for example 'tying' and 'bundling'. These forms of abuse are interesting because they have both lawful[154] and unlawful forms. Both practices involve making the sale of one good (A) dependent upon the purchase of a second distinctive item (B). The items can be sold separately but the consumer is forced to buy an unwanted product from the same supplier in order to obtain the desired product. Such tying agreements are an issue of concern in particular where the supplier holds a dominant position in the marketplace because they are then in a strong position to 'extract two monopoly prices, one from the tying and one from the tied product'.[155] They

---

[152] C-6 and 7/73 *Istituto Chemioterapico Italiano and Commercial Solvents v Commission* [1974] ECR 223
[153] C-241/91 P and C-242/91 P *RTE and ITP / Commission* (Magill) [1995] ECR I-743
[154] 'BOGOF' (Buy One, Get One Free) schemes use tying as a form of 'freebie' marketing.
[155] Michelle Cini and Lee McGowan, *Competition Policy in the European Union*, 2nd edn, Palgrave MacMillan, 2008, p. 115

not only restrict competition and undermine choice but can also fragment the market. Tying can be both contractual and technical. The case of *Tetrapak*[156] provides an example of contractual tying.

a) Contractual tying

The Tetra Pak group specialises in equipment for the packaging of liquid or semi-liquid food products in cartons. Its activities consist essentially in manufacturing cartons and carton-filling machines. Tetra Pak also manufactured the 'Tetra Brik' system, designed for 'aseptic' packaging used for long-life UHT milk. In that sector, PKL was the only competitor that manufactured a comparable system of packaging for long-life products. Possession of a filling technique is the key to market entry both for long-life machines and cartons. In contrast, 'non-aseptic' carton packaging used less sophisticated equipment. The 'Tetra Rex' carton, used by Tetra Pak on the market for basic cartons, had direct competition from the 'Pure-Pak' carton produced by Norwegian firm Elopak.

Tetrapak enjoyed a 'quasi-monopoly' on the aseptic market: it held a 90–95 per cent share with the remaining 5–10 per cent held by PKL. It also had a 'leading position' on non-aseptic markets, which was found to be oligopolistic:

> [45] At the time when the contested decision was adopted, Tetra Pak held 50 to 55 per cent of the market in the Community. In 1985, Elopak held some 27 per cent of the market in non-aseptic machines and cartons, followed by PKL which had approximately 11 per cent of that market. The remainder of the market in cartons was divided between three companies, and the remainder of the market in non-aseptic machines between ten or so small manufacturers.

Standard contracts issued by Tetrapak contained, among others, clauses obliging purchasers of machines in all countries to obtain supplies of packaging materials solely from Tetrapak:

> (ix) the purchaser must use only Tetra Pak cartons on the machines (all countries);

> (x) the purchaser must obtain supplies of cartons from Tetra Pak or a supplier designated by Tetra Pak (all countries).[157]

Tetrapak also reserved the right to impose penalties on any leaseholder who infringed the obligations contained in the contract, the amount being set at its discretion.

In 1983, Elopak Italia filed a complaint with the Commission against Tetra Pak Italiana and its associate companies in Italy, accusing it of having abused Article 102 by engaging in trading practices such as predatory pricing, imposition of unfair conditions on the supply of machines for filling cartons and, in certain cases, the sale of that equipment at prices which were also predatory. Five years later, in 1988, the Commission began proceedings and adopted a decision which upheld these and other abuses. The Commission ordered Tetra Pak to adopt measures to end the infringements and imposed a fine of ECU 75 million. The appeals by Tetrapak to the GC and CJ were dismissed.

---

[156]T-83/91 *Tetra Pak* v *Commission* [1994] ECR II-755; C-333/94
[157]Tetra Pak standard contract paragraph 2

This contractual tying is common. It can have serious financial consequences for individual entrepreneurs as seen in the case of *Crehan v Courage*[158] which first came before the CJ in 2001. The dispute arose from a pub lease. Mr Crehan had signed a contract with Inntrepreneur for the lease of two pubs. The lease contract stipulated that all beer sold must also be bought exclusively from Courage. This made Mr Crehan a 'tied tenant'. As a direct result of having to buy his beer at more expensive prices, the venture failed and Crehan abandoned the leases. Courage sued him for arrears in the region of £15,000 for unpaid deliveries of beer. He sought damages for the loss before the court in England, claiming that the beer-tie was an abuse.

The problem was that the Commission had provided Courage and its partners with an exemption under Article 101(3)[159] and Crehan was a willing party to the agreement. In the English courts doubts arose as to whether a party privy to an anti-competitive agreement could claim damages: however the CJ enthusiastically affirmed that Crehan could claim damages. Drawing upon the fundamental nature of competition law, the CJ defended Crehan's ability to rely on Article 101(1) before a national court 'even where he is a party to a contract that is liable to restrict or distort competition within the meaning of that provision'.[160] The Court then went further to identify a right for Crehan to claim damages from Courage:

> [26] The full effectiveness of Article 85 of the Treaty [101 TFEU] and, in particular, the practical effect of the prohibition laid down in Article 85(1) would be put at risk if it were not open to any individual to claim damages for loss caused to him by a contract or by conduct liable to restrict or distort competition.

> [27] Indeed, the existence of such a right strengthens the working of the Community competition rules and discourages agreements or practices, which are frequently covert, which are liable to restrict or distort competition. From that point of view, actions for damages before the national courts can make a significant contribution to the maintenance of effective competition in the Community.

> [28] There should not therefore be any absolute bar to such an action being brought by a party to a contract which would be held to violate the competition rules.[161]

b) Technical tying

Tying can also be technical: two products can be put together so that they only work with each other. Technical tying is similar to bundling – products are incorporated into each other and so intertwined that they can only be sold together. A seminal decision concerning technical tying and bundling was the Commission Microsoft Decision.[162] This long and complicated case began in the United States, where Microsoft had to face charges

---

[158] C-453/99 *Bernard Crehan v Courage Ltd and Others* [2001] ECR I-6297

[159] [8]

[160] [24]

[161] When the case returned to the English courts, the Court of Appeal awarded Crehan £131,336 in damages for the losses he suffered, but on appeal to the House of Lords the claim failed.

[162] Microsoft COMP/C3/37, 792 [2005] 4 CMLR

under the US Sherman Act of monopolistic behaviour. In *US* v *Microsoft,* the giant software company faced four charges under section 2 Sherman Act[163] of

i. unlawful exclusive dealing arrangements;
ii. unlawful entwining of Microsoft Internet Explorer Web browser to its Windows 95 and Windows 98 PC operating systems;
iii. unlawful maintenance of a monopoly in the market for PC operating systems;
iv. unlawful attempted monopolisation of the Web browser market.

In 2007, Microsoft launched a new version of its software. An audio package, Windows Media Player, was sold already integrated into Microsoft 2007. The technical tying of these distinct products preyed upon the apathy of consumers – purchasers were disinclined to explore other audio players that existed on the market. A second problem concerned Microsoft's refusal to provide other designers of software with the information required to ensure that their products would be interoperable with Microsoft systems. This raised the intellectual property question of whether dominant firms must give competitors access to proprietary technology.

The Commission developed a cumulative test for tying and bundling: was there dominance in the tying product market: were the products distinct (tying and tied); was there coercion (consumers had no option to buy products separately); and was there foreclosure of the tied market (competition kept out)?[164] The Commission also considered whether there might be objective justifications for this related to transaction, production or distribution cost savings; protection of intellectual property rights; or quality assurance. None of these were upheld.

The Commission's long investigation concluded that these products were in fact divisible and by bundling them together, Microsoft foreclosed competition and secured an advantage unrelated to merits of product. In addition, the refusal to share essential proprietary information hindered interoperability between programmes and excluded competition. It gave Microsoft an advantage by closing the market to creators of other audio programmes. This ensured Microsoft's continued dominance based upon size rather than merit. The Commission therefore ordered Microsoft to disclose the specifications and also place on the market a version of Windows 2007 without Windows Media Player.[165]

Antitrust authorities in the United States may soon have to consider tying in the virtual world: Facebook has been charged by Kickflip, its rival in the market of virtual currency, of forcing social-game developers to use Facebook's virtual currency rather than that produced by Kickflip. Kickflip claims that Facebook banned its virtual currency, Gambit, from its platform in 2009 and from 2011 obliged game developers to use Facebook's virtual currency to host games on its site. Kickflip claims that Facebook's anti-competitive actions destroyed its Gambit game currency business. Facebook allegedly earned $557 million for this business for half of 2011. Kickflip also claims that Facebook used its market position to persuade social-game developers to end their contractual relationships.[166]

---

[163]Sherman Act 1890 section 2: 'Every person who shall monopolize, or attempt to monopolize, or combine or conspire with any other person or persons, to monopolize any part of the trade or commerce among the several States, or with foreign nations, shall be deemed guilty of a felony . . .'
[164]Microsoft COMP/C3/37, 792 [2005] 4 CMLR [842]
[165]T-201/04 *Microsoft* v *Commission* [2007] ECR II-3601
[166]*Kickflip* v *Facebook* Case 1:12-cv-01369-LPS, Delaware, USA

ii.   Refusal to supply goods/withholding of essential facilities

An undertaking can infringe the idea of a special responsibility when they refuse, for no good reason, to provide access to an essential or indispensable facility[167] needed to provide a new and innovative service. An example of this arose in the case of *Magill*. Mr Magill had spotted a gap in the market for television listings: each network – RTE, BBC and ITV – produced their own programme listings but there was no composite catalogue for consumers. The copyright to this information was owned by the networks, and although the information was readily available, they refused to supply it to Magill so that he could exploit this viable business idea. In order to prevent him doing so, the companies began national proceedings to obtain injunctions for breach of copyright. Magill argued that their behaviour constituted an abuse under Article 102. The case was somewhat complicated by the fact that intellectual property rights were at issue but ultimately the Commission agreed with him and the decision was upheld when challenged before the CJ. The CJ stated that in 'exceptional circumstances' refusal to supply – even when IP rights arose – could breach Article 102. It furthermore drew a distinction between the use of Article 102 to prevent the distortion of competition and to protect the position of competitors.

This distinction was more clearly articulated in the case of *Oscar Bronner*,[168] where it clarified that the former was the priority. Mr Bronner owned a small newspaper, Der Standard, in Austria where he enjoyed a small (3.6 per cent) market share of the daily newspaper market and a larger (6 per cent) market share of advertising. His position was dwarfed by Mediaprint, which published two daily newspapers in Austria securing a 46.8 per cent share of national circulation and 42 per cent share of advertising revenues. Their two papers reached 53.3 per cent of the population aged over 14 in private households and 71 per cent of all newspaper readers.[169] This dominant position was secured by a nationwide delivery system. Mr Bronner could not afford to set up his own delivery network and approached MediaPrint with the request to use its delivery system. Mediaprint refused, even for payment.

Bronner alleged Mediaprint was abusing its dominant position and discriminating against him. He sought an order requiring Mediaprint to include *Der Standard* in its home-delivery service for a reasonable fee. He argued that postal delivery, was not an equivalent alternative to home delivery, because it took place late in the morning and furthermore, given the small number of subscribers, it would be entirely unprofitable for him to organise a separate home-delivery service. Bronner also claimed discrimination by Mediaprint, as it had agreed to include another daily newspaper in its home-delivery scheme that was also not published by Mediaprint.

Although the facts of the case were confined to a single member state – Austria – it was admissible.[170] In its reply to the assertions by Bronner, the CJ took the opportunity to draw a red line between his situation and cases such as *Commercial Solvent* and *Magill*. The decision reads like the *Keck*[171] of EU competition law:

> [38] Although in *Commercial Solvents v Commission* and *CBEM* . . . the Court of Justice held the refusal by an undertaking holding a dominant position in a given

---

[167]Phillip Areeda, 'Essential Facilities: An Epithet in Need of Limiting Principles', *Anti Trust Law Journal* 58(3), 1990, p. 841; Spencer Weber Wallace, 'Areeda, Epithets and Essential Facilities', *Wisconsin Law Review* 359 (2008)
[168]C-7/97 *Oscar Bronner* [1998] ECR I-7791
[169][4–6]
[170][17–19]
[171]C-267/91 *Keck and Mithouard* [1993] ECR I-6097

market to supply an undertaking with which it was in competition in a neighbouring market with raw materials . . . and services . . . respectively, which were indispensable to carrying on the rival's business, to constitute an abuse, it should be noted, first, that the Court did so to the extent that the conduct in question was likely to eliminate all competition on the part of that undertaking.

[39] Secondly, in *Magill*, at paragraphs 49 and 50, the Court held that refusal by the owner of an intellectual property right to grant a licence, even if it is the act of an undertaking holding a dominant position, cannot in itself constitute abuse of a dominant position, but that the exercise of an exclusive right by the proprietor may, in exceptional circumstances, involve an abuse.

The Court based its finding in *Magill* upon the existence of four 'exceptional circumstances':

1. the refusal concerned a product which was indispensable for creating the business in question (publication of a general television guide) – without that information, production and sale of such a publication would be impossible;
2. the refusal prevented the appearance of a new product for which there was a potential consumer demand;
3. the refusal was not justified by objective considerations; and
4. it would have the effect of excluding all competition in the secondary market of television guides.[172]

If Bronner were to succeed in his claim, he would have to demonstrate that such facts existed in his case. The CJ was unconvinced of this – the Mediaprint distribution system was not 'indispensable – other methods such as post or via newsagents existed and Bronner was not prevented from utilising these. If cost were a concern, he could cooperate with dailies in a similar position to create a delivery scheme. The *Magill* judgment could not be relied upon:

> For such access to be capable of being regarded as indispensable, it would be necessary at the very least to establish, as the Advocate General has pointed out at point 68 of his Opinion, that it is not economically viable to create a second home-delivery scheme for the distribution of daily newspapers with a circulation comparable to that of the daily newspapers distributed by the existing scheme.

Bronner had not demonstrated this – Mediaprint's refusal of access to the only nationwide newspaper home-delivery scheme in Austria was therefore not an abuse of a dominant position.

ANALYSING THE LAW

Explain the different outcomes in *Magill* and *Bronner*. How clear is the idea of a 'special responsiblity'?

---

[172][40]

6. Enforcement of EU competition law

Enforcement of EU competition norms was initially solely the job of the Commission supported by the CJ but this is no longer the case – the task is shared with national courts, national competition authorities and specialist national regulators: in the UK the Office of Fair Trading, the Competition Commission, the Competition Appeal Tribunal[173] and the Supreme Court[174] all enforce EU competition law.[175] Each member state has its own network of authorities overseeing competition law.

Although these norms are enforced separately to the internal market rules, the procedures have similar features: centralisation and decentralisation, multiple agencies and a network – all national competition authorities have been brought together into the 'European Competition Network'. However, in contrast to the internal market rules they operate in parallel at the national and EU level. This means enforcement of EU competition law avoids some of the problems of street level compliance. Also, there is a multi-level system of appeal: enforcement can begin at the national level and conclude there or at the EU level with a Commission decision; this decision can be sent upon appeal to the General Court and further on appeal to the CJ, which is the court of last instance. For example, *British Airways*[176] began when Virgin Airways complained to the Commission; the Commission decision (IV/D-2/34.780, OJ L 30/1) was appealed to the General Court (T-219/99) and then to the Court of Justice (C-95/04). In *GSK*,[177] the Spanish Tribunal decision led to a Commission decision (2001/791/ EC OJ L302/1) that was appealed to the GC (T-168/01) and finally the CJ (C-501/06P, C-513/06P, C-515/06P and C-519/06). A company with sufficient resources can bring proceedings simultaneously in the national and EU courts. HB/Masterfoods,[178] a case concerning ice-creams, fridges and an exclusivity clause, is an example of this:

ACTION IN IRISH COURTS	Masterfoods appears in Irish ice cream market; HB enforces exclusivity clause	Masterfoods and HB action in High Court		High Court judgment against Masterfoods; Masterfoods appeal to Supreme Court		Irish Supreme Court Article 267 TFEU reference to CJ
YEAR	1989	1990	1991	1992	1993	1998
ACTION IN THE EU			Masterfood lodges complaint against HB with the Commission		1st Commission decision against HB	2nd Commission decision against HB; HB Article 263 TFEU application

---

[173]The Competition Appeal Tribunal is a specialist judicial body with cross-disciplinary expertise in law, economics, business and accountancy whose function is to hear and decide cases involving competition or economic regulatory issues.
[174]*BCL Old Co Limited and others (Appellants)* v *BASF plc and others (Respondents)* [2012] UKSC 45
[175]Prohibitions (EU and UK): Agreements restricting competition; Abuse of dominance and Merger control (EU and UK); Market investigations (UK); State aid control (EU)
[176]BA appealed arguing that the Commission lacked competence to take this decision.
[177]GSK appealed arguing failure to give reasons.
[178]C-344/98 *Masterfoods Ltd* v *HB Icecreams* [2000] ECR I-11369

These cases also illustrate how long, complicated, and therefore costly, competition law proceedings tend to be. The system also features financial sanctions, but as will be seen these are significantly larger than the sums levied under Article 260 TFEU. After discussing the structure of enforcement of competition law, the modernisation in the form of Regulation 1/2003 will be discussed.

i.   The Treaty provisions

Article 105 TFEU provides the Commission with the authority to oversee EU competition law:

> (1) *Without prejudice to Article 104, the Commission shall ensure the application of the principles laid down in Articles 101 and 102. On application by a Member State or on its own initiative, and in cooperation with the competent authorities in the Member States, which shall give it their assistance, the Commission shall investigate cases of suspected infringement of these principles. If it finds that there has been an infringement, it shall propose appropriate measures to bring it to an end.*
>
> (2) *If the infringement is not brought to an end, the Commission shall record such infringement of the principles in a reasoned decision. The Commission may publish its decision and authorise Member States to take the measures, the conditions and details of which it shall determine, needed to remedy the situation.*

This responsibility was activated by Regulation 17.[179] For 50 years, the Commission used this Regulation to develop a competition policy and disseminate a competition culture in the member states. Doing so, however, required a highly centralised enforcement that required the Commission to oversee all aspects of the administration of EU competition law in all member states. This was an enormous task and DG Competition was under-resourced to fulfil it. It had to respond to any complaint of anti-competitive practices, resulting in to unstrategic, inefficient and ineffective enforcement. It also had to respond to notifications of agreements under Article 101(3) as well as approve any request for exemptions from firms. Often, by the time the Commission was able to assess these requests, the firms affected had begun their collaboration; in some instances their exemption application was not approved, they became subject to proceedings under Article 101(1). Frustration and delay undermined economic activity and growth in the EU, creating uncertainty and making the single market unattractive to investment. It also left the Commission unable to focus on the most egregious infringements, allowing serious market distortions to continue with impunity and leaving EU law enforced unevenly. Enforcement was unpredictable and patchy, and led to accusations of politically motivated action by the Commission. The loudest voices of protest against the centralised scheme came from Germany and the UK: Germany urged more transparency on the part of the Commission while the UK promoted greater involvement of the national competition authorities.

---

[179]Council Regulation No 17 of 6 February 1962, OJ 13/204/62 1962. Last amended by Regulation (EC) No 1216/1999, OJ L 148/5 1999

These demands were finally answered in 2003, when a modernised enforcement regime was introduced by Regulation 1/2003. The most important reform introduced by this regulation was the removal of the obligation to notify agreements to the Commission and the removal of the Commission's exclusive right to grant exemptions for firms. The broader effect has been to usher in a decentralised enforcement system with much broader scope for private enforcement. The new regulation retains use of the Advisory Committee set up under Regulation 17.

A major effect of modernisation has been to allow the Commission to focus EU action on the most significant abuses, making enforcement of competition law more goal-oriented. It has undertaken sector specific projects, such as the project to increase competition in the energy sector. It has also produced guidance on its enforcement priorities.[180] The focused strategy is all the more effective because the Commission has also been given stronger investigation, decision-making and fining powers.

ii. Regulation 1/2003

Article 1 of this regulation makes Articles 101 and 102 TFEU directly applicable in the EU in their entirety. Under Article 2, any firm seeking to benefit from the Article 101(3) exemption bears the burden of proving that the conditions are fulfilled. This was confirmed in *GSK* – when dealing with an application for annulment the GC can conduct a limited review.[181] Firms must now conduct a self-assessment based on EU guidelines.

The centrepiece of the decentralised regime is Article 3 – this establishes the principle of mirror provisions in EU and national competition law so that whenever national courts apply national competition law, they also apply EU competition law and any decision taken under national law, may not contradict a decision taken under EU law:

3(1) Where the competition authorities of the Member States or national courts apply national competition law to agreements, decisions by associations of undertakings or concerted practices within the meaning of Article 81(1) of the Treaty [Article 101(1) TFEU] which may affect trade between Member States within the meaning of that provision, they shall also apply Article 81 of the Treaty to such agreements, decisions or concerted practices. Where the competition authorities of the Member States or national courts apply national competition law to any abuse prohibited by Article 82 of the Treaty, they shall also apply Article 82 of the Treaty [Article 102 TFEU].

(2) The application of national competition law may not lead to the prohibition of agreements, decisions by associations of undertakings or concerted practices which may affect trade between Member States but which do not restrict competition within the meaning of Article 81(1) of the Treaty, or which fulfil the conditions of Article 81(3) of the Treaty [Article 101(3) TFEU] or which are covered by a Regulation for the application of Article 81(3) of the Treaty.

---

[180]Communication from the Commission, 'Guidance on Enforcement Priorities in Application of Article 82', COM(2009)/C45/02
[181]C-501/06 [84]

In the UK this means that provisions in the Competition Act 1998 (CA98) mirror Articles 101 and 102 TFEU: Chapter I and Chapter II use almost identical wording. In addition, section 60 CA 98[182] lays out that:

> *The purpose of this section is to ensure that so far as is possible (having regard to any relevant differences between the provisions concerned), questions arising under this Part in relation to competition within the United Kingdom are dealt with in a manner which is consistent with the treatment of corresponding questions arising in Community [Union] law in relation to competition within the Community. [Union]*

The obligation to avoid conflicting decisions was emphasised in *Masterfoods Ltd v HB Icecreams*[183] where the CJ said national courts must 'avoid giving decisions which would conflict with a decision contemplated by the Commission . . .'. *Racecourse Association* suggests this obligation is adhered to:

Section 2 is modelled on Article 81(1) of the EC Treaty [Article 101(1) TFEU]. Section 60 requires that questions arising under the Act are to be determined, so far as possible, and having regard to any relevant differences, in a manner consistent with Community law.[184]

However, EU competition law must not always be applied – only where there is a cross-border element to the case. Member states may for this purpose apply stricter laws which prohibit or sanction conduct engaged in by individual national undertakings.

Uniform application of EU competition law is also mandated under Article 16 of Regulation 1/2003. This is necessary because Article 6 of the Regulation empowers national courts to apply Articles 101 and 102 TFEU. The same power and obligation as to uniformity applies to the national competition authorities.[185] They may also, acting on their own initiative or following a complaint, adopt decisions requiring that an infringement be brought to an end, and order interim measures, accept commitments and impose fines or penalty payments. It should be noted that the national competition authorities have no power to adopt negative decisions concluding no infringement of Article 101 TFEU.[186]

Cooperation between national competition authorities – such as the exchange of confidential information – is encouraged in Article 11. Avoidance of duplicate proceedings is stressed in Article 13 – any competition authority or the Commission may reject a complaint on the grounds that it is being dealt with or has already been dealt with by another authority in the EU. This cooperation is facilitated by the European Competition Network (ECN), which not only facilitates exchange of best practice (especially important in those member states with limited experience with competition law) but also allows the Commission to disseminate a competition culture.

The risks of decentralisation are clear – it may undermine coherence. Effective enforcement is now dependent upon the capacities of national competition authorities and national courts – they are unlikely to share the same resources and levels of knowledge

---

[182]Amended by the Enterprise Act 2002
[183]C-344/98 *Masterfoods Ltd v HB Icecreams* [51–52]
[184]*The Racecourse Association and Others & The British Horseracing Board v The Office of Fair Trading* [2005] CAT 29 [11]
[185]See Articles 5 and 16 Regulation 1/2003
[186]C-681/11 *Bundeswettbewerbsbehoerde and another v Schenker and Co AG and Others* [2013] WLR (D) 245; C-375/09 *Prezes Urzędu Ochrony Konkurencji i Konsumentów v Tele2 Polska sp. z o.o., devenue Netia SA (Tele2 Polska)* [2011] ECR I-3055

of EU competition law. Lack of knowledge may lead to incorrect rulings resulting in cross national uncertainty rather than certainty. The ECN may, however, ameliorate these difficulties – all competition authorities will learn from and support each other. This may be idealistic but is in theory possible if the network functions to ensure this.

The biggest advantage of decentralisation is that it frees the Commission to set its own agenda – it no longer has to respond to every agreement notified to it.[187] The Commission retains arm's-length oversight and control. In particular it has the power to remove any case from the national authorities – regardless of whether the national authorities agree with this. Article 11(6) states that:

> *The initiation by the Commission of proceedings for the adoption of a decision under Chapter III shall relieve the competition authorities of the Member States of their competence to apply Articles 81 and 82 of the Treaty. If a competition authority of a Member State is already acting on a case, the Commission shall only initiate proceedings after consulting with that national competition authority.*

In relation to national court proceedings, the Commission may request a copy of the written judgment and submit written or oral observations.[188]

APPLYING THE LAW

Which body should anti-competitive practices between firms in the same member states be reported to: the Commission or the national competition authority?

---

a) Procedure before the Commission

Proceedings before the Commission can be separated into three stages. Stage one includes an initial assessment, which may conclude with the case being reassigned to a national competition authority or discarded as unworthy of further action. Alternatively, proceedings may be opened and an investigation of the complaint may ensue, using powers in Regulation No. 1/2003. The Commission will not always conduct a detailed assessment:

> [22] . . . there may be circumstances where it is not necessary for the Commission to carry out a detailed assessment before concluding that the conduct in question is likely to result in consumer harm. If it appears that the conduct can only raise obstacles to competition and that it creates no inefficiencies, its anti-competitive effect may be inferred. This could be the case, for instance, if the dominant undertaking prevents its customers from testing the products of competitors or provides financial incentives to its customers on condition that they do not test such products, or pays a distributor or a customer to delay the introduction of a competitor's product.[189]

The complainant must be informed of the Commission's response.

---

[187]Cini and McGowan 2008, p. 218
[188]Article 15, Regulation No 1/2003
[189]COM(2009)C45

Stage two includes production of a 'Statement of Objections', further collection of data, comments by third parties and responses from the infringer(s). Oral hearings are held and conducted by a 'Hearing Officer'. These meetings are not public – attendance must be notified. They are not minuted but recorded – copies are available only to attendees. The purpose of these is to give parties in the proceedings an opportunity to expand upon the arguments submitted in writing before the Commission services and representatives of the competition authorities of the member states. 'Commitments', or agreements to change practices, can be presented at this stage – these are subjected to market analysis before acceptance and the Commission can decline them. The hearing is also a time for the Commission to explain the preliminary findings contained in the Statement of Objections. Meetings can be held *in camera* with sufficient justification. The main outcome of stage three is the finding of the Commission. The Commission will consult with the Advisory Committee before deciding the outcome.

The Commission can take three forms of action: it can make a finding of infringement and require this to be brought to an end – in so doing it may impose on the undertakings concerned any reasonable behavioural or structural remedies necessary in its opinion to effectively end the infringement.[190] The member states may lodge a complaint against such action, as may natural and legal persons if they can show a legitimate interest.[191] Interim measures can also be ordered and renewed under Article 8 if there is a risk of 'serious and irreparable damage to competition'. Under Article 9 the Commission may accept 'commitments' from firms in place of a decision under Article 7:

---

(1) Where the Commission intends to adopt a decision requiring that an infringement be brought to an end and the undertakings concerned offer commitments to meet the concerns expressed to them by the Commission in its preliminary assessment, the Commission may by decision make those commitments binding on the undertakings. Such a decision may be adopted for a specified period and shall conclude that there are no longer grounds for action by the Commission.

However, the Commission may reopen the proceedings if new information is brought to light, the Article 9 commitment is broken or the decision was based on 'incomplete, incorrect or misleading information provided by the parties'.[192] If so, the Commission can impose a fine without proving violations of any kind.[193] Commitments have been effective in sectors such as energy, where structural changes are often required, or in fast moving markets such as communications and technology, where fast decisions that can have an immediate impact are necessary.[194] Finally, it can find that EU competition law is inapplicable because the conditions of Articles 102 and 101(1) are not fulfilled or on the contrary because the conditions of Article 101(3) of the Treaty are satisfied.

---

[190]See settlement decisions at http://ec.europa.eu/competition/elojade/isef/index.cfm?fuseaction=dsp_result&case_title=E.ON
[191]Article 7, Regulation No 1/2003
[192]Article 9 (2), Regulation No 1/2003
[193]The first fine of this kind was imposed on Microsoft in 2013 for 561 million euros.
[194]See E-Book Decision with Penguin – Press Release IP/13/746 25/07/2013

> **VIEWPOINT:**
>
> Is use of Article 7 or Article 9 preferable from the perspective of a) the Commission, or b) the undertaking?

b) Financial sanctions for anti-competitive practices

An Article 7 infringement finding can be accompanied by a fine, and this is usually the case. Initially these fines were only lump sum sanctions and came in three levels: 'minor', 'serious' and 'very serious'.[195] The fining policy was refined in 2006[196] to remove these somewhat vague categories and replace them with a clearer basis for the calculation of fines. Although the Commission retains full discretion its calculation of sanctions will take two aspects into consideration: the gravity and the duration of the infringement. In setting the fine, the Commission will also consider the value of the goods or services related to infringement. A penalty payment was also introduced to act as a deterrent and the power to impose a 'symbolic' fine.[197] The fines will therefore continue to be variable, calculated according to the role of each firm in the infringement. This rationale also allows for harsher punishment of repeat offenders.

It is partly because of the level of fines that EU competition law has grown into one of the most significant and controversial regulatory areas of the single market. The Commission may fine a company up to 10 per cent of its annual turnover[198] – the highest fine to date on a single company is the 1.1 billion euros demanded of Intel in 2009.[199] Significant fines can also be imposed for interference with a Commission investigation: in *E.ON Energie* v *Commission* the General Court confirmed the fine of 38 million euros imposed by the Commission[200] on E.ON 'because a seal that Commission officials had affixed to a door during a dawn raid at E.ON Energie's premises in May 2006 had been found slightly displaced on the following day and had shown markings of 'Void'.'[201] Suez Environnement/Lyonnaise des Eaux France (LDE) was therefore relatively lucky to have a fine of 8 million euros.

There are two routes to escape a fine. The first is to demonstrate on the basis of objective information an inability to pay – the Commission will grant a reduction if presented with evidence that the fine 'would irretrievably jeopardise the economic viability of the undertaking concerned and cause its assets to lose all their value'.[202] The second escape route is to make use of the leniency programme.

---

[195] 1998 Guidelines, OJ C9 (1998)
[196] Guidelines on the method of setting fines imposed pursuant to Article 23(2)(a) of Regulation No 1/2003 (2006/C 210/02)
[197] Section 36, 2006 Guidelines
[198] Article 23 Regulation 1/2003 empowers the Commission to impose fines on undertakings and associations of undertakings who infringe Articles 101 and 102 TFEU. For each undertaking and association of undertakings participating in the infringement, the fine shall not exceed 10 per cent of its total turnover in the preceding business year. Article 31 Regulation 1/2003 gives the CJEU 'unlimited jurisdiction' to review these fines.
[199] http://news.bbc.co.uk/1/hi/8047546.stm. See also Alex Barker, 'Google revises Brussels Offer', *Financial Times,* 17 July 2012, p. 17
[200] Decision of 30 January 2008 (COMP/B-1/39.326—E.ON Energie AG) OJ C240/6 2008
[201] T-141/08 *E.ON Energie AG* v *Commission of the European Communities* [2010] ECR II-5761. E.ON appealed to the CJEU. C-89/11 P *E.ON Energie/Commission* Reported in Kallaugher and Weitbrecht 2011
[202] Section 35, 2006 Guidelines

c) The leniency programme

A key way for authorities to identify and gather the evidence required to tackle anti-competitive practices is with the help of 'whistle-blowers'. Employees at any level can take this action – the CEO of Olympus became a whistle-blower when he discovered years of accounting fraud[203] – but the cost may be the loss of job, career and livelihood. As events in the British National Health Service demonstrate, the more secretive the organisational culture, the more likely that there is something to hide.[204] In many countries, laws[205] exist to protect individual whistle-blowers from punitive reprisal action such as dismissal, but these do not always work well.

The leniency programme shields any member of a cartel from fines if it cooperates with the Commission and provides information which helps to bring anti-competitive practices to an end.[206] Individual whistle-blowers are not protected in EU law[207] but a leniency programme[208] protects whistle-blowing undertakings – a company that provides information leading to the prosecution of their fellow cartel members is shielded from financial penalties.[209] In a case concerning a cross-EU soap powder cartel, the whistle-blowing firm, Henkel, was not fined while its cartel partners Unilever and Procter & Gamble were fined 104 million euros and 211 million euros respectively.[210] The three companies were part of a cartel lasting three years, during which time customers in eight countries paid inflated prices for soap powder.

VIEWPOINT:

Why are whistle-blowers important in EU competition law? Does EU law offer adequate incentives to individual and organisational whistle-blowers?

A leniency application may be the first piece of evidence of cartel activity obtained by a competition authority.[211] Application of the leniency programme can be reviewed by the CJEU.[212] The EU leniency programme is important because there is no space for clemency

---

[203]Michael Woodford, *Exposure: Inside the Olympus Scandal: How I Went from CEO to Whistleblower,* Penguin, 2012
[204]http://www.theguardian.com/uk/2013/feb/14/nhs-whistleblower-quit-gagged
[205]For example section 47B Employment Rights Act 1996. The Public Interest Disclosure Act 1998 (PIDA) is a piece of legislation, incorporated into the Employment Rights Act 1996 that provides a remedy for workers who have been dismissed or suffered a detriment as a result of raising a concern either internally and/or externally to regulatory bodies, the media and campaigning NGOs. Section 43B PIDA identifies a broad range of categories by which workers can raise concerns about wrongdoing: criminal offences, failures to comply with a legal obligation, miscarriages of justice, health and safety dangers, damage to the environment or an attempt to cover-up one of the preceding categories. http://www.halsburyslawexchange.co.uk/whistleblowing-whats-in-the-public-interest/
[206]Section 34, 2006 Guidelines
[207]See C-145/83 *Adams* v *Commission* ECR 3539
[208]For details on the Model Leniency Programme see http://ec.europa.eu/competition/ecn/mlp_revised_2012_en.pdf. In relation to complaints on the level of reduction see C-501/11 P *Schindler Holding Ltd and Others* v *European Commission* [146–161]
[209]26 EU member states currently operate a leniency programme.
[210]http://www.reuters.com/Article/2011/04/13/us-eu-cartel-idUSTRE73C1XV20110413
[211]Antonio Gomes, Zsofia Tari and Yonatan Cwikel, 'Unannounced Inspections in Antitrust Investigations', OECD Competition Division paper presented at the Latin American Competition Forum, 3–4 September 2013, p. 19
[212]C-501/11 P *Schindler* [155]

under Article 101 TFEU, even if the action is based upon erroneous legal advice.[213] Companies that passively engage in behaviour that gives rise to suspicion of collusion can find themselves subject to hefty fines:

[95] . . . Once an undertaking's participation in meetings has been proved, it may be concluded that it participated in the anti-competitive scheme. It is then incumbent on any undertaking which claims that it dissociated itself from decisions reached on agreed action to provide express proof thereof. Any failure to put the concerted decisions into effect is another matter and does not suffice to refute such participation.[214]

In the EU and beyond, leniency programmes are the most effective method to obtain the evidence required in competition law proceedings.[215] The EU leniency programme is so important that access to documents submitted under it is restricted. In *Pfleiderer*,[216] a company that had been the victim of a price-fixing cartel requested access to the materials submitted voluntarily by the cartel members in order to reduce their fines. Pfleiderer wished to use these documents in its action for damages against the cartel members. However, the German competition authorities refused access and this was supported by the Commission who argued that it would undermine the usefulness of the leniency procedure in uncovering and ending infringements if documents relating to it were to be disclosed.

The protected nature of leniency documents was supported by the CJ and reiterated in the subsequent case of *Donau Chemie*.[217] Nonetheless, while recognising the public interest of effective leniency programmes, the CJ stressed that by itself, this argument 'cannot justify a refusal to grant access to that evidence' as actions for damages are also important in ensuring effective competition.[218] It concluded that national procedural rules which make third party access to cartel documents dependent upon the agreement of all parties to the proceedings is incompatible with the principle of effectiveness in EU law. A blanket ban is precluded – access or refusal of access must be determined in each individual case so as to enable cartel victims to exercise their right to compensation.

It has, however, been argued that this decision creates an ambiguity which may deter applicants for leniency and undermine effective regulation of competition.[219] There is concern that it may make disclosure disputes more complex:

The court does not offer a definition of what it means by documents in a case file – does this include only those documents made specifically for a leniency application, such as corporate statements, or also pre-existing documents? Regardless, the statements of the court do lead to the conclusion that, were it essential for evidencing a damages claim, victims ought to have access to leniency applicants' self-incriminating corporate

---

[213]C-681/11 *Bundeswettbewerbsbehoerde and another* v *Schenker and Co AG and Others*
[214]C-49/92 P *Commission* v *Anic Partecipazioni* [1999] ECR I-4125
[215]Gomes *et al*. 2013, p. 29
[216]C-360/09 *Pfleiderer AG* v *Bundeskartellamt*
[217]C-536/11 *Donau Chemie*. See also the AG opinion in C-365/12 *European Commission* v *EnBW Energie Baden-Württemberg*
[218]*Donau Chemie* [46]
[219]Di Stefano 'Access of damage claimants to evidence arising out of EU cartel investigations: a fast evolving scenario', *Global Competition Litigation Review* 5(3), 2012, p. 95. See also Chris Brown 'Pfleiderer Re-visited' at http://eutopi-alaw.com/2013/02/22/pfleiderer-revisited-the-ag-opinion-in-donau-chemie/#more-1787

statements . . . the Court of Justice emphasises in *Donau Chemie* that national courts weigh each document when assessing whether to disclose it (para. 48). As a result, disputes as to disclosure in follow-on claims are likely to become more complex and burdensome for parties in the absence of EU legislation.[220]

ANALYSING THE LAW

Read the short note by Hirst on *Donau Chemie*. Identify three ways that EU legislation can help reduce the complexity of disclosure disputes in EU competition law.

It has been left to the national authorities to determine when documents submitted under the leniency programme should be made available to parties in private follow-on cases for damages. Disclosure will remain controversial as the project to encourage private enforcement of competition law continues – in the United States, 90 per cent of antitrust enforcement is private.

iii. Private enforcement of EU competition law

According to the Commission:

> . . . public and private enforcement are complementary tools to enforce competition law and [that] we need both types of enforcement. The practices forbidden by Articles 101 and 102 of the Treaty harm competition and consumer welfare. This harm is not abstract or theoretical. Customers who pay an overcharge because of a cartel and businesses that suffer a loss of profit because of illegal foreclosure feel the negative effects of these infringements directly in their pockets and balance sheets. That is real harm.[221]

As discussed above, disclosure is necessary to enable claims for damages for such harm.

The question of private actions under EU competition law first arose in a dispute concerning a pub lease.[222] Mr Crehan agreed with Inntrepreneur to lease two pubs. He signed a contract agreeing to buy his beer exclusively from Courage. The business was unsuccessful. Crehan then sought damages for the loss of a business from Inntrepreneur on the basis that the contractual tying prevented him from buying cheaper beer elsewhere which would have allowed him to make a profit. In the English courts, doubts arose as to whether a party voluntarily privy to an anti-competitive agreement could claim damages. When asked about this, the CJ enthusiastically endorsed the idea – the loss was caused by anti-competitive tying and Crehan should be able to claim damages for loss caused. When the case returned to the English courts, the Court of Appeal awarded Crehan £131,336 in damages for the losses he suffered, but on appeal to the House of Lords the claim failed.

---

[220]Nicholas Hirst, 'Donau Chemie: National Rules Impeding Access to Antitrust Files Liable to Breach EU law', *Journal of European Competition Law and Practice* 4(6), 2013
[221]Alexander Italianer, Director General, DG Competition, 'Public and private enforcement of competition law', Paper delivered at 5th International Competition Conference, 17 February 2012, Brussels
[222]C-453/99 *Courage* v *Crehan*

The CJ had another chance to develop the right to damages under competition law in *Manfredi*.[223] Consumers in Italy had paid inflated prices for vehicle insurance as a result of collusion between insurers. The Italian competition authority found an infringement of Italian competition law. In a follow-on claim, affected Italian consumers then sought damages under EU competition law as an easier alternative to national competition law: rather than bring a claim before the Italian Court of Appeal for damages for breaches of Italian competition, a more informal, quicker and cheaper claim under Article 101 can be taken to a small claims court. The Court of Justice agreed that although the cartel was national, it affected trade between member states and thus allowed the application of Article 101. It found that there was no national law prohibiting such an action.

What role can private enforcement play in the ecology of EU competition law enforcement? Arguably, facilitating follow-on damage claims will not only make it easier for those who have suffered damages arising from an infringement of the competition rules to recoup their losses from the infringer but beyond this strengthen the enforcement of competition law in general. The Commission has approached this idea with as much enthusiasm as the CJ. However, what would the logic and logistics of such enforcement be?

In 2005 the Commission produced a Green Paper proposing that private actions could be used as punishment to deter future infringements; a subsequent White Paper of 2008[224] laid out a compensatory logic. Which of these should it be?

> If . . . public antitrust enforcement is the superior instrument to pursue the objectives of clarification and development of the law and of deterrence and punishment, whereas private actions for damages are superior for the pursuit of corrective justice through compensation, then the optimal antitrust enforcement system would appear to be a system in which public antitrust enforcement aims at clarification and development of the law and at deterrence and punishment while private action for damages aim at compensation . . .[225]

This separate tasks approach is not supported by all:

> . . . a public enforcement-centric view, under which national courts only deal with follow-on actions to compensate for damages is theoretically inconsistent with the system. Since courts are bound to enforce Articles 81 and 82 [101 and 102 TFEU] to protect subjective rights, they must also be prepared to address stand-alone actions, and therefore to ascertain alleged antitrust infringements.[226]

An integrated approach would broaden the application of competition law while reducing the burden on the Commission and national competition authorities. Private actions would complement public enforcement. Fines could include payment of compensation as part of the settlement of a public antitrust action. For example, in the *Independent Schools* case the infringers paid a fine of £10,000 per school but also had to create a public fund to benefit pupils at the schools.

---

[223]C-295-98/04 *Vincenzo Manfredi and others* [2006] ECR I-6619
[224]European Commission, 'Damages Actions for Breach of the EC antitrust rules', White Paper, COM(2008) 165 final. A Staff Working Paper and a concise summary of the existing *acquis communautaire* on this point were published alongside the White Paper.
[225]W. Wils, 'The relationship between public antitrust enforcement and private actions for damages', *World Competition* 32(1) 2009, p. 12
[226]G. Bruzzone and G. Boccaccio, 'Taking Care of Modernisation After the Startup: A View from a Member State', *World Competition* 31(1), 2008, p. 89

The logistics of private enforcement are also unclear. If claimants will be able to choose whether to go to competition authorities or national courts, this will increase the burden on the courts. It would require either all national judges to have in-depth training in EU competition law and economic analysis, or the creation of specialist competition courts in the member states to deal with these cases. Will national judges have to look at all cases or will a *de minimis* rule apply? Will 'national procedural autonomy' be a guiding principle?

A suggestion from Britain has been to promote alternative dispute resolution (ADR) in competition law so that courts are an option of last resort:

> While it is essential that wrong-doers can practically be taken to court, it is also right that businesses and consumers are encouraged to resolve their differences outside of court. The use of ADR can reduce costs and allow swifter resolution for all parties. We are therefore consulting on how to ensure ADR is the default option when bringing cases in the CAT and whether to grant the OFT a power to encourage companies found to have breached competition law to provide restitution to those they have wronged.[227]

Would this 'privatise' competition law disputes by removing them from the public realm of litigation? If this were to happen, EU competition law may move from being a part of constitutional law to a plank of economic and industrial policy.

Beyond the logic and logistics, the larger question is whether private actions will be more successful than public enforcement in reducing competition law violations – this would be an important justification for increasing private enforcement of competition law:

> How much antitrust enforcement is desirable depends of course on how much value society attaches to the avoidance of anti-trust violations, but that value is certainly not infinite, given the multitude of other societal concerns. Moreover, effective deterrence does not require that each and every violation is detected and punished, but rather, that the expected penalty, which is a function both of the probability of detection and punishment and of the size of the penalties imposed, exceeds the expected gains of anti-trust infringements.[228]

PUBLIC and PRIVATE ENFORCEMENT OF EU COMPETITION LAW	
PUBLIC: goals = clarification and development of law, punishment and deterrence	**PRIVATE: goal = compensation**
Driven by public interest – social interests drive actions Effective investigation More effective sanctions More optimal sanctions Broader range of sanctions Broader application of outcome	Driven by private interests – rise in 'unmeritorious actions'? Weaker investigation – limited discovery rules Only monetary sanctions Damages calculated by reference to losses Weaker deterrent effect

---

[227]Department for Business, Innovation and Skills, 'Private actions in competition law: a consultation on options for reform', April 2012, pp. 5–6
[228]Wils 2009, p. 10

The Commission has now proposed a directive to harmonise the private enforcement regime.[229] Ultimately private follow-on actions will only increase if injured parties think it is worth the effort of pursuing them. They are likely to be discouraged if they are denied access to documents that can help. On the other hand the public enforcement regime will be undermined if this is granted: companies, who play a vital role at the national and EU level, are unlikely to whistle blow if the information they provide can later be used against them.

ANALYSING THE LAW

Does private enforcement of EU competition law complement or compete with public enforcement?

---

7. Conclusion

Antitrust activities are everyday occurrences. They can appear in any product market, whether it be dairy goods, soap powder, tobacco, music, online search engines or energy. While competition law is focused on economic activity and financial gain, competitiveness also has important social consequences: put simply, if the price of bread or basic foodstuffs is too high, people will be hungry and unable to work; in the absence of labour, productivity declines and social unrest increases. Competition is therefore of social and economic consequence.

The breadth of EU competition law is similar to that of Article 34 TFEU after *Dassonville*. It appears absolute and this gives rise to a great deal of criticism and concern: not only does it potentially cover almost every field of commercial activity, but it is a very sensitive area of EU law that can in fact be triggered by a range of commercial practices beyond those listed in the Treaty. The range is likely to grow as deregulation of economic sectors continues. The relationship between health services and competition law will be debated for some time to come.[230] There is no clear answer on when competition law will apply to this field.

While there is little evidence of a rule of reason in Article 101(1) TFEU, the case law seems to suggest a slightly different test where the undertaking is performing a public service. The CJ will examine the activities of the undertaking – especially the purpose of purchasing – to determine if the competition rules apply. Where there is no public interest concern, the CJ will look at the 'object' and if necessary also the 'effect' of the practice. The burden of proof falls on the undertakings to show their activities are covered by Article 101(3) TFEU.

Article 102 TFEU is central to the battle against monopolies and cartels. Abuses of a dominant position weaken competition and raise prices for the consumer. The Commission will check closely, even if there appears to be lively competition. As the CJ stated in *United Brands* and *Hoffman la Roche*, the existence of lively competition on a particular market does not rule out the possibility of dominance.[231] However, market responsiveness

---

[229]European Commission, 'Directive on Antitrust Damages Actions', COM(2013) 404 final
[230]See Oke Odudu, 'Competition law and the National Health Service' at http://competitionbulletin.com/2012/10/08/competition-law-and-the-national-health-service/
[231]*Hoffman la Roche* [70]

will be taken into account. The notion of a 'special responsibility' emphasises the importance of the market structure and indicates the continued Harvard approach promoted by the CJ. It also illustrates the public interest focus of competition law.

A new front in the debate between the Harvard and Chicago approaches has appeared in the form of discussions on the role of private enforcement in EU competition law.[232] Whether this will strengthen competition law is another question.

Taken together, the above considerations should make clear that ensuring fair competition in the EU is a time-consuming, lengthy and intensive process requiring detailed market studies for each individual case. It is perhaps therefore not surprising that the Commission has chosen to decentralise its enforcement.

Although the Commission remains the overall 'Guardian of the Treaties', decentralisation has allowed it to establish strategic priorities[233] for its guardianship role. Sector specific action is now possible. In relation to competition law, it has announced that it will focus on ensuring a competitive process:

> [6] The emphasis of the Commission's enforcement activity in relation to exclusionary conduct is on safeguarding the competitive process in the internal market and ensuring that undertakings which hold a dominant position do not exclude their competitors by other means than competing on the merits of the products or services they provide. In doing so the Commission is mindful that what really matters is protecting an effective competitive process and not simply protecting competitors. This may well mean that competitors who deliver less to consumers in terms of price, choice, quality and innovation will leave the market.

The Commission retains discretion to reject a complaint when in its view the case lacks priority on 'grounds of lack of Community interest'. Intervention is likely where 'on the basis of cogent and convincing evidence, the allegedly abusive conduct is likely to lead to anti-competitive foreclosure' – that is where it finds exclusionary conduct or single dominance.[234] It has also identified a new priority of standard-setting – this facilitates a horizontal approach:

> . . . standards are becoming increasingly important in facilitating innovation (in particular in the IT sector) and efficient standard-setting plays a key role in the desired shift towards a knowledge-based economy.[235]

Whether this ensures administrative accountability, especially given the tensions between the joint goals of leniency and private actions in competition law, remains to be seen.

---

[232]In the United States 90 per cent of antitrust enforcement is private.
[233]Communication from the Commission, 'Guidance on Enforcement Priorities in Application of Article 82', (COM)2009 C45/02
[234][4]
[235]DG Competition Management Plan 2010, p. 20

Further reading

On competition law in general:

David J. Gerber, *Global Competition: Law, Markets and Globalization*, Oxford University Press, 2010

Vivien Rose and David Bailey, *Bellamy and Child: EU Law of Competition*, 7th edn, Oxford University Press, 2013

On Article 101 TFEU:

Alexei Alexandrov, George Deltas and Daniel F. Spulber, 'Antitrust And Competition In Two-Sided Markets', *Journal of Competition Law and Economics* 7(4), 2011, pp.775–812

Julian Joshua, 'Single Continuous Infringement of Article 81 EC: Has the Commission Stretched the Concept Beyond the Limit of Its Logic?', *European Competition Journal* 5(2), 2009, p. 451

Okeoghene Odudu, 'The Last Vestiges of Overambitious EU Competition Law', *Cambridge Law Journal* 69(2), 2010, pp. 248–250

On Article 102 TFEU and dominance:

Phillip Areeda, 'Essential facilities: An Epithet in need of a limiting principles', *Anti Trust Law Journal* 58, 1990, p. 841

Ioannis Lianos and Evgenia Motchenkova, 'Market Dominance and Quality of Search Results in the Search Engine Market', CLES Working Paper series 2/2012, p. 4

Mark R. Patterson, 'Google and Search-Engine Market power', *Harvard Journal of Law and Technology* Occassional Paper Series, July 2013, p. 4

Spencer Weber Wallace, 'Areeda, Epithets and Essential Facilities', *Wisconsin Law Review*, 2008, p. 359

On approaches to competition law:

Doris Hildebrand, 'The European School in EC Competition Law', *World Competition* 25(1), 2002, pp. 3–23

Herbert Hovenkamp, 'Antitrust Policy After Chicago', *Michigan Law Review* 84, 1986, p. 213

Alberto Pera, 'Changing views of competition, economic analysis and EC Anti-Trust law', *European Competition Journal* 4(1), June 2008, pp. 127–168

Richard A. Posner, 'The Chicago School of Antitrust Analysis', *University of Pennsylvania Law Review* 127, 1979, p. 925

On non-economic objectives of competition law:

Suzanne Kingston 'Integrating Environmental Protection and EU Competition law', *ELJ* 16(6), November 2010, pp. 780–805

On enforcement of competition law:

Marco Botta 'Testing the Decentralisation of Competition Law Enforcement: Comment on Toshiba' *European Law Review* 38(1) 2013, 107

Nicholas Hirst, 'Donau Chemie: National Rules Impeding Access to Antitrust Files Liable to Breach EU law', *Journal of European Competition Law and Practice* 4(6), 2013

Wouter P.J. Wils, 'The relationship between public antitrust enforcement and private actions for damages', *World Competition* 32(1), 2009, p. 12

Index

Hague Summit, 10
Harvard school, 477
Healthcare services, receipt of, 432–44
 hospital care, undue delay in, 438–42
 hospital costs, reimbursement of, 436–8
 hospital treatment, scheduled *vs.* unsched-
  uled, 442–4
 overriding reason in the general interest,
  434–6
High Authority, 4–5
Highway Code, 389
Horizontal co-administration, 156–9
Horizontal direct effect of directives,
 210–13
Hospital care, undue delay in, 438–42
Hospital costs, reimbursement of, 436–8
Hospital treatment, scheduled *vs.* unsched-
 uled, 442–4
Housing Act, 343
Human rights. *See* Fundamental rights
Human Rights Act, 171, 231, 235

ICCPR. *See* International Covenant on Civil
 and Political Rights (ICCPR)
ICERD. *See* International Convention on the
 Elimination of All Forms of Racial Dis-
 crimination (ICERD)
ICTY. *See* International Criminal Tribunal
 on Former Yugoslavia (ICTY)
IGC. *See* Intergovernmental Conference
 (IGC)
IMPALA. *See* Independent Music Publishers
 and Labels Association (IMPALA)
Imperative requirements in general interest,
 418–21
Implementing acts, 82–4
Independence, 175–7
Independent Music Publishers and Labels
 Association (IMPALA), 123
Indirect access under Article 267 TFEU,
 127–32
Indirect effect, 213–16
Individual concern, test for, 122–7
Infringement of EU law. *See* Enforcement of
 EU law
Institutional agenda setting, 25–6
Institutions of EU. *See* Central institutions
 of EU
Integration in EU, levels of, 359–60
Intergovernmental Conference (IGC), 13–14
 Constitutional Treaty and, 24, 25
 Nice Treaty and, 22, 235

Treaty of Amsterdam and, 20
International Convention on the Elimination
 of All Forms of Racial Discrimination
 (ICERD), 234
International Covenant on Civil and Political
 Rights (ICCPR), 247
International Criminal Tribunal on Former
 Yugoslavia (ICTY), 13
Invalidity, declarations on, 184–7
Ireland
 abandonment of EFTA by, 9–10
 Lisbon Treaty 'No,' 29–30
 Nice Treaty 'No,' 21–2
Iron Curtain, 11–12

JHA. *See* Justice and Home Affairs (JHA)
Judicial deliberation, structure of, 111–16
 Advocate General, 113–16
Judicial protection of fundamental rights,
 253–61
Justice and Home Affairs (JHA), 18, 52, 53,
 144

K

KVN. *See* German Association of Dental
 practitioners of Social Security Schemes
 (KVN)

Legal acts of the Union, 74–6
Legal basis, 95–7
Legal services, 395, 407, 447
Legislative functions
 Council of Ministers, 51–2
 European Commission, 59
 European Parliament, 39–40
Legislative procedures, 76
 consent, 80
 consultation, 79–80
 ordinary legislative procedure,
  76–9
Legislative processes, 73–106
 introduction, 74
 legal acts of the Union, 74–6
 legislative procedures, 76
 makers of EU law, 105–6
 non-legislative procedures, analysis of,
  80–4
 regulatory environment in EU, understanding, 84
Leniency programme, 500–2